Second Edition

CONTEMPORARY HUMAN RESOURCE MANAGEMENT Text and Cases

Tom Redman

Adrian Wilkinson

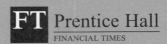

FT Prentice Hall

FINANCIAL TIMES

An imprint of **Pearson Education**
Harlow, England • London • New York • Boston • San Francisco • Toronto • Sydney • Singapore • Hong Kong
Tokyo • Seoul • Taipei • New Delhi • Cape Town • Madrid • Mexico City • Amsterdam • Munich • Paris • Milan

Pearson Education Limited
Edinburgh Gate
Harlow
Essex CM20 2JE
England

and Associated Companies throughout the world

Visit us on the World Wide Web at:
www.pearsoned.co.uk

First published 2001
Second edition published 2006

© Tom Redman and Adrian Wilkinson 2001, 2006

ISBN 0-273-68663-1
ISBN 978-0-273-68663-7

British Library Cataloguing-in-Publication Data
A catalogue record for this book is available from the British Library

Library of Congress Cataloging-in-Publication Data
Contemporary human resource management : text and cases / [edited by] Tom Redman,
   Adrian Wilkinson. — 2nd ed.
        p. cm.
   Includes bibliographical references and index.
   ISBN 0-273-68663-1 (pbk.)
   1. Personnel management. 2. Personnel management—Study and teaching. 3. Personnel
management—Case studies. I. Redman, Tom, 1952- II. Wilkinson, Adrian, 1963-

HF5549.15.C66 2006
658.3—dc22

                                                                                    2005047014

10 9 8 7 6 5 4 3
10 09 08 07 06

Typeset in 10/12 Minion by *71*
Printed and bound by Ashford Colour Press, Gosport

The publisher's policy is to use paper manufactured from sustainable forests.

To: Edwina, Rachel and Rosie
Jackie, Erin and Aidan

CONTENTS

CASE STUDIES

EDITORS

Tom Redman is Professor of Human Resource Management at University of Durham Business School. He is the editor of *Personnel Review* and his books include *Managing Managers* (1993) and *Managing through TQM: Theory and Practice* (1998). He is a Fellow of the Chartered Institute of Personnel and Development.

Adrian Wilkinson is Professor of Human Resource Management at Loughborough University Business School. His books include *Making Quality Critical* (1995), *Managing Quality and Human Resources* (1997), *Managing through TQM: Theory and Practice* (1998), *Understanding Work and Employment: Industrial Relations in Transition* (2003) and *Human Resource Management at Work* (2005). He is a Fellow of the Chartered Institute of Personnel and Development. He is Joint Chief Editor of the *International Journal of Management Reviews*.

CONTRIBUTORS

Peter Ackers	Professor in Employment Relations, Loughborough University Business School
Stephen Ackroyd	Professor of Organisational Behaviour, University of Lancaster
Nick Bacon	Professor of Human Resource Management, Nottingham Business School
Sheena Bevitt	Head of HR, Compass Services
Catherine Cassell	Professor of Organisational Behaviour, Manchester Business School
Alistair Cheyne	Lecturer in Organisational Psychology, Loughborough University Business School
Allen Clabaugh	Lecturer in Human Resource Management at the School of Management, Edith Cowan University
Laurie Cohen	Senior Lecturer in Organisational Behaviour, Loughborough University Business School
Graeme Currie	Professor of Organisational Behaviour, Nottingham University
Tony Dundon	Lecturer in Human Resource Management, Department of Management, National University of Ireland, Galway
Amal El-Sawad	Lecturer in Human Resource Management, Loughborough University Business School
Paul J. Gollan	Lecturer in Industrial Relations, Department of Industrial Relations, London School of Economics
Irena Grugulis	Professor of Human Resource Management, Management School, Bradford University
Philip Hancock	Lecturer in Organisational Behaviour, Warwick Business School
Donald Hislop	Lecturer in Organisational Behaviour, University of Sheffield Management School
Sue Hutchinson	Teaching Fellow, School of Management, University of Bath

Nick Kinnie	Reader in Human Resource Management, School of Management, University of Bath
Philip Lewis	Principal Lecturer in Human Resource Management, Cheltenham and Gloucester College of Higher Education
John Loan-Clarke	Senior Lecturer in Organisational Development, Loughborough University Business School
Samantha Lynch	Lecturer in Human Resource Management, Kent Business School, University of Kent
Sue Newell	Professor of Management, Bentley College, Boston, MA
Stephen Procter	Alcan Professor of Management, School of Management, University of Newcastle
John Purcell	Professor of Human Resource Management, School of Management, University of Bath
Douglas Renwick	Lecturer in Human Resource Management, University of Sheffield Management School
Maxine Robertson	Senior Lecturer in Organisational Behaviour, Warwick Business School
Viv Shackleton	Senior Lecturer, Aston Business School
Ed Snape	Professor, Department of Management, Hong Kong Polytechnic
Juani Swart	Lecturer in Human Resource Management, School of Management, University of Bath
David Thompson	Associate Professor, Department of Management, Hong Kong Polytechnic
Melissa Tyler	Lecturer in Organisation Studies, Loughborough University Business School
Geoffrey Wood	Professor of Comparative Human Resource Management Sheffield University Management School

ACKNOWLEDGEMENTS

As with any book, the list of acknowledgements is extensive. But these are the most important. Thanks to our editor Jacqueline Senior for her patience and encouragement. Rebecca White was responsible for putting the manuscript together and coordinating communication of contributors and we are grateful to her for the work she has done. As usual family and friends make the major contribution and Tom and Adrian are grateful to their families for their support while the book was being written. Jackie Wilkinson helped with some of the research material in the book.

Publisher's acknowledgements

We are grateful to the following for permission to reproduce copyright material:

The Society for Human Resource Management, Alexandria, VA for an extract from 'Selecting a diversity consultant' by M. Frase-Blunt, published in *HR Magazine*, Vol. 49, No. 6, June 2004; The Progressive for an extract from 'Big Bad Welfare' by Ruth Coniff, published in *The Progressive,* 409 E Main Street, Madison, WI 53703, www.progressive.org; Human Resource Management Journal for extracts from 'Managing performance-related pay based on evidence from the financial services sector' by Philip Lewis, published in *Human Resource Management Journal*, Vol. 8, No. 2, 1998, and 'Introducing Cellular Manufacturing: Operations, Human Resources and High-Trust Dynamics' by Stephen Proctor, John Hassard and Michael Rowlinson, published in *Human Resource Management Journal,* Vol. 5, No. 2, Winter 1994/5; Lexis Nexis Butterworths for an extract from 'Variable pay accord in banking' published in *European Industrial Relations Review,* October 2003; Reed Elsevier (UK) Ltd trading as Lexis Nexis Butterworths for an extract from *Work Councils for the UK? Assessing the impact of the employee consultation directive* by Mark Hall, Andrea Broughton, Mark Carley and Keith Sisson, © IRS / Industrial Relations Research Unit, Warwick Business School; Elsevier for an extract from 'Managing Culture at British Airways: hype, hope and reality' by Irena Grugulis and Adrian Wilkinson, published in *Long-Range Planning: International Journal of Strategic Management,* Vol. 35, No. 2, 2002, pp. 179–94; Palgrave Macmillan for an extract from *The Experience of Managing* by C. Clegg, K. Legge and S. Walsh, published by Palgrave Macmillan 1999; Blackwell Publishing Limited for extracts from 'Shareholder primacy and the trajectory of UK Corporate Governance' by J. Armour, S. Deakins and S. Konzelmann, published in *British Journal of Industrial Relations,* Vol. 41, No. 3, and 'An assembly line in the head: work and employee relations in the call centre' by P. Taylor and P. Bain, published in *Industrial Relations Journal,* Vol. 30, No. 2; The Chartered Institute of Personnel and Development, London, for an extract from *Redundancy*, CIPD 2002; Department of Trade and Industry for an extract from *High Performance Workplaces: Informing and Consulting Employees*, published by the Department of Trade and Industry 2003; Citizens Advice Bureau for an extract from *Flexibility Abused: A CAB Evidence Report on Employment Conditions in the*

Labour Market 1997, published by National Association of Citizens Advice Bureaux, London; and Pearson Education Limited for an extract from 'HRM and commitment: a case study of teamworking' by Paul Edwards and Martyn Wright, published in *Human Resource Management: The New Agenda*, edited by Paul Sparrow and Mick Marchington.

Table 1.1, from *Developments in the Management of Human Resources*, Blackwell Publishing (Storey, J. 1992); Table 1.2, from *Human Resource Management*, p.7, Thomson Learning (EMEA) Ltd (Storey, J. 2001); Table 1.5, reprinted by permission of Harvard Business School Press, from *Human Resource Champions* by Ulrich, D., Boston MA, 1998, pp.20–1, copyright © 1998 by the Harvard Business School Publishing Corporation, all rights reserved; Table 1.6, from 'Rhetoric, facts and self-fulfilling prophecies: exploring practitioners' perceptions of progress in implementing HRM', *Industrial Relations Journal*, Vol.35, No.3, Blackwell Publishing (Caldwell, R. 2004); Box 2.1, taken from *People and Performance in Knowledge Intensive Firms*, J. Swart, N. Kinnie and J. Purcell (2003), with the permission of the publisher, the Chartered Institute of Personnel and Development, London; Table 4.1, from SKT 27 *The Returns to Academic, Vocational and Basic Skills in Britain*, 2000, DfES, © Crown copyright, reproduced with the permission of the Controller of HMSO and the Queen's Printer for Scotland; Figure 5.1, from 'The new pay: a strategic approach', *Compensation and Benefits Review*, July–August, Sage Publications (Lawler, E. 1995); Table 7.1, from *Britain at Work*, p.110, Taylor & Francis Group (Culley, M., Woodland, S., O'Reilly, A. and Dix, G. 1999); Table 7.2, from 'Why do people join unions in a period of membership decline?', *British Journal of Industrial Relations*, Vol.35, No.4, Blackwell Publishing (Waddington J. and Whitson C. 1997); Table, chapter 8, unnumbered, adapted with permission from 'Exploring the relationship between HR and middle managers', by Graham Currie and Stephen Proctor, published in *Human Resource Management Journal*, Vol.11, No.3, 2001; Table 8.5, from 'Line manager involvement in HRM: an inside view', *Employee Relations*, Vol.25, No.3, Emerald Group Publishing Limited (Renwick, D. 2003); Table 9.1, from *Leadership for Competitive Advantage*, Georgiades, N. and Macdonell, R., copyright 1998, copyright © John Wiley and Sons Ltd, reproduced with permission; Table 11.2, reprinted by permission from Arnold, J., *Managing Careers into the Twenty-first Century*, copyright © Sage Publications Ltd, 1997; Table, chapter 14, unnumbered from 'Strategies for successful organizational downsizing', *Human Resource Management*, (1994) Vol.33, No.2, p.192, K. S. Cameron, copyright © (1994, John Wiley & Sons, Inc.), reprinted with permission of John Wiley & Sons, Inc.; Box 14.3, from *Redundancy Survey Report*, CIPD (2002), with the permission of the publisher, the Chartered Institute of Personnel and Development, London; Table 15.1, from *The 1998 Workplace Employee Relations Survey: First Findings*, p.10, Taylor & Francis Group (Culley, M., O'Reilly, A., Millward, N., Forth, J., Woodland, S., Dix, G. and Bryson, A. 1998); Table 16.2, adapted with permission from 'Finders, keepers? Attracting, motivating and retaining knowledge workers', by Frank M. Horowitz, Chan Teng Heng and Hesan Ahmed Quazi, published in *Human Resource Management Journal*, Vol.13, No.4, 2003; Figure 18.1, 'from United we stand, or else? Exploring organizational attempts to control emotional expression by employees on September 11, 2001', *Journal of Organizational Change Management*, Emerald Group Publishing Limited (Driver, M. 2003); Figure 19.1, from 'Manpower strategies for flexible organizations', *Personnel Management*, September, People Management magazine (Atkinson, J. 1984).

Part I FUNDAMENTALS OF HUMAN RESOURCE MANAGEMENT

Chapter 1

HUMAN RESOURCE MANAGEMENT: A CONTEMPORARY PERSPECTIVE

Tom Redman and Adrian Wilkinson

Introduction

This book is about human resource management and is concerned with the way in which organisations manage their people. In this introductory chapter we discuss our own approach to the study of HRM and the rationale underpinning the ordering and presentation of material in the book. Our aim is to chart some of the broad terrain of a rapidly developing field of study in order to prepare the reader for the more finely grained treatment of specific HRM topics to be found in the individual chapters. In particular we examine the rise of HRM, the effects of the changing context of work on HRM, what it involves, the strategic nature of HRM practice, its impact on organisational performance and the changing role of the HRM function. The chapter concludes with a consideration of our views on the audience at which the book is targeted and some thoughts on how it may best be used.

The development of HRM

The last twenty years or so has seen the rise of what has been called the Human Resource Management (HRM) new orthodoxy (Guest 1998; Bacon 2003; Marchington and Wilkinson 2005). In the mid-1980s in the UK, and earlier in the US, the term HRM became fashionable and started gradually to replace others such as 'personnel management', 'industrial relations' and 'labour relations'. The practitioners of people management are no longer personnel officers and trainers but are HR managers and human resource developers (and importantly line managers). The 1990s saw the launch of new journals and the flourishing of university courses in HRM. The then Institute of Personnel Management, the main professional body for Personnel practitioners, re-launched its journal *People Management,* but subtitled it *'the magazine for human resources professionals'.* The millennium has now witnessed the professional body receiving a Royal Charter to become Chartered Institute of Personnel and Development. The HRM bandwagon is well and truly rolling.

Early contributions on the implications of the rise of HRM were concerned to define it and to compare it with the more traditional British approach to personnel management (e.g. Guest 1987). HRM was in turn both heralded as 'a new era of humane people oriented employment management' (Keenoy 1990, p.375) and derided as a 'blunt instrument to bully workers' (Monks 1998). There has been considerable ambiguity in the use of the term, with various commentators using 'HRM' as simply a more modern label for traditional personnel management, as a 're-conceptualising and re-organising of personnel roles', or as a new and distinctive approach, attempting to develop and utilise the potential of human resources to the full in pursuit of the organisation's strategic objectives. It is the promise that is held by this latter view that has most excited practitioners and attracted the attention of management academics (Storey 2001; Marchington and Wilkinson 2005).

There has long been a debate over whether HRM is no more than a re-labelling of personnel management, the 'old wine in new bottles' critique, or something more fundamental (Legge 1995; Gennard and Kelly 1997). Traditionally, personnel management is often characterised as having little focus on broader business links and being overly concentrated on the activities of personnel professionals and a range of operational techniques. Thus personnel management was seen as a low-level record keeping and 'people maintenance' function. The HRM stereotype, in contrast, is characterised as being much more concerned with business strategy, and linkages with HR strategy, taking the view that HR is a, if not *the* most important organisational resource. Thus there has been much talk of an HRM 'revolution'. However, although evolution is less exciting than revolution, Torrington *et al.*'s (2002) view that HRM is merely the next stage in the development of personnel management is persuasive. Torrington (1993), a staunch defender of 'good' personnel management, has also suggested that much of what is now labelled 'HRM' may be seen much more simply as longstanding good people management practice while what was less effective has been relegated to remain, rather unfairly it seems, with the 'personnel management' brand.

To a large extent the rise of HRM reflects the changing concerns of management more generally. In the 1970s, following the Donovan (1968) report, senior management tended to concentrate on formalisation of relations with unions and national issues such as incomes policies put personnel into a position of entrenchment. In the 1980s, with a changing balance of power in the workplace following from reforming Conservative governments with an ideological distaste for trade unions, management concerns turned to efficiency and productivity which many felt were best dealt with at line management level and interest in employer practices became more prevalent.

Even the more 'upbeat' HRM work such as that of Storey (1992) indicates that changes in the arena of HRM did not come from initiatives designed directly to do this. Change was driven by broader organisational initiatives and personnel specialists have not been seen as the key drivers of change. Similarly Wood's (1999) work on high commitment practices suggests that innovations in HRM tend to accompany changes in production concepts and that innovations on humanistic grounds are unrealistic. Thus in part HRM can be seen as a consequence of managing in 'uncharted territory' with new rules governing the employment relationship (Beardwell 1998). Furthermore, the changing nature of the context of work clearly has had a significant effect on the development of HRM. The next section briefly sketches some the main developments in this area.

The changing context of work

Things are happening in employment that are neither a cause nor an effect of HRM but which could have some impact on it. These include the intensification of work, the choices of work location provided by technology and the divisive nature of a society in which many are idle and impoverished while many others are seriously over-worked (Guest 1998, p.51).

In the main developments in HRM, as we argue above, have been driven by large-scale organisational changes as employers adjust to a much more competitive global economic environment. To meet some of the challenges posed by intense competition organisations have been downsized, delayered and decentralised (Wilkinson 2004). Organizations are now less hierarchical in nature; have adopted more flexible forms; and have been subjected to continuing waves of organisational change programmes such as total quality management, business process re-engineering, performance management, lean production, learning organisations and a seemingly relentless series of culture change initiatives. The type of staff employed and the way they are organised has also undergone considerable change in the new organisational form. Employees are often now more likely to be female, work part-time, away from the workplace (e.g. teleworking and the so-called 'hot desking'), and be subcontractors, consultants, temps and interims. The boundaries between work and home are now much more blurred (Cully *et al.* 1999) and employment now has to be managed across organisational boundaries, public, private, partnerships, franchises, agencies and other forms of inter-firm contractual relations which have a major impact on work and employment (Marchington *et al.* 2004).

Such pressures have not been restricted to the private sector and we have seen the rise of the so-called 'new public management' with its emphasis on economy and efficiency (Exworthy and Halford 2002). The public sector has undergone many similar changes with new organisational forms emerging in wake of 'marketisation', compulsory competitive tendering and 'best value'. For example, the civil service has experienced delayering, market testing, citizens' charters as well as the creation of next step agencies and most recently has been targeted for major downsizing and restructuring. The NHS has seen the advent of Trusts, the creation of an internal market via the separation of purchasers from providers of healthcare, and the introduction of performance league tables and patients' charters. Major organisational change has continued unabated in the NHS with the creation of a primary care sector, the abolishing of health authorities and the launching of foundation hospitals. The suggestion is that healthcare provision has changed from being a citizen's right to a customer service. The traditional NHS culture has moved from one based on professionalism to one imbued with the rhetoric of the market with hospitals and clinics 'franchised' by the Department of Health to sell healthcare services (see Dent 1995).

Some of these changes are seen as facilitating more discretion for staff while at the same time retaining control of performance. Here the relevance of HRM comes to the fore; new forms of work and organisation demand new HRM strategies and practices. The new work context also brings new HRM challenges; not the least of these derives from the impact of such changes on the stresses and strains involved in working under such conditions. Here the growing literature on stress at work paints a rather disconcerting picture of organisational life in the new workplace. Typical of this work is the series of biennial surveys of safety reps by the TUC (TUC 2004). These show the number of workers suffering from stress has steadily increased over the series with three in five workers (58 per cent) now complaining of being stressed at work. The main reasons cited for stress are increased workloads, change at work, staff cuts, long hours, bullying and job insecurity. Interestingly, given the changes highlighted above, it is the public sector where the highest stress levels are found. The TUC surveys found nearly two-thirds (64 per cent) of public sector workers complained of stress at work, compared to less than half (48 per cent) in the private sector. Similarly, results from the Bristol Stress and Health at Work Study report 5 million workers in the UK as having very high levels of stress at work (Smith 2001).

It is perhaps thus hardly surprising that much research reports a decline in organisational commitment and employee engagement at work. Taylor (2003) notes a significant deterioration that has taken place among workers in having any sense of personal commitment to their company. Despite all the HRM rhetoric there is no widespread belief in any sense of obligation to the firms who employ them. Green's research (2005) shows a significant downturn in job satisfaction since the early 1990s despite rising wage levels and a generally tight labour market. Green notes people receiving less control and autonomy, with more targets, rules and greater stress. High workload allied to little control over work is liable to cause stress.

While HRM practices (e.g. employee assistance programmes, workplace counselling schemes etc.), are used in some organisations to provide a more supportive environment and there is some evidence that these appear to have some potential to ease but not cure the impact of workplace stress, the general picture is rather bleak. Indeed, HRM practices may have added considerably to the stresses of modern worklife with the increased use such practices as performance management systems, contingent pay and flexibilisation. For example, in relation to flexibility, the Citizens' Advice Bureau reports find numerous accounts of worker exploitation with unilateral changes in contracts, and forced reduction in hours and pay. Recent times have also witnessed the growth of 'zero hours contracts', particularly in retailing, whereby employers do not guarantee that any work will be offered but should they require labour the employee is expected to be available. The impact of organisational change on employees has been so considerable that commentators now argue there is a need to radically reconstruct the nature of the 'psychological contract' between employer and employee (Brotherton 2003). The search is now on for new deals for new times (Herriot and Pemberton 1995).

Thus HRM is clearly not a simple panacea, and even may contribute directly to some of the above problems, but it is relatively safe to speculate that it looks likely to play an increasingly important role in the workplaces of the future. However, in this discussion we must also be careful not to overstate the case for HRM. There is a danger that accounts of change in organisations are always portrayed as major paradigm shifting events when the reality is rather different. The rhetoric of organisational change often relies too heavily on hype from unrepresentative examples (Thompson and O'Connel Davidson 1995; Beynon *et al.* 2002). Managers, it seems often perceive themselves to be in the midst of massive organisational change. Eccles and Nohira's (1992) historical account of post-Second World War management traces how it has been the norm rather than the exception for practitioners and writers to view their organisational environment as turbulent and characterised by transformative change or as Sorge and van Witteloostuijn (2004) put it, the nature of the change hype changes regularly just as flu viruses mutate over time. Thus issues of continuity are in many respects overlooked in the brave new world of HRM (Noon and Blyton 2002). As we note above, poor people management practice is not just a product of old management systems, such as that attributed to personnel management by HRM advocates. It may be that many commentators have been rather blinded by the glossy nature of the new HRM vision, but we would suggest that talk of the end of traditional career jobs and the demise of trade unions and the like is somewhat premature (Taylor 2003). History generally has a fairly cruel way of treating such rash predictions.

In particular the 'rose tinted' managerial accounts of HRM in practice have recently been tempered somewhat by a literature examining HRM 'from below'. Surprisingly, the voice of the worker in evaluating HRM's achievements has been relatively silent. Where there is mention of workers, for example in Storey's work, the impression is one of scepticism that they would gain benefits. Workers' responses to HRM initiatives have generally been limited in early studies to anecdotal evidence and some limited case study work (Snape *et al.* 1993; Scott 1994; Collinson *et al.* 1997; Wilkinson *et al.* 1997; Mabey *et al.* 1998; Pass 2004; Glover 2005) with broader survey-based work taking some time to emerge (Guest and Conway 1999; Guest, 1999).

Thus there here is a danger, apparent in much of the prescriptive literature in HRM (Armstrong 2004), of focusing almost exclusively on the initiatives of management and thereby seeing employees as essentially passive beings, whose attitudes and behaviour are there to be moulded by HR strategy in the pursuit of competitive advantage. The feasibility of a 'top–down' approach to the management of organisational culture has already been challenged by a number of authors (Grugulis and Wilkinson 2002). Employees too may respond to changes in the competitive environment, and this suggests that the effective implementation of HRM may be more than simply a matter of management will. However, there is some evidence the employee experience of HRM is not always negative and exploitative. According to Guest (1999, p.23): 'it appears that workers like their experience of HRM. The more HR practices they are currently experiencing in their employment, the more satisfied they seem to be and the better their psychological contract.' Indeed work by Guest and Conway (1999) found that management practices are more important than union membership in determining whether staff feel fairly treated. Interestingly they argue that union leaders should overcome their natural scepticism and pressure management to adopt progressive HRM practices. Clearly more research is needed in this area.

What then is HRM?

In order to address this question we examine some of the key works on HRM theory. Storey's (1992) study of HRM identifies twenty-seven points of difference between HRM and PM (see Table 1.1) and divides this into four broad categories: beliefs and assumptions, strategic qualities, the critical role of managers and key levers (see Table 1.2). Sisson (1990) sees HRM in terms of four aspects of employment practice: an integration of HR policies with business planning; a shift in responsibility of HR issues from personnel specialists to line managers; a shift from the collectivism of management–trade union relations to the individualism of management–employee relations and, finally, an emphasis on commitment.

The definition of HRM by Storey emphasises a particular set of policies now identified with 'high commitment management' or 'high performance work systems':

> Human resource management is a distinctive approach to employment management which seeks to achieve competitive advantage through the strategic deployment of a highly committed and capable workforce, using an integrated array of cultural, structural and personnel techniques (Storey 1995, p.5).

A broader definition is provided by Boxall and Purcell:

> HRM includes anything and everything associated with the management of employment relationships in the firm. We do not associate HRM solely with a high-commitment model of labour management or with any particular ideology or style of management (Boxall and Purcell 2000, p.184).

Thus Bacon suggests that if HRM is defined exclusively as high commitment management then the subject marginalises itself to the discussion of a relatively small number of distinct companies since many organisations pursue a 'low wage path'. The above 'exclusive' definition thus identifies HRM in contrast to other forms of labour management (industrial relations or traditional personnel management) whereas the second inclusive definition covers all forms of labour management (Bacon 2003, p.73).

Of course, the term HRM disguises as much as it enlightens. For the purposes of this book it is important to distinguish HRM as a generic term for managing people, from the specific 1980s supervariant associated with a particular prescriptive approach, differentiated from personnel management (Storey 1992). Slippage between these terms is the cause of considerable confusion, generating more heat than light in debates on HRM and its meaning. Our view is that HRM is part of the gradual development of personnel management, but rather

Table 1.1 The twenty-seven-item checklist

Dimension	Personnel and IR	HRM
Belief and assumptions		
1. Contract	Careful delineation of written contracts	Aim to go 'beyond contract'
2. Rules	Importance of devising clear rules/mutuality	'Can do' outlook: impatience with 'rule'
3. Guide to management action	Procedures/consistency control	'Business need'/flexibility/commitment
4. Behaviour referent	Norms/custom and practice	Values/mission
5. Managerial task vis-à-vis labour	Monitoring	Nurturing
6. Nature of relations	Pluralist	Unitarist
7. Conflict	Institutionalised	De-emphasised
Strategic aspects		
8. Key relations	Labour–management	Business–customer
9. Initiatives	Piecemeal	Integrated
10. Corporate plan	Marginal to	Central to
11. Speed of decisions	Slow	Fast
Line management		
12. Management role	Transactional	Transformational leadership
13. Key managers	Personnel/IR specialists	General/business/line managers
14. Communication	Indirect	Direct
15. Standardisation	High (e.g. 'parity' an issue)	Low (e.g. 'parity' not seen as relevant)
16. Prized management skills	Negotiation	Facilitation
Key levers		
17. Selection	Separate, marginal task	Integrated, key task
18. Pay	Job evaluation: multiple, fixed grades	Performance-related: few if any grades
19. Conditions	Separately negotiated	Harmonisation
20. Labour–management	Collective bargaining contracts	Towards individual contracts
21. Thrust of relations with stewards	Regularised through facilities and training	Marginalised (with exception of some bargaining for change models)
22. Job categories and grades	Many	Few
23. Communication	Restricted flow/indirect	Increased flow/direct
24. Job design	Division of labour	Teamwork
25. Conflict handling	Reach temporary truces	Manage climate and culture
26. Training and development	Controlled access to courses	Learning companies
27. Foci of attention for interventions	Personnel procedures	Wide-ranging cultural, structural and personnel strategies

Source: Storey 1992 (www.blackwell-synergy.com)

Table 1.2 The HRM model

1. Beliefs and assumptions
- That it is the human resource which gives competitive edge.
- That the aim should not be mere compliance with rules, but employee commitment.
- That therefore employees should, for example, be very carefully selected and developed.

2. Strategic qualities
- Because of the above factors, HR decisions are of strategic importance.
- Top management involvement is necessary.
- HR policies should be integrated into the business strategy – stemming from it and even contributing to it.

3. Critical role of managers
- Because HR practice is critical to the core activities of the business, it is too important to be left to personnel specialist alone.
- Line managers are (or need to be) closely involved as both deliverers and drivers of the HR policies.
- Much greater attention is paid to the management of managers themselves.

4. Key levers
- Managing culture is more important than managing procedures and systems.
- Integrated action on selection, communication, training, reward and development.
- Restructuring and job redesign to allow devolved responsibility and empowerment.

Source: Storey 2001, p.7

---

broader and associated rather less with personnel managers than line managers (Legge 1995; Torrington 1998; Ackers and Wilkinson 2003, p.16).

Guest (1987) theorises HRM as having four key dimensions: commitment, flexibility, quality and integration. Commitment is sought in the sense that employees are expected to identify closely with the interests of the organisation, and to go beyond mere compliance to management by internalising the goals of the organisation and behaving accordingly. Flexibility involves the ability and willingness of staff to adapt to change, within the context of flexible organisation structures. The quality of staff and management is also seen to be important in achieving high levels of performance. Finally, integration refers to the matching of human resource strategies to the needs of the business strategy, and requires that the various elements of human resource management are themselves consistent and mutually supportive. Integration also implies that line managers should be fully involved in the management of their staff. Such a transformation would involve the pursuit of each of the four goals, with the adoption of a longer-term, strategic perspective, and the treatment of staff as a resource to be utilised to the full, rather than simply as a cost to be minimised (Guest 1987).

Legge (1995) finds more common ground between the ideal types of personnel management and HRM than other commentators but also identifies three significant differences in the HRM literature. HRM concentrates on managers rather than on what managers do with shopfloor staff; it emphasises the key role of line managers rather than personnel managers and the responsibility of top management for managing culture. All these approaches in adopting stereotypical conceptualisations, however, tend to thus exaggerate the difference between HRM and PM in practice. Indeed it could be said that HRM is depicted as aspirational, whereas PM is what is actually happens in practice in many organisations, so like is not being really compared with like.

It is certainly true that HRM has encouraged a greater emphasis on efficiency and competitiveness. However, this need not spell neo-unitarism, but simply recognise what is obvious to most workers and trade unions, that employees and organisations have common as well as divergent interests. It is possible, therefore, to see efficiency and cooperation as worthwhile issues to explore without having a managerial intellectual agenda; to study management without studying 'for management'. There is a danger, evident in some writing, that all practical reforms to improve organisations and the lot of workers are doomed and await the abolition of capitalism and total emancipation of the human spirit. This approach absolves its adherents from having examined complex realities and from relating their theories to pressing practical problems, such as low pay or declining job satisfaction (Ackers and Wilkinson 2003, p.17).

A strong central theme of HRM in these accounts is that of linking the people management practice to business strategy and we examine this in the next section of this chapter.

Strategy and HRM

More recently the study of HRM has adopted a cross-functional approach and expanded its breadth of analysis beyond the staple concerns of selection, training, reward etc. In particular one stream of research, strategic human resource management (SHRM), has emerged as being particularly influential in this respect. In essence SHRM theory posits that an organisation's human resource assets are potentially the sole source of sustainable competitive advantage. Much of the work in this area draws from the resource-based theory (RBT) of the firm (Barney 1991, 1995; Boxall and Purcell 2003). Here RBT suggests that competitive advantage depends ultimately on an organisation having superior, valuable, rare, non-substitutable resources at its disposal and that such resources are not easily imitated by others. The non-imitable nature of resources is a key aspect, otherwise competitors would be able to replicate and the advantage would rapidly disappear.

The subtleties of the human resource value creation process, however, are extremely difficult for competitors to imitate. The ambiguities and complexities associated with even the 'strongest' of organisational cultures, and how HRM practices are related to culture, are considerable and cannot be easily teased out by would-be imitators. Equally, any competitive advantage located in a codified and explicit set of HRM practices is also much less likely to be non-imitable than one based on the complex interaction of HRM policies and an organisation's 'social architecture' (Mueller 1996). By social architecture Mueller is referring to skill formation activities, cooperative behaviour and the tacit knowledge organisations possess. Thus the value creation process arising from HRM competencies does appear to meet the criteria set out by RBT and consequently a growing body of empirical and theoretical work has emerged on SHRM see (Boxall and Purcell 2003 for reviews of this literature). Thus RBT perhaps helps us explain some the contradictions in HRM, and provides answers to questions such as that posed by Guest and King (2001, p.11), namely 'If good people management is self-evidently beneficial to organisations, why do not more of them adopt it?'

Nevertheless, our knowledge base of SHRM is still rather limited, not least by its somewhat fragmented nature and there is, as yet, little consensus in the empirical findings. However, a particular concern in applying the RBT to HRM is that it lacks a theory of the employment relationship because it assumes internal resources do not have interests which may conflict or require negotiated alignments (Bacon 2003, p.80). In the discussion below we review some of the more influential debates and findings of SHRM research.

A classic early work by Kochan *et al.* examined the nature of 'strategic choice' in HRM and provides an example whereby changes in the competitive environment lead to business decisions which 'reverberate through the organisation and its industrial system' (1983, p.13). While such a response is clearly connected with business changes, Miller (1987) is undoubtedly right to question whether, in such circumstances, strategy is an appropriate term. The strategic management of human resources must be more than a mere knock-on effect: most business decisions will have some effects on the management of people, but such effects are not necessarily strategic decisions. For Miller, operational linkages between the business strategy and the policy towards employees are the key, or in his words, the 'fit of HRM with the strategic thrust of the organisation'. This is clearly an important point, but Miller's definition of SHRM:

> those decisions and actions which concern the management of employees at all levels in the business and which are directed towards creating and sustaining competitive advantage (p.352),

while important in demanding that human resources be a corporate level concern, has a significant weakness because of its concentration on linkages to the neglect of content.

If we return to the work of Porter (1985), from which Miller borrows, we find that competitive advantage can be achieved *either* through cost leadership or differentiation. Thus Miller's definition of SHRM would cover firms adopting either of these two approaches, as long as there was a 'fit' of HRM with the business policy followed. Yet these two approaches are likely to embody very different strategies for the management of human resources: one being based on seeing employees as a commodity, with the emphasis on cost control while the other may emphasise differentiation in terms of quality, with employees as a resource to be developed.

A more useful approach might be to characterise SHRM as entailing strategic integration and a 'positive' approach to the management of employees with an emphasis on staff as a resource rather than a cost. Thus strategic integration is a necessary but not sufficient component of SHRM. The emphasis on staff as a resource would be likely to embody policies designed to achieve the goals Guest (2001) (see above) has identified as being important, namely flexibility, quality and commitment, although Guest himself appears to regard integration as an outcome rather than a process. However, we would argue that an emphasis on staff as a resource without strategic integration is not SHRM either. For instance, the many customer care and employee involvement programmes owe much to the fact that other companies are doing them rather than relating to the business strategy of the organisation concerned. Thus in circumstances whereby HRM programmes become ends in themselves it is hard to credit them with being strategic. Equally, it clearly fails one of the tests of resource-based theory, namely being non-imitable. In contrast, an 'accounting' view of labour management may well be strategic in that it may be related to competitive advantage through cost leadership and as such strategically integrated, but this is not what SHRM is supposed to be about. Hence the latter approach sees the importance of staff in a 'negative' sense of not hindering existing business strategy as opposed to actively contributing towards it. Of course many companies would fit neither category in that the management of staff may not be considered a strategic issue at all, and not integrated into the strategic planning process nor considered as a resource (see Table 1.3). Thus there is generally much academic criticism of failure of SHRM in practice but we must ask whether our expectations are rather too high of what SHRM can deliver.

One recurrent theme in the SHRM literature is that organisations need to 'match' their human resource strategies to their business strategies, so that the former contribute towards

Table 1.3 Strategic HRM

	Strategic	Non strategic
People as resource	SHRM	PM
People as cost	Cost-driven SHRM	Traditional management

the successful implementation of the latter (Miller 1987; Lengnick-Hall and Lengnick-Hall 1988; Schuler and Jackson 1989; Boxall 1992). A number of sectoral and company-level studies have shown how organisations facing change in their competitive environment have responded with new business strategies, which in turn have required a transformation in the organisation's approach to the management of staff (see, for example, Hendry and Pettigrew 1992; McKinlay and Starkey 1992; Snape *et al.* 1993; Boxall and Steenveld 1999).

This approach, the so-called 'matching model' by Boxall (1992), argues for a fit or match between business strategy and a human resource strategy, which fosters the required employee attitudes and behaviour. In this sense, human resource strategy flows from the initial choice of business strategy (Purcell 1989). Furthermore, to the extent that changes in the corporate environment evoke a particular business strategy response, human resource strategies can also be seen as being strongly influenced by environmental change (Hendry *et al.* 1988). As Sparrow and Hilltrop (1994, p.628) argue 'HRM strategies are all about making business strategies work'. A closely related body of work has recently called for a *configurational* approach to SHRM. Here it is argued that it is the pattern of HRM practices that supports the achievement of organisational goals and that in line with the contingency approach argues that fit with strategy is vital to explaining the HR-performance nexus. The configurational approach takes the best fit view a step further in that it argues there are a number of specific ideal types that provide both horizontal fit, between HR practices, and vertical fit, between HR practices and business strategy (Ferris *et al.* 1999). The configuration of practices which provides the tightest fit is then seen as being ideal for the particular strategy. Although this work is still in its infancy there has been some recent theorising on the nature of the 'ideal types' of configurations for customer, operations, product, etc. led organisations (Sheppeck and Militello 2000).

Nevertheless, there is an issue as to how far human resource strategies can simply be 'matched' with the requirements of a changing business strategy. As Boxall (1992, p.68) notes, much of the 'matching' literature has implicitly assumed that employee attitudes and behaviour can be moulded by management strategy in the pursuit of strategic fit. However, human resource outcomes cannot be taken for granted, and whatever the merits of the view that personnel managers must increasingly see themselves as 'business managers' (Tyson 1987, 1995), it is important to recognise that personnel management and industrial relations are about more than simply selecting the appropriate fit with a given business strategy. Thus the best-fit approach can be criticised for failing to acknowledge the importance of social norms and legal rules in the search for alignment. Indeed the notion of fit is somewhat static and an inappropriate metaphor in a fast-changing corporate world.

A commonly expressed view is that since businesses exist to produce profit, not good HRM, and to the extent that such practices are essentially facilitative and not 'stand alone' activities but must flow from corporate strategy, it is inevitable that they are indeed second or third order (Boxall and Purcell 2003). However, the discussion on much of this debate has been relatively unhelpful because of the assumption that it is only first order strategies that are really 'strategic', and other concerns relate essentially to operational considerations and are hence non-strategic. This is potentially misleading as it assumes strategies are of one kind (partly stemming from the view that strategy relates to product market issues) and other matters are either strategic or non-strategic, whereas in fact it may be better to think of degrees of strategy. It is clear, for instance, that HR is downstream from the overall corporate mission, be it a return on assets or profits through business decisions. The common argument posed above is undoubtedly correct: businesses are not formed to create good HR practice. However, this is less than helpful in examining the significance of the relationship with business issues. What is being called for is that such matters should be considered within the overall business strategy of the organisation rather than separately from it. In other words, HR should not merely be affected in a knock-on manner, but be located much further up in the business strategy process. As Purcell notes, once strategy is recast, moving from outside the firm to inside to look at resources, processes and behaviour, the strategic potential of HRM is much more easily defined (Purcell 2001, p.74).

What appears to be demanded is integration at two levels: first at the level of implementation, where it is argued that much of the success of policy implementation depends on the effective management of human resources. Second, it is argued that this is not in itself adequate, that human resources should actually be considered further up the planning process, so that rather than just flowing from the business strategy, it should be part of it, in that the human resource dimension may constrain the type of business strategy adopted or provide opportunities. It is no good making a business decision (strategic) to relocate if the organisation finds it cannot recruit the workforce in the area. The existing skills of the workforce may well constrain business growth, etc. Either or both of these approaches would be consistent with SHRM. In other words, the first approach suggests that the human resource strategy should be consistent with business strategy and implementation should take account of human resource factors. The second approach demands rather more: that human resource factors not only be considered in the implementation of policy but actually influence which business strategy is adopted.

As Boxall and Purcell note (2003, p.197), inconsistent application of well-designed HR policies often undermines their desired impact. This is very evident in the work of Gratton *et al.* (1999) and their study of 7 leading-edge UK organisations. Hence according to Boxall and Purcell 'there is no such thing as *the* single HR practice of the firm. It is more accurate to imagine the HR practices of the firm as norms around which there is variation due to the idiosyncratic behaviour of line managers' (2003, p.198). Truss (2001) notes the importance of 'agency', thus we should not assume that simply having a particular human resource policy will necessarily lead to a desired outcome. Problems of implementation and interpretation occur alongside people's sometimes unpredictable responses and actions.

Performance and HRM

For years, HR professionals have yearned for evidence to show that people were really the most important asset a company had and that good HR practice delivered in terms of organisational performance. By the mid-1990s their prayers appeared to have been answered in that a growing number of studies appeared to demonstrate just that. For example, in research undertaken on behalf of the then Institute of Personnel and Development in the UK the Sheffield Effectiveness Programme (based on 100 SMEs in manufacturing) concluded that people management is not only critical to business performance but is also much more important than an emphasis on quality, technology, competitive strategy or R&D in terms of influence on the bottom line. Thus according to Patterson *et al.* (1998) this finding in one sense validates the oft quoted claims of CEOs that people are the most important asset but is also paradoxical in that it is one aspect of business that is the most neglected:

> Overall, the results of this study clearly indicate the importance of people management practices in influencing company performance. The results are unique, since no similar study has been conducted, comparing the influence of different types of managerial practices upon performance. If managers wish to influence the performance of their companies, the results show that the most important area to emphasise is the management of people. This is ironic, given that our research has also demonstrated that emphasis on HRM practices is one of the most neglected areas of managerial practice within organisations (Patterson *et al.* 1998, p.21).

These findings have been replicated in the public sector. In a well-cited study of the NHS, UK, West *et al.* (2002) reported that practices associated with High Performance Work Systems (HPWS), particularly the extent and sophistication of appraisal systems, the extent of teamworking and the quality and sophistication of training were associated with lower patient mortality. However, the Chartered Institute of Personnel Development sponsored research studies have also underscored the broad scale of the implementation problems of 18 'high-commitment' practices in 237 UK companies. Only 1 per cent used more than three-quarters of the practices, 25 per cent used more than half and 20 per cent used fewer than a quarter (Guest 2000). These findings and others have become a source of increasing concern to both HR practitioners and academics (Caldwell 2004).

There are various terms used in these studies, for example, high-performance management, high commitment management, best practice HRM, high involvement management, but a common message: the adoption of HRM practices pays in terms of where it matters most, the bottom line (Huselid 1995) (see Kinnie *et al.* in Chapter 2 of this volume). An exhaustive review by Ichniowski *et al.* (1996, p.299) concluded that a 'collage of evidence suggests that innovative workplace practices can increase performance, primarily through the use of systems of related practices that enhance worker participation, make work design less rigid and decentralise managerial tasks'. They also note that individual work practices have no effect on economic performance but 'the adoption of a *coherent and integrated system* innovative practices, including extensive recruiting and careful selection, flexible job definitions and problem solving teams, gainsharing-type compensation plans, employment security and extensive labour–management communication, substantially improve productivity and quality outcomes'. The general argument is that piecemeal take-up of HR practices means that many managements miss out on the benefits to be gained from a more integrated approach (Marchington and Wilkinson 2005). Thus such collections of re-enforcing HR practices have begun to be referred to as a 'bundle', and the task of HR managers is to identify and implement such HR systems.

However, this appears to be rather more easily prescribed than achieved. Many authors produce lists of HR practices which should be included in these bundles. Unfortunately, there is as yet little consistency and we still await a definitive prescription of the best 'bundle'. As Wood and de Menezes (1998) point out reviewing these studies indicates that there a somewhat 'pick and mix' approach to the HRM bundle. Storey (1992, p.35) identified aspects such as integrated selection systems, performance-related pay, harmonisation, individual contracts, teamworking and learning companies. Pfeffer (1994, pp.30–59) provides a list of 16, which includes employment security, selectivity in recruitment, incentive pay, employee ownership, participation and empowerment, teamworking, training and skill development, wage compression and promotion from within. These are held together under an overarching philosophy with a long-term commitment and a willingness to engage in consistent measurement of whether or not high standards are being achieved. Dyer and Reeves (1995) counted 28 HR practices across four studies of the human resource–performance link, of which only one practice, formal training, was common to all. Similarly Becker and Gerhart (1996) found 27 practices, none of which was common across five studies of the human resource management–performance link. Delaney *et al.* (1989) identified 10 practices, Huselid (1995) 13, Wood (1999) 17, while Delery and Doty (1996) appear quite miserly in comparison in only identifying seven strategic practices. All this must seem at the very least confusing to the practitioner but more than this there appear to be some quite contradictory notions in the various lists. For example, on the one hand formal grievance systems appear in some bundles as an indicator of best practice but are associated in others with trade unionism and thus seen as part of the bureaucratic 'personnel management' approach.

Aside from the inconsistencies in the HRM bundle, the best practice and universalistic approach has received considerable criticism. Purcell, for example, is wary of the claim for a universal application:

> The claim that the bundle of best practice HRM is universally applicable leads us into a utopian cul-de-sac and ignores the powerful and highly significant changes in work, employment and society visible inside organisations and in the wider community. The search for bundles of high commitment work practices is important, but so too is the search for understanding of the circumstances of where and when it is applied, why some organisations do and others do not adopt HCM, and how some firms seem to have more appropriate HR systems for their current and future needs than others. It is only one of many ways in which employees are managed, all of which must come within the bounds of HRM (Purcell 1999, p.36).

Whitfield and Poole (1997, p.757) point out there are unresolved issues of causality, problems of the narrow base of the work undertaken (largely manufacturing), concerns that much of the data is self-reported by single management respondents, as well as doubts about measures of performance which are used. Even if the data does indicate a causal link, we lack understanding of the processes involved and the mechanisms by which practices translate into desired outcomes. Equally problematic is the implicit assumption that a particular bundle of practices is feasible for all organisations. Some organisational structures and cultures will provide major difficulties in implementing certain HRM practices, for example high involvement practices in highly bureaucratic and formal organisations will be particularly problematic. The notion of a re-enforcing bundle of practices also cannot be fully convincing given the variation in the bundles noted above. It cannot yet be dismissed that the different HR practices have a differential impact on firm performance. The best practice approach thus appears somewhat of a black box and many questions remain as yet unanswered. Why is there a linkage? What is it about having these practices that delivers performance? What is the process by which these outcomes have occurred? It is unlikely say that the very act of introducing practices X, Y and Z will deliver benefits directly. Much will depend on the context of its introduction, the way it is implemented, the support provided, etc.

As Pass notes,

> the mechanisms involved in the 'causal chain' are rarely specified and are, in general, based upon assumptions or beliefs in 'employee outcomes' of commitment, motivation and increased competence. As a result, a 'black box' has been created with organisations left wondering 'how it works' – they are, instead, prescribed to follow a make believe scenario whereby they borrow Dorothy's ruby slippers from the Wizard of Oz (the appropriate bundle

of HR practices), click them together three time and then arrive at their destination (high organisational performance with happy workers) (Pass 2004, p.1).

Some writers (e.g. Godard 2004, p.371) argue that the conflicts embedded in the structure of the employment relation may limit the effectiveness of the high-performance paradigm for employers, and render it highly fragile, and it is this that may explain its variable adoption depending on workplace context. These same conflicts may also explain why high-performance practices are often implemented in ways that tend to have negative effects for workers and unions. In other words, it may be in the interests of only a minority of employers to adopt high-performance management and, even when it is adopted, it may not have positive implications for workers or their unions. Thus there is a need to recognise that there may not be a universal coincidence of interests here, in which what is good for employers is also always good for workers and their unions.

The changing role of HRM

Despite the growing recognition of the importance of effective people management for organisational success, discussed above, there are still a number of concerns about the future for HRM. At a surface level the HRM function seems to be in good health. The CIPD now claims over 100,000 members (CIPD 2004) and Workplace Employment Relations Survey (WERS) data found that the proportion of workplaces with personnel specialists, defined as managers whose job titles contain personnel, HR or industrial, employee or staff relations and who spent at least a quarter of their time on such matters, rose by a third during the 1990s. In 1998, 20 per cent of workplaces employed a personnel specialist, up from 14 per cent in 1984 (Cully *et al.* 1999). However, deeper worries about the effectiveness of the HR function linger on.

According to Peter Drucker, there has been a tendency in the past for the HR department to be seen as something of a 'trash can' function, a repository for all those tasks which do not fit neatly anywhere else:

> Personnel administration . . . is largely a collection of incidental techniques without much internal cohesion. As personnel administration conceives the job of managing worker and work, it is partly a file-clerk's job, partly a housekeeping job, partly a social worker's job and partly fire-fighting to head off union trouble or to settle it . . . the things the personnel administrator is typically responsible for . . . are necessary chores. I doubt though that they should be put together in one department for they are a hodge-podge . . . They are neither one function by kinship of skills required to carry out the activities, nor are they one function by being linked together in the work process, by forming a distinct stage in the work of the managers or in the process of the business (Drucker 1961, pp.269–70; quoted in Legge 1995, p.6).

Table 1.4 lists some of the key functions that HR departments now provide. In part Drucker's critique that the HR function lacks coherence has been moderated by some recent organisational changes. In particular the practice of outsourcing during the 1980s and 1990s saw many of the more peripheral HR responsibilities, such as catering arrangements and security, subcontracted to specialist firms. Equally the practice of decentralising HR responsibility from corporate central departments to business unit level departments and further still to line management has seen much 'streamlining' of HR responsibilities. However, perhaps more worrying for the HR function is that these trends have also seen some traditional core personnel areas, such as recruitment, training and employee welfare management, also outsourced to HR consultants. In some accounts these trends have been seen as part of a

Table 1.4 Functions performed by the HR department
Job analysis
Human resource planning
Recruitment and selection
Training and development
Pay and conditions of employment
Grievance and disciplinary procedures
Employee relations and communications
Administration of contracts of employment
Employee welfare and counselling
Equal opportunities policy and monitoring
Health and safety
Outplacement
Culture management
Knowledge management

'crisis' as HR struggled for legitimacy and status in cost-conscious times and the function has been described as being 'under siege from external consultants' (Clark and Clark, 1990). In Torrington's view this 'crisis' is nothing new and its recent intensity may owe rather more to critical academics than actual reality in the profession:

> There is a crisis of confidence among personnel specialists, as there always has been. Their results are almost impossible to measure and their successes and failures are largely the successes and failures of other people. Furthermore, they operate in a field – how people behave – in which everyone else is an expert with a personal point of view from which they will not depart. The difficulty for personnel people is that they know how intractable some of the people problems really are. They are not helped by the persistent disparagement of HRM academics, who go to considerable lengths to explain how badly their job is done (Torrington 1998, p.36).

Others have interpreted the increasing use of consultants as reflecting a sign that HR is now seen as being much more important and thus merits additional investment. Management consultants are argued to be an important conduit along which new and more sophisticated HR practices flow between organisations. However, some recent trends suggest that a 'crisis' interpretation may be more in tune with the facts. In particular the reduction of the HR domains appears to have been taken one step further and there is now a considerable debate on the benefits of outsourcing the entire HR function. In part such changes have been driven by further cost pressures in a period of corporate downsizing, but more worrying for the HR function is that outsourcing may also have been fuelled by senior management concerns about the quality and responsiveness of in-house HR functions (Greer *et al.* 1999).

For example, from one of the CIPD's own studies of a survey of senior executives, non-HR managers rated the HR profession poorly, seeing it as 'bureaucratic' and 'isolated from the outside world' (Guest and King 2001) Perhaps more worrying is that this 'news' does not appear to be new to the HR profession. The survey canvassed the views of over 3,000 HR managers in the UK and found that:

■ just a quarter think HR is respected by other managers, is seen as a key function of senior management, or has strong input at board level;

■ 85 per cent agree that the profession 'struggles to get a voice at the highest level in organisations' and a similar number admit that it is 'often overlooked by executives'.

Yet, when asked to rate themselves and the contribution they make, the respondents have been more diametrically opposed:

■ over 85 per cent of HR managers believe that HR will be vital to the continued success of an organisation;

■ over 75 per cent of respondents believe HR has a strategic business focus and acts as internal consultant and enabler.

Thus there is a large gap between what HR professionals see their role as and how other managers in the organisation see it. Thus the rising recognition that HR issues are vitally important in organisations has, paradoxically, not been all good news for the HR department given their 'Cinderella' image. It seems many senior managers may be of the view that people management is far too important to be left to the HR department. Thus in a *Fortune* article one commentator urged CEOs to 'Blow the sucker (HR) up' (Stewart 1996). While others have not been as forthright as this, the HR function appears to be at a dangerous crossroads with some suggesting ascendancy to a full business partner while others predict a painful demise. On the one hand the ascendancy school sees the rise of HR following hard on the success of SHRM and the creation of competitive advantage for organisations. In contrast the formula for demise often involves the failure of HR to understand the broader business agenda. The literature typically sees a need for the 're-invention' of HR along such lines, and that HR must simply evolve or die. However, Ulrich (1997) has also warned that the literature is replete with premature death notices of the HR function.

What then is the 'formula' for HR success? First, in addressing this question there is a real danger in slipping into unrealistic, wishful thinking – of which there is already an ample supply in the prescriptive HR literature. Second, there is rather more consistency in the literature on what the future for HR should *not* be based on than that on what it should be. Thus Rucci (1997) has suggested that the worst-case scenario for HR survival is a department that does not promote change, does not identify leaders, does not understand the business, does not know customers, does not drive costs and does not emphasise values. According to Pfeffer (1998, p.195) 'if human resources is to have a future inside organisations, it is not by playing police person and enforcer of rules and policies, nor is it likely to be ensured by playing handmaiden to finance'.

In contrast there are a wide variety of suggestions for what the HR department should do in the future. The future agenda according to Brockbank (1997) is that a successful HR department needs to be involved in framing not only HR strategy but also business strategy, promoting growth rather than downsizing and building more credible relationships with key shareholders and board members. Beer and Eisenstat (1996) emphasise the need for a comprehensive HR vision and that in the future HR managers will require coordination skills across functions, business units and borders following the increased globalisation of business, and general management, communication leadership, creativity and entrepreneurship competencies. Research by Eichinger and Ulrich (1995) on the top priorities that HR professionals believe need to be addressed in the future emphasises organisational redesign, attracting new leaders, customer focus, cost containment, rejecting fads, addressing diversity and becoming a more effective business partner with their line management customers. Ulrich (1998) also reports the results of survey research on the key competencies managers believe will be necessary for future success in HR roles – see Table 1.5. The ability to manage culture and change coupled with personal credibility are seen as critical.

Table 1.5 Key competencies of HR professionals

Relative importance to effectiveness	%
Understanding of business	14
Knowledge of HR practices	17
Ability to manage culture	19
Ability to manage change	22
Personal credibility	27

Source: Ulrich 1998, pp.20–1. Reprinted by permission of
Harvard Business School Press. From *Human Resource
Champions* by Ulrich, D., Boston, MA, 1998, pp.20–1.
Copyright © 1998 by the Harvard Business School Publishing
Corporation; all rights reserved

According to Hamel, HR has to lead the way in making businesses more like communities and less bureaucratic in the quest for business resilience. HR is seen as having a historic opportunity to create organisations 'in which people can bring all their humanity to work every day'. This would involve breaking down traditional hierarchies and creating forums where everyone can analyse where things have gone wrong, and offer '1,000 wacky ideas'. 'As long as it's mostly bureaucracy, there will be an upper limit on human effort,' he said. 'Resilience depends on initiative, creativity and passion.' However, HR would first have to get managers to 'escape the denial trap', and look at the world 'in the way it is, and not in the way we want it to be' (Millar 2004).

Thus a key theme in much of the work is that HR needs to earn its place at the top, i.e., senior management, table. One danger in these accounts is that the emphasis is very much on the strategic and business aspects of the HR role. In particular the 'bread and butter' issues of effectively managing the recruitment, selection, appraisal, development, reward and involvement of staff have been rather pushed to the periphery. What is interesting about Table 1.5 is the relatively low rating of knowledge of HR practices. There is thus a real concern that HR managers could be neglecting 'the basics' in their search for legitimacy and status with senior managers. In short, HR could be accused of ignoring employees. Indeed HR 'futurologists', it seems, need to be reminded of Giles and Williams' (1991) rejoinder to accept that the HR role is to serve their customers and not their egos. We feel that there is a danger that the senior management and shareholder customers will still be getting rather better service than the 'employee customer' in the HR department of the future.

Perceived from the perspective of HR practitioners, 'progress' in implementing HRM is an unfinished process. The six areas where practitioners believe most policy progress has been made are the areas they consider less important (Table 1.6). Caldwell (2004, p.211) argues that a plausible interpretation of this is to suggest that the idea of 'most progress' tends to correlate with the easier to deliver, softer and less high-level strategic aspects of HRM. Improvements in employee communications for example are achievable through the relatively low-level interventions associated with 'traditional' personnel management. In contrast, the areas where 'least progress' appears to have been made towards implementation seem to be associated with the more strategic aspects of HRM. For example, the shift towards treating people as assets, productivity improvements and competitiveness, requires that HRM becomes an integral aspect of strategic decision making at the highest level.

Thus one of our aims in the presentation of material in this book has been to balance the discussion in terms of both employee expectations and management expectations of the HR

Table 1.6 Policy importance and progress in implementing HRM

Most important, least progress

Managing people as assets which are fundamental to the competitive advantage of the organisation

Developing a close fit of personnel policies, procedures and systems with one another

Creating a flatter and more flexible organisation capable of responding more quickly to change

Encouraging team working and co-operation across internal organisational boundaries

Creating a strong customer-first philosophy throughout the organisation

Increasing line management responsibility for personnel management and HR policies

Least important, most progress

Improving employee involvement through better internal communication

Aligning HRM policies with business planning and corporate strategy

Empowering employees to manage their own self-development and learning

Developing reward strategies designed to support a performance-driven culture

Developing the facilitating role of managers as enablers

Building greater employee commitment to the organisation

Source: Caldwell 2004, p.200 (www.blackwell-synergy.com)

function. For example, in accounts of topics such as downsizing, empowerment, performance management, reward, flexibility, etc. the aim has been not only to critically examine HR's strategic role in the process but also to review the impact of these practices on employees. The last section of this chapter now discusses in more detail the layout of the book and some suggestions on its use.

The book

This book has been written primarily as a text for students of business and management, who are studying HRM. It aims to be critical but pragmatic: we are wary of quick fixes, slogans, prescriptive checklists and bullet points of 'best practice'. The authors are all prominent researchers and draw from a considerable depth of research in their field. Each chapter provides a critical review of the topic bringing together theoretical and empirical material. The emphasis is on analysis and insight and areas of growing significance are also included in each chapter. At the same time we wish to look at the implications of HRM research and theory development for practice and to do so in a readable, accessible manner. The book does not assume prior knowledge on the part of the reader but seeks to locate issues in a wider theoretical framework. It is suitable for MBAs, and undergraduates who these days may be doing business studies as well as degrees in engineering, humanities, social sciences, etc. As such this is appropriate for modular degree courses.

Each chapter is accompanied by a combination of case studies, role-plays and exercises for students. The intention is that students should be actively involved in the study of HRM. We believe in this sense the book is unique in the UK, the trend has been for the publication of separate text and case books. Our aim in combining these elements in a single volume is to permit a smoother integration of the topic material and supporting cases and exercises. In all chapters the authors have provided both text and cases, although in some we also include additional material from other authors. The cases and exercises are of different lengths, level and type in order to serve different teaching and learning purposes, e.g., a long case study for students to read and prepare prior to seminars/tutorials as well as shorter cases and exercises which can be prepared in the session itself. The aim is to provide a good range of up-to-date, relevant material based upon actual HRM practice.

The book is divided into two parts; the first one, the 'Fundamentals of HRM', examines the core elements of HR practice (see Table 1.3 above). In this section there are chapters on selection and recruitment, performance appraisal, employee training, reward, industrial relations, line managers. The second half of the book, 'Contemporary Themes and Issues', addresses some key areas of rising importance in HRM practice. Here there are chapters on careers, downsizing, participation, ethics and diversity management. All these were topics covered in the first edition of the book.

To reflect the ever-changing nature of HRM, this second edition of the book has been substantially revised in several key respects, in particular we have added some new chapters on topics that have grown in importance since the publication of the first edition. First, given the changing structure of industrial economies with the decline of manufacturing and the rapid growth of service work, we have included chapters examining the implications of managing emotion at work and on knowledge management and HRM. In response to the increasing importance of a global perspective on HRM we have included a chapter on international HRM.

As we note above, HRM practices are often shaped by the changing context of work and two aspects of this have been sufficiently prominent in debates of late to merit expansion into full chapters in this new edition. First, the importance of organisational culture and the role of HRM in managing and changing cultures is now seen as critical to organisational success. Second, there have been major concerns recently about the problems of long-hours working cultures and a decline in life satisfaction in industrial societies. Thus we have included a new chapter examining issues involved in balancing work and family life. Finally, as organisations react to the increasingly competitive business environment and question the contribution of the HR function to the bottom line we have included a full chapter examining the relationship between HRM and organisational performance.

References

Ackers, P. and Wilkinson, A. (eds) (2003) *Understanding Work and Employment: Industrial Relations In Transition,* Oxford: Oxford University Press.

Armstrong, M. (2004) *A Handbook of HRM,* London: Kogan Page.

Bacon, N. (2003) 'Human resource management and industrial relations', in P. Ackers and A. Wilkinson (eds) *Understanding Work and Employment: Industrial Relations In Transition,* Oxford: Oxford University Press.

Barney, J. (1991) 'Firm resources and sustained competitive advantage', *Journal of Management,* Vol.17, No.1, pp.99–120.

Barney, J. (1995) 'Looking inside for competitive advantage', *Academy of Management Executive,* Vol.9, No.4, pp.49–61.

Beardwell, I. (ed.) (1998) *Contemporary Industrial Relations,* Oxford: Open University Press.

Becker, B. and Gerhart, B. (1996) 'The impact of human resource management on organizational performance: progress and prospects', *Academy of Management Journal,* Vol.39, pp.779–801.

Beer, M. and Eisenstat, R. (1996) 'Developing an organisation capable of implementing strategy and learning', *Human Relations,* Vol.49, No.5, pp.297–619.

Beynon, H., Grimshaw, D., Rubery, J. and Ward, K. (2002) *Managing Employment Change, The New Realities of Work,* Oxford: Oxford University Press.

Boxall, P. (1992) 'Strategic human resource management: beginnings of a new theoretical sophistication?', *Human Resource Management Journal,* Vol.2, No.3, pp.60–793.

Boxall, P. and Purcell, J. (2000) 'Strategic Human Resource Management: Where have we come from and where should we be going?' *International Journal of Management Reviews*, Vol.2, No.2, pp.183–203.

*Boxall, P. and Purcell, J. (2003) *Strategy and Human Resource Management*, London: Palgrave.

Boxall, P. and Steenveld, M. (1999) 'Human resource strategy and competitive advantage: a longitudinal study of engineering consultancies', *Journal of Management Studies*, Vol.36, No.4, pp.443–63.

Brockbank, W. (1997) 'HR's future on the way to a presence', *Human Resource Management*, Vol.36, No.1, pp.65–9.

Brotherton, C. (2003) 'Industrial relations and psychology', in P. Ackers and A. Wilkinson (eds) *Understanding Work and Employment: Industrial Relations In Transition*, Oxford: Oxford University Press.

Caldwell, R. (2004) 'Rhetoric, facts and self-fulfilling prophecies: exploring practitioners' perceptions of progress in implementing HRM', *Industrial Relations Journal*, Vol.35, No.3, pp.196–215.

CIPD (2004) National Conference, Harrogate.

Clark, I. and Clark, T. (1990) 'Personnel management and the use of executive recruitment consultancies', *Human Resource Management Journal*, Vol.1, No.1, pp.46–62.

Collinson, M., Edwards, P., Rees, C. and Innes, L. (1997) *Involving Employees in Quality Management*, London: DTI report.

Cully, M., Woodland, S., O'Reilly, A. and Dix, G. (1999) *Britain at Work*, London: Routledge.

Delaney, J.T., Lewin, D. and Ichniowski, C. (1989) 'Human resource policies and practices in American firms', Washington, DC: US Government Printing Office.

Delery, J. and Doty, D. (1996) 'Modes of theorizing in strategic human resource management: tests of universalistic, contingency and configurational performance predictions', *Academy of Management Journal*, Vol.39, No.4, pp.802–35.

Dent, M. (1995) 'The new National Health Service: a case of postmodernism?', *Organization Studies*, Vol.16, No.5, pp.875–99.

Donovan (1968) 'The Royal Commission on trade unions and employers' associations, 1965–1968', Report, Cmnd. 3623.

Drucker, P. (1961) *The Practice of Management*, London: Mercury.

Dyer, L. and Reeves, T. (1995) 'Human resource strategies and firm performance: what do we know and where do we need to go?', *International Journal of Human Resource Management*, Vol.6, pp.656–70.

Eccles, R. and Nohira, N. (1992) 'Beyond the hype: rediscovering the essence of management', Boston, MA: Harvard Business School Press.

Eichinger, B. and Ulrich, D. (1995) 'Are you future agile?', *Human Resource Planning*, Vol.18, No.4, pp.30–41.

Exworthy, M. and Halford, S. (2002) *Professionals and the New Managerialism in the Public Sector*, Buckingham: Open University Press.

Ferris, G. Hochwarter, Buckley, M.R., Hamell-Cook, G. and Frink, D.D. (1999) 'Human Resource Management: Same New Directions', *Journal of Management*, Vol.25, No.3, pp.385–416.

Gennard, J. and Kelly, J. (1997) 'The unimportance of labels: the diffusion of the personnel/HRM function', *Industrial Relations Journal*, Vol.28, No.1, pp.27–42.

Giles, E. and Williams, R. (1991) 'Can the personnel department survive quality management?', *Personnel Management*, April pp.28–33.

Glover, L. (2005) 'Listening to the shopfloor: broadening our conceptualization of the relationships that shape responses to quality management', Working Paper, De Montfort University.

Godard, J. (2004) 'A critical assessment of the high-performance paradigm', *British Journal of Industrial Relations*, Vol.42, No.2, pp.349–78.

Gratton, L., Hope Hailey, V., Stiles, P. and Truss, C. (1999) *Strategic Human Resource Management*, Oxford: Oxford University Press.

Green, F. (2005, forthcoming) 'Why is work effort becoming more intense?' *Industrial Relations*.

Greer, C.R., Youngblood, S.A. and Gray, D.A. (1999) 'Human resource management outsourcing: the make or buy decision', *Academy of Management Executive,* Vol.13, No.3, pp.85–96.

Grugulis, I. and Wilkinson, A. (2002) 'Managing culture at British Airways: hype, hope and reality', *Long-Range Planning,* Vol.35, pp.179–94.

Guest, D. (1987) 'Human resource management and industrial relations', *Journal of Management Studies,* Vol.24, No.5, pp.503–21.

Guest, D. (1998) 'Beyond HRM: commitment and the contract culture', in M. Marchington and P. Sparrow (eds) *Human Resource Management: The New Agenda,* London: Pitman.

*Guest, D. (1999) 'Human resource management: the workers' verdict', *Human Resource Management Journal,* Vol.9, No.3, pp.5–25.

Guest, D. (2000) 'Piece by piece', *People Management,* 20 July, pp.26–31.

Guest, D. and Conway, N. (1999) 'Peering into the black hole: the downside of the new employment relations in the UK', *British Journal of Industrial Relations,* Vol.37, No.3, pp.367–90.

Guest, D. and King, Z. (2001) 'Voices from the boardroom report: state of the profession survey', *Personnel Today,* pp.10–11.

Hendry, C. and Pettigrew, A. (1992) 'Patterns of strategic change in the development of human resource management', *British Journal of Management,* Vol.3, pp.137–56.

Hendry, C., Pettigrew, A. and Sparrow, P. (1988) 'Changing patterns of human resource management', *Personnel Management,* November, pp.37–41.

Herriot, P. and Pemberton, C. (1995) *New Deals: The Revolution in Management Careers,* London: Wiley.

Huselid, M. (1995) 'The impact of human resource management practices on turnover, productivity and corporate financial performance', *Academy of Management Journal,* Vol.38, No.3, pp.635–72.

Ichniowski, C., Kochan, T., Levine, D., Olsen, C. and Strauss, G. (1996) 'What works at work: overview and assessment', *Industrial Relations,* Vol.35, No.3, pp.299–333.

Keenoy, T. (1990) 'HRM: rhetoric, reality and contradiction', *International Journal of Human Resource Management,* Vol.1, No.3, pp.363–84.

Kochan, T., McKersie, R. and Cappelli, P. (1983) 'Strategic choice and industrial relations theory', *Industrial Relations,* Vol.23, No.1, pp.16–39.

Legge, K. (1995) *Human Resource Management: Rhetorics and Realities,* Basingstoke: Macmillan.

Lengnick-Hall, C.A. and Lengnick-Hall, M.L. (1988) 'Strategic human resources management: a review of the literature and a proposed typology', *Academy of Management Review,* Vol.13, No.3, pp.454–70.

Mabey, C., Clark, T. and Skinner, D. (eds) (1998) *The Experience of Human Resource Management,* Milton Keynes: Open University Press.

*Marchington, M. and Wilkinson, A. (2005) *Human Resource Management at Work* (3rd edn), London: CIPD.

Marchington, M., Rubery, J., Grimshaw, D. and Willmott, H. (2004) *Fragmenting Work: Blurring Organizational Boundaries and Disordering Hierarchies,* Oxford: Oxford University Press.

McKinlay, A. and Starkey, K. (1992) 'Competitive strategies and organizational change', in G. Salaman (ed.) *Human Resource Strategies,* London: Sage.

Millar, M. (2004) 'HR must reduce bureaucracy to reduce business resilience', *Personnel Today,* 2 November 2004, p.2.

Miller, P. (1987) 'Strategic industrial relations and human resource management: distinction, definition and recognition', *Journal of Management Studies,* Vol.24, No.4, pp.347–61.

Monks, J. (1998) 'Trade unions, enterprise and the future', in P. Sparrow and M. Marchington (eds) *Human Resource Management: The New Agenda,* London: FT/Pitman.

Mueller, F. (1996) 'Human resources as strategic assets: an evolutionary resource based theory', *Journal of Management Studies,* Vol.33, No.6, pp.757–85.

*Noon, M. and Blyton, P. (2002) *The Realities of Work,* London: Palgrave.

Pass, S. (2004) 'Looking inside the 'Black Box': employee opinions of HRM/HPWS and Organisational Performance', BUIRA Conference, Nottingham University, 1–3 July.

Patterson, M., West, M., Hawthorn, R. and Nickell, S. (1998) 'Impact of people management practices on business performance issues', *Institute of Personnel Management*, No.22, IPD.

Pfeffer, J. (1994) *Competitive Advantage Through People*, Boston, MA: Harvard Business School Press.

*Pfeffer, P. (1998) *The Human Equation*, Boston, MA: Harvard Business School Press.

Porter, M. (1985) *Competitive Advantage*, New York: Free Press.

Purcell, J. (1989) 'The impact of corporate strategy on human resource management', in J. Storey (ed.) *New Perspectives on Human Resource Management*, London: Routledge.

Purcell, J. (1999) 'Best practice and best fit: chimera or cul-de-sac?', *Human Resource Management Journal*, Vol.9, No.3, pp.26–41.

Purcell, J. (2001) 'The meaning of strategies in human resource management', in J. Storey (ed.) *Human Resource Management: A Critical Text* (2nd edn), London: Routledge.

Rucci, A.J. (1997) 'Should HR survive? A Profession at the crossroads', *Human Resource Management*, Vol.36, No.1, pp.169–75.

Schuler, R.S. and Jackson, S.E. (1989) 'Determinants of human resource management priorities and implications for industrial relations', *Journal of Management*, Vol.15, No.1, pp.89–99.

Scott, A. (1994) *Willing Slaves?* Cambridge: Cambridge University Press.

Sheppeck, M.A. and Militello, J. (2000) 'Strategic HR configurations and organizational performance', *Human Resource Management*, Vol.39, No.1, pp.5–16.

Sisson, K. (1990) 'Introducing the Human Resource Management Journal', *Human Resource Management*, Vol.1, No.1, pp.1–11.

Smith, A. (2001) 'Perceptions of stress at work', *Human Resource Management*, Vol.11, No.4, pp.74–86.

Snape, E., Wilkinson, A. and Redman, T. (1993) 'Human resource management in building societies: making the transformation?', *Human Resource Management*, Vol.3, No.3, pp.43–60.

Sorge, A. and van Witteloostuijn, A. (2004) 'The (non)sense of organizational change: an essay about universal management hypes, sick consultancy metaphors, and healthy organization theories', *Organization Studies*, Vol.25, pp.1205–31.

Sparrow, P. and Marchington, M. (1998) *Human Resource Management: The New Agenda*, London: FT/Pitman.

Sparrow, P. and Hilltrop, J. (1994) *European Human Resource Management in Transition*, London: Prentice Hall.

Stewart, T. (1996) 'Taking on the last bureaucracy', *Fortune Magazine*, pp.105–8.

Storey, J. (1992) *Developments in the Management of Human Resources*, Oxford: Blackwell.

Storey, J. (ed.) (1995) *Human Resource Management: A Critical Text*, London: Routledge.

*Storey, J. (ed.) (2001) *Human Resource Management: A Critical Text* (2nd edn), London: Routledge.

Taylor, R. (2003) *Britons World of Work: Rights and Realities*, Swindon: ESRC.

Thompson, P. and O'Connel Davidson, J. (1995) 'The continuity of discontinuity: managerial rhetoric in turbulent times', *Personnel Review*, Vol.24, No.4, pp.17–33.

Torrington, D. (1993) 'How dangerous is human resource management?', *Employee Relations*, Vol.15, No.5, pp.40–53.

Torrington, D. (1998) 'Crisis and opportunity in HRM: the challenge for the personnel function', in P. Sparrow and M. Marchington (eds) *Human Resource Management: The New Agenda*, London: Prentice Hall.

Torrington, D., Hall, L. and Taylor, S. (2002) *Human Resource Management*, London: FT/Prentice Hall.

Truss, C. (2001) 'Complexities and controversies in linking HRM with organizational outcomes', *Journal of Management Studies*, Vol.38, No.8, pp.1121–49.

TUC (2004) *Workers are More Stressed than Ever*, London: TUC.

Tyson, S. (1987) 'The management of the personnel function', *Journal of Management Studies*, Vol.24, No.5, pp.523–32.

Tyson, S. (1995) *Human Resource Strategy: Towards a General Theory of Human Resource Management*, London: Pitman.

Ulrich, D. (1997) *Tomorrow's Human Resource Management*, New York: Wiley.

Ulrich, D. (1998) *Human Resource Champions*, Boston, MA: Harvard Business School Press.

West, M., Borrill, C., Dawson, J., Scully, J., Carter, M., Anelay, S., Patterson, M. and Waring, J. (2002) 'The link between the management of employees and patient mortality in acute hospitals', *International Journal of Human Resource Management*, Vol.13, No.8, pp.1299–311.

Whitfield, K. and Poole, M. (1997) 'Organizing employment for high performance', *Organization Studies*, Vol.18, No.5, pp.745–764.

Wilkinson, A. (2004) *Downsizing, Rightsizing or Dumbsizing? Human Resources, Quality and Sustainability*, Paper presented at the 9th World Congress for Total Quality Management, September, 2004, Abu Dhabi, UAE.

Wilkinson, A., Godfrey, G. and Marchington, M. (1997) 'Bouquets, brickbats and blinkers: total quality management and employee involvement', *Organization Studies* Vol.18, No.5, pp.799–820.

Wood, S. (1995) 'The four pillars of human resource management: are they connected?', *Human Resource Management*, Vol.5, No.5, pp.49–59.

Wood, S. (1999) 'Getting the measure of the transformed high performance organisation', *British Journal of Industrial Relations*, Vol.37, No.3, pp.391–417.

Wood, S., and de Menezes, L. (1998) 'High commitment management in the UK', *Human Relations*, Vol.51, pp.485–515.

* Useful reading

Chapter 2

HUMAN RESOURCE MANAGEMENT AND ORGANISATIONAL PERFORMANCE

Nicholas Kinnie, Sue Hutchinson, John Purcell and Juani Swart

Introduction

Research into the links between HR policy and organisational performance has become one of the main areas, some would say *the* main area of study, in the field of human resource management (Guest 1997). The claims made, especially in the mid–late 1990s, for the impact of HR policies on business performance raised the profile of the issue among practitioners and policy makers. However, debate rages among academics over these claims and their theoretical, empirical and methodological underpinnings. While some authors regard the evidence as the Holy Grail they have been searching for, others question the basis of the research (Legge 2001). They say the research is too narrowly focused on business performance at the expense of other important measures such as employee well-being and corporate responsibility (Delaney and Godard 2001; Marchington and Grugulis 2000). Others warn of the risks of methodological weaknesses and confusion which cast doubt on the robustness of the relationship between HR and performance (Purcell 1999).

It is not difficult to see the reasons for the increased interest in the field. Senior managers were looking for ways to improve their performance by becoming more flexible and responsive in markets that became increasingly competitive because of globalisation and deregulation (Becker and Gerhart 1996; Boxall and Purcell 2003, pp.18–19). The rise of the knowledge economy where firms rely almost completely on their human and intellectual capital for their competitive advantage elevated the importance of people management still further. In this context, managers of HR saw the opportunity to demonstrate their contribution to the business more convincingly than in the past. Some researchers in the field, it has been suggested, were motivated by the desire to demonstrate the policy relevance of their research (Legge 2001).

It is against this background that we aim in this chapter to:

- Review the research in the field critically;

- Identify the key schools of thought and trace their evolution;

- Examine some of the available data;

- Provide case study examples.

OUR APPROACH

Our aim is not, however, simply to describe and evaluate all the available research in the field. This is a self-defeating task because the reader will quickly become lost in a mass of detail. Indeed, there are already a number of excellent detailed reviews to be found elsewhere (Purcell 1999; Richardson and Thompson 1999; Marchington and Wilkinson 2002; Boxall and Purcell 2003). One recent review of the research (Wood and Wall 2004) examined the 26 most cited studies published since 1994 and identified a number of characteristic features. Half were based in the industrial sector, most used a single respondent and were cross-sectional in design. Just over half the measures of performance were self-reported and were from the same source as the HRM measures.

We take a thematic approach to the research referring to key studies as illustrations. More importantly, we use a much needed theoretical framework based on the concept of human resource advantage (Boxall 1996, 1998; Boxall and Steeneveld 1999) to guide us through the maze of research findings. We use this framework to examine the research thematically in the following way. The next major section outlines the concept of HR advantage and explains how it will be used to structure our analysis. This is followed by an examination of the research into the two forms of HR advantage referred to as HUMAN CAPITAL ADVANTAGE and Organisational Process Advantage. The chapter concludes by considering the theoretical, methodological and practical implications of our discussion. Before all of this we complete our introduction by providing the background to our discussion.

BACKGROUND TO THE RESEARCH

There has always been an intuitive feeling that the way employees are managed affects the performance of the organisation. This is an unstated assumption behind much of the research stretching back to the theories of scientific management, the Hawthorne studies and total quality management movement. However, much of this early work lacked a strategic focus (Legge 1978; Golding 2004).

In the early to mid-1980s there were studies, mostly in the US, which looked in a more focused way at the possible links between HR and performance. The texts by Beer *et al.* (1985) and by Fombrun *et al.* (1984) were thought to be particularly influential and in some ways represented a major leap forward in the area. However, these studies were not based on empirical research and as Truss notes (2001, p.1122) there were no attempts at this stage to measure performance in any well-defined or systematic way.

It is only relatively recently that studies have explicitly focused on the performance issue and the data has been available and shown a positive relationship between the presence of key HR policies and organisational performance. Much of the recent interest can be traced back to the work of Huselid (1995) and Pfeffer (1994, 1998) in the US (which itself can be linked back to Peters and Waterman (1982)). Huselid (1995) in particular sought to measure the contribution of HR to performance in much more well-defined and precise ways than in the past. Drawing on a survey of 968 US firms and taking financial performance (although other outcome measures were also used, for example, employee turnover and retention) as his dependent variable he used sophisticated statistical techniques to consider the impact of high performance work systems. Huselid found that 'the magnitude of the returns for investments in High Performance Work Systems is substantial'. Indeed, 'A one standard deviation increase in such practices is associated with a relative 7.05% decrease in (labour) turnover, and on a per employee basis, $27,044 more in sales and $18,641 and $3,814 more in market value and profits, respectively' (Huselid 1995, p.667).

Research in the UK (Patterson *et al.,* 1997) came up with similar findings. Using a sample of sixty-seven UK manufacturing businesses studied over time they found that 18 per cent of the variation in productivity and 19 per cent of profitability could be attributed to people management practices. These were a better predictor of company performance than strategy, technology and research and development.

It is this kind of research which has stimulated the vigorous debate we referred to earlier. However, before we explore the findings of this research in more detail we need to establish our framework for analysis.

Human Resource Advantage

Much of the research in the field has been criticised for its excessive emphasis on the quantitative analysis of data collected by the survey method. For example, Guest (1997, p.264), commenting on the early research, noted that 'While these studies represent encouraging signs of progress, statistical sophistication appears to have been emphasized at the expense of theoretical rigour. As a result the studies are non-additive, except in a very general way.' More precisely, Wood (1999, p.408), argued that 'The empirical work . . . has concentrated on assessing the link between practices and performance with increasing disregard for the mechanisms linking them.'

The work by Peter Boxall and his colleagues can be regarded as an exception to this with their development of the concept of Human Resource Advantage (Boxall 1996, 1998; Boxall and Steeneveld 1999; Boxall and Purcell 2003). This is the series of policies, practices and processes that together contribute to the competitive advantage of the organisation. It is comprised of a HUMAN CAPITAL ADVANTAGE (HCA) and an Organisational Process Advantage (OPA). Although there are a variety of forms of capital which are critical to organisational performance (see Box 2.1 for further details) our discussion focuses on the generation of HCA which involves developing superior policies in key areas such as recruitment, selection, training and team building designed to ensure the best people are employed and these staff develop high levels of skill. However, there is unlikely to be a competitive advantage in the policies themselves because they are easily copied (Mueller 1996). It is the processes and routines required to put these policies into operation as intended that are more difficult to replicate and form the OPA (Boxall 1996, p.267). These processes, such as team-based learning and cross-functional cooperation, develop over time, are socially complex and causally ambiguous (Boxall and Purcell 2003, p.86).

Both HCA and OPA can generate competitive advantage, but they are most effective when they are combined together. The form of HR Advantage is likely to change as the firm grows through the establishment, mature and renewal contexts (Boxall 1998). Thus 'While knowledge of individual HR policies is not rare, the knowledge of how to create a positively reinforcing blend of HR philosophy, process, practice and investment *within* a particular context is likely to be very rare' (Boxall and Purcell 2003, p.86). This 'social architecture' is created and re-created at all levels in the firm and is therefore especially difficult to imitate (Mueller 1996, p.177).

For our purposes this creates a dual focus on the design and content of HR policies *and* the role of line managers and employees in putting these into action. We use this framework as a way of organising our discussion of the links between HR and performance. We look first at the research conducted into the influences shaping the HR policies that comprise the HCA. This can be broken down into two schools of thought typically referred to as 'best practice'

Box 2.1: Forms of capital

There are a variety of forms of capital which are likely to be central to organisational performance. These are especially important in knowledge intensive firms which rely heavily on these forms of capital for their success. The main forms of capital we can recognise are:

Human capital	Human intellect. Individual tacit knowledge, i.e., inarticulable skills necessary to perform their functions. Innovation, creativity and problem solution.
	Combination of genetic, education, experience and attitudes toward life and business.
Social capital	Knowledge embedded within the organisational relationships and routines (Organisational tacit knowledge.)
Structural capital	Structures that support the social relationships, i.e., networks or project teams.
Organisational capital	Technologies and processes, e.g., customer segmentation, software, customisation.
Customer capital	Knowledge about marketing channels and customer relationships held by customers and the firm.

Source: Swart *et al.* 2003a. This material is taken from *People and Performance in Knowledge Intensive Firms*, J. Swart, N. Kinnie and J. Purcell (2003), with the permission of the publisher, the Chartered Institute of Personnel and Development, London

and 'best fit'. Attention is then turned to studies of OPA looking at the role of employees and line managers.

Human Capital Advantage

Research into the impact of HR policies on performance can be divided into two groups. First, those who argue that a set of HR policies can be identified which can be applied in a wide variety of circumstances and will have a positive effect on business performance. The second view is that the effectiveness of HR policies depends on the external and internal context of the organisation. We review each of these using illustrations from the principal studies.

BEST PRACTICE

There is a long history of researching individual best practices, for example psychology-based research into psychometric testing (Boxall and Purcell 2003, p.61). What is new is the concept of looking for a 'bundle' of practices which need to be combined together (Huselid 1995; MacDuffie 1995; Guest 1997). Making changes to individual practices will, it is argued, have a very limited effect whereas making changes together will have a more powerful effect. This suggests there is a set of practices that can and should be adopted by firms, which will lead to improvements in performance. In practical terms not only must firms become aware of these policies, but they also need support from top-level managers to adopt these policies. Researchers have also highlighted the need to avoid what they referred to as 'deadly' combinations, for example the introduction of individual performance pay and teamworking (Delery 1998).

The terms for these bundles vary, indeed there is an array of acronyms used which seem designed to confuse the practitioner and the academic including HR System, High Commitment Management (HCM), High Performance Work Systems (HPWS), High Involvement Management (HIM).

What these approaches have in common is that they identify a distinctive set of successful HR policies that can be applied successfully to all organisations irrespective of their setting. Pfeffer (1994, 1998) is perhaps the best known of these, developing a list of sixteen best practices which were subsequently narrowed down to seven (1998). The seven practices are: employment security, selective hiring, self-managed teams/teamworking, high compensation contingent on organisational performance, extensive training, reduction of status differentials and sharing information.

As we noted earlier, Huselid (1995) highlighted the need for an integrated system of work practices to fit the needs of the organisation. This research involved counting the number of practices a firm employs with data usually collected by means of a postal questionnaire completed by a single respondent representing the company as a whole. Impressive results are available linking the number of practices and various forms of performance – typically profit and market value.

Rather more mixed results have emerged from recent research by Guest *et al.* (2003) drawing on a survey of 366 UK firms. They found that greater use of HR practices was associated with lower labour turnover and higher profit per employee, but not with higher productivity. However, these associations ceased to be significant once profitability in earlier years is taken into account (Guest *et al.* 2003, p.306). Although the association between HR practices and organisational performance is confirmed, there is no evidence to show that the presence of HR practices causes a change in performance (Guest *et al.* 2003, p.307).

This type of research has a number of advantages because it focuses the debate on the role of HR practices but also raises various problems (Purcell 1999; Boxall and Purcell 2003, p.63). Two kinds of problems have been identified: methodological and theoretical. Let us look at methodological problems first.

Methodological problems

Perhaps the easiest way of summarising the criticisms of this research is to pose a series of questions.

What is the direction of causation? It is possible that the direction of causation is in the opposite to that which is proposed since it may only be the successful firms that can afford these HCM practices (Guest *et al.* 2003, p.309). There is also the possibility that respondents might believe that HR practices are good simply because the performance of their organisation is good (Gerhart 1999, p.42; Wright and Gardener 2000, p.8). Moreover, it is highly likely that there will be multiple causes of any improvement in performance and it is very difficult to unpick these satisfactorily.

What measures should be used? The measures of performance are typically narrowly focused on financial criteria with very few studies examining the broader issue of employee attitudes and well-being. Similarly, there are issues over the extensiveness of HR practices: should they, for example, apply to all employees or only a selection? One study may examine whether the organisation has self-managed teams (i.e., yes or no), while another may look at the proportion of employees working in a self-managed team. Linked to this is the profound problem, discussed in more detail when we look at organisational process advantage, which has either been ignored or side-stepped by much of this research, that the policies that are being so carefully counted are not actually implemented in practice.

How should the data be collected, analysed and presented? Many studies rely on postal surveys where the main problem is mis-reporting by single respondents who have limited knowledge of the extent and use of the policies themselves (Gerhart 1999). Much of the research makes use of highly sophisticated statistical techniques that produce results that are hard for the practitioner, as well as many students and academics, to understand.

Theoretical problems

As we have mentioned there have been strong criticisms of the lack of theoretical development. This poses another set of questions that need to be addressed.

Best practice for whom? Is there room for an employee voice in this discussion or is the emphasis simply on the perspective of shareholders and managers? (Boxall and Purcell 2003, p.64). Marchington and Grugulis (2000, pp.1105–6) consider the impact of these practices on employees and argue that these practices, such as teamwork or performance-related pay,

> which appear superficially attractive may not offer universal benefits and empowerment but actually lead to work intensification and more insidious forms of control; in other words quite different and more worrying interpretations from that portrayed in the 'upbeat' literature – such as that by Pfeffer.

They are in short 'nice words and harsh realities'. Ramsay *et al.* (2000) investigated the labour process explanation which argues that improvements in productivity are the result of the intensification of work using the data from the *Workplace Employee Relations Survey* (Cully *et al.* 1999). However, they could not find support for either the labour process or the high commitment management explanations.

More generally the absence of an independent employee voice is noted (Marchington and Grugulis 2000, p.1119) reflecting more generally a set of unitarist assumptions underpinning Pfeffer's work. Thus emphasis tends to be on the psychology-based techniques such as recruitment and selection, training, performance appraisal and pay rather than those based on pluralist assumptions, for example employee involvement practices and collective bargaining.

Which practices should be included? It is relatively easy to spot so called 'bad' practices, for example the use of unstructured selection interviews or a poorly conducted performance appraisal. However, it is difficult to get agreement on what the good practices are, apart from the most obvious statements such as the need for careful planning. The lists of practices themselves vary (Boxall and Purcell 2003, p.63) and there is no agreement on what constitutes the best practices, such that 'studies of so-called high performance work systems vary significantly as to the practices included and sometimes even as to whether a practice is likely to be positively or negatively related to high performance' (Becker and Gerhart 1996, p.784). Guest and Hoque (1994), for example, list 23 practices, MacDuffie (1995) has 11 items and Pfeffer has seven. Marchington and Grugulis (2000, p.1114) note that employment security is included by Pfeffer but not by a number of other authors; similarly the importance of employee voice varies: some include it but Pfeffer does in a very limited way. Arthur (1994) gives low emphasis to variable pay whereas Huselid (1995) and MacDuffie emphasise this (Truss 2001, p.1124). Consequently, both Boxall and Purcell (2003) and Youndt *et al.* (1996, p.839) argue there is a need for this kind of research to be more selective in the way findings are presented.

Do you need all of these practices and are they all equally important? The argument put forward by MacDuffie (1995), based on bundles of HR practices, suggests that these practices need to be combined and just taking one or two is likely to be ineffective. Marchington and Grugulis (2000, pp.1112–15) argue that in practice we often find weak links between these practices or simply contradictory practices – one person's job security might be at the expense of another person's whether in the employing firm or a subcontractor.

Are all employees treated in the same way? Are these practices just reserved for a minority of supposedly core employees or are they applied to all? (Marchington and Grugulis 2000, p.1117). This is not just an issue of differences between manual and staff employees but applies more widely in times of the decline of the internal labour market and the externalisation of the workforce through subcontracting and network relations. Early work into the 'flexible firm' suggested that employees would be treated differently based on how central they were to the core of the firm (Atkinson 1984). More recent work by Lepak and Snell (1999), discussed below, also addresses this issue.

What is the level and unit of analysis? The question of the level and unit of analysis is an important one. In some cases the research has been carried out at the level of the corporate head office (Huselid 1995) where the gap between HR policy, the employees they are intended for and performance is wide. Other research has collected data at the level of the business unit where the gap between the HR policy and performance data is narrowed (Wright *et al.* 2003). This issue is addressed to some extent by the sectoral studies discussed below.

If these policies are so effective why are they not used more widely? Evidence from the *Workplace Employee Relations Survey* (Cully *et al.* 1999) found that only 14 per cent of workplaces used HCM and while in the US (Osterman 1994), only 35 per cent of firms used two or more HCM practices, a finding confirmed by Gittleman *et al.* (1998). Guest *et al.* (2000) found that only 1 per cent of their firms used three-quarters of eighteen progressive policies and 20 per cent use less than a quarter. It is possible that just putting policies in on their own does not change very much leading to a loss of enthusiasm because of the difficulty in identifying results.

More generally Guest *et al.* (2000) tell us that there were relatively few firms in their survey that had an HR strategy and a long tail of firms that did not. They found that while two-thirds of firms rely on people as their source of competitive advantage only about 10 per cent gave people a priority above that of marketing and finance and in most companies people are not viewed by top managers as their most important asset.

How important is the context? Both national context where customers, laws, cultures and styles vary (Boxall and Purcell 2003, p.64) and organisational sectoral contexts pose questions about the suitability of these practices, although multi-national companies will attempt to standardise their practices across countries (Boxall and Purcell 2003, pp.66–7). There may well be circumstances where employers simply cannot afford these practices, most commonly in labour intensive organisations, where arguably the difficulty of controlling costs is greatest (Marchington and Grugulis 2000, p.1117).

To sum up, we can see from these questions that although the best-practice view has gained a great deal of publicity because of the simplicity of the message it has also attracted widespread criticism. Indeed, Purcell (1999) has characterised research in this area as leading into a 'cul-de-sac' where no forward progress is possible. Many of the critics argue that what works in one organisational setting, for example a small, knowledge-intensive firm, will be quite different from what is effective in another, for example a low-cost manufacturing company, or an NHS Trust. This leads them to argue that in order to maximise performance managers must tailor their HR policies and practices to the contexts within which they are working – a view typically referred to as 'best-fit'.

BEST-FIT

Types of strategy?

This perspective is derived from the contingency view that argues that the effectiveness of HR practices depends on how closely they fit with the external and internal environment of the organisation. Business performance, it is argued, improves when HR policies mutually re-enforce the choice of competitive strategy. This is the concept of vertical integration between the competitive strategy, the objectives of the firm, the HR policies and individual objectives (Fombrun *et al.* 1984; Wright *et al.* 1994) and it helps to explain lack of diffusion because the appropriate practices will depend on the context.

There are different views on the importance of particular contexts: some stress the stage in the life-cycle whereas others draw attention to the 'outer context' of the competitive strategy or the 'inner context' of existing structures and strategy (Hendry and Pettigrew 1992).

Some authors (Kochan and Barocci 1985; Baird and Meshoulam 1988) argue that there needs to be a fit between the HR policies and the stage in the business life-cycle. They suggest that the HR policies needed during the start up phase are quite different from those needed during growth, maturity and decline. However, most organisations will have a series of products that are at different stages in their life-cycles producing the situation familiar to many managers whereby certain parts of their business are growing whereas others are shrinking, producing quite different pressures on HR policies.

A second view draws on the classic analysis (Porter 1980) of the sources of competitive advantage. It argues that HR policies work best when they are adapted to the competitive strategy. The best-known exponents of this view are Miles and Snow (1978, 1984) and Schuler and Jackson (1987). For example a strategy based on cost leadership will result in minimal levels of investment in human capital with low standards for recruitment and poor levels of pay and training. In contrast a strategy based on differentiation calls for HR policies that encourage risk taking and cooperative behaviour.

This is perhaps best shown in studies carried out in a single sector where most firms are operating within the same industrial context. Arthur (1994) showed how steel mini-mills firms pursuing cost leadership business strategies adopted cost minimisation command and control type approaches. Those pursuing product and quality differentiation pursued HCM or HPWS approaches with emphasis on training, employee problem solving, team working, higher pay, higher skills and attempts to create a work community. Batt and Moynihan (2004) examined call centres in the US telecommunications industry and found that HR policies emphasising investment in employees were more successful in the parts of the industry that required employees to exercise their discretion.

Thompson (2000) conducted two surveys of firms in the UK aerospace industry. His first survey in 1997 found that establishments with higher levels of value added per employee tended to have higher penetration of innovative working practices among their non-management employees. These workplaces tended to be more heavily engaged in specialist production for niche markets and employed a richer mix of technical and professional employees. The second survey in 1999 revealed 'compelling evidence that firms introducing a greater number of high performance work practices have much improved business performance' (Thompson 2000, p.10). Indeed, firms moving from less than five to more than six innovative practices made a 34 per cent gain in value added per employee.

Other research has highlighted the influence of the network of relationships within which firms, especially knowledge intensive and professional service firms are working (Swart and Kinnie 2003b; Beaumont *et al.* 1996; Sinclair *et al.* 1996). Firms increasingly form relationships with clients, suppliers and collaborators and often these other parties will influence the HR policies pursued by the focal firm both directly and indirectly, as shown by the example in Box 2.2. They may influence these policies directly, for example, through shaping recruitment and selection criteria or through requiring certain types of training to be conducted, or more

Box 2.2: Tocris Cookson

Tocris Cookson, with sixty employees, is a specialist chemical company with experience in the synthesis of a wide variety of compounds. They employ teams of skilled chemists (mainly at postdoctoral level) and operate from one site in the UK and one site in the USA. HR policies in Tocris Cookson can be understood only in the context of the network in which they operate (see Figure below).

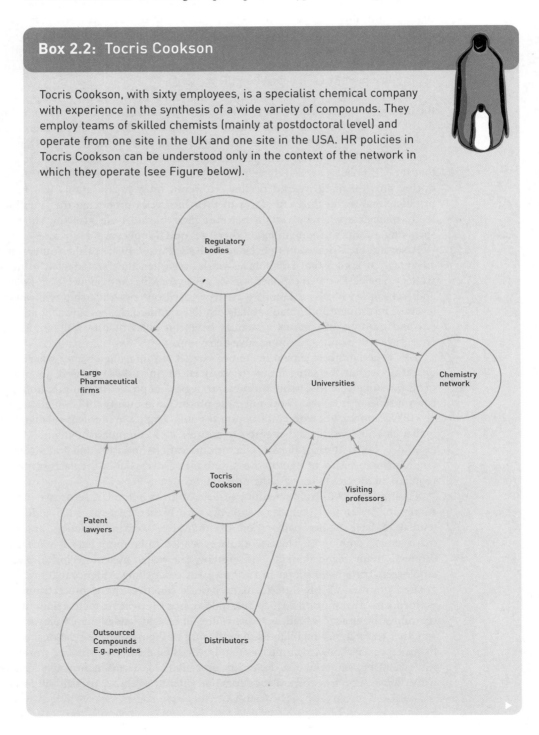

Tocris Cookson's key clients are life science researchers at universities or other research institutes. In order to build these client relationships and make the compounds, they need to maintain very strong ties with large pharmaceutical companies, patent lawyers and academics in the field. Pharmaceutical firms often have patents on some of the chemicals that need to be synthesised, however these could lapse in an 8–10-year period. If a 'cool chemical is spotted' the patent rights need to be negotiated with the relevant firm. A senior manager in Tocris Cookson said, 'once our key to success was developing compounds, now it is building relationships'. Relationships with universities also need to be maintained to:

(i)   update employee's skills in the pharmacological discipline;
(ii) build client relationships, where the universities are often users of the compounds made;
(iii) build an external recruitment pool by making top-performing research chemists aware of the business.

The process of building external relationships was regarded as 'an art' which could only be mastered over several years of experience: first as a doctoral chemist, then as a postdoctoral researcher and finally as a negotiator with major pharmaceutical firms. Tocris Cookson recruits its employees during a postdoctoral placement at the company and this is often their first full-time employment. Managers regard this as a threat because of the majority of their workforce is young, highly qualified and mobile (single). The threat is managed through the strong organisational culture, which employees describe as a family or home away from home.

Most formalised HR practices originated from an elaborate HR policy, which was written by the part-time HR manager. The drive toward more formalised HR systems coincided with the company objective of 'becoming more corporate'. Within the set of formalised practices, performance management was central to other HR practices both practically, given its links to reward and development, and also politically, because it influenced the career development of this group of knowledge workers. Furthermore, the performance appraisal process was questioned by research chemists and there was a push to develop an in-house system because it is particularly difficult to appraise the outcome of research. This resulted in sets of HR practices evolving from formalised practices that may have originated outside the firm to sets of practices that grew from within the community of knowledge workers.

indirectly by setting performance targets that can be reached only by adopting, for example, team based forms of work organisation (Kinnie and Parsons 2004).

Labour markets are also likely to be important because in certain industries and geographical areas firms find they have to compete much more intensively than others. Tight labour markets, as seen where call centres are concentrated, will put pressure on particular HR policies such as recruitment and selection and reward (Kinnie *et al.* 2000).

Others argue that HR policies need to fit with and complement other important strategies and structures within the organisation. The size of the organisation will be important – larger firms will have complex internal structures often with multiple layers and more generally the resources needed to fund certain approaches, for example a formalised salary structure or recruitment scheme. There is also a need to take account of the influence of the manufacturing strategy of the firm (Baron and Kreps 1999; Purcell 1999; Boxall and Purcell 2003, pp.56–8).

The best-fit approach has been subject to extensive review (see Boxall and Purcell 2003, pp.54–6; Purcell 1999, p.32 for further details) and a number of issues have been raised concerning the impact of the outer and the inner context. Perhaps the most basic point of all is the assumption that firms have a competitive strategy with which HR policies can fit (Legge 1995; Ramsay et al. 2000). Even if the firm does have a strategy this view assumes that the one they have is the most appropriate for them. This may not be the case if firms do not have sufficient knowledge of their external environment or if they have misinterpreted the information that they have gathered.

Multiple contingencies

Perhaps the biggest problem is that most firms exist within complex external environments with multiple contingencies that cannot all be isolated or identified. There are particular problems with modelling the influences, with understanding what happens if the influences do not all pull in the same direction and with coping with change (Purcell 1999, p.34). This raises the issue of the dynamic fit between policy and context: if the external environment changes should firms keep changing their policies to fit the market circumstances? There are strong arguments against this because HR practices are quite slow to change. Consequently, Purcell (1999) has argued that firms seeking a best-fit are effectively chasing a 'chimera'.

In response to criticisms of the best-fit approach Wright and Snell (1998) argue for the need to have both fit and flexibility (Boxall and Purcell 2003, p.56). This is not just the ability to move from one best-fit to another, but to be able to adapt to the situation where the need to change is virtually continuous. 'Flexibility provides organisations with the ability to modify current practices in response to non-transient changes in the environment' (Wright and Snell 1998, p.757). In particular there is a need to achieve fit between the HR system and the existing competitive strategy while at the same time achieving flexibility in a range of skills and behaviours needed to cope with changing competitive environments.

More broadly, there may be some characteristics of successful organisations that are impossible to model, usually referred to as idiosyncratic contingency or causal ambiguity (Purcell 1999, p.35). These are the patterns and routines of behaving or the cultural norms that have been built up slowly over a long period associated with success. It may simply not be possible to disentangle what exactly are the key factors in success when looking at a large complex organisation.

Treating employees differently

The need to respond to external pressures creates problems of treating employees with consistency especially over time (Baron and Kreps 1999; Boxall and Purcell 2003, pp.56–8). In reality it is likely that a combination of policies will be needed depending on external circumstances: as products grow and decline there may need to be redundancies for some employees but also the need to retain good employees and to develop them (Boxall and Purcell 2003, p.51).

In response to some of these criticisms we have seen the development of the HR architecture model (Lepak and Snell 1999). This is based on the configurational view which argues that it is unlikely that a company will use a single approach for all its employees. It suggests that the best-fit approach is too simple because there is a need to focus on the combination or patterns of practices which are needed – putting horizontal fit together with vertical fit (Delery and Doty 1996). Most organisations employ different groups of employees who will need to be treated differently and in effect there are different configurations of policies for different types of employees.

The Lepak and Snell model of HR architecture expresses these ideas in a more accessible form. They argue that,

> To date most strategic HRM researchers have tended to take a holistic view of employment and human capital, focusing on the extent to which a set of practices is used across all employees of a firm as well as the consistency of these practices across firms. We believe that the most appropriate mode of investment in human capital will vary for different types of capital (Lepak and Snell 1999, p.32).

Their model distinguishes between employees on the basis of the value they create for the organisation (the extent to which they contribute towards the creation of competitive advantage) and the extent to which their knowledge and skills are specific to that organisation (uniqueness).

This approach represents a step forward but also raises various questions. In particular there is the issue of consistency here: if an employer wishes to pursue an inclusive culture-based approach why should they treat employees differently? If certain activities are externalised there is a danger that the core competences of organisation will be lost. There is also a moral issue here – why should different groups be treated differently?

Recent work (Purcell 2004, pp.14–15) has examined this is in a slightly different way looking at the attitudinal outcomes such as organisational commitment and job satisfaction for different occupational groups. It was found that an increase in the commitment of professional employees, first line managers and shopfloor employees is associated with different HR policies (see Box 2.3 for further details).

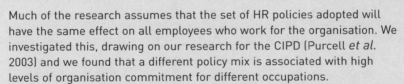

Box 2.3: Influences on the attitudes of different employee groups

Much of the research assumes that the set of HR policies adopted will have the same effect on all employees who work for the organisation. We investigated this, drawing on our research for the CIPD (Purcell *et al.* 2003) and we found that a different policy mix is associated with high levels of organisation commitment for different occupations.

Professional employees want excellent communication about the business with good rewards and recognition for good work. They want to know how well they are doing, enjoy working hard but need to get on with their boss and want a good work–life balance.

Front line managers want good communications and an opportunity to be involved in decision making. They show commitment if they have good rewards, find the firm helps them achieve a work–life balance and they believe they are not stuck for ever in their current job.

Workers value communication, want praise and reward, the ability to discuss grievances and personal problems and a good work–life balance.

Source: Kinnie *et al.* 2005

In summary, we have considered the best-practice and best-fit approaches towards the generation of HRA and examined the criticisms which have been made of these. It is possible, however, that these approaches can be reconciled. Boxall and Purcell (2003, p.69) conclude that some general principles can be established, for example, on selection interviewing, but that policies themselves are likely to be influenced by best-fit considerations at national and organisational levels. This combination of views remains, however, incomplete because it is still looking only at the formal policies and we now need to consider how these policies are actually used.

Organisational Process Advantage (OPA)

The key theme running throughout our discussion has been that the acquisition of HRA depends on developing both a capital and a process advantage (Purcell 1999, p.36; Boxall and Purcell 2003, p.22). We need therefore to understand how HR polices are actually translated into operation before we can begin to thoroughly understand the links between HR and performance. It is important to look at the routines and processes, or using another language, both the formal and informal practices which make up the day-to-day realities of organisational life.

Studying OPA is much more difficult than looking at policies because these processes are often tacit and intangible; they are immune to data collection by postal questionnaire and analysis by sophisticated statistical packages. In fact OPA is only seen most clearly when it is absent, when things go wrong: there is infighting between departments, poor knowledge sharing within and between project teams, or people do not work to their full potential.

The concept of OPA is derived from research carried out into the resource-based view (RBV) of strategy.

RESOURCE-BASED VIEW (RBV)

This draws attention to the intangible assets of the firm which make up its distinctive competencies and organisational routines (Purcell 1999, p.35). The resource-based view has developed from business strategy literature that competitive advantage is based on what is difficult to imitate not on what can be copied. There is a need to develop an exclusive form of fit. This is particularly important for knowledge intensive firms that rely almost entirely on their human and intellectual capital for their success and is effectively rebalancing an over dependence on the Porter approach (Boxall and Purcell 2003, pp.74–5).

The RBV involves looking at the internal resources of the firm and considering the ways in which HR can maximise their contribution to development of competitive advantage. This focuses on how human resources can become scarce, organisation specific and difficult to imitate (Barney 1991; Barney and Wright 1998) and draws on the research into core competencies (Hamel and Prahalad 1994).

In particular this view involves looking at how HR can develop the following (Barney and Wright 1998; Golding 2004, p.51):

Value – how does the firm seek to distinguish itself from its competitors? What part does HR play in this?

Rarity – is the firm doing something with its employees that its competitors are not?

Inimitable – causal ambiguity means that the unique history of each firm makes it difficult to ascertain what causes the advantage and therefore make it difficult to copy.

Organisation – these internal resources need to be integrated into coherent systems so advantage is sustainable.

Research into the resource-based view tends to be associated with unpredictable environments and emphasises what is distinctive. However, we need to remember that firms also need to have the base-line characteristics right before developing distinctive characteristics, what Hamel and Prahalad (1994) and Boxall (1996) refer to as 'table stakes', the resources and skills needed simply to play the game. Once these have been established it is the differences between firms which are important.

Truss (2001) notes that one of the problems with the RBV is its emphasis on the importance of synergy and fit between the various elements of the HR system and asks how compatible is a systems-based approach with flexibility (Becker and Gerhart 1996, p.789).

The RBV has looked at the intangible sources of competitive advantage in general terms. If we are to understand this in the HR context we need to consider what has come to be known as the 'black box' research.

APPLICATION TO HR: EXAMINING THE 'BLACK BOX'

The importance of examining the implementation of HR policies was noted by Becker and Gerhart (1996, p.793) when they argued that 'future work on the strategic perspective must elaborate on the black box between a firm's HR systems and the firm's bottom line'. Moreover, 'more effort should be devolved to finding out what managers are thinking and why they make the decisions they do' (1996, p.794). This emphasis suggests there is a need to understand how and why HR policies influence performance and to move away from the simple input–output models which have policy inputs on the left-hand side of the model and outcomes on the right-hand side.

When we begin to look inside the 'black box' we find that there are clearly differences between the espoused policies and the policies in use. For example, Truss (2001) draws on her research in Hewlett-Packard to highlight the importance of the informal processes that exist alongside the formal practices. There were clear gaps between what the company claimed they were doing and what was actually experienced by employees: 'in areas such as appraisals and training and development the results obtained were not uniformly excellent; in fact some were highly contradictory' (Truss 2001, p.1143). Although the formal appraisal processes in HP rewarded employees' performance against targets related to the company's objectives 'informally what counted was visibility and networking if people wanted to further their careers' (Truss 2001, p.1144). Despite espousing the value of training less than half said they got the training they needed to do their job, fewer than half felt the appraisal system was working well and less than one-third felt their pay was fair. 'These are all examples of a strong disconnect between the "rhetoric" of human resource management as expressed by the human resource department, and the reality as experienced by employees' (Truss, 2001, p.1143). This 'highlights the importance of the informal organization as mediator between policy and the individual' (Truss, 2001, p.1144).

These findings were repeated in a study of 12 organisations where there was a clear gap between formal HR policy statements and practice in areas such as performance appraisals, training, involvement and communication (Purcell *et al.* 2003). For example in organisations which claimed to have formal employee involvement schemes (such as team briefs) for all their employees, not all staff were aware of the existence of these initiatives and an even lower proportion of employees claimed to have been practically involved in such schemes (Hutchinson and Purcell 2003, p.36).

Research into formal and informal practices has a long tradition in the industrial relations literature (Brown 1972, 1973; Terry 1977) and sheds important light on contemporary concerns about the processes that are actually important. This makes a focus solely on formal policies inappropriate, and in particular we need to consider the role of the 'individual manager as agent, choosing to focus his or her attention in varying ways' (Truss 2001, p.1145). We examine this under the heading of discretionary behaviour. However, before we do this we need to consider the role of employees when engaging in discretionary behaviour.

Employee discretionary behaviour

Research in the US steel, clothing and medical equipment industries highlights the importance of employee discretionary behaviour (Appelbaum *et al.* 2000). Drawing evidence from managers and shopfloor employees as well as a study of formal HR policies, they found that the willingness of employees to engage in discretionary behaviour depended on the creation of opportunities to participate, skill development and motivation and incentives (Appelbaum *et al.* 2000, pp.118–20).

Their key finding was the positive effects of HPWS on plant performance, most importantly through increased discretionary effort by employees and the increased rate of knowledge accumulation. Moreover, these practices had a different effect on performance in different industries (Appelbaum *et al.* 2000, p.227). In steel there was evidence that quality and employment security raised 'up time' by 8 per cent, incentives by 13 per cent and work organisation by 14 per cent and HPWS as a whole by 17 per cent (Appelbaum *et al.* 2000, p.108). In clothing, modular production involving self-directed teams reduced sewing time by 94 per cent and led to substantial cost savings. In medical equipment the opportunity to participate is closely linked to value added per dollar and profits and quality (Appelbaum *et al.* 2000, p.108). The likelihood of employees engaging in this discretionary behaviour is also influenced more generally by the role of line managers.

Role of line managers in bringing policies to life

Recent research has looked at the discretionary behaviour of managers, especially first line managers and their contribution towards the development, or absence, of an organisational process advantage.

Numerous studies have observed how, over the last decade, line managers have played a more prominent role in the delivery of HR practices such as performance management, team leadership and communications as an increasing number of people management activities have been devolved to them (Hutchinson and Wood 1995; Renwick 2000; Larsen and Brewster 2003). The importance of the role of line managers has been recognised by both recent research (Marchington and Wilkinson 2002, pp.232–7) and earlier work on the 'forgotten supervisor' (Thurley and Wirdenius 1973; Child and Partridge 1982) and the role of the line manager in the emergence of informal practices (Brown 1972, 1973; Terry 1977; Armstrong and Goodman 1979).

A recent study (Purcell *et al.* 2003) shows that the way line managers implement and enact HR policies by 'bringing them to life' and show leadership strongly influences employees' attitudes. Employees' perceptions of line management behaviour (in terms of how they carry out their HR activities such as responding to suggestions from employees) was the most important factor in explaining variations in both job satisfaction and job discretion – or the choice people have over how they do their jobs. There is also evidence that a pattern can be traced between line manager activities, employee attitudes and the performance of comparable business units and in changes over time. The Selfridges and Omega cases (Case studies 2.1 and 2.3) illustrate this well.

Bartel (2000) examined these issues in the banking industry in Canada and found that when controlling for environment and branch and managerial effects, the HR environment (as measured by the quality of feedback and communications) has a significant positive effect on loan sales. Although there were common HR practices it was clear that there was discretion over how these were applied. One standard deviation increase in managerial effectiveness accounts for a 16–26 per cent increase in loan sales. Thus the discretion exercised by branch managers has a direct effect on performance through the education and motivation of branch staff.

These differences between 'espoused' and 'enacted' policies can be partly attributed to the line manager for a variety of reasons (McGovern *et al.* 1997; Marchington 2001; Hutchinson and Purcell 2003). Line managers may suffer from work overload partly because of organisational restructuring and the demise of the middle manager and simply lack the time to carry out all their duties. They may have inadequate training on how to operate the policies, lack commitment to them (Marchington 2001), be doubtful about the claimed benefits, or simply be ignorant of what is expected of them.

In an attempt to analyse this role Purcell *et al.* (2003) develop a model which places the discretionary behaviour exercised by line managers at the centre of the analysis, as shown in Box 2.4. In particular it sees the link between HR policies and performance as being the interaction between line manager behaviour and employee attitudes and behaviour. Line managers are important because of the key role they play in the generation of operational process advantage: most employees experience work through their contacts with their immediate team and their team leader.

Box 2.4: Bath People and Performance Model

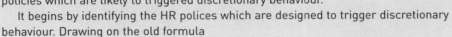

Many of the attempts to link HR policy and performance pay insufficient attention to the linking mechanisms. Although it is relatively easy to draw up a list of HR policies, as we have seen, we cannot assume that these are implemented as intended. The Bath model (below) attempts to overcome this by looking in detail at this 'Black Box'. It draws on the work of people such as MacDuffie (1995) and Appelbaum *et al.* (2000) to identify the HR policies which are likely to triggered discretionary behaviour.

It begins by identifying the HR polices which are designed to trigger discretionary behaviour. Drawing on the old formula

$$P = f(A, M, O)$$

(Where P is performance, A is ability, M is motivation and O is opportunity) it argues that people perform well when:

- they are able to do so (they *can do* the job because they possess the necessary knowledge and skills);
- they have the motivation to do so (they *will do* the job because they are adequately incentivised); and
- their work environment provides the necessary support and avenues for expression (e.g., functioning technology and the opportunity to be heard when problems occur).

This allows us to identify 11 HR policies which our research suggests stimulate discretionary behaviour. However, the model also shows the key role that line managers play in implementing, enacting, leading and controlling and the impact this has on employee attitudes and their behaviour.

Source: Purcell *et al.* 2003

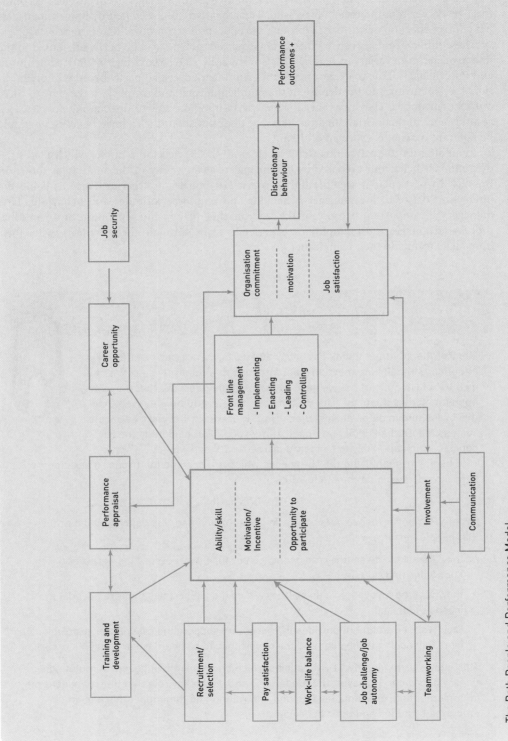

The Bath People and Performance Model

The key role played by line managers opens up further lines of inquiry concerning how these line managers are themselves managed. Research (Kinnie *et al.* 2005) suggests that the key factors influencing line managers' commitment and their willingness to engage in discretionary behaviour are their opportunities to be involved in decision making and the existence of career opportunities. In addition, work–life balance, and good rewards and communications are associated with organisational commitment (Kinnie *et al.*). (See also Box 2.3.)

More broadly this suggests that the values and culture of the organisation can be a form of organisational process advantage. There are positive links between this form of OPA and organisational commitment, for example, employees in firms which exhibit 'strong values' or who have a clear, well-established Big Idea have higher levels of commitment compared to employees in firms without these strong values (Purcell *et al.* 2003). Box 2.5 provides more details of this and again the Selfridges case (Case study 2.3) illustrates this well. This supports the argument made by Barney (1986, p.656) some time ago that 'Firms with sustained superior . . . performances typically are characterised by a strong set of core managerial values that define the way they conduct business.'

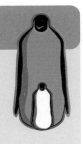

Box 2.5: The Big Idea

In some companies it is not just the senior managers but also employees at all levels who identify strongly with the values and mission of the organisation. We came to call this the 'Big Idea' since it seemed there was something simple or easy to explain that captured the essence of the firm and clearly informed or enthused HR policy and practice. The essence of this is:

'A clear sense of mission underpinned by values and a culture expressing what the firm is and its relationship with its customers and employees.'

The Big Idea had a number of attributes:

- **Embedded** – it was embedded throughout the organisation, for example quality in Jaguar

- **Connected** – it connected, and derived from the same root, the way customers were treated and employees managed, for example mutuality in Nationwide

- **Enduring** – it was enduring, not a flash in the pan, not the product of a board discussion on an away day and had clear historical roots, for example a long-standing commitment to 'have fun and make money' in AIT

- **Collective** – it was encapsulated in routines about the way work was done and people behaved. In that sense it was collective, combining people in processes and routines in the sense of a taken for granted, everyday activity as seen in Nationwide

- **Measured and managed** – it was measured and managed often using broad measures of performance as we found in Selfridges.

Source: Purcell *et al.* 2003

Conclusions and implications

We have examined research into the links between HR and performance using the concept of HRA. This has highlighted the importance of gaining both a human capital and a process advantage. Our discussion has implications for method, theory and practice.

The methodological debates referred to here are likely to continue. The approach based on the sophisticated analysis of quantitative data collected by questionnaires is likely to remain popular especially where it is supported by a wider research tradition and higher education infrastructure, as in the US. However, the implication of this discussion is that this approach is unlikely to gain insights into the organisational processes that are clearly crucial to successful organisations. These critical processes and routines can only be effectively examined by means of the case study approach. However, the problems of generalisability of case study findings will remain. One possible way forward is the collection of a combination of quantitative and qualitative data perhaps within a restricted number of industries.

A whole series of theoretical issues are thrown up by our discussion. Perhaps the most basic issues of all revolve around questions such as: what do we mean by performance? Whose performance? How do we measure this? Delaney and Godard (2001) have argued that it is time for the research to move outside the narrow confines of financial performance. Not only should the narrow measures of organisational performance be broadened, but also concern should be given to wider measures such as employee well-being. We also need to explore the concept of HRA in more detail, particularly the sources of organisational process advantage or disadvantage. We need to understand more clearly why gaps between espoused and operational policy emerge and what the consequences of this are for all parties. If line managers are critical to this, we need to know more about how they are managed and what factors influence their attitudes and behaviour. This raises the much broader issue of widening the focus of study away from human resource management to people management, from the tendency to study formal HR policies to a range of factors that impinge directly on the employee experience of work and which trigger discretionary behaviour. This would include the role of line managers in the operation of policy, the cultural context and work organisation and job design.

The policy implications of this discussion are profound. The 'best-fit–best-practice' debate has largely been sidelined by the realisation that both fit and flexibility are needed. The most likely way of getting this is by employing staff who carry out the HR policies most closely to the way that they were intended. More generally the implication is that simply developing the appropriate policies is not in itself going to be enough because HR advantage also depends on how these policies are implemented. Consequently, looking for a link between HRA policies and performance is a misguided activity because the main focus needs to be on the links between policy, processes, implementation and performance.

This focus on process has potential benefits for HR specialists because these processes have to be carefully developed internally and cannot simply be copied from a textbook in the way that policies might be. Here the HR practitioner role becomes key because the development of what we might call 'best processes' can become a core competence which is embedded within the thinking and acting of the organisation such that it cannot be imitated or outsourced.

CASE STUDY 2.1

UNDERSTANDING PERFORMANCE IN RETAILING:
The Case of Omega Supermarkets[1,2]

SUE HUTCHINSON

Omega is a successful growth company and one of the largest supermarket chains in the UK, employing a large number of staff in stores across the country. Although the industry has seen very little growth in recent years Omega has successfully increased its market share through a policy of lowering prices (the company claims to have reduced prices by 7.5 per cent over the last four years) and improving customer service. It currently holds a dominant share of the UK market in its core business and is growing rapidly in related areas. The company plans to continue expanding in the UK, opening up new stores on brownfield sites in regeneration areas.

The organisation underwent considerable change in the mid-1990s in order to improve its competitive position, with a much greater emphasis on a customer-facing culture. As a senior human resources manager remarked, '1995 saw the evolution of a customer-focused business. With quality and price being very much the same across the sector, people and our service were seen as a differentiator.' One of the many changes introduced at this time was the balanced scorecard approach (Kaplan and Norton 1992) which helped define the business more strongly and bring about this culture change. The scorecard has four quadrants – people, finance, customers and operations and each store's performance is measured against specific targets in each area. In the people quadrant, for example, targets include recruitment, development, retention, labour turnover, absence and staff morale (taken from the staff attitude survey). Although the four quadrants are not weighted, one retail director we interviewed considered the 'people' quadrant to be the most important, as he explained 'if we can recruit, maintain and deliver fantastic people then operationally we can deliver'. The measures are updated each quarter and link to the corporate measures which underpin the organisations strategic objectives. The introduction of this approach brought about a much greater focus on people and customer issues in the stores which historically had been driven by financial and operational results. Delayering also took place as part of the restructuring in the mid-1990s and within the stores there are currently four levels: store manager, senior managers (mostly operational managers), section managers and general assistants. Each store is run by a store manager whose job it is to provide coaching, guidance and support and to deliver the Omega 'standard'. As one store manager explained 'my role is to mobilise the team with a goal, to be energetic and to be able to motivate people'. There is a senior management team which includes operational managers responsible for departments and in an average-sized store (employing around 400 staff) this would comprise five or six managers which typically would include the store manager, personnel manager, customer services manager and operations managers. Each member of this team, including the personnel manager, takes a turn in managing the store for around 20 per cent of their working time so that they gain an understanding of the wider business issues. The personnel function within the stores

---

[1] Some details of the case have been change or omitted to preserve the anonymity of the organisation.
[2] Research for this case was undertaken as part of a project sponsored by the Chartered Institute of Personnel and Development.

(over two-thirds of stores have their own personnel manager) has undergone considerable change over the last five or six years, moving from a predominantly administrative and welfare role to a store-level senior management position. The role of the personnel manager includes taking responsibility for the payroll and controllable expenses and ensuring that the store maintains productivity levels. This means focusing on the people measures such as absence management, employee appraisal and development, resourcing and succession planning. One of the benefits of the balanced scorecard approach has therefore been to make the role of the personnel manager much clearer within the stores and enabled the function to measure themselves against specific goals.

A more recent change within Omega has been the drive for consistency across stores and all policies, procedures and processes are centrally determined and their implementation closely monitored. Each store is governed by the company routines handbook which provides detailed information on how every task is to be performed – this is down to the minutest detail even including details on office layout, such as where pictures should go on the wall. On the HR side all policies and procedures are highly centralised and controlled – the wages budget for example is fixed for each store and there is no local flexibility on pay – something which was obviously a cause of great frustration in some of the stores where recruitment, retention and staff quality are on-going major problems. Although the stores cannot function without these routines it is the way in which the rules and routines are implemented that is considered a key ingredient to success. It is management, in particular store managers, who are responsible for how the policies and processes are implemented and their behaviour is therefore critical to a store's performance.

Section managers occupy first line manager position within the store. Spans of control are normally 12 general assistants to each section manager and in a large store there may be about 20 section managers covering different areas of the store. In addition to being responsible for the day-to-day running of their areas section managers take responsibility for a range of people management tasks such as recruitment, training, performance appraisal, disciplinary and grievance issues, and pay enquires. The nature of the job is very demanding – these staff have to work long hours, perform a wide range of tasks and struggle to fill vacancies and absences on the shop floor. As one store manager explained:

> Section managers have to work bloody hard . . . they are more task orientated than the senior team . . . ideally section managers should spend 70–80% of their time managing, but they do not always do this because of the demands of the job.
> Especially if they have gaps. It's one of the more pressurised roles.

This may partly explain why many stores face recruitment and retention difficulties with this position.

We focus on four stores in a single region. All are in market towns with similar socio-economic profiles, in other words demographic, labour market and income patterns in these towns are broadly similar. A total of 43 section managers were interviewed using a structured questionnaire, representing over two-thirds of the section manager population in those stores. Their views were sought on their job, the HR policies practiced, the way their senior managers behaved and more general attitudes towards their work. Some of the results are summarised in Table 2.1.

We would expect to find low levels of variation in terms of exercise of management discretion at store level because Omega is a highly centralised organisation with clear routines and policies. However as Table 2.1 shows there are wide variations in satisfaction with certain HR policies, the controlling dimension of discretion and in the way these managers themselves are managed as well as variations in more general attitudes such as job satisfaction, motivation and commitment. In particular it is clear that Store C is out of line with the others. For example section managers in Store C, in comparison to the other stores, consistently have a poorer perception of the way senior managers carry out their people management roles – or leadership. Only 18 per cent for example of section managers in Store C feel their managers (i.e., the senior managers) are good at responding to suggestions compared to 82 per cent in Store B, 60 per cent in Store D and 27 per cent in Store A.

Table 2.1 Employee satisfaction with aspects of HR policy and practice: Omega – four stores compared. Percentage of respondents who said 'very satisfied' or 'satisfied' (n = 43)

	Store A	Store B	Store C	Store D
(a) *HR policies*	%	%	%	%
Training	46	82	36	90
Career opportunities	64	91	55	70
Pay	46	64	9	60
Appraisal	50	82	64	90
(b) *Controlling*				
Influence over how job is done (% a lot)	64	64	27	50
Job influence	82	82	36	100
Sharing knowledge (% good)	64	82	18	70
(c) *Leadership % good*				
Chance to comment on changes	53	72	18	30
Respond to suggestions	27	82	18	60
Deal with problems	73	82	55	70
Treating employees fairly	64	100	64	70
Provide coaching/guidance (% to a great extent)	46	55	27	40
Respect received from your boss	100	91	64	90
(d) *Outcomes*				
Job satisfaction	64	73	64	80
Motivation (% 'very' & 'fairly' motivated)	55	46	36	40
Commitment (% proud to tell people who I work for)	91	73	46	90

Table 2.2 shows some key operational performance measures for the stores. It is clear that again Store C was the poorest performer in a number of key areas. For example its expenses were 28 per cent higher than the average and its profit contribution was 34 per cent lower. It was particularly poor at managing wastage (shrinkage), which at the time was one of the key indicators used by Omega. In contrast, Store B had expenses which were 2.3 per cent lower than average and profits which were 20 per cent higher.

Table 2.2 Omega Performance Data Year 1 (2000/01). Percentage variation from regional average (20 stores)

	Store A	Store B	Store C	Store D
Availability	-0.1	0.6	-0.8	0.3
Waste/known loss	-5.5	4.7	-11.8	7.1
Shrinkage/unknown loss	5.4	63.5	-59.5	44.6
Operating expenses as % of sales	2.4	2.4	-28.2	-11.7
Waiting to be served	2.4	-6.9	-0.6	-3.3
Payroll costs as % of sales	-4.3	14.8	4.3	0.1
Profit contribution	-13.0	21.4	-33.7	-0.1
Turnover £m	42.6	71.1	48.2	54.8

NB. Data has been corrected to ensure that positive figures reflect better than average performance and negative figures show worse than average performance.

Questions

1. How might the differences between the stores shown in Table 1 be explained?

2. How might the differences in performance between the stores (Table 2) be explained?

3. How does the case study help illustrate the concept of Organisational Process Advantage (OPA) and the link with performance?

References

Kaplan, R. and Norton, D. (1992) 'The balanced scorecard–measures that drive performance', *Harvard Business Review*, Vol.70, No.1 p.71.

HUMAN CAPITAL IN THE SOFTWARE INDUSTRY: The Case of MPC Data[3]

CASE STUDY 2.2

JUANI SWART

This small software house is located on two sites in the southwest of England and originated 16 years ago. It was the brainchild of three software engineers who wanted to focus their commercial work on bespoke software development in embedded systems.

[3]Research for this case was carried out as part of a project sponsored by the Chartered Institute of Personnel and Development.

A conscious decision was made at the outset by the owners to grow their business organically and to value quality of life. As the Managing Director put it: 'The quality of life is the most important thing for us. You have to remember our people are all we have. We don't have products, only people.'

The organisation has managed to maintain a flat structure (only three levels: five directors, senior software engineers and software engineers) through periods of growth. The market focus has also remained on bespoke software development and commercial efforts are directed toward the development of modules, subcomponents and hardware–software interfaces for multi-national clients.

A clear strategy is to steer away from the product route (a current trend in software development) because it is believed that this will have a devastating effect on their culture and staff retention. Their specific suite of software services means that it is difficult to recruit the right skills in the current labour market: this is intensified by universities taking a commercial approach, rather than technical specialist, in their education of software engineers.

This software house is cash rich with no funds owing to venture capitalists. According to the chairman it is due to their financial success that they can afford to be less traditional in their management approach. They are also successful at retaining both employees and clients: only four employees have resigned since the start of the business. Finally, the organisation occupies a dominant position within a niche market, with their main competitors being independent consultants.

Human capital

MPC employ 30 software engineers who specialise in systems software solutions. These employees are fluent in computing languages such as ANSI C and C++, Java, Visual Basic and Delphi (to name but a few). Most of these employees are recruited via their university placements, thereby maintaining strong links with software education and influencing the quality of human capital upwards through the supply chain. Although most employees are software engineers, with only a couple of administrative staff, it would be incorrect to assume homogeneity. This is due to specific specialisms in software solutions. This causes software engineers to specialise in certain areas and almost to 'speak different languages', which then develops centres of expertise.

Organisational and organisational structure and clients

The particular substructures in the wider organisational structure that underpin the HR practices include:

(i)   The mentoring structure, where each senior software engineer has 2–3 protégés whom they 'coach'. None of the protégés report to a mentor within the project structure (see (iii) below). In other words, no employee will be mentored by a senior software engineer who is working with them on a project. All mentors belong to a mentoring committee, which forms part of the second major organisational structure within which HR is practised.
(ii) The committee structure devolves what would be otherwise known as more traditional functions and all employees are members of at least two committees.

(iii) The third 'dynamic' structure, which facilitates HR practices, is the project structure. This structure is fluid with either a software engineer, a senior software engineer or a director managing the project and employees tend to circulate between projects over time.

This software house has a history of maintaining clients over long periods of time with contracts being renewed several times. Its key clients include: Hitachi Microsystems, Psion Dacom, Sony, Varian Oncology systems and Remote Metering Systems. Customer contact is not restricted to one level in the organisation and it is a common occurrence for student software engineers to have continuous contact with a client. However, one particular senior software engineer is responsible for new business development and uses the client knowledge base in the organisation to market new business.

The lengths of contracts vary with both short- and long-term projects running parallel: some contracts are shorter than two man-months while others can exceed ten man-years. Customers include both small and large multi-national organisations and span several markets including telecommunications, retail, instrumentation and consumer electronics.

HUMAN CAPITAL ADVANTAGE and organisational process advantage

Most HR practices are formalised[4] and the core HR roles are divided between several positions in the organisation. The business development director oversees recruitment and selection together with one other senior software engineer. He works closely with the Chief Technical Officer (CTO) who oversees the performance management system, which is regarded central to other formal HR processes (skill enhancement and remuneration). Through involvement in the mentoring committee another senior software engineer suggested and implemented an induction programme, which has been running in this more formalised manner for the last three to four months. The responsibility for skill enhancement rests with mentors. The directors jointly determine pay levels and make decisions about increases based on the recommendations made by the mentors as the outcome of performance appraisal discussions.

Although HR practices are more formalised and the responsibility is split between directors and senior software engineers, the implementation of the HR processes is a lot more informal and the responsibility of these processes rest with mentors and project managers. Through the mentoring system the *mentors*, acting in a line management capacity, are responsible for the implementation of HR processes: focusing on personal and career development via the performance management system. Project managers take a leading developmental role in a technical skill enhancement capacity. A director could be reporting to a software engineer on a project and consequently be trained by a younger and more junior member of staff.

The HR architecture can therefore be presented as the relationship between HR practices (formalised with distributed responsibilities) and HR processes (informal and 'practised' by mentors and project managers). This is reflected in the presentation of the organisational structure (which reflects mentoring responsibility and sharing of cultural knowledge) alongside the project structure (which reflects technical development and houses software (skills) knowledge sharing).

---

[4]The processes of formalisation takes place through the committee structure, where suggestions from directors, senior software engineers and software engineers are published on the intranet, discussed at a formal gathering, and approved by directors at their monthly meeting.

Questions

1. To what extent would you say that MPC data establish a HUMAN CAPITAL ADVANTAGE?

2. Given that MPC is a knowledge intensive organisation, what are the particular challenges that the organisation is faced with regarding the establishment of a HUMAN CAPITAL ADVANTAGE?

3. Identify and describe the various ways in which an Organisational Process Advantage has been created and established.

4. How do the HCA and the OPA work together to facilitate improved knowledge sharing?

5. How would the unique HCA and OPA of MPC Data be transferred to a larger organisation? What are the key lessons that larger organisations could learn from MPC Data in the establishment of HRA?

CASE STUDY 2.3

HRM AND ORGANISATION TURNAROUND AT SELFRIDGES & CO.[5]

SUE HUTCHINSON

Background

The Selfridges story is one where human resource management has played a vital role in delivering high performance, enabling the company to emerge in the late 1990s as an expanding and very successful, up-market retail department store. Formerly part of the Sears Group, Selfridges was widely described as the embodiment of the 'Grace Brothers'[6] having acquired a rather old-fashioned, stuffy image in the 1980s and early 1990s and become, in the words of one senior manager, 'an organisation headed by senior managers with no logistical support, no idea of supply chain relationships, no use of technology and extremely hierarchical'. A process of renewal and growth began in the mid-1990s with the appointment of a visionary chief executive, Vittorio Radice (formally with Habitat) and a new senior management team. Almost three-quarters of senior managers left the organisation (then just a single site store in Oxford Street, London), to be replaced by a younger, predominantly female team. In 1998 Selfridges de-merged from the Sears group and was launched as a public limited company investing £100 million in the Oxford Street site and opening a second store in Trafford Park, Manchester. Further stores subsequently opened in Manchester City centre (2002) and Birmingham (2003).

The vision of the company was 'to become the best and most exciting department store chain in Europe, by meeting the needs of customers in a unique and theatrical

---

[5]Research for this case was carried out as part of a project sponsored by the Chartered Institute of Personnel and Development.
[6]Grace Brothers was the retail department store portrayed in the 1970s television comedy 'Are You Being Served?'.

way whilst maximising operational efficiency' (Mission statement, 1999). Staff, especially staff associates who serve customers, were seen to be central to creating and achieving this ambience and experience. As the Commercial Director explained 'Selfridges see themselves at the upper end of the price market with customers prepared to pay a little bit more so the service must be good – people will be critical to that.' This emphasis on employees was not new to the organisation and could be traced back to the founder of the store, Harry Gordon Selfridge, as this extract from a company document illustrates:

> **The aim of our Education Department is to develop to the utmost the human resource of the business. It aims at being a progressive force which seeks to promote happiness in work and, through happiness true efficiency. For the work of the department rests on the conviction that efficiency is the normal outcome of happiness, rather than an achievement accomplished through a system of instruction or mental gymnastics.** (The Selfridges Education Department, 1920)

What is remarkable about this quote is not only its recognition of the importance of having a contented workforce, but its reference to 'human resources' a term only popularised in the 1980s.

Selfridges re-invented itself as the 'House of Brands', and as part of the transformation process made major changes in almost every aspect of the business including:

- A new approach to leadership and management style which was to be 'aspirational, friendly and accessible';

- Managers would need to take more responsibility for people management (in the past even first-level disciplinary matters were sent to the Personnel/HR Department);

- Integrated IT Systems linking suppliers to Selfridges and improved communication within the company;

- A new team of retail operations managers meeting weekly;

- A new approach to buying with buyers taken off the department floor and no longer reporting to a senior manager in the department;

- Moving to seven-day-a-week trading with longer opening hours;

- New and more accurate performance measures especially in relation to profit per square foot, data on 'foot-fall' and Key Performance Indicators (KPIs). The financial information and data were to be made available down to the lowest level so that economic literacy would improve;

- A different, more partnership-based relationship with concessionaires and their staff.

At the same time the company consciously set out to change the internal brand image of Selfridges among its staff making it identical to, and consistent with the revitalised external image, introducing such values as 'brand champions', and 'brand experts'. The goal was to turn 'values into value' by acting out the values. These values were expressed in a more articulated form under four goals: 'Selfridges should be aspirational, friendly, accessible and bold.' These goals were, in turn, translated into statements so that all stakeholders (employees, customers, shareholders, suppliers and the community) could clearly understand what this meant for them. For example, the value 'everyone is friendly' was translated in to the following

Employee values:	How does this make me want to work here?
Customer values:	How am I encouraged to shop?
Community values:	How does Selfridges reflect the spirit of the city?
Shareholder values:	Why should we invest in the store?
Supplier values:	What makes Selfridges an interesting proposition?

An example of how these questions are to be answered is provided in Table 2.3.

A number of HR initiatives were adopted to facilitate this change in culture. For example culture surveys were undertaken, employee focus groups organised and a new performance appraisal system was introduced. The old Hay job evaluation scheme was abandoned in favour of a broadbanding pay arrangement replacing age and length of service with performance-based progression. A 'mystery shopper' programme was introduced to monitor staff effectiveness based on the acronym SHINE (Smile, Help, Inform, New product push, End the sale). The mystery shopper survey forms part of the monthly key performance indicators (KPIs) for each department which also includes measures on stock control, labour turnover and absence. A new staff forum was created including staff representatives from the union USDAW and National Vocational Qualifications (NVQs) were introduced for sales associates with financial rewards for advancement.

Selfridges, Trafford Park, Manchester

The Trafford Park, Manchester store was the first store to be opened outside London and became a test bed for the development of future stores. Located in the Trafford Centre, a shopping mall 3 miles outside Manchester, Selfridges was the anchor store for the site which houses around 280 stores. Visitors tend to come from a very wide geographic area (the site has good motorway connections), and the centre is perceived more as a leisure complex, providing restaurants and cinemas in addition to the shopping experience. The location however presents difficulties for staff as local transport is very poor with all buses stopping at 8pm.

The store sells an extensive range of branded merchandise in fashion, cosmetics and homeware, in addition to providing specialist services such as hairdressing, a beauty salon, and a personal shopping department. In 1999 the workforce comprised 318 full- and part-time staff employed directly, and 250 full- and part-time staff employed by concessionaires. These staff are employed by concession owners who are responsible for their recruitment, pay, training and development, and discipline. They wear identical name badges to Selfridges' staff and mostly operate to Selfridges' policies and procedures. For example, if Selfridges are having a sale or promotion the concession staff will have an identical event, and they also promote and sell Selfridges account cards. The aim is to have these staff presenting an identical presence to the customer as Selfridges' staff. Concession staff are included in all Selfridges business and social activities and attend daily pre-opening store briefings.

The store opens 364 days a year, 7 days week up from 10am until 9pm most days (which was subsequently extended to 10pm opening on some days). All staff work a range

Table 2.3 Selfridges: an example of the values matrix – Friendly – everyone is welcome

Employee values	Customer values	Community values	Shareholder values	Supplier values
– how does this make me want to work here?	– how am I encouraged to shop?	– how does Selfridges reflect the spirit of the city?	– why should we invest in the store?	– what makes Selfridges an interesting proposition?
Selfridges is a very friendly place to work. I like my boss and my team.	People at Selfridges are always smiling and helpful – they seem to enjoy working there.	Selfridges promote an inclusive spirit.	Their annual reports are inviting and easy to read.	We help each other in the continuous improvement of our relationship.
I know my opinion and contribution is welcomed.	I like to buy and browse in Selfridges – I never feel under pressure but rarely come home empty handed.	It is a microcosm of all the different cultures and communities which make up the city.	Their financial information is transparent and their directors are open to any questions.	Their wide and diverse range of quality products adds value to my product.
I feel welcomed and this makes me welcome others.	Selfridges represents the good things about city living.	Through its managers and staff Selfridges gets involved in community projects.	I feel welcome when I attend shareholders' meetings.	My concession staff are treated well and made to feel welcome.

of shifts with part-timers working as little as one day a week. Nearly 65 per cent of staff work on a part-time basis. Temporary workers, a high proportion of whom are students, are employed to cover peaks in the workload and absences, including holidays. This heavy reliance on concessionary staff, part-timers and to a lesser degree temporary staff undoubtedly presents strong challenges to the store in terms of managing people.

HR policies and procedures in Trafford Park

The HR department initially had a lot of autonomy from head office in terms of developing their own HR policies and procedures. Before the store opened to the public around 650 staff had to be recruited and trained off-site. Initially the need was to recruit staff who had deep product knowledge and were able to create a relationship with the customer. Preference was therefore given to those with retail experience and only a handful of staff transferred from the London store. Many managers, including team leaders, had previously worked for House of Fraser stores in Manchester and as a consequence were initially keen to adopt 'the House of Fraser way' in terms of policies and procedures. The store soon discovered that many of these people did not 'fit' with Selfridges' values and culture and the recruitment process was subsequently changed to focus on employee attitudes and behaviours, rather than experience. Concession staff were responsible for their own recruitment but had to obtain approval from the HR department in the store before they could appoint.

The store is committed to the training and development of all of its employees and in 1999 was awarded Investors in People (IiP) accreditation. The responsibility for training and development lies with line managers, with the HR department acting as a support function. Formal training is provided at the end of the week in the morning and also at the weekend. All new staff (full- and part-timers) undertake a two-day induction programme covering an overview of the company, its mission and values, security, health and safety and store familiarisation.

A great deal of emphasis is placed on communication and each day, for example, there is a 10-minute team talk prior to the store opening which details daily targets, the previous day's performance, and important events for the day (a second team talk session was subsequently added later in the day to ensure coverage of some part-time staff). The mission statement (see earlier) is regularly referred to within the communication process and is on display in all staff areas and covered in the induction programme. Trade unions (USDAW is the main union) are involved in the consultation and communication process through the staff forum (although it is sometimes hard to get enough employee represen- tatives to sit on the forum). Negotiations, however, do not take place over pay which is decided by the employers. Pay rates are average for the area and sales associates are paid an annual salary based on an hourly rate – overtime is normally paid at time and a half the hourly rate. Team leaders receive a bonus based on departmental targets (KPIs). Staff are not allowed to discuss pay and to do so is considered a disciplinary offence. There is also a generous staff discount of 35 per cent for all staff and a good pension scheme.

In 2000 a staff attitude survey was conducted in the store as part of a study looking at the link between people management and performance (Purcell *et al.* 2003). This showed very high levels of organisational commitment among sales associates (including conces- sionary staff) which compared very favourably with commitment levels in the other 11 organisations in the study. When compared with attitudes of retail trade staff nationally (taken from *WERS* 98)[7] the levels were even more impressive. For example:

- 97 per cent were proud to tell people who they worked for (*WERS* 56 per cent)
- 93 per cent were loyal to Selfridges (*WERS* 70 per cent)
- 72 per cent shared the values of the organisation (*WERS* 50 per cent)

There were no major differences between the views of concessionary staff and those of Selfridges' employees and 92 per cent felt the relationship between Selfridges' staff and concessionary staff to be good. These figures suggest that the emphasis on people management was working in terms of delivering positive employee attitudes. Further analysis of the survey findings showed a positive relationship between various HR practices and employee attitudinal outcomes (job satisfaction, commitment and motivation). For example, teamworking, career opportunities, performance appraisal, involvement and communication and line management behaviour showed positive correlations with job satisfaction and/or organisation commitment.

Team leaders

Despite these very positive findings, the store felt improvements could be made to certain aspects of HR policy and practice which had been identified as areas of possible weakness in the survey. This mainly concerned the delivery of people management by team leaders and the performance appraisal system. As a consequence the team leader role was redefined and team leaders were asked to re-apply for their positions through a new selection process which focused on behaviours as well as skill sets, which resulted in some losing their position. Improvements were also made to the performance appraisal process by linking it to succession planning and therefore working more on career opportunities. This ensured that team leaders took greater ownership of the process, and that appraisals actually got done properly. The second attitude survey (conducted in 2001) showed even more impressive results with improved employee attitudes in terms of job satisfaction, commitment and job discretion, as shown in Table 1. These changes coincided with improved employee perceptions of team leaders' behaviour and better employee attitudes towards some HR policies (Table 2). As one sales associate remarked 'we now have a manager that gets appraisals done . . . and we get praise now and little gifts, such as perfume'.

These were significant changes over a relatively short period of time and could be explained by changes to the team leader position and the appraisal scheme since these were the only key changes that took place over this time period. Performance also improved in the store with sales increasing by 23 per cent compared to the previous year, payroll costs down 5 per cent and 'contribution' – the key measure of sales against payroll costs – up 31.7 per cent.

Significantly, senior store managers themselves believed that these improvements (to performance and attitudes) were due to the changes made to the team leader role and continued to focus on this group of managers. In 2002 the role was again re-defined by issuing team leader role guides in order to give greater clarity to the role and more emphasis to the people management aspects. In terms of recruitment and selection, a task formally undertaken by the HR department, team leaders are now required to

[7]*Workplace Employee Relations Survey 1998*, as detailed in Cully *et al.* 1999.

Table 2.4 Employee attitudes (sales associates) in Selfridges

Employee Outcomes	% of Employees Year 1 (2000) (n=40)	% of Employees Year 2 (2001) (n=40)
A lot of influence over the job	35	56
Satisfied with level of job influence	68	73
Satisfied with sense of achievement	68	83
Commitment: 'I feel proud to tell people who I work for' (% agree)	98	97
'I would recommend a friend or relative to work in Selfridges' (% agree)	83	90

Table 2.5 Employee attitudes (sales associates) in Selfridges

Views on Certain HR Policies and Practices	% of Employees Year 1 (2000) (n=40)	% of Employees Year 2 (2001) (n=40)
Managers are good at:		
– Keeping everyone up to date about proposed changes	58	61
– Responding to suggestions from employees	43	59
– Treating employees fairly	58	68
Satisfied with respect from immediate line manager	88	92
Line manager provides coaching and guidance to help improve your performance (% to a great extent or some extent)	58	78
Satisfied with performance appraisal	59	84
Satisfied with career opportunities	70	88

interview applicants, advise on the job evaluation and make the final decision to select. Team leaders also have a 'coaching and counselling' role. Coaching involves regularly observing sales associates, sometimes on a weekly basis, and providing instant feedback (rather than waiting for the formal development review). Counselling is concerned with monitoring absence, sickness, lateness and attitudes on a monthly bias, and conducting disciplinary meetings (team leaders can discipline up to the first level of written warning). In order to prepare them for this new role, all team leaders went through eight days of training in 2002, covering mainly aspects of people management such as discipline, recruitment, and selection, training, coaching and development.

In addition to these people management activities team leaders have other responsibilities. These include:

- Ensuring excellent customer services, including dealing with customer complaints;

- Ensuring effective communication and team working – including communicating on a daily basis with team members, attending weekly management meetings and planning weekly rotas;

- Ensuring excellent standards on the shop floor–for example ensuring that all staff wear badges and adhere to the dress code.

Team leaders are also responsible for key performance indicators which are incorporated into their performance reviews.

Selfridges' effort to improve the performance of team leaders also included addressing how the team leaders themselves were managed. Four areas in particular were focused on: involvement, coaching and guidance, career opportunities and management support. A team leader forum was set up (at their initiative) which meets twice a month to discuss, and try and resolve common issues and problems. Assistant sales managers (ASMs – those who manage the team leaders) have taken on the role of coaching and developing team leaders through both formal and informal means. On the formal side, for example, development reviews are conducted twice yearly which focus on monitoring team progress against performance indicators. In addition, weekly formal meetings are held with team leaders to assess their training needs. On a more informal basis the ASMs do weekly floor walks with the team leaders to assess sales and performance issues.

The whole process of re-defining the role of team leaders, particularly in terms of giving them more responsibility for people management activities has been acclaimed a success by the store. As one senior manager rather bluntly explained, 'forcing the team leaders to be more disciplined, more planned and forcing them to be less reactive . . . partly because the HR team are no longer available on site to wipe their back sides!'

Questions

1. What are the main sources of HUMAN CAPITAL ADVANTAGE (HCA) demonstrated in the case study?

2. Explain how the case study illustrates the concept of Organisational Process Advantage (OPA).

3. How and why did the company try to influence team leaders' behaviour?

4. Explain how HCA and OPA were combined together to improve organisational performance.

5. What wider lessons do you draw from this case concerning the links between people management and performance, especially the importance of changes over time?

References

Cully, M., Woodland, S., O'Reilly, A. and Dix, G. (1999) *Britain at Work. As Depicted by the 1998 Workplace Employee Relations Survey*, London: Routledge.

Purcell, J. Kinnie, N. Hutchinson, S. Rayton, B. and Swart, J. (2003) *Understanding the People and Performance Link: Unlocking the Black Box*, London: Chartered Institute of Personnel and Development.

References

Appelbaum, E., Bailey, T. and Berg, P. (2000) *Manufacturing Advantage: Why High-Performance Systems Pay Off*, Ithaca, NY: ILR Press.

Armstrong, P. and Goodman, J. (1979) 'Management and supervisory custom and practice', *Industrial Relations Journal,* Vol.10, No.3, pp.12–24.

Arthur, J. (1994) 'Effects of human resource systems on manufacturing performance and turnover', *Academy of Management Journal,* Vol.37, No.3, pp.670–87.

Atkinson, J. (1984) 'Manpower strategies for flexible organisations', *Personnel Management,* August 28–31.

Baird, L. and Meshoulam, I. (1988). 'Managing two fits of strategic human resource management', *Academy of Management Review* 13(1), pp.116–28.

Barney, J. (1986) 'Organizational culture: Can it be a source of competitive advantage?', *Academy of Management Review,* Vol.11, No.3, pp.56–65.

Barney, J. (1991) 'Firm resources and sustained competitive advantage', *Journal of Management,* Vol.17, No.1, pp.99–120.

Barney, J. and Wright, P. (1998) 'On becoming a strategic partner: the role of human resources in gaining competitive advantage', *Human Resource Management,* Vol.37, No.1, pp.31–46.

Baron, J. and Kreps, D. (1999) 'Consistent human resource practices', *California Management Review,* Vol.41, No.3, pp.29–53.

Bartel, A. P. (2000) 'Human resource management and performance in the service sector: the case of bank branches', *NBER Working Paper Series,* Cambridge, MA: National Bureau of Economic Research.

Batt, R. and Moynihan, L. (2004) 'The viability of alternative call centre models', in S. Deery and N. Kinnie (eds) *Call Centres and Human Resource Management,* Basingstoke: Palgrave.

Beaumont, P.B., Hunter, L.C. and Sinclair, D. (1996) 'Customer–supplier relations and the diffusion of employee relations change', *Employee Relations,* Vol.18, No.1, pp.9–19.

Becker, B. and Gerhart, B. (1996) 'The impact of human resource management on organizational performance: progress and practice', *Academy of Management Journal,* Vol.39, No.4, pp.779–801.

Beer, M., Spector, B., Lawrence, P., Quinn Mills, D. and Walton, R. (1985) *Human Resource Management: A General Manager's Perspective,* New York: Free Press.

Berg, P. (1999) 'The effects of high performance work practices on job satisfaction in the United States Steel Industry', *Relations Industrielles,* Vol.54, No.1, pp.111–34.

Berg, P., Appelbaum, E., Bailey, T. and Kalleberg, A. (1996) 'The performance effects of modular production in the apparel industry', *Industrial Relations,* Vol.35, No.3, pp.356–73.

Boselie, P., Paauwe, J. and Jansen, P. (2000) 'Human resource management and performance lessons from the Netherlands', *International Journal of Human Resource Management,* Vol.12, No.7, pp.1107–25.

Boxall, P. (1992) 'Strategic human resource management: beginnings of a new theoretical sophistication?', *Human Resource Management Journal,* Vol.2, No.3, pp.60–79.

Boxall, P. (1994) 'Placing HR strategy at the heart of business success', *Personnel Management,* Vol.26, No.7, pp.32–5.

Boxall, P. (1995) 'Building the theory of comparative HRM', *Human Resource Management Journal,* Vol.5, No.5, pp.5–17.

Boxall, P. (1996) 'The strategic HRM debate and the resource-based view of the firm', *Human Resource Management Journal,* Vol.6, No.3, pp.59–75.

Boxall, P. (1998) 'Achieving competitive advantage through human resource strategy: towards a theory of industry dynamics', *Human Resource Management Review,* Vol.8, No.3, pp.265–88.

Boxall, P. (1999) 'Human resource strategy and industry-based competition: a conceptual framework and agenda for theoretical development', in P. Wright, L. Dyer, J. Boudreau and G. Milkovich (eds) *Research in Personnel and Human Resource Management (Supplement 4: Strategic Human Resources Management in the Twenty-First Century)*, Stamford, CT and London: JAI Press.

Boxall, P. and Purcell, J. (2000) 'Strategic human resource management: where have we come from and where should we be going?', *International Journal of Management Reviews,* Vol.2, No.2, pp.183–203.

*Boxall, P. and Purcell, J. (2003) *Strategy and Human Resource Management,* Basingstoke: Palgrave MacMillan.

Boxall, P. and Steeneveld, M. (1999) 'Human resource strategy and competitive advantage: a longitudinal study of engineering consultancies', *Journal of Management Studies,* Vol.36, No.4, pp.443–63.

Brown, W. (1972) 'A consideration of custom and practice', *British Journal of Industrial Relations,* Vol.10, No.1, pp.42–61.

Brown, W. (1973) *Piecework Bargaining,* Oxford: Heinemann.

Child, J. (1997) 'Strategic choice in the analysis of action, structure, organizations and environment: retrospect and prospect', *Organization Studies,* Vol.18, No.1, pp.43–76.

Child, J. and Partridge, B. (1982) *Lost Managers,* Cambridge: Cambridge University Press.

Cully, M., Woodland, S., O'Reilly, A. and Dix, G. (1999) *Britain at Work: as Depicted by the 1998 Workplace Employee Relations Survey,* London: Routledge.

Delaney, J.T. and Godard, J. (2001) 'An industrial relations perspective on the high performance paradigm', *Human Resource Management Review,* Vol.11, pp.395–429.

Delery, J. (1998) 'Issues of fit in strategic human resource management: implications for research', *Human Resource Management Review,* Vol.8, No.5, pp.289–309.

Delery, J. and Doty, H. (1996) 'Modes of theorising in strategic human resource management: tests of universalistic, contingency and configurational performance predictions', *Academy of Management Journal,* Vol.39, No.4, pp.802–35.

Dyer, L. and Reeves, T. (1995) 'Human resource strategies and firm performance: what do we know and where do we need to go?', *International Journal of Human Resource Management,* Vol.6, No.3, pp.656–70.

Dyer, L. and Shafer, R. (1999) 'Creating organizational agility: implications for strategic human resource management', in P. Wright, L. Dyer, J. Boudreau and G. Milkovich (eds) *Research in Personnel and Human Resource Management (Supplement 4: Strategic Human Resources Management in the Twenty-First Century)*, Stamford, CT and London: JAI Press.

Fombrun, C., Tichy, N. and Devanna, M. (eds) (1984) *Strategic Human Resource Management,* New York: Wiley.

Fox, A. (1974) *Beyond Contract: Work, Power and Trust Relations,* London: Faber.

Gerhart, B. (1999) 'Human resource management and firm performance: measurement issues and their effect on casual and policy inferences', in P. Wright, L. Dyer, J. Boudreau and G. Milkovich (eds) *Research in Personnel and Human Resource Management (Supplement 4: Strategic Human Resources Management in the Twenty-First Century)*, Stamford, CT and London: JAI Press.

Gittleman, M., Horrigan, M. and Joyce, M. (1998) '"Flexible" workplace practices: evidence from a nationally representative survey', *Industrial and Labor Relations Review,* Vol.52, No.1, pp.99–115.

Golding, N. (2004) 'Strategic Human Resource Management' in I. Beardwell, L. Holden and T. Claydon, (eds) *Human Resource Management,* Harlow: Pearson.

Goshall, S. and Napahiet, J. (1998) 'Social capital, intellectual capital and the organizational advantage', *Academy of Management Review,* Vol.23, No.2, pp.242–66.

Gratton, L., Hope-Hailey, V., Stiles, P. and Truss, C. (1999a) 'Linking individual performance to business strategy: the people process model', *Human Resource Management,* Vol.38, No.1, pp.17–31.

Gratton, L., Hope-Hailey, V., Stiles, P. and Truss, C. (1999b) *Strategic Human Resource Management: Corporate Rhetoric and Human Reality,* Oxford: Oxford University Press.

Guest, D. (1987) 'Human resource management and industrial relations', *Journal of Management Studies,* Vol.24, No.5, pp.503–21.

Guest, D. (1995) 'Human resource management, trade unions and industrial relations', in J. Storey (ed.) *Human Resource Management: A Critical Text,* London: Routledge.

Guest, D. (1997) 'Human resource management and performance: a review and research agenda', *International Journal of Human Resource Management,* Vol.8, No.3, pp.263–76.

Guest, D. (1999) 'Human resource management and performance: the workers' verdict', *Human Resource Management Journal,* Vol.9, No.3, pp.5–25.

Guest, D. and Hoque, K. (1994) 'The good, the bad and the ugly: employment relations in new non-union workplaces', *Human Resource Management Journal,* Vol.5, No.1, pp.1–14.

*Guest D., Michie, J., Conway, N. and Sheehan, M. (2003) 'Human resource management and corporate performance in the UK', *British Journal of Industrial Relations,* Vol.41, No.2, pp.291–314.

Guest, D. Michie, J., Sheehan, M. and Conway, N. (2000) *Effective People Management: Initial Findings of the Future of Work Study,* London: Chartered Institute of Personnel and Development.

Hall, L. and Torrington, D. (1998) 'Letting go or holding on: the devolution of operational personnel activities', *Human Resource Management Journal,* Vol.8, No.1, pp.41–55.

Hamel, G. and Prahalad, C. (1994) *Competing for the Future,* Boston, MA: Harvard Business School Press.

Hendry, C. and Pettigrew, A. (1992) 'Strategic choice in the development of human resource management', *British Journal of Management,* Vol.3, No.1, pp.37–56.

Huselid, M. (1995) 'The impact of human resource management practices on turnover, productivity and corporate financial performance', *Academy of Management Journal,* Vol.38, No.3, pp.635–72.

Hutchinson, S., Kinnie, N., Purcell, J., Collinson, M., Scarbrough, H. and Terry, M. (1998) *Getting Fit, Staying Fit: Developing Lean and Responsive Organisations,* London: Chartered Institute of Personnel and Development.

Hutchinson, S., Kinnie, N., Purcell, J., Rees, C., Scarbrough, H. and Terry, M. (1996) 'The people management implications of leaner ways of working', *Issues in People Management No.15,* London: Institute of Personnel and Development.

Hutchinson, S. and Purcell, J. (2003) *Bringing Policies to Life,* London: Chartered Institute of Personnel and Development.

Hutchinson, S. and Wood, S. (1995) *Personnel and the Line: Developing the New Relationship: The UK Experience,* London: Institute of Personnel and Development.

Ichniowski, C., Shaw, K. and Prennush, G. (1995) 'The impact of human resource management practices on productivity', Working Paper 5333, Cambridge, MA: National Bureau of Economic Research.

Ichniowski, C., Kochan, T., Levine, D., Olson, C. and Strauss, G. (1996) 'What works at work: overview and assessment', *Industrial Relations,* Vol.35, No.3, pp.299–333.

Jackson, S. and Schuler, R. (1995) 'Understanding human resource management in the context of organizations and their environments', *Annual Review of Psychology,* Vol.46, pp.237–64.

Kinnie, N. and Parsons, J. (2004) 'Managing client, employee and customer relations: constrained strategic choice in the management of human resources in a commercial call centre', in S. Deery and N. Kinnie (eds) *Call Centres and Human Resource Management,* Basingstoke: Palgrave.

Kinnie, N., Hutchinson, S., Purcell, J., Rayton, B. and Swart, J. (2005, forthcoming) 'One size does not fit all: employee satisfaction with HR practices and the link with organisational commitment: a disaggregated analysis', *Human Resources Management Journal.*

Kinnie, N., Purcell, J. and Hutchinson, S. (2000) 'Human resource management in telephone call centres', in K. Purcell (ed.) *Changing Boundaries,* Bristol: Bristol Academic Press.

Kochan, T. and Barocci, T. (1985) *Human Resource Management and Industrial Relations,* New York: Basic Books.

Larsen, H.H. and Brewster, C. (2003) 'Line management responsibility for HRM: what is happening in Europe?', *Employee Relations,* Vol.25, No.3, pp.228–44.

Legge, K. (1978) *Power, Innovation, and Problem-solving in Personnel Management,* London: McGraw-Hill.

Legge, K. (1995) *Human Resource Management: Rhetorics and Realities,* Basingstoke: Macmillan.

Legge, K. (2001) 'Silver bullet or spent round? Assessing the meaning of the High Performance Commitment Management/Performance Relationship', in J. Storey (ed.) *Human Resource Management: A Critical Text* (2nd edn), London: Thompson Publishing.

Leonard, D. (1992). 'Core capabilities and core rigidities: a paradox in managing new product development', *Strategic Management Journal,* Vol.13, pp.111–125.

Leonard, D. (1998). *Wellsprings of Knowledge: Building and Sustaining the Sources of Innovation.* Boston, MA: Harvard Business School Press.

Lepak, D. and Snell, S. (1999) 'The strategic management of human capital: determinants and implications of different relationships', *Academy of Management Review,* Vol.24, No.1, pp.1–18.

Lowe, J., Delbridge, R. and Oliver, N. (1997) 'High-performance manufacturing: evidence from the automotive components industry', *Organization Studies,* Vol.18, No.5, pp.783–98.

MacDuffie, J.P. (1995) 'Human resource bundles and manufacturing performance: organizational logic and flexible production systems in the world auto industry', *Industrial and Labor Relations Review,* Vol.48, No.2, pp.197–221.

MacDuffie, J.P. and Pil, F.T. (1997) 'Changes in auto industry employment practices: an international overview', in T. A. Kochan, R. D. Lansbury and J. P. MacDuffie (eds) *After Lean Production: Evolving Employment Practices in the World Auto Industry,* Ithaca, NY: ILR Press.

Marchington, M. (2001) 'Employee involvement at work', in J. Storey (ed.) *Human Resource Management: A Critical Text* (2nd edn), London: Thompson.

*Marchington, M. and Grugulis, I. (2000) '"Best practice" human resource management: perfect opportunity or dangerous illusion?', *International Journal of Human Resource Management,* Vol.11, No.6, pp.1104–24.

Marchington, M. and Wilkinson, A. (2002) *People Management and Development,* London: Chartered Institute of Personnel and Development.

McGovern, P., Gratton, L., Hope-Hailey, V., Stiles, P. and Truss, C. (1997) 'Human resource management on the line?', *Human Resource Management Journal,* Vol.7, No.4, pp.12–29.

Miles, R. and Snow, C. (1978) *Organizational Strategy, Structure and Process,* New York: McGraw-Hill.

Miles, R. and Snow, C. (1984) 'Designing strategic human resources systems', *Organizational Dynamics,* Vol.13, No.1, pp.36–52.

Miles, R. and Snow, C. (1999) 'The new network firm: a spherical structure built on human investment philosophy', in R. Schuler, and S. Jackson (eds) *Strategic Human Resource Management,* Oxford: Blackwell.

Miller, D. and Shamsie, J. (1992) 'The resource-based view of the firm in two environments: the Hollywood film studios from 1936 to 1965', *Academy of Management Journal,* Vol.39, No.3, pp.519–43.

Millward, N., Bryson, A. and Forth, J. (2000) *All Change at Work: British Employment Relations 1980–1998 as portrayed by the Workplace Industrial Relations Survey Series,* London: Routledge.

Mueller, F. (1996) 'Human resources as strategic assets; an evolutionary resource-based theory', *Journal of Management Studies,* Vol.33, No.6, pp.757–85.

Osterman, P. (1987) 'Choice of employment systems in internal labor markets', *Industrial Relations,* Vol.26, No.1, pp.46–67.

Osterman, P. (1994) 'How common is workplace transformation and who adopts it?', *Industrial and Labor Relations Review,* Vol.47, No.2, pp.173–88.

Osterman, P. (2000) 'Work reorganization in an era of restructuring: trends in diffusion and effects on employee welfare', *Industrial and Labor Relations Review*, Vol.53, No.2, pp.179–96.

Patterson, M., West, M., Lawthom, R. and Nickell, S. (1997) 'Impact of people management practices on business performance', *Issues in People Management No.22*, London: Institute of Personnel and Development.

Peters, T. and Waterman, R.H. (1982) *In Search of Excellence: Lessons from America's Best-Run Companies*, New York: Harper & Row.

Pfeffer, J. (1994) *Competitive Advantage Through People*, Boston, MA: Harvard Business School Press.

*Pfeffer, J. (1998) *The Human Equation: Building Profits by Putting People First*, Boston, MA: Harvard Business School Press.

Pfeffer, J. and Salancik, G.R. (1978) *The External Control of Organizations: a Resource Dependence Perspective*, New York: Harper & Row.

Pil, F.K. and MacDuffie, J.P. (1996) 'The adoption of high involvement work practices', *Industrial Relations*, Vol.35, No.3, pp.423–55.

Porter, M. (1980) *Competitive Strategy*, New York: Free Press.

Prahalad, C. and Hamel, G. (1990) 'The core competence of the corporation', *Harvard Business Review*, May–June, Vol.68, No.3, pp.79–91.

*Purcell, J. (1999) 'The search for "best practice" and "best fit": chimera or cul-de-sac?', *Human Resource Management Journal*, Vol.9, No.3, pp.26–41.

Purcell, J. (2004) 'The HRM-Performance Link: why, how and when does people management impact on organisational performance?', John Lovett Memorial Lecture, University of Limerick (available from the author).

Purcell, J., Kinnie, N., Hutchinson, S., Rayton, B. and Swart, J. (2003) *Understanding the People and Performance Link: Unlocking the Black Box*, London: Chartered Institute of Personnel and Development.

Ramsay, H., Scholarios, D. and Harley, B. (2000) 'Employees and high-performance work systems: testing inside the black box', *British Journal of Industrial Relations*, Vol.38, No.4, pp.501–31.

Renwick, D. (2000) 'HR-line work relations: a review, pilot case and research agenda', *Journal of European Industrial Training*, Vol.24, Nos2–4, pp.241–53.

Richardson, R. and Thompson, M (1999) 'The impact of people management practices on business performance: a literature review', *Issues in People Management*, London: Chartered Institute of Personnel and Development.

Schuler, R. (1989) 'Strategic human resource management and industrial relations', *Human Relations*, Vol.42, No.2, pp.157–84.

Schuler, R. (1996) 'Market-focussed management: human resource management implications', *Journal of Market-Focussed Management*, Vol.1, pp.13–29.

Schuler, R. and Jackson, S. (1987) 'Linking competitive strategies and human resource management practices', *Academy of Management Executive*, Vol.1, No.3, pp.207–19.

Sinclair, D., Hunter, L. and Beaumont, P.B. (1996) 'Models of customer–supplier relations', *Journal of General Management*, Vol.22, No.2, pp.56–75.

Snell, S., Youndt, M. and Wright, P. (1996) 'Establishing a framework for research in strategic human resource management: merging resource theory and organizational learning', *Research in Personnel and Human Resources Management*, Vol.14, pp.61–90.

Snell, S., Lepak, D. and Youndt, M. (1999) 'Managing the architecture of intellectual capital: implications for human resource management', in P. Wright, L. Dyer, J. Boudreau and G. Milkovich (eds) *Research in Personnel and Human Resources Management: Strategic Human Resource Management in the Twenty-First Century*, Stanford, CA and London: JAI Press.

Swart, J. and Kinnie, N. (2001) 'Human resource advantage within a distributed knowledge system: a study of growing knowledge intensive firms', paper presented at ESRC Seminar: 'The Changing Nature of skills and knowledge'. Manchester School of Management, September 2001 (available from the authors).

Swart, J. Kinnie, N. and Purcell, J. (2003a) *People and Performance in Knowledge Intensive Firms*, London: Chartered Institute of Personnel and Development.

Swart, J. and Kinnie, N. (2003b) 'Knowledge intensive firms: the influence of the client on HR systems', *Human Resource Management Journal*, Vol.13, No.3, pp.37–55.

Swart, J. and Kinnie, N. (2004) *Managing the Careers of Knowledge Workers*, London: Chartered Institute of Personnel and Development.

Terry, M. (1977) 'The inevitable growth of informality', *British Journal of Industrial Relations*, Vol.15, No.1, pp.76–90.

Thompson, M. (2000) *Final Report: the Bottom Line Benefits of Strategic Human Resource Management, The UK Aerospace People Management Audit*, London: Society of British Aerospace Companies.

Thurley, K. and Wirdenius, H. (1973) *Approaches to Supervisory Development*, London: Institute of Personnel Management.

Truss, C. (2001) 'Complexities and controversies in linking HRM with organizational outcomes', *Journal of Management Studies*, Vol.38, No.8, pp.1121–49.

Ulrich, D. (1998) *Human Resource Champions*, Boston, MA: Harvard Business School Press.

Ulrich, D. (1997) 'Measuring human resources: an overview of practice and a prescription for results', *Human Resource Management*, Vol.36, No.3, pp.303–20.

Wood, S. (1996) 'High commitment management and payment systems', *Journal of Management Studies*, Vol.33, No.1, pp.53–77.

*Wood, S. (1999) 'Human resource management and performance', *International Journal of Management Reviews*, Vol.1, No.4, pp.367–413.

Wood, S. and Albanese, P. (1995) 'Can we speak of high commitment management on the shop floor?', *Journal of Management Studies*, Vol.32, No.2, pp.215–47.

Wood, S. and Wall, T. (2004) 'A critical analysis of quantitative studies of HRM and performance', Human Resource Management Research, 1st Annual Conference, University of Bath, 5–6 April (available from the authors).

Wright, P, and Gardener, T.M. (2000) 'Theoretical and empirical challenges in studying the HR practice–firm performance relationship', paper presented at the Strategic Human Resource Management Workshop, European Institute for Advanced Studies in Management, INSEAD, March (available from the Center for Advanced Human Resource Studies Working Paper Series No.00-04, Cornell University).

Wright, P. and Snell, S. (1998) 'Toward a unifying framework for exploring fit and flexibility in strategic human resource management', *Academy of Management Review*, Vol.23, No.4, pp.756–72.

Wright, P.M., Gardener, T.M. and Moynihan, L.M. (2003) 'The impact of HR practices on the performance of business units', *Human Resource Management Journal*, Vol.13, No.3, pp.21–36.

Wright, P., McCormick, B., Sherman, W. and McMahan, G. (1999) 'The role of human resource practices in petrochemical refinery performance', *International Journal of Human Resource Management*, Vol.10, No.4, pp.551–71.

Wright, P., McMahan, G. and McWilliams, A. (1994). 'Human resources and sustained competitive advantage: a resource-based perspective', *International Journal of Human Resource Management*, Vol.5, No.2, pp.301–26.

Youndt, M., Snell, S., Dean, J. and Lepak, D. (1996) 'Human resource management, manufacturing strategy, and firm performance', *Academy of Management Journal*, Vol.39, No.4, pp.836–66.

* Useful reading

Chapter 3

SELECTION AND ASSESSMENT

Sue Newell

Introduction: selection from a decision-making perspective

A given topic can always be viewed from a number of different perspectives. Traditionally, selection and assessment have been viewed from a psychometric perspective. They are treated as representing a measurement problem. There are clearly individual differences (both physical and psychological), which mean that certain people will be more suited to some jobs than others. From a psychometric perspective then, selection and assessment are concerned with finding methods to measure these individual differences more accurately so that individuals and jobs can be appropriately matched.

In this chapter, while not ignoring this psychometric tradition, we will adopt a rather different perspective, which can help us to explore some issues in selection and assessment that may be underemphasised by the traditional perspective. We will view selection and assessment from a decision-making perspective (Brunsson 1982, 1989), where a decision is a conscious choice between at least two alternative actions. We will also consider decisions that are made in respect of both selection and development, both of which involve making decisions based on the assessment of individuals. Thus, in terms of selection, a representative (or group of representatives) of the recruiting organisation chooses between a number of candidates in order to select the individual who best fits the requirements of a particular job for which there is a vacancy. These decisions are made on the basis of some kind of assessment of the relative suitability of a group of potential individuals who might fill the vacancy.

While selection involves decisions about who will best fit a particular job vacancy, the same or similar processes of assessment are also increasingly used within organisations to make developmental decisions related to the promotion potential of internal employees. Thus, it is recognised that it is necessary to prepare current employees for taking on more senior roles within the organisation, so that leadership crises are averted. However, it is also recognised that not all existing employees will be suitable for these more senior roles. Assessment methods are therefore used to identify the developmental potential of existing employees. The result is that choices are made about who will be groomed and developed and for which senior jobs.

The emphasis in the selection literature has typically been on the decision made by the recruiting organisation. However, it is also the case that candidates are making decisions – to apply (or not) for a particular job vacancy, to turn up (or not) to an interview, or to take (or decline) an offered job. In terms of assessment for developmental purposes there has always been more recognition that the candidate is making decisions as well as the assessors. Indeed, with the increasing emphasis on self-direction, assessment exercises are used as much to provide the individual with evidence to make career path choices as they are for the organisation to make promotion decisions. In this chapter we will consider the selection and assessment decision-making processes from the perspective of both the organisation and the candidates.

The decision-making perspective has been dominated by normative research, which prescribes how decisions should be made (Brunsson 1982, 1989). This assumes that the desire is to make decisions as 'rational' as possible. The prescription for making decisions rational is to follow a sequence of specified steps: understand the situation and identify the problem(s); generate potential solutions to the problem(s); systematically evaluate each solution; select the best solution; monitor and evaluate the results; identify the problem(s) etc. This rational, decision-making model has also implicitly underpinned selection and assessment research. Thus, in selection or development decisions, the objective has been to make this decision as objective and rational as possible in order to select the 'right' or 'best' person for the job. It is possible therefore to look at the steps prescribed in the rational, decision-making process and apply them to the literature on selection and assessment. Here we critically apply this rational model to the selection and assessment decision-making processes. In so doing, we also identify the limitations of this rational model and suggest an alternative way of viewing these processes that may bear more relation to what actually happens in practice.

This chapter does not deal with recruitment and election in general.[1] Recruitment and selection involves making predictions about future behaviour so that decisions can be made about who will be most suitable for a particular job. It can be viewed as a process by which the organisation tries accurately to match the individual to the job and can be compared to completing a jigsaw puzzle. Recruitment and selection is a process of selecting the correct jigsaw piece (the 'right' individual) from the incorrect pieces (the 'wrong' individuals) to fit into a particular hole in a jigsaw puzzle (Newell and Shackleton 2001).

Selection and assessment as a rational decision-making process

Each of the steps in the rational decision-making model can be applied to the steps in selection and assessment.

UNDERSTAND THE SITUATION AND IDENTIFY THE PROBLEM(S): ORGANISATIONAL REVIEW AND JOB ANALYSIS

The first step typically identified in the selection process is to undertake a review of the situation to determine that a recruitment need actually exists. Even if an individual has left a job, this should not automatically mean that a job vacancy is presumed. It is necessary to establish that there are not alternative and more effective ways of filling the gap left by the departing employee. For example, this may be a chance for reassigning these tasks to other employees and in so doing provide opportunities for employee development. Alternatively,

---

[1]Several different recruitment methods can be used (internal and external) including advertising in newspapers and trade journals, placing notices in job centres, employing agents, attending careers fairs and posting job advertisements on the internet. Survey evidence shows, however, that the most significant single recruitment method is word of mouth. Decisions about which method or combination of methods to use have to be based on the budget available, the number of applicants considered necessary and the current size of the labour market concerned (Taylor 2002, p.209). The documentation used in the recruitment exercise has a wider impact in that it conveys images of the organisation, its products and its overall philosophy. Legal issues have to be borne in mind when recruiting, particularly in the design and wording of adverts and in on-line channels (Taylor 2002). Furthermore, if the recruitment process generates insufficient applications, or too may unsuitable ones, it will prove expensive (Marchington and Wilkinson 2005). However, the purpose of this chapter is not to dwell on the subject of recruitment. This is well covered in other texts – e.g., Torrington *et al.* 2002; Beardwell *et al.*; Marchington and Wilkinson 2005 – and there is extensive guidance provided by ACAS on their website and in their guidebooks.

the tasks may be automated so that human resources are no longer required. Prior to developmental assessment, the rational model would prescribe succession planning be undertaken to identify the predicted gaps at senior levels for which people need to be groomed.

Once the situation has been reviewed to ensure that a job vacancy or succession gap actually exists, the next step is to conduct a thorough analysis of the particular job. Job analysis is used to gather information about a job in order to determine the key tasks and role requirements and so specify the kind of person most likely to be successful in that job. A problem with traditional job analysis is that it collects information about the job as it currently exists on the assumption that it will be similar in the future (Schneider and Konz 1989). Unfortunately, given the dynamic environment in which organisations operate, this is increasingly an unwarranted assumption. As a result, there is a need to develop new methods of job analysis which can identify the key tasks and the associated knowledge, skills and abilities (KSAs) that are required for jobs that are changing (Hough and Oswald 2000). Unfortunately, this aspect of the selection process has not been adequately scrutinised by scholars, so that job analysis techniques that are used are often problematic (Robertson and Smith 2001). One of the few examples to date of collecting data that is more future-oriented is provided by Landis *et al.* (1998). They begin with a traditional job analysis, collecting relevant information about the target jobs as they currently exist and then use panel discussion groups to develop a comprehensive list of tasks and KSAs. Then subject-matter expert groups are involved to identify how these tasks and KSAs are likely to change in the future.

The traditional person specification has given way to a focus on competencies (Boam and Sparrow 1992). Competencies are behavioural indicators that have been identified as relevant to a particular context. Roberts (1997, p.6) defines competence as 'all work-related personal attributes, knowledge, experience and skills and values that a person draws on to perform their work well'. There are a number of different approaches to identifying competencies, but they have a common focus on specifying 'outputs'. These are 'couched in terms of what an individual achieves and produces from a situation by managing it effectively' (Sparrow and Bognanno 1993, p.51). For example, Alldredge and Nilan (2000) describe the global leadership competency framework that was developed and used by 3M for assessment, development and succession.

Example: **The competencies needed for a diversity consultant**

Diversity consultants should:

- Understand the concept of diversity as it impacts four inter-related layers of the organization – individual, group and work team, interpersonal and organisational.
- Understand the client's business.
- Be able to connect diversity back to work processes and work design.
- Understand what drives their own personal biases and biases regarding individual differences.
- Understand systemic issues of discrimination, and apply an expansive definition of diversity.
- Discern the differences in the concepts of equal opportunity and affirmative action and diversity and inclusion.
- Understand both people and business issues and be prepared to confront difficult issues.
- Demonstrate constant renewal of technical knowledge and skills in the diversity area.

Source: Frase-Blunt 2004

The advantage of using a competency framework is that the focus is on actual behaviour – what a person can do or needs to be able to do – and there is no need to make inferences about personal qualities that might underpin this. Theoretically, this should allow for the fact that different individuals can achieve the same output, but using a rather different approach because of different knowledge, skills and abilities. Unfortunately, while this is true in theory, in practice competency approaches are often used in ways which specify process criteria as well as output or task criteria. In other words, the person is assessed not simply in terms of whether they successfully completed the task but also in terms of dimensions that are 'normally' expected to underpin successful task completion. This means there is a presumption of 'the right way' to complete a task, and the individual will be assessed against this 'right way', as well as against the task output itself.

Nevertheless, whether a job analysis (traditional or future-oriented) or competency analysis is undertaken, the goal is to describe the particular job, identify the task requirements and specify the kind of person most likely to fulfill these requirements.

GATHER INFORMATION AND MATERIALS TO HELP SOLVE THE PROBLEM: IDENTIFY APPROPRIATE ASSESSMENT METHODS

Once the job analysis has been completed, the next step is to identify methods that will allow individuals to be assessed and compared on the various KSAs or competencies identified as crucial for job success. Much effort has been devoted to this step from the psychometric perspective. The reason for this is that traditional assessment methods – unstructured interviews and references – have been shown to be very poor at measuring these important individual differences. The development of newer methods of assessment is considered in more detail below.

GENERATE POTENTIAL SOLUTIONS TO THE PROBLEM: RECRUITMENT

Once this initial phase has been completed and there is a clear idea about the kind of person wanted and the methods to be used to assess individuals, the next step is to attract a pool of applicants from which the 'right' person can be chosen. Where assessment is used for developmental purposes, recruitment will be internal and typically based on information gathered during appraisals as to which individuals are 'ready' and have the potential to be developed. Where an organisation is selecting for a particular job vacancy, recruitment can be internal or external. Internal recruitment, often involving promotion, may often be the better option since this reduces information uncertainty as candidates can be directly observed in the workplace over an extended period; the internal recruit will also already have firm-specific knowledge (Staffsud 2003). Moreover, external recruitment is expensive (Merrick 1997) and often does not produce the quality of candidates required (Fish and Mackim 2004). Nevertheless, companies will often need to recruit externally.

Matthews and Redman (1998) found that, despite such a large amount being spent on recruitment advertising, recruiters were not making the most effective use of it, because generally the advertisements were not well tailored to managerial requirements. In particular, they argue that recruitment advertisements need to be more specifically targeted to the group they are trying to attract. They advocate that this targeting should be done on the basis of market research to identify what the potential applicant is looking for in a recruitment advertisement. With regard to the content of advertisements they suggest that many do not contain enough information to attract the initial interest, especially of the casual job seeker.

For example, they found that one in five advertisements gave no details of salary level and job location, which have been shown to be key to gaining attention. Once attracted, potential applicants then seek further information from the advertisement to decide whether to apply. However, 59 per cent of the advertisements gave no information on minimum qualifications, which is useful to help applicants self-screen. At the same time, 71 per cent did give information on personal attributes required, despite this being condemned by prescriptive models of 'good' adverts (Redmond 1989).

Increasingly, companies are using the internet for advertising job vacancy information. This has the advantage of reaching a global audience, at least of potential recruits with access to this technology. Similarly, applicants are using the internet to submit their CVs, thus potentially speeding up the process of applying. A key advantage of such electronic applications is that CVs can be coded (e.g., in terms of the applicants' competencies) and stored electronically so that they can be easily searched, both for current job vacancies and for jobs in the future. This search can be done on a global basis provided that a company has a shared electronic database for storing and retrieving applicant information. Beyond recruitment, firms are also using the internet for actual selection, for example using computer-based testing that can be done virtually (Anderson 2003). For example, Bingham *et al.* (2002) describe how the Washington State Department of Personnel has introduced online application submissions and instant online screening and testing processes which score and identify candidates suitable for different positions. This has cut down the recruitment and selection process from several weeks to a few hours. The use of the internet for both recruitment and selection is likely to increase as accessibility and familiarity with this medium grow (Batram 2000, 2004).

SYSTEMATICALLY EVALUATE EACH SOLUTION: ASSESSMENT METHODS APPLIED TO CANDIDATES

Once a pool of recruits has been attracted, the assessment methods are applied in order to evaluate each individual against the KSAs or competencies identified as important for job success. For selection, presuming that there are more applicants than vacancies, a first step will be to pre-select those applicants who look potentially suitable. This is done typically on the basis of the application form and/or CV that has been sent in. Despite the widespread use of such pre-screening methods, research evidence suggests that they are not designed or used systematically (Keenan 1995). New methods of pre-screening are now being introduced, for example, as already indicated, pre-selection is often also done using online testing to screen potential applicants (Mooney 2002; Konradt *et al.* 2003). Other methods are also being introduced to get more direct detail about a candidate's background, for example using telephone interviews. Telephone interviews, however, can be costly, especially if there are large numbers of applicants to be contacted. Bauer *et al.* (2004) compared three types of selection screening methods – face-to-face interviews, telephone interviews and interactive voice response (IVR) screening (non-interpersonal screening). They found that although the IVR screening was rated lower on certain variables such as interpersonal treatment and openness, this method was no different in terms of structural fairness. Given the significantly lower costs of IVR screening they suggest that companies should evaluate which types of screening methods fit the recruitment strategy for a particular type of employee. From this initial screening, a smaller number of applicants will be assessed more fully, using whatever is considered to be the appropriate assessment method(s). The different methods of assessment are considered more fully later in the chapter.

SELECT 'BEST' SOLUTION: SELECTION OR DEVELOPMENT DECISION

This step in the decision-making cycle is seen to be the logical outcome of the previous steps. Once each candidate has been measured using the particular assessment methods, the data can be evaluated in a logical manner in order to select the 'best' candidate. Each candidate can be rated against the person specification or competency profile. The candidate who has all the specified essential characteristics and the most desirable characteristics should be selected for the job. Where assessment is used for developmental purposes the decision is more about which candidates are suitable for which senior positions within the organisation. Nevertheless, there is the same assumption that this can be done rationally and logically on the basis of the data accumulated from the assessment exercises.

MONITOR AND EVALUATE RESULTS: VALIDATION

Ratings of employee potential estimated during the selection or developmental assessment process can be compared with subsequent performance on the job. This provides the measure of validity. High correlations between the selection or development ratings (referred to as the predictor) and performance ratings (referred to as the criterion) would indicate that the decisions made during the assessment process were valid (and hence rational). Low correlations would indicate that decisions were not valid. Evidence of the criterion-related validity of traditional methods used to make selection decisions, i.e., the unstructured interview and references, suggests that neither of these methods results in valid predictions.

One particular problem with such validity studies is that the criteria against which the selection or development decisions are compared (i.e., measures of job performance) may themselves be inaccurate (Campbell 1990). The most typical criterion used is supervisory ratings, but research has demonstrated that these may vary widely in terms of accuracy. For example, Sundvik and Lindeman (1998) found that accuracy was dependent on the opportunity the supervisor had to observe the subordinate, especially in terms of the length of the supervisor–subordinate relationship. They also found that female supervisors are more accurate at rating than are males. More recently, Kacmar *et al.* (2003) similarly reported that job-performance ratings by supervisors were affected by communication frequency although they also found that this was moderated by the relationship between the supervisor and the subordinate.

From the rational, decision-making perspective, however, the key issue is to identify where selection or development decisions have been made that have not been good (i.e., where validity is poor) and to take this as the starting point for repeating the decision-making cycle in order to improve validity.

IDENTIFY PROBLEM

And so the cycle repeats itself!

The selection and assessment decision-making process in practice

While the rational, decision-making model can be applied to the selection and assessment process, and indeed underpins much of the literature on improving the validity of such decisions, research evidence suggests that, in practice, the decision process is often far removed from this ideal. This is true for decisions of all kinds, not just selection and development decisions. Thus, research has demonstrated that such rational decision making does not equate with reality. Rather, empirical research gives mostly examples of irrational decisions when compared to the normative standard (Cyert and March 1963; March and Olsen 1976; Nisbett and Ross 1980; Buchanan and Huczynski 2004). This is the case even where the decision is taken by a group rather than an individual. Indeed, Janis (1972) demonstrated how groups making extremely important strategic decisions failed to adopt the rational, normative approach. Janis used the term 'groupthink' to refer to the fact that, within the decision-making groups he observed, disturbing information was suppressed, immense and unjustified risks taken, and individuals censored their own concerns. The result was an illusion of unanimity for the decision taken, despite individual group members not really agreeing. The concept of groupthink has been used to explain more recent decision fiascos, suggesting that the political nature of decision making is still very evident (e.g., Yetiv 2003).

Given that research evidence does not support a rational, decision-making process in practice, other models have been developed which attempt to mirror reality rather than idealism. Simon (1960) introduced the concept of bounded rationality, which acknowledged the fact that decision makers, in practice, were under pressure to make decisions so that they did not have time to search exhaustively for all possible solutions. He coined the term 'satisficing' to describe how the search for solutions was not exhaustive, but continued only until a satisfactory solution had been found. Another model of decision making that has attracted attention recently has been the intuitive, decision-making model (e.g., Agor 1989; Behling and Eckel 1991). This assumes that managers make decisions by relying on past experiences and their general sense of the situation. Intuition is essentially an unconscious process created out of distilled experience. When managers face complex decisions and cannot get accurate information, they tend to rely on hunches, intuitions and general experiences. As Bazerman (1994) concludes: 'Most significant decisions are made by judgement, rather than by a defined prescriptive model.' Such intuition, however, is not really acceptable in cultures where rational analysis is the approved way of making decisions, such as North America and the UK. So intuition is often disguised or hidden. For example, one of the executives in the study by Agor (1986) commented: 'Sometimes one must dress up a gut decision in "data clothes" to make it acceptable or palatable, but this fine-tuning is usually after the fact of the decision.'

A final, non-rational model of the decision-making process is the garbage can model developed by Cohen *et al.* (1972). They described decision-making processes in terms of a 'garbage can', rather than a rational process. This model suggests that decisions have a random and haphazard element to them – that is, decisions are sometimes made from the random interaction of problems, solutions, choice situations and participants, rather than from intentions, plans and consistent decisions. Various kinds of problems, solutions and energy ('garbage') are dumped into a garbage can by participants. The decision process may then just as well start with the solution as the problem.

These models of decision making acknowledge the limits or 'bounds' to rational decision making, including:

1. Perceptual limitations and biases.
2. Limited availability of information.
3. Prediction is an art not a science so it is not possible to evaluate options as rationally as proposed.
4. Organisational goals constrain decisions.
5. Conflicting goals of different stakeholders mean that interpersonal conflicts, personal biases and power struggles are an inherent part of the decision process.

The irrationality of the selection and assessment decision-making process

The irrationality of decision-making processes has been confirmed in studies focusing on selection and assessment decisions. A brief look at the steps in the decision-making cycle and evidence of what happens at each stage highlights the continued 'irrationality' of the selection process in practice.

UNDERSTAND THE SITUATION AND IDENTIFY THE PROBLEM

The idea that someone leaving an organisation should be used as an opportunity to rationally consider whether or not a replacement is 'really needed', ignores the political realities of organisations (Pfeffer 1981; Contu and Willmott 2003). Power within organisations is at least partly a function of resources that are controlled, including human resources. While individuals are recruited to work for a particular company, in reality they are recruited to particular departments or divisions. A department is unlikely to admit voluntarily that they do not need to replace a particular person since that will diminish their 'empire'. The department may actually be more likely to argue that they 'need' two people to replace the one leaver! Someone leaving may be an opportunity for a renegotiation of resources within the organisation, but this needs to be understood as an inherently political process. 'Need' is not something that can be established as fact, but is socially constructed through a process of negotiation and sense making until a 'workable version of reality' is produced (Weick 1990).

GATHER INFORMATION AND MATERIAL TO HELP SOLVE THE PROBLEM

Despite the extensive effort put into developing new, more valid methods to measure and assess individuals during the selection process, evidence suggests that unstructured interviews and references remain the most dominant methods (Shackleton and Newell 1991; Keenan 1995). This can be related to the human fallacy of us each believing that we are a 'good judge of people', despite evidence to the contrary (see section below on person perception errors). Later in this chapter we will also consider another reason for the continued use of the interview – that is, that selection is not simply about 'valid' selection, but also about commitment and motivation to follow up the decision with behaviours that encourage the individual selected to integrate into the organisation. A recruiter who feels that they have personally selected the candidate is much more likely to feel committed and motivated to helping achieve that integration. Similarly, the selected candidate may well be more committed to the organisation because unstructured interviews are more likely to provide the opportunity to negotiate a 'mutually agreeable psychological contract' (Dipboye 1997).

GENERATE POTENTIAL SOLUTIONS

While the rational model of selection suggests that the recruitment stage is about generating the widest search possible in order to ensure the 'best' pool of applicants, evidence suggests that, in reality, the alternatives considered are often less than exhaustive. For example, some organisations only go to Oxford and Cambridge universities to recruit graduates. While these universities may well have some of the brightest graduates, there will certainly be bright graduates at other universities. Other evidence suggests that the so-called 'old boy network' is still actively used across organisations (Coe 1992; O'Higgins 2002). In other words, it is very often personal contacts, one's social capital (Adler and Kwon 2002) that lead to job opportunities rather than systematic recruitment and selection procedures.

SYSTEMATICALLY EVALUATE EACH SOLUTION

The evidence suggests that assessors, whatever method they are using, do not systematically use the evidence that is collected. For example, the evidence about assessment centres, reviewed below, suggests that assessors are unable to distinguish between different aspects of behaviour within a given exercise, but instead give ratings based on their overall assessment of the candidate's performance on that particular exercise. Research on interviews suggests that decisions are often made very quickly and are subjective, unreliable and vulnerable to bias (Janz 1989; Arvey and Faley 1992; Dipboye 1992).

SELECT BEST SOLUTION

A truly rational decision process would have assessors numerically rate each candidate on each dimension or competency; give the different dimensions or competencies specific weightings depending on their relative importance for the job in question; and then total the score for each candidate, taking into account the relative weightings. The candidate with the highest total would be selected. This can be described as the actuarial method as it is based purely on a numerical calculation of the collected data (although the ratings themselves are subjective). In practice, however, the decision is much more likely to be based on a process of clinical judgement. The ratings may be numerical but these will be evaluated subjectively by the assessors and weightings will be assigned to justify decisions rather than to make the decisions. So leadership skills become more important than numerical skills, if this allows the favoured candidate to come out top! As Beach (1990, p.xiii) states: 'most decisions are made quickly and simply on the basis of "fittingness", and only in particular circumstances are they made on the basis of anything like the weighing and balancing of gains and losses that is prescribed by classical decision theory'.

MONITOR AND EVALUATE RESULTS

In practice it seems that very few organisations carry out a systematic evaluation of their selection process (or indeed any other human resource practice). Moreover, where validity studies have been conducted, they demonstrate low levels of validity even when using methods that can potentially provide reasonable or good levels of validity (see below). These results confirm that selection methods are not used in the prescribed way and that efforts to improve validity have had rather limited impact on actual practice.

The conclusion drawn from such research is that the prescriptive, rational, decision-making process does not typically equate with what happens in practice and that methods of selection actually used by practitioners are often not high on criterion-related validity, despite the fact that evidence now demonstrates that criterion-related validity can be significantly improved using the newer, more structured and systematic approaches (Ryan and Tippins 2004). Exactly the same points could be made with reference to decisions made during developmental assessment processes. The response from those researching and writing about selection and assessment has been to attempt to improve the validity of the methods used to measure individual differences. In other words, the focus has been on trying to find ways of improving the extent to which the rational, normative, decision-making model is actually followed.

Improving the validity of selection and assessment decisions

In particular, attention has focused on introducing methods which provide a better basis on which to make rational decisions. Considerable progress has been made here, which demonstrates how the validity of the selection and assessment decision-making process can be improved (Robertson and Smith 2001).

STRUCTURED INTERVIEWS

The interview is the most common selection tool used within organisations across many countries (DiMilia *et al.* 1994; Shackleton and Newell 1994). Early research demonstrated that the traditional unstructured interview had very low validity (e.g., Mayfield 1964; Ulrich and Trumbo 1965). Given the ubiquity of the interview, effort has been devoted to improving its validity, primarily by increasing the structure of the interview, so that at least all candidates are asked the same sorts of questions (if not the identical questions) and all interviewers use the same dimensions to assess candidates. Research looking at the validity of structured interviews suggests that they can indeed improve validity (McDaniel *et al.* 1994).

There are two main varieties of structured interviews – behavioural and situational interviews. In a behavioural interview, hypothetical situations are posed to the candidate (the same questions to each candidate) and the candidate is asked to say how they would react to this situation. In a situational interview, candidates are asked to identify where they have experienced certain job-relevant situations and to report how they responded to these situations.

Example: **Situational and behavioural interviews: examples of interview questions for a head teacher of an inner-city secondary school**

An example of a situational interview question: You are working in your office when your secretary tells you that there is a gentleman to see you. You invite him into your office, and he tells you that he is a parent of one of your pupils. He says that he wants his daughter to leave school and start work immediately. The daughter is one of your brightest pupils and you know that she is working hard to go to medical school next year. You start to explain this to the parent but he clearly does not place any value on higher education. What would you do?

An example of a behavioural interview question: Can you give me some examples of when you have had to deal with parents who do not value higher education for their children; how have you managed this situation?

Both types of structured interview have been found to be effective. For example, Barclay (2001) uses empirical data from UK organisations to illustrate the advantages of behavioural interviews. Advantages included the ability to gather better information which leads to improved selection decisions, improved consistency between interviewers, and the increased ability for candidates to demonstrate their skills. Similarly, Sue-Chan and Latham (2004) examined the validity of the situational interview and demonstrated its power in predicting both academic and team-playing behaviour of professionals and managers. However, there is some evidence that for complex jobs behavioural interviews are more effective than situational interviews (Heffcut *et al.* 2004). Structuring interviews can therefore potentially improve the quality of decisions made, although there appears to be a ceiling on this, beyond which increasing structure does not improve validity (Heffcutt and Arthur 1994).

BIOGRAPHICAL MEASURES

Biographical measures, or biodata, attempt to capture directly the past behaviour of a person and use this as the basis for predicting future behaviour. Since they are based on actual behaviour, the idea is that they are less prone to misinterpretation, resistance and distortion (Stricker and Rock 1998). Research has indeed demonstrated that biographical measures can produce good levels of predictive validity (e.g., Mumford and Stokes 1992; Stokes *et al.* 1993; Hesketh 1999; Oswald *et al.* 2004). Nevertheless, there remain a number of concerns about the appropriate item content and about test construction methods (Mael 1991). For example, in terms of content many biographical measures contain questions which are indistinguishable from items on an attitude scale (e.g., What is your attitude towards working mothers?); or items that call for subjective judgements (e.g., How punctual are you?); or items that are not under the control of the assessee and so are dubious on ethical grounds (e.g., How many sisters and brothers have you got?). In terms of test construction, a key problem is that because most measures are empirically keyed to predict particular criteria, they cannot be used in different settings. Nevertheless, more recently, research has demonstrated that a biodata form can be designed to predict performance in a variety of organisational settings (Carlson *et al.* 1999).

PSYCHOMETRIC TESTS

Essentially, there are two kinds of tests used for selection or developmental assessment – cognitive and personality tests. Cognitive tests, especially tests of general intelligence, have typically been found to have high predictive validity across a wide range of jobs (Hunter and Hunter 1984), but it is debatable how much additional information they provide since there are other ways of estimating ability, especially from academic qualifications. For example, McManus *et al.* (2003) Showed that 'A'-level score was a good predictor of success in medical training and subsequent career progress, but that a test of ability added no additional predictive validity.

Personality tests have typically been found to have a low validity for predicting job performance (Ghiselli 1973; Schmitt *et al.* 1984). However, more recently, evidence has been established to suggest that personality measures can be valid predictors of job performance (e.g., Day and Silverman 1989; Robertson and Kinder 1993; Salgado 1996). One reason for the early pessimism was that there was no generally accepted model of personality. More recently, the so-called 'Big 5' have emerged, around which there is substantial agreement (the 'Big 5' personality traits are openness, conscientiousness, extraversion, agreeableness and neuroticism). Research using the Big 5 model has shown that measurement of these five traits can help to predict job performance. For example, Barrick and Mount (1991) found that conscientiousness is a valid predictor for all occupational groups and all criterion types. And Hough *et al.* (1990) found that neuroticism is negatively related to general performance measures. Moreover, researchers have begun to consider more thoughtfully the relationship between particular aspects of personality and particular aspects of performance that might logically be related; not assuming that a measure of personality will be related to just any criterion measure. For example, Tett *et al.* (2003) demonstrated that using broad measures of personality obscured potentially useful linkages between specific aspects of personality and performance. Thus they advocate focusing on specific personality traits and specific measures of performance in order to improve predictive validity.

ASSESSMENT OR DEVELOPMENT CENTRES

Assessment or development centres make use of a variety of exercises over a period of time (typically two days) to assess a small group of candidates on a number of dimensions (often defined in terms of competencies) that are deemed relevant to the particular job and organisation. Ratings are made by a small group of trained assessors who observe the candidates on the different exercises. Exercises might include: a group decision-making exercise, a presentation, a role play, an in-basket test, psychometric tests and interviews. In the UK, the use of assessment centres is increasing more rapidly than any other selection procedure, with 65 per cent of large firms (over 1,000 employees) using them (Industrial Relations Service 1997). Research evidence using meta-analysis demonstrates that they can have a relatively high level of predictive validity (Hough and Oswald 2000) and are seen as fair and thorough by candidates (Macan *et al.* 1994; Salgado 1999).

Despite this good predictive validity, research has demonstrated that assessment and development centres do not have good construct validity (Goldstein *et al.* 1998). In particular, research has demonstrated that within each exercise, ratings across the different dimensions are not clearly differentiated, while correlation of a given dimension across exercises is low (Kauffman *et al.* 1993; Joyce *et al.* 1994; McCredie and Shackleton 1994). One suggested reason for this is that the information-processing load on assessors is too high, so that they selectively attend to only certain behaviours, misinterpret key behaviours, and/or confuse categorisation of behaviours by dimensions (Thornton 1992; Fleenor 1996). Schema-driven theory suggests that this occurs because people use established schemata to interpret and evaluate the observed behaviour of others (Zedeck 1986; Fiske and Taylor 1991). Schemata refer to the mental representations that an individual has built up over time to structure and cluster their understanding of perceived phenomena. Any new input will be interpreted on the basis of the assumptions which underpin these schemata. Traditionally, the recommended way to overcome this problem has been to separate the steps of observation and classification – recording behaviours longhand while observing, classifying behaviours according to the defined dimensions for the exercise, and only then rating the individual on each dimension (Bray and Grant 1966; Boyle *et al.* 1995). While this does help to overcome some of the perceptual problems of assessors, the requirement to write detailed notes of the observation can be a distraction and means that the assessor might miss some behavioural information. Similarly, the suggestion by Kolk *et al.* (2002) of having each assessor rate only one exercise and one dimension per exercise is likely to be practically difficult to implement.

Hennessy *et al.* (1998), in an attempt to overcome this problem, experimented with the use of a behavioural coding method of assessment. This provides a list of key behaviours for each of the dimensions rated and requires observers to code the frequency of behaviours as they occur. They are not required actually to note the behaviours per se, but only tally the frequency of the specified behaviours. This has the advantage that information-processing demands are reduced and also limits the extent to which personal schemata will direct the observation. The results of their research demonstrated that this behavioural coding method was as accurate as the traditional method of assessment and reduced differences between raters in their judgements. They suggest that its simplicity in comparison with the traditional method, and its theoretical basis in schema-driven theory, may make this a preferred method for overcoming the construct validity problem of assessment or development centres.

On the basis of reviewing a number of studies which have attempted to improve the construct validity of assessment and development centres, Lievens (1998) makes a number of practical recommendations. For example, in terms of:

1. Dimensions: use only a small number of conceptually distinct dimensions and define these in a concrete and job-related way.
2. Assessors: ensure assessors are trained, especially in relation to understanding the dimensions and categorisation schemes used.
3. Situational exercises: develop exercises which generate a large amount of dimension-related behaviour and avoid exercises which elicit behaviours potentially relevant to many dimensions.
4. Systematic observation, evaluation and integration procedures: provide assessors with an observation aid (a checklist), which operationalises each dimension with 6–12 key behaviours.

While an assessment centre can be improved by observing these types of recommendations, organisations should also think very carefully about using such a method, given the expense of doing so and the fact that other methods may provide as good predictions much more cost-effectively (Robertson and Smith 2001).

The rhetoric versus the reality of the selection and assessment decision-making process

These newer assessment methods appear to offer significant benefits since they can improve objectivity and criterion-related validity. However, as seen, research into actual practice suggests that, in reality, selection and development decisions continue to be dominated by more subjective approaches (Anderson 2003). Moreover, even where so-called 'objective' approaches are used, their interpretation remains highly subjective. That is, the fact that a structured interview or an assessment centre has the potential to reach high levels of validity does not mean that it will be used in ways to guarantee this. For example, DiMilia and Gorodecki (1997) evaluated the reliability and use of a commercially available structured interviewing system. They found that, in practice, the reliability achieved was much lower than considered in the literature to be an acceptable level. This was because there was a lack of role clarity for interviewers, interviewers had different expectations of the job specification and there was inconsistency in the application of the rating system. They conclude that: '. . . whilst an interviewing system can have a number of features described in the literature as necessary conditions for better validity, the actual result of the system is in the hands of the user' (DiMilia and Gorodecki 1997, p.198).

Similarly, while psychometric tests can potentially add valid information to the selection or development decision, it is also clear that this will only occur if tests are used appropriately (Newell and Shackleton 1993). Rees (1996) identifies a number of common misunderstandings among test users which suggest that tests are not always used in a valid and ethical way. For example, a frequent misconception is that it is acceptable to use a poor test to structure a subsequent interview. Rees concludes that such misunderstandings may, over time, undermine the case of those attempting to use psychometric tests 'effectively and appropriately in the occupational setting'. He argues that there are too many test users who are unable to recognise technically poor test material and so use such tests inappropriately to help them make decisions that affect both individuals and organisations.

These observations are not confined to selection decision methods. Other attempts to improve the rationality of decision making, for example by introducing cost–benefit analysis, computer-based information systems or other decision support systems, demonstrate that, in practice, these solutions are not used in the prescribed way (e.g., Ackerman *et al.* 1974; Argyris 1977). Essentially, the normative model of the selection and assessment decision-making process does not equate to reality because selection and assessment is a process that inherently depends on an interaction between two or more parties. Such interpersonal *interactions* involve two (or more) parties who are simultaneously providing input (which the other is evaluating) and evaluating the other. Such interactions are inherently subjective, involving processes of impression management and interpretation.

IMPRESSION MANAGEMENT

Decisions made about candidates during selection and assessment depend on the concrete experiences that are provided. These experiences of the 'target person' (i.e., the candidate) may be indirect (e.g., information from an application form or a personality test) or direct (e.g., behaviour exhibited during an interview). The newer methods of assessment attempt to ensure that the event provides assessors with an accurate reflection of the person being assessed. This assumes that the candidate is passively responding to the various assessment experiences. In reality, of course, candidates are actively attempting to create a certain image of themselves. This is especially the case in the 'high stakes' selection situation. Candidates will attempt to create and maintain a particular impression of themselves which coincides with what they believe the assessor is looking for. Thus, to some extent at least, the assessor only sees what the target person wants them to see. This is referred to as 'impression management' (Rosenfeld *et al.* 1995). Arnold *et al.* (1997) identify a variety of techniques that can be used to convey a particular impression. For example, ingratiation ('I have always wanted to work for this firm'), selective description of events (candidate ignoring details of failed examinations they have taken), positive descriptions of self ('I am a very hard-working person'). For example, Griffin *et al.* (2004) demonstrated that faking was a real issue when personality measures are used for selection, with job applicants responding significantly differently to students on a conscientiousness measure. While it might be obvious to appreciate that candidates are engaging in impression management tactics, it is also the case that assessors are simultaneously attempting to 'create an impression' because they want to attract or retain the 'best' candidates.

INTERPRETATION

The assessor has to make sense of the data that is accumulated about the candidate and this sense-making process is inherently subjective. At the same time, the candidate is also trying to 'make sense' of the situation – what would it be like to work for this company, or what would my colleagues be like, or what are my implied career opportunities? For both parties, there is a stimulus ('evidence' from the candidate to the assessor and vice versa) and a response (a job offer or an acceptance of a job offer). However, the key to understanding this is that between these two observable phenomena are the unobservable processes of perception.

Perception, by definition, is a subjective process by which individuals attend to, organise and so interpret their sensory input in order to give meaning to their environment. Subjective processes, including selective attention, personal judgement and interpretation, will therefore affect the decision. Behaviour is based on the world as it is perceived and a number of factors operate to shape and sometimes distort perception, including personal characteristics, motives, interests, past experiences, and expectations. This will result in biases, such as:

1. **Selective attention** – as we cannot attend to everything, we only attend to some things, but this is not random. Rather, what we attend to is chosen according to our interests, background, experience and attitudes. This allows us to draw conclusions from an ambiguous situation.

2. **Halo/horn effect** – we tend to draw a general impression about an individual on the basis of a single characteristic, such as intelligence.

3. **Contrast effects** – evaluations of a person's characteristics can be affected by comparisons with other people recently encountered. So, in an interview situation, if someone has just been interviewed who was judged very poor, the next candidate may be more positively evaluated in contrast. Conversely, following a very good candidate, an average candidate may be rated poorly.

4. **Projection** – there is a tendency to attribute one's own characteristics to other people. So if I want challenge and responsibility in a job, I assume that others want the same.

5. **Stereotyping** – this involves judging someone on the basis of one's perceptions of the group to which that person belongs.

6. **Heuristics** – these are judgemental shortcuts in decision making. Two common heuristics are availability and representativeness. The availability heuristic is the tendency for people to base their judgements on information that is readily available to them. For example, if there is an internal and an external candidate, the internal candidate may be preferred simply because more information is readily available about them ('better the devil you know!'). The representative heuristic is the tendency to assess the likelihood of an occurrence by drawing analogies and seeing identical situations where they do not exist. So, for example, if four graduates from the same college had all been recruited but none had been very satisfactory, then another applicant from this college might be rejected on the assumption that they also would not be good.

It is just these sorts of impression management problems and perceptual biases that 'new' assessment methods have attempted to overcome. They structure and standardise the information gained during the assessment process, so that decisions are less likely to be biased by these perceptual shortcuts that we use in our everyday judgements of other people, to a greater or lesser extent. To the extent that these new assessment methods can reduce these biases, they can improve validity. The research evidence presented earlier suggests that this is indeed the case. However, as we have also seen, while newer, more valid assessment methods have been developed, and can improve the validity of selection and development decisions, in practice they are often not used in quite the 'rational' way anticipated. Human subjectivity and the political reality of organisations mean that the normative decision model can never be an entirely realistic account of decision-making in practice (Anderson 2003).

Unfounded assumptions: selection as an interactive process

While human perception and organisational politics limit the extent to which a selection or development decision can ever be entirely rational, there is an even more fundamental problem with the normative decision model. The normative approach makes the assumption of a 'right' or 'best' person for the job and assumes that there is one key decision, i.e., to select or reject the candidate, which is the crucial point. The important issue is to select the 'right' person and then this will solve the organisational problem because this person will be able successfully to carry out the particular tasks where there is currently a vacancy (although this may be only after training has been given). However, this ignores the fact that successful performance on a job is rarely, if ever, dependent solely on a particular individual. The individual job exists within a complex network of structures, processes and relationships, which will affect and interact with the actions of the particular individual employee. So a potentially very competent recruit can be thwarted in their ability to perform to a high standard by a whole multitude of events – a lack of adequate resources, poor training, an unhelpful supervisor, colleagues who are not supportive, etc. On the other hand, a barely competent recruit can perform to a high standard if they are exposed to a supportive or benign situation.

In other words, it is not helpful to look at the selection decision itself in isolation from the stream of events that occur both before and after this. Vaughan (1996, 1997) made a similar point in analysing the Challenger space shuttle disaster. She points out that the explosion should not be viewed as the unfortunate result of one bad decision to launch on that day in January 1986. Rather, it was the outcome of an accumulation of many launch decisions over the course of the shuttle programme. Thus instead of focusing on single decisions, she advocates the analysis of cycles of decisions or networks of decisions. This is equally the case in terms of analysing selection or development decisions. Thus, whether a decision to select (or reject) can be described as 'good' or 'bad' is the result of a network of interacting decisions. These decisions are made by both the individual and the organisational representatives, over a period of time, starting well before the actual advertisement of a job. For example, individuals will form an impression of a particular company based on what they know about its products and services or what they know about the organisation itself. These impressions may be formed either on the basis of direct experience (e.g., good or bad experience of service as a customer) or indirect experience (e.g., reading something good or bad about the company in the press). These impressions will influence how an individual responds to a recruitment advertisement. So a potentially ideal candidate may not even apply if they have formed a negative impression. Moreover, decisions made subsequent to the selection decision, will have a considerable impact on the extent to which the recruit performs the job effectively. Particularly important in this respect is the socialisation experience of the new recruit (Anderson and Ostroff 1997). This suggests the need to see selection as an interactive process in which the expectations of both parties are intertwined in a process of continuous exchange, which does not begin and end at the point of the selection decision (Shintaku 2004). Again, exactly the same points can be made with reference to development decisions. Whether the 'right' career path is chosen for and by a particular individual on the basis of evidence from a development centre will depend on a host of decisions made prior and subsequent to this choice.

What this analysis implies is that the normative, rational model of decision making isolates the decision from subsequent action, including subsequent decisions (Brunsson 1982, 1989). Brunsson argues that the normative decision-making perspective fails to recognise that a decision is not an end product but simply a step towards action of some kind. In the case of selection, this equals the effective deployment of human resources. More importantly, Brunsson points out that rational decisions are not always good bases for appropriate and successful actions: 'Since decision processes aim at action, they should not be designed solely according to such decision-internal criteria as the norms of rationality; they should be adapted to external criteria of action' (1982, p.32). The selection or development decision per se is only one episode in the successful integration of the individual in the organisation. Successful integration is more likely to occur where there are positive expectations, motivation and commitment from both parties (Scholarios *et al.* 2003). Thus, the stronger the expectation, motivation and commitment expressed in a decision, the more power that decision exerts as a basis for action. However, Brunnson argues that to achieve such expectation, motivation and commitment breaks all the rules for rational decision making:

1. Few alternatives should be considered: while the rational model assumes that many (all) alternatives should be considered, from a decision–action perspective parsimony is more appropriate. Considering multiple alternatives generates uncertainty and this reduces commitment and motivation.

2. Only positive consequences of the chosen decision should be analysed: the rational model advocates considering all consequences of a decision, both positive and negative. From a decision–action perspective it may be more sensible to search for consequences in only one direction since this reduces inconsistency which can stimulate doubt.

3. Objectives should not be pre-defined: the rational model assumes that objectives should be pre-defined so that all alternatives can be considered against these objectives. For producing action, a better strategy may be to start from the consequences and invent the objectives afterwards (Lindblom 1959).

This action-oriented perspective can help to explain some of the research findings on the selection and assessment decision process, which suggest that it remains less rational than prescribed best practice would advocate. Examples of this are given below.

1. Continued use of unstructured interviews – the belief that 'I am a good judge of character' allows the interviewer to be confident in their decision and so increases commitment and motivation to make the chosen individual 'fit'.

2. Continued use of subjective (clinical) rather than objective (actuarial) choice criteria – again this empowers the assessor to believe that they were influential in the decision and so makes them more committed to ensuring the decision translates into effective action, i.e., successful integration of the chosen candidate within the organisation.

3. Less than exhaustive search of alternatives – making decisions quickly makes life more comfortable for managers. It allows them to use heuristics or 'shortcuts' to solving problems. Pre-defined recipes for successful selection decisions can increase confidence in the decision and so raise expectations of subsequent success by the candidate.

4. Little systematic evaluation of selection decision – while academic research has focused on establishing the predictive validity of selection decisions, in practice few organisations systematically monitor the success of their decisions. Again, from an action perspective this is sensible since it allows those involved to be confident in their decision-making qualities and so more confident about and committed to the decisions they make. It also reduces the possibility of cognitive dissonance (Festinger 1957). Cognitive dissonance is the uncomfortable feeling that occurs when people hold inconsistent or conflicting beliefs – I made the decision to hire this person, I am good at making these kinds of decisions, this person is not a good employee. Cognitive dissonance can be avoided if systematic evaluation of selection decisions is avoided.

5. Overemphasis of negative data – research has demonstrated that negative information about a candidate is given more weight than positive information. Many of the newer assessment methods are aimed at reducing this effect. However, from a decision–action perspective this is entirely rational. Negative information raises doubts about the suitability of a candidate and so will undermine confidence that the person can be successful. So if there are two candidates, and from an objective evaluation of the evidence, candidate A is 'better', having more of the essential and desirable characteristics than candidate B, then rationally that candidate should be selected. However, if there is also one piece of negative information

about candidate A (for example a question mark over their willingness to collaborate), while there is nothing negative about candidate B, then from an action–decision perspective, candidate B would be preferable. If candidate A were selected there would remain doubts, which might undermine motivation and commitment to the decision.

In each case, the decision–action criteria improve the positive expectations of those involved over the purely rational decision criteria. This is important since expectations can become self-fulfilling prophecies. For example, Eden and Shani (1982) informed the instructors of a command course for the Israeli Defence Forces that one-third of the 105 soldiers on the course had high potential, one-third had normal potential and the rest were of unknown potential. In reality, the soldiers had been randomly assigned to one of these three groups. However, at the end of the 15-week course, those trainees who were given the high potential label scored significantly higher on objective achievement tests and exhibited more positive attitudes to the course and the instructors, than did the rest.

Interactive action-oriented perspective, fairness and justice

One particular problem in selection and development decisions has been the issue of 'fair' discrimination. Thus, while selection is based on making discriminations between people, the objective has been to make these discriminations on the basis of relevant criteria, i.e., ability to do the job effectively, rather than irrelevant criteria like sex, ethnicity and disability. One of the key benefits of the psychometric perspective is that it presents a very rational and objective view of the whole process. It assumes that the 'best' person for the job can be clearly specified in advance, with selection and assessment processes essentially presented as a set of 'rational' choices based on objective evidence gained about the candidates from the various selection methods deployed. This allowed companies to defend against claims of unfair discrimination. Essentially, the traditional approach may be considered to have a high level of procedural justice (Lind and Tyler 1988) since it theoretically treats everyone the same. In this chapter, we have argued that this semblance of rationality is actually a myth. Moreover, it could be argued that the psychometric perspective actually increases the opportunity for distributive injustice (Singer 1993), because its starting premise is that there is one 'best' way to do the job. This 'best' way is likely to be a reflection of the way previous job incumbents have done the job. So if the previous job incumbents have all been white males who have adopted fairly autocratic management styles, worked long hours, relied on a lot of electronic communication, etc., then the assumption will be that these are the characteristics to look for in a replacement. This may perpetuate the status quo and thus the segregation that exists within organisations, although the process may look procedurally 'fair' (Truxillo *et al.* 2004).

Adopting the interactive, action-oriented perspective provides the opportunity to break through this barrier by recognising that people can do jobs in very different ways but equally effectively. The problem with this perspective, however, is that it acknowledges the subjectivity of the selection process and so could be used as a vehicle to increase unfair discrimination even more. This is entirely true but it will depend on the motives of those involved. If there is a belief in equal opportunities, or, perhaps even better, in the advantages of diversity in the workforce, then this perspective can help to increase these opportunities. The psychometric perspective simply hides behind a façade of objectivity so that it remains easy to perpetuate discrimination even while presenting the whole process as fair. The interactive action-oriented perspective does not have this façade to hide behind so that any continuation of segregated workforces must, by implication, be the result of prejudice and unfair discrimination.

Conclusion

Understanding the selection and assessment process from a decision-making perspective highlights issues that are otherwise not brought into focus. In this chapter, this perspective has been used to contrast the traditional psychometric perspective with its implicit acceptance of the normative rational decision-making model, with an interactive decision–action perspective. The decision–action perspective leads us to recognise both that the process of selection and assessment can never be entirely rational and objective and that the decision per se (to accept or reject) is not necessarily the crucial point in the process. Rather, it is a stage in the ultimate goal of achieving the effective integration and socialisation of an individual within the organisation. Effective integration is clearly unlikely if an entirely unsuitable person is chosen for a job. However, the assumption that there is a fixed type of person for a particular job and that the only goal of selection and assessment is to ensure accurate measurement in order to be able to identify this right type, is inappropriate. It is inappropriate both because of its assumptions about individual differences and our ability to assess these accurately in a selection or development situation and because it ignores the criteria for translating the decision into action. Successful performance on the job is dependent on motivation as well as ability. Ability is dependent not only on fixed characteristics, but also on opportunities for training and development that are provided. An 'ideal' person selected for a job but then given no training or development opportunities is more likely to fail than a moderately suitable person who is given such opportunities.

More importantly, in terms of motivation, success or failure will depend on both the individual's own self-beliefs and on the beliefs of those around them. If these significant others have been involved in the selection and assessment process and believe that the person selected is 'the best', then they will be committed to ensuring they are successful, regardless of whether or not they are best according to some objective, rational decision criteria. An entirely rational, actuarial evaluation of data collected during an assessment centre that results in the selection of a person that those involved do not 'like' or do not think is 'best' (for whatever reason), is unlikely to translate into active commitment aimed at helping that individual succeed. As seen, such commitment is more likely to follow a selection decision process that is less than entirely rational, but that allows those involved to believe that they have chosen someone who will be successful. Similarly, motivation is likely to be high if the selection or development experience results in positive but realistic expectations on the part of those assessed. Self-efficacy beliefs, an individual's belief that they are capable of performing the task they have been selected for (Bandura 1977) will be high, and these beliefs have been shown to be important in influencing the persistence and effort that someone will put into ensuring success (Gist 1987).

An action–decision perspective can help to identify those selection and assessment processes that can generate such high levels of self- and other belief and expectation that lead, in turn, to high levels of commitment and motivation. Of course, measurement of individual differences will remain important in selection and development decisions. However, the recognition that accurate measurement per se is not enough (even if it were possible), can help us focus on the ultimate goal of successful person–organisation fit, rather than just valid and rational decisions that might not readily translate into action. The decision–action perspective, therefore, complements the more traditional psychometric perspective and can help to ensure not only that decisions are made on the basis of reasonably good individual assessment but also that those decisions get translated into successful organisational performance.

CASE STUDY 3.1

ASSESSMENT AT NEWSCO, PHARMCO, RETAILCO AND SCIENCECO

SUE NEWELL, VIV SHACKLETON[*] AND MAXINE ROBERTSON[†]

Taking a decision–action perspective suggests that processes involved in selection and assessment should differ depending on the particular context and, in particular, on the intended action outcome. In order to demonstrate this diversity, we consider three separate cases in the following section. Each had a different objective and so a different design.

Newsco

Introduction

The first example of the application of the assessment techniques we have talked about in this chapter concerns Newsco, a large and successful company in the business of selling news and information. It is a truly international company, operating as it does in most countries of the world. It divides the world up into three zones. We are concerned here with the European part of the operation.

The brief

The company decided to assess the top 50 or so of its managers in this region. The stated purpose was assessment for development. That is to say, the managers would go through a development centre (an assessment-type centre designed with development in mind) in order for them to assess what sort of development they needed. 'Development' is a word that is frequently misunderstood. Here, it does not necessarily mean promotion or acquiring new responsibilities. It means training in techniques or skills, or acquiring new information, that would help them in their present or future roles. The traditional 'sheep dip' approach to management development, training and learning, where everyone receives the same training, regardless of need, is often not appropriate at any level in an organisation. It can be particularly inappropriate for senior people where the opportunity-cost of having them away from their desks on a course is very high. This organisation wanted to target training only on those who needed it, in the areas they most needed.

The role of those participating in the development centre was mostly that of 'country manager', the people who headed up the business in each country, although there were also specialists of various kinds.

The design

The start of the process of designing the development centre was an assessment of competencies, just as we described in the section on the traditional approach to assessment in this chapter. This involved interviewing people in the organisation to establish what the competencies were, both for the present job and for the ways in which the jobs might develop. The interviews were based on in-depth reviews of the role in question and how the organisation might develop. Two other kinds of interview were also used, the repertory

---

[*] Co-author on 'Newsco', 'Pharmco' and 'Retialco'.
[†] Co-author on 'Scienceco'.

grid technique and the critical incident technique. The repertory grid technique asks the interviewee to think of a number of people known to them who do, or have done, the job and to compare the way that they perform that role. From this information, the interviewer can work out the key skills, knowledge, abilities or competencies that effective job holders need and which differentiate the effective from the less effective. The critical incident technique asks interviewees to think of times in the job when they or their team were particularly successful or unsuccessful. The interviewee is encouraged to say what it was that made this particular incident successful or unsuccessful. From this evidence, the experienced interviewer can work out some of the competencies needed in the job.

Some of the competencies in this case were:

■ *Managing change*
  ● Continually challenging the status quo.
  ● Generating innovative ideas and solutions.
  ● Driving change through and overcoming resistance.

■ *Thinking for the future*
  ● Anticipating future trends and identifying new opportunities.
  ● Thinking strategically.
  ● Retaining a global perspective.

■ *Working with customers*
  ● Building partnerships with customers by knowing their business.
  ● Consulting with customers to understand needs and provide the best service.
  ● Promoting a positive image of the company.

Exercises were then designed to provide the opportunity to assess these and the other competencies. Exercises included:

■ A role play with a customer, where the customer had a serious complaint about the level of service and support they were receiving.
■ A competitor analysis, where participants were given information about three competitors and asked to do a SWOT (strengths, weaknesses, opportunities and threats) analysis of their own organisation and the competition.
■ Giving a presentation on issues of their own choosing from their own country business to the top management from the head office.
■ A group discussion on a strategic issue facing the whole organisation.
■ Some psychometric tests.

The workshop

Each development centre lasted two days. Managers from all corners of Europe and North Africa arrived, eight at a time, for the programme. There were external consultants and managers from head office running the programme and assessing the participants on the competencies. A crucial element of the two days was a one-to-one feedback, lasting around an hour, conducted by the external consultant with each of the participants. The purpose of this meeting was to review the performance of the participant on each of the exercises and competencies, and to get their agreement on the accuracy of the assessment. Most importantly, it was also an opportunity to discuss what the participant proposed to do about developing the strengths and remedying the weaknesses exposed by the programme.

The outputs

Following the workshop, the consultant wrote a report on the participant, summarising their performance and outlining a development plan. In effect, the report summarised and formalised the one-to-one discussion at the end of the centre. The report was sent to the participant and to their human resources manager. Participants themselves only showed it to their line manager or others in the organisation if they so wished. It was a confidential report and the recommendations were to be implemented by the participant in the manner most likely to achieve the development proposed. Development methods included secondments, job shadowing, training courses, self-directed learning, distance learning, job changes, and even withdrawal from the organisation if this was what the participant wanted.

After the development centre, there was no follow-up to check that the participants at the workshop had done any development after the event, and no attempt to evaluate the benefits of the programme. It was sufficient for the participants to say that the workshop had been useful and enjoyable. The feedback was essentially positive. This is not to say that the development centre was anodyne. There was some indication of how they could do even better. It pointed out that, where the participant had demonstrated excellent skills, they might coach others in these skills or seek opportunities to use them even more. Where there were skills that needed improving, suggestions were made on how this might be accomplished. But the whole development centre, and the feedback in particular, was geared to reinforcing, motivating and encouraging, rather than assessing and measuring. The participants were generally very positive about the event, after some initial reservations. They pointed out the many considerable advantages of the programme, including the opportunity to meet others in similar roles, to reflect on their own progress in the organisation, to think about themselves for a change, rather than the job in hand, and to consider how they might change or reinforce certain aspects of their own behaviour. In summary, the opportunity to reflect and learn was very motivating and satisfying for them.

Pharmco

Introduction

The second case concerns a long-established German corporation, Pharmco. Its early beginnings were in the traditional 'smokestack' industries of iron and steel, but since the Second World War it has moved into pharmaceutical manufacture and retail, along with the manufacture of medical and other technical equipment and a number of other businesses. In the more recent past, it has also started to expand beyond its national border and acquire and develop businesses in other European countries, including Britain, France and Spain. It is still predominantly a German company, however, with 90 per cent of its manufacturing and retail business conducted within the country.

The brief

We met up with the company at the point when it was thinking of investing in the development of its young managers to groom them for more senior appointments. In typical German style, it placed great emphasis on the importance of formal, high-quality education. It planned to offer the chance for some of the young managers to broaden their education and experience outside their technical and functional expertise and into a general management education. They would offer the opportunity to enrol in a part-time MBA at a prestigious international business school for those who were assessed as having the potential to profit from it. But who would benefit?

The design

The method they chose to select those who would be offered the opportunity was an assessment centre. Germany, like Britain and America, has a long tradition of using assessment centres, right back from the days of officer selection in the Second World War. Here, however, there was the additional complication of having to design an assessment centre for candidates from a number of different European countries. Although the language of the centre would be English, the exercises would be taken by people from four or five different countries. Whereas Newsco was a very international group, and consideration was given to designing exercises that would not favour one culture rather than another, here the cultural fairness issue was considered even more carefully by the designers. This is because this centre was seen as more akin to a traditional assessment centre, where fairness of treatment and equal opportunity to display skills are paramount.

Once again, the first issue was what knowledge, skills and abilities should be assessed. And again, the favoured means of acquiring that knowledge was a competency analysis. Methods adopted to decide on the required competencies were very similar to those already described for Newsco. Competencies included:

■ *Cross-cultural sensitivity*
  - Demonstrating curiosity and open-mindedness about other national cultures.
  - Acting to promote mutual understanding of other cultures.
  - Demonstrating sensitivity when working with people from other cultures.

■ *Leadership*
  - Focusing a group on generating a range of new ideas and possibilities.
  - Demonstrating confidence and a sense of responsibility.
  - Developing subordinates by making demands on them.

■ *Orientation to the task*
  - Agreeing clear and realistic actions.
  - Prioritising.
  - Taking decisions.
  - Reviewing progress towards achieving the task.

Participants were nominated by their line managers and by human resource professionals in their separate companies, in whichever country they worked. Participants were assessed at the centre by both company managers and by outside consultants, using competency-based rating scales.

Exercises were designed with the multi-cultural audience in mind. They included one on cultural sensitivity, where participants discussed their perception of their own culture and the German culture, as they had experienced it. They had to meet to discuss what recommendations they would make to improve cross-cultural working and how they would know if their recommendations were effective.

When designing assessment centre exercises, it is important to keep these and other cultural dimensions in mind. So, for example, it is important to make sure that exercises have many routes to success for a participant. An example of this need to provide many routes to success (and failure) in a multi-cultural environment is provided by an exercise used in this case. The exercise involved a customer service manager who was new to the post, and a subordinate, a customer service team leader, who had been in post for a long time. This was a role play exercise. An 'actor', a manager who had been in that post in the past, played the team leader. The participant played the superior, the customer service manager. There was some written material on the team leader, such as previous performance appraisal reports and statistical data on the subordinate's performance, available to the new boss. The issues were that the team leader was very good with customers, being liked and respected by them, but not good at developing the team, in part because they spent so much time with customers. In addition, they were not good at organising the work of the team since they were too busy doing the work themselves. The exercise could be done in a number of ways. It could be done from a relationships-building point of view, where, for example, the new boss could coach or mentor the old hand into new ways of working. Or it could be done from a very task-focused point of view, such as saying that this style and level of performance is not acceptable and you should be working in a different way and here are some targets and a timetable to achieve a different level of achievement. Or it could be successfully tackled in ways between those two extremes, such as helping the individual to explore alternative ways of doing the job over the next month and coming back to discuss progress after that time interval. What was important was that the individual was guided to seeing that the job involved two sets of customers, internal and external, and that it was important for the team leader to give attention to both. How participants achieved that aim was up to them.

Retailco

Introduction

The third case is a British-based retailer, Retailco. Like many large retailers in Britain, it was finding organic growth within Britain hard to achieve. It was already market leader, with the market dominated by about five players. Growth in its main market was less than 5 per cent a year, with it achieving this or a little more, year by year. This was likely to be the case for the foreseeable future. It was innovative in expanding in other businesses, but its main core business was unlikely to grow substantially.

An obvious route for a company in this position is growth by acquisition. While this was an option, a few big players dominated the market, so, realistically, a major acquisition in its home market was unlikely. Another route was expansion into other markets, which it was pursuing. A third route was expanding overseas, and it is this route which concerns us here.

Recently, the markets of eastern Europe have opened up considerably. Our case organisation saw this as an opportunity. In four or five countries in that part of the world, it acquired small businesses in its market sector, or, in some cases, developed those businesses from scratch.

The brief

However, this presented the organisation with a difficulty from a human resources point of view. It was completely new to the issue of recruiting and employing a non-British workforce. To start with, it sent experienced, specialist managers from Britain and recruited skilled and semi-skilled workers locally. But this was only a stopgap measure. For the longer term it needed to develop indigenous managers. In Britain, it had a well-designed and long-standing assessment centre for the selection of graduates who would become the senior managers of the future. This selection centre was regularly revised and checked for criterion validity. But could this centre be used for the assessment and selection of foreign graduates?

The design

The answer was a firm 'no'. The exercises and tests were not appropriate for candidates from outside Britain. It was not just the obvious differences, such as use of the English language or measurements in miles and gallons rather than kilometres and litres. It was the nature of the exercises themselves. Topics for group discussion, such as use of drugs by young people, have different meanings and importance for people from other cultures. Exercises dealing with the design of supermarkets are unlikely to work as well in countries less familiar with them. Tests not only have to have local norms and validation studies, but may not be as appropriate in countries where the whole concept of testing is unfamiliar and even disapproved of.

There was also the issue of whether the competencies were the same for graduates being selected for a post within their own country and for a well-established, brand name company in its local market, compared to a start-up enterprise for a company which was small and unknown in its local market. Obviously, the competencies were different. A competency analysis, similar to that described in the first two cases, was conducted. This revealed that being able to be independent of much day-to-day support was important. These managers would be big fish in small ponds, the opposite of new recruits in Britain. So they needed considerable confidence to back their own judgements and to act independently, when they were hundreds or thousands of miles from their head office in England. Similarly, the capacity for innovation and entrepreneurialism was much more important in eastern Europe than it was in the home country. In effect, these managers would be in charge of their own business in a more fundamental way than they would be if running a store in Britain. Finally, a capacity for cultural awareness was important. The candidates would be groomed for the role of international manager. They would spend time in Britain, getting to know the business. They would spend time in their home country, learning about and, hopefully, expanding the business there. But this organisation had big expansion plans. It was considered likely that the European managers would often be transferred to foreign postings outside their home market. So it was important for them to have not just the capacity to work in English, the international business language, but to be able to have some cultural sensitivity and awareness to be able to relate to, and work with, people from a wide range of different cultures. This was not a fundamental requirement for most of the British graduates being recruited in the organisation's home country.

So the whole assessment process was redesigned. Out went those stalwarts of the assessment centre, psychometric tests, since appropriate norms of sufficient sample size were not available. In addition, there were doubts about their acceptability in cultures unfamiliar with such things.

Exercises which could assess the required competencies, such as cultural sensitivity, entrepreneurialism and independence, were designed. An exercise designed for the cultural issue was a group discussion, which involved candidates describing how they saw their own culture and the cultures represented in the group. Observers were trained to look for behaviours which indicated that a candidate was open-minded towards different views of their own culture, and aware of the ways in which their own culture could be viewed. Defensiveness about others' negative perceptions of one's own culture was a contraindication.

This approach is very much in the psychometric tradition: job analysis, followed by description of the job in competency terms, then design of exercises to assess that competency. What is different from the usual approach to the design of selection centres, though, is the cross-cultural dimension. This brings enormous challenges, as described in the case of Pharmco. Once again, the exercises were designed so that there was more than one route to success. How candidates tackled the exercise was much less important than the outcome.

Even here, though, the rational decision-making model was not adopted to the full. Candidates were expected to gain an 'acceptable' score on all competencies, but this was not always adhered to. Rules were 'broken' when a candidate was seen to perform exceptionally well in one or two exercises. There was no attempt to base decisions on a statistical or mathematical calculation of marks (sometimes called the actuarial method) whereby scores given for each competency are summed or weighted in some way. The decision was much more an intuitive feel (sometimes called the clinical approach) for what final grade a candidate should be given based on an impression of the suite of marks. In the early centres the assessors were a mix of expatriates and indigenous managers. The power and influence in contentious decisions about a certain candidate tended to lie with the expatriate. As the company became more established in the foreign market, and more and more expatriates became replaced with indigenous managers, the power shifted. So, even in this more traditional example, the rational, decision-making model is found not to explain all purposes and outcomes.

ScienceCo

Introduction

The final case is of a medium-sized, science and technology-based consultancy company, located in the UK. It was established, in 1986, by a founder and two senior consultants. This 'Group of 3' had previously worked together in a large global consultancy but had become increasingly dissatisfied with what they saw as the 'stifling bureaucracy'. As a result the 'Group of 3' had decided to start their own business. Since 1986, ScienceCo has grown from a small entrepreneurial business, employing a handful of scientific consultants specialising in engineering and communications, to a medium-sized company employing about 200 people (75 per cent consultants, with the rest being technical and administrative support staff) and incorporating other scientific disciplines such as bio-technology, applied sciences and information systems. It operates today on a global basis.

At the time of its inception, the founder – himself a leading, internationally respected scientist – wished to create a consultancy environment that would not only develop solutions in response to client problems, but also stimulate invention and innovation more freely among its employees. The workforce consists of highly educated scientists and technologists, who rely primarily on their expertise and knowledge, rather than equipment or systems, to provide inventions and innovative solutions for manufacturing, engineering and pharmaceutical companies around the world.

The brief

A major issue for management has always been attracting and, just as importantly, retaining a highly skilled, expert workforce of international standing, in order for the firm to grow and successfully compete on a global basis. To a significant extent this has been achieved. Generally far more candidates apply for positions with the firm than there are posts, and turnover rates are only around 6 per cent. Developing and sustaining an appropriate organisational environment in which expert consultants are highly motivated, and perform optimally, has always been considered to be the most important strategic issue. For many years, the firm did not employ a dedicated human resources (HR) manager. However, two years ago, based on predicted project work, and management discussions around the requirements of floating on the stock market, the management team decided to recruit an HR manager. The remit of this HR manager was to increase the expert workforce by 15 per cent (a figure that was projected to continue annually) in order to meet market demand, to develop a more formalised recruitment and selection process, and to develop ways of motivating consultants and maintaining high retention rates across the firm.

The design

In the past, consultants had typically been recruited, informally, by word of mouth, drawing upon consultants' global personal networks of colleagues and contacts. However, according to the HR manager, 'this only works if the person you happen to want to get hold off is on the end of the phone at the time, and able to remember who you should talk to – we miss on opportunities to get great people because we don't have any formal systems to contact them with'. In order to formalise the recruitment process, the HR manager contracted two international recruitment agencies. Once provided with a person specification and a brief that described very broadly the type of work carried out by the firm, they provided shortlists of candidates on an ongoing basis. In terms of the selection process, the founder had always insisted that candidates take an AH6 intelligence test and Cattell's 16PF personality test because, as he put it, 'it is important to use our own scientific knowledge in the science of selecting others'. However, given that the majority of candidates short-listed by the agencies generally had a PhD in a scientific discipline, it was virtually impossible for any candidate to fail the AH6 intelligence test. It was also difficult to 'fail' to qualify on the 16PF because *Science Co* did not actually have an 'ideal' personality profile for any job, other than 'openness' and a 'willingness to experiment'. Indeed, a major group norm was that diversity should be encouraged and so a mix of personality types should be welcomed. The 16PF was used, therefore, simply because consultants were curious to see what sort of personality profile candidates had. Thus, almost all candidates who had been shortlisted qualified on the basis of these tests and proceeded to an initial short interview with the HR manager and the relevant divisional manager.

During this preliminary interview, the HR manager stated that candidates were expected to demonstrate a strong understanding of their own, and more importantly other disciplines, because of the need to work in inter-disciplinary teams sharing knowledge. They were also expected to be 'almost naturally innovative', have a strong commercial awareness, be fluent in English, and be prepared to adopt the role of a consultant. This role involves marketing their own, and more generally, the firm's abilities and expertise. It is therefore a relatively unique set of characteristics which are sought in candidates. The HR manager stated: 'It's quite a unique mix we are looking for. All the way through the selection process, we give out big indicators to say the sort of organisation we are. It's quite aggressive maybe, and I'm sure interviewees will pick up quite a lot of arrogance on the part of the company. But the messages we are giving out are more about confidence in what we do and how we do it rather than us thinking we are better than anyone else.'

The majority of candidates were rejected at this initial interview stage and only approximately 25 per cent (typically equating to four candidates) progressed to a second interview. While the management team were not overly concerned about the high numbers of rejections (seeing it as a reflection of their high standards), the HR manager found it extremely frustrating. The second interview focused on assessing the candidate's ability to market to clients, their overall level of expertise, and their ability to work within inter-disciplinary project teams. This second interview was a panel interview involving any number of consultants from several divisions who wished to be involved in 'quizzing' the applicant in some depth on their knowledge of their own, and other, science- or technology-based fields. Panel members were randomly drawn from across the firm, based on availability at the time of the interview. If the panel agreed on a candidate, then the candidate would be recommended for appointment to the MD.

Typically 16 candidates were interviewed for each post, and for each of those interviewed, approximately 10 CVs would have been received from the recruitment agencies. While the selection process was described as 'rigorous' by the HR manager, he emphasised that the interviews focused primarily on the candidates' ability to 'fit in' to the ScienceCo way of working – 'You get a CV, and the person has a PhD, and they've worked for a pretty high-powered research agency, and that's brilliant. You've got to see them, but you know that there is a pretty strong chance that the moment you meet them you're going to know what they're not – they're not one of us.' However, beyond a willingness and ability to share knowledge and collaborate across different science and technology-based fields, it wasn't at all clear what 'fitting in' actually meant. Yet, even though 'fitting in' was a movable feast, anyone on the panel had a right to veto any candidate that did not 'fit in' – another major source of frustration to the HR manager who commented 'with criteria as loose as this I don't know how we can ever say yes to anyone'. As a result, the HR manager had attempted to formalise the recruitment process further by asking divisional managers to nominate a consultant within their division to act as an HR liaison and to sit on all relevant panels. However, despite numerous promptings, a list of nominated liaisons had yet to appear.

Questions

1. Compare the four cases according to how far they conform to the rational decision-making perspective (i.e., the psychometric tradition) or to the interactive action-oriented perspective described in this chapter.

2. On the surface, the case of Newsco illustrates the design of a fairly standard assessment for development workshop in the psychometric tradition. What evidence is there to suggest that assessment is not the sole purpose? What other purposes might the centre serve?

3. In what ways is Pharmco an example of an assessment centre, a development centre, or a mix of the two?

4. Why is it important to consider the national/cultural dimension in the design of centres?

5. Why might the rejection of such high numbers of candidates at ScienceCo actually be an important positive aspect of their recruitment and selection process?

References

Ackerman, B., Ross-Ackerman, S., Sawyer, J. and Henderson, D. (1974) *The Uncertain Research for Environmental Quality,* New York: Free Press.

Adler, P. and S-W. Kwon (2002) 'Social capital: prospects for a new concept', *Academy of Management Review,* Vol.27, No.1, pp.17–40.

Agor, W. (1986) 'The logic of intuition: how top executives make important decisions', *Organizational Dynamics,* Winter, pp.5–15.

Agor, W. (1989) *Intuition in Organizations,* Newbury Park, CA: Sage.

Alldredge, M. and Nilan, K. (2000) '3M's leadership competency model: an internally developed solution', *Human Resource Management,* Vol.39, Nos2–3, pp.133–46.

*Anderson, N. (2003) 'Applicant and recruiter reactions to new technology in selection: a critical review and agenda for future research', *International Journal of Selection and Assessment,* Vol.11, Nos2–3, pp.121–37.

Anderson, N. and Ostroff, C. (1997) 'Selection as socialization', in N. Anderson and P. Herriot (eds) *International Handbook of Selection and Assessment,* Chichester: Wiley.

Argyris, C. (1977) 'Organizational learning and management information systems', *Accounting, Organizations and Society,* Vol.2, pp.113–23.

Arnold, J., Cooper, C. and Robertson, I. (1997) *Work Psychology: Understanding Human Behaviour in the Workplace,* London: FT/Pitman Publishing.

Arvey, R.D. and Faley, R.H. (1992) *Fairness in Selecting Employees* (2nd edn), Reading, MA: Addison-Wesley.

Bandura, A. (1977) 'Self-efficacy: toward a unifying theory of behavioural change', *Psychological Review,* Vol.84, No.2, pp.191–215.

*Barclay, J. (2001) 'Improving selection interviews with structure: organizations' use of behavioural interviews', *Personnel Review,* Vol.30, Nos1–2, pp.81–103.

Barrick, M. and Mount, M. (1991) 'The big five personality dimensions and job performance: A meta-analysis', *Personnel Psychology,* Vol.44, pp.1–26.

Batram, D. (2000) 'Internet recruitment and selection: kissing frogs to find princes', *International Journal of Selection and Assessment,* Vol.8, No.4, pp.261–74.

Batram, D. (2004) 'Assessment in organizations', *Applied Psychology: An International Review,* Vol.53, No.2, pp.237–50.

Bauer, T., Truxillo, D., Paronto, M., Weekley, J. and Campion, M. (2004) 'Applicant reactions to different selection technology: Face-to-Face, Interactive Voice Response, and Computer-Assisted Telephone Screening Interviews', *International Journal of Selection and Assessment,* Vol.12, Nos1–2, pp.135–48.

Bazerman, M. (1994) *Judgement in Managerial Decision-making* (3rd edn), New York: Wiley.

Beach, L. (1990) *Image Theory: Decision Making in Personal and Organizational Contexts,* Chichester: Wiley.

Beardwell, I., Holden, L. and Claydon, T. (2004) *Human Resource Management,* London: FT/Prentice Hall.

Behling, O. and Eckel, N. (1991) 'Making sense out of intuition', *Academy of Management Executive,* Vol.5, pp.46–54.

Bingham, B., Ilg, S. and Davidson, N. (2002) 'Great candidates fast: online job application and electronic processing', *Public Personnel Management,* Vol.31, No.1, pp.53–64.

Boam, R. and Sparrow, P. (1992) *Designing and Achieving Competency: A Competency-Based Approach to Managing People and Organizations,* London: McGraw-Hill.

Boyle, S., Fullerton, J. and Wood, R. (1995) 'Do assessment/development centres use optimal evaluation procedures?', *International Journal of Selection and Assessment,* Vol.3, pp.132–40.

Bray, D. and Grant, D. (1966) 'The assessment centre in the measurement of potential for business management', *Psychological Monographs,* Vol.80, No.17 (Whole No.625).

Brunsson, N. (1982) 'The irrationality of action and action rationality: decisions, ideologies and organizational actions', *Journal of Management Studies,* Vol.19, No.1, pp.29–44.

Brunsson, N. (1989) *The Organization of Hypocrisy, Talk, Decisions and Actions in Organizations,* Chichester: Wiley, pp.242.

Buchanan, D. and Huczynski, A. (2004) 'Images of influence', *Journal of Management Inquiry,* Vol.13, No.4, pp.312–24.

Campbell, J.P. (1990) 'Modeling the performance prediction problem in industrial and organizational psychology', in M.D. Dunnette and L.M. Hough (eds) *Handbook of Industrial and Organizational Psychology* (2nd edn), Vol.1, Palo Alto, CA: Consulting Psychologists Press.

Carlson, K., Scullen, S., Schimdt, F., Rothstein, H. and Erwin, F. (1999), 'Generalisable biographical data validity can be achieved without multi-organizational development and keying', *Personnel Psychology,* Vol.52, pp.731–55.

Coe, T. (1992) *The Key to the Men's Club: Opening the Doors to Women in Management,* Corby: IM Foundation.

Cohen, M., March, J. and Olsen, J. (1972) 'A garbage can model of organizational choice', *Administrative Science Quarterly,* Vol.17, No.1, pp.1–25.

Contu, A. and Willmott, H. (2003) 'Re-embedding situatedness: the importance of power relations in learning theory', *Organization Science,* Vol.13, No.3, pp.283–97.

Cyert, R. and March, J. (1963) *A Behavioural Theory of the Firm,* Englewood Cliffs, NJ: Prentice-Hall.

Day, D. and Silverman, S. (1989) 'Personality and job performance: evidence of incremental validity', *Personnel Psychology,* Vol.42, pp.25–36.

DiMilia, L. and Gorodecki, M. (1997) 'Some factors explaining the reliability of a structured interview at a work site', *International Journal of Selection and Assessment,* Vol.5, No.4, pp.193–9.

DiMilia, L., Smith, P. and Brown, D. (1994) 'Management selection in Australia: a comparison with British and French findings', *International Journal of Selection and Assessment,* Vol.2, pp.80–90.

Dipboye, R. (1992) 'Selection interviews: Process perspectives', Cincinnati, OH: South-Western.

Dipboye, R. (1997) 'Structured selection interviews: Why do they work? Why are they underutilized?', in N. Anderson and P. Herriot (eds), *International Handbook of Selection and Assessment,* Chichester: Wiley.

Eden, D. and Shani, A. (1982) 'Pygmalion goes to boot camp: Expectancy, leadership and trainee performance', *Journal of Applied Psychology,* Vol.67, No.2, pp.194–9.

Festinger, L. (1957) *A Theory of Cognitive Dissonance,* New York: Harper Row.

*Fish, A. and Mackim, R. (2004) 'Perceptions of executive search and advertised recruitment attributes and service quality', *Personnel Review,* Vol.33, No.1, pp.30–55.

Fiske, S. and Taylor, S. (1991) *Social Cognition,* New York: McGraw-Hill.

Fleenor, J. (1996) 'Constructs and developmental assessment centres: Further troubling empirical findings', *Journal of Business and Psychology,* Vol.10, pp.319–33.

Frase-Blunt, M. (2004), 'Selecting a diversity consultant', *HR Magazine,* Vol.49, No.6, pp.147–53.

Ghiselli, E. (1973) 'The validity of aptitude tests in personnel selection', *Personnel Psychology*, Vol.26, pp.461–77.

Gist, M. (1987) 'Self-efficacy: implications for organizational behaviour and human resource management', *Academy of Management Review*, Vol.12, pp.472–85.

Goldstein, H., Yusko, K., Braverman, F., Smith, D. and Chung, B. (1998), 'The role of cognitive ability in the subgroup differences and incremental validity of assessment centre exercises', *Personnel Psychology*, Vol.51, pp.357–74.

Griffin, B., Hesketh, B. and Grayson, D. (2004), 'Applicants faking good: evidence of item bias in the NEO PI-R', *Personality and Individual Differences*, Vol.36, No.7, pp.1545–54.

Heffcut, A.I. and Arthur, W. (1994) 'Hunter and Hunter (1984) revisited: interview validity and entry level jobs', *Journal of Applied Psychology*, Vol.79, pp.184–90.

Heffcut, A.I., Roth, P., Conway, J. and Klehe, U.-C. (2004) 'The impact of job complexity and study design on situational and behaviour description interview validity', *International Journal of Selection and Assessment*, Vol.12, No.3, pp.262–73.

Hennessy, J., Mabey, B. and Warr, P. (1998) 'Assessment centre observation procedures: an experimental comparison of traditional, checklist and coding methods', *International Journal of Selection and Assessment*, Vol.6, No.4, pp.222–31.

Hesketh, B. (1999) 'Introduction' to the International Journal of Selection and Assessment special issue on biodata, *International Journal of Selection and Assessment*, Vol.7, No.2, pp.55–6.

Hofstede, G. (1984) *Culture's Consequences: International Differences in Work-related Values*, London: Sage.

Hough, L., Eaton, N., Dunnette, M., Kamp, J. and McCloy, R. (1990) 'Criterion-related validities of personality constructs and the effect of response distortion on those validities', *Journal of Applied Psychology*, Vol.75, pp.581–5.

Hough, L. and Oswald, F. (2000) 'Personnel selection: Looking toward the future–remembering the past', *Annual Review of Psychology*, Vol.51, pp.631–64.

Hunter, J. and Hunter, R. (1984) 'Validity and utility of alternative predictors of job performance', *Psychological Bulletin*, Vol.96, pp.72–98.

Industrial Relations Service (1997) 'The state of selection: an IRS survey', *Employee Development Bulletin*, Vol.85, pp.8–18.

Janis, I. (1972) *Victims of Groupthink*, Boston, MA: Houghton-Mifflin.

Janz, T. (1989) 'The patterned behaviour description interview: the best prophet of the future is the past', in R.D. Eder and G.R. Ferris (eds) *The Employment Interview: Theory and Practice*, London: Sage.

Joyce, L., Thayer, P. and Pond, S. (1994) 'Managerial functions: An alternative to traditional assessment centre dimensions?', *Personnel Psychology*, Vol.47, pp.109–21.

Kacmar, M., Witt, L., Ziznuska, S. and Gully, S. (2003) 'The interactive effect of leader-member exchange and communication frequency on performance ratings', *Journal of Applied Psychology*, Vol.88, No.4, pp.764–72.

Kauffman, J., Jex, S., Love, K. and Libkuman, T. (1993) 'The construct validity of assessment centre performance dimensions', *International Journal of Selection and Assessment*, Vol.1, pp.213–23.

Keenan, T. (1995) 'Graduate recruitment in Britain: A survey of selection methods used by organizations', *Journal of Organizational Behaviour*, Vol.16, pp.303–17.

Kolk, N., Born, M. and van der Flier, H. (2002), 'Impact of common variance on construct validity of assessment centre dimension judgements', *Human Performance*, Vol.15, No.4, pp.325–38.

Konradt, U., Hertel, G. and Joder, K. (2003), 'Web-based assessment of call-centre agents: Development and validation of a computerized instrument', *International Journal of Selection and Assessment*, Vol.11, Nos 2–3, pp.184–94.

Landis, R., Fogli, L. and Goldberg, E. (1998) 'Future-oriented job analysis: a description of the process and its organizational implications', *International Journal of Selection and Assessment*, Vol.6, No.3, pp.192–7.

Landy, F., Shankster-Cawley, L. and Moran, S. (1995) 'Advancing personnel selection and placement methods', in A. Howard (ed.) *The Changing Nature of Work*, San Francisco, CA: Jossey-Bass.

Lievens, F. (1998) 'Factors which improve the construct validity of assessment centres: a review', *International Journal of Selection and Assessment,* Vol.6, No.3, pp.141–52.

Lind, E. and Tyler, T. (1988) *The Social Psychology of Procedural Justice,* New York: Plenum.

Lindblom, C.E. (1959) 'The science of "muddling through"', *Public Administration Review,* Vol.19, pp.79–88.

Macan, T.H., Avedon, M.J., Paese, M. and Smith, D.E. (1994) 'The effects of applicants' reactions to cognitive ability tests and an assessment centre', *Personnel Psychology,* Vol.47, No.4, pp.715–38.

Mael, F. (1991) 'A conceptual rationale for the domain and attributes of biodata items', *Personnel Psychology,* Vol.44, pp.763–92.

March, J. and Olsen, J. (1976) *Ambiguity and Choice in Organizations,* Bergen: Universitetsforlaget.

Marchington, M. and Wilkinson, A. (2005) *Human Resource Management at Work,* London: CIPD.

Matthews, B. and Redman, T. (1998) 'Managerial recruitment advertisements – just how market-orientated are they?', *International Journal of Selection and Assessment,* Vol.6, No.4, pp.240–8.

Mayfield, E.C. (1964) 'The selection interview: A re-evaluation of published research', *Personnel Psychology,* Vol.17, pp.239–60.

McCredie, H. and Shackleton, V.J. (1994) 'The development and interim validation of a dimensions-based senior management assessment centre', *Human Resources Management Journal,* Vol.5, No.1, pp.91–101.

McDaniel, M.A., Whetzel, D.L., Schmidt, F.L. and Maurer, S.D. (1994) 'The validity of the employment interviews: a comprehensive review and meta-analysis', *Journal of Applied Psychology,* Vol.79, pp.599–616.

McManus, I., Smithers, E., Partridge, P., Keeling, A. and Fleming, P. (2003) 'A levels and intelligence as predictors of medical careers in UK doctors: 20 year prospective study', *British Medical Journal,* Vol.327, No.7407, pp.139–43.

Merrick, N. (1997) 'Big thaw shows up on recruitment market', *People Management,* Vol.3, No.2, pp.10–11.

Mooney, J. (2002) 'Pre-employment testing on the internet: put candidates a click away and hire at modem speed', *Public Personnel Management,* Vol.31, No.1, pp.41–52.

Mumford, M. and Stokes, G. (1992) 'Developmental determinants of individual action: Theory and practice in applying background measures', in M. Dunnette and L. Hough (eds) *Handbook of Industrial and Organizational Psychology* (2nd edn), Vol.3, Palo Alto, CA: Consulting Psychologists Press, pp.61–138.

*Newell, S. and Shackleton, V. (1993) 'The use (and abuse) of psychometric tests in British industry and commerce', *Human Resource Management Journal,* Vol.4, No.1, pp.14–23.

Newell, S. and Shackleton, V. (2001) 'Selection and assessment as an interactive decision process', in T. Redman and A. Wilkinson (eds) *Contemporary Human Resource Management,* London: Prentice Hall, pp.24–56.

Nisbett, R. and Ross, L. (1980) *Human Inference,* Englewood Cliffs, NJ: Prentice-Hall.

O'Higgins, E. (2002) 'Non-executive directors on boards in Ireland: co-option, contributions and characteristics', *Corporate Governance: An International Review,* Vol.10, No.1, pp.19–29.

Oswald, F., Schmitt, N., Kim, B., Ramsay, L. and Gillespie, M. (2004), 'Developing a biodata measure and situational judgement inventory as predictors of college student performance', *Journal of Applied Psychology,* Vol.89, No.2, pp.187–206.

Pfeffer, J. (1981) *Power in Organisations,* Marshfield, MA: Pitman.

Redmond, S. (1989) *How to Recruit Good Managers,* London: Kogan Page.

Rees, C. (1996) 'Psychometrics: topical misunderstandings amongst test users', *International Journal of Selection and Assessment,* Vol.4, No.1, pp.44–8.

Roberts, G. (1997) *Recruitment and Selection: A Competency Approach,* London: IPD.

Robertson, I. and Kinder, A. (1993) 'Personality and job competences: the criterion-related validity of some personality variables', *Journal of Occupational and Organizational Psychology,* Vol.66, pp.225–44.

*Robertson, I. and Smith, M. (2001) 'Personnel selection', *Journal of Occupational and Organizational Psychology,* Vol.74, pp.441–72.

Rosenfeld, P., Giacalone, R.A. and Riordan, C.A. (1995) *Impression Management in Organizations,* London: Routledge.

Ryan, A. and Tippins, N. (2004) 'Attracting and selecting: what psychological research tells us', *Human Resource Management,* Vol.43, No.4, pp.305–19.

Salgado, J. (1996) 'Personality and job competences: a comment on Robertson and Kinder's (1993) study', *Journal of Occupational and Organizational Psychology,* Vol.69, pp.373–5.

Salgado, J. (1999), 'Personnel selection methods', in C. Cooper and I.T. Robertson (eds) *International Review of Industrial and Organizational Psychology,* New York: Wiley.

Schmitt, N., Gooding, R., Noe, R. and Kirsch, M. (1984) 'Meta-analyses of validity studies published between 1964 and 1982, and the investigation of study characteristics', *Personnel Psychology,* Vol.37, pp.407–22.

Schneider, B. and Konz, A. (1989) 'Strategic job analysis', *Human Resource Management,* Vol.28, pp.51–63.

Scholarios, D., Lockyer, C. and Johnson, H. (2003) 'Anticipatory socialisation: the effects of recruitment and selection on career expectations', *Career Development International,* Vol.8, No.4, pp.182–98.

Shackleton, V. and Newell, S. (1991) 'Management selection: a comparative survey of methods used in top British and French companies', *Journal of Occupational Psychology,* Vol.64, pp.23–6.

Shackleton, V. and Newell, S. (1994) 'European selection methods: a comparison of five countries', *International Journal of Selection and Assessment,* Vol.2, pp.91–102.

Shintaku, R. (2004), 'Invited reaction: understanding the experience of college graduates during their first year of employment', *Human Resource Development Quarterly,* Vol.15, No.1, pp.25–30.

Simon, H. (1960) *The New Science of Management Decision,* New York: Harper Row.

Singer, M. (1993) *Fairness in Personnel Selection,* Aldershot: Avebury.

Sparrow, P. and Bognanno, M. (1993) 'Competency requirement forecasting: issues for international selection and assessment', *International Journal of Selection and Assessment,* Vol.1, No.1, pp.50–8.

Staffsud, A. (2003) 'Recruitment policy versus recruitment process: espoused theory versus theory-in-use', *Academy of Management Proceedings,* pG1, 6p.

Stokes, G., Hogan, J. and Snell, A. (1993) 'Comparability of incumbent and applicant samples for the development of biodata keys: the influence of social desirability', *Personnel Psychology,* Vol.46, pp.739–62.

Stricker, L. and Rock, D. (1998) 'Assessing leadership potential with a biographical measure of personality traits', *International Journal of Selection and Assessment,* Vol.6, No.3, pp.164–84.

Sue-Chan, C. and Latham, P. (2004) 'The situational interview as a predictor of academic and team performance: a study of the mediating effects of cognitive ability and emotional intelligence', *International Journal of Selection and Assessment,* Vol.12, No.4, pp.312–21.

Sundvik, L. and Lindeman, M. (1998) 'Performance rating accuracy: convergence between supervisor assessment and sales productivity', *International Journal of Selection and Assessment,* Vol.6, No.1, pp.9–15.

*Taylor, S. (2002) *Employee Resourcing,* London: CIPD.

Tett, R., Steele, J. and Beauregard, R. (2003) 'Broad and narrow measures on both sides of the personality–job performance relationship', *Journal of Organizational Behaviour,* Vol.24, No.3, pp.335–57.

Thornton, G. (1992) *Assessment Centres in Human Resource Management,* Reading, MA: Addison Wesley.

Torrington, D., Hall, L. and Taylor, S. (2005) *Human Resource Management,* London: FT/Prentice Hall.

Trompenaars, F. (1993) *Riding the Waves of Culture: Understanding Cultural Diversity in Business,* London: Nicholas Brealey.

Truxillo, D., Steiner, D. and Gilliland, S. (2004), 'The importance of organizational justice in personnel selection: defining when selection fairness really matters', *International Journal of Selection and Assessment,* Vol.12, Nos 1–2, pp.39–54.

Ulrich, L. and Trumbo, D. (1965) 'The selection interview since 1949', *Psychological Bulletin,* Vol.53, pp.100–16.

Vaughan, D. (1996) *The Challenger Launch Decision: Risky Technology, Culture, and Deviance at NASA,* Chicago, IL: University of Chicago Press.

Vaughan, D. (1997) 'The trickle-down effect: policy decisions, risky work and the Challenger tragedy', *California Management Review,* Vol.39, No.2, pp.80–102.

Weick, K.E. (1990) 'Technology as equivoque: sensemaking in new technologies', in P.S. Goodman, L.S. Sproull and Associates, *Technology and Organisations,* Oxford: Jossey-Bass.

Yetiv, S. (2003) 'Groupthink and the gulf crisis', *British Journal of Political Science,* Vol.33, No.3, pp.419–43.

Zedeck, S. (1986) 'A process analysis of the assessment centre method', in B. Shaw and L. Cummings (eds) *Research in Organizational Behaviour,* Vol.8, pp.259–96, Greenwich, CT: JAI Press.

* Useful reading

Chapter 4

TRAINING AND DEVELOPMENT

Irena Grugulis

Introduction

Training, development and skills are key aspects of economic life. At the levels of the firm and the national economy training offers the hope of increased competitiveness through raising skill levels, productivity and 'value added'. For trade unions and professional associations, training enhances members' expertise, facilitating negotiations for pay and status. While for individuals, given that life chances are still heavily influenced by the job a person does and the wages they earn, education and training can increase knowledge and opportunities, give access to more highly rewarded work and reduce the prospect of unemployment. Small wonder then that consensus exists in this area, that governments encourage training through regulation or exhortation, or that employers praise its importance in surveys. Yet despite this support, the levels and quality of vocational education and training in Britain are neither as high, nor as evenly distributed, as might be hoped. Excellent practice exists, but rarely 'trickles down' to less well-provided areas. This chapter, drawing on international practice, explores some of the advantages of developmental systems of vocational education and training (VET) and sets them against both positive and negative aspects of the British experience. It argues that, in common with other human resource practices, training should not be considered in isolation. Its effectiveness, or otherwise, hinges on the wider economic and organisational context.

The case for training and development

The advantages of training and development are not illusory. Within organisations, it can equip workers to carry out tasks, monitor quality and manage complex products and services. Arthur's (1999) research into US steel mini-mills describes the way that switching between different types of steel or different shapes required close monitoring by melt-shop employees. The exact nature of changeover activities was difficult to predict and down-time was expensive so the quality and quantity of production relied heavily on the skills of operators and maintenance workers who had a considerable amount of discretion managing these shifts. Here, as elsewhere, quality products relied heavily on workers' expertise.

Training and development safeguards such productivity as well as supporting it, by preparing employees for future jobs and insulating firms from skills shortages. When jobs can be filled internally, firms are less dependent on the outside labour market and do not risk appropriate

Box 4.1: Biscuits and skill: biscuit making in Britain and Germany

This is taken from a study of biscuit manufacture in ten British and eight German firms.

The type of biscuits produced varied greatly between the two countries, largely owing to national tastes and demand. In Britain, demand concentrated on relatively basic biscuits: either plain or with one simple coating of chocolate, cream or jam. In Germany, there was a much higher demand for decorated and multi-textured products (soft biscuits with jam filling in chocolate cases or layered variegated biscuits). Since this affected the type of biscuits that each firm produced, relative output figures were not easy to measure. On crude output figures, productivity per employee hour was 25 per cent higher in Britain than in Germany, largely because British firms produced large quantities of simple, low-quality biscuits. However, when these productivity figures were adjusted for quality, the British advantage disappeared with German firms 40 per cent more productive per employee hour.

In Germany 90 per cent of process workers were craft-trained bakers and could work in all of the main areas of operations (mixing, biscuit forming and oven control). This multi-skilling meant that three-person teams could be responsible for at least two oven lines at the same time. In German firms, employees were focused in areas that added value to the product. Maintenance staff were highly qualified and, in addition to undertaking regular maintenance, they worked with supervisors to customise equipment and increase productivity. In Britain, no process workers and few supervisors were vocationally qualified. As a result, each individual production line needed a three-person team to cover mixing and baking since workers were narrowly trained and tended to stick to their own jobs. Few firms had any regular system of machine maintenance since shift work meant that equipment was rarely scheduled to stop but breakdowns were frequent and high staffing levels in areas such as wrapping were needed to sort out problems caused by equipment breakdown and malfunction. On the line, narrow training restricted the ability of shop-floor workers to anticipate problems (such as machine malfunctioning) and take appropriate action.

Source: Mason *et al.*1996

recruits not being available (or not being available at the price the organisation wishes to pay). Such security is welcome. According to Hillage *et al.*, 8 per cent of employers in England have skill-shortage vacancies and 23 per cent report internal skills gaps (in which not all employees are fully proficient at the work that they do). The problems reported as a result of these gaps include difficulties with customer service, delays developing new products, increases in operating costs or problems introducing new working practices, difficulties with quality standards, the withdrawal of products or services and loss of business (2002, pp.48 and 84).

Within firms, training and development is a key element of human resource management, indeed Keep (1989) argues that it is the litmus test against which other aspects of management practice should be gauged. When firms compete on the basis of quality and adopt high-commitment work practices such as employee involvement, teamworking or merit-based pay; developing employees is the key element in performance. It can raise the capacity of the individuals and groups employed, enabling them to participate meaningfully in systems where their contribution is encouraged (Keep and Mayhew 1996). Arthur (1999) links the 'commitment'-oriented human resource practices in steel mini-mills to the strategic focus on quality and batch production, contrasting it with less developmental 'control' mechanisms in organisations where production was routine and where human resource practices focused on minimising labour costs.

Training also allows organisations to adapt to changes in the business environment. A point somewhat evangelically made in writings on the Learning Organisation (see, for example, Senge 1992). While this literature is problematic, focusing more on evangelical rhetoric, anecdote and prescription rather than considered evaluations of the ways that people learn in organisations, and while it is unlikely that a Learning Organisation either has or could have existed (Keep and Rainbird 2000), job design and organisational structure influence the way that people work and the amount they can learn. At the most basic level, as Hillage *et al.* (2002) reveal, organisations with skills shortages report difficulties introducing new products and working practices.

In addition to these substantive factors, training and development also serves an important and very positive symbolic function. Everything that a firm does sends messages (of one kind or another) to its employees (one of the key elements of the positive side of HRM). Organisations that spend money on raising skills are, quite literally, investing in their workers. Employees who participate in firm-sponsored training are more likely to see themselves as having better career prospects and say that they are intending to stay with their employer than those that do not (Heyes and Stuart 1996) – a finding that raises interesting questions on current discussions about 'employability' as a substitute for employment security.

However, while training and development can have an extremely positive impact on the quality of production, can insulate firms from skills shortages and is a pivotal element of most models of high-commitment human resource management, its links to productivity and profit are much harder to gauge. This is not to argue that such links do not exist, or that well-trained experienced workers do not out-perform novices; rather, it is that the data that is collected is neither coherent nor robust enough for a convincing case to be made. At a national level Britain's lack of vocational preparation is consistently cited as one of the main reasons for its under-performance. Manufacturing productivity in the US is 81 per cent higher than in the UK, Germany is 59 per cent higher and Sweden 72 per cent (cited in Nolan and Slater 2003). However, VET here is one element of a much wider system and it is difficult to separate its impact from that of other factors, such as technology.

At the level of the firm, employers believe in the links between training, performance and profitability (Coopers and Lybrand 1985; DTZ Pieda Consulting 1999). And, according to some of the most recent estimates, firms spend around £23.5 billion on VET (Spilsbury 2001). However, cross-firm comparisons are difficult to make since figures between (and occasionally within) firms are rarely consistent. Some organisations include costs of room hire and employees' salaries in their calculations, others give only the cost of training departments or external consultants and the costs of on-the-job training are almost impossible to collate. These inconsistencies, coupled with the fact that many organisations simply did not know how much they spent on training, were pointed out to employers by Coopers and Lybrand (1985). Most revealed that they would rather true figures were not collated since this would result in pressure to reduce training spend, a response which reveals the vulnerability of UK training, rather than its centrality.

To make this issue more confusing, organisations may use training as a means to escape from an economic downturn, increasing spending when profit levels are low; or symbolically, to motivate and reward. From the perspective of encouraging training and development, both of these approaches are welcome; but they do cause problems for academics attempting to establish links between an organisation's training activities and its performance. Then too, official measures of training success such as increases in employment (a factor of key interest to governments), may not be welcomed by individual organisations whose managers are more concerned with the impact practice has on profitability and share-price (for a fuller discussion of these issues see Keep *et al.* 2002).

The benefits to organisations are matched by advantages that individuals can gain. According to human capital theory (Becker 1964) the more investment an individual makes in themselves, the greater their lifetime returns, through increased earnings, fewer (and shorter) periods of unemployment and access to more interesting work. As Table 4.1 shows, male graduates can expect to earn 28 per cent more than men with 'A' levels (the figures are cumulative) while women graduates gain 25 per cent on average over women with 'A' levels. (Since men tend to earn more than women, this table gives the premiums against only either male or female earnings, which explains why a teaching qualification adds 27 per cent to women's earnings but has a nil return for men. It is not that women teachers are more highly paid than their male colleagues but rather that, for women teaching is a comparatively well-paid option, whereas well-qualified men are likely to be in more highly paid work.) Training that leads to formal certification (qualifications) has the additional advantage of helping the labour market to function more efficiently. Qualifications are an uneasy proxy for skills, but they are simple to check and so, particularly in recruitment and selection, they tend to serve as a form of shorthand that enables individuals and employers to find one another.

Table 4.1 Wage premium (%) from obtaining qualifications, Labour Force Survey

	Men	Women
CSEs / lower GCSEs	9	5
'O' level / higher GCSEs	21	19
'A' level	17	19
First degree	28	25
Higher degree	8	18
Professional qualifications	35	41
Nursing	13	21
Teaching	Nil	27
Level 1–2 NVQs	Nil	Nil
BTEC First	Nil	Nil
Level 3–5 NVQs	6	5
RSA Higher	4	12
C&G Craft	7	Nil
C&G Advanced	7	Nil
ONC/ONC BTEC National	10	8
HND/HNC	15	9

Notes:
1. The wage premiums are additive, so, for example, a man with 'O' levels/higher GCSEs and 'A' levels and a first degree will earn 66 per cent more than a man with no qualifications
2. Lower level NVQs and the BTEC First have a significantly positive effect on *employment* rates for women, but not for men
3. Controls for age, ethnicity, region, firm size, public/private sector

Source: Dearden *et al.* 2000; cited in Machin and Vignoles 2001, p.8. SKT 27, *The Returns to Academic, Vocational and Basic Skills in Britain, 2000*, DfES. © Crown copyright. Reproduced with the permission of the Controller of HMSO and the Queen's Printer for Scotland

Individuals can benefit at a collective level too, as members of a particular profession or craft. Indeed, many of the most respected forms of training (medical, engineering, apprenticeships) are designed to lead to full membership of an occupation. Professional bodies and trade unions then develop, market and defend the skills of their members, and are among the most active supporters of VET in Britain. Several professional bodies even have mandatory schemes to ensure that members' training is up-dated (Keep, 1994; Rainbird, 1994, 1990).

VOLUNTARIST AND REGULATED APPROACHES

While there is a consensus over the importance and value of training and development, this is not matched by agreement on how best to encourage good practice. At a national level the two principal approaches are voluntarist (market-based) and regulated (educational). Both the USA and Britain are broadly voluntarist. The principal assumption behind such systems is that organisations operate more effectively when unfettered by regulation. Market pressures (to remain competitive, produce quality goods and run efficiently) will ensure that, where training is appropriate, firms will invest in it and, in the absence of expensive and cumbersome official bureaucracy, investment can be accurately targeted to respond to market needs.

By contrast, in a regulated system, as in much of continental Europe, vocational education and training is supported by the state. Regulation may take a variety of forms. In France, employers are required to support training or pay a levy to the state while in Germany there is a system of extensive and rigorous apprenticeships for young people entering the labour market, coupled with 'licences to practice' for particular occupations. The assumption behind this approach is that vocational education and training is a public good and it is in the long-term interests of all to have a highly skilled workforce. But left to themselves individual firms will prioritise profitability and may not invest in skills development or may fund only short-term and low-level training. Training and development is, after all, only one way of securing skilled workers and firms may choose to recruit workers trained elsewhere or de-skill production instead. By providing an appropriate infrastructure (or a system of levies, or by regulating practice) the state ensures robust skills development.

Both voluntarist and regulated approaches can be successful. Silicon Valley, California provides an excellent example of the way that skills can be developed in a market-based system. Silicon Valley is famously the site of a cluster of extremely high-tech computing firms. These are supported by the proximity of universities (University of California campuses in Berkeley, San Francisco, San Diego and Los Angeles and private institutions such as Stanford, USC and CalTech) that supply expert labour, share research and stimulate start-up companies. Stanford (whose graduates include William Hewlett and David Packard) even set up the first university science park to provide fledgling firms with support services. The infrastructure is conducive to growth with good local transport, an international airport and a state-of-the-art telecommunications system while the availability of venture capital, low levels of regulation and limited penalties on bankruptcy encourage start-ups. These small and often highly focused firms prosper through inter-dependency, forming partnerships with other organisations and participating in employer groups to pursue initiatives such as improving technical training in city colleges, which are to their mutual benefit. Individuals also collaborate through professional associations, continuing education courses and alumni associations. In firms there is little formal training but skills and expertise are developed through project work on cutting-edge technical challenges. Even labour mobility, a point of concern elsewhere, assists knowledge diffusion and increases personal and professional networks (Finegold 1999).

Such an unstructured 'ecosystem' is very successful at developing and supporting the most expert who work at the cutting edge of their profession. However, the USA as a whole is far less successful in training and development for the majority and it is here that a more regulated system triumphs. The highly regarded German apprenticeship system is one of the best-known routes to achieving vocational qualifications. Full apprenticeships last three years and trainees are taught technical skills in the classroom which are subsequently developed through participation in a series of problem-solving activities, graded in terms of difficulty. Care is taken to ensure that apprentices are exposed to a full range of different work situations with central training centres supplementing workplace experience and providing additional workplace settings for trainees to learn in; an arrangement which gives smaller employers the capacity to offer high level training. Technical training is supplemented with knowledge of work control and design (manufacturing qualifications involve familiarity with costs, design and planning, and administration and production) and, in addition to this, all apprentices are required to continue to participate in further education for the duration of their vocational studies (Streeck *et al.* 1987; Lane 1989; Marsden and Ryan 1995; though see also Culpepper 1999).

The German system is made possible by close, collaborative links between employers' associations, trade unions and regional governments cooperating on creating a system that works for the benefit of all. Taiwan is different, its economy is dominated by small and medium-sized enterprises (SMEs), that successfully resisted the introduction of a levy for vocational education and training in the 1970s. Yet, despite this it has managed to introduce extensive vocational skills development, increasing the amount of technical, vocational education and the numbers of scientists and engineers through the education system. Demand for education was for academic education (and this would have been cheaper to provide) but access to academic courses was officially restricted, more than half of schoolchildren were channelled into technical training and, at university level, more courses were made available for scientists and engineers and new Institutes of Technology launched. Student numbers, textbooks and curricula were state-controlled and this meant that Taiwan succeeded in both the growing low-cost industrial products for export and also managed the transition from this to higher value-added production across many if not all sectors without significant reported skills shortages (Green *et al.* 1999).

Each system has its strengths and limitations. The 'high skills eco-system' of Silicon Valley is highly responsive to developing new and expert skills in a sector that the German apprenticeship system has struggled to provide qualifications for since the tripartite arrangements for agreeing standards are so time-consuming that qualifications in fast-developing fields may be out of date before they are launched (although this development process has been considerably shortened and the dominance and longevity of systems like Microsoft mean that computing skills that do not date rapidly can be supported). However, regulation, as in Germany, does mean that skilled workers are widely available with two-thirds of workers holding intermediate qualifications or above. By contrast, in unregulated systems some occupations neglect training even when this is to their detriment. After construction was deregulated in the USA, training levels fell dramatically – as did investment in physical capital and productivity (Bosch 2003).

Perhaps the most notable feature of these examples is that they are systemic, success here goes beyond the simple provision of high quality training (indeed, in the US example, formal training is one of the least significant elements of skills development). The high-skills eco-system of Silicon Valley is made possible by the fact that recruits are already extremely highly educated on entry (and many of them are IT experts). In Germany, the existence of employers' associations, trade unions and vocational colleges that are prepared to collaborate; and in Taiwan the government's readiness to both pay for skills development and take decisions that may be unpopular with individual students and their families, facilitate good intermediate skills training.

Box 4.2: Expansive and restrictive approaches to training and development

Systemic approaches to training and development can also be observed *within* firms. One manufacturer of bathroom showers, described by Fuller and Unwin (2004), took an *expansive* approach to development. It had a long-established apprenticeship programme and many ex-apprentices had progressed to senior management. Apprentices were rotated around different departments to gain wider knowledge of the business and improve their skills. They also attended college on day release, working towards knowledge-based qualifications which would give them access to higher education, went on residential courses designed to foster team working and were involved with local charities through the company's apprenticeship association. Contrast this with the *restrictive* environment of a small steel polishing company where apprentices had been reluctantly taken on only when managers were unable to recruit qualified staff. After less than a year, the two apprentices who had learned on the job, had gained all the skills necessary for their work. There was no system of job rotation and formal training was limited to 10 half-day courses on steel industry awareness (the sum total of apprentices' outside involvement) and an NVQ.

Source: Fuller and Unwin 2004

This is an important point and a key element of the success of each of these approaches. It also has implications for attempts to identify and transplant 'best practice', which generally focus only on one narrow element of a successful system. Korea's attempts to replicate the German apprenticeship system are a case in point (Jeong 1995). This had government support and experienced German advisors were engaged, but little financial support was available, the firms employing the apprentices provided little training, and used them as low-paid and low-skilled workers, few college tutors were sufficiently skilled to make up this deficit and seniority, rather than skill, remained the key element in promotion. As a result, the initiative failed.

Voluntary intervention

The difference between voluntarist and regulated approaches to VET is clearer in theory than it is in practice. Even in Britain, where successive governments have argued that decisions on training and development should be left to employers, officials are not passive. Indeed, policy documents regularly exhort employers to train and official reports stress the importance of VET (DfES/DTI/HM Treasury/DWP 2003). A state-funded infrastructure exists to promote 'best practice' in training and development, provide limited funding or subsidies for particular groups (some of the unemployed, young people, SMEs) and help occupational sectors to develop and market qualifications. There is currently one national Learning and Skills Council, 47 Local Learning and Skills Councils, a Sector Skills Development Agency and a network of Sector Skills Councils. In addition, various government bodies have an interest in

VET including the Department for Work and Pensions, the Department for Education and Skills, regional development associations and local authorities. The infrastructure is extensive, but it is also liable to re-organisation (earlier attempts to encourage training and raise skills include Training and Enterprise Councils, the Manpower Services Commission and Industry Lead Bodies, all of which are now defunct). This fluidity is also reflected in the high number of (generally short-lived) initiatives. According to the Cabinet Office's Performance and Innovation Unit, in 2001 there were 54 separate workforce development initiatives (PIU 2001). Unsurprisingly, employers have great difficulty negotiating this complex, confusing and changeable system.

Official activity generally stops short of actual legislation with regulation limited to areas such as health and safety, food standards and care work. Although there is extensive regulation in one area that has a significant impact on VET, the education system. Realistically, the lines between schooling and VET have always been blurred. The success of Silicon Valley rests on the influx of bright, well-educated graduates; the expert workers in Arthur's (1999) steel mini-mills depend on US universities' engineering courses since employer-provided VET tends to be weak; and Taiwan's skills base is largely supported by government investment in technical schools and colleges. Schooling certainly influences VET provision, not least because an influx of well-educated recruits into the labour market makes VET far more effective. In Britain, a combination of factors (including high youth unemployment, benefit changes and the introduction of criterion-referenced rather than norm-referenced qualifications) has resulted in a dramatic rise in educational participation. As recently as 1975, 62 per cent of 16-year-olds left full-time education at the first moment they could legally do so, most without any formal qualifications (Keep and Rainbird 2000, p.179). By 2003 there had been a dramatic change and 72 per cent of 16-year-olds were in full-time education with a further 15 per cent undertaking some form of training (DfES 2004). This is not to argue that the main role of the education system is (or should be) to equip students with vocational skills and several commentators have been highly critical of the transfer of responsibilities from employers to taxpayers that this implies (Keep 2001). Rather it is that the education and abilities of recruits impacts on the way jobs are designed and the VET that is offered.

It is also worth considering in a little more detail two of the most widely known official structures to encourage VET in firms: Investors in People and National Vocational Qualifications (NVQs). Both are voluntary and, while some official funds are provided, to market these schemes and (occasionally) subsidise accreditation, each relies on advertising rather than compulsion.

Investors in People is a quality kitemark awarded to firms that meet certain standards in human resource provision. Specifically these include linking training to business strategy, ensuring that practices such as appraisal, involvement and communication are in place for the whole workforce and checking that these are appropriate by evaluating the processes implemented. By May 2004 just over 36,000 organisations covering 28 per cent of people in employment had gained Investors in People accreditation (http://www.iipuk.co.uk). Successes have been reported in terms of employee motivation and morale (Hillage and Moralee 1996) and reduced levels of absenteeism and turnover (Alberga *et al.* 1997). Tamkin *et al.* (2000), in a comparison between firms with and without Investors in People accreditation, report that those with the award enjoy higher levels of profit. However, it is not clear whether these differences are attributable to Investors in People, or to the nature of the firms that seek accreditation. It may be that accredited firms are those that were already actively engaged in training and development and that the kitemark simply rubber-stamped existing practice (Grugulis and Bevitt 2002). Moreover, the impact that Investors in People has on practice is not necessarily positive. Ram (2000), in a study of three SMEs that had either gained or were working towards Investors in People argues that the award was valued because it could help them to gain business from government bodies, rather than for the impact it might have on skills. Indeed, changes tended to be sham exercises. One company director, who had pinned mission statements onto the office walls before an assessor's vist commented:

> We had a mission statement devised very quickly for Investors in People and basically we had to have all these statements stuck around the room, so that when the assessor came in he was able to see these, which really I think qualifies my argument that we are doing it for a paperwork exercise. I am sure if he walks round this building and says to people 'What is our mission statement?' I can almost guarantee that 90 per cent, maybe 95 per cent, of our employees would not know what it was (Ram 2000, p.80).

It was not that these organisations did not value training and development. They did and all actively engaged in it, but rather that the accreditation process was bureaucratic and did not fit their current practice particularly readily. As a result, gaining the Investors in People award became a 'mock' exercise with the activities necessary for accreditation divorced from reality. It seems that, while the Investors in People award can be valuable, it does not necessarily extend training and development activities beyond organisations that already actively train and that the bureaucracy involved in accreditation may cause problems.

While Investors in People is targeted at the level of the firm, NVQs provide a system of qualifications that cover almost all occupations and all levels of achievement for level 1 (the most basic) to level 5 (the most complex). By March 2004 nearly 4.5 million NVQs had been awarded, over 75 per cent of which were at levels 1 and 2 (http://www.qca.org.uk). NVQs were originally intended to provide an umbrella framework against which all vocational awards could be measured (Raggatt and Williams 1999). Such clarity was (and is) badly needed since vocational qualifications in Britain are a cottage industry, designed, delivered and accredited by a range of bodies including professional associations, colleges, trade unions and employers. As a result, provision is often fragmented. In 1990 there were 279 different certificates available for secretaries at five different levels (Employment Department 1992, cited in Keep 1994, p.311). However, in practice, NVQs became a radical new form of qualification themselves. Their distinctive feature was lists of the behaviours workers should demonstrate, so that people who had become competent through years of experience on-the-job could be assessed as easily as those who had undertaken formal training.

This structure created problems. Senker (1996) observed that NVQ level 3 in engineering covered only two-thirds of the requirements of the traditional apprenticeship. Since an NVQ could be achieved after two years, while the 'full apprenticeship' typically took three-and-a-half to four years, this estimate probably errs on the side of generosity. Other studies note the lowering of standards in construction (Callendar 1992), hairdressing (Raggatt 1994; 'Dispatches', Channel 4, 1993), management (Grugulis 1997) and electrical engineering (Smithers 1993).

Work done by Smithers (1993), which contrasts the old City and Guilds plumbing certificate with the plumbing NVQ provides a dramatic illustration of the differences between the two qualifications. The City and Guilds qualification not only required a higher level of practical, technical expertise, it also tested knowledge of physics, electronics, maths, technical drawing and technology. The background to technology included physical qualities, electricity and magnetism, forces, pressure, heat, thermal movement, energy, principles of tool construction and materials technology, concepts in chemistry, applied chemistry and materials for industry. The NVQ which replaced it specified none of these and the lists of behaviours (or 'competences') NVQs prescribed proved cumbersome. According to Eraut *et al.* (1996) even at the lowest level, NVQs involved around 1,000 separate assessment decisions.

To what extent have NVQs succeeded? Qualifications have been awarded to many previously excluded from the system, which is praiseworthy. However, they have been widely criticised (see, among others, Hyland 1994; Wolf 1995; Grugulis 2003) and, outside the public sector, the armed services and retailing, proved unpopular with employers. Moreover, as Table 4.1 shows, compared to other qualifications, NVQs produce few financial benefits with levels 1 and 2 giving no salary premium at all. In part this is because they are targeted at those at the lowest end of the achievement scale (many advantages of higher-level qualifications stem from the fact that they mark individuals as belonging to the brightest group in society or the highest social class, Crouch *et al.* 1999). However, HNDs and HNCs also serve previous low achievers yet they consistently produce financial gains. The explanation for this is probably that HNDs and HNCs have syllabi and attempt to teach candidates new skills while NVQs simply accredit what workers already do. Indeed, in Munro and Rainbird's (2001) research into low-skilled workers, none said they had learned anything from the NVQs they had taken. Qualifications need to be achievable, but they should also develop skills and it is here that NVQs fail. As Young (2001) argues, making the qualifications that those at the lowest level of the workforce do so different from those at the highest simply reinforces disadvantage.

It seems that government intervention UK-style has a mixed record. The education system is certainly producing higher numbers of more highly qualified people (though possibly at the expense of standards) but official involvement in workplace activity is less successful. Investors in People tends to be well received by organisations that have gained accreditation, but it may simply certify existing good provision rather than extend it. NVQs have helped many workers to gain certification, but do little to actively build skills.

Training and development in the workplace

While there are many reasons to support training and development, and while both voluntarist and regulated approaches can work, the value of state intervention in Britain is limited. This may not matter. If employers are already providing extensive high quality training and development for staff, to enhance their competitive position and foster a reputation for being a 'good employer' this may compensate for limitations in state provision. But even here there are problems. Excellent provision exists, but is rather unevenly distributed and not all training is developmental.

According to the Labour Force Survey, 15.6 per cent of workers in Britain received either on- or off-the-job training (DfES 2003, p.63). But this experience of training (and particularly of the duration and content of training) varies greatly according to both occupation and sector. Employees in the public sector, younger workers, people who are new to the job and those working in professional or clerical occupations are far more likely to receive training than older workers in 'blue collar' jobs (Cully *et al.* 1999). While 14 per cent of managers and 25 per cent of professionals had received training, only 6.5 per cent of process, plant and machine operatives had done so. Overall, 29 per cent of training lasts for less than five days.

This is particularly significant when we step back from the data and recall what training is provided for. One of the main advantages of training and development was that it could enhance the skills base, equip workers with expertise and change the way that they worked. Given this, the overall statistics are of concern for, while training figures have risen since the 1980s, there is some evidence that this has been achieved by shorter training courses more evenly distributed. Clearly, duration is not a proxy for quality, but it is unlikely that fundamental changes to the skills base can be achieved in less than five days.

The content of training is also important. Workplace training can cover a multitude of activities. Graduate trainee accountants with major accountancy firms spend three years on a mixture of formal courses, guided work experience and personal study, leading to a prestigious professional qualification. By contrast, call centre workers can expect far more basic workplace training. In Callaghan and Thompson's (2002) study, one call centre worker, who had let his voice drop slightly during a conversation with a customer, was sent on a training course to teach him to keep intonation even and enthusiastic. Both of these activities count as training and both may increase organisational effectiveness, but the advantages they confer on workers are very different.

Reinforcing this, the two types of training most commonly funded by employers are health and safety and induction, a factor that may explain why temporary workers are more likely to receive training than their permanent colleagues (20 per cent as opposed to 15 per cent, DfES 2003, p.63). Heyes and Gray (2003), in their survey of SMEs after the introduction of the national minimum wage found that training spend had risen, but that this was because employers were hiring younger (and cheaper) workers rather than up-skilling existing staff. Clearly it is important that workplaces are healthy and safe places to be and that new recruits receive adequate induction. However, it is highly unlikely that such forms of training will affect productivity, product quality or individual career development.

Training and development may also serve a social function, helping workers to form friendships and distracting them from alienating work. Two call centres investigated by Kinnie et al. (2000) used employee teams, games and spot prizes to motivate employees. These organisations also had three-week induction and technical training but their on-going investment was in activities described by one supervisor as 'fun and surveillance'. An interesting modern variant on Adam Smith's (1993) approval of publicly funded education for the working poor, who engaged only in simple, de-humanising and repetitive tasks, the better to support a 'decent and orderly' society (p.436).

PERSONAL QUALITIES AND GENERIC SKILLS

The type of training identified by Kinnie and his colleagues, the focus on games and the development of 'soft' or generic skills is becoming more widespread. In part it reflects attempts to alleviate repetitive work, increase commitment or foster a particular organisational culture. But it also stems from the fact that workforce skills are increasingly being defined in attitudinal terms. The Department for Education and Employment's Skills Task Force included communication, problem solving, teamworking, an ability to improve personal learning and performance, motivation, judgement, leadership and initiative in its list of skills (DfEE 2000, p.24). The CBI's (1989) earlier suggestions included values and integrity and interpersonal skills; Whiteways Research (1995) extended this to cover self-awareness, self-promotion, political focus and coping with uncertainty. These are not isolated instances and some of the lists produced can be extremely long. Hirsch and Bevan (1988) drawing on lists of managerial skills came up with 1,745 different items.

To a certain extent there is little here that is novel. Employers have always demanded appropriate qualities and attributes from their workers and this may be simply a modern variant of that. Moreover, the increasing numbers of service jobs demand very different qualities of those who carry them out than manufacturing work. In services, the process of being served is as much a part of the purchase as any product being sold and customers may conflate their delight at service levels with their appreciation of the product (Korczynski 2002). As a result, the way that employees look and feel and the impressions and emotions they provoke in others are important (see among others, Hochschild 1983; Leidner 1993). However, couching this in the language of skill causes a number of problems. Unlike formally accredited technical skills, it is not clear that soft skills are either transferable or give their holders power in the labour market. The communication skills needed to tell a customer which aisle the baked beans are in are very different from those needed to describe the rules of cricket or explain complex statistics. In each of these areas (just as for the exercise of judgement, leadership or problem solving), efficacy demands technical and local knowledge, a factor neglected by the compilers of generic lists. This is particularly worrying since there is some evidence that organisations attempting to train their staff in soft skills are neglecting the technical aspects of work (Grugulis and Vincent 2005).

Then too, soft skills may be reciprocal and relational rather than individual. In his study of the skills required by US employers Lafer (2004) draws on research by Moss and Tilly (1996) in two warehouses in the same district of Los Angeles both of which employed present and past gang members. While managers in one complained of high turnover, laziness and dishonesty, in the second, which paid several dollars per hour more, managers had few complaints and turnover was a modest 2 per cent. As Lafer (2004, p.117) argues: 'traits such as discipline, loyalty and punctuality are not "skills" that one either possesses or lacks; they are measures of commitment that one chooses to give or withhold based on the conditions of work offered'.

Focusing on motivation as an individual skill presupposes that people are unaffected by their conditions of work or the way that they are treated. Factors once considered the responsibility of management or personnel are individualised such that the emphasis on control systems, job design, pay rates or being a 'good employer' becomes the straightforward problem of hiring the most appropriately 'skilled' people (Keep 2001; Grugulis et al. 2004).

Nor is the exercise of soft skills particularly clear. Employers value them but often judge their presence or their absence through sexual and racial stereotypes. Women are favoured for call centres and reception desks (Collinson et al. 1990; Taylor and Tyler 2000; Hebson and Grugulis 2005). Asian women are not considered to be career-minded and men's marital status may be taken as a proxy for their reliability (Oliver and Turton 1982; Collinson et al. 1990). As Ainley (1994, p.80) argues, 'at rock bottom, the real personal and transferable "skills" required for preferential employment are those of whiteness, maleness and traditional middle-classness'. It is difficult to escape from the conclusion that in some environments focusing on soft skills can be used to legitimise prejudice and reinforce disadvantage.

This is a conundrum. At one level most jobs clearly require a mixture of both technical and soft skills and, given the existing lack of recognition for women's skills, rhetorical support for their importance should advantage them. At another, as Bolton (2004) argues, these skills – regardless of their complexity – seem to be the exception to the normal laws of supply and demand in the sense that, no matter how much employers require them, they are seldom highly rewarded when not accompanied by high levels of technical skill. The advantages that soft skills offer seem precariously dependent on their being noted, appreciated

Box 4.3

During the first week [of a US state funded training programme] about a dozen women and two men sit around a conference table at the Dane county job centre. The instructor, who introduces herself as Kelly, shows flashcards. One flashcard says, *You'll never amount to anything.*

'Has anybody ever heard this in your life?' she asks.

No response.

'Good! Because it's not true!'

She holds up another flashcard: *You can do anything you set your mind to.*

'How about this one, how often do we hear this?'

No one says anything.

This is day three of the two-week . . . session. The topic: communication. From Kelly's point of view, things aren't going so well. 'People aren't talking a lot', she says.

Several participants are clearly trying though. Kelly holds up a flashcard that says *I'm so proud of you.* 'How do we feel when someone says this to us?' she asks.

'Good?', one participant offers.

'Yeah!', says Kelly. She hands out pieces of paper and asks everyone to write down the names of two people who have had a positive influence on their lives.

'It's the person who believes in you', she says.

She writes 'belives' in magic marker on a flip chart, then crosses it out and writes 'beleives'.

'Don't tell her,' the woman in front of me whispers.

'What?', Kelly asks, 'Don't tell me what?'

'You still spelled "believes" wrong', someone says.

Kelly stares at the flip chart.

'It's I before E except after C', another participant explains.

'That's okay', the woman in front of me says. 'That's a hard one.'

After a short break, Kelly lists some more rules for good communication. 'Here are two of the hardest things to say in the English language', she says, and writes 'Thank you' and 'I'm sorry' on the flip chart . . .

I interview some participants after class. 'I don't want to knock the programme or anything – maybe someone is getting their self-esteem raised', says one. . . . 'But . . . they've given me an ultimatum: you either go to this class or it's your check.'

Source: Conniff 1994, pp.18–21; quoted in Lafer 2004, p.121

and rewarded by senior management (Grugulis and Vincent 2005). In isolation they provide workers with few of the labour market advantages of technical skills (Payne 1999, 2000; Keep 2001).

In part this is a systemic issue. A focus on soft skills (such as communication, loyalty or even punctuality) in low-level work confers few advantages on workers because it equips them only to perform low-level tasks. Whereas an emphasis on teamworking, problem solving and responsibility for production integrated with technical skills in Thompson *et al.*'s (1995) cross-national comparisons of vehicle production provided employees with opportunities for progression. Similarly, in NUMMI's plant in Freemont, California, soft skills are combined with the development of technical skills and workers are given a great deal of discretion to address workplace problems (Rothenberg 2003). However, while integrating these generic qualities with challenging work may make them more 'skilful' and advantage those workers who possess or develop them, it does not overcome the tendency to read these virtues into gender, race, class, age or marital status.

THE DISADVANTAGES OF TRAINING AND DEVELOPMENT

The overall picture of training and development is not clear cut. Some courses, qualifications and on-the-job training are excellent at developing workforce skills which can then be integrated into the way work is designed and controlled. But developmental provision is set alongside narrow qualifications and training courses that serve only to entertain. At one level such behaviour is difficult to explain. If training and development is universally believed to have a positive impact then why are so few firms training and why are the ones that do confining much of their activity to short courses, health and safety and induction? Equally, why do not individual employees respond to this by filling the gap themselves? Such lack of activity appears, at best, irrational.

There is, however, an explanation. Training and development does not occur in a vacuum, rather it is one aspect of an organisation's activities and exists to support the other activities. As Keep and Mayhew (1999) argue, training is a third-order issue, following on from decisions about competitiveness, product specification and job design. For organisations that choose to compete on the basis of quality, highly skilled workers are essential; for ones that compete on cost, they are an unjustifiable extravagance – and large sections of the British economy still compete on cost (Bach and Sisson 2000). The second reason, and this is related to the first, is that many jobs are designed to be tightly controlled with employee discretion (and with it skill) taken away. One employer, interviewed by Dench *et al.* (1999) said that their ideal worker had two arms and two legs. When this is what jobs demand, it is difficult to see how training will help. Job design is not set in stone and it is perfectly possible to construct skilled work from the same jobs, the same market conditions and the same strategy. Boxall and Purcell (2003) provide an interesting example from two firms competing with one another in delivering bottled gas. British Oxygen decided to compete by using delivery drivers as key staff. Drivers were trained in customer relations, cab-based information systems and product knowledge, ensuring that customers were satisfied and encouraging them to trade up wherever possible. By contrast Air Products, a rival firm in the same industry facing the same pressures, decided to compete by outsourcing its haulage and distribution to an independent contractor. Their drivers were not expected to know anything about bottled gas beyond the standard health and safety guidelines. When large numbers of employers design jobs to be done without skill, pay low wages and workers with little purchasing power buy products of low price and low quality we have all the elements of what Finegold and Soskice describe as a 'low skills equilibrium' (1988).

Box 4.4

McDonald's famously and relentlessly standardise every aspect of their product in order to eliminate the need for human input. The Operations and Training Manual (known to staff as 'the Bible') provides detailed prescriptions on every aspect of working life. Its 600 pages include full colour photographs illustrating the proper placement of ketchup, mustard and pickle on every type of burger, set out the six steps of counter service and even prescribe the arm motions that should be used in salting a batch of fries. Kitchen and counter technology reinforce these instructions as lights and buzzers tell workers when to turn burgers or take fries out of the fat, ketchup dispensers provide measured amounts of product in the requisite 'flower' pattern and lights on the till remove the need for serving staff to write out orders as well as prompting them to offer additional items.

For more information on this see Leidner 1993; Ritzer 1998

Then too, it is instructive to consider the areas of job creation; 78 per cent of UK jobs are now in the service sector (Labour Market Trends 2004). Service work includes many of the most highly skilled and knowledgeable workers such as medics, teachers and IT professionals but it also, and in far greater numbers, covers care workers, security staff and personal services, numbers of which are rising far faster. The sector as a whole is dominated by low-paid, part-time workers, few of whom are either highly skilled or allowed to exercise their skills in their work. This need not be the case. McGauran's (2000, 2001) research into retail work in France and Ireland shows how French employers expect their workers to be experts in the products sold and French customers request advice on products and product care when shopping. However, it is not clear that this skilled variant of shop-work influences behaviour elsewhere. Rather, pressure for hyper-flexibility, described by Gadrey (2000, p.26) as 'tantamount to a personnel strategy based on zero competence', zero qualifications, zero training and zero career, means that retail work is dominated by poorly paid part-time workers and the flexibility demanded of them is availability for shift work at short notice. In Germany, this is threatening long-established traditions of training and qualifications as employers avoid training employees, since this would make them expensive to hire and rely instead on large numbers of low-paid staff supported by small numbers of highly skilled 'anchor' workers (Kirsch *et al.* 2000).

At an individual level too there are good and sound reasons for not taking up vocational training. Human capital theory is neither as straightforward, nor as axiomatic as some commentators argue. While some qualifications do indeed bring high returns, others do not and it is the low-level vocational qualifications that bring least reward. Then too, not all skills are equal and the status and labour market power of job holders influence the way their skills are perceived (Rubery and Wilkinson 1994). In practice this means that women's work, even when technically and objectively more complex than men's, tends to be under-valued (Phillips and Taylor 1986). Mechanistically assessing workers as a supply of skills neglects both this social construction and factors such as trust and motivation that are needed to put skills into practice at work (Brown 2001). Human capital theory also individualises the responsibility for acquiring and developing skills. Nor is it clear that highly skilled workers create their own demand. As the UK skills survey consistently demonstrates, more than a third of workers report that their skills are under-utilised in employment (Felstead *et al.* 2002).

Re-thinking training and development

This chapter has deliberately extended the debate on training and development beyond the confines of formal courses and qualifications. These are important factors but, for students of HRM, they are only one aspect of a wider issue, the development of 'resourceful humans'. A knowledgeable workforce is the product, not of excellent training in isolation, but of a combination of a range of factors including training, job design, status, control systems and discretion. As Cockburn (1983) and Littler (1982) argue, skill reposes in the individual, in the job and in the social setting. In practice, this means that for development to be effective, individuals need enough discretion and challenge in their work to exercise their skills.

Given this, there are some reasons for optimism in Britain. Between 1986 and 2001 skills in work have risen against almost every indicator. Employers are demanding more (and more advanced) qualifications, training periods for jobs are rising and the amount of experience that employees need to do their work well is also rising (Felstead *et al.* 2002). However, while this trajectory is encouraging, it starts from a low base and most work still demands few skills with 61 per cent of jobs requiring less than three months' training and 20 per cent less than one month's experience to do well (compared to 26 per cent which require more than two years', Felstead *et al.* 2002, p.28). *iMac* jobs have not yet entirely replaced *McJobs* (Warhurst and Thompson 1998).

This skills survey also reveals two extremely worrying developments. The first emerged in the 1990s as more individuals gained qualifications and workplace demand failed to keep pace. The most recent results show that at an aggregate level the number of workers holding level 4 qualifications (roughly equivalent to degree level, though here degrees themselves are treated as a separate group within this category) equals the number of jobs that require workers educated to level 4, with supply only slightly exceeding demand (7.1 million jobs set against 7.4 million individuals). However at levels 2 and 3 (GCSEs and 'A' levels respectively) there are far more workers with qualifications than work that demands this input and, most dramatically there are 6.5 million jobs which require no qualifications at all but only 2.9 million economically active people without qualifications (Warhurst and Thompson 1998, p.31; see also Green and McIntosh 2002).

This under-utilisation of skills is apparent in Rainbird and Munro's (2003) research. Drawing on an extensive study of low-paid workers they found that rigid hierarchies, narrow

Box 4.5

I've actually got the convenor saying to me, 'we've got to watch this multi-skill thing, because it's too interesting for them'.

Source: Managing Director, GKN Hardy Spicer; cited in Hendry 1993, p. 92

job descriptions and cost constraints all acted as barriers that employees, who were often highly educated, skilled or anxious to progress, could not overcome. Nor was there any sign, despite the very significant differences that good managers could make, that this might change. Indeed, the structural innovations observed, such as contracting out by the public sector, often reduced employees' areas of influence and took away aspects of their work that were interesting or skilful.

The second area for concern is the sharp decline in discretion employees can exercise, a trend that was particularly marked for professional workers. In 1986, 72 per cent of professionals reported that they had 'a great deal' of choice over the way that they worked. By 2001 this figure had fallen to 38 per cent (Rainbird and Munro 2003, p.71; see also Evetts 2002; Grugulis *et al.* 2003). Yet discretion is a pre-requisite for skills to be put into practice.

Discussion and conclusions

It has frequently been argued that training is the 'litmus test' of human resource management (Keep 1989). The pivotal element of a system designed to harness the talents of those it employs (through well-designed jobs, team working, employee involvement and other human resource practices) is ensuring that employees are developed for their roles. However, the reverse also applies and human resource practices are the test of training. There is little point in training and developing employees if the jobs they are to undertake are tightly controlled with no trust or discretion given. Skill is an aspect of jobs as well as a part of individuals and a highly skilled individual put in a job where they have little control, discretion or responsibility and which they have little power to change is likely to become frustrated. This means that, just as many excellent analyses of human resource management have queried the extent to which its ambitious rhetoric has been matched by its lived reality (see, among others, Legge 1995; Wilkinson and Willmott 1995) so training and development needs to be subjected to the same scrutiny. Good training and development has the capacity to significantly change lives. It can equip people for more interesting, better paid and more demanding work; help to mitigate the discrimination in the labour market experienced by women and members of minority groups and provide an effective route out of poverty for people working in unskilled and low-paid jobs. However, just because some forms of training can do this does not mean that all can. Training and development is not straightforwardedly a 'good thing' – not all training is developmental and not all development is integrated into work. Before according our approval we really do need to examine what is involved in particular training systems, the effect it has on individuals and the way it is integrated into work. If this is not the case there is a danger that effort and resources will be put into systems which simply reinforce disadvantage and equip people only for minimum wage employment (Lafer 2004) or horizontal movement between a range of low-skilled jobs (Grimshaw *et al.* 2002).

DEVELOPING RESOURCEFUL HUMANS

IRENA GRUGULIS

Chapter 4 showed the way that training and development is systemic and linked to product strategies, job design, the way that work is controlled and the level of discretion workers can use. For each of the jobs listed below set out:

(a) how people are trained to do the job
(b) what (if any) continuing development they have on the job (remember that a challenging job provides opportunities for development just as formal training does)
(c) how much discretion they can exercise
(d) what other human resource policies you would expect (on pay rates, involvement, career ladders, etc.)
(e) what would happen to these jobs if recruits received more developmental training or were more highly educated?

> A secondary school teacher
> A call centre worker
> An anaesthetist
> An accountant
> A gardener
> A shop assistant
> A junior manager in a chain restaurant
> A bank cashier
> A factory worker
> A cleaner

SOFT SKILLS AND PERSONAL QUALITIES

IRENA GRUGULIS

In surveys of employers, the 'skills' that are most highly valued are often 'soft' skills or personal qualities and attributes such as customer handling, communication and problem solving (Hillage *et al.* 2002) or discipline, loyalty, punctuality and work ethic (Lafer 2004). For each of the jobs below consider:

(a) how important 'soft' skills are for doing the job
(b) the advantages to the employer
(c) the advantages to the employee
(d) how complex these skills are
(e) to what extent these are individual attributes and to what extent they are reactions to the way that people are treated
(f) are all skills with the same name the same skill (are they interchangeable between jobs)?

A worker on a building site
A receptionist
A waiter/waitress
A chief executive
A university lecturer
A nurse
A computer programmer
A lawyer
A TV repairman/woman
A chef

INVESTING IN PEOPLE IN THE NHS

IRENA GRUGULIS AND SHEENA BEVITT

Introduction

This case study is set in a hospital trust in the north of England. At the time of the research the trust employed a workforce of just over 2,000 covering a wide range of skill levels. Employees operated across 36 different sites and the research was carried out at the main district general hospital incorporating trust headquarters, health promotion, occupational health units and the post-graduate education centre as well as the hospital itself.

The hospital was going through a major change process following a decision to merge with a nearby Acute Services Health Authority, a merger which would increase the workforce to approximately 6,000. There was evidence that this was creating feelings of insecurity and instability at all staff levels though this may have been a reflection of the point in the merger process that had been reached rather than the merger itself. The new organisational structure had been agreed, but few of the top-level posts filled and the appointments that had been made were mainly from this particular trust (as opposed to their partners in the merger). Most of the units were still waiting to find out which directorates they would report to.

The trust had first gained Investors in People accreditation in 1996 and, at the time of the research, was beginning to prepare for reassessment. Management certainly believed that these were positive, indeed, the very fact that they were seeking re-accreditation was an expression of confidence in the impact that the standard had. As the assistant chief executive (personnel) said:

> I think it is important to demonstrate to both the world outside and the staff within that we do have the HR/personnel policies and procedures – training and development policies and procedures – that are designed to support them in the work that they are doing and to help them achieve.

Motivation and morale

Staff motivation, job satisfaction and commitment were extremely high. In a survey of several different departments 91 per cent of respondents said that they were highly motivated, and none that they were not motivated; 46 per cent reported that they were highly satisfied with their jobs, 50 per cent that they were satisfied; 27 per cent that they were highly committed to the trust and 69 per cent that they were committed. Moreover, the loyalty and pride many felt in the trust went beyond its status as an employer:

> I want [the trust] to work. I want it to be the best because it's my hospital at the end of the day . . . I've got an invested interest for my family as well as myself [Intensive Care Sister, female].

Essentially the trust was valued because it helped people and served a key role in the community. Helping people was also a major source of job satisfaction. Six employees, both skilled and unskilled, indicated they were motivated to work because they 'enjoyed doing their jobs' and five that job satisfaction increased their commitment to their jobs:

> I enjoy it. If I didn't enjoy it I wouldn't like coming and I enjoy coming to work . . . I wouldn't change [jobs] unless I really, really needed to. I've got job satisfaction and that's the main thing with me . . . I put my satisfaction before earning a lot more money [Call Order Cook, female].

The reasons workers gave for this job satisfaction varied on the survey but included colleagues, the nature of the work and job satisfaction as well as pay, pensions and holidays, convenient hours of work, relationships with other people and working as part of a team. Job satisfaction appeared to be particularly powerful in influencing both motivation to work and organisational commitment and was itself influenced by the way that work was designed both positively and negatively. In the linen services department, where employees frequently damaged their hands on heavy fire doors receiving deliveries and a lack of space increased the amount of heavy lifting that staff had to do to keep work areas tidy and fresh stock accessible, staff did not feel 'invested in'.

Pressure of work and under-staffing was the most potent source of discontent for all staff. Its effect was particularly negative when employees felt that it impacted on the service they gave to patients. Job insecurity also provoked negative feelings and the proposed merger, described by one male team leader as a 'big black cloud' hanging over their heads, was felt to be particularly threatening.

However, there was little evidence that employees felt motivated because of the Investors in People 'badge'. Indeed, less than 13 per cent agreed with the statement that Investors in People had made them feel more motivated or that it had increased their job satisfaction and over a third disagreed in both cases. Just under a quarter of those surveyed agreed that they were proud to work for an organisation with an Investors in People award, but the majority (61 per cent) had no opinion, choosing neither the agree nor the disagree option. Even these may have exaggerated the award's positive effect. In the survey some 86 per cent of employees claimed to have heard of Investors in People and 76 per cent that the trust held the award. In interviews, where questions were to continue and ignorance might be exposed, only half did. No employee directly mentioned Investors in People as something which gave them job satisfaction, motivated them to do their job or increased their commitment or loyalty to the trust. Some directly denied that Investors in People had had any effect:

> To me I don't think it makes a lot of difference. You're not going to change your own attitude just because you've got that thing against your hospital, you know, like our hospital has got Investors in People, what difference does it make what so ever [Call Order Cook, female].

And again:

> It didn't really affect me. I don't think it affected anybody. And I still don't know if it affects anybody [Superintendent Sonographer, female].

Training and development

The trust, in common with much of the NHS, had a good record of vocational education and training and this training was supported by qualifications as well as internal career paths. Interviews revealed evidence of progression from unskilled ancillary posts to skilled nursing positions, while the survey responses showed employee qualification levels improving.

Training was received positively by staff at almost all levels of the organisation for a range of reasons. One senior member of the medical staff argued that it increased his ability to work:

> I think they affect your ability to do your job efficiently, which is part and parcel of your motivation to work for me. I feel that – if I felt that I was falling behind the times or wasn't providing a good service with the work I did – that would affect my motivation rather than the other way around . . . they actually affect your motivation through an enabling process rather than through a direct effect [Staff Grade Anaesthetist, male].

At lower levels NVQ qualifications were viewed by many as a 'seal of approval' to their competence in the workplace, providing a welcome boost to both confidence and self-esteem. One male team leader reported feeling 'on a real high' after attending a training course on line management and a domestic services supervisor explained how her sister-in-law felt 'thrilled to bits' when she achieved her NVQ. Another commented that:

> I felt like I had achieved something because I never did any exams at school or anything like that. I said to my husband it must be the first thing I've ever done and completed really [Domestic worker, female].

Given these interview comments it is hardly surprising that employees undertaking training were more likely to report positively on their own motivation and commitment. Having training needs identified, being offered training courses and 'a chance to better yourself', all major aspects of Investors in People, did influence the way that people felt about their jobs. Over two-thirds (68 per cent) believed it affected their motivation to work and just over half (56 per cent) felt that training affected their commitment to the trust. A larger number of employees who were currently receiving training or had received training in the last four weeks had higher commitment levels than their colleagues who had not received training. More dramatically, nearly 90 per cent of those who were currently receiving training experienced high or very high job satisfaction compared to less than three-quarters of those who had received no training for over 12 months. Two employees who reported receiving no training at all both had low job satisfaction.

However, not all training was positively received and disillusionment was felt when qualifications simply certified existing skills rather than increasing them. One catering employee explained that she already knew all the things on her NVQ qualification because they had been part of her job for so long. Similarly, in the sewing department workers complained that:

> No one can teach us anything about a sewing machine we don't already know . . . There's no new technology here like they have in other departments so there are no changes to the job so we don't need new training . . . We've only got four or five years to go anyway, we don't want to do anything [Linen Services Officer, female].

Investors in People is also designed to link human resource practices to business strategy and in the trust, this link was interpreted in the narrowest and least developmental way. Most employees were to be trained to the level of competence that was required by their current job and no further. Such training was often extremely low-level. A domestic services manager pointed out that, while her staff had completed NVQ level 1, all were perfectly capable of achieving more but did not have the opportunity to do so; while a supervisor, who had just completed training equivalent to an NVQ level 3 and was offered the chance to do an NVQ level 1 related to the work she was currently doing, described the process as a 'bit daft'. Nor was training related to the current job welcomed where workers had been de-skilled. In linen services, employees who had once performed quite complicated and integrated tasks were required only to pack, unpack and dispatch orders. Here there was little positive response to training since this required fewer skills than staff had previously exercised.

Emphasising business need also had extremely unfortunate repercussions for the old policy of staff development, particularly since each individual business unit within the trust was invoiced for training and assessment. One cleaner, who hoped to become a nursing auxiliary, was refused access to training on the grounds that it was not necessary for her current job. Her manager then went on to point out that she would not be likely to approve any training for a member of staff which resulted in their leaving that department. As one female theatre manager protested, training is 'the most important thing, yet it is the first thing to go and Investors in People doesn't prevent this'.

Nor did the extensive development of various business plans affect employees, though they were positively regarded by top management. For employees, the majority reaction was one of ignorance. Over half of those surveyed reported they had never seen or never read a copy of the trust's business plan summary, staff or training charter, training and development policy or value statement, all of which were key elements of the trust's assessment portfolio. In interviews, when 14 employees were shown copies of the documentation, recognition was even lower with half recognising the staff development policy but only four the training charter and staff charter. Recognition of the value statement card by nine employees was more encouraging but, despite the fact that the trust had issued a copy to all employees as part of the Investors in People process, only one-quarter said they had seen or received a copy in the questionnaire survey. Far from improving employee attitudes to work the value statement attracted only negative attention. Described as 'wishy washy', and 'very managementy' and containing 'yucky modern language' it was criticised for being 'someone else's value statement'. Some complained that they had had no input in developing these statements, but for others the problems were rather more fundamental:

> I think they're a waste of time personally. I mean the object of a hospital is to treat people and get them better, you don't really need it written down do you . . ., we don't need to be *told* we need to treat them to the best of our ability because it doesn't *make* you treat them to the best of your ability by telling you that you need to do it [Radiology Sister, female].

Questions

1. What human resource practices did the trust adopt and what effect did they have?

2. What systems did the trust use to train and develop staff?

3. What impact did Investors in People have?

4. Is there a conflict between increasing employees' skills and linking training to business strategy?

Source: Reproduced with permission from *Human Resource Management Journal*, Vol.12, No.3, pp. 44–60, July 2002

References

Ainley, P. (1994) *Degrees of Difference*, London: Lawrence & Wishart.

Alberga, T., Tyson, S. and Parsons, D. (1997) 'An evaluation of the investors in people standard', *Human Resource Management Journal*, Vol.7, No.2, pp.47–60.

Arthur, J.B. (1999) 'Explaining variation in human resource practices in US steel mini-mills', in P. Cappelli (ed.) *Employment Practices and Business Strategy*, Oxford and New York: Oxford University Press.

Bach, S. and Sisson, K. (2000) 'Personnel management in perspective', in S. Bach and K. Sisson (eds) *Personnel Management* (3rd edn), Oxford: Blackwell.

Becker, G.S. (1964) *Human Capital*, Chicago, IL: University of Chicago Press.

Bolton, S.C. (2004) 'Conceptual confusions: emotion work as skilled work', in C. Warhurst, I. Grugulis and E. Keep (eds) *The Skills that Matter*, Basingstoke: Palgrave Macmillan.

Bosch, G. (2003) 'Skills and innovation – a German perspective', paper presented at the Future of Work/SKOPE/Centre for Organisation and Innovation Conference on Skills, Innovation and Performance, Cumberland Lodge, Windsor Great Park 31 March–1 April.

Boxall, P. and Purcell, J. (2003) *Strategy and Human Resource Management*, London: Palgrave.

Brown, P. (2001) 'Skill formation in the twenty-first century', in P. Brown, A. Green and H. Lauder (eds) *High Skills: Globalization, Competitiveness and Skill Formation*, Oxford: Oxford University Press.

*Callaghan, G. and Thompson, P. (2002) 'We recruit attitude: the selection and shaping of routine call centre labour', *Journal of Management Studies*, Vol.39, No.2, pp.233–54.

Callendar, C. (1992) *Will NVQs Work? Evidence from the Construction Industry*, Sussex: University of Sussex/Institute of Manpower Studies.

CBI (Confederation of British Industry) (1989) *Towards a Skills Revolution – A Youth Charter*, London: CBI.

Cockburn, C. (1983) *Brothers: Male Dominance and Technological Change*, London: Pluto Press.

Collinson, D., Knights, D. and Collinson, M. (1990) *Managing to Discriminate*, London and New York: Routledge.

Conniff, R. (1994) 'Big, bad welfare: welfare reform politics and children', *The Progressive*, Vol.58, No.8, pp.18–21.

Coopers and Lybrand (1985) *A Challenge to Complacency*, London: Manpower Services Commission.

Crouch, C., Finegold, D. and Sako, M. (1999) *Are Skills the Answer? The Political Economy of Skill Creation in Advanced Industrialised Countries*, Oxford: Oxford University Press.

Cully, M., Woodland, S., O'Reilly, A. and Dix, G. (1999) *Britain at Work*, London: Routledge.

Culpepper, P.D. (1999) 'The future of the high-skill equilibrium in Germany', *Oxford Review of Economic Policy*, Vol.15, No.1, pp.43–59.

Dench, S., Perryman, S. and Giles, L. (1999) *Employers' Perceptions of Key skills*, IES Report 349, Sussex: Institute of Manpower Studies.

Department for Education and Employment (2000) *Skills for All: Research Report from the National Skills Task Force*, Suffolk: DfEE.

Department for Education and Skills (2003) *Statistics of Education: Education and Training Statistics for the United Kingdom*, London: TSO.

Department for Education and Skills (2004) 'First release: participation in education, training and employment by 16–18 year olds in England: 2002 and 2003', July.

Department for Education and Skills / DTI / H M Treasury / Department for Work and Pensions (2003) *Twenty-first Century Skills, Realising our Potential: Individuals, Employers, Nation*, Norwich: HMSO.

DTZ Pieda Consulting (1999) *Evaluation of the IiP Small Firms Development Projects*, Research Report RR135, Nottingham: DfEE Publications.

Eraut, M., Steadman, S., Trill, J. and Parkes, J. (1996) *The Assessment of NVQs*, Research Report No.4, Brighton: University of Sussex.

Evetts, J. (2002) 'New directions in state and international professional occupations: discretionary decision making and acquired regulation', *Work, Employment and Society*, Vol.16, No.2, pp.341–53.

Felstead, A., Gallie, D. and Green, F. (2002) *Work Skills in Britain 1986–2002*, Nottingham: DfES Publications.

Finegold, D. (1999) 'Creating self-sustaining, high-skill ecosystems', *Oxford Review of Economic Policy*, Vol.15, No.1, pp.60–81.

Finegold, D. and Soskice, D. (1988) 'The failure of training in Britain: analysis and prescription', *Oxford Review of Economic Policy*, Vol.4, No.3, pp.21–43.

Fuller, A. and Unwin, L. (2004) 'Expansive learning environments: integrating organisational and personal developments', in H. Rainbird, A. Fuller and A. Munro (eds) *Workplace Learning in Context*, London and New York: Routledge.

Gadrey, J. (2000) 'Working time configurations: theory, methods and assumptions for an international comparison', in C. Baret, S. Lehndorff and L. Sparks (eds) *Flexible Working in Food Retailing: A Comparison Between France, Germany, the UK and Japan*, London and New York: Routledge.

Green, F. and McIntosh, S. (2002) *Is There a Genuine Under-utilisation of Skills amongst the Over-qualified?*, SKOPE Research Paper No.30, University of Oxford and University of Warwick: SKOPE.

Green, F., Ashton, D., James, D. and Sung, J. (1999) 'The role of the state in skill formation: evidence from the republic of Korea, Singapore and Taiwan', *Oxford Review of Economic Policy*, Vol.15, No.1, pp.82–96.

Grimshaw, D., Beynon, H., Rubery, J. and Ward, K. (2002) 'The restructuring of career paths in large service sector organisations: "delayering", up-skilling and polarisation', *Sociological Review*, Vol.50, No.1, pp.89–116.

Grugulis, I. (1997) 'The consequences of competence: a critical assessment of the Management NVQ', *Personnel Review*, Vol.26, No.6, pp.428–44.

*Grugulis, I. (2003) 'The contribution of National Vocational Qualifications to the growth of skills in the UK', *British Journal of Industrial Relations*, Vol.41, No.3, pp.457–75.

Grugulis, I. and Bevitt, S. (2002) 'The impact of Investors in People on employees: a case study of a hospital trust', *Human Resource Management Journal*, Vol.12, No.3, pp.44–60.

Grugulis, I. and Vincent, S. (2005) 'Changing boundaries, shaping skills: the "new" organisational form and employee skills', in M. Marchington, D. Grimshaw, J. Rubery and H. Willmott (eds) *Fragmenting Work: Blurring Organisational Boundaries and Disordering Hierarchies*, Oxford: Oxford University Press.

Grugulis, I., Vincent, S. and Hebson, G. (2003) 'The rise of the "network organisation" and the decline of discretion', *Human Resource Management Journal*, Vol.13, No.2, pp.45–59.

Grugulis, I., Warhurst, C. and Keep, E. (2004) 'What's happening to skill?', in C. Warhurst, I. Grugulis and E. Keep (eds) *The Skills that Matter*, Basingstoke: Palgrave Macmillan.

Hebson, G. and Grugulis, I. (2005) 'Gender and new organisational forms', in M. Marchington, D. Grimshaw, J. Rubery and H. Willmott (eds) *Fragmenting Work: Blurring Organisational Boundaries and Disordering Hierarchies*, Oxford: Oxford University Press.

Hendry, C. (1993) 'Personnel leadership in technical and human resource change', in C. Clark (ed.) *Human Resource Management and Technical Change*, London: Sage.

*Heyes, J. and Gray, A. (2003) 'The implications of the national minimum wage for training in small firms', *Human Resource Management Journal*, Vol.13, No.2, pp.76–86.

Heyes, J. and Stuart, M. (1996) 'Does training matter? Employee experiences and attitudes', *Human Resource Management Journal*, Vol.6, No.3, pp.7–21.

Hillage, J. and Moralee, J. (1996) *The Return on Investors, The Institute of Employment Studies Report 314*, Brighton: IES.

Hillage, J., Regan, J., Dickson, J. and McLoughlin, K. (2002) *Employers Skill Survey 2002, Research Report 372*, Nottingham: DfES.

Hirsch, W. and Bevan, S. (1988) *What Makes a Manager?* Brighton: IMS.

Hochschild, A.R. (1983) *The Managed Heart*, Berkeley, CA: University of California Press.

Hyland, T. (1994) *Competence, Education and NVQs*, London: Cassell.

Jeong, J. (1995) 'The failure of recent state vocational training policies in Korea from a comparative perspective', *British Journal of Industrial Relations*, Vol.33, No.3, pp.237–52.

Keep, E. (1989) 'Corporate training strategies: the vital component?', in J. Storey (ed.) *New Perspectives on Human Resource Management*, London: Routledge.

Keep, E. (1994) 'Vocational education and training for the young', in K. Sisson (ed.) *Personnel Management*, Oxford: Blackwell.

Keep, E. (2001) 'If it moves, it's a skill', paper presented at an ESRC seminar on *The Changing Nature of Skills and Knowledge*, Manchester, 3–4 September.

Keep, E. and Mayhew, K. (1996) 'Evaluating the assumptions that underlie training policy', in A. Booth and D.J. Snower (eds) *Acquiring Skills*, Cambridge: Cambridge University Press.

Keep, E. and Mayhew, K. (1999) 'The assessment: knowledge, skills and competitiveness', *Oxford Review of Economic Policy*, Vol.15, No.1, pp.1–15.

*Keep, E. and Rainbird, H. (2000) 'Towards the learning organisation?', in S. Bach and K. Sisson (eds) *Personnel Management: A Comprehensive Guide to Theory and Practice* (3rd edn), Oxford: Blackwell.

Keep, E., Mayhew, K. and Corney, M. (2002) *Review of the Evidence on the Rate of Return to Employers of Investment in Training and Employer Training Measures*, SKOPE Research Paper No.34, Universities of Oxford and Warwick: SKOPE.

Kinnie, N., Hutchinson, S. and Purcell, J. (2000) 'Fun and surveillance: the paradox of high commitment management in call centres', *International Journal of Human Resource Management*, Vol.11, No.5, pp.967–85.

Kirsch, J., Klein, M., Lehndorff, S. and Voss-Dahm, D. (2000) 'The organisation of working time in large German food retail firms', in C. Baret, S. Lehndorff and L. Sparks (eds) *Flexible Working in Food Retailing: A Comparison Between France, Germany, the UK and Japan,* London and New York: Routledge.

Korczynski, M. (2002) *Human Resource Management in Service Work,* Basingstoke: Palgrave.

Labour Market Trends (2004) *Employment by Occupation and Industry,* Office for National Statistics, London, June, http://www.statistics.gov.uk

*Lafer, G. (2004) 'What is skill?', in C. Warhurst, I. Grugulis and E. Keep (eds) *The Skills that Matter,* Basingstoke: Palgrave Macmillan.

Lane, C. (1989) *Management and Labour in Europe,* Aldershot: Edward Elgar.

Legge, K. (1995) *Human Resource Management: Rhetorics and Realities,* Basingstoke: Macmillan.

Leidner, R. (1993) *Fast Food, Fast Talk: Service Work and the Routinization of Everyday Life,* Berkeley and Los Angeles, CA: University of California Press.

Littler, C. (1982) *The Development of the Labour Process in Capitalist Societies,* London: Heinemann.

Machin, S. and Vignoles, A. (2001) 'The economic benefits of training to the individual, the firm and the economy: the key issues', London: Performance Innovation Unit.

Marsden, D. and Ryan, P. (1995) 'Work, labour markets and vocational preparation: Anglo-German comparisons of training in intermediate skills', in L. Bash and A. Green (eds) *Youth, Education and Work,* World Yearbook of Education, London: Kogan Page.

Mason, G., van Ark, B. and Wagner, K. (1996) 'Workforce skills, product quality and economic performance', in A. Booth and D.J. Snower (eds) *Acquiring Skills,* Cambridge: Cambridge University Press.

McGauran, A-M. (2000) 'Vive la différence: the gendering of occupational structures in a case study of Irish and French retailing', *Women's Studies International Forum,* Vol.23, No.5, pp.613–27.

McGauran, A-M. (2001) 'Masculine, feminine or neutral? In-company equal opportunities policies in Irish and French MNC retailing', *International Journal of Human Resource Management,* Vol.12, No.5, pp.754–71.

Moss, P. and Tilly, C. (1996) 'Soft skills and race: an investigation into black men's employment problems', *Work and Occupations,* Vol.23, No.3, pp.252–76.

Munro, A. and Rainbird, H. (2001) 'Access to workplace learning and trade union voice under different regulatory regimes: cleaning and care work', paper presented at the *British Universities Industrial Relations Association* conference, Manchester, 7–9 July.

Nolan, P. and Slater, G. (2003) 'The labour market: history, structure and prospects', in P. Edwards (ed.) *Industrial Relations: Theory and Practice* (2nd edn), Oxford: Blackwell.

Oliver, J.M. and Turton, J.R. (1982) 'Is there a shortage of skilled labour?', *British Journal of Industrial Relations,* Vol.20, No.2, pp.195–200.

Payne, J. (1999) *All Things to all People: Changing Perceptions of 'Skill' Among Britain's Policymakers Since the 1950s and their Implications,* SKOPE Research Paper No.1, Oxford and Warwick Universities: SKOPE.

Payne, J. (2000) 'The unbearable lightness of skill: the changing meaning of skill in UK policy discourses and some implications for education and training', *Journal of Education Policy,* Vol.15, No.3, pp.353–69.

Performance and Innovation Unit (2001) *In Demand: Adult Skills for the Twenty-first Century,* PIU, Cabinet Office, www.cabinet-office.gov.uk

Phillips, A. and Taylor, B. (1986) 'Sex and Skill', *Feminist Review,* Vol.6, pp.79–83.

Raggatt, P. (1994) 'Implementing NVQs in colleges: progress, perceptions and issues', *Journal of Further and Higher Education,* Vol.18, No.1, pp.59–74.

Raggatt, P. and Williams, S. (1999) *Government, Markets and Vocational Qualifications: An Anatomy of Policy,* London: Falmer Press.

Rainbird, H. (1990) *Training Matters: Union Perspectives on Industrial Restructuring and Training,* Oxford: Basil Blackwell.

Rainbird, H. (1994) 'Continuing training', in K. Sisson (ed.) *Personnel Management* (2nd edn), Oxford: Blackwell.

Rainbird, H. and Munro, A. (2003) 'Workplace learning and the employment relationship in the public sector', *Human Resource Management Journal,* Vol.13, No.2, pp.30–44.

*Ram, M. (2000) 'Investors in People in small firms: case study evidence from the business services sector', *Personnel Review,* Vol.29, No.1, pp.69–91.

Ritzer, G. (1998) *The McDonaldisation Thesis,* London: Sage.

Rothenberg, S. (2003) 'Knowledge content and worker participation in environmental management at NUMMI', *Journal of Management Studies,* Vol.40, No.7, pp.1783–802.

Rubery, J. and Wilkinson, F. (1994) 'Introduction', in J. Rubery and F. Wilkinson (eds) *Employer Strategy and the Labour Market,* Oxford: Oxford University Press.

Senge, P. (1992) *The Fifth Discipline: The Art and Practice of the Learning Organisation,* London: Century Books.

Senker, P. (1996) 'The development and implementation of National Vocational Qualifications: an engineering case study', *New Technology, Work and Employment,* Vol.11, No.2, pp.83–95.

Smith, A. (1993) *Wealth of Nations,* Oxford and New York: Oxford University Press.

Smithers, A. (1993) *All our Futures,* London: Channel 4 Television.

Spilsbury, M. (2001) *Learning and Training at Work 2000, DfES Research Report No.269,* Nottingham: DfES.

Streeck, W., Hilber, J., van Kevalaer, K., Maier, F. and Weber, H. (1987) *The Role of the Social Partners in Vocational Education and Training in the FRG,* Berlin: CEDEFOP.

Tamkin, P., Hillage, J., Cummings, J., Bates, P., Barber, L. and Tackey, N.F. (2000) *Doing Business Better: The Long-Term Impact of Investors in People,* London: FOCUS Central London.

Taylor, S. and Tyler, M. (2000) 'Emotional labour and sexual difference in the airline industry', *Work, Employment and Society,* Vol.14, No.1, pp.77–96.

Thompson, P., Wallace, T., Flecker, J. and Ahlstrand, R. (1995) 'It ain't what you do, it's the way that you do it: production organisation and skill utilisation in commercial vehicles', *Work, Employment and Society,* Vol.9, No.4, pp.719–42.

Warhurst, C. and Thompson, P. (1998) 'Hearts, hands and minds: changing work and workers at the end of the century', in P. Thompson and C. Warhurst (eds) *Workplaces of the Future,* London: Macmillan.

Whiteways Research (1995) *Skills for Graduates in the Twenty-first Century,* London: Association of Graduate Recruiters.

Wilkinson, A. and Willmott, H. (eds) (1995) *Making Quality Critical,* London: Routledge.

Wolf, A. (1995) *Competence-Based Assessment,* Buckingham and Philadelphia, PA: Open University Press.

Young, M. (2001) 'Conceptualising vocational knowledge', paper presented at a joint Network/SKOPE/TLRP international workshop, Sunley Management Centre, University College, Northampton, 8–10 November.

* Useful reading

Chapter 5

REWARD MANAGEMENT

Philip Lewis

Introduction

Reward is an exciting area of HRM that is changing rapidly. What was once little more than a procedural issue, concerned with the technicalities of complex pay structures and job evaluation, is now in many organisations no longer the 'Cinderella' topic it once was (Smith 1993). The HRM movement has prompted many managers to think that reward has the potential to do much more than simply compensate employees for the time that they sell to their employer.

The term 'reward' rather than 'pay' is used in this chapter. This is an important point because employees expect more than pay for their efforts, so the definition of reward used in this chapter includes non-pay benefits, such as recognition and pensions, as well as wages and salaries. This broad definition of reward is examined in the first part of the chapter.

This chapter continues with an analysis of the expectations that the parties to the employment relationship have of reward. There follows an examination of the changes that are taking place in reward management throughout the world. This examination covers new systems of reward and the management rationales underpinning these systems. However, it would be wrong to think that traditional forms of reward have been subject to wholesale reform, therefore the reasons why in many organisations well-established forms of reward persist are analysed. The chapter then concludes with a discussion of some of the ethical concerns which attend new types of reward, not the least of which is the threat to equality.

What is reward?

Armstrong (2002, p. 3) defines reward as 'how people are rewarded in accordance with their value to the organisation. It is concerned with both financial and non-financial rewards and embraces the philosophies, strategies, policies, plans and processes used by organisations to develop and maintain reward systems.'

It is worth spending a little time studying this definition because it provides a strong underpinning for the chapter. The first part of the definition notes that 'people are rewarded in accordance with their value to the organisation'. This is a significant point because it immediately raises the central concept in new reward thinking that it is *people* that are the focus of concern, not *jobs*. This is reflected, for example, in individual performance-related pay schemes.

FINANCIAL AND NON-FINANCIAL REWARDS

Armstrong's (2002) definition notes the importance of both financial and non-financial rewards. Including both financial and non-financial rewards in the reward system is recognition by the employer that non-financial rewards may play an important part in attracting, and more particularly retaining employees. It also suggests a view of humanity which recognises that individuals require more for their efforts than simply monetary reward.

Armstrong (2002) notes that there are five areas where employees' needs may be met by non-financial rewards: achievement, recognition, responsibility, influence and personal growth. Of these, it is likely that the first two, achievement and recognition, will apply to virtually all employees. Responsibility, influence and personal growth will apply to many more employees than may be realised. Everyone likes to feel that they have accomplished something in their work; pride being derived from their achievement. In addition, most managers realise that a simple 'thank you' and a pat on the back for a job well done has enormous motivational power. It has to be recognised that not all employees seek greater responsibility in their jobs, or greater influence over decisions which directly or indirectly influence those jobs. This may be related to the individual's personal characteristics. But it may also be a consequence of a history of organisations not giving people the opportunity to exercise responsibility or influence. Semler's (1993) account of the management style in his Brazilian company is an excellent example of how employees accept responsibility when they are treated in such a way that they are obviously valued. The desire of many individuals to seek opportunities for personal growth through their work is very powerful. It may seem odd that this could be termed an employee reward rather than a vital pre-requisite of organisational success. Yet many individuals rate the opportunity for personal growth higher than financial reward.

Non-financial rewards may be particularly important as motivational tools for some employees. Meeting these needs increases the possibility of more positive employee attitudes and behaviours. Policies of employee involvement figure significantly in the array of means by which these need may be met. A communication strategy which broadcasts the successes of individuals and teams is a good example. Many organisations do this through their in-house magazines. This combined with special 'thank you' prizes (e.g. a weekend in Paris) often will have more motivational influence than direct financial rewards. Most of us like our colleagues to know when we are successful! Performance appraisal systems also have a significant role to play in meeting employees' needs for recognition and a feeling of achievement. Goal-setting and giving feedback to employees about their performance in pursuit of those goals are key performance appraisal activities. A developmental perspective to performance appraisal, rather than seeing it as a management control mechanism, is likely to result in employees defining their own training and career development needs. However, this approach to performance appraisal does depend on line managers having the appropriate attitudes and skills to manage in such a way that the individual is given sufficient autonomy for personal growth to be developed. This implies a clear training need for managers to shed the 'technician' label they often possess and embrace new ways of managing which have leadership and facilitation as their guiding principles. These 'new ways of managing' are central to the concept of change given the key role line managers play in managing the change process. Employees' needs for responsibility, influence and personal growth may also be met through imaginative job design. Among the elements of job design which Armstrong (1993) advocates to enhance the interest and challenge of work are: greater responsibility for employees in deciding how their work is done; reducing task specialisation; allowing employees greater freedom in defining their performance goals and standards of performance and introducing new and more challenging tasks. In addition, more opportunities for employee involvement may also foster responsibility, influence and personal growth among employees. Achievement may be the result of involvement in such activities as quality circles and problem-solving groups.

TOTAL REWARD

Non-financial rewards are the cornerstone of the concept of total reward. This emerged from the US in the late 1990s when a war for talent, and the consequent need to retain the most effective employees, was the result of an internet-inspired booming economy (IRS 2003a). Total reward combines the traditional pay and benefits elements with the other things that employees gain from employment: skills, experience, opportunity and recognition. Therefore it is more than a flexible benefits package or a consideration of the combined value of basic pay, incentives and benefits. Total reward takes into account the less tangible benefits of employment (IRS 2003a). The total reward package may differ between organisations, employee groups or individual employees. It may contain such considerations as a competitive base salary, development opportunities or flexible working hours. The aim is to construct the total reward package in such a way that it is tailored to the desires of individual employees with the cost implications for the employer being minimal.

THE LINK WITH ORGANISATIONAL STRATEGY

Armstrong (2002) also notes in his definition that reward embraces the philosophies, strategies, policies, plans and processes used by organisations to develop and maintain reward systems. More particularly, writers such as Lawler (1995) have stressed the need for reward systems to play an important part in changing employee behaviours in order to complement business strategy. Such behaviours may be, for example, the acquisition of more 'commercially aware' attitudes and behaviours and greater preparedness and ability to undertake a wider range of tasks. This sits easily with the strategic HRM literature (see, for example, Mabey *et al.* 1998) which also emphasises changed employee behaviours as the outcome of strategic HRM activities.

The strategic reward model in Figure 5.1 suggests that reward strategy starts with a consideration of the business strategy. This is based upon the organisation's external and internal operating environments. Armstrong (1993) notes that the internal environment consists of the organisation's culture, structure, technology, working arrangements, processes and systems.

Lawler's model proposes that the compensation strategy can make a valuable contribution to the development of these employee behaviours. As such compensation is, of course, only part of the wider HR strategy. Lawler (1984) argues that there should be congruence between these various aspects of the HRM strategy in that the reward system needs to fit the other features of the HR strategy, such as job design and managers' leadership styles, to ensure that total human resource management congruence exists.

According to Lawler (1995) the reward strategy consists of three components:

the organisation's core reward values;

structural issues; and

process features.

The organisation's core reward values are what the organisation stands for, which inform the principles on which the reward strategy is founded. Structural issues include the strategy features (e.g., performance-related or profit-related pay) and the administrative policies surrounding these features. Process features include principally how the strategy is communicated and implemented and the extent to which employees are involved in the

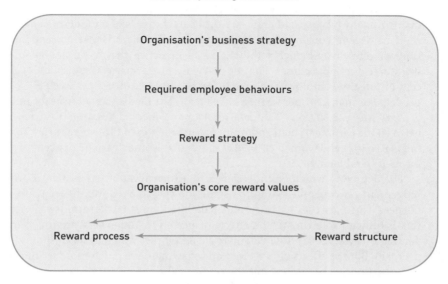

External operating environment

Internal operating environment

Figure 5.1 Key elements of reward system design

Source: Developed from Lawler 1995

design and implementation of the strategy. Lawler makes the point that the stronger the alignment between the core reward values, structural features and processes, the more effective the reward strategy will be. He argues that the key consideration is the level of consistency between what organisations say and what they do. In the event of inconsistency, Lawler notes that there is likely to be employee misunderstanding about how the reward strategy works with a consequence being a failure to generate the required behaviours.

What are the expectations that the parties to the employment relationship have of reward?

Reward is a highly sensitive area and has the potential for considerable employment relations problems. Therefore it is important for reward specialists to be clear about the expectations that the differing parties to the employment relationship have of reward systems.

EMPLOYEES

It would be too simple to assume that employees always want to earn the biggest possible salary. Most employees are more realistic about their earning potential and seek a balance between what they estimate to be that potential, the level of effort expended and inconvenience suffered. Torrington and Hall (2002) suggest that employees have a number of specific pay objectives. Three of these are analysed here: purchasing power, felt-fairness and relativities.

Purchasing power is the most basic objective of all: all employees want to earn sufficient money to support the lifestyle to which they aspire. From this flows many of the basic rights many of many of us would argue are the characteristics of a modern, democratic society: the right to decent housing, food, transport and the dignity that accompanies the ability to support oneself and one's family. It is an objective that a substantial proportion of the workforce does not achieve. The 2001 New Earnings Survey (Jenkins 2002) shows that 25 per cent of full-time employees in the UK earned less than £267 per week (£13,884 p.a.), and 10 per cent less than £207 per week (£10,764 p.a.). The median weekly rate for full-time employees in 2001 was £23,607 p.a. The data masks more inequalities, one of which is the difference between the earning of men and women. Comparison of the average gross annual earnings for men (£24,102) and women (£19,922) shows that women earn 83 per cent of the median wage for men (Grabham 2003).

The degree to which employees feel that their level of pay is 'fair' is a highly subjective judgement. Two people doing the same job may have quite different notions of pay 'felt fairness' (Jacques 1962) as a result of their different backgrounds and aspirations. While this is difficult to estimate, the effects of perceived 'unfairness' are much more predictable. Torrington *et al.* (2002) note that there are employees who may feel dishonest because they are overpaid. But the effects of perceived underpayment are much more serious. The employee in this situation is likely to exhibit the traditional signs of dissatisfaction: e.g., lateness, lack of cooperation, absence. However, as Torrington *et al.* (2002) note: the more serious problem of resentment exists with employees who feel underpaid and unable to move to another job. Clearly, for them the employment relationship is likely to be an unfulfilling one.

The issue of felt-fairness raises the question of 'fair in relation to what?' All employees derive their judgement of what feels fair from comparisons with other individuals and groups. These comparisons at an individual level may be related to the qualifications and experience of a colleague, or to the level of performance which the employee thinks that colleague delivers. At a group level it may be felt that higher-earning colleagues in a different function or geographical region have an easier life. At a national level, trade union negotiators use comparative data to promote the cause of their members. An example of this is a dispute at Eurostar over pay in 2001. This involved some train managers in London who wanted higher pay to bring them in line with drivers. Drivers can earn £40,000 a year, while train managers received between £23,000 and £24,000, according to the union which represents both groups.

'When Eurostar was established the differential between train managers and train drivers was £5,000 to £6,000 a year. Now the gap has widened to about £17,000,' said Andrew Murray, a spokesman for the Associated Society of Locomotive Engineers and Firemen (BBC Online, 2001).

EMPLOYERS

The principal reward objective for the employer is to set levels of reward to attract, retain and motivate the type of employees needed to run an effective organisation (Lupton and Bowey 1983). The key to this is to establish the reward levels of similar organisations in the employer's area. For this purpose, employers may enlist the help of consultants, fellow HR managers in 'pay clubs' (Armstrong 2002) and even trade union officials. While it is not necessarily the case that employees will always be attracted to the highest payer in a defined labour market, the generous employer is in a strong competitive position.

Torrington *et al.* (2002) include control as one of the employer's reward objectives. In essence, this means using rewards as a tool to direct employee behaviours in a way that suits the purposes of the employer. The traditional way of doing this has been incentive schemes based typically upon work output although it may be argued that the type of 'new' reward schemes outlined in this chapter are equally 'controlling'. It is clear from Armstrong's (2002) definition of reward cited earlier that having clear objectives for the pay bill is gaining more importance in many organisations. But whether making reward more 'strategic' is simply a more attractive wrapper for old-fashioned control initiatives is a moot point.

In a survey of employers' reasons for introducing individual performance-related pay (IPRP) (Thompson 1992) 46 out of 48 employers said that IPRP had been introduced to motivate employees. This suggests an unproblematic causal relationship between pay and motivation. However, this relationship is a highly complex one which is beyond the scope of this chapter. But Lawler (1984) suggests that employees tend to behave in whatever way they perceive leads to rewards they value. This suggests that motivation is a highly individual affair. What may motivate one employee may not have the same effect on another. Similarly, what may motivate an employee now (e.g., high earnings and promotion opportunities) may not have the same effect when they are in their 50s when they may be more concerned with the pension element of the reward package. Given the simplistic assumptions of many employers and the complex reality of pay and motivation it is hardly surprising that pay remains the most frequently cited reason for employee relations disputes in the UK.

A significant influence behind any employer's reward strategy is the need to keep a tight control on the budget so that the organisation can afford what it pays. This is particularly important in organisations where the ratio of labour costs to total costs is very high. Consequently, management negotiators often place importance on explaining the current economic position of the organisation to employees and their trade unions at the time of the annual pay review. This is an attempt to suppress the level of any claim. Similarly, senior managers spend time monitoring the decisions of line managers about incentive scheme payments they propose to award their employees to ensure affordability within budgets. To some extent this explains the rise in popularity of self-financing schemes such as gainsharing and profit-related pay.

GOVERNMENT

As part of a strategy to control inflation in recent decades governments in the developed economies have played a major role in pay policy. This has been done in two main ways. First, through government's role as employer. In developed market economies, government acts as employer of upwards of 20 per cent of the total workforce (Hollinshead and Leat 1995). The relationship between governments and their employees has been an uneasy one as greater productivity and accountability has been sought from public sector agencies that have passed this pressure to their employees. Strict controls have been put on annual pay budgets with the consequence that the pay of some employee groups has continually fallen behind inflation. The second way in which governments have played a major role in pay policy is through exerting pressure on the private sector. This is done generally by the example that is set in the public sector and by economic pronouncements. More particularly in the UK there was a series of incomes policies in the 1970s (see Kessler and Bayliss 1998) which controlled the amount of pay increases that employers could give to their employees.

TRADE UNIONS

The pay objectives of trade unions may seem straightforward. As former TUC General Secretary John Monks argued 'it is only reasonable that workers are entitled to take home a living wage for an honest day's work' (Monks 1998, p.178). This may represent a share in the profits of private sector companies or a fair allocation of resources in the public sector. Not surprisingly, the trade unions have been very supportive of the introduction of the national minimum wage, since this, they hope, will drive up what Monks calls the 'unacceptable' level of wages for some workers.

But, increasingly, pay bargaining is not the sole aim of trade unions. As the emphasis switches to unions seeking partnerships with employers, the aims are becoming wider, encompassing such issues as employment security, employability, employee voice and investment in training.

Nonetheless, even with the increasing tendency for employers to move from 'rate for the job' pay systems to those which are related to the individual employee, trade unions still have a role to play in pay bargaining. There is now more emphasis upon negotiating the size of the annual pay 'pot' with managers making decisions on how this 'pot' is to be allocated. This means that the highly visible 'annual pay round' battle between employers and unions may become a thing of the past. Pay negotiations will become far more complex with pay becoming just one of a series of items on the collective bargaining agenda.

The reformed reward agenda

The examination of some background issues to reward above note that in many organisations reward systems are changing, with particular importance being attached to the link between performance and reward. In this section some of these major changes are explored.

PAYING FOR PERFORMANCE

Rewarding performance, either individual job performance, team performance or organisational performance, is, for many organisations, at the heart of a reward strategy. This raises what for many employees is a highly contentious issue: the putting at risk of a proportion of their salary. Most employees think about reward in terms of base pay (Schuster and Zingheim 1992): the fixed amount which traditionally has increased yearly to reflect inflation and, often, length of service. Base pay will also change, of course, upon promotion to a more responsible job. This embodies the values of predictability, security and permanency – none of which is a characteristic consistent with the desire to change employee behaviours. From a managerial perspective, it is not necessarily the best form of reward strategy. The very permanency which employees value is expensive. Increasingly employers are asking themselves why they should build into their fixed salary costs a permanent salary bill which takes little account of changing external, organisational and individual circumstances. Reward strategies which rely exclusively on base pay enshrined in salary scales through which employees move annually until the top of the scale is reached, or promotion achieved, are typical in public sector employment. Such strategies assume that length of service equates with experience and loyalty. Neither tends to be as prized by organisations now as in the past. Such is the pace of change that yesterday's experience may be an impediment to change. It is accepted that loyalty to one employer, typified by a career spent with that employer, is an increasingly outdated concept in an age where employees may have a number of different careers as well as employers. In addition, reward strategies which rely on promotions for employees to increase their salaries do not take into account the fact that organisations now have flatter structures with the consequence that promotion is less available.

For some organisations base pay is of declining importance. This raises the question: 'how can the traditional reward objectives of attracting, retaining and motivating people be achieved while making the pay budget more cost effective?' The answer for many organisations has been to make base pay reflect the market rate for the job and to supplement this with a variable pay element related to individual performance, team performance, organisational performance and individual competence acquisition – or a combination of these. One of the key decisions that needs to be taken into account is whether to pay the variable element as a lump sum bonus or to consolidate this into salary. The trend in both the USA and the UK has been for a move towards one-off cash bonuses. This is hardly surprising given the cost saving that the organisation enjoys. By not raising base pay, one-off cash bonuses do not affect future base pay increases or other associated payments such as overtime, and, of course, pensions.

A shift from all base pay to a combination of base and variable pay does, of course, signal the organisation's desire to move from paying for the job to paying the person. Therefore, the reliance on traditional bureaucratic forms of job evaluation is less pronounced. However, job evaluation is still relevant. Base pay still needs to be set at a level consistent with jobs throughout the organisation and the external labour market. Therefore, some method of determining the relative importance of jobs is needed. It is that definition of importance that is likely to be different in the organisation which places more significance in a combination of base and variable pay. Such a definition is likely to reflect the changed employee behaviours the organisation wishes to encourage in order to meet its changed organisational circumstances. What is clear, according to Schuster and Zingheim (1992), is that internal equity will no longer be the dominant consideration. The market value of jobs, and employees' skills and their impact on the organisation's strategy will take precedence over internal equity.

REWARDING INDIVIDUAL PERFORMANCE

Individual performance-related pay

Individual performance-related pay (IPRP) is defined by ACAS as: 'a method of payment where an individual employee receives increases in pay based wholly or partly on the regular and systematic assessment of job performance' (ACAS 1990, p.2).

It was adopted throughout the 1990s in the USA and the UK with great enthusiasm in many areas of white-collar employment, for example education, local government and financial services. There is some evidence that the popularity of IPRP is spreading to many countries. In a survey of 460 organisations in 13 European countries by Towers Perrin it was reported that only 25 per cent of non-management employees in the firms surveyed had general, across-the-board pay increases, while 93 per cent of the respondent firms had variable bonus schemes (Brown 1999).

Even in Japan, well known for its inclination towards rewards based upon seniority and length of service, survey evidence noted by Ornatowski (1998) suggests that some of the leading organisations are paying their managers based upon their job performance, albeit that these are called annual salary systems (*nen poesi*). For example, Fujitsu is changing to merit-based pay and promotions for all its 47,000 employees. The chairman of the company labour union summed up the thinking behind the change when he said: 'The seniority system made possible one era, now we need to have a system that meets the times' (Zukis and Ushida 1998). However, as the research of Shibata (2002) confirms, in general the changes to reward practice in Japan are limited.

IPRP has been introduced in many organisations to change the culture to reflect the 'new' values which senior managers think are necessary. Lawler (1984, p.128) argues that reward systems can 'cause the culture of an organisation to vary quite-widely. For example they can influence the degree to which it is seen as a human-resource oriented culture, an entrepreneurial culture, an innovative culture, a competence-based culture, and a participative culture'. There is also a strong thread of felt-fairness about IPRP. Most employees (Kessler 1994) agree with the principle of IPRP: that the able and industrious employee should be rewarded more generously for that ability and industry than the idle and incompetent.

Hand (2000) notes the growth of IPRP in Ireland. But he is not alone in commenting on some of the difficulties experienced by Irish organisations. Among these are:

- poor design, implementation and communication;

- too much emphasis upon individual performance over a short-time scale;

- an excessive focus on financial results;

- inadequate salary differentiation (particularly a problem in times of low inflation).

Lewis (1998) in a study of PRP for first-level managers in three UK financial services organisations found other implementation problems. Perceived unfairness was one which had a variety of causes. There was evidence of managers imposing objectives with the result that the objective setting process was 'something that was done to them rather than something in which they played an active part' (Lewis 1998, p.70).The employees interviewed by Procter *et al.* (1993) in an electronics plant expressed concerns about favouritism, in particular the arbitrary way in which managers applied measurement criteria and the ways in which grades were distributed. In two of the three organisations Lewis (1998) researched he noted little attention paid to the giving of performance feedback to employees. This may be because managers are put in a position where they must differentiate between the level of reward of their team members, a position many find uncomfortable. This decision process effectively creates increased dependency of the team member on the line manager, and less dependency on, for example, the trade union (Kessler 1994). Consequently, some organisations have seized this opportunity to expect greater management accountability. ACAS (1990, p.8) point out that the role of managers and supervisors is critical to the implementation of PRP. It is they who must define the required standards of performance and behaviour; explain these to their team members; take tough decisions about assessments; communicate these decisions to team members and defend their judgements if asked (Storey and Sisson 1993). But often managers find this differentiation difficult with the result that they produce statistical distributions that concentrate on the middle rank of performance, thus defeating the object of paying for differentiated performance.

The outcome of these implementation weaknesses is that the value of paying for performance is not practised. What seems a good idea in principle becomes overtaken by perceived problems with the result that employees and managers lose faith in the concept.

Competence-related pay

Competence-related pay can be defined as 'a method of rewarding people wholly or partly by reference to the level of competence they demonstrate in carrying out their roles. It is a method of paying people for their ability to perform' (Armstrong 2002, p.289). It is predictable that interest in competence-related pay should grow given the enormous amount of attention given to the definition of competencies for purposes of selection, training and

Box 5.1: Introducing individual performance-related pay at Sinoelectronics

China is the world's fastest growing economy and management practices are changing to reflect this growth. HR practices are not excluded from this and there is a growing interest in tying reward to employee performance.

   This case is about Sinoelectronics, a large manufacturer of consumer electronics located in the south of China. It has five manufacturing plants with over 7,000 employees. Eighty per cent of the employees are production operatives and the remaining 20 per cent are in managerial, administrative and technical positions. Although ownership of Sinoelectronics is shared between the state and a foreign investor it is not subject to close government control. The company's commercial record in recent years has been impressive. This is mainly because it has demonstrated expertise in production and marketing. It has achieved 50 per cent annual growth since 1993 and developed a strong export market in developing countries such as India. This is mainly due to the cost advantage the Chinese have over their main competitors, the Japanese. But Sinoelectronics is reluctant to move too quickly into the export market. This is due to the vast sales potential for consumer electronic appliances in the Chinese domestic market of 1.3 billion people and the self-confessed lack of management expertise in the company.

   Sinoelectronics is keen to introduce individual performance-related pay. However, the research literature suggests that the history of egalitarianism in China provides obstacles to a move to greater individualisation of pay. The situation is similar at Sinoelectronics. The company's senior managers are aware of the move in the West increasingly to relate the pay of their employees to individual job performance. The company's senior managers claim that they operate an element of performance-related pay. But it is operationalised in a different way from the West. Pay is related to the performance of individual employees in few of the departments, and even in those the relationship is fairly loose.

   The research and development department provides a typical example of the way reward works at Sinoelectronics. The salary of R&D engineers comprises four elements:

1. monthly base pay;
2. a monthly production bonus;
3. an annual profit-related bonus; and
4. an annual bonus.

The monthly base pay is approximately 1,000 yuan (approximately £76). This amount differs between engineers but such was the veil of secrecy surrounding pay levels (there were no published pay scales) that nobody seemed to understand the basis on which base pay was differentiated. The monthly production bonus equates to an amount somewhere between 500 and 1,000 yuan. This figure was derived from the level of production achieved by the factory. The individual employee R&D engineer has no direct control over the level of production but managers justify the large proportion of an individual's pay devoted to the production bonus in terms of the sense of community that exists in Chinese organisations, a claim with which Sinoelectronics' employees generally agree. The annual profit-related bonus generates for each employee approximately 50 per cent of the base salary. The fourth element of salary, the annual bonus, yields an amount equivalent to another two months' base pay. This is paid in February, at the time of the Annual Spring Festival, a family time which makes similar financial demands upon Chinese as Christmas does upon Westerners. Therefore, the annual salary of the typical the research and development engineer may be around 26,000 yuan (approximately £2,000). This is summarised in Table 5.1

Table 5.1   Annual salary of typical R and D engineer at sinoelectronics

	Monthly/ One-off amount	Annual amount
Monthly base pay	1,000 yuan	12,000 yuan
Monthly production bonus	500–1000 yuan	6,000 yuan
Annual profit-related bonus	6,000 yuan	6,000 yuan
Annual bonus	2,000 yuan	2,000 yuan
Total per annum		26,000 yuan

Source: Derived from company data

The history of egalitarianism in China is clearly part of the 'old' values which still are influential in Chinese organisations. So-called 'red eye disease' (jealousy) is evident at Sinoelectronics where there is resentment over differing levels of pay. The resistance to the principle of paying individuals differently according to their performance also highlights another difficulty which the CEO at Sinoelectronics bemoans: the absence of any real employee understanding of entrepreneurialism. It seemed as if individual performance-related pay serves as an embodiment of the tension that exists in China between the 'old' values and the realisation that economic necessity dictates a set of 'new' values, a set in which old egalitarianism plays little part. Part of this set of 'new' values is using job effectiveness as a pay differentiator. This poses practical barriers in Sinoelectronics (e.g., the absence of an effective performance management system) and cultural barriers. However, the newer, younger generation of Sinoelectronics managers are keen to embrace the 'new' values.

Source: Adapted from Lewis 2003

appraisal in recent years. There is some evidence, however, that take-up of competence-related pay is low. Only 14 per cent of the 460 organisations in the Towers Perrin study noted above (Brown 1999) reported that they related base pay increases to employees' competences.

Managers often tend to concentrate on the 'hard' outputs (i.e., those performance indicators that can be calculated numerically) rather than the 'soft' processes (e.g., processes such as working with other team members) when measuring employee performance. All too often managers are not too concerned with how the job is done provided that results are achieved.

Competence-related pay overcomes this alleged weakness of IPRP by ensuring that, usually, both processes and outputs are taken into account when pay-related measurement is made.

Armstrong's definition of competence-related pay captures the most important difference between competence-related pay and IPRP. This is that IPRP is essentially retrospective in that it measures performance over the past pay period (often one year). However, competence-related pay is more forward-looking. It identifies those competencies that are likely to be associated with effective current and future job performance.

Flannery *et al.* (1996, p.92) define competencies as 'sets of skills, knowledge, abilities, behavioural characteristics, and other attributes that, in the right combination and for the right set of circumstances, predict superior performance'. So the technical skill to do the job is clearly not enough. The successful job-holder must ally this skill (e.g., introducing clients to new products) with other attributes (e.g., the desire to enhance the performance of the branch or team). In other words, competence-related pay is highly contextual. It also has, potentially, strong links to organisational strategy. The question which may be asked at business strategy level is 'what competencies do we want our people to demonstrate in order that we may achieve our business goals?'

Managers concerned with 'hard' outputs would be comforted by the fact that many organisations introducing competence-related pay accompany competence-related ratings with performance output measurements, the market rate for the job, and the position of the individual on the pay scale in determining salary level. (Á good example of such a reward programme is that of US giant Dow Chemical (Risher 2000)).

It is noted above that managers can apply IPRP measurement criteria in an arbitrary way which creates in employees problems of a lack of felt-fairness. This is no less true of competence-related pay. In fact, the more the approach moves from one where identifying discernible skills and outputs is possible, the more subjective the measurement process becomes. As yet, little empirical research has been done on the operation of competence-related pay but it would be surprising were it to uncover anything other than the same sort of employee dissatisfactions as IPRP. However, the measurement criteria themselves may be more acceptable to employees than in the case of IPRP. This is often because there is some form of employee involvement in the development of the competence statements (Armstrong and Murlis 1998), albeit that line managers are making the assessment of the extent to which they have been demonstrated. This is unlike IPRP where it is usually the manager who defines the performance objectives and assesses performance.

REWARDING TEAM PERFORMANCE

In team-based pay, payments, or other forms of non-financial reward, are made to team members on the basis of some pre-determined criteria. These criteria may reflect some difference of individual contribution to the team's performance. Armstrong (2002, pp.336–7) notes that the purposes of team-based pay are to, reinforce the sort of behaviour that leads to and sustains effective team performance by:

1. providing incentives and other means of recognising team achievements;
2. clarifying what teams are expected to achieve by relating rewards to the attainment of pre-determined and agreed targets and standards of performance or to the satisfactory completion of a project or the stage of a project;
3. conveying the message that one of the organisation's core values is effective teamwork.

Thompson (1995) identified the types of teams that may be associated with team-based pay. He categorised these as temporary and permanent. The former may be a team set up to achieve a specific project-related goal. The team would consist of employees in different functions operating at different levels in the organisation. Permanent teams may be those based on a specific function (e.g., HR), a process (e.g., in manufacturing plants), a product market or a geographical area. What seems to be important for team-based pay to have a chance of success is that the team has a clear identity, a sense of autonomy, consists of members whose work is inter-dependent and who are flexible, multi-skilled and good team players (Roberts 1997, p.570).

Although in recent years there has been increased interest in employees working in teams this has not necessarily been reflected in actual change. Research by UK bodies such as IRS, CIPD, the Institute for Employment Studies and the Industrial Society suggest that, at most, 10 per cent of UK organisations operate team pay schemes although the figure noted in the European-wide study by Towers Perrin was more than double that (see IRS 2001).

IRS (2001) argue that the slow take-up of team-based pay may be for five reasons: the problem of identifying teams; the difficulty is assessing individual contributions; the effect that it may have in encouraging employees to stay in high-performing/rewarding teams thus prejudicing organisational flexibility; group norms which encourage teams to perform at the level necessary to trigger the financial reward and the 'peaking out' effect where teams reach a performance peak from which they decline after two or three years.

REWARDING ORGANISATIONAL PERFORMANCE

In addition to rewarding individual and team performance many organisations link the rewards of their employees to company performance. The most popular way of doing this is through employee share-ownership schemes in which employees obtain shares in the company's stock.

EMPLOYEE SHARE-OWNERSHIP SCHEMES

In the UK employee share-ownership schemes are part of the drive towards a 'property-owning democracy' that was launched by the 1980s Thatcher government and reinforced by Chancellor Gordon Brown in his 1998 pre-budget report:

> I want to remove, once and for all, the old 'them and us' culture in British industry. I want to encourage the new enterprise culture of teamwork in which everyone contributes and everyone benefits from success. . .we will make it easier for all employees. . .to become stakeholders in their company. I want to double the number of firms in which all employees have the opportunity to own shares (Cited in Hyman 2000).

Hyman argues that there are three principal management rationales for the introduction of employee share schemes. First, they offer property rights to employees; second, they help to unite employee and employer interests with resultant enhancements in employee satisfaction and, therefore, productivity; and third, they buttress management attempts to seek control over the regulation of the employment relationship through, for example, moving pay away from pre-determined formulae such as cost of living and connecting it more directly with company performance. Hyman is dubious about the effect of the first two of these rationales. In general, the amount that is added to employees' salaries is modest, such that employees tend to see the share allocation as a bonus. In addition, there are usually no means for influencing corporate decision making. Given these points is it is unlikely that significant gains in employee identification with the interests of the employer will result. That said, Hyman points out that there is some evidence to suggest the management ambition to retain key employees through the introduction of employee share-ownership schemes is being realised. This view receives some support in a recent IRS study (IRS 2003b). However, the same study notes a considerable disadvantage to such schemes reported by employers – the administrative burden they impose.

Granting employee share ownership is a growing reward trend in China. One recent survey for general industry showed around 10 per cent of companies grant stock options to their employees (Lee and Shao 2000). Lee and Shao report that most of the organisations in the hi-tech industry, where employee share-ownership schemes are most prevalent, perceive such schemes as a means of enhancing competitiveness and retaining employees.

This finding is borne out by the study of international reward practices conducted with 2,000 managers in ten countries by Lowe *et al.* (2002). Respondent managers were asked the extent to which pay in their organisations was contingent upon group and organisational performance. However, only managers in China and Taiwan reported 'relatively high' scores.

But there is some evidence that in Europe the granting of employee shares is growing. Carrol *et al.* (2000) detail the trends in Germany, Italy, Spain and Sweden. In all these countries there has been a rise in the granting of employee shares. They argue this has been due to five factors:

■ globalisation of large organisations with the consequent need to attract key managers and specialists on the international labour market;

■ increasing pressure for shareholder value creation;

■ privatisation of large former state-owned organisations;

■ growth of the stock market;

■ the opportunity for employees to reap tax advantages.

In the main Carrol *et al.* note that management employees are the main recipients of such plans although in Germany eligibility is wider in some companies (e.g. Deutsche Bank and Dresdner Bank).

For illustrative purposes the current available employee share-ownership schemes in the UK are summarised below.

Share Incentive Plans (SIP)

SIPs were introduced in the 2000 Finance Bill. Before October 2001 they were known as All-Employee Share Ownership Plans (AESOPs). SIPs provide for four types of share provision:

■ free shares: given by the company to employees up to a limit of £3,000 in any tax year;

■ partnership shares: purchased by employees out of their salary before it is subject to tax or national insurance to a limit of £125 per month (or 10 per cent of salary whichever is the lower);

■ matching shares: companies match partnership shares purchased by employees up to a limit of two matching shares for each partnership share purchased;

■ dividend shares: dividends may be re-invested tax-free up to a limit of £1,500 per year depending on the rules in the company plan.

Employees who keep their shares in the scheme for five years pay no income tax or national insurance contributions on the shares. If the shares are withdrawn after three years, income tax and national insurance contributions must be paid in the initial market value of the shares. In addition, employees do not have to pay capital gains tax if their shares are kept in the scheme for five years.

SIPs offer companies a high degree of flexibility because they may combine the four types of share provision. In addition, for the first time, companies are able to link a share-ownership scheme to individual employee performance. Of the 27 large UK employers which participated in an IRS study in 2003 (IRS 2003b) four were operating SIPs schemes.

One of these was the financial services organisation National Australia Group Europe, where 90 per cent of its employees participate in the scheme. The minimum monthly employee purchase of partnership shares is £10 and additional free shares are allocated, based on the company's performance (no matching shares are allocated as part of the scheme). The company's latest allocation of shares through the scheme exceeded Aus$10 million (£4.1 million) providing each employee with an allocation worth Aus$956 (£394) (IRS 2003b).

Save-As-You-Earn (SAYE) or Savings-Related Share Option Schemes

The savings-related share option scheme requires a contribution from the employee. In such schemes the employee saves for a specified period of three, five or seven years. The scheme specifies that employees can buy shares at the end of the savings period with the savings fund accumulated. The price of the shares will be the market price at the start of the savings contract or at an agreed discount at the start of the contract. The shares bought at the end of the savings contract attract tax relief.

With the three-year savings contract the employee saves a fixed amount monthly (it cannot exceed £250) and at the end of the term a cash bonus of 2.75 months' payment is added. At the end of a five-year contract a cash bonus of 7.5 months' payment is added. At the end of the three- or five-year term the employee uses the amount saved and the bonus to buy shares in the company. For employees who have saved for five years there is the option of extending the term to seven years, in which case 13.5 months' payments is added as a cash bonus. Employees who choose a seven-year contract do not have to make monthly contributions after five years but agree to leave their savings untouched for the final two years to qualify for the higher bonus.

The price at which employees have the opportunity to purchase shares must not be below 80 per cent of the market value at the start of the contract. This seemed to be the typical price determined by employers in an Incomes Data Services study (Incomes Data Services 1998). At the end of the contract period employees also have the option to have their contributions returned if the share price is not favourable, rendering the scheme risk-free.

As with profit-sharing schemes, all employees who have been employed by the company for five years must be eligible to participate in savings-related share option schemes if the scheme is to gain Inland Revenue approval.

The UK bank First Direct's SAYE scheme has a 61 per cent take-up among eligible employees (those with at least six months' service). Participating employees must make a minimum monthly payment of £5, and the company offers a discount of up to 20 per cent on the market price of the shares purchased. Three- and five-year period options are available (IRS 2003b).

Gainsharing

Gainsharing is more popular in the USA than in Britain. In a gainsharing scheme the relationship between employees' efforts and their eventual reward is more direct than with employee share ownership schemes. Gainsharing plans are designed so that employees share the financial results of improvements in productivity, cost saving or quality. The resultant payment is paid from costs savings generated as a result of such improvements. For example, the American ceramics manufacturer Zircoa based its scheme on the speed at which jobs are done, the quantity of product produced and the spend required to achieve these factors (IRS 1998).

The gainshare plan payment may be made in three ways: as a percentage of base pay; as a one-off cash bonus or as a payment per hour worked. At Zircoa a flat rate payment is made to all relevant employees and the gains are divided 50:50 between the employees and the company.

Schuster and Zingheim (1992) are careful to point out that the organisation must design safeguards to ensure that it derives financial value from the results generated from the project linked to gainsharing. This type of gainsharing differs from more traditional forms of gainsharing which have operated in manufacturing under the heading of Scanlon and Rucker plans. The principal difference is that the foundation of this new type of gainsharing is the future goals of the organisation whereas that of more traditional gainsharing plans is the historical performance standards of the participating employees. The key point here, of course, is that historical performance standards may be achieved or exceeded while the organisation's overall goals are not met.

Box 5.2: Reward changes in the German banking industry

The principle of variable pay has been considered by German bank employers for over 30 years but little progress was made with its introduction. However, interest sharpened in the late 1990s as employers increasingly saw it as a means of the banks becoming more competitive. Negotiating a national agreement between the employers and trade unions still proved difficult as the trade unions saw variable pay, in particular individual performance-related pay, as threatening employee income levels and the quality of customer service as employees concentrated upon short-term sales targets rather than meeting customer needs.

In 2002 an agreement was reached to cover all employees (except trainees) in the public and private banking sector. It commenced in July 2003. The 'collective agreement on performance and/or success-related variable remuneration for the private and public banking sector' is innovative and contains the strong strand of voluntarism that the trade unions were demanding while meeting employer demands for variable pay. The main points of the collective agreement are listed below:

Any scheme will be agreed at local level between company management and the works council (Betriebsrat) in the private sector or the employees council (Personalrat) in the public sector.

Schemes may cover all the employees in a company or just particular employee groups. Those employees not covered by the agreement will receive the standard pay increase applicable for the period.

Performance-related pay schemes may be agreed for individuals or teams.

Employees covered by the variable pay scheme will contribute 4 per cent of monthly pay (12 monthly contributions per year) to be placed in a variable pay budget which will then be distributed as variable performance-related pay. The employer will also

▶

contribute to the variable pay budget (the amount is not defined but it is anticipated that this will be an amount equal to the employee contribution). All money in the variable pay budget must be distributed to employees annually as a 13-month bonus.

For the 13-month bonus there are two options. Which option is chosen must be agreed at local level. The first option is simply to take the 12-monthly 4 per cent employee contributions (48 per cent of a month's pay) together with the employer's contribution (say, another 12-monthly 4 per cent contributions equalling another 48 per cent of a month's pay, totalling 96 per cent of a month's pay). To this is added a further contribution from the employer which means that the 13-month bonus is just over one month's additional pay. The second option puts the 13-month bonus at greater risk for the employee. In this option the bonus is based upon the annual pay award. In 2003 this was 5.1 per cent. The 13-month bonus may be either 100 per cent of the month's pay plus double the annual pay award (100% + 10.2% = 110.2%) or 100 per cent of the month's pay less the annual pay award (100% − 5.1% = 94.9%).

Performance targets are agreed at the local level between management and employees. There will usually be no more than four or five targets and must be based on demonstrable evidence. They can be a mixture of 'hard' quantitative targets (e.g., sales) and 'softer' targets (e.g., quality of customer service) and are assessed jointly by supervisors and employees. Target achievement level will determine the level of payment of the 13-month bonus.

Source: Developed from *European Industrial Relations Review* 2003

The case for a reformed reward agenda and the speed of its adoption

The point is made above that reward strategy is increasingly being driven by the overall business strategy of the organisation which is shaped by the external and internal environment in which the organisation operates. There is little doubt that the case for reform of reward strategy is a compelling one. Several factors suggest themselves as key drivers. These are summarised in Table 5.2.

Compelling though these drivers may be, the reality in most organisations may not reflect the 'leading edge' practice of the few. Lowe *et al.*'s (2002) international survey showed that the move to variable pay may not be as pronounced as it is tempting to think. Only three countries' managers (China, Japan and Taiwan) rated pay incentives as an important part of their current reward systems, much higher than USA and Australia. However, all managers in all 10 countries were of the opinion that there should be greater dependence upon pay incentives in their reward systems. This suggests that actual reward practice is running behind management ambitions. When asked if incentives were a significant amount of pay only Korea scored highly whereas USA, Canada and Australia were low. This last finding is surprising given the national cultural value of individualism in these three countries. Again managers in all 10 countries thought incentives should be a more significant amount of pay. A similar result was evident when the focus turned to reward being contingent upon organisational or group performance. Again only China and Taiwan reported relatively high dependence on reward contingent upon organisational or group performance.

Table 5.2 Reformed reward strategy driver and its relationship to reward strategy

Reformed reward strategy driver	Relationship to reward strategy
More competitive product markets.	Greater employee productivity needs to be generated through making it a key driver of reward strategy.
More competitive product markets dictating need for greater cost control.	Greater emphasis upon cash bonuses (e.g., in team pay or IPRP schemes) which are not consolidated into base pay.
The drive for more customer-focused organisational cultures.	Greater need for reward strategies which emphasise the demonstration of customer-focused behaviours as a key performance criteria.
More competitive product markets in key occupations.	Reward strategies which are designed to attract and retain key employees (e.g., paying for competence acquisition, high performance). (See Schuster and Zingheim 1999)
Low inflation economies.	Greater need for self-financing reward mechanisms, e.g., output-related performance-related pay, gainsharing.
Adoption of new technologies.	Reward strategies which are designed to pay employees for acquiring new competences become more important.
Increase in flexible organisation structures and work practices.	Enhanced importance of flexible reward practices.
Flatter organisational structures resulting in fewer promotion opportunities.	Alternative ways of rewarding employees who are effective need to be adopted (e.g., IPRP).
Changing career expectations of employees.	Declining likelihood of employees staying with organisations most of their careers means loyalty less important than effectiveness so rewards schemes need to reflect individual effectiveness. Less attention paid to service-related pay.
The decline of collective bargaining.	Less emphasis upon across-the-board pay settlements to apply to all employees means greater opportunity for managers to differentiate between the pay of individuals and teams.
The rise of HRM and high commitment work practices.	Increase in initiatives such as employee involvement and teamwork lead to search for reward initiatives which complement these.

In addition, Brown (1999) notes that although 94 per cent of the respondent organisations in the Towers Perrin study referred to above report that they had made 'significant' changes to their reward policies in the preceding three years and even more had changes planned,

> the reward package of the average European worker, in fact, looks very similar to that of three, five or even ten years ago, with base pay levels set using a job evaluation system in three-quarters of the companies; pay managed within ranges averaging between 20 and 40 per cent in width; an annual profit-sharing scheme; and an increasingly comprehensive bundle of benefits (Brown 1999, p.53).

The picture that emerges from this study, argues Brown, is one of incremental change with, for example, competences being used to improve traditional job evaluation schemes and team pay introduced alongside, rather than in place of, individual bonus schemes.

The lack of radical reform does raise the question of the impediments there may be to its introduction. Brown (1999) argues that there may be two such impediments. The first is the lack of skill and commitment that many line managers have when it comes to the implementation of reward initiatives, particularly (as noted earlier in this chapter) when they are linked to performance management. The second impediment is the poor grasp that many employees have of such basic issues as how their base pay is set and the value of their reward packages. This is what Lewis *et al.* (2002) found in a study of the introduction a new reward scheme in a large UK company. Only eight of the 460 respondents to the Towers Perrin survey noted above were able to say that their employees had a strong understanding of the basic pay issues that relate to them.

Ethical concerns of strategic reward management

While there may be a compelling business case for strategic reward reform, these reforms do promote ethical concerns. Heery (1996) argues that there are three concerns with new pay. First, strategic reward management poses a threat to the well-being of employees. New pay advocates suggest reducing the proportion of pay that is fixed, thus putting a proportion of the pay packet 'at risk' through techniques such as performance-related pay. Well-being is threatened by an increased amount of insecurity and unpredictability that is potentially harmful both economically and psychologically. Additionally, putting a proportion of employees' income at risk may lead to such behaviours as overwork which may damage both mental and physical health.

Second, Heery argues that new pay may be unjust. This may be at two levels. It may be procedurally unjust in terms of the way in which the element of pay at risk is determined, usually by line managers. It also may be unjust in a distributive sense. New pay theory has it that employees take their share of the hardship when the organisation is doing less well, for example, through lower share values. In this way employers are transferring an element of risk from the main body of their shareholders to their employees. But as Heery points out, shareholders are often better equipped to spread their risks than employees who often are dependent on their salary as the sole source of income.

Third, Heery (1996, p.62) suggests that strategic reward reform has an essentially unitarist flavour. As such it 'affords little scope for the exercise of democratic rights by citizens at the workplace'. If it is assumed that there is no essential conflict of interest between employer and employees then the right of employees to have their views represented is of little importance. Indeed, trade unions and collective bargaining have little coverage in the strategic reward literature. On the other hand, there is emphasis on employee involvement, but this tends to focus on securing commitment of employees to the goals of the organisation and the reward reforms rather than representing the interests of employees. In this sense, new pay may be seen as part of a sophisticated edifice to marginalise the democratic rights of employees at the workplace and the mechanisms for securing those rights. There is little evidence, however, of such a sophisticated level of strategic thinking in the UK. Wood's (1996) survey of UK manufacturing plants found little systematic association between pay systems such as performance-related pay and profit-related pay and so-called high commitment work practices such as teamworking, quality circles, employee communication, multi-skilling and single status terms and conditions. These are the sort of HR practices, when aligned with new reward techniques, which one would expect to see if management were making concerted efforts to ensure employees adopted the goals of the organisation.

CHANGING REWARD STRUCTURES: The Case at Airbus UK

PHILIP LEWIS

Airbus UK is part of the giant European aerospace group EADS and is jointly owned by EADS and Britain's BAE Systems. It is the only European manufacturer of aircraft. Airbus UK competes with the American manufacturer Boeing; the world's only other major aircraft producer. Airbus has European manufacturing facilities in Germany, France and Spain as well as in the UK. In the UK the company operates on two sites: Filton (Bristol) and Broughton, Cheshire.

Airbus UK has approximately 9,200 employees operating on the two sites. Approximately one-half of these are blue-collar manufacturing operatives. The other half of the workforce consists of white-collar employees: managers, professional, technicians and support staff. Much the biggest employee group is the design and manufacturing engineers. Other groups include procurement, finance, information technology, human resources, production support, programmes and administration. This case study is concerned with the 2,500 white-collar employees who make up the professional, technician and support staff population.

The case is set against the background of a very difficult product market for the word's air industry, due in the main to the events of 11 September 2001 and the consequent reluctance of travellers to use air transport. Airbus profits declined by 60 per cent in the third quarter of 2003. However, despite the decline in plane deliveries, Airbus confirmed it achieved its target to deliver 300 aircraft. As a result it has overtaken rival Boeing for the first time in three decades of fierce competition. A company statement said: 'Our performance during the first nine months of 2003 is in line with our plans. We continue to reinforce our position in the industry's competitive environment and lay the foundation for future profitable growth through investments such as the Airbus A380 programme.' (BBC Online 2003). One of the consequences of this tighter financial climate has been the need to generate HR responses which match the strategic need to be more cost effective. As far as reward is concerned Steve Dumbleton, the compensation and benefits specialist, says 'we need to breed a performance culture. It is not now enough for people to come and work, even for ten hours a day. They have to perform, make a difference. It's not how long you are here, or what qualifications you have: it's what you actually do that counts.'

Reward structures 1991–2001

The Airbus reward structure had been very traditional. There were 13 grades for white-collar staff up to executive level. This was devised using a job evaluation system which, according to Steve Dumbleton, was perceived by some as intensely bureaucratic. In addition, he noted that 'at one stage it seemed as if we had more job descriptions than employees'. The result was an inflexible structure which meant that when employees wanted to progress they had to seek promotion to a higher grade. Were this not possible, discontent would be the obvious result. This was a particular problem if managers wished to retain those employees. In these circumstances it was necessary to inflate the importance of the job as part of the job evaluation re-grading appeal process.

This 13-grade reward structure was revised in 1996 following consultation with the two trade unions representing white-collar employees: AMICUS and the T&GWU. For the first time a broad-banded structure was introduced. This reduced the 13 grades to five: technician, advanced technician, professional, advanced professional and professional leader. (Advanced professional and professional leader are management grades and hence outside of the scope for this case study.) The result of this was that managers had a good deal more flexibility to progress employees within the band without the need for promotion or submitting job evaluation appeals. In addition to an annual general award, employees could earn a merit increase based upon their performance. However, the 1996 reward structure was not deemed to be wholly successful and at the 2001 pay negotiations the trade unions registered 'a failure to agree'. The unions' objections were three-fold:

1. They were unhappy with inconsistencies produced as a result of the job evaluation system where, they felt, some jobs were incorrectly positioned in the structure;
2. They felt that the merit pay system bred unfairness as managers were inconsistent in the awards they made to employees. Only 25 per cent of employees received the merit increase in any one year. They would have preferred a system where all employees received an increase.
3. They were dissatisfied with the way in which some new entrants were given a higher salary than existing employees in the same band performing the same duties. Company managers defended this on the basis that in order to attract the best staff, particularly engineers, in a market where demand for high calibre staff exceeds supply, it is sometimes necessary to pay a premium in addition to the market rate for any given specialism.

Reward structure post-2001: 1. Failure to agree and ensuing research.

Following the failure to agree in 2001 it was agreed that a project team should be appointed to recommend a revised grading and reward structure and process. The team consisted of five senior trade union representatives from both of the recognised trade unions, five senior line managers from across the business and human resource specialists. The three main aims of the project team were to:

1. review pay bands taking into account external market rates to support recruitment and retention;
2. reintroduce performance-related pay using a process that rewards employees fairly;
3. introduce processes that, supported by training, can ensure results are thought to be fair, equitable and transparent.

Over a period of 18 months the project team undertook a good deal of research to ensure that the aims were met. This entailed the trade unions sounding out their members who confirmed that the over-riding concern was the potential for inconsistency in application of the current scheme. In addition, a questionnaire was sent to all managers within the company. The results showed that they too felt that the current processes could result in inconsistencies. Moreover, it demonstrated that rewarding employees fairly was the managers' main concern. The research also involved benchmark visits to a number of organisations similar in size and nature to Airbus to seek their views on grading and reward. Three common themes emerged from the visits:

a) the feeling that limiting to three the number of operating bands across the white-collar reward population could be unduly restrictive;

b) rewarding high performers and applying external market rates were critical determinants of pay levels;

c) communication and training were vital to the consistent application of the scheme.

Reward structure post-2001: 2. Project team recommendations

As a result of the project team's research a number of recommendations were made. These were:

■ The technician and advanced technician broad bands should remain unaltered;

■ The one professional band should be divided into two: in addition to 'professional' there would be a new band for newly qualified high potential graduates to be titled advanced professional developing (APD) (see further details below). The recommended reward and grading structure is shown in Figure 5.2.

As illustrated in Figure 5.2, the professional, advanced technician and technician bands all contain three pay zones, enhanced zone, target zone and incremental zone. The intention is that eventually all fully competent performing employees should be in the target zone pay range. This runs from 95–110 per cent of the mid-point market rate and thus represents the external market value for jobs within the band. Recently appointed employees who do not possess all the skills and knowledge to be considered fully capable in their role, or existing staff who for whatever reason have not progressed to the target zone pay range, are placed in the incremental zone pay range. The aim of management is to move effective employees from incremental zone pay range to target zone pay range as quickly as possible in order that they may receive a salary which is competitive with external market rates, thus aiding retention. This is achieved through awarding employees in this zone an incremental increase each year in addition to any general award. However, to receive an increment employees must be developing towards full competence in their role as assessed in the annual personal development review (appraisal). The incremental zone pay range runs from 70–95 per cent of the target zone pay for each job with an increment being worth 3 per cent at the lower end of the scale and 2 per cent at the upper end. The enhanced zone pay range is designed for those employees operating in the upper part of the band, for example, those staff who have jobs considered to be larger than normal for the grade due to additional responsibilities. The enhanced zone pay range covers the range from 110–130 per cent of the target zone pay for each job. In the professional band this range is extended to 150 per cent.

The advanced professional developing band is a new grade for employees who are in a development role and are destined for advanced professional status. They are normally expected to possess a minimum of an upper second class honours degree and studying for chartered professional status. Approximately 250 employees are in this grade. It is important that pay is competitive in this grade as competition for the services of young engineers in the external labour market is fierce. Unlike the other grades, there is no overtime in the advanced professional developing band. However, incumbents are eligible for non-consolidated variable pay and can benefit from higher salary increases for high levels of performance as the company moves towards a performance culture. The APD pay band consists of a series of increments. There are no target or enhanced zones because within three years incumbents are expected to have achieved advanced professional status. Advanced professional is recognised as the first management grade within the company.

Professional

£33300		£28009		£21090	Enhanced zone pay range
[ ]		[ ]		£20646	Target zone pay range
[ ]		[ ]		£20202	Incremental zone pay range
[ ]		[ ]		£19758	
[ ]		[ ]		£19315	
[ ]		[ ]		£18870	
		[ ]		£18204	
				£17538	
				£16872	
				£16206	
				£15540	

Advanced Professional Developing **Advanced Technician**

£30870	£24119		£20140		£17256	Enhanced zone pay range
£30248	[ ]		[ ]		£16885	Target zone pay range
£29622	[ ]		[ ]		£16514	Incremental zone pay range
£29000	[ ]		[ ]		£16143	
£28376	[ ]		[ ]		£15771	
£27752	[ ]		[ ]		£15215	
£27129			£17628		£14658	
£26505					£14102	
£25881					£13545	
£25258					£12989	
£24634						
£24011						
£23387						
£22763						
£21827						

Technician

£19612		£16214		£13708	Enhanced zone pay range
[ ]		[ ]		£13413	Target zone pay range
[ ]		[ ]		£13118	Incremental zone pay range
[ ]		[ ]		£12823	
[ ]		[ ]		£12529	
[ ]		[ ]		£12087	
		£14003		£11664	
				£11203	
				£10760	
				£10318	

Figure 5.2 Pay band–professional, technician and advanced technician

Pay progression through the lower end of the technician, advanced technician and professional pay bands will be by increments. The criteria for awarding increments will be the development of the individual employee towards the skills and behaviours required by the job as listed in the job description. These increments are in addition to those determined by the collective bargaining process. Normally one increment per year will apply, but this could be two increments or, indeed, none. Determination of whether the employee possesses the skills and behaviours required by the job is by performance appraisal in which the employee's immediate manager rates the employee according to pre-determined criteria. Some of the trade union's fears about inconsistencies are allayed by virtue of the 'grandfather' system whereby the manager's manager ratifies the rating and resultant increment that is awarded to the employee.

The guiding principle of the scheme that employees lower in any pay band will be more likely to receive a salary increase for a given level of performance than an employee higher in the band does raise the possibility of employees higher in the band becoming 'stuck' with reduced scope for pay progression. To overcome this potential problem there is a possibility to award a pay increase to individuals in the target and enhanced zones in return for additional responsibility. Employees in the enhanced zone are only eligible for a payment if their job is also considered to be larger than normal for the grade. However such an increase is likely to be restricted to approximately 25 per cent of the population in the target and enhanced zones with increases likely to be somewhere between 1 and 4 per cent.

In addition, a variable pay scheme is being devised where all employees in the target zone and above for any band will be eligible to receive a one-off payment, not consolidated into salary. The criterion will be the individual's performance over the previous year. Airbus intends to introduce this scheme in 2005 following further negotiations with the trade unions.

Employees who feel that they have been unfairly treated may invoke an appeals procedure. Perceived unfairness may be due to employees feeling that either the job has been located in the wrong band or that the rating and increment given as a result of the performance appraisal process is inappropriate. The appeals procedure has two stages, as illustrated in Figure 5.3.

It is hoped that appeals will be kept to a minimum due to the fact that training will be provided for all managers to ensure that they understand the new structure and processes. This will play an important part in developing a rewards scheme that will meet all the aspirations of both Airbus managers and trade union representatives.

Stage one	Meeting between employee, the employee's manager's manger and the trade union representative
Stage two	Meeting between employee, the head of the employee's department, an HR advisor and the trade union representative

Figure 5.3 Reward scheme appeals procedure

Questions

1. What may be the advantages and disadvantages of the new reward structure at Airbus?

2. The new reward structure was designed to help the generation of a performance culture. Which other HR initiatives would be consistent with this aim?

3. Which other HR initiatives complement the new reward structure?

4. To what extent may fairness and inconsistency co-exist in the Airbus (or any other organisation's) reward structure without harmful consequences?

5. A key finding of the reward project team was that 'communication and training were vital to the consistent application of the scheme'. What should be the form and content of the communication and training programmes?

References

ACAS (1990) *Appraisal Related Pay,* London: ACAS.

Armstrong, M. (1993) *Managing Reward Systems,* Buckingham: Open University Press.

*Armstrong, M. (2002) *Employee Reward* (3rd edn), London: Chartered Institute of Personnel and Development.

Armstrong, M. and Murlis, H. (1998) *Reward Management: A Handbook of Remuneration Strategy and Practice* (4th edn), London: Kogan Page.

BBC Online (2001), 'Pre-Christmas strikes hit Eurostar', 21st December. Available from http://news.bbc.co.uk/1/hi/business/1719389.stm

Brown, D. (1999) 'States of pay', *People Management,* 25 November, pp.52–3.

Carrol, A., Holscher, C., Signorotto, E. and Linares, A. (2000) 'Stock option practices in Germany, Italy, Spain and Sweden', *Benefits and Compensation International,* Vol.32, No.1, January/February, pp.53–65.

European Industrial Relations Review (2003) 'Variable pay accord in banking', No.357, October, pp.15–18.

*Flannery, T., Hofrichter, D. and Platten, P. (1996) *People, Performance and Pay,* New York: Free Press.

Grabham, A. (2003) 'Composition of pay', *Labour Market Trends,* No.297, pp.397–405.

Hand, D. (2000) 'Remuneration in the Republic of Ireland', *Benefits and Compensation International,* Vol.29, No.7, March, pp.21–4.

Heery, E. (1996), 'Risk, representation and the new pay', *Personnel Review,* Vol.25, No.6, pp.54–65.

Hollinshead, G. and Leat, M. (1995) *Human Resource Management: An International and Comparative Perspective,* London: Pitman.

Hyman, J. (2000) 'Financial participation schemes', in G. White and J. Druker (eds) *Reward Management: A Critical Text,* London: Routledge.

Income Data Services (1998) *Profit sharing and share options,* Study No. 641, January.

IRS Employment Trends (1998) 'Gainsharing drives improvement process at Zircoa', No.656, pp.12–13.

IRS Employment Review (2001) 'Whatever happened to team reward?', No.732.

IRS Employment Review (2003a) 'Totally rewarding', No.782, pp.34–6.

IRS Employment Review (2003b) 'Sharing the spoils: profit-share and bonus schemes', No.784, pp.28–32.

Jacques, E. (1962), 'Objective measures for pay differentials', *Harvard Business Review*, January/February, pp.133–7.

Jenkins, J. (2002) 'Patterns of pay: results of the 2001 New Earnings Survey', *Labour Market Trends*, March, pp.129–39.

Kessler, I. (1994) 'Performance pay', in K. Sisson (ed.) *Personnel Management*, Oxford: Blackwell.

Kessler, S. and Bayliss, F. (1998) *Contemporary British Industrial Relations* (3rd edn), Basingstoke: Macmillan.

Lawler, E.E. (1984) 'The strategic design of reward systems', in C. Fombrun, N.M. Tichy and M.A. Devanna, *Strategic Human Resource Management*, New York: Wiley.

*Lawler, E. (1995) 'The new pay: a strategic approach', *Compensation and Benefits Review*, July–August, pp.14–22.

Lee, M. and Shao, G. (2000) 'Compensations and benefit trends–report from China', *Benefits and Compensation International*, Vol.29, No.6, January/ February, pp.12–18.

Lewis, P. (1998) 'Managing performance-related pay based on evidence from the financial services sector', *Human Resource Management Journal*, Vol.8, No.2, pp.66–77.

Lewis, P. (2003) 'New China–old ways?: a case study of the prospects for implementing human resource management practices in a Chinese state-owned enterprise', *Employee Relations*, Vol.25, No.1, pp.42–60.

Lewis, P., Thornhill, A. and Saunders, M. (2002) 'Family breakdown: developing an explanatory theory of reward system change', paper presented to 'HRM in a changing world' conference, Oxford Brookes University, April.

Lowe, K., Milliman, J., De Cieri, H. and Dowling, P. (2002) 'International compensation practices: a ten country comparative analysis', *Human Resource Management*, Vol.41, No.1, pp.45–66.

Lupton, T. and Bowey, A. (1983) *Wages and Salaries* (2nd edn), Aldershot: Gower.

Mabey, C. , Salaman, G. and Storey, J. (1998) *Human Resource Management: A Strategic Introduction*, Oxford: Blackwell.

Mabey, C. , Salaman, M. and Storey, J. (1998) *Human Resource Management: A Strategic Introduction* (2nd edn), Oxford: Blackwell.

Monks, J. (1998) 'Trade unions, enterprise and the future', in P. Sparrow, and M. Marchington, (eds) *Human Resource Management: The New Agenda*, London: Financial Times/Pitman.

Ornatowski, G. (1998) 'The end of Japanese-style Human Resource Management?', *Sloan Management Review*, Vol.39, No.3, Spring, pp.73–84.

Procter, S., McArdle, L., Rowlinson, M., Forrester, P. and Hassard, J. (1993) 'Performance-related pay in operation: a case study from the electronics industry', *Human Resource Management Journal*, Vol.3, No.4, pp.60–74.

Risher, H. (2000) 'Dow Chemical's salary program: a model for the future?', *Compensation and Benefits Review*, May–June, pp.26–34.

Roberts, I. (1997). 'Remuneration and reward', in I. Beardwell and L. Holden (eds) *Human Resource Management: A Contemporary Perspective*, London: Pitman.

Schuster, J. and Zingheim, P. (1992) *The New Pay: Linking Employee and Organisational Performance*, New York: Lexington.

*Schuster, J. and Zingheim, P. (1999) 'Dealing with scarce talent: lessons from the leading edge', *Compensation and Benefits Review*, Vol.31, No. 2, March/April, pp.31–44.

Shibata, H. (2002) 'Wage and performance appraisal systems in flux: a Japan–United States comparison', *Industrial Relations*, Vol.41, No. 4, pp.629–52.

Semler, R. (1993). *Maverick! The Success Story Behind the World's Most Unusual Workplace*, London: Arrow Business Books.

Smith, I. (1983) *The Management of Remuneration: Paying for Effectiveness*, London: Institute of Personnel Management.

Smith, I. (1993) 'Reward Management: a retrospective assessment', *Employee Relations*, Vol.15, No. 3, pp.45–59.

Storey, J. and Sisson, K. (1993) *Managing Human Resources and Industrial Relations*, Buckingham: Open University Press.

Thompson, M. (1992) *Pay and Performance: The Employer Experience,* Brighton: Institute of Manpower Studies.

Thompson, M. (1995) *Team Working and Pay,* Institute of Employment Studies Report No. 281, Brighton: University of Sussex.

Thorpe, R. and Homan, G. (2000) *Strategic Reward Systems,* Harlow: Pearson Education.

Torrington, D., Hall, L. and Taylor, S. (2002), *Human Resource Management* (5th edn), Harlow: FT/Prentice Hall.

White, G. and Druker, J. (eds) (2000) *Reward Management: A Critical Text,* London: Routledge.

Wood, S. (1996) 'High commitment management and payment systems', *Journal of Management Studies,* Vol.33, No. 1, pp.53–77.

Zukis, B. and Ushida, M. (1998) 'Japan's changing compensations and benefits structure', *Benefits and Compensation International,* Vol.29, September, pp.6–13.

*Useful reading

Chapter 6

PERFORMANCE APPRAISAL

Tom Redman

Introduction

The practice of performance appraisal has undergone many major changes over the last decade or so. In the main, developments have been driven by large-scale organisational change (see Chapter 1) rather than theoretical advances in the study of performance appraisal. Particularly prominent here are the advent of downsizing, decentralisation and delayering, flexibilisation of the workforce, the move to teamworking, wave after wave of culture change programmes and new managerial initiatives such as total quality management (TQM), business process reengineering (BPR), competency and, in particular, Investors in People. The most recent Workplace Employee Relations Survey (WERS) data finds organisations who are recognised as an Investor in People were significantly more likely to have a performance appraisal scheme in use (Cully *et al.* 1999). Changes in payment systems have also fuelled the growth and development of performance appraisal. Developments in integrated reward systems, harmonisation and the increased use of merit- and performance-based pay have been strongly associated with the growth of performance appraisal.

Two main implications for performance appraisal practice arise from the new organisational context. First, it would be clearly inappropriate to expect those appraisal schemes operating 10 years or so ago to be effective in many organisations today (see Case study 6.1 at the end of this chapter). Second, rather than new developments heralding the end of performance appraisal or diminishing its importance, they appear to have enhanced its contribution to helping achieve organisational objectives and stimulated considerable experimentation and innovation in its practice. Performance appraisal, as we discuss below, has in fact become more widespread. It has grown to include previously untouched organisations and occupational groups. In particular, performance appraisal has moved down the organisational hierarchy to encompass blue-collar, secretarial and administrative staff and from the private to the public sector. New forms of appraisal have also emerged. We thus now have competency-based appraisal systems, staff appraisal of managers, team-based appraisal, customer appraisals and '360°' systems. Old systems of performance appraisal have also been dusted down and re-emerged in new forms (see Box 6.1).

This chapter's main aim is to critically review some of the key developments in the practice of performance appraisal. First, a brief history of performance appraisal is presented and its current practice examined by considering how widespread it is, what it is used for, and its role as a managerial control tool within broader performance management systems. Second, we

Box 6.1: Performance appraisal in hard times: ranking and yanking

A growing number of organisations are reported as having adopted a performance appraisal system in which best-to-worst ranking methods are used to identify poor performers. Such appraisal systems rank employees along a normal distribution curve in which the top 10 per cent typically receive an A grade or equivalent, the middle 80 per cent earn a B, and the bottom 10 per cent earn a C and dismissal if they do not improve. Such systems gained popularity in the 1990s, and about a third of companies now use them in the US, up from 13 per cent in 1997, according to *Time* Magazine (Fonda 2003). Equally a large number of multi-national companies in India appear also to be using such schemes. The poor performers thus identified are first given help and a period of time to improve. If they fail to rise in the ranking, they must leave. The exit may be 'encouraged' with a redundancy package, but if the poor performer refuses to leave voluntarily, they face the possibility of termination without compensation. This strategy has become known as the 'rank and yank' system after the nickname given to the scheme by former Enron employees where it appears to have first emerged.

An example of the rank and yank appraisal is provided by Sun Microsystems. The company ranks its 43,000 employees into three groups. The top 20 per cent are rated as 'superior', the next 70 per cent as 'standard'. At the bottom is a 10 per cent band of 'under-performers'. The under-performers are told that they must improve and are provided with one-on-one coaches. The ultimate fate of these employees is clear from the CEO's view that these under-performers must be 'loved to death'. Informal variants of rank and yank appraisal systems seem to be emerging in some UK university departments in the run up to the next Research Assessment Exercise (RAE). The RAE ranks a department's research from sub-national to world-class levels (0 to 4*). In some mock assessment exercises university managers have ranked the research output and esteem of employees on this grading system, with 4* performers receiving 'retention packages' while those rated 1* and 0 rated have been made to feel, in the words of one dean, 'very unloved and uncomfortable'.

The advocates of rank and yank believe that forced rankings make managers and supervisors take the unpleasant but tough decisions that otherwise they would seek to avoid as being too fraught with conflict. Some organisations see the forced ranking approach as a way to create a continuously improving workforce. The view is that an annual culling system produces a 'hotbed of over-achievers' who increase the overall calibre of an organisation. However, despite its obvious Darwinian managerial appeal, there are many problems with the system. First, someone must always fall into the lower or under-performing category, even if everyone has performed at a very high level. It is also possible that those rated as 'poor performers' in highly productive departments may contribute more to the overall progress of the organisation than those rated as 'good performers' in other low-performing departments. Forced ranking thus does little for teamwork and can encourage high levels of in-fighting and dysfunctional internal competition as employees seek to protect their own position at the expense of their co-workers. The legality of such dismissals in many countries must be open to question and some ranking and yanking systems have been abandoned in the US following legal challenge. It must also be questioned whether the level of churn induced by such a system with an annual culling is good for the stable employee networks required to produce innovation and creativity, and whether it justifies the increased administrative costs associated with replacement recruitment and training. However, it is not clear that 'yanked' employees have been always replaced and some critics have suggested the schemes are thinly disguised smoke screens for downsizing or to get rid of older workers who often populate the lower rankings. Thus the US has also seen forced ranking systems subject to a rising number of age discrimination lawsuits.

review some of the major innovations in the practice of performance appraisal. Third, some of the problems of performance appraisal in practice are considered, in particular here we examine the compatibility of performance appraisal with TQM, continuous improvement and customer service initiatives. Finally, in light of the growing criticisms, we conclude by considering whether performance appraisal has a future in HRM practice. ↘ New Cont. of development of HRM

Development of performance appraisal

Informal systems of performance appraisal have been around as long as people have worked together; it is a universal human tendency to make evaluations of our colleagues at work. Formal performance appraisals have a shorter but still considerable history. Grint (1993) traces it back to a third-century Chinese practice. In the UK Randell (1989) identifies its first use via the 'silent monitor' in Robert Owen's textile mills. Here a multi-coloured block of wood was hung over the employee's workspace with the front colour indicating the foreman's assessment of the previous day's conduct, from white for good through to black for bad. Owen also recorded a yearly assessment of employees in a 'book of character'.

Since these early developments, performance appraisal has now become a staple element of HRM practice. Personnel managers themselves, however, have tended to be much keener on it than their line manager colleagues (see Chapter 8). Accompanying practitioner interest in performance appraisal has seen a mushrooming of academic research, notably by occupational psychologists. A key thrust of much of this research has been on improving performance appraisal's effectiveness and in particular, its accuracy in assessing employee performance. We know rather less about a more strategic use of performance appraisal as an organisational change lever and managerial control tool. There is now a wealth of academic studies on performance appraisal. Computer literature searches on the topic show over 20 academic articles per month appearing with 'performance appraisal' in their titles. Despite the large and growing volume of research work on the subject, however, it is debatable how much influence such studies have had on the actual practice of performance appraisal. It seems that managers are peculiarly reluctant to heed the advice of researchers in this area of business practice and there is an increasing 'gap' between research and practice (Banks and Murphy 1985; Maroney and Buckley 1992).

This lack of impact of research on practice is not simply a question of general managerial indifference to the academic researcher, especially when compared to the wide influence of consultants and popular management 'gurus'. Rather, one explanation is that little of the research has considered the implications for practitioners who are faced with a plethora of organisational constraints not encountered in the research laboratory. More damning perhaps is the view that much of the research has had little to offer HR managers, except for the recommendation to train appraisers, as it has generally been unable to provide much improvement in terms of accuracy at least, over the simplest of supervisory ratings systems.

The practice of performance appraisal

HOW WIDESPREAD IS PERFORMANCE APPRAISAL?

Performance appraisal has become more widespread in Western countries. For example, surveys report performance appraisal in the US increasing from 89 per cent of organisations surveyed in the mid-1970s to 94 per cent by the mid-1980s (Locher and Teel 1988). In large and medium-sized US organisations performance appraisal systems are now virtually universally present (ASTD, 1996). Similar surveys in the UK by the Chartered Institute of Personnel and Development report increasing coverage of formal performance appraisal arrangements (Long 1986; Armstrong and Baron 1998; IPD 1999). Performance appraisal is also now more common in many other non-Western countries such as China (Chow 1994), Hong Kong (Snape *et al.* 1998), Japan in the form of *Satei* (Endo 1994); Africa (Arthur *et al* 1995) and India (Lawler *et al.* 1995). Performance appraisal appears to be one of the most commonly adopted HR practices in high performance work systems (ILO 2002).

Appraisal is particularly prominent in some industrial sectors in the UK such as financial services (IRS 1999) and it has grown rapidly in the public sector of late. It is now widespread in schools, hospitals, universities, local authorities, the civil service, etc. For example, some 80 per cent of local authorities surveyed either operated or were currently introducing performance appraisal (IRS 1995a). It has also grown from its main deployment in the middle of organisation hierarchies, particularly in middle management and professional occupations, to include a much broader group of manual and clerical employees (Cully *et al.* 1999). Increasingly it seems, in line with harmonisation policies, all employees in an organisation are included in the performance appraisal system. An IRS survey found that 39 per cent of organisations' appraisal applied to every employee (IRS 1994) and a replication of the survey five years later found 75 per cent to do so (IRS 1999). The coverage of employees in the public sector, given the relative infancy of many schemes, is still rather more limited than the private sector. The IRS found only 17 per cent of public sector organisations surveyed included all employees in the scheme. However, these claims can be misleading. Employers who include the growing numbers of 'contingent' or 'peripheral' workers, such as part-time and contract staff, in performance appraisal schemes appear to be exception rather than the rule.

HOW IS APPRAISAL CONDUCTED?

There is a wide range of methods used to conduct performance appraisals, from the simplest of ranking schemes through objective, standard and competency-based systems (see below) to complex behaviourally anchored rating schemes (see Snape *et al.* 1994). The nature of an organisation's appraisal scheme is largely a reflection of its managerial beliefs (Randell 1994), the amount of resources it has available to commit and the expertise it possesses. Thus smaller organisations with limited HR expertise tend to adopt simpler ranking and rating schemes while the more complex and resource consuming systems, such as competency based and 360° appraisal, are found mainly in larger organisations.

Most employers use only one type of appraisal scheme, often a 'hybrid form' of a number of methods and a few companies even provide employees with a choice of methods in how they are appraised. The IRS surveys (IRS 1994, 1999) found many organisations with more than one system of performance appraisal operating. The main reason behind multiple systems was the wish to separate out reward and non-reward aspects of appraisal, different systems for different occupational groups (e.g., managerial and non-managerial employees) and separate systems for different parts of the organisation.

WHAT IS IT USED FOR?

Organisations use performance appraisal for a wide range of different purposes. Surveys commonly report the use of performance appraisal for clarifying and defining performance expectations, identifying training and development needs, providing career counselling, succession planning, improving individual, team and corporate performance, facilitating communications and involvement, allocating financial rewards, determining promotion, motivating and controlling employees and achieving cultural change (Bowles and Coates 1993; IRS, 1994, 1999).

Recent trends suggest that the more judgemental and 'harder' forms of performance appraisal are on the increase and that 'softer' largely developmental approaches are declining (Gill 1977; Long 1986; Armstrong and Baron 1998; IPD 1999). Thus there has been a shift in performance appraisal away from using it for career planning and identifying future potential and increased use of it for improving current performance and allocating rewards. Here the arrival of flatter organisations has given rise to the need to uncouple, to some extent at least, performance appraisal and promotion while competitive pressures have emphasised the need to incentivise improvements in short-term performance.

There are both advantages and disadvantages to such broad demands upon performance appraisal systems. A wide use helps to integrate various, often disparate, HRM areas into a coherent package of practices. For example, by providing a link between performance and rewards, and development needs and succession planning, more effective HRM outcomes are possible. However, it also gives rise to the common criticism that performance appraisal systems are simply too ambitious in that managers expect them to be able to accommodate a very wide a range of purposes. The breadth of use thus results in appraisal becoming a 'blunt instrument that tries to do too much' (Boudreaux 1994).

Further, many of the above purposes of appraisal are seen as being in conflict. Thus recording the past and influencing future performance is difficult to achieve in a single process. The danger is that appraisal, particularly given the trends identified above, concentrates on the past at the expense of the future performance with a common analogy here being that this is rather like using the rearview mirror to drive future performance. Similarly, allocating rewards and identifying training needs are often seen as being incompatible objectives in a single appraisal scheme. The openness required for meaningfully assessing development needs is closed down by the need for the employee to 'explain away' performance problems in order to gain a merit rise. However, the danger of disconnecting reward allocation from appraisal is that appraisers and appraised would not treat the process as seriously because without it appraisal lacks bite and 'fires blank bullets' (Lawler 1994). Increasingly, as we now examine, performance appraisal is used as one element of a much broader performance management system.

PERFORMANCE MANAGEMENT

Performance management, like many HRM innovations is a US import that has been a major driver in the increased use of performance appraisal by British organisations. Performance management has been defined as 'systems and attitudes which help organizations to plan, delegate and assess the operation of their services' (LGMB 1994, p.6). Bevan and Thompson (1991) describe a 'textbook' performance management system thus:

- a shared vision of the organisation's objectives communicated via a mission statement to all employees

- individual performance targets which are related to operating unit and wider organisational objectives

- regular formal review of progress towards targets

- a review process which identifies training and development needs and rewards outcomes

- an evaluation of the effectiveness of the whole process and its contribution to overall organisational performance to allow changes and improvements to be made

A principal feature of performance management is thus that it connects the objectives of the organisation to a system of work targets for individual employees. In such models of performance management, objective setting and formal appraisal are placed at the heart of the approach. The development of performance management systems has had major implications for performance appraisal. A key trend has been away from 'stand-alone' performance appraisal systems and towards individual appraisal becoming part of an integrated performance management system.

There is a growing critique of performance management systems. First, they are seen as adding more pressure to a short-term view among British managers, which may well hamper organisational performance over the long term. Second, they are often proffered in a very prescriptive fashion with many writers advocating a single best way for performance management, to the neglect of important variables such as degree of centralisation, unionisation, etc. This is in contrast to the actual practice of performance management in the UK, which is 'extremely diverse' (Fletcher and Williams 1992). The real danger is that performance management systems cannot be simply 'borrowed' from one organisation and applied in another, as many advocates appear to suggest. Third, it is supposed to be line management 'driven' but case studies of its practices report the motivating forces in organisations as being chief executives and HR departments with often questionable ownership and commitment from line managers (Fletcher and Williams 1992). Fourth, there is a growing concern that performance management systems, because of their dedicated focus on improving the 'bottom line' have added unduly to the pressures and stresses of work–life for many employees. Many systems have been introduced with scant regard for employee welfare (see Box 6.1) and there is increasing concern that employees are now being performance managed to exhaustion (Brown and Benson 2003) and burnout (Gabris and Ihrke 2001). Lastly, and perhaps more damning, is the view that it is ineffective. The main driver of performance management is the improvement of overall organisational effectiveness. However, there is little support from various studies for the view that performance management actually improves performance. For example, Bevan and Thompson's (1991) survey of performance management in the UK found that there was no relationship between high-performing UK companies (defined as those demonstrating pre-tax profit growth over a five-year period) and the operation of a performance management system.

PERFORMANCE APPRAISAL AS MANAGERIAL CONTROL

With the decline of careers in the flat, delayered organisation, HRM techniques such as performance appraisal have become more important managerial tools in motivating and controlling the workforce. Appraisal is now seen by some commentators as being much more important in maintaining employee loyalty and commitment than in directly managing performance (Bowles and Coates 1993). Its use provides managers with a major opportunity to reinforce corporate values and attitudes and thus it appeals as an important strategic instrument in the control process. Thus we find an increasing use of appraisal systems for non-managerial employees that are based on social, attitudinal and trait attributes (Townley 1989). Employees are increasingly being appraised not only on 'objective' measures such as attendance, timekeeping, productivity and quality but also on more subjective aspects such as 'dependability', 'flexibility', 'initiative', 'loyalty', etc.

Recent analyses of performance appraisal, based upon the work of Foucault, have given particular emphasis to the power relations implicit in performance appraisal (Townley 1993, 1999; Coates 1994). For Townley performance appraisal has the potential to act as the 'paper equivalent' of the panopticon with its 'anonymous and continuous surveillance' (1993, p.232). Thus recent developments in appraisal, which have both broadened the range of, and increased the number of appraisers, via 360° appraisal, upward appraisal and the use of external customers, have increased the potential for managerial control and the utilisation of the panoptical powers of performance appraisal. In such systems the employee is now continually exposed to the appraisers 'constant yet elusive presence' (Fuller and Smith 1991, p.11). Every customer, peer, subordinate and colleague is now also a potential appraiser. Thus it is hardly surprising that employees have nicknamed peer reviews of performance 'screw your buddy' systems of appraisal.

Managers themselves are not immune from the disciplinary 'gaze' of performance appraisal (see below). Managerial attitudes, especially at middle-management levels have often been identified as a barrier to the introduction of new ways of managing, such as introducing employee involvement and empowerment. Upward appraisal of managers by staff is increasingly being used to link managerial behaviour more closely with corporate values and mission statements by incorporating questions on these into appraisal instruments which are completed by the employee (Redman and Snape 1992). Thus at one and the same time organisations promote their required values to their employees and evaluate the commitment of their managers to these. Managers scoring badly in such appraisals are often 'culled' (see Redman and Mathews 1995). Thus, for example, at Semco, the much discussed Brazilian company, managers are upwardly appraised every six months using a scale up to 100. The results are then posted on a noticeboard and those who consistently under-perform are squeezed out or simply 'fade away'.

Recent developments in performance appraisal

As we noted in the introduction there have been many innovations in performance appraisal practice. In this section we discuss some of the more influential of these.

UPWARD APPRAISAL

Upward appraisal is a relatively recent addition to performance appraisal practice in the UK. Although still far from common, the 1990s have witnessed the introduction of upward appraisal in a range of UK companies. Upward appraisal is more common in the US and appears to have spread from US parent companies to their UK operations (e.g., at companies such as Federal Express, Standard Chartered Bank and AMEX) and from these to UK companies such as WHS Smith, The Body Shop and parts of the UK public sector (see Redman and Mathews 1995). Upward appraisal involves the employee rating their manager's performance via, in most cases, an anonymous questionnaire. The process is anonymous to overcome employees' worries about providing honest but unfavourable feedback on managerial performance. Anonymity limits the potential for managerial 'retribution' or what is termed the 'get even' factor of upward appraisal.

Advocates claim significant benefits for upward appraisal (Redman and Snape 1992; Bettenhausen and Fedor 1997) including improved managerial effectiveness and leadership through 'make-you-better feedback' and increased employee voice and empowerment. Equally, upward appraisal is seen as being more in tune with the delayered organisation where managerial spans of control are greater and working arrangements much more diverse. In such situations employees are in much greater contact with their manager than the manager's manager and thus traditional top–down boss appraisal is seen as being less effective. Upward appraisal, because of the use of multiple raters, is also seen as being more robust to legal challenge of performance judgements. Given the increasingly litigious culture in the UK and US, it is surprising that performance appraisal methods and the systems in which they are embedded are not attacked in the courts more often (Lee *et al.* 2004).

Managers have been reported as not being especially fond of upward appraisal systems. In part this may stem from the career-threatening use of upward appraisal schemes in some organisations. For example, one of BP Exploration's objectives in introducing upward appraisal was to return to individual contribution roles those managers 'clearly not cut out to manage people' (Thomas *et al.*1992). Often it appears to the manager on the receiving end of upward appraisal that, according to Grint (1993), 'the honest opinions of subordinates look more like the barbs on a whale harpoon than gentle and constructive nudges'. Such a lack of managerial acceptance of upward appraisal, especially at middle and junior levels of management, may go some way to explaining its relatively low uptake in the UK after a flurry of activity in the early 1990s.

360° PERFORMANCE APPRAISAL

The so-called 360° appraisals appear to be taking root and becoming an established form of appraisal in the UK (see Box 6.2). A survey by consultants Pilat reported up to 40 per cent of FTSE companies are now using it. Although considerable, such a usage rate is somewhat behind the three-quarters of *Fortune 500* companies reported as employing 360° appraisal in a similar US survey (*Personnel Management*, July 1995, p.15). Dudgill (1994) traces the origins of 360° appraisal to the US army in the 1970s. Here military researchers found that peers' opinions were more accurate indicators of a soldier's ability than were those of superiors.

The term 360° is used to describe the all-encompassing direction of feedback derived from a composite rating from peers, subordinates, supervisors and occasionally customers. It is again normally conducted via an anonymous survey although some recent innovations include the use of audio and videotape to record feedback answers. Some organisations also use online computerised data-gathering systems as well as more informal systems where managers simply pass a disk around a number of appraisers. One management consultancy, in order to encourage responses, is experimenting with 'fun' methods of collecting data such as using short statements comparing individual managers with well-known characters (CPCR 1995).

There is a wide variation in what is appraised in 360° feedback. Many companies use fully structured questionnaires based upon models of managerial competency. Others, such as Dupont's use of 360° appraisal in its individual career management programme employ a much less structured approach. Here appraisers respond to open questions, which ask for descriptions of the appraiser's 'major value-adding areas for the year'; summaries of the manager's strengths; descriptions of key improvement needs and a call for other general comments. Unstructured systems of appraisal have advantages in tapping into key aspects of

Box 6.2: 360-degree appraisal at Northumbrian Water

Following the hot, dry summers and accompanying water shortages, adverse public relations and intense media interest, life has been particularly difficult for managers in the privatised water companies. One company, Northumbrian Water, has been helping its managers to cope with a range of management development practices, including 360-degree appraisal.

Northumbrian Water introduced a 360-degree feedback programme for its managers via a pilot group of 35 managers. A key reason behind the introduction was to provide data for the company's development centre for senior managers. The development centre was designed to enable managers to move to a position of managing their own career development. It was considered important that individual managers should have a view from their colleagues about their performance, potential and development needs in order to facilitate sound career decisions. The 360-degree appraisal instrument consists of a bank of questions asking respondents to comment on the effectiveness and performance of the appraised manager against three main categories: competence, style and role. Appraisers, for example, are asked to say how often they see the candidate behave in a particular fashion which is consistent with the behaviours listed for a senior manager. Space is also provided for open comments on the manager's performance and the company feels it is often these which prove the most enlightening.

The system is based upon a refined competency model originally developed in the early 1980s. The competencies model was further developed following privatisation of the industry as the roles and styles of management appropriate to the company's new values were developed. For example, commercial awareness and customer care were not present in the original formulation. A study of HRM practices in the post-privatisation water industry considers Northumbria to have introduced the 'most dramatic changes' of all the companies (IRS 1992).

The feedback forms are distributed to 10–12 of the managers' colleagues in some form of distribution such as 2 above, 5 sideways and 4 below by the individual manager. Internal customers are often part of the process but the company has yet to incorporate external customers. The forms are returned directly to the company's consultants who produce a summary data booklet, discuss the results with the manager, and help prepare them for the development centre.

The main benefit the company perceives it has obtained from 360-degree feedback is in providing individual managers with vital insights into some of their shortcomings, which would otherwise remain unaddressed. Although it has been somewhat of a shock for some, managers are considered to be much more self-aware about their leadership qualities and are felt to be working better with their staff. Also, 360-degree appraisal is seen as making a valuable contribution in encouraging managers to engage in continuous professional development and encouraging an approach where performance problems can be positively tackled through training and development. The main problems the company has found with its implementation are that in the early programmes there was some difficulty in convincing managers that such feedback was of value because their development and career planning was within their own remit rather than that of their of boss. A few individuals also had great difficulty in accepting the feedback and searched for reasons to rationalise their opposition.

Source: interviews with managers

managerial performance. However, the danger of using an unstructured approach is that the popular but incompetent manager may well fare better than one who is highly effective but not particularly pleasant. Mostly the appraisers remain anonymous but some systems, such as Dupont's, leave the option open to the appraiser whether or not to add their name to the appraisal form. However, unless a composite rating only is presented to the manager, and this tends to counter the value of having multiple perspectives in 360°, it is very difficult to provide the immediate supervisor with anonymity.

It seems that 360° appraisal is edging away from a management development tool and towards a broader organisational role (Toegal and Conger 2003). Increasingly, and controversially, it seems organisations are also experimenting with linking 360° and managerial remuneration. Given that 360° appraisal is now so popular for managers and professionals that some see it as replacing traditional performance appraisal systems, this trend to widening its remit raises some concerns. Toegal and Conger (2003) suggest that 360° appraisal is being 'overstretched' by including such broader administrative concerns and that these additions blunt its usage as a feedback tool. The solution, it seems, its to develop two distinct 360° appraisal tools, one for management development and one for performance feedback, a solution that, as we note above, could raise as many problems as it solves.

Rather a lot is claimed for 360° appraisal and like many new initiatives we have seen a rash of articles announcing how it can 'change your life' (O'Reilly 1995); and deliver competitive advantage for the organisation (London and Beatty 1993). Because of its use of multiple raters with different perspectives, a sort of safety in numbers approach, it is often suggested that it provides more accurate and meaningful feedback. However, as Grint (1993) notes this often simply replaces the subjectivity of a single appraiser with the subjectivity of multiple appraisers.

Undoubtedly, many organisations have gained some advantages from using it, particularly in management developmental terms. It has proved especially useful for providing feedback for senior managers who are often neglected at the top in appraisal terms. One key benefit of the broad group of appraisers used in 360° is that it can provide a more meaningful appraisal for employees with little contact with their workplace. In such situations traditional top–down appraisals are of little value. A strength of 360° is that management consultants proffering systems will tailor a basic questionnaire to meet the organisation's characteristics such as culture, mission, business values and structure and management practices. It remains to be seen whether the benefits gained are outweighed by the considerable time, effort and costs involved. Indeed, it seems some management consultants are 'gravy training' on the back of the current enthusiasm for 360° with week-long feedback courses, facilitated by themselves, recommended to debrief managers.

Thus a number of questions remain unanswered about 360° appraisal, not least whether the data generated is accurate, valid and more importantly meaningful for the appraisee and whether the organisation stands to benefit from it. Ratings are only as good as the questions asked and often the interpretation of question wording is far from clear in many instruments. Such questions as 'does the manager deal with problems in flexible manner' are not uncommon in appraisal instruments. Items need to be clear, easy to understand and easy to rate given the raters' contact with the appraisee. One particular criticism of many 360° systems is that all raters are given the same instrument, despite the different nature of the contact with the appraisee. Some issues are clearly more visible to the rater from different vantage points and questionnaires should ideally be constructed accordingly. Items based on actual behaviours – key organisational competencies or critical incidents observed in the workplace indicative of superior performing managers – tend to be more effective. However, respondents will usually provide ratings on whatever questions are asked, whether or not they are in a position to do so.

There is also a certain tendency to produce overly bureaucratic systems. The danger here is that one common cause of failure generally in performance appraisal, that of requiring participants to fill in large quantities of paperwork, is being ignored. Making the feedback meaningful is also a challenge many users of 360° fail to rise to. To ensure meaningful feedback a process of self-appraisal, comparison against other managers' ratings and follow-up with facilitators and those who provided the ratings is the minimum required. Also there is an implicit expectation on the part of those providing the ratings that such feedback will lead to improvements and that managers will change their behaviour for the better. There is, however, yet little evidence that this actually occurs.

Lastly, many so-called 360° degree appraisal systems are actually far from an all round view of managers; the external customer as a reviewer is often left out, but, as we discuss in the next section, customers are an increasingly heard voice in the assessment of employee performance. It seems 360° degrees appraisal is also only a starting point and as management consultants 'discover' new sources of raters we can look forward to such innovations as 450° and even 540° appraisal.

CUSTOMER APPRAISAL

TQM and customer care programmes are now very widespread in both private and public sectors in the UK. One impact of these initiatives is that organisations are now increasingly setting employee performance standards based upon customer care indicators and appraising staff against these. A mix of 'hard' quantifiable standards such as 'delivery of a customer's first drink within two minutes' and soft qualitative standards such as 'a warm and friendly greeting', as used at Forte Roadside Restaurants, are now used in performance appraisal systems (IRS 1995b). The use of service guarantees, which involve the payment of compensatory moneys to customers if the organisations do not reach the standards has also led to a greater use of customer data in performance appraisal ratings.

Customer service data for use in appraising employees is gathered by a variety of methods. First, there is the use of a range of customer surveys, such as via the completion of customer care cards, telephone surveys, interviews with customers and postal surveys. Organisations are now using such surveys more frequently and are increasingly sophisticated in how they gather customer views. Second, there is a range of surveillance techniques used by managers to sample the service encounter. Here the electronic work monitoring of factory workers is being extended into the services sector (Laabs 1992). For example, customer service managers at Mercury Communications spend some 30 hours of their time each month reviewing staff performance by taping staff–customer conversations and giving immediate feedback as well as using the data for the regular formal review process.

Third, and even more controversial, is the increasing use of the so-called 'mystery' or 'phantom' shopping. For some commentators, customer service can only be really effectively evaluated at the boundary between customer and organisation and this view has fuelled the growth of mystery shopping as a data capturing process. Here staff employed by a specialist agency purport to be real shoppers and observe and record their experience of the service encounter. It is now commonly used in banks, insurance companies, supermarkets and parts of the public sector. For example, an element of the Citizen's Charter requires the setting of performance indicators on answering telephone calls and letters. Some local authorities evaluate the quality of telephone responses by employing consultants to randomly call the authority and assess the quality of the response (IRS 1995b).

Mystery shopping is argued to give a company a rich source of data that cannot be uncovered by other means, such as customer surveys. Such surveys, although useful for some purposes, are often conducted many months after the service encounter and thus exact service problems are difficult to recollect. Mystery shopping is also seen as being particularly useful in revealing staff performance that causes customers to leave without purchasing. In many service sector organisations a natural consequence of the use of mystery shoppers has been to utilise the data in the performance evaluations of staff (Fuller and Smith 1991). Although as yet relatively understudied, there are a number of concerns with mystery shopping, not least the psycho-metric quality of data collected in comparison to customer surveys. Few studies have addressed this issue but recent work by Kayande and Finn (1999) report that mystery shopping provides 'reasonably reliable ratings' of performance and that such data can be produced at considerably less cost than customer surveys. All this suggests that mystery shopping is very likely to grow in use in the future.

However, these data gathering methods are, as one could well expect, not very popular with staff. Employees often question the ethics of introducing mystery shoppers and feel that it represents a distinct lack of managerial trust in them (Shing and Spence 2002). Thus employees describe shoppers in terms of 'spies' and 'snoopers' and react with hostility and 'shopper spotting' to their introduction. The introduction of mystery shopping for largely negative reasons of catching staff performing poorly only fuels such reactions. Cook (1993) advises that using them to reward staff for good performance rather than punish them for poor performance can help their acceptance. Staff who obtain good mystery shopping ratings should be rewarded and recognised while those who obtain poor ones should use them as a source of identifying training needs.

In an increasing number of organisations internal service level agreements are also being established. The introduction of compulsory competitive tendering and subsequently 'Best Value' has given considerable impetus to such agreements in the public sector. Often in such agreements there is an internal customer-service 'guarantee' stating the level and nature of services the supplier will provide. It thus has been a natural progression of such a development for organisations, such as at Federal Express and Digital, to incorporate performance data from service level agreements into the appraisal process (e.g., Milliman *et al.* 1995). A key advantage claimed for using internal customers in this way is that joint goal setting helped provide both internal customer and provider with greater understanding of the roles that individuals and departments provide. It thus helps in breaking down internal barriers between departments.

TEAM-BASED APPRAISAL

Work is increasingly being restructured into highly interdependent work teams yet despite this performance appraisal often remains stubbornly based on the individual. In some cases teams are increasingly being given responsibility for allocating work tasks, setting bonuses, selecting new staff, and even disciplining errant members. For such organisations it has thus been seen as entirely appropriate that performance appraisals should also be based upon and even conducted by the team themselves.

Two main variants of team appraisal can be identified. In some approaches the managers appraise the team as a whole. Targets are set, performance measured and assessments made, and rewards allocated as with traditional individual appraisals. The manager makes no attempt to differentiate one member from another in performance terms, in fact the creation of internal inequity with respect to rewarding performance is a deliberate aspect (Lawler 1994). Equal ratings and rewards ensue for all the team regardless of performance. The team are then encouraged to resolve internally any performance problems or competence deficiencies in order to facilitate overall team performance and development. Team members themselves may then provide informal awards or recognition of superior performance. The other main variant is whereby individual appraisals of each team member are still made but not by management. Rather, in a form of peer appraisal, team members appraise each other usually via the use of anonymous rating questionnaires.

COMPETENCY-BASED APPRAISAL

Interest in the concept of competency has been one of the major HR themes of recent times. Connock (1992) describes it as one of HRM's 'big ideas'. One consequence of this has been the attempt by some organisations to use the competency approach to develop an integrated human resource strategy. This has been particularly pronounced in HR practices targeted at managers but is also growing for non-managerial groups. A consequence of the development of organisational competency models has been that employers have increasingly extended their use from training and development, selection and reward uses into the area of appraisal (e.g. Mitrani *et al.* 1992). For example, the most widely reported innovation in performance appraisal systems during the 1990s has been the linking of appraisals to competency frameworks (IRS 1999).

The assessment of competencies in the appraisal process has a number of benefits. The evaluation of competencies identified as central to a good job performance provides a useful focus for analysing the progress an individual is making in the job rather than the static approach of many ability- or trait-rating schemes. Thus competency-based assessment is especially useful in directing employee attention to areas where there is scope for improvement. The use of competencies broadens appraisal by including 'how well is it done' measures in addition to the more traditional 'what is achieved' measures. It also helps concentrate the appraisal process on the key area of performance and effectiveness and provides a language for feedback on performance problems (Sparrow 1994, p.9). This latter benefit overcomes one of the problems of traditional objective-based appraisal systems in which the appraiser is often at a loss as to how to counsel an employee on what they should do differently if the appraisal objectives have not been achieved. However, these benefits must be counterbalanced against the development and running costs involved and the wider critical debate surrounding the 'competency movement' in general.

Problems of performance appraisal

Performance appraisals appear to be one human resource activity that everyone loves to hate. Carroll and Schneier's (1982) research found that performance appraisal ranks as the most disliked managerial activity. It is frequently suggested in the popular management literature that most managers would prefer having a dental appointment rather than conduct a performance appraisal. Many appraisees, it seems, would also prefer this! According to Grint (1993, p.64) 'rarely in the history of business can such a system have promised so much and delivered so little'.

The critics of performance appraisal argue that it is expensive, causes conflict between appraised and appraiser, has limited value and may even be dysfunctional in the improvement of employee performance, and despite the rhetoric its use contributes little to the strategic management of an organisation. It is also argued to be riddled with so many distorting 'effects' that its accuracy in providing an indicator of actual employee performance must also be called into question (see Box 6.3). Some appraisal systems, especially the more judgemental, those tied into merit pay systems and those with forced distributions are argued to be especially problematic in these respects. Thus for many writers performance appraisal is 'doomed' (Halachmi 1993); a managerial practice 'whose time has gone' (Fletcher 1993; Bhote 1994) and whose end is imminently predicted (Roth and Ferguson 1994).

> ## Box 6.3: Cronies and Doppelgangers in performance appraisal
>
> The search for accurate performance appraisals is a seemingly illusory one with many pitfalls and distorting effects strewn in the appraiser's path. Some of the main ones are:
>
> *'Halo effects'.* This is where one positive criterion distorts the assessment of others. Similarly the *'horns effect'* is where a single negative aspect dominates the appraisal rating.
>
> *'Doppelganger effect'* is where the rating reflects the similarity between appraiser and appraised.
>
> *'Crony effect'* is the result of appraisal being distorted by the closeness of the relationship between appraiser and appraised.
>
> *'Veblen effect'* is named after Veblen's practice of giving all his students the grade C irrespective of the quality of their efforts. Thus all those appraised received middle-order ratings.
>
> *'Impression effect'* is the problem of distinguishing actual performance from calculated 'impression management'. The impression management tactics of employees can result in supervisors liking them more and thus rating their job performance more highly. Employees often attempt to manage their reputations by substituting measures of process (effort, behaviour, etc.) for measures of outcome (results), particularly when the results are less than favourable.

Why does performance appraisal not work? One reason is that despite their widely held belief to the contrary most managers are not naturally good at conducting performance appraisals. According to Lawler (1994, p.17), it is an 'unnatural act' for managers, a result of which is that if they are not trained properly it is done rather poorly. Appraisal meetings are thus reported as being short-lived, ill-structured and often bruising encounters. Studies find that appraisers are ill-prepared, talk too much, and base much of the discussion on third-party complaints with many of the judgements made on 'gut feelings' (e.g., Finn and Fontaine 1993). It is then of little surprise when we find reports of how it takes the average employee six months to recover from it (Peters 1987).

Being subject to 'political' manipulation also discredits appraisals. Managers it seems frequently play organisational games with performance ratings (Snape *et al.* 1994). Longenecker's (1989) research found that managers' appraisal ratings are often manipulated to suit various ends. Sometimes ratings were artificially deflated to show who was the boss; to prepare the ground for termination; to punish a difficult and rebellious employee and even to 'scare' better performance out of the appraisee. One manager we interviewed described how he deflated the performance ratings of all new graduate trainees for their first few years of employment in order to 'knock some of the cleverness out of them' and show them that they 'did not know everything'. Equally a poor performer may be given an excellent rating in order that they will be promoted up and out of the department and managers may inflate ratings in the hope that an exemplary set of appraisals reflects favourably on the manager responsible for such a high-performing team.

The move to more objective forms of performance appraisal, particularly encouraged by performance management models, and increasingly reported for managerial grades is often argued to overcome some of the above 'subjective' problems. Legal challenges to personality- and trait-based performance appraisal schemes, particularly in North America and increasingly in the UK (Townley 1990; Lee *et al.* 2004) have also encouraged the move away from personality- and trait-based systems. However, the so-called objective-based schemes are not without difficulties. First, measurement is often difficult and according to Wright (1991) 'there are a number of jobs where the meaningful is not measurable and the measurable is not meaningful'. The tendency is also to simplify measurement by focusing on the short rather than the long term. Second, since objectives are set for individual employees or teams under such systems it can be especially challenging to achieve equitable ratings. Equally problematical is that the actions of the employee may account for little of the variability in the outcomes measured (a key criticism of the quality gurus – see p.000) and thus the extent to which they are achievable is not within the employee's control. This has posed real problems with appraisals in industries such as financial services where the economic climate and general business cycle arguably affect outcomes far more than individual effort. The potential here is thus for employee demotivation and disillusionment, especially when many such systems are now linked to reward structures.

Kessler and Purcell (1992) identify a range of further specific problems with objective-based systems. These include the difficulty in achieving a balance between maintenance and innovator objectives; in setting objectives that cover the whole job so that performance does not get skewed to part of it; and the lack of flexibility to re-define objectives as circumstances change during the appraisal cycle. The introduction of performance appraisal into the public sector has also given rise to many concerns. In particular there are worries about its potential to undermine professional autonomy, with this concern being strongly expressed by clinicians in the NHS. A more general concern is that such a 'managerialist' intervention would undermine the public service values and public accountability of employees (Redman *et al.* 2000).

A range of more practical difficulties also results in problems with performance appraisal. Often the paperwork used to support the system can become excessive and give rise to a considerable bureaucratic burden for managers, particularly as spans of control grow. Some organisations have attempted to reduce this problem by designing paperless systems, requiring the employee to complete the bulk of the paperwork or moving to a computer-based system. A real danger in many systems is that the paperwork dominates and the process is reduced to an annual 'cosy chat' and a ritual bureaucratic exercise devoid of meaning or importance for all concerned. Thus according to Barlow (1989, p.503) the performance appraisal of managers is little more than the 'routinized recording of trivialities'. Appraisers and appraised go through the motions, sign-off the forms and send them to a central personnel department who simply file them away rather than utilising the data in a meaningful way (Snape *et al.* 1994). Given the lack of follow up in many appraisal systems it is hardly surprising when they fall into disrepute and eventual decay.

Lastly, the growth of TQM and customer care programmes has triggered a considerable debate and a re-assessment of the organisational value of appraisal. On the one hand there has been a high-profile barrage of criticism rejecting appraisal as being incompatible with TQM. In its strongest formulation it is suggested that managers face a stark choice between choosing either TQM or performance appraisal (Aldakhilallah and Parente 2002). On the other hand some have suggested that appraisal may play a key role in developing, communicating and monitoring the achievement of quality standards (Fletcher 1993) and many organisations have been spurred by the introduction of TQM to revise their appraisal schemes in more customer-focused ways.

TQM has thus focused attention on some old as well as highlighting some new problems with performance appraisal. In relation to old problems some of the quality gurus, most notably Deming (1986), maintain that performance appraisal is inconsistent with quality improvement. He argues that variation in performance is attributable mainly to work systems rather than to variations in the performance of individual workers. Quality improvements are thus found mainly by changing processes rather than people, and the key is to develop cooperative teamwork. This, he claims, is difficult to do where the focus is on 'blaming' the individual, as in traditional appraisal, and where as a result there is a climate of fear and risk avoidance, and a concern for short-term, individual targets, all of which undermines the cooperative, creative, and committed behaviour necessary for continuous improvement.

Deming is careful to argue, in rejecting performance appraisal, not that all staff perform equally well but that appraisers are incapable of disaggregating system effects from individual staff effects. Thus what is needed for TQM is a shift away from the traditional focus on results and individual recognition, towards processes and group recognition. The TQM critics also raise some new problems with performance appraisal, in particular that it 'disempowers' employees by reducing variety and increasing homogenisation of the workforce while for meaningful customer care we need the 'empowered' employee.

Conclusions

Performance appraisal is now more widespread that at any time in its history and the organisational resources consumed by its practice are enormous. At the same time its critics grow both in number and in the ferocity of their attacks. It is thus tempting to adopt a somewhat sceptical view of the value of performance appraisal. Following the rise of TQM and the prominence of its, mainly American, management gurus it has become rather fashionable of late to reject performance appraisal outright. Pathological descriptions of performance appraisal as a 'deadly disease' and an 'organisational virus' are increasingly common.

However, it would appear that the danger here is that such views are often based on little more than anecdote rather than solid empirical research. For example, one survey of employer reasons for introducing appraisal systems in the UK found that in over a third of cases it was developed to provide support for quality management initiative (IRS 1994). Our studies of managers' actual experience of being appraised finds many reporting its overall value to them and the organisation with few suggesting it should be discarded altogether (e.g., Redman and Mathews 1995; Redman *et al.* 2000). Many of the criticisms are based upon a hard and uncompromising model of performance appraisal that is now less commonly found in practice and the ineffective way that many organisations implement appraisal. The critics all too often have rather conveniently ignored many of the new developments we discuss above, which act to ameliorate some of these problems. Many of the problems of performance appraisal can be ironed out over time as experience with its practice accumulates. Indeed, there is some evidence to suggest that employers who have utilised performance appraisal for longer report fewer problems (Bowles and Coates 1993).

Further, performance appraisal's detractors are usually silent on what should replace it. A common response is to suggest this is an unfair question in that it is the organisational equivalent of asking, 'what you would replace pneumonia with?'(e.g., see *People Management,* 13 July 1995, p. 15). The question of how to assesses individual performance, determine rewards and promotion, provide feedback, decide training and career needs and link business and individual goals without a performance appraisal system, however, cannot be so easily shrugged off.

Performance appraisal emerged in the first place to meet such needs and employees still need guidance in focusing their skills and efforts on important organisational goals and values. Hence we would suggest that performance appraisal will continue to have an important role in HRM practice. A good example here is that organisations often struggle to get managers committed to taking health and safety management as seriously as other aspects of their jobs. Tombs (1992) reports that 'safety leaders' in the chemical industry ensure that managers give safety management the attention it deserves by developing a 'safety culture', a key part of which is achieved by incorporating safety objectives into their performance appraisals. Thus the first objective of all ICI plant managers is always a safety one.

This is not to argue that the current practice of performance appraisal is unproblematic. Certainly some of the evidence also presented above would suggest that there are many concerns with its application. However, these are persistent but certainly not insurmountable nor terminal problems and it is argued strongly that organisations should think very carefully before abandoning it altogether. Rather, the evidence would seem to support the view that the key task facing most organisations in the millennium is the upgrading, renewal and reinvention of performance appraisal such that it is more compatible with new business environments. The evidence above and elsewhere (e.g., IRS 1999) suggests that many employers are rising to such a challenge.

CASE STUDY 6.1

PERFORMANCE APPRAISAL AT NORTH TRUST

TOM REDMAN, ED SNAPE AND DAVID THOMPSON

Organisation background[1]

This case study examines the practice of performance appraisal in an NHS trust hospital. North Trust is a whole district trust in the north-east of England serving a community of a quarter of a million people. It provides 32 major healthcare services, including the full range of in-patient, day case and out-patient services alongside a comprehensive primary care service including health visiting and district nursing services. It employs some 2,200 'whole time equivalent' (wte) staff. The trust has recently been relatively successful, meeting all its financial targets thus far. However, at the time of the study – the late 1990s–early 2000s – it was, similar to many other trusts, experiencing increasing difficulties in meeting the demand for healthcare services within the constraints of its current resources.

The development of appraisal at NT

Appraisal at North Trust, a variant of the national Individual Performance Reviews (IPR) scheme was first implemented for senior managers in 1988. Between 1988 and 1994 it was largely restricted to managerial and senior professional groups. In 1994 a review of IPR was conducted. An initial analysis found patchy coverage of IPR and a half-hearted commitment to it. Following the review a decision was taken to revise and re-launch the IPR scheme and 'roll it out' to a wider group of staff. There were two key influences underpinning this decision. First, a new chief executive with a much greater belief in the value of performance management was appointed. Second, a decision to pursue the Investors in People award resulted in a decision to commit more time and effort to making IPR work. The next 18 months thus saw the revising of policy, the redesigning of supporting paperwork, and the committing of major training resources to IPR.

Final written agreement was secured in March 1995 and the new policy and procedure were 'signed off' by the chief executive in June 1995. The key aims of IPR at NT were articulated in the new policy document as ensuring all staff understand the Trust's goals and strategic direction; are clear about their objectives, how these fit with the work of others and the organisation as whole and are aware of the tasks they need to carry out; are given regular feedback and explicit assessment of performance; and are developed to improve their performance. The revised policy document made an explicit commitment to implement IPR for all employees.

The revised IPR policy at NT placed greater emphasis on measurability as a key aspect of the setting of individual objectives. The policy document outlines the principles underpinning individual objective setting as following the acronym 'SMART'. Here objectives should be specific, measurable, agreed/achievable, realistic and time-bound with the form of measurement for each objective to be agreed at the time that they are set. According to the CEO, when he first arrived, this aspect was perceived as being very weak in practice:

> Most people didn't know what an objective was if it sat up and bit them on the backside. Objectives here tended to be half-a-dozen or so generalised statements with no measurable outcome, no timescale, no agreement about how something is to be judged and whether it has been done or not with the result that there is little accountability.

For the CEO the result of this was major problems in 'getting things done' at the trust:

> We don't have a performance culture here. This place was just great for talking about things. Only talking about things, not actually doing them.

Thus a key aim for the CEO was to 'toughen up' IPR. This was to be attained in part by an increased emphasis on the evaluation of the achievement of work objectives and to encourage detailed measures to be established for all new objectives. However, the CEO's view of the direction that IPR should go in did not seem to be shared by its 'owners'; the personnel department. Here a softer, more developmental focus for IPR was envisioned:

> What is important is the manager taking the time out to talk to the individual about how they are progressing. How they feel things are going. And talk about training and development. These things really help morale. Forget the form filling and objectives, and all the other bits. It is these things that really make the difference.

In the remainder of this chapter we describe the practice of performance appraisal in North Trust.

The IPR process

Mechanics

IPR at NT is designed to cascade downwards through the organisation. The business plan is formulated by December/January each year and reviews conducted during February and March for senior managers. The majority of appraisals for other staff take place during April and May. A minority of managers, because of the large number of appraisals they conducted, in one case over 50, scheduled the appraisals over the full year, which in effect largely undermined the direct link with business planning for the majority of their staff. However, linkages with the business plan, especially for lower levels of staff, were also difficult to discern in the accounts of the IPR reviews conducted by those managers who did these in phase with the business planning process. Here managers' descriptions of how they appraised healthcare assistants, porters, domestics, catering staff, laundry workers and nurses rarely mentioned anything other than the loosest of connections with the business plan.

The IPR policy specifies a very much a 'top–down' process, noting that only occasionally it might be beneficial to involve another manager closely involved with the objectives being measured (such as a project manager). In practice no examples of this were found. A particular problem reported by the interviewees was that of continuity of appraisers between appraisal cycles. Due to high levels of managerial turnover, caused by resignations, promotions, transfers, and secondments, etc., of both appraisees and appraisers, nearly a third of interviewees reported having different appraisers from one cycle to the next. This level of managerial change, because of the need for a close working relationship between manager and employee for appraisal to be effective (see below), was generally felt to limit IPR's potential. Interviewees described how continuity between appraiser and appraisee was important because reviews were generally perceived as improving as both parties got to know each other better and the discussion became more useful and open.

Coverage

There was an uneven application and use of IPR. Despite the avowed intention of the new policy to 'roll out' IPR uniformly over the trust, its use appeared to be distinctly patchy. The personnel department estimated only around 25–30 per cent of staff received a performance review and that below management levels 'huge swathes' of staff were not involved. One of the tools to encourage its greater uptake was that senior managers were now being given personal objectives in their own appraisals to introduce IPR for all their staff. However, this strategy alone did not seem sufficient in gaining their commitment to making IPR process effective. As one manager explains:

> Appraisal for lower level staff is a five minute wonder, get it out of the way. The supervisors say . . . 'I have got to go through this with you. You haven't been too bad a lad this year have you. See you next year.' We get the odd constructive thing coming out of it but the main thing is that the director will be happy that he can report we have now appraised all the staff in our department when he has his next IPR.

Such cynical attitudes were a source of irritation to the majority of managers who spent considerable time and effort on conducting IPRs in their departments. Here it was particularly resented that their managerial colleagues either did not conduct appraisals ('its not fair that I have to do it if others don't'; 'other staff feel they are missing out because they are not getting it') or gave mere lip service to them ('it brings the whole IPR process into disrepute and makes it much more difficult for me to get my staff to take it seriously').

Documentation

The standard trust documentation was used for less than half of our interviewees' appraisals. The standard forms were felt to be too cumbersome and somewhat of an administrative chore, especially for use with employees at lower levels in the organisation. Thus those responsible for IPR often tailored the forms, usually reducing their length. A problem with some of the customised forms was that questionable performance categories, such as an appraisee's 'personality', featured prominently in these versions. In contrast, some professional groups found the forms rather too simplistic to capture the nature of their roles and again customised the standard forms to suit their needs. In a number of departments reviews were conducted without the aid of either customised or standard forms, and in one case an appraiser admitted that this was because he had never got round to actually reading them.

The IPR encounter

The heart of the IPR process, and the main source of participants' evaluation of it as either a success or failure, is the face-to-face meeting between appraiser and appraisee. Here for IPR is its 'moment of truth'. Table 6.1 shows that the majority of our appraisees reported interviews of at least 30 minutes, with 47 per cent having interviews of more than an hour. Judging from Table 6.2, appraisers were not usually dominating the interviews. The impression gained is that the majority of appraisees were having a sufficiently long and participative appraisal interview, an encouraging finding when we note that those who reported longer and more participative interviews also tended to report greater satisfaction with the appraisal process.

Table 6.3 sets out the extent to which various issues were discussed during the appraisal, as reported by our appraisees. The main emphasis appears to be on the achievement and planning of work objectives and on the planning of training and development. Not surprisingly, given the absence of performance-related pay for most

Table 6.1 How long did the appraisal interview last?

	(Percentages)
Less than 30 minutes	11
Between 30 minutes and an hour	43
Between one and two hours	35
More than two hours	12

Table 6.2 During the appraisal interview approximately what proportion of the time did you and the appraiser talk?

	(Percentages)
Mainly me (more than 75%)	13
Approximately 60% me	26
Approximately equal	48
Approximately 60% appraiser	12
Mainly the appraiser (more than 75%)	1

Table 6.3 To what extent were the following issues covered in your appraisal?

	Percentages		
	3	2	1
	Thoroughly discussed	Briefly discussed	Not discussed at all
Your achievement of work objectives	63	32	5
Your future work objectives	65	31	4
Your personality or behaviour	17	42	42
Your skills or competencies	35	52	13
Your training and development needs	45	43	12
Your career aspirations and plans	30	43	27
Your pay or benefits	3	12	85
Your job difficulties	24	57	19
How you might improve your performance	16	40	44
How your supervisor might help you to improve your performance	15	45	40
Your personal or domestic circumstances	4	20	76

staff, pay and benefits were only discussed in any detail during the appraisal interview. Overall, the approach seems to be one of performance management and development rather than of judgement and reward allocation.

A strong theme in the accounts of those who were positive about the overall IPR process was the notion that the interview represented 'quality time' between manager and managed. For some it was an 'employee's right' to have meaningful 'one-on-one time' with their manager and:

> People value quality time to talk through with their immediate manager what they are doing, why they are doing it, and what they need to do in the future.

As we have seen, in these 'quality-time' appraisals, which were often between two to three hours' duration for managers, appraisees reported that a broad range of issues were discussed.

In contrast, the focus for lower-level grades was much more restricted and our in-depth interviews suggested that for such staff the time spent on the IPR interview varied between 10 to 45 minutes. Typical descriptions of the nature of appraisals for lower-grade staff were:

> I discuss with them how they have worked this year. I say 'You've been a bit slack in these things. You are bloody good at that. You are one of my key workers for this. But your time-keeping wants pulling up a bit and your general attitude is not what should it be.'

> To be honest there is very little to say to someone who feeds sheets into a machine five days a week. I have found it hard to think of positive things.

One manager reported the difficulty of getting lower-grade staff to relax during their review because prior to IPR's introduction the only time such staff were called to her office was for a 'rugging'. Perhaps unsurprisingly given such an approach, lower-grade staff were often reported as being 'indifferent' and 'uninterested' with the IPR process.

> It's the lower grades that feel 'Do I have to go through this again. I don't know why. I only want to do the job I'm doing and get my money at the end of the week.' These tend to be short interviews, most are less than 10 minutes.

Managers appeared to be coping with this lack of interest via a number of strategies. First, by renewing efforts in an attempt to encourage active staff participation and using develop-mental 'carrots'. Second, individual sceptics were labelled 'lost causes' and managers simply went through the motions in IPR and waited for such staff to leave. A more difficult problem was with 'clusters' of IPR-resistant employees. Here a coping strategy, often sold under the guise of self-development, appeared to be one of 'sharing the misery' more evenly with more junior managers and supervisors. The responsibility for conducting IPRs for 'difficult', 'obstructive' and 'awkward' staff was spread around the managerial team.

Generally, appraisees felt that their managers were good at giving performance feedback but fewer felt that they received regular feedback on their progress towards objectives (Table 6.4). The need for appraisal to be an ongoing, year round exercise was emphasised in the IPR system (see below). It seems that at NT, significant minorities of appraisers were neglecting to do the expected follow-up. Judging from our interviews, constructive feedback was especially welcomed by the appraisees in providing direction ('you realize you are getting there'; 'gives me some comfort I am getting there') and helping to boost confidence ('you know what you are doing is being done correctly'). Critical feedback was also valued but not often received by the interviewees, who in part blamed appraisal training here, which overly emphasised the 'positive' nature of IPR. Around a third of interviewees said they often 'watered down' their feedback in the reviews to ensure a positive IPR event and 'harmony' within their work-teams. Appraisees, especially female managers, emphasised the value of constructive criticism and 'meaningful' appraisals, with cosy chats being seen as a waste of their time.

Sound personal relationships between appraiser and appraised were emphasised by our interviewees as being a necessary but not sufficient condition for the review to be effective. The large majority of appraisees felt that their managers were professional enough not to reward favourites, were confident that appraisers were objective, felt they could talk freely, were confident enough to challenge their appraisal, and that keeping on good terms with their manager was not a requirement in order to obtain a good appraisal (see Table 6.4). However, this still leaves a minority of appraisers whose appraisal

Table 6.4 Perceived supervisor behaviour

Percentages	5 Strongly agree	4 Agree	3 Neither agree nor disagree	2 Disagree	1 Strongly disagree
POSITIVE ASPECTS					
My supervisor is good at giving me feedback on my performance	7	51	19	19	4
I receive regular informal feedback from my supervisor regarding my progress towards agreed targets and objectives	4	37	19	30	9
My supervisor takes my appraisals very seriously	21	50	15	12	2
My supervisor takes my career aspirations very seriously	5	50	24	17	3
I am confident that my supervisor is as objective as possible when conducting appraisals	10	60	20	8	1
NEGATIVE ASPECTS					
I have to keep on good terms with my supervisor in order to get a good appraisal rating	2	10	21	52	14
Supervisors use appraisals to reward their favourites	2	6	16	54	23
I am not entirely happy about challenging my supervisor's appraisal of my performance	3	18	17	52	11
I found it difficult during my performance appraisal to talk freely with my supervisor about what I wanted to discuss	4	14	9	52	21

behaviour was less positively rated by appraisees. Thus, some interviewees reported a poor relationship with their manager, describing IPR reviews in terms of conflict, verbal confrontation, point scoring, and 'edging about the real issues'. At its worst, this came down to appraisers using IPR to list what the appraisee had done wrong or badly over the year. A few appraisers, particularly those in clinical posts, described the problems of achieving an appropriate environment for conducting appraisal in a busy, emergency-led hospital.

> When I had my IPR the phones were going, people were coming in and out of the office, the manager got called away. It spoke volumes to me about the value that was attached to IPR here.

> Conducting IPRs on nights, at 2 am, when people are not at their best, is hardly conducive to a quality process.

Mini-reviews

The formal annual reviews are supported by 'mini-reviews'. The policy document sees these as a 'crucial element' of IPR providing constant review and monitoring such that the annual review itself becomes 'mainly a confirmation of agreements made during the year' or as the title of the IPR training video suggests, appraisees should experience '*No Surprises*'. However, these appear to be rather sporadic in practice and, as we saw in Table 6.4, only 41 per cent of survey appraisees said that they received regular feedback from their supervisor on their progress towards their objectives.

A few departmental heads formally scheduled three-monthly reviews for all employees. The norm for the mini-reviews was a six-monthly, informal discussion, with a minority of interviewees receiving only the annual appraisal. Below management and professional levels, the impression gained was that mini-reviews were extremely rare or very ad hoc and rushed at best – 'corridor and canteen chats' – with managers struggling to find the time to conduct even the annual appraisal for some groups. However, the interviewees themselves often stressed the value of mini-reviews not only in providing a measure of progress and attainment but in a general updating of performance objectives. Several interviewees reported requesting, and receiving, additional mini-reviews. Here mini-reviews were especially useful to fine-tune, and often to replace personal objectives that had been rendered obsolete by a rapidly changing organisational environment. Given the current level of change and 'churn' in the NHS we suggest that it may now be appropriate to consider it a 'high-velocity' environment requiring fast, strategic decision making. In such circumstances static yearly objectives are clearly inappropriate. Interviewees reported how objectives set in April of one year were often irrelevant and obsolete by the following year. Mini-reviews allowed for individual objectives to be kept in line with changes in business strategy.

Objective setting

As we have seen, the increased emphasis on work objectives and measurability desired by the CEO is reflected in the issues covered in the appraisal process, with appraisees reporting that the achievement and planning of work objectives were the most thoroughly discussed issues in the appraisal process. Generally, appraisees found the emphasis on objectives a useful part of the IPR process. A picture that emerges from the survey findings is that objectives are generally clear, cover the most important parts of the job, and that appraisees are actively involved in the objective setting process (see Table 6.5). Interviewees reported being reassured they were on the 'right track', 'working along the right lines', 'on-line', and 'knowing where they stood' ('you might think you are doing a good job but you need someone to tell you that and vice versa') in their jobs. For example:

> Without IPR it would be so easy for you to drift and not do anything. It keeps you on your toes. It keeps you focused. You know exactly what you are aiming for. It makes you look at what you do and what the organisation's trying to achieve. If you didn't have appraisal it would be so easy just to not do anything. You'd just drift. It makes you think about where you are going and where you would like to be.

The setting of objectives provided direction in an increasingly complex and fast-moving organisational environment. The view of one manager was that by appraising her staff she:

> Gives them something to hang onto. The job description is so vast and we are facing so many changes. The objectives give direction. It's a stepping stone for them. They give staff guidance and something to aim for, something constructive to aim for.

Interviewees reported how they often tended to 'push' and 'challenge' themselves to make 'progress', attain 'personal development' and 'growth' via the objective-setting process.

Table 6.5 Objectives and feedback

Percentages	5 Strongly agree	4 Agree	3 Neither agree nor disagree	2 Disagree	1 Strongly disagree
The goals that I am to achieve are clear	8	61	13	15	2
The most important parts of my job are emphasised in my performance appraisal	3	58	24	13	2
The performance appraisal system helps me understand my personal weaknesses	5	48	19	26	3
My supervisor allows me to help choose the goals that I am to achieve	13	65	10	10	1
The performance appraisal system helps me to understand my job better	3	37	27	31	1
The performance appraisal system gives me a good idea of how I am doing in my job	6	55	23	14	2

The general view was that in this respect the objectives they set for themselves were more challenging (and interesting) than those produced by their managers. For example:

> Generally I can take them in my stride. There are one or two demanding ones but they are actually objectives I have brought forward myself. I probably tend to push myself harder than the organisation does.

> I always put a new really challenging one in each time, like reducing sickness absence. I tend to challenge myself.

However, for some interviewees their accumulated experience of objective setting had taught them not to challenge themselves 'too much' and restrict both the scope and the number of the objectives they set for themselves. Here we find managerial appraisees becoming sensitised to the objective-setting 'game'. For example:

> What I've learnt, as time goes by, is you've got to be careful, right at the outset, how you set your objectives because you can be over optimistic, unrealistic. There's a danger of sitting down and thinking of all the things you'd love to do, or ideally should do, forgetting that you've got lots of constraints and you couldn't in a month of Sundays achieve it. So I think quite a few of us have learnt there is a skill in setting objectives which are reasonable and stand a chance of being achieved. I think that that bit is probably more important than anything else. There is nothing more demoralising than being measured against something which you yourself have declared as being in need of being done and finding that you couldn't possibly do it.

Some appraisees felt that objectives were 'imposed' on them but most accepted that this was 'just part of the job'. However, occasionally this caused some considerable irritation and anger, particularly in the clash with IPR's espoused developmental focus. One manager described 'ending up with nothing you really wanted to do' from his IPR and another described how when she pushed her appraiser to include a particular objective that she perceived as being a key issue for the department and which fitted well with her personal development needs, she was told 'either forget it or fit it into your own time'. The danger with imposing objectives on staff reluctant to accept them was that all that was achieved was lip service and half-hearted commitment, accompanied by subsequent 'fudge' in the appraisal review on the measures of achievement. For example:

> I've got to do them [objectives]. I don't not do them but I don't give them the commitment they need if I don't feel it's right. And it never gets picked up at the next appraisal.

Measuring achievement

The use of data in measuring and evaluating individual performance was reported by interviewees as being very reactive on the part of appraisers. Here if the appraisee did not produce data there tended to be very little use of anything other than informed opinion in assessing whether objectives had actually been achieved. An effect of this lack of data use appears to be that although a majority appraisees felt that IPRs represented an accurate measure of their performance, a substantial number were unclear on the standards used to evaluate performance (see Table 6.6).

Table 6.6 Measuring performance

Percentages	5 Strongly agree	4 Agree	3 Neither agree nor disagree	2 Disagree	1 Strongly disagree
My performance appraisal for this year represents a fair and accurate picture of my job performance	7	68	11	13	1
My supervisor and I agree on what equals good performance in my job	6	67	14	12	1
I know the standards used to evaluate my performance	2	40	26	29	4

Some appraisees were prolific in their use of data in the IPR process. Interviewees who had also undertaken NVQ management programmes described a considerable use of reports and the production of memorandums to measure their achievement of objectives. Here, it seems that the NVQ requirement to produce a portfolio causes managers to start to document their work – at least until they attain the award. Our findings suggest this new found enthusiasm for the memorandum and report generated by NVQs found a further outlet in the IPR process. Further, such documentation and the generally greater level of preparation on the part of the appraisee enabled them to control, to a considerable extent, the content and outcomes of the IPR process. For example:

> I took lots of things along [to the IPR meeting]. One of my objectives was to set up team objectives on the ward. I copied examples of these objectives and took them along. I showed reports I had done on the empowerment of patients' and gave her copies of patients' meetings. I used information to show that I had done things. I used these things to prove to her that I had achieved them.

In contrast, other managers usually reported a much less documented measuring process under IPR. The effective use of documentation by this group of managers and professionals thus raises the issue of 'impression management' in the performance measurement process. Impression management is a process by which people attempt to create and sustain desired perceptions of themselves in the eyes of others. In the employment context such others are colleagues, peers, internal customers, clients and especially bosses. The theory of impression management suggests that employees attempt to control, sometimes consciously and sometimes unconsciously, information on themselves which positively shapes others' perceptions of them. The performance-appraisal process is a particular important arena for the creation of favourable impressions at work. The effective use of performance documentation on the part of appraisees thus appears to be a very powerful tool in the production of an overall favourable impression of their managerial capability. A number of appraisers appeared to be very aware of staff's attempts at impression management via the IPR process. Such appraisers reported how they supplemented data from the IPR interview with views from an appraisee's peers and the 'grapevine'. Some declared that they were very wary of the accuracy of views offered by 'mouthy' and 'gobby' staff. For example:

> A nurse who's an extrovert, who does a lot of mouthing off, may give the impression that they are doing a really wonderful job and the lass who is quiet could be doing an even better job. But because she's not there selling herself, telling you how wonderful she is, she often loses out here.

> I am always wary of the gobby ones. Those who are always telling you how wonderful she is and how hard worked she is.

It appears the key for managers in measuring individual performance under IPR was distinguishing between 'real' and 'created' performance achievements, the danger being that managers may actually measure an employees ability to perform in 'theatrical' rather 'task-oriented' sense.

Objectives and teamwork

The CEO was also keen to encourage wider sharing of objectives, particularly between managers. Here the IPR policy's emphasis on the confidential nature of the appraisal process and its individual nature was seen as discouraging the formal communication of personal objectives with others. The individualistic nature of IPR thus fitted rather uneasily with the considerable growth in teamwork across the trust. For example, according to one manager:

> My boss knows how my objectives fit in with my colleagues, but I don't because I never see them.

The CEO was attempting to introduce change here by leading by example and then encouraging other managers to do the same. After setting objectives for his executive directors, all objectives for each manager, including his own were circulated to the entire senior management team and also sent out to the clinical divisions. However, there generally did not seem to be much formal sharing of objectives among other managers and professionals. Many of our interviewees felt greater sharing of objectives would be valuable, not least in creating a better understanding of performance priorities within and between departments. On informal levels some staff were actively sharing objectives. One manager describes how she encourages this at team meetings with her managers and supervisors:

> I'll say at meetings 'have you looked at your IPR lately. Who's got that in their IPR. Somebody's got that in their IPR'.

Interviewees expressed how they found it easier to prepare their own objectives when their appraising manager provided copies of his or her own objectives in advance of the review process. Appraisees also reported that much of their work was now conducted in teams, and many felt that more team-based appraisals and the setting of team objectives would helpfully supplement the individualistic nature of IPR. For example:

> I think IPR needs to achieve a better balance between individual performance and team performance. We need a much greater emphasis on team performance. Nowadays at NT we are all about teamwork. The IPR approach is too preoccupied with individual performance. It can become too narrow and it is often divisive.

A number also suggested that wider collaboration on the setting of objectives with other managers, project leaders, working parties, etc., would be beneficial in encompassing the full range of their activities.

IPR outputs

In this last section we report our findings on what the IPR process actually achieves. Here we structure our discussion under four main headings; management control; employee motivation; training and development; and rewards.

Management control

Clearly, as we discuss above, the setting and measuring of work objectives facilitates a direct form of managerial control over the labour process. Despite the rhetoric and policy of development, appraisers seemed to use IPR to exert their managerial authority. Occasionally, this was done in a very crude way. For example, a number of interviewees reported problems with managers waiting for the IPR to 'settle scores' for past conflicts. IPR was thus perceived as a vehicle by some appraisees for the line manager to 'tell me what I should be doing', and to 'tell me what I am not doing right in my job'. There is also evidence that IPR acts as a less manifest and more indirect form of managerial control. Here IPR appears to act as a vehicle to encourage 'self-discipline' and 'responsibility' among staff and to thus promote the reshaping of staff attitudes to fit new managerial values and beliefs in line with the changing form of work organisation. For example, even some of the sternest critics of IPR noted its subtle effects on them:

> I achieve nothing from it. I suppose the main benefit is I actually discipline myself more with my time management. I think 'oh I have got to do so and so', and I chart out my work better so that I'll take all that in. I give myself deadlines for my work saying 'I'll achieve that by March.'

The direction of control in the IPR process, however, is far from one way. Some managers described how their staff turned the IPR 'tables' on them:

> The cooks use IPR to say 'This is why I cannot do my job. This is why I cannot achieve this objective'. And then they trot out a great list of problems with the job.

One manager described why he hated doing appraisals with lower-level staff because it reduced to 'a managerial witch-hunt and a general gripe and groan session about what I had or hadn't done over the year'. The manager became so fed up with being on the receiving end of this that he had written to all staff reminding them of the nature of the IPR process and asking for a more positive attitude and less moaning about perceived managerial inadequacies. However, the memorandum had only served to highlight his discomfort with the process and to increase the level of complaining behaviour from appraisees, such that he now admitted to merely 'going through the motions with IPR to get it over with as quickly as possible'.

It's good to talk motivation and morale

IPR, as we discuss above, was often perceived by appraisers and appraised as a good opportunity for managers and managed to talk meaningfully, and engage in 'quality time' together. Not only did IPR visibly and symbolically demonstrate to staff their value and importance to the organisation but the manager also personally cared about their well-being. In some of the accounts of appraisers there were classic human-relations descriptions of the IPR encounter going well beyond the boundaries of work relations. Here interviewees reported appraisals discussing broader personal and social issues and referred to this as 'getting to know your staff'.

> **IPR helps people in knowing where their professional career and their lives are going.**

> **It's your time that you devote to them. And some of them have aspirations that you wouldn't know about until you sit down and talk to them. You show that you are genuinely interested in them as people as well as nurses.**

The language used to describe these encounters was often heavily redolent of the unitary ideology of human relations. Appraisees and appraisers stories were littered with references to 'progress', 'going forward together', 'participation', 'empowering the appraisee', 'boosting morale', 'becoming a proactive team', 'harnessing our collective energies' via IPR. Interviewees emphasised the importance of good communication, listening and being listened to particularly, as being a manager was often described as being a 'lonely job'. Thus some two-thirds of interviewees felt that they performed the duties of the post better and that IPR contributed positively to their personal motivation and job satisfaction:

> **If they scrapped it tomorrow, I don't think I would go home in tears but I would miss it. It helps me keep going, helps me keep motivated. It gives me some comfort, considering all the problems we have at the moment – I've got a service with a lot of problems – that I am achieving what I am supposed to do in my job.**

In contrast other managers, again especially in relation to lower-level staff, were not convinced that IPR reviews delivered much other than a lot of 'hot air' and wasted time that could have been much more profitably employed doing other things. For example:

> **I have 49 staff. Appraisal takes at least 30–40 minutes each. That's a lot of man-hours to get nothing out of it other than hot air.**

> **Senior management would like to think that if you appraise everybody it would instill in them some kind of belonging, some kind of corporate feeling. But for the rank and file they are just not interested.**

Training and development

Despite the emphasis of IPR on training and development by the personnel department, as we can see from Table 6.3, the discussion of an appraisee's training needs takes second place to that on work objectives. Some 12 per cent of appraisees reported that training and development issues were not discussed at all. The majority of those interviewed emphasised training and development as an output of the IPR process. All interviewees claimed to have discussed their own 'personal development plan' (PDP) during the interview. However, this was often reported to be a relatively unfocused and vague discussion. Indeed, few interviewees, under persistent probing, could actually give details of what was in their PDP. The impression gained was that the PDP title signified a much more formalised, more detailed and rather grander training and development document in theory at least if not in practice. Many of the interviewees described a rather mechanical process whereby training and development was discussed as a distinct, almost stand-alone issue. The appraiser was often perceived as running through a checklist of items to be covered in the interview, of which training and development was one, rather than the identification of training needs emerging from a grounded discussion of appraisee performance. The large majority of interviewees felt that much of the training and development that was taking place would still have occurred without the use of IPR but possibly less systematically and at a slower pace.

Managers reported problems with the IPR process – especially coupled with the decision to pursue the IiP award – giving rise to appraisees producing training and development 'wish lists'. Here the key difficulty was finding the training resources to fund costly external courses in the face of increasingly tight training budgets. The demand for degree and diploma courses – particularly amongst nursing staff – fuelled in part by IPR, was causing managers problems in maintaining staff commitment to the appraisal process given few employees could be supported in this way. Managers described a coping strategy here of encouraging employees to consider alternative, and less costly, development activities such as short secondments, work shadowing and job exchanges. Interviewees were also critical of the personnel department pushing the current training 'flavour of the month' via the IPR process. At the time of our study this was reported as being the managerial NVQ programme running in-house in conjunction with a local university.

Rewards

The PRP element of IPR was not particularly popular with either appraisers or appraisees. Whereas the general view of IPR was that a majority of both appraisees and interviewees considered it to be an overall positive experience, at least for managers and professionals, the views expressed in relation to performance-related pay were largely all negative. A strong view from those receiving PRP was that it was a lot of 'hassle' for little reward; more influenced by quotas than real performance; did little to motivate yet was often de-motivating; unfair; arbitrary; inequitable; highly subjective; bias laden; ineffective and detrimental to professionalism; created dysfunctional interpersonal competition; and undermined the developmental focus of IPR. For some IPR was 'sullied' by its linkage with PRP. At best appraisees felt PRP might possibly work with better and more stringent guidelines, where performance targets were clear and easily measurable rather than subject to an assessment based on ratings, and when they got on well with their line manger. PRP also ensured that appraisals were treated seriously. Many of these issues are very familiar 'moans and groans' from the growing PRP literature. A particular problem identified at NT was that performance was highly dependent on team effort and that work was increasingly being re-organised along teamwork lines yet PRP was individually based. The team – individual conflict in PRP may be at least partially resolved by including team-work objectives in the appraisal process but as we discuss above this was rarely done at NT. Thus:

> To achieve my objectives I have to rely on all my heads of departments. I have to rely on people outside of our division to co-operate or to take things on board. It's a team effort yet I receive an individual reward that's largely determined on things beyond my control.

Equally, those who did not receive PRP were not keen to be subject to it. This seems to contradict the view that PRP is like an extra-marital affair where those with no experience of such things think they are missing out on something terribly exciting and rewarding while those who were involved simply felt miserable. For example:

> I don't need someone wielding a financial stick to tell me how to do my job or push myself.

> PRP wouldn't affect me in the slightest. A few hundred pounds is neither here nor there for me.

Only one of the non-PRP managers was concerned that he was not receiving PRP. In essence this stemmed from his belief that it was unfair for some managers to receive PRP while others (such as himself) did not, rather than any great desire to be subject to it himself:

> IPR was first introduced here for senior managers and was linked to their pay. Then they brought it down to other managers. This is not sour grapes, but when it got down to my level of management the pay was wiped out and just the appraisal was left.

Questions

1. Is IPR a failure at North Trust?

2. Should IPR be retained by the organisation? If you recommend retention, what changes would you advise? If you recommend it should be scrapped, what would you advise should replace it?

3. According to Wright (1991) a paradox of performance management systems is that the meaningful is rarely measurable and the measurable is rarely meaningful. What evidence is there to support such a criticism in North Trust?

4. A key for managers in measuring individual performance under systems of performance appraisal is distinguishing between 'real' and 'created' performance achievements. The danger is that managers may actually measure an employee's 'ability to perform in the theatrical rather than task oriented sense' (Randle and Rainnie, 1997). What evidence is there that this is a problem at North Trust? How can the problems of 'impression management' be minimised?

5. It has been suggested that the key challenge currently facing performance appraisal systems is their upgrading, renewal and re-invention such that they are more compatible with business environments. To what extent does IPR fit the business environment of the 'new, modern and dependable NHS' (Department of Health 1997)?

6. Some analysts have suggested that the NHS is moving from a bureaucratic mode of organisation to a network mode of organising. What are the implications of such a development for IPR practice?

Note 1

This case study draws on four main sources of data: interviews with managers and professionals, a fully structured postal questionnaire administered to a sample of 270 managers and professionals, the analysis of internal documents and procedures manuals and, fourth, the observation of training workshops on appraisal and several senior management meetings reviewing appraisal practice at the organisation (see Redman *et al.* 2000).

References

Aldkakhilallah, K. and Parente, D. (2002) 'Re-designing a square peg: Total quality management performance appraisals', *Total Quality Management,* Vol.13, No.1, pp.39–51.

Armstrong, M. and Baron, A. (1998) *Performance Management,* London: IPD.

Arthur, W., Woehr, D.J., Akande, A. and Strong M.H. (1995) 'Human resource management in West Africa: practices and perceptions', *International Journal of Human Resource Management,* Vol.6, No.2, pp.347–67.

ASTD (1996) 'Training industry trends 1996', *Training and Development,* November, pp.34–8.

Banks, C.G. and Murphy, K.R. (1985) 'Toward narrowing the research–practice gap in performance appraisal', *Personnel Psychology,* Vol.38, pp.335–45.

*Barlow, G. (1989) 'Deficiencies and the perpetuation of power: latent functions in management appraisal', *Journal of Management Studies,* Vol.26, No.5, pp.499–517.

Bettenhausen, K.L. and Fedor, D.B. (1997) 'Peer and upward appraisals: a comparsion of their benefits and problems', *Group and Organizational Management,* Vol.22, No.2, pp.236–63.

Bevan, S. and Thompson, M. (1991) 'Performance management at the crossroads', *Personnel Management,* November, pp.36–9.

Bhote, K.R. (1994) 'Boss performance appraisal: a metric whose time has gone', *Employment Relations Today,* Vol.21, No.1, pp.1–8.

Bowles, M.L. and Coates, G. (1993) 'Image and substance: the management of performance as rhetoric or reality', *Personnel Review,* Vol.22, No.2, pp.3–21.

Boudreaux, G. (1994) 'What TQM says about performance appraisal', *Compensation and Benefits Review,* Vol.26, No.3, pp.20–4.

Brown, M. and Benson, J. (2003) 'Rated to exhaustion? Reactions to performance appraisal processes', *Industrial Relations Journal,* Vol.34, No.1, pp.67–81.

Carroll, S.J. and Schneier, C.E. (1982) *Performance Appraisal and Review Systems: The Identification, Measurement, and Development of Performance in Organizations,* Glenview, IL: Scott, Foresman and Company.

Chow, I. (1994) 'An opinion survey of performance appraisal practices in Hong Kong and the Peoples' Republic of China', *Asia Pacific Journal of Human Resources,* Vol.32, pp.62–79.

Coates, G. (1994) 'Performance appraisal as icon: Oscar-winning performance or dressing to impress?' *International Journal of Human Resource Management,* Vol.5, No.1, pp.165–91.

Connock, S. (1992) 'The importance of "big ideas" to HR managers', *Personnel Management,* Vol.21, No.11, pp.52–6.

Cook, S. (1993) *Customer Care,* London: Kogan Page.

CPCR (1995) *The Right Angle on 360-degree Feedback,* Newcastle: CPCR.

Cully, M., Woodland, S., O'Reilly, A. and Dix, G. (1999) *Britain at Work,* London: Routledge.

Deming, W.E. (1986) *Out of the Crisis: Quality, Productivity and Competitive Position,* Cambridge: Cambridge University Press.

Department of Health (1997) *The New NHS: Modern, Dependable,* London: The Stationery Office.

Dugdill, G. (1994) 'Wide angle view', *Personnel Today,* 27 September, pp.31–2.

Endo, K. (1994) '*Satei* (personal assessment) and interworker competition in Japanese firms', *Industrial Relations,* Vol.33, No.1, pp.70–82.

Finn, R.H. and Fontaine, P. A. (1993) 'Performance appraisal: Some dynamics and dilemmas', *Public Personnel Management,* Vol.13, No.4, pp.335–43.

Fletcher, C. (1993) 'Appraisal: an idea whose time has gone?', *Personnel Management,* September, pp.34–8.

Fletcher, C. and Williams, R. (1992) 'The route to performance management', *Personnel Management,* 42–7.

Fonda (2003) 'It's the B Team's Time to Shine: Under-appreciated corporate foot soldiers may be quick to bolt when the economy rebounds', *Time,* September 15, pp.62–4.

Foucault, M. (1975) *Discipline and Punish: The Birth of the Prison*, New York: Vintage Books.

Fuller, L. and Smith, V. (1991) 'Consumers' reports: management by customers in a changing economy', *Work Employment and Society*, Vol.4, No.1, pp.1–16.

Gabris, G.T. and Ihrke, D.M. (2001) 'Does performance appraisal contribute to heightened levels of employee burnout', *Public Personnel Management*, Vol.30, No.2, pp.157–72.

Gill, D. (1977) *Appraising Performance: Present Trends and the Next Decade*, London: IPD.

*Grint, K. (1993) 'What's wrong with performance appraisals? A critique and a suggestion', *Human Resource Management*, Vol.3, No.3, pp.61–77.

Halachmi, A (1993) 'From performance appraisal to performance targeting', *Public Personnel Management*, Vol.22, No.2, pp.323–44.

ILO (2002) *Supporting Workplace Learning for High Performance Working*, Geneva: ILO.

IPD (1999): *Training and development in Britain 1999, IPD Survey Report*, London: IPD.

IRS (1992) 'Industrial relations developments in the water industry', *Employment Trends*, No.516, pp.6–15.

IRS (1994) 'Improving performance? A survey of appraisal arrangements', *Employment Trends*, No.556, pp.5–14.

IRS (1995a) 'Survey of employee relations in local government', *Employment Trends*, No.594, pp.6–13.

IRS (1995b) 'The customer is boss: matching employee performance to customer service needs', *Employment Trends*, No.585, pp.7–13.

IRS (1999) 'New ways to perform appraisal', *Employment Trends*, No.676, pp.7–16.

Kayande, U. and Finn, A. (1999), 'Unmasking the phantom: a psychometric assessment of mystery shopping', *Journal of Retailing*, Vol.75, No.2, pp.135–217.

Kessler, I. and Purcell, J. (1992) 'Performance related pay: objectives and application', *Human Resource Management Journal*, Vol.2, No.3, pp.16–33.

Laabs, J. (1992) 'Measuring work in the electronic age', *Personnel Journal*, Vol.71, No.6, p.35.

Lawler, E.E. (1994) 'Performance management: the next generation', *Compensation and Benefits Review*, May–June, pp.16–28.

Lawler, J.J., Jain, H.C., Ratnam, C.S.V. and Atmiyanandana, V. (1995) 'Human resource management in developing economies: a comparison of India and Thailand', *International Journal of Human Resource Management*, Vol.6, No.2, pp.320–46.

Lee, J., Havighurst, L. and Rassel, G. (2004) 'Factors related to court references to performance appraisal fairness and validity', *Public Personnel Management*, Vol.33, No.1, pp.61–77.

LGMB (1994) *Performance Management and Performance-Related Pay. Local Government Practice*, London: LGMB.

Locher, A.H. and Teel, K.S. (1988) 'Appraisal trends', *Personnel Journal*, Vol.67, No.9, pp.139–43.

London, M. and Beatty, R.W. (1993) '360-degree feedback as a competitive advantage', *Human Resource Management*, Vol.32, Nos 2–3, 353–72.

Long, P. (1986) *Performance Appraisal Revisited*, London: IPD.

*Longenecker, C. (1989) 'Truth or consequences: politics and performance appraisals', *Business Horizons*, November–December, pp.76–82.

Maroney, B.P. and Buckley, P.P.M. (1992) 'Does research in performance appraisal influence the practice of performance appraisal? Regretfully not', *Public Personnel Management*, Vol.21, No.2, pp.185–96.

Milliman, J.F., Zawacki, R.A., Schulz, B., Wiggins, S. and Norman, C. (1995) 'Customer service drives 360-degree goal setting', *Personnel Journal*, June, pp.136–41.

Mitrani, A., Dalziel, M.M. and Fitt, D. (1992) *Competency Based Human Resource Management*, London: Kogan Page.

O'Reilly, B. (1995) '360-degree feedback can change your life', *Fortune Magazine*, 17 October, pp.55–8.

Personnel Management (1995) Vol.1, No.7, p.15.

Peters, T. (1987) *Thriving on Chaos*, London: Macmillan

Poon, J. (2004) 'Effects of performance appraisal politics on job-satisfaction and turnover intention', *Personnel Review*, Vol.33, No.3, pp.322–4.

*Randell, G. (1994) 'Employee Appraisal', in K. Sisson (ed.) *Personnel Management: a Comprehensive Guide to Theory and Practice in Britain,* Oxford: Blackwell.

Randle, K. and Rainnie, A. (1997) 'Managing creativity, maintaining control: a study in pharmaceutical research', *Human Research Management Journal,* Vol.7, No.2, pp.32–46.

Redman, T. and Snape, E. (1992) 'Upward and onward: can staff appraise their managers?', *Personnel Review,* Vol.21, No.7, pp.32–46.

Redman, T. and Mathews, B.P. (1995) 'Do corporate turkeys vote for Christmas? Managers' attitudes towards upward appraisal', *Personnel Review,* Vol.24, No.7, pp.13–24.

*Redman, T., Snape, E., Thompson, D. and Ka-ching Yan, F. (2000) 'Performance appraisal in the national health service: a trust hospital study', *Human Resource Management Journal,* Vol.10, No.1, pp.1–16.

Roth, W. and Ferguson, D. (1994) 'The end of performance appraisals?', *Quality Digest,* Vol.14, No.9, pp.52–7.

Shing, M. and Spence, M. (2002) 'Investigating the limits of competitive intelligence gathering: is mystery shopping ethical', *Business Ethics: a European Review,* Vol.11, No.4, pp.343–44.

Snape, E., Redman., T. and Bamber, G. (1994) *Managing Managers,* Oxford: Blackwell.

*Snape, E., Thompson, D., Ka-ching Yan, F. and Redman, T. (1998) 'Performance appraisal and culture: practice and attitudes in Hong Kong and Great Britain', *International Journal of Human Resource Management,* Vol.9, No.5, pp.841–61.

Sparrow, P. (1994) 'Organizational competencies: creating a strategic behavioural framework for selection and assessment', in N. Anderson and P. Herriot (eds) *Assessment and Selection in Organizations,* Chichester: Wiley.

Thomas, A., Wells, M. and Willard, J. (1992) 'A novel approach to developing managers and their teams: BPX uses upward feedback', *Management Education and Development,* Vol.23, No.1, pp.30–2.

Toegel, G. and Conger, J. (2003) '360-degree feedback: time for reinvention', *Academy of Management Learning and Education,* Vol.2, No.3, pp.297–311.

Tombs, S. (1992) 'Managing safety: could do better . . .', *Occupational Safety and Health,* Vol.26, No.1, pp.9–12.

Townley, B. (1989) 'Selection and appraisal: reconstituting "social relations"', in J. Storey (ed.) *New Perspectives on Human Resource Management,* London: Routledge.

Townley, B. (1990) 'A discrimination approach to appraisal', *Personnel Management,* December, pp.34–7.

Townley, B. (1993) 'Performance appraisal and the emergence of management', *Journal of Management Studies,* Vol.30, No.2, pp.221–38.

Townley, B. (1994) *Reframing Human Resource Management,* London: Sage

Townley, B. (1999) 'Practical reason and performance appraisal', *Journal of Management Studies,* Vol.36, No.3, pp.287–306.

Tziner, A. (1999) 'The relationship between distal and proximal factors and the use of political considerations in performance appraisal', *Journal of Business and Psychology,* Vol.14, No.1, pp.217–31.

Wright, V. (1991) 'Performance related pay', in F. Neale (ed.) *The Handbook of Performance Management,* London: IPM.

* Useful reading

Chapter 7

INDUSTRIAL RELATIONS

Nick Bacon

Introduction

The terms 'industrial relations' and more recently 'employee relations' are used to indicate those areas of the employment relationship in which managers deal with the representatives of employees rather than managing employees directly as individuals (Edwards 1995). Where employees seek collective representation they generally join trade unions and the reaction of managers to this potential challenge to management authority provides valuable insights into the nature of employment. As the membership of trade unions has declined over the past two decades a critical debate has developed around the nature of employment relations in non-union workplaces. The purpose of this chapter is to chart the changes in the collective regulation of labour and consider the implications of the increasing number of workers who are not represented by trade unions.

Management frames of reference and management style

The suggestion that employees may need some form of collective protection from employers provokes a strong response in many managers. Behind this response are a set of assumptions about the right to manage (frequently termed the management prerogative) and the correct power balance in the employment relationship. These assumptions held by managers are the mixture of a complex blend of experiences, pre-dispositions, learned behaviour and prejudice. They combine to create management frames of reference (Fox 1966, 1974) that capture the often deeply held assumptions of managers towards a labour force. Three separate frames of reference can be identified: unitarism, pluralism and radical. Each of these differs in their beliefs about the nature of organisations, the role of conflict and the task of managing employees. Managers holding a unitarist frame of reference believe the natural state of organisations is one of harmony and cooperation. All employees are thought to be in the same team, pulling together for the common goal of organisational success. The employee relations task of management is to prevent conflict arising from misunderstandings that result if they fail to adequately communicate organisational goals to employees. Any remaining conflicts are attributed to mischief created by troublemakers. A pluralist frame of reference recognises that organisations contain a variety of sectional groups who legitimately seek to express divergent interests. The resulting conflict is inevitable and the task of managers is to establish a system of structures and procedures in which conflict is institutionalised and a negotiated order is established. The radical critique of pluralism is not, strictly speaking, a frame of reference for understanding management views of the employment relationship. It draws upon Marxism and explains workplace conflict within a broader historical and social context and places a stress upon the unequal power struggle of opposing social classes.

There are no simple methods to assess the frame of reference held by managers – indeed, they usually hold a complex set of ideas rather than falling neatly into a single and possibly over-simplistic frame of reference. However, insights into management attitudes can be gained through their responses to questions about trade unions. From comparable questions posed to managers at the start of the 1980s and 1990s, Poole and Mansfield (1993) suggested the underlying pluralistic preferences of British managers were remarkably consistent. Another question posed more recently indicated a majority of workplace managers do not have a single frame of reference. In the 1998 *Workplace Employee Relations Survey* (WERS 98) most managers (54 per cent) were 'neutral' about union membership, whereas 29 per cent were 'in favour' with 17 per cent 'not in favour' (Cully *et al.* 1999, p. 87). However, when managers are asked more directly whether they prefer to manage employees directly or through unions then unitarist preferences emerge. For example, 72 per cent of managers agreed with the statement 'we would rather consult directly with employees than with unions', whereas only 13 per cent disagreed (ibid., p.88). Consequently, management approaches to industrial relations are often characterised as a mixing and matching between unitarism and pluralism in the 'time-honoured' British fashion (Edwards *et al.* 1998). Many managers accept such a view on the grounds that it merely reflects the reality of managing employees who may at times need representation. The evidence suggests, however, that managers can deter or encourage employees from joining trade unions. In the 1998 *Workplace Employee Relations Survey* pro-union management attitudes were significantly associated with union presence in the workplace (Cully *et al.* 1998, p.19).

Frames of references are also important because they underlie the management style adopted in organisations towards the workforce. Many authors have attempted to classify management styles (Fox 1974; Purcell and Sisson 1983; Storey and Bacon 1993; Purcell and Ahlstrand 1994) and as the resulting models have become increasingly complex Some now doubt the usefulness of producing yet more typologies (Kitay and Marchington 1996). The most recent typologies attempt to highlight the interaction between HRM and industrial relations. The central question raised is the extent to which HRM and industrial relations are alternative or complementary systems for managing employees. If they are alternatives then HRM may provide a 'unitarist' alternative to managing with unions (Bacon 2003). Whether managers recognise trade unions indicates the extent to which a 'collective' approach to managing employees is preferred and it does capture a key factor in distinguishing between management approaches. In addition, the extent to which managers invest in and develop employees indicates the extent to which they stress 'individualism'. In Figure 7.1 Purcell and Ahlstrand (1994) use the dimensions of 'collectivism' and 'individualism' to identify six different management styles of employee relations.

Individualism and collectivism have recently become popular terms in employee relations. In comparison with the traditional management frames of reference–unitarism and pluralism–these concepts have 'common sense' meanings and appear grounded in everyday management vocabularies and thinking about employee relations. Individualism in employment relations is traditionally used to denote non-unionism and/or a HRM-style investment approach to employees (Purcell 1987; Marchington and Parker 1990; Storey and Sisson 1993). Correspondingly, collectivism in industrial relations in the 1970s is counter-posed with individualism and HRM in the 1990s (Storey and Sisson 1993). The 'collectivism' dimension includes a unitarist position where trade unions are not recognised, an adversarial position of conflict with unions and a cooperative position of partnership with unions. The 'individualism' dimension includes a cost minimisation approach to employees, a 'paternalist' position of care for employee welfare and an employee development scenario.

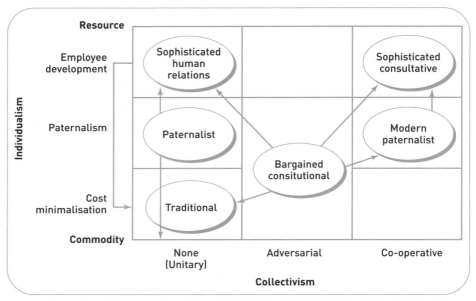

Figure 7.1 Movements in management style in employee relations
Source: Storey and Sisson, 1993, adapted from Purcell and Ahlstrand, 1994

Initial studies of the adoption of HRM policies in unionised workplaces (Storey 1992) suggested little fit between HRM and industrial relations as managers attempted to bypass industrial relations processes and deal directly with employees. This comes as no great surprise as personnel management in the UK is commonly described as pragmatic and largely opportunistic (Sisson and Marginson 1995). In seeking the appropriate recipe for managing employees during the 1980s many managers saw an opportunity to reduce the influence of unions. This involved a secular (if disputed) shift towards unitarism as managers reasserted their prerogative over employees at work. Initially, in the 1980s this appeared in an aggressive form of 'macho-management' as senior executives, often in state-owned industries, attacked unions and the customs and practices entrenched in many workplaces (Purcell 1982). However, most companies did not derecognise unions and commentators noted that 'the lack of clarity about how industrial relations fits with the new initiatives will sooner or later have to be addressed' (Storey and Sisson 1993, p.27). In short, the main issue on the employee relations agenda appeared to be how to combine the individual and collective approaches in a complementary fashion.

Employee views on work

A widespread criticism of management during the 1960s and 1970s, a point which still holds today, is that employees may not feel everyone shares the same goals in their workplace and they may reject a unitarist perspective. In many, if not most, workplaces employees talk of 'us' and describe managers as 'them', believing there are two sides with partially conflicting interests (Clegg 1979). Thus, many employees subscribe to a pluralist perspective and feel workers and managers are on different sides with separate interests, rather than feeling that working for an organisation is like playing for a football team where all groups supporting a club are on the same side and pursuing a common goal (Ramsey 1975).

Where employees feel they have different interests from managers they often join trade unions. Trade unions have approximately 320 million members world-wide which amounts

Table 7.1 What reasons do employees give for joining unions?	
Support if I had a problem at work	72%
Improved pay and conditions	36%
Because I believe in trade unions	16%
Free legal advice	15%
Most people at work are members	14%

Source: Waddington and Whitston 1997, p.521 (www.blackwell-synergy.com)

to between one fifth and one quarter of the global labour force (Visser 2003). Significant variation exists between countries. For instance, Russia, Ukraine and Belarus (58 per cent) and China (42 per cent) have high rates of union membership; around one quarter (26 per cent) of European workers are union members, whereas a smaller proportion of workers in North America (13 per cent) and Asia (10 per cent) belong to unions.

Employees may choose to join trade unions for a wide range of reasons (Schnabel 2003, p.19). They may feel dissatisfied with their work situation (termed the frustration-aggression thesis), joining a union may bring benefits such as higher wages that outweigh the costs of membership (a rational choice explanation), or they may be encouraged to join by the traditions and opinions of their work group (an interactionist explanation). In a survey of almost 11,000 union members in the UK conducted by Waddington and Whitston (1997) employees revealed they continued to join unions for collective protection and to improve their terms and conditions (Table 7.1). Some studies suggest that HRM initiatives introduced over the past 20 years have had little impact on workers' perceptions of 'them' and 'us' (Kelly and Kelly 1991; D'Art and Turner 1999).

The decline of collective regulation

In a majority of countries union membership has fallen over the past twenty years, especially in Europe and North America. The decline in the numbers of union members suggests employment relations have been transformed and we have witnessed 'the end of institutional industrial relations' (Purcell 1993). In the UK, for example, the *Workplace Industrial Relations Surveys* (WIRS) since 1990 record fundamental changes with industrial relations no longer characterised by adversarial collective bargaining at workplace level (Millward *et al.* 1992). Figure 7.2 illustrates this change as captured by these surveys in terms of changes to union presence (the presence of one or more union members in a workplace), union membership density (percentage of employees who are union members), union recognition for negotiating pay and conditions of employment, coverage of collective bargaining (the proportion of employees in workplaces with recognised unions covered by collective bargaining) and joint consultative committees.

The decline in union recognition in the UK since the 1980s is mainly due to the failure of unions to organise workers and gain recognition for collective bargaining in new firms and workplaces (Machin 2000). Responding to heightened competitive pressures managers have proved reluctant to recognise unions for fear of higher wages, and unions have found it difficult to recruit the growing numbers of female and service sector workers. As the number of large manufacturing plants and manual workers declined the traditional habitat for the UK's system of industrial relations based on adversarial collective bargaining began to disappear (Millward *et al.* 1992).

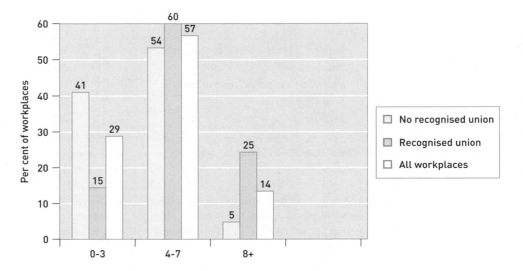

Figure 7.2 Number of high commitment management practices, by trade union recognition.
Source: Cully *et al.* 1999

Table 7.2	The decline of collective regulation in the workplace industrial relations surveys*			
	1980	**1984**	**1990**	**1998**
Union presence	73%	73%	64%	54%
Union membership density	65%	58%	47%	36%
Union recognition	65%	65%	53%	42%
Coverage of collective bargaining	–	70%	54%	41%
Joint consultative committees	34%	34%	29%	29%

Source: Workplace Industrial Relations Surveys; see Cully *et al.* 1999

*Figures related to percentages of workplaces

Trade union influence appears even lower than current levels of union recognition indicate when we consider the scope and depth of joint consultation and bargaining. It is difficult to assess the extent to which managers rely upon collective agreements with trade unions in workplaces. One study comparing collective agreements at the start and end of the 1980s outlined a relative stability in procedural agreements covering how issues are handled between management and labour (Dunn and Wright 1994). A rather different picture emerged from case studies at plant level, indicating managers were increasingly exercising their prerogative to make important changes, particularly in working methods (Geary 1995). Data from the 1998 *Workplace Employee Relations Surveys* indicates a deeper 'hollowing out' of collective agreements. In workplaces where union representatives are present only a 'modest' level of joint regulation occurs. No negotiations occurred over any issues in one half of the workplaces with worker representatives present (Cully *et al.* 1999, p.110). In a further 13 per cent of workplaces negotiations only occurred on non-pay issues, in 17 per cent negotiations only covered pay, and in 22 per cent negotiations occurred over pay and one other issue. Managers in many workplaces appear to regard certain HR issues as 'off limits' to union representatives and do not even involve unions in providing information. In 53 per cent of workplaces with union representatives, representatives played no role at all in performance appraisals, in 52 per cent no role in recruitment, in 46 per cent no role in payment systems, and in 43 per cent no role in training. This evidence suggests that in many cases trade union influence has 'withered on the vine' and where union representatives remain in place this resembles a unionised approach to industrial relations which in fact is little more than a 'hollow shell' (Hyman 1997). Given these findings traditional debates on the most appropriate levels for collective bargaining (at the workplace, corporate or industry levels) and the balance between collective bargaining and joint consultation are giving way to the broader question of whether and on what terms trade unions are involved in any degree of joint workplace governance. The central role played by collective industrial relations has certainly declined but what types of non-union workplaces have emerged?

Non-union workplaces

According to one estimate the majority of UK workplaces had become non-union by 1995 (Cully and Woodland 1996). In the classic account by Fox (1974) it was necessary for managers to enforce management prerogative by coercive power to justify a unitarist ideology and non-union status. Managers have often used a wide-ranging web of defences against unionisation that in their more extreme variants in the United States could combine 'sweet stuff' to make management policies more acceptable to employees, 'fear stuff' to discourage union joining and 'evil stuff' to demonise unions (Roy 1980). A unitarist ideology can therefore include a variety of different management techniques. Returning to Figure 7.1 we can see that Purcell and Ahlstrand (1994) classify three non-union management styles in terms of whether an organisation recognises and develops individual employees. Companies adopting a 'sophisticated human relations' approach invest in staff development and use a wide range of human resource management policies to substitute for the services unions provide for members (a union substitution approach). Other non-union companies adopt a 'paternalist' approach and seek the loyalty and commitment of staff through consideration for employee welfare. Finally, some organisations maintain a 'bleak house' strategy of cost minimisation and avoid union recruitment.

Several key commentators in the late 1980s identified the non-union sector as the most likely location for the development of HRM in the UK, foreseeing a growth in the 'sophisticated human relations' approach (Sisson 1989). As some HRM models, but not all, are fundamentally unitarist, a non-union environment appeared well suited to the demands of developing committed and flexible employees as demonstrated by several large non-union US multinationals such as IBM, Hewlett Packard and Mars (Foulkes 1980; Kochan et al. 1986). For example, IBM had combined corporate success, a positive employee relations climate of low conflict, low labour turnover and long service, with good pay and conditions. In addition, the company provided procedures to fulfil many of the functions met by unions, including a complex array of alternative procedures (a no-redundancy policy, single status, equal opportunities policies, merit pay and performance assessments), a strong emphasis on internal communications and a grievance system.

Empirical support for the apparent link between sophisticated HRM and non-unionism was also provided by several case studies in the UK outlining a union-substitution approach. In the case of 'Comco' explored by Cressey et al. (1985) employees identified strongly with the company and enjoyed 'greater benefits' and 'less disciplinary pressure'. Most employees working at an IBM plant in the UK studied by Dickson *et al.* (1988) were positively attached to the individualistic ethos of the company and perceived little need for union protection. Scott (1994) outlined a 'golden handcuffs' approach whereby employees in a chocolate works received good terms and conditions in return for accepting a high rate of effort and strict rules. Despite this evidence, initial studies indicated that non-union companies with a sophisticated approach to managing employees may remain the exception. A study of high-tech companies in the southeast of England where we might expect companies to reproduce the IBM non-union model uncovered little evidence of sophisticated HRM, with companies either opportunistically avoiding unions or adopting the style of 'benevolent autocracies' (McLoughlin and Gourlay 1994). Furthermore, the assumed benefits of a 'sophisticated human relations' approach have more recently come under closer scrutiny. Blyton and Turnbull (1994) suggest that Marks and Spencer, so often held up as an exemplar non-union company, simultaneously pursued a 'union substitution' strategy in retail outlets while forcing suppliers into a cost-minimisation approach. In another case study, a steel plant had widely publicised the introduction of an HRM approach and subsequently derecognised trade unions. However, employee gains proved illusory, with managerial strategy geared towards attitudinal compliance, work intensification and the suppression of any counterbalancing trade union activity (Bacon 1999).

As almost one half of workplaces are effectively union-free a 'representation gap' (Towers 1997) may have developed where managers operate without any independent employee voice. Three in five workplaces have no worker representatives at all (either union or non-union representatives), and this increases to nine out of ten workplaces where unions are not present (Cully *et al.* 1999, p.95). The absence of representation is important because if dissatisfied workers cannot express their grievances then their only option may be to leave the organisation (Hirschman 1971). In the absence of union recognition managers can provide employee voice through direct channels by communicating with workers in team briefings and problem solving, and there is evidence managers are more responsive to these communications than in listening to unions (Bryson 2004). However, as we will see below many organisations fail to provide either union or direct channels for employee voice.

HRM: A union or non-union phenomena?

The evidence from the latest UK workplace survey (WERS98) confirms the finding of the 1990 survey (WIRS3, see Sisson 1993, p.206) that sophisticated HRM practices are to be found alongside union recognition mainly in larger workplaces and those in the public sector. In short, these surveys indicate 'an active and strong union presence is compatible with the broad suite of high commitment management practices' (Cully *et al.* 1999, p.111). Furthermore, higher union density (the proportion of employees who are trade union members) is also associated with greater joint regulation and more high commitment management (HCM) practices. Figure 7.2 indicates that of the workplaces with no recognised unions, 41 per cent had between nought and three HCM practices, 54 per cent four to seven HCM practices, and 5 per cent for eight or more. This compares unfavourably with 25 per cent of workplaces with recognised unions reporting eight or more high commitment management practices.

However, only 4 per cent of workplaces in the workplace survey combine a majority of the workforce in unions, collective negotiations over issues and at least one half of the measured list of high commitment work practices in place. There is, nevertheless, evidence from the

1998 *Workplace Employee Relations Survey* that the combination of union recognition and HCM practices has a powerful effect on workplace performance. In the words of the WERS98 team 'workplaces with a recognised union and a majority of the HCM practices . . . did better than the average, and better than workplaces without recognition and a minority of these practices' (Cully *et al.* 1999, p.135). Sceptics of the impact of trade unions may still like to believe that adopting a wide range of HCM practices in a non-union environment may lead to higher performance still, but the fact that WERS98 could find so few such organisations casts some doubt upon this belief. Managers continuing to recognise unions are seeking new approaches to industrial relations involving 'partnership agreements'.

Partnership and the 'New Unionism'

The election of 'New Labour' in the UK in 1997 has resulted in a new public policy environment. The government's Employment Relations Act 1999 and 'Fairness at Work' programme have introduced new rights for trade unions and individual employees (Undy 1999; Wood and Godard 1999). In sum, this legislative programme involves a statutory route for union recognition, an extension of rights for individual employees, a national minimum wage and closer engagement with the social policies of the European Union. A central aim of this legislative programme is to 'replace the notion of conflict between employers and employees with the promotion of partnership in the longer term' (DTI 1998). The influence of a European approach was already felt as legislation obliged companies to establish a European works council if they employed over 1,000 employees in Europe and a minimum of 150 employees in at least two member states. The partial Europeanisation of British industrial relations shows no sign of slowing. The European Union Directive for informing and consulting employees will be phased in from 2005 providing rights for employees to be informed about the economic situation of their employer's business, employment prospects and substantial changes in work organisation or employment contracts. In sum, these changes now make it commonplace to call for less destructive conflict and more cooperation to improve organisational productivity.

The issue of the respective balance between cooperation and conflict in union – management relations is a long-standing tension in employee relations. As the employment relationship encapsulates both shared and contrary interests the relationship between management and unions will contain elements of conflict and cooperation. As management and unions have begun to use the word 'partnership' it has become a contested term that appears inherently ambiguous and at times has no agreed meaning (Ackers and Payne 1998; Undy 1999). As Undy (1999, p.318) has pointed out 'What one party, or commentator, means by "partnership" is not necessarily shared by others'. As with so many terms in the area of employment relations, key pressure groups such as the TUC, the CBI and the Institute of Directors (IoD) have sought to provide 'widely differing interpretations' of partnership (Undy 1999, p.318), defining the term for their own ends. The Institute of Personnel and Development, for example, explains that partnership 'has more to do with an approach to the relationship between employers and employees, individually and in groups, than it has to do with trade unions' (IPD 1997, p.8). Partnership can therefore be defined in both unitarist and pluralist terms. Rather unsurprisingly, the definition favoured by the TUC is pluralistic, with the stress placed on respecting union influence, whereas the Institute of Directors prefers a unitarist definition, whereby employees identify with the employer and trade unions are compliant to the wishes of management.

The Involvement and Participation Association, an independent pressure group, developed an influential definition of partnership with leading companies and trade union leaders. This approach was endorsed by leading figures including representatives from J Sainsbury plc, the Boddington Group, the Post Office and the leaders of several trade unions (Involvement and Participation Association 1992). This definition requires managers to declare security of employment as a key corporate objective; 'gainsharing' the results of success, and recognise the legitimacy of the employees' right to be informed, consulted and represented. In return, trade unions are required to renounce rigid job demarcations and commit to flexible working, give sympathetic consideration to the Continental model of representation of the whole workforce by means of election of representatives to new works councils, and recognise and then co-promote employee involvement methods. Case 7.2 invites you to consider the extent to which you feel companies and unions are able to sign-up to a partnership agenda.

Given the lack of a general consensus on the meaning of industrial relations partnerships, it may be surprising that the term has acquired such a topical currency. A principal reason the concept has taken hold is that it offers an industrial relations solution to the low competitiveness of much of UK industry. In this respect, partnership is no different from previous legislative changes that have sought to improve organisational performance through changes in industrial relations. Influential US literature suggests that in some companies managers may be able to forge a strategic linkage between industrial relations and HRM initiatives to create 'mutual gains enterprises' (Appelbaum and Batt 1994; Kochan and Osterman 1994). In such enterprises important changes are introduced in the reorganisation of work to enhance productivity, to the mutual benefit of employees, unions and management acting in coalition.

The signing of partnership agreements is of potential importance (IRS 1997) although to date there is little evidence they have become widespread beyond around forty companies. If partnerships are to become further established in UK industrial relations then managers and unions must find a workable balance between a number of key tensions beyond the above-mentioned disputes as to the meaning of the concept. The first tension is that workable partnership agreements appear to require a strategic and long-term commitment by managers to working closely with unions in the tradition of companies labelled 'sophisticated moderns' by Fox (1974). If managers are simply behaving in a short-term, contradictory or opportunistic manner then genuine industrial relations partnerships are unlikely to endure. For example, at the Royal Mail several partnership initiatives have struggled, primarily because some managers in the company are not firmly behind the partnership approach (see Bacon and Storey 1996, 2000).

The second tension, not unconnected to the first, is to what extent management and unions are able to commit fully to a single strategy of cooperative industrial relations. If partnerships do not secure the types of compliant trade unionism required in the CBI's definition of partnership then management commitment to such agreements may prove half-hearted. Similarly, at the same time as the TUC is supporting partnership agreements it is also pursuing an organising and campaigning approach to membership growth (Heery 1998). It may prove difficult for unions to convince a company to sign a meaningful partnership agreement in one plant while actively recruiting union members against the wishes of the same or a similar company in another plant.

The third tension is whether partnership agreements form part of a longer term strategy to marginalise trade unions rather than an alternative. Many observers critical of the cooperative relationships between managers and unions that are central to partnership agreements have highlighted continued employer attacks on unions (Claydon 1989, 1996; Smith and Morton 1993; Gall and McKay 1994; Kelly 1996). Although partnerships are frequently presented as a step change away from attempts to de-recognise trade unions this may not be the case. Evidence on this matter is not yet conclusive. Whereas one recent review of partnership agreements in six organisations reported 'none gave serious consideration to ending recognition' (IDS 1998, p.4), a study of management attempts to restructure industrial relations in ten organisations (Bacon and Storey 2000) revealed de-recognition had been more seriously explored. In the latter study, the new agreements signed with trade unions did not appear to reflect long-term commitments to working with trade unions nor sophisticated moves towards derecognition. Managers appeared to display unitarist preferences. However, for pragmatic reasons – for instance, the desire to maintain the trust of employees – they were willing to involve unions in joint regulation albeit within parameters managers attempted to control. In many workplaces union representatives feel they have no option but to accept management terms and union support for partnership resembles a resigned compliance. For example, in the case of United Distillers trade unions either signed the partnership agreement on offer or faced '*de facto* de-recognition' (Marks *et al.* 1998, p.222). The statutory provisions for union recognition contained in the Employment Relations Act 1999 did mark an increase in union recognition agreements suggesting trade unions may have turned a corner in their decline (Gall 2004) with employers showing greater approval of unions (Oxenbridge *et al.* 2003). However, according to Oxenbridge *et al.* (2003) this involved employers seeking union assistance in implementing organisational change and did not restrain the rate at which employers were excluding unions from bargaining over issues such as pay.

Finally, it is not yet clear whether partnership agreements will deliver greater returns for managers and trade unions. If returns are not forthcoming for either party then enthusiasm for the partnership approach may wane. Kelly (1996) has argued that, *a priori*, a union strategy of moderation is inferior in many respects to a militant stance. Union moderation is associated by Kelly with: eroding the willingness and capacity of union members to resist employers; inhibiting the growth of workplace union organisation; generating apathy among union members; involving union 'give' and management 'take'; and resulting in attempts to drive down terms and conditions of employment and failing to genuinely represent member grievances. The key differences between militant and moderate union positions are highlighted in Case study 7.3.

The extent to which Kelly is correct, and neither unions nor employees will benefit from partnership agreements, is an interesting question. Kelly (2004) compared similar UK companies with and without partnership agreements and found that partnership firms shed jobs at a faster rate than non-partnership firms in industries marked by employment decline. In contrast, partnership firms in expanding sectors created jobs at a faster rate than non-partnership firms. Partnership appeared to have no impact on wage settlements or union density. The number of partnership agreements signed between unions and management remains low overall and this may reflect the extent to which such agreements deliver job security and higher wages for employees and the flexibility that managers seek. Gains for employees from partnership appear to be particularly elusive. In a study of 54 companies, Guest and Peccei (2001, p.207) discovered that the balance of advantage from partnership at work 'is skewed towards management' and was associated with positive estimates of employment relations, quality and productivity.

Conclusions

In this chapter we have argued that managers in the majority of workplaces no longer appear to support or utilise collective industrial relations in their employee management strategies. Sisson and Storey (2000, p. x) have recently restated that 'managing the employment relationship will demand both an individual and a collective perspective' in forthcoming years. However, recent evidence suggests that managers in few workplaces have sought to balance an individual and collective approach to employee management. Figure 7.3 presents a summary drawing upon the findings from WERS98 of the current pattern of employee relations. The predominant employee relations style in the British workplace is not to manage both individualism and collectivism, it is to manage neither. Considering all the workplaces who fall into the bottom left hand quadrant of the dotted lines, approximately seven in ten (68 per cent) operate fewer than one-half of 15 high-commitment management practices and do not involve trade unions in negotiations on matters other than pay. Fifty-two per cent of workplaces in this quadrant do not recognise trade unions.

Approximately 14 per cent of workplaces could be described as pursuing an HRM approach but only 5 per cent appeared to combine individualism with either a union exclusion or partnership approach. The majority of workplaces appear to be marginalising unions, and although they remain present significant negotiations do not occur. It is tempting to classify organisations falling into the four corner boxes as having an apparently settled employee relations strategy that is unlikely to change in the near future. The numerous workplaces which fall into the 'Bleak House' classification (approximately 22 per cent) are focused upon cost reduction and will resist any attempts at unionisation. In such 'Bleak House' workplaces employees report lower levels of job satisfaction, organisational commitment, trust in management and experience unfair treatment (Guest and

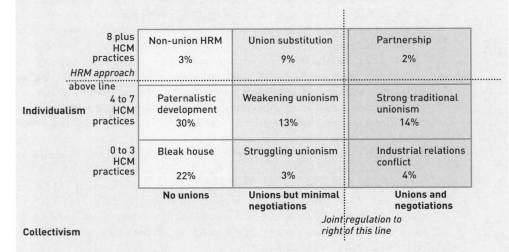

Figure 7.3 New patterns of employee relations

Conway 1999). The small number of organisations which negotiate with unions but eschew developing employees ('industrial relations traditional') may be resigned to dealing with unions in the absence of a more sophisticated approach to managing employees. A few genuine examples of partnership may flourish in the current political climate but the overall number of such workplaces remains small. Companies adopting non-union HRM are likely to feel they have permanently resolved the union issue.

This leaves approximately 69 per cent of organisations (in the shaded areas of Figure 7.2) who currently operate with an opportunistic mixture of labour management policies. Organisations currently occupying these different positions face somewhat different dilemmas. Those currently using HRM policies to substitute for negotiating with unions but still recognising unions ('union substitution') may at some point in the future sign partnership deals with trade unions to share more decision-making and/or further erode union influence. Companies with 'strong traditional unionism' may further develop HR policies either to substitute for unions or develop a partnership approach. From an industrial relations perspective the most significant developments may occur within the 'weakening unionism' category. Although trade unions in these workplaces are involved in fewer negotiations managers have not developed high commitment management practices to replace the services unions provide for members in terms of voicing collective grievances and seeking to improve terms and conditions. It would appear to be in this category of workplaces that trade unions may target recruitment to increase union density and exert greater influence. The Employment Relations Act 1999 encourages union recruitment and organising efforts as it provides a statutory recognition procedure. As so few organisations appear to have resolved the issue of managing employees through individual or collective means they are likely to face continued pressure from individual employees for increased training and more satisfying work and from employee representatives for a greater say in workplace governance.

CASE STUDY 7.1

UNION RECOGNITION IN THE PRIVATE SECTOR

NICK BACON

Below is a list of the largest private sector employers in the UK taken from *Labour Research.* Which do you think: do not recognise trade unions; recognise and negotiate with trade unions; or recognise trade unions but only for the purposes of consultation or to represent individual employees? Explain your decisions.

Tesco	153,800	Retail – supermarkets
J Sainsbury	150,700	Retail – supermarkets
BT	125,800	Telecommunications
Lloyds-TSB	82,000	Banking and finance
Whitbread	80,000	Food and drink
Boots Co.	75,000	Retail and pharmaceuticals
Asda Group	73,700	Retail – supermarkets
Safeway Group	70,400	Retail – supermarkets
Kingfisher	69,600	Retail
Bass	67,500	Brewing and leisure
National Westminster	66,000	Banking and finance
Rentokil Initial	65,000	Business services
Barclays	60,800	Banking and finance
Granada Group	58,000	Leisure
Marks & Spencer	54,900	Retail
General Electric Co.	52,300	Electronics
HSBC Holding (Midland Bank)	50,000	Banking and finance
British Airways	47,700	Banking and finance
Allied Domecq	46,500	Food and drink
Somerfield	45,700	Retail – supermarket
Burton Group	43,700	Retail
British Steel	43,400	Steel manufacturers
Ladbroke Group	42,000	Leisure
John Lewis Partnership	41,100	Retail – department stores
BMW-Rover Group	39,000	Motor manufacture
Scottish & Newcastle	39,000	Brewing and leisure
British Aerospace	38,500	Aerospace and engineering
MacDonald's Restaurants	36,700	Food retail
Halifax	36,000	Banking and finance
Ford	35,900	Motor manufacturing
Compass Group	35,700	Catering
Co-operative Wholesale Society	35,000	Banking, insurance, retail
OCS Group	35,000	Cleaning
Sears	32,600	Retail
Rolls Royce	31,200	Aerospace and engineering
Rank Organisation	30,300	Leisure and films
Greenhalls Group	30,100	Brewing, food, hotels
WH Smith	30,000	Retail
Royal & Sun Alliance	27,800	Insurance
Securicor Group	27,500	Security services
Wm Morrison Supermarkets	27,000	Retail – supermarkets
Unigate	27,000	Food manufacture
Lucas Varity	26,800	Engineering
BTR	26,600	Industrial conglomerate
Kwik Save Group	26,000	Retail

THE PRINCIPLES AND PRACTICES OF PARTNERSHIP WITH TRADE UNIONS

NICK BACON

As explained in Chapter 7, one option for managers and trade unions is to establish a partnership agreement. However, successful agreements depend upon a serious commitment to the principles and practices of partnership. Thinking of the last organisation you worked for, an organisation you know well or your own personal 'frame of reference', to what extent do you agree or disagree with the following statements? Your answers indicate whether organisations could be committed to a partnership agreement. (Circle one number for each statement.)

	Agree	Neutral	Disagree
Personnel managers worry about trade unions, most other senior managers would rather they disappear	1	2	3
Trade unions don't have a useful function in organisations	1	2	3
All managers should share all information, however sensitive, with unions	1	2	3
Managers can get employees to work hard without making concessions to unions	1	2	3
Job security is a myth in today's world	1	2	3
To attract top managers organisations have to offer extra incentives, such as private health insurance, that are too expensive to give to all employees	1	2	3
Companies should train all employees to a high level even though some will leave	1	2	3

MILITANCY OR MODERATION?

NICK BACON

In Chapter 7 we outlined Kelly's (1996) argument that trade unions would benefit from a militant rather than a moderate stance. Reading through the following statements, indicate the extent to which you believe trade unions should adopt a moderate and militant stance. Explain your choices.

Trade unions should:

Union militancy		Union moderation
Make ambitious demands	or	Make moderate demands
Offer few concessions	or	Offer many concessions
Rely on members' activity	or	Rely on managers' goodwill
Rely on collective bargaining	or	Rely on consultation
Frequently threaten industrial action	or	Rarely threaten industrial action
Believe in a basic conflict of interests	or	Believe a basic common interest

CASE STUDY 7.4

THE CHALLENGE FOR UNION AND EMPLOYER PARTNERSHIP: THE EUROTUNNEL EXPERIENCE

PAUL J. GOLLAN

How will the impending law on information and consultation affect a union–management partnership? Eurotunnel's experience could spell problems and opportunities for both unions and employer.

Recent developments at Eurotunnel could have serious implications for the future of the partnership approach in the UK and of the likely success of the European Information and Consultation Directive.

The story of employee relations at this company shows that putting in place a consultation mechanism does not in itself necessarily give employees an effective 'voice'.

Eurotunnel has a 99-year lease to operate the Channel Tunnel link between Britain and France, running freight trains and maintaining the infrastructure. It consists of two legal entities for the UK and France and employs 3,400 staff, about 1,400 of them based in Britain on UK contracts.

To harmonise the workforce, it set up a company council for UK-contracted employees in December 1992, broadly similar to the French comité d'entreprise. Until June 2000, Eurotunnel (UK) recognised only the company council for consultation. This had one representative and one deputy elected from each of eight constituencies including: Technical Engineering, Shuttle Services, Tourist Division, Train Crew, Freight Division, Corporate (Administration), Technical Railway and the Call Centre.

With the introduction of the Employment Relations Act in 1999, the company signed a recognition and partnership agreement with the Transport and General Workers Union (TGWU) to cover all non-managerial staff. This conferred negotiation rights, confirmed the acceptance of the existing consultation framework and established a joint management – trade union forum. As a result, there are two representation structures: a modified company council with eight representatives meeting six times a year and representing all employees and the joint trade union forum representing union members at Eurotunnel covering all issues of concern, with sole negotiating rights over UK pay and conditions.

The then director of HR indicated that the impetus for change was the threat of industrial action by train drivers in late 1999. This was considered important due to the company's £6.5 billion debt and the perishable nature of service delivery, as industrial action could potentially cost millions of pounds a day in lost revenue. It was felt by management that the legislation could be a catalyst for a number of diverse union arrangements within Eurotunnel, leading the company to opt for a single union agreement with the TGWU rather than a traditional rail union.

The author has conducted research at the company for five years using employee surveys, interviews and focus groups. Employees were surveyed before union recognition from December 1999 to January 2000, and 18 months after union recognition in December 2002, to find out their attitudes towards the company council and the trade union.

Over this period, the TGWU had some success in recruiting members and increasing its presence with some 35 per cent of employees in the second survey indicating they were a trade union member compared to only 12 per cent in the first survey. More than half of respondents in the second survey suggested they had an active union presence in their workplace compared to only 6 per cent from the first survey.

However, the second survey revealed the lack of progress the union had made with many employees suggesting that the trade union had not met their expectations. In the first survey there had been strong support for trade unions in all sections of Eurotunnel with the majority of workers suggesting that a trade union would improve their position over pay and benefits, work conditions, health and safety and employee grievances. For example, in relation to pay and benefits, just over 70 per cent of respondents suggested that trade unions would improve their position. There was a similar finding regarding work conditions, with three-quarters of employees suggesting that trade unions would improve their position over work conditions.

But in the second survey, less than a third of respondents suggested that the union was effective or very effective in representing general employee interests. Furthermore, when asked if the trade union had improved their position on pay and benefits, only around one in ten respondents agreed. This attitude was also reflected with other issues, such as work conditions, health and safety, training, individual grievances and job security.

While the TGWU ambitions and aims were understood and supported, it could be argued that this highlights the risks for trade unions when employees' expectations are unrealistic, which could potentially undermine the impact of unions and their effectiveness in the bargaining process. The vast majority of all respondents suggested that the company council should retain a consultation role even though they wanted union recognition. This view increased in the second survey. However, this is not a vote for the existing company council to replace unions, because nearly two-thirds of employees in both surveys stated that the company council was not effective in representing general employee interests either.

These findings would suggest that the previous company council (before recognition) could not be seen as a substitute for union representation, due to employees' perception of the limited role it played in the bargaining and decision-making processes. In general, it would seem that its prime focus was on information about performance or 'business' issues (improving quality, productivity, customer service and/or sales) rather than issues based on meeting workers' expectations. Managers also saw the company council as a means to communicate the benefits of change and to encourage the need for such change.

The research findings also seem to indicate that while the majority of employees were in favour of union recognition, they are not yet convinced that union representation alone will achieve greater benefits for them. Some employees at Eurotunnel would like the company council to be given greater powers to play an important part in representing the workforce, with its role ranging from an information channel on some issues to a genuine negotiating body on others.

The challenge for the union at Eurotunnel is that increased trade union membership and presence has not made the majority of employees more positive about union effectiveness – one could term this 'seduction without love'. The lack of belief in its ability to achieve traditional union objectives on pay, fairness, protection in disciplinary action, support in making a complaint and changes in employees' immediate workplace. Some respondents suggested they were best able to deal with such issues as individuals. The Eurotunnel employees' perception of a lack of effective union voice could undermine the union's influence on management. This could be seen as the challenge for partnership.

Given the devolution of decision-making in many organisations and the greater focus on employee commitment and effective organisational change, these findings are of particular interest. They suggest that if employers wish to encourage an alignment of interests between employee behaviour and organisational goals, they need to place greater emphasis on giving employees a real voice.

These findings are particularly important given the provisions of the European directive on information and consultation. The directive encourages a more formalised approach, expanding on existing information and consultation rights within enterprises.

The developments at Eurotunnel may signal difficulties for trade unions and employers in satisfying the requirements of the legislation. While the draft legislation and regulations reject a 'one-size-fits-all' approach, arrangements need to meet certain requirements. In particular, they set out processes that force employers to establish an information and consultation framework when a valid request has been initiated by 10 per cent of employees in a firm. If there are existing arrangements, 40 per cent or more must endorse the request in a ballot. If existing arrangements do not satisfy the directive's requirements, the employer must seek to reach a negotiated agreement with 'genuine employee representatives'.

Importantly for trade unions, these existing agreements must cover all the employees in a firm and cannot have been unilaterally imposed by management without discussion with employees and a chance for them to voice disapproval. In other words, 'sweetheart' deals with unions over the heads of employees are threatened.

Also important are the issues on which management must provide information and consult under the directive. They include the economic situation of the enterprise, the structure of and potential threat to employment, and, most significantly, 'decisions likely to lead to substantial changes in work organisation or in contractual relations', on which consultation must take place 'with a view to reaching agreement'. Consultation is defined as enabling information and consultation representatives (elected by all employees and not limited to trade union representatives) to put forward their views and to 'obtain a reasoned opinion from the employer'.

In my view, issues concerning 'contractual relations' may include rewards, such as performance related pay or career structures and procedures etc. 'Changes in work organisation' may also affect workplace restructuring such as teamwork systems. Consultation 'with a view to reaching agreement on decisions within the scope of the management's powers' may be little different to traditional trade union activities of collective bargaining. In addition, they do not provide any automatic participatory rights to union representatives who must stand for election alongside other non-union representatives. Potentially such arrangements may operate with, against, or in the absence of, union structures, threatening the traditional role of unions in collective bargaining.

Experience tells us that any representative structures within firms need to have full support of the majority of employees and to be seen as organic to the workplace rather then an imposed arrangement between management and trade unions. Without such a bottom-up approach, the legitimacy and respect for such arrangements will diminish, creating obstacles for developing meaningful dialogue and trust between management, staff and unions.

The clear message from this research and the requirements under the information and consultation directive is that a mechanism for communication between management and employees at the workplace may not be enough. Voice, the right to be heard and have a true say over workplace issues and at times an acknowledgement of differing interests may be essential for achieving greater employee satisfaction and commitment. These results would suggest that while trade unions may provide greater voice than non-union arrangements, the strength of voice is dependent on the legitimacy and effectiveness of trade unions in representing employees' interests at the workplace.

And that in turn depends on the union being perceived by the workforce as both representative and able to act independently. If it isn't, it will not meet the needs of either employees or management and could run the risk of being supplanted under the provisions of the new directive.

Questions

1. Why was the company council not a 'substitute' for union representation?

2. Can union–management partnership actually succeed? Why?

3. In what way/why could the process of union recognition be handled differently?

4. What can management do to increase union effectiveness?

5. Why could Eurotunnel employees' perception of a lack of effective union voice undermine the union's influence on management?

6. In what way could the new information and consultation legislation affect the union–employer partnership at Eurotunnel?

References

Ackers, P. and Payne, J. (1998) 'British trade unions and social partnership: rhetoric, reality and strategy', *International Journal of Human Resource Management*, Vol.9, pp.529–50.

Appelbaum, R. and Batt, R. (1994) *The New American Workplace*, Ithaca, NY: ILR Press.

*Bacon, N. (1999) 'Union derecognition and the new human relations: a steel industry case study', *Work, Employment and Society*, Vol.13, No.1, pp.1–17.

Bacon, N. (2003) 'Human resource management and industrial relations', in P. Ackers and A. Wilkinson (eds) *Understanding Work and Employment*, Oxford: Oxford University Press, pp.71–88.

Bacon, N. and Storey, J. (1996) 'Individualism and collectivism and the changing role of trade unions', in P. Ackers, C. Smith and P. Smith (eds) *The New Workplace and Trade Unionism*, London: Routledge, pp.1–40.

*Bacon, N. and Storey, J. (2000) 'New employee relations strategies: towards individualism or partnership', *British Journal of Industrial Relations*, Vol.38, No.3, pp.407–28.

Blyton, P. and Turnbull, P. (1994) *The Dynamics of Employee Relations,* Houndmills: Macmillan.

Bryson, A. (2004) 'Managerial responsiveness to union and nonunion worker voice in Britain', *Industrial Relations,* Vol.43, No.1, pp.213–42.

Claydon, T. (1989) 'Union de-recognition in Britain in the 1980s', *British Journal of Industrial Relations,* Vol.27, pp.214–23.

Clegg, H. (1979) *The System of Industrial Relations in Great Britain,* Oxford: Blackwell.

Cressey, P., Eldridge, J. and MacInnes, J. (1985) *Just Managing: Authority and Democracy in Industry,* Milton Keynes: Open University Press.

Cully, M. and Woodland, S. (1996) 'Trade Union membership and recognition: an analysis of data from the 1995 Labour Force Survey', *Labour Market Trends,* May, London: HMSO, pp.215–25.

Cully, M., Woodland, S., O'Reilly, A., Dix, G., Millward, N., Bryson, A. and Forth, J. (1998) *The 1998 Workplaces Employee Relations Survey: First Findings,* London: Department of Trade and Industry.

Cully, M., Woodland, S., O'Reilly, A. and Dix, G. (1999) *Britain at Work,* London: Routledge.

D'Art, D. and Turner, T. (1999) 'An attitudinal revolution in Irish industrial relations: the end of "them and us"?', *British Journal of Industrial Relations,* Vol.37, No.1, pp.101–16.

Dickson, T., McLachlan, M.V., Prior, P. and Swales, K. (1988). 'Big Blue and the Union: IBM, individualism and trade union strategy', *Work, Employment and Society,* Vol.2, pp.506–20.

DTI (1998) 'Fairness at Work', White Paper, London: HMSO.

Dunn, S. and Wright, M. (1994) 'Maintaining the "status quo": An analysis of the contents of British collective agreements 1979-1990', *British Journal of Industrial Relations,* Vol.32, pp.23–46.

Edwards, P. (1990). 'The politics of conflict and consent', *Journal of Economic Behaviour and Organization,* Vol.13, pp.41–61.

Edwards, P. (1995) 'The employment relationship', in P. Edwards (ed.) *Industrial Relations,* Oxford: Blackwell, pp.3–26.

Edwards, P., Hau, M., Hyman, R., Marginson, P., Sisson, K., Waddington, J. and Winchester, D. (1998) 'Great Britain: from partial collectivism to neo-liberalism to where?', in A. Ferner and R. Hyman (eds) *Changing Industrial Relations in Europe,* Oxford: Blackwell, pp.1–54.

Flanders, A. (1970) *Management and Unions: The Theory and Reform of Industrial Relations,* London: Faber.

Foulkes, F. K. (1980) *Personnel Policies in Large Non-union Companies,* Englewood Cliffs, NJ: Prentice Hall.

Fox, A. (1966) *Industrial Sociology and Industrial Relations,* Royal Commission Research Paper No.3, London: HMSO.

Fox, A. (1974) *Beyond Contract: Work, Power and Trust Relations,* London: Faber and Faber.

Freeman, R.B. and Medoff, J.L. (1984) *What Do Unions Do?,* New York: Basic Books.

Gall, G. (2004) 'Trade union recognition in Britain, 1995–2002: turning a corner?', *Industrial Relations Journal,* Vol.35, No.3, forthcoming.

Gall, G. and McKay, S. (1994) 'Trade union de-recognition in Britain 1988–94', *British Journal of Industrial Relations,* Vol.32, pp.433–48.

Geary, J. (1995) 'Work practices: the structure of work', in P. Edwards (ed.) *Industrial Relations,* Oxford: Blackwell, pp.368–96.

Guest, D. (1987) 'Human resource management and industrial relations', *Journal of Management Studies,* Vol.24, No.5, pp.503–21.

Guest, D. (1989) 'Human resource management: its implications for industrial relations and trade unions', in J. Storey (ed.) *New Perspectives on Human Resource Management: a critical text,* London: Routledge, pp.41–55.

Guest, D. (1990) 'Human resource management and the American Dream', *Journal of Management Studies,* Vol.27, No.4, pp.378–97.

Guest, D. (1995) 'Human resource management, trade unions and industrial relations', in J. Storey (ed.) *Human Resource Management: A Critical Text,* London: Routledge, pp.110–41.

*Guest, D. and Conway, N. (1999) 'Peering into the black hole: the downside of the new employment relations in the UK', *British Journal of Industrial Relations,* Vol.37, No.3, pp.367–89.

Guest, D. and Hoque, K. (1994) 'The Good, The Bad and the Ugly: employment relations in new non-union workplaces', *Human Resource Management Journal*, Vol.5, pp.1–14.

*Guest, D.E. and Peccei, R. (2001) 'Partnership at work: mutuality and the balance of advantage', *British Journal of Industrial Relations*, Vol.39, No.2, pp.207–36.

Heery, E. (1996) 'The new new unionism', in I. Beardwell (ed.) *Contemporary Industrial Relations*, Oxford: Oxford University Press, pp.175–202.

Heery, E. (1998) 'The re-launch of the Trades Union Congress', *British Journal of Industrial Relations*, Vol.36, pp.339–60.

Hirschman, A. (1971) *Exit, Voice and Loyalty*, Cambridge, MA.: Harvard University Press.

Hyman, R. (1987) 'Strategy or structure? capital, labour and control', *Work, Employment and Society*, Vol.1, No.1, pp.25–55.

Hyman, R. (1997) 'The future of employee representation', *British Journal of Industrial Relations*, Vol.35, No.3, pp.309–36.

IDS (1998) *Partnership Agreements. IDS Study 656, October,* London: IDS.

Institute of Directors (1994) Evidence presented to the Employment Committee Enquiry, *The Future of Trade Unions*, HMSO, HC 676-II, London: HMSO.

Involvement and Participation Association (1992) *Towards Industrial Partnership: A New Approach to Management Union Relations*, London: IPA.

IPD (1997) *Employment Relations into the Twenty-first Century*, London: Institute of Personnel and Development.

IRS (1997) Partnership at work: a survey, *Employment Trends*, Vol.645, December, pp.3–24.

Kelly, J. (1996). 'Union militancy and social partnership', in P. Ackers, C. Smith and P. Smith (eds) *The New Workplace and Trade Unionism*, London: Routledge, pp.41–76.

Kelly, J. (2004) 'Social partnership agreements in Britain: labour cooperation and compliance', *Industrial Relations*, Vol.43, No.1, pp.267–92.

Kelly, J. and C. Kelly (1991) 'Them and us: social psychology and the "new industrial relations"', *British Journal of Industrial Relations*, Vol.29, No.1, pp.25–48.

Kitay, J. and Marchington, M. (1996) 'A review and critique of workplace industrial relations typologies', *Human Relations*, Vol.49, No.10, pp.1263–90.

Kochan, T. and Osterman, P. (1994) *The Mutual Gains Enterprise*, Cambridge, MA: Harvard Business School Press.

Kochan, T., Katz, H. and McKersie, B. (1986) *The Transformation of American Industrial Relations*, New York: Basic Books.

Machin, S. (2000) 'Union decline in Britain', *British Journal of Industrial Relations*, Vol.38, No.4, pp.631–45.

Marchington, M. and Parker, P. (1990) *Changing Patterns of Employee Relations*, Hemel Hempstead: Harvester Wheatsheaf.

*Marks, A., Findlay, P., Hine, J., McKinlay, A. and Thompson, P. (1998) 'The politics of partnership? innovation in employment relations in the Scottish spirits industry', *British Journal of Industrial Relations*, Vol.36, No.2, pp.209–26.

McLoughlin, I. and Gourlay, S. (1994) *Enterprise Without Unions: Industrial Relations in the Non-Union Firm*, Milton Keynes: Open University Press.

Millward, N., Stevens, M., Smart, D. and Hawes, W.R. (1992) *Workplace Industrial Relations in Transition*, Dartmouth: Aldershot.

Monks, J. (1998) 'Trade unions, enterprise and the future', in P. Sparrow and M. Marchington (eds) *Human Resource Management: The New Agenda*, London: Pitman, pp.171–9.

Oxenbridge, S., Brown, W., Deakin, S. and Pratten, C. (2003) 'Initial responses to the Statutory Recognition Provisions of the Employment Relations Act 1999', *British Journal of Industrial Relations*, Vol.41, No.2, pp.315–34,

Poole, M. and Mansfield, R. (1993) 'Patterns of continuity and change in managerial attitudes and behaviour in industrial relations 1980–90', *British Journal of Industrial Relations*, Vol.31, No.1, pp.11–36.

Purcell, J. (1982) 'Macho managers and the new industrial relations', *Employee Relations*, Vol.4, No.1, pp.3–5.

Purcell, J. (1993) 'The end of institutional industrial relations', *Political Quarterly*, Vol.64, pp.6–23.

Purcell, J. (1987). 'Mapping management styles in employee relations', *Journal of Management Studies*, Vol.24, No.5, pp.533–48.

Purcell, J. (1991) 'The rediscovery of management prerogative: the management of labour relations in the 1980s', *Oxford Review of Economic Policy*, Vol.7, No.1, pp.33–43.

Purcell, J. (1993) 'The end of institutional industrial relations', *Political Quarterly*, Vol.64, No.1, pp.6–23.

Purcell, J. and Ahlstrand, B. (1994) *Human Resource Management in the Multi-Divisional Company*, Oxford: Oxford University Press.

Purcell, J. and Sisson, K. (1983) 'Strategies and practice in the management of industrial relations', in G. Bain (ed.) *Industrial Relations in Britain*, Oxford: Blackwell.

Ramsey, H. (1975) 'Firms and football teams', *British Journal of Industrial Relations*, Vol.13, No.3, pp.396–400.

Roy, D. (1980) 'Fear stuff, sweet stuff and evil stuff: management's defences against unionization in the south', in T. Nichols (ed.) *Capital and Labour: A Marxist Primer*, Glasgow: Fontana, pp.395–415.

Schnabel, C. (2003) 'Determinants of trade union membership', in J.T. Addison and C. Schnabel (eds) *International Handbook of Trade Unions*, Cheltenham: Edward Elgar, pp.13–43.

Scott, A. (1994) *Willing Slaves?*, Cambridge: Cambridge University Press.

Sisson, K. (1989) 'Personnel management in transition?', in K. Sisson (ed.) *Personnel Management in Britain*, Oxford: Blackwell.

Sisson, K. (1993) 'In search of HRM', *British Journal of Industrial Relations*, Vol.31, No.2, pp.201–10.

Sisson, K. (1994) *Personnel Management*, Oxford: Blackwell.

Sisson, K. (1995) 'Human resource management and the personnel function', in J. Storey (ed.) *Human Resource Management: A Critical Text*, London: Routledge, pp.87–109.

Sisson, K. and Marginson, P. (1995) 'Management: systems, structures and strategy', in P. Edwards (ed.) *Industrial Relations*, Oxford: Blackwell, 89–122.

*Sisson, K. and Storey, J. (2000) *The Realities of Human Resource Management*, Buckingham: Open University Press.

Smith, P. and Morton, G. (1993) 'Union exclusion and decollectivization of industrial relations in contemporary Britain', *British Journal of Industrial Relations*, Vol.31, No.1, pp.97–114.

Storey, J. (1989) *New Perspectives on Human Resource Management*, London: Routledge.

Storey, J. (1992) *Developments in the Management of Human Resources*, Oxford: Blackwell.

Storey, J. (1995) *Human Resource Management: A Critical Text*, London: Routledge.

Storey, J. and Bacon, N. (1993) 'Individualism and collectivism: into the 1990s', *International Journal of Human Resource Management*, Vol.4, No.3, pp.665–84.

Storey, J. and Sisson, K. (1993) *Managing Human Resources and Industrial Relations*, Milton Keynes: Open University Press.

Storey, J., Bacon, N., Edmonds, J. and Wyatt, P. (1993) 'The "new agenda" and human resource management: a roundtable discussion with John Edmonds', *Human Resource Management Journal*, Vol.4, No.1, pp.63–70.

Towers, B. (1997) *The Representation Gap*, Oxford: Oxford University Press.

TUC (1993) Evidence presented to the Employment Committee Enquiry, *The Future of Trade Unions*, HMSO, HC 676-II, London: HMSO.

Undy, R. (1999) 'Annual review article: New Labour's "Industrial Relations Settlement": the Third Way?', *British Journal of Industrial Relations*, Vol.37, No.2, pp.315–36.

Visser, J. (2003) 'Unions and unionism around the world', in J.T. Addison and C. Schnabel (eds) *International Handbook of Trade Unions*, Cheltenham: Edward Elgar: 366–414.

Waddington, J. and Whitston, C. (1997) 'Why do people join unions in a period of membership decline?', *British Journal of Industrial Relations*, Vol.35, No.4, pp.515–46.

Wood, S. (1997) *Statutory Union Recognition*, London: Institute of Personnel and Development.

Wood, S. and Godard, J. (1999) 'The statutory union recognition procedure in the Employment Relations Bill: a comparative analysis', *British Journal of Industrial Relations*, Vol.37, pp.203–44.

* Useful reading

Chapter 8

LINE MANAGERS

Douglas Renwick

BACKGROUND

The involvement of line managers in HR work seems such a common occurrence in work organisations today that it is perhaps seen as an (obvious) core part of an HRM approach to the employment relationship. The logic of why line managers are used in HRM seems simple: they are closest to employees and customers and occupy a key role in the general management job of managing people. This includes them having some input into communicating, motivating, rewarding, disciplining and releasing people at work. HR specialists are therefore left to form policies and procedures in HRM and engage in the more strategic and complex parts of HR work (e.g., employment law). But research in the field of line manager involvement in HRM has revealed that numerous issues appear – calling into question the assumptions contained in the thinking above. This chapter aims to unravel some of the developments, questions and challenges that surround involving line managers in HRM in a pragmatic fashion, and contains cases to test student's knowledge in this field. This chapter proceeds by reviewing developments in the relevant literature and questions arising from it. This is followed by outlining some challenges the key stakeholders face by involving line managers in HRM. Some ideas for future research are then discussed, and then some conclusions are put forward.

DEFINITION

Line managers are defined by some as those who engage in 'general management work – rather than being specialists in a particular functional area, like HRM, marketing or sales' (Legge 1995). But different studies focus on different types of manager working at different work levels in the literature. For example, some studies have examined the role of middle managers (Fenton-O'Creevy 1998, 2001; Currie and Procter 2001), the role of front line and first line managers (Storey 1992), supervisors (Lowe 1992), and/or both of these groups in HRM (Marchington 2001). Differences also exist in terms of what aspects of HRM these managers work on (which are examined later in this chapter), and other differences include how line managers engage in HRM, as different authors use different terms. For example, 'involvement' is used by some (Marsh and Gillies 1983; Gibb 2003; Renwick 2003), and

Table 8.1 Why do work organisations want to involve line managers in HRM?

1. Pressure on firm costs to include the management of people in a line role
2. To provide a more comprehensive HRM: which is arguably best achieved by including HR responsibilities with those (line) managers responsible for them
3. The growing influence of the service industries, where responsibility for customer management is most sensibly placed with the manager responsible
4. That waiting for HR specialists to handle HR issues may be too slow
5. Changes in philosophy and organisational structure, where 'devolution' may be an alternative to outsourcing the HR function

Source: Adapted from Larsen and Brewster 2003

'responsibility' is used by others (Thornhill and Saunders 1998; Larsen and Brewster 2003; Whittaker and Marchington 2003).

RATIONALE

The reasons why line managers are perhaps most 'involved' in HRM is linked to the issue of devolution. In recent years the line's involvement in HRM has been more noticeable as HR work has been specifically 'devolved' to them (Storey 1992, 2001; Ulrich 1997, 1998, 2001; Brewster and Larsen 2000; Currie and Procter 2001; Guest and King 2001). Some of the thinking behind line involvement in HRM is illustrated in Table 8.1.

But involving line managers in managing people in the UK is not a totally new development. There has always been a notion that line managers have had responsibility and accountability for managing people at work (Marsh and Gillies 1983; Guest 1987; Storey 1992; Legge 1995). However it is the greater degree of line involvement in the HRM in the UK today (due in part to the devolution of some HR work to the line) that seems to make the headlines. For example:

> The shift of responsibility to the line as opposed to personnel departments has been overstated. To be sure, at least in respect of *actual practice*, the pattern in Britain at least seems to be typically one of line dominance, but this has almost certainly been historically the case rather than it representing a new wave or a 'new movement' associated with the rise of HRM itself (Poole and Jenkins 1997, pp.353–4).

Indeed, some research studies in the literature have recognised that the increased role of non-specialist managers in HRM is a subject worthy of discussion in its own right (see Cully *et al.* 1999; Millward *et al.* 2000). But while the complexities that surround the devolution of HR work to the line may well seem to serve only in clouding our understanding of the role of involving line managers in HRM, some clear developments in the literature on this topic can be identified. These are now outlined.

Developments in the literature

THE EUROPEAN DIMENSION

Brewster and Larsen (1992) found that devolution to the line in the UK and Ireland was low compared to other EU states, and this was confirmed in the update to this work nearly a decade later in Larsen and Brewster (2003). However, the latter study found that although there are moves across the EU to hand the line more responsibility for staff management, the extent of line autonomy varies by subject (in recruitment and selection, health and safety, and expansion/reduction of workforce numbers). They argue that the most frequent pattern is of shared responsibilities between HR and the line, with many organisations still very centralised in a lot of aspects of HRM. However, they also state that anecdotal evidence suggests that the line do not accept devolution willingly, and neither do HR (Brewster and Larsen 2000).

The dominant pattern across Europe (the EU) is of sharing HR work between HR and the line (Brewster and Larsen 2000) and this has continued up to and including some of the most recently published studies in the field (Larsen and Brewster 2003). Indeed, the latter study is interesting as it examines developments in this field in the EU for nearly the last decade.[1] Two parts of their study stand out. First, what they call 'differences in assignment' or what we might label as changes in *who* is doing *what*? Their findings are summarised in the following Tables 8.2 and 8.3.

As we can see, in the three areas of pay, training and Industrial Relations (IR), line management responsibility for them has increased, and has also increased for most of the other EU states reported here, with only Denmark (DK) showing a slightly lower growth rate

Table 8.2 % change in responsibility of line management over 3 years to 1999/2000

	D	F	UK	E	DK	Fin
For pay						
Increased	18	32	22	25	31	31
Decreased	3	2	5	4	6	5
For training						
Increased	34	48	47	40	31	41
Decreased	4	1	5	7	11	5
For IR						
Increased	13	23	24	14	24	23
Decreased	4	4	4	10	8	6

Key: IR = Industrial Relations

Table 8.3 A decade of assignment rankings for European countries (1991–2000)

	Least devolved								Most devolved			
1991	I	UK	F	E	D	NL		S	CH		DK	
1992	Irl	F	UK	E	D	N	NL	S	P	Fin	DK	
1995	E	UK	F	Irl	D	NL		N	S	Fin	DK	
1999 / 2000	F	I	Irl	E	UK	P D	T	S	CH N	NL	DK	Fin

Legend: Germany (D), France (Fr), United Kingdom (UK), Spain (E), Denmark (DK), Finland (Fin), Italy (I), Ireland (Irl), Portugal (P), Turkey (T), Switzerland (CH), Norway (N), Netherlands (NL), and Sweden (S).

Source: Tables 8.2 and 8.3 copyright of Larsen and Brewster 2003. Reproduced with permission

---

[1] Their study is based on survey data from the Cranet-E survey, which covered 22 countries, drawing on a sample of 4,050 respondents (see Larsen and Brewster 2003).

in training, and Spain (E) showing a lower one in IR. The authors also detail a second area of interest, what they call 'assignment rankings', which are the levels of devolution of HR work to the line. These are represented in Table 8.3.

As we can see from Table 8.3, the Nordic states of Denmark and Finland are the ones that have devolved the most HR work to the line in the EU, while France and Spain are at the least devolved end, along with Italy. The UK and Ireland continue to practice relatively low levels of devolution. The authors concluded their study stating that in the EU:

> There is a clear evidence here of a convergence of trends – the movement to a greater assignment of HRM responsibilities to line managers. However, there is also evidence that the comparative position of the countries has not changed in a decade; and that could be taken as evidence, if not of divergence, then at least of stasis (Larsen and Brewster 2003, pp.240–1).

THE UK

Line managers have always been involved in managing people at work in the UK, especially since trade union influence decreased in the 1980s and 1990s, as this trend gave line managers increased ability to re-assert their prerogative to improve organisational performance via the manipulation and control of the labour resource. Although, as we have just seen, devolution to the line in the UK is still comparatively low when compared to the practices of other European countries, the extensive Workplace Employee Relations Survey of 1998 (WERS '98)[2] notes that in the handling of employee relations issues, line managers outnumber employee relations specialists at British workplaces (Millward *et al.* 2000, pp.52–3). Thus some empirical research in Britain has found a key role for the line in handling some HR work, notably in the area of employee relations. This development was reflected in the language writers used in the HR literature in Britain and North America from the mid to late 1990s onwards, of 'partnerships' being formed between HR and the line (Hutchinson and Wood 1995; Eisenstat 1996; Ulrich 1997, 1998, 2001), so that HR could 'add value' and 'deliver results' for work organisations (Ulrich 1997, 1998). At this time, cost/benefit analyses of devolution were also detailed (Storey 2001; Sisson and Storey 2000), but the main thinking here was that the line should engage in HR processes, which span 'boundaries outside the organisation', where 'they have freedom to experiment rather than being excluded from decision making' (Currie and Procter 2001, p.57).

Specific developments in the UK

In the UK, studies in the field have (historically) revealed that chief production managers did not view themselves as formal negotiators between management and unions. Instead, they wanted to pass personnel and industrial relations (IR) activity onto factory administrators as they considered it an inefficient use of their time (Marsh 1971, p.22). These managers did recognise that IR work was a discrete part of their workload, but preferred to rely on the advice given to them by personnel/IR specialists – even though they were not keen to be directed by them (Marsh and Gillies 1983, pp.32–8). Such ambiguity by managers towards managing people is still seen today. Lynch (2003) for example examines the role managers play in the recruitment and selection of new staff. She quotes one retail store manager saying:

> The least flexible workers are women with children who have child-care restrictions. It is a difficult decision when recruiting new staff and you are faced with a very capable person

---

[2]WERS '98 refers to the 1998 Workplace Employee Relations Survey.

who can do the job well, but will be limited in the flexibility which they can offer. It is a big issue and if you do offer them a job you usually end up shooting yourself in the foot (Store manager, HomeCo).

Hence the line's role in the recruitment and selection of new staff is not always a positive one. The keenness of line managers to rely on the advice specialist HR managers can offer them in HRM is particularly notable in the area of performance management and appraisal. Harris (2001, pp.1182–90) notes managers disliking the 'bureaucracy' that surrounds such initiatives which may lead managers to engage in 'abdication management', i.e., being reluctant to accept responsibility for decisions they have made regarding people's performance. Similarly, Redman's (2001) work saw the line rating themselves highly in performance appraisal (even though it is perhaps one of the managerial activities they wish they could avoid doing), but concluded that they tend not to do it very well. In addition, Guest and King (2001, p.26) find that managers tend not to do performance management properly, unless they receive a 'kick' to do so.

That the line give the impression of taking a 'learning by doing' approach to HRM is seen in the way they train and develop others. Brewster and Larsen (1992) for example found the line using such experiential approaches. Some managers seem to go a little further and argue that training in HRM is not necessarily needed for them to gain expertise in HRM. Thus:

Most of this is common sense anyway. We have had some training, but when an issue comes up it's always in an area were you have had no preparation . . . you can deal with it if you consider matters carefully . . . If I went for a personnel manager's job, I would know what to do . . . I have had no formal training in these matters – it has just been on-the-job experience using manuals (managers quoted in Cunningham and Hyman 1995, p.18).

However, Gibb's (2003) review and analysis of the notion of 'managers as developers' found that specialist HR advice is still needed by the line, as he argues that there is a need to re-align work, organisation and management in an era where Knowledge Management (KM) comes to the fore. Indeed, MacNeil's (2003) review and analysis of line managers as facilitators of sharing knowledge in teams reveals that line managers may play a role in 'capturing' employees' tacit knowledge, which may be able to be transferred into specific organisational competencies. But understanding what the barriers to the transfer of tacit knowledge between individuals and teams are, and the skills the line will need to develop to take on a facilitator role, both need development. There is also a need for greater understanding of the role of the line in the field of the development and assessment of management and employee skills. This may contain a gender dimension, as Green and James' (2003, p.63) study found that in cases where the manager is male and the worker female 'there is a tendency for the boss to underestimate and/or the worker to overestimate their skill level by comparison with other gender combinations'.

In employee involvement (EI), research by Fenton-O'Creevy (1998, p.67) found 'middle-management resistance' producing less positive outcomes in EI, and in a later study (2001), he found that in failing EI schemes, senior managers may be blaming middle managers for their demise, while middle managers may view any resistance to change as a 'pragmatic adaptation' (Fenton-O'Creevy 2001, pp.24, 38). Marchington's (2001) work on EI revealed a series of 'unintended impacts' from involving non-specialist managers in EI. These include a lack of commitment and ability in it, some deficiencies in training and time to do it, and some scepticism about why it needs to be done. This sense of line expediency towards some aspects of HR work may also be seen in grievance and discipline cases. One study by Rollinson *et al.* (1996) found that HR managers had been asked to 'sit in' on these meetings because they were needed to 'police' the practices of line managers so that good outcomes emerged, and IRS (2001) found that the line were less involved than their HR counterparts in taking responsibility for disciplinary procedures.

That the line are being given more scope in some areas of HRM is apparent in the area of pay. Currie and Procter (2001, pp.58–9, 63–6) found that greater discretion was being given to the line in 'implementing' HR strategies, and that they had a key role in 'synthesising information'. But other studies still indicate a lack of line enthusiasm to the operation of performance-related pay schemes. Harris' (2001, p.1184) study for example found that there is a 'lack of ownership of the processes of performance-related pay' by some line managers, and that the line view HR in a negative light by trying to introduce such changes, as they feel it may result in work overload for line managers.

The limitations of line involvement in HRM are perhaps sharply illustrated in the work of Cunningham, James and Dibben (2004) on how the line manage long-term sickness and disability cases. They found that there was a lack of line willingness to attend training in this area, that what training that was provided was inadequate, and that the line were being asked to handle some cases in it without specialist HR help. Similar findings appeared in absence management, as Dunn and Wilkinson's (2002, p.245) study found that some organisations had an 'ad hoc' approach to it, with unclear responsibilities, resulting in 'muddling through' in some instances. Even trying to use new technologies in HRM to provide HR services to the line (like HR call centres and e-HR) has seen some commentators noting limitations. Issues like a lack of line willingness to take on extra HR work was noted at Marks and Spencer, and the affect using such technologies was seen to have an effect on line manager perceptions of their workloads at British Nuclear Fuels (Deeks 2000).

That difficulties occur for the line in HRM are perhaps exacerbated in cases where the devolution of specific HR tasks to the line has taken place. Lynch (2003) for example found a department manager in retailing arguing that in employee development:

> All the staff now have Personal Development Planners to improve the level and standards of training and development. But we just don't have the time to sit down with staff to work through them, so they're often just ignored (Department manager, GroceryCo).

Indeed, Whittaker and Marchington's (2003) study found that senior line managers had been given more HR responsibilities, but they still wanted specialist help from HR, as they found doing HRM difficult as other business pressures took priority. They conclude that while 'partnership' working between HR and the line is a useful way to tackle such problems, firms may lose long-term strategic advantage if the line are asked to take on more HR work alone.

But what of the views of line managers themselves on their role in HRM? Renwick's (2003) empirical study gave some detail here, and a summary of some of the views of line managers towards doing HR work is detailed in Table 8.4 from his work.

SUMMARY

This review has identified that the lack of capability and commitment to HRM by line managers identified by Brewster and Larsen (1992) still resonates today, as do the costs and benefits of greater line involvement in HRM. Both are presented in Table 8.5.

The studies mentioned in the review above can perhaps be used to paint a picture of line manager involvement in HRM being characterised by their reluctance and unwillingness to do specific HR-related tasks, and their lack of ownership, capacity and amateurism, along with a general scepticism from them towards doing such tasks. However, another picture also emerges of the factors that inhibit the line from displaying their knowledge and skills in the HR field. These include a lack of training and time to prepare in it, the conflicting demands placed on them by senior managers, colleagues and employees in it, the lack of visible help towards them from HR, and the pressing need for them to deliver on the business targets they

Table 8.4 Case findings scorecard on line manager involvement in HRM

Positives
- The line are taking on responsibility and accountability in HR work.
- Flexibility is forthcoming from the line to do HR work.
- The line are keen to take part on doing HR work.
- The line are managing large numbers of employees.
- The line take a professional and serious attitude to doing HR work.
- Line managers are relatively happy doing some HR work.
- The line are considerate of employee needs and wishes.
- The line see HR as positive helpers in HR work.
- The line see career benefits for them in doing HR work.

Negatives
- The line have many duties, and lack time to do HR work well.
- The line don't see themselves as experts in HRM.
- Doing HR work dilutes the line's generalist managerial focus.
- Significant line inadequacies exist when handling HR duties.
- Tensions between line and HR over transfer and completion of HR duties.
- The line need to reflect and be critical of their performance in HR work.
- The line are reliant on HR to do HR work properly.
- Differing line commitment and discipline levels to doing HRM.
- The line have responsibility and accountability in HRM, but little authority.
- Little appreciation of line flexibility in doing HR tasks from firms.

General
- The line want reciprocity from HR to deliver business targets if the line do HR work.

Table 8.5 Benefits and costs of adopting more line manager involvement in HRM

Benefits of adoption
- HR problems are solved at source.
- Better change management is achieved.
- Increased speed of decision making.
- More scope for HR managers to focus on strategic HRM.
- HR issues receive a business focus.
- Line managers 'own' HR issues, are aware of them and thus can't ignore them.
- Line managers are more likely to be committed to their 'own' HR decisions.
- Promotes local management accountability and responsibility for HR issues.
- Reduces costs.
- Promotes the case that HRM can't always be transferred to specialists.

Costs of adoption
- Increased pressure to train and/or re-skill line managers in HRM.
- A need for strict HR auditing.
- Problems in maintaining consistency in decision making.
- Risk of falling standards, or abuse of position (discrimination).
- Problems in maintaining balance of power between line and HR specialists.
- Potential for the HR/ER management role to be marginalised.
- Low line capability/commitment when doing HR work.
- Little time for line to perform HR duties well due to operational demands on them.
- Risks of job overload/stress as line manager workloads are increased.

Source: Adapted from various authors (see Renwick 2003). Republished with permission, Emerald Group Publishing Limited (www.emeraldinsight.com)

have been set. So, from a line viewpoint, any inconsistencies that may emerge from their role in HRM are perhaps predictable, and not solely due to their own intransigence in HRM. Hence these are some of the reasons why some line managers may subscribe to the following kinds of negative stereotypes of HR managers that appear in the literature:

> If personnel specialists are not passive administrative nobodies who pursue their social work, go-between and fire-fighting vocations with little care for business decisions and leadership, then they are clever, ambitious power seekers who want to run organisations as a kind of self-indulgent personnel playground (Watson 1986, p.204).

General questions arising

The literature reviewed above highlights some important questions regarding line manager involvement in HRM. In addition to the issues of line capability and commitment in HRM that have dominated the literature in the last decade (Brewster and Larsen 2000; Larsen and Brewster 2003), the pressure on the line to focus on the 'hard stuff', the 'numbers' has increased (Whittaker and Marchington 2003). This circumstance has left some line managers having to complete operational tasks (like managing a team, delivering to customer expectations and maintaining high-quality product) and HR tasks as well (like performance appraisal, training/development, employee relations and pay and reward). It is difficult to imagine such non-specialist (line) managers doing all of these tasks equally well. So a question arises as to which tasks they see as their priority, and what effects the choices they make have in terms of HRM in general, and on employee well-being (EWB) in particular.

Some studies are quite positive on such questions, and note the role of the line in making HR strategies 'come to life' (Hutchinson and Purcell 2003; Purcell *et al.* 2003). For example, Lazenby argues that at the Nationwide:

> Our research has demonstrated that line manager behaviour has a significant impact on employee commitment, which has an impact on customer commitment, which has an impact on business performance (Lazenby, quoted in Hutchinson and Purcell 2003, p.55).

But other studies question the logic of making such connections (Renwick 2003), or argue that there are significant limitations in trying to make such connections in practice, as they reveal that involving line managers in HRM makes for poorer organisational performance in general terms (Gibb 2001). Moreover, others like Gratton *et al.* (1999) argue that the incentives for the line to develop people at work need to be thought through, while other studies have found that line managers tend to 'marginalize, under-use and under-develop part-timers' (Edwards and Robinson 2001). In addition, some subordinates mention line incapability in HRM as a significant and specific factor contributing to explaining why they left their old jobs (Taylor 2002).

Specific questions emerging

THE UTILITY OF HR MODELS

That better outcomes in corporate performance and employee well-being are not necessarily guaranteed from more use of the line in HRM perhaps serves as a reminder to us to question some models of HRM that have line involvement in HRM at their core. For example, Jackson and Schuler's (2000) American 'HR triad' model of HR, the line and employees all working together to generate increased organisational performance, perhaps looks like an 'ideal type' when contrasted with some of the results on line involvement in HRM in the UK. Two problems seem to emerge. First, that HR specialists do not necessarily give useful advice to the line in HRM (Guest *et al.* 2001, p.67). Second, that line managers themselves may be putting a brake on achieving such outcomes by their incapability and lack of commitment in HRM (Harris 2001; Redman 2001; Cunningham *et al.* 2004). A specific question arising from the literature here is whether line managers do act in a professional way when doing HR work, especially in terms of how they treat one employee compared to another. The over-riding impression from the research studies (above) is that this question is still unanswered (Cunningham and Hyman 1999; Marchington 1999; Budhwar 2000), and that more work needs to be done to give greater insight here.

HR, THE LINE AND EMPLOYEES

Whether there are specific disputes going on between HR and the line in terms of who does what in HRM is not something that we can make much comment on, as we have little empirical work in this area. What work does exist on such intra-management work relations tends to tread the sort of 'partnership' line of Jackson and Schuler (2000) above (Hutchinson and Wood 1995, for example; see Currie and Procter 2001). But increased rewards and career development for employees do certainly seem to be the sorts of decisions that line managers take, and they need to have more skills in HRM to make informed choices here (Tyson and Fell 1995; Marchington 1999). So, from an employee perspective, that HR managers may want to 'give up' responsibility for the more operational side of HR work may be a big issue. This is because a (relative) lack of line skill in HRM may have negative consequences for employees. Thus the dynamics of intra-management work relations need to be assessed because they have the potential to decide how people are managed and treated at work. Auditing line skills in HRM may be one way forward to determine the effects of line capability and commitment in HRM. Other options include 'giving' the more operational aspects of HR work back to HR specialists if the outcomes the line produce in HRM prove to be poor ones in years to come.

LINE CAREERS

The effects of increasing line manager involvement in HRM on the careers of line managers themselves needs assessing. One study has revealed some tensions arising with HR managers from greater line involvement in HRM due to HR work being seen to belong only in the HR domain (Bach 1995). It may be tempting to view this as an example of the beginning of a 'turf war' between HR and the line in HRM – as some line groups have historically held HR work in disdain as low-status, low-paid work – and not something to either be associated with, never mind involved in (Renwick 2000). This is the 'Cinderella' tag for HR that appears in many textbooks on HRM. But this line view of HR may have altered, as recent developments that have charted the rise of 'partnerships' between HR and the line could be used to state that the line now view HR and HR work in a more positive light. Further work is needed here to support such an interpretation. Either way, we need to assess exactly what rewards and career development the line get from doing more HRM, and if the line feel that doing more HR work makes them 'generalist' managers. We need to know if this new role for them is one they embrace or fear, as they feel it makes them more easy to replace. We need an answer to the question of whether they feel that doing HR work is one step for them on the road to redundancy, or (in the context of the de-layering of some middle management jobs in general), it is one step on the road to recovery for them. In short, does doing HR work give the line new skill sets and a new expert knowledge-base to add to their portfolio, and does having such knowledge and skills make them more marketable?

TOWARDS MORE LINE INVOLVEMENT IN HRM?

In the literature, some chief executives are positive about increased line manager involvement in HRM as they see it as 'good people management' (Guest and King 2001, p.25). So whether the line are keen on doing more HR work or not, their increased involvement in HRM seems to be with us in some firms for the immediate period, as their senior managers take the strategic choice of viewing it as a useful way of managing people at work. This impression is further reinforced by the number of cases reported in the literature (earlier) where increased line involvement in HRM has occurred in recent years (Hutchinson and Purcell 2003; Larsen and Brewster 2003; Purcell *et al.* 2003). Such recent increased involvement by the line in HRM follows a pattern of involvement by non-specialist managers in the UK mentioned earlier (Marsh and Gillies 1983).

But whether involving line managers more in HRM is a good thing may well be a debatable matter, as the specific contingencies of different work contexts seem to account for a lot here. For example, people may be managed poorly in work organisations that have moved to full devolution of HRM to the line, or those that have no HR specialist employed to 'police' line practices in HRM – which may be the case in some small to medium-sized enterprises (SMEs). Alternatively, the people management practices found in SMEs may be better than in larger firms. This may be because as line managers in SME environments may know their employees very well, they may be better able to motivate them, and to communicate with them. Similarly, SME firms may be more successful in creating a family atmosphere that some workers respond to. We need more data to draw more definitive conclusions here. But what data does exist reminds us to be cautious. There is one striking feature in all of the research studies in the literature reviewed above, and this is that there are very few examples of the 'excellent' outcomes that involving line managers in HRM has produced, or many quotes of the 'my great boss' sort from employees!

Challenges

EMPLOYEE WELL-BEING

A key challenge for line managers doing HR work is to deliver organisational targets and to pay the requisite attention to the needs of employees who help them deliver such targets. As non-specialist managers are the largest group who handle employee relations issues in the UK (Millward *et al.* 2000, pp.52–3), they have a key role in maintaining employee well-being. But in doing so, the line are perhaps stuck between a rock and a hard place. They need to balance requests from their employer to make employees subject to strict performance criteria to help deliver increasing customer expectations. But they also need to develop people at work as resourceful humans to ensure that they are motivated, have some form of job satisfaction and also feel fairly rewarded. This is the (classic) challenge of reconciling the soft and hard parts of HRM in practice (Legge 1995). Too strict an approach from the line manager may result in claims of harassment/bullying, and cases of stress, anxiety and depression, and too soft an approach could see managers foregoing the benefits of efficiency that holding people to account may deliver. Any lack of line skill (capability), interest (commitment) or fairness (consistency) in managing people could adversely affect employee opinion, which in turn may affect productivity and absenteeism. For example, employees may leave their work organisation if they feel that their managers are not up to the job in managing them (Taylor 2002).

While being involved in HR work may or may not help advance the careers of the line, how managers manage employees may perhaps affect employee careers (Walton 1999), as managers are asked which employees to recommend for development, rewards and promotions. So, while the line may be the people that make HR strategies 'come to life' (Purcell *et al.* 2003), they may also be the people that potentially make employee careers take off or flounder. Managing people effectively takes time and consideration, and it is not clear whether line managers are being given the scope and opportunity to do HRM properly. Developing people at work requires managers to make a mental leap away from using control and direct styles of management, and embracing ones of tutoring, coaching and facilitating. Making such adjustments may not be easy for them:

> The general analytical conclusions from this study are that (c.f. Brewster and Larsen, 2000) the line do have the 'desire' to do HR work, and may have both the 'capacity' and the 'ability' to do it well if adequately trained and assisted by HR, but not if they try do it without significant HR help . . . *it could be argued that they are making HR work seem mentally a simple common-sense exercise, even though their lived experience of doing it is perhaps that it is not* (Renwick 2003, pp.274–5, italics added).

HR AND THE LINE

Generating excellent outcomes in people management from involving line managers in HRM seems to rest on one key requirement – that HR managers support line involvement in it and also give them good advice in it (Brewster and Larsen 2000). Marchington and Wilkinson (2002) quoting Currie and Procter (2001) argue that there are ways in which HR managers can provide support to middle managers. These are detailed below:

How HR managers can support middle managers

- HR strategies should be composed of broad themes that can then be contextualised by middle managers at an operational level.
- Middle managers should be encouraged to contribute towards an elaboration of these broad themes.
- Opportunities should be provided for middle managers to span boundaries within the organisation through membership of project groups.
- The HR function should be organised to allow HR professionals to work closely with middle managers at the point of delivery.
- The development of middle managers is directed towards their contribution to strategic change.

Source: Marchington and Wilkinson 2002; adapted with permission from 'Exploring the relationship between HR and middle managers' by Graham Currie and Stephen Proctor, published in *Human Resource Management Journal*, Vol.11, No.3, 2001

However, it is not clear whether such support for the line is forthcoming from HR:

> Ideally, the transfer of responsibilities to line management would involve substantial commitment, preparation and support by personnel management . . . It is not certain, to say the least, that this occurs in all cases (Brewster and Larsen 2000, p.208).

And:

> A simple, seamless transfer of responsibility between HR managers and line managers is, at best, proving difficult to achieve . . . on the part of HR managers, there appears to be a desire to keep hold of at least some of their operational responsibilities . . . the HR function's successful execution of operational responsibilities is seen as important for the credibility needed to exercise influence at a strategic level (Currie and Procter 2001, p.54).

HR MANAGERS

It is logical that some HR managers fear losing their *raison d'être* if they seek to devolve too much operational HR work to the line, and other stakeholders may object to such a move if it generates poor outcomes in employee well-being. However, some HR managers may welcome the chance to use such changes to engage in more strategic and holistic HR activity, and have some opportunity to 'move on up' in their work organisations into a more senior role (Kelly and Gennard 2001). Thus involving line managers in HRM has some implications for HR managers too. The stakes are high for HR. If, over the next few years, greater line involvement in HRM fails, then HR's strategic contribution will need to be complimented by a more operational one. But if involving the line more in HRM is successful, then other HR managers may be able to pursue more strategic career paths. Some theorising may need to be done on these questions to guide us. Achieving this link between theory and practice in this field requires us to establish a wide research agenda on line manager involvement in HRM. This is now detailed.

Future research

While some works in the field of involving line managers in HRM are positive on the question of the usefulness of involving line managers in HRM (see Hutchinson and Purcell 2003; Purcell *et al.* 2003), most of the works reviewed above suggest that there are limitations is using the line to manage people at work. This fact needs to be acknowledged in future research in this field.[3] To paraphrase Guest, in the simplest terms, we need to know whether involving the line in HRM is a good, bad or ugly development, and we need to know whether or not the line are capable, committed and consistent in HRM. To gain answers to these questions, we need more studies to be done to produce a more definitive picture, especially comparative and international ones, and those that give us insights into line practices in SMEs. Of particular importance is a need to seek the views of the key actors in HRM: the line, HR and employees.

More research is needed on how the line cope with the conflicting demands placed on them in operations and people management (Lynch 2003), and more work is needed on how line managers are recruited, inducted, trained, appraised and rewarded in the HR aspects of their jobs, and what leadership roles senior line managers play in developing people at work (Whittaker and Marchington 2003). Similarly, more research is needed on how these managers can develop new management styles when managing people, i.e., tutor, coach or mentor (Gibb 2003).

---

[3]Further detail on other research ideas for the field of line involvement in HRM are detailed in Renwick (2003).

Conclusions

In today's work organisations, involving line managers in HRM requires them to manage in work environments that are characterised by high levels of change and uncertainty to meet the performance demands thrust upon them from internal and external stakeholders. These managers have to reconcile the demands of higher levels of responsibility for financial and people management with a search for cost-control and innovation in HRM. Choices need to be made and taken by them in how they manage people at work, which involve the pursuit of hard or soft HRM strategies within work contexts of high or low commitment. Coping with such demands and expectations places great pressure on these managers, and this fact needs to be recognised. However, there is also a need to recognise the need for these managers to practise people management in a more professional and consistent manner, as line expediency in HRM has been exposed (Cunningham and Hyman 1995; McGovern *et al.* 1997). Thus today's employers face a series of questions. How do they want to manage people at work? What roles should HR specialists and non-specialists take in HRM? And is involving the line in HRM a useful development for all stakeholders in HRM? Gaining answers to these questions will help us understand whether involving the line in HRM is part of a cost-cutting exercise by employers, or one they are pursuing to add value for all those involved in the management of people at work.

CASE STUDY 8.1

LINE MANAGERS AND HRM AT RETAILCO

SAMANTHA LYNCH

Background

Retailco plc operates in the multiple store grocery retailing sector and employs over 10,000 staff across 700 branches throughout the UK. Retailco's corporate strategy is focused on improving customer service and cutting costs. The company is divided into three divisions: head office, distribution and retail. This case study concentrates on the retail division, particularly focusing on a supermarket called The Riverside.

The Riverside store is open 100 hours each week, including evenings and weekends. Four hundred and fifty staff work at the store, of whom 71 per cent work part-time. Just over half of the workforce is female, with the majority of these working part-time. Overseeing store operations is the general manager, who is supported by four senior store managers: customer services manager, personnel manager, and two trading managers. Senior store managers are responsible for their designated departments in addition to taking responsibility as duty manager in the general manager's absence. The personnel manager is no exception with over a third of their working week spent as the

▶

duty manager. No prior HR experience or knowledge is required to become a store personnel manager and the role is perceived to be no more specialist than any of the other senior store management roles. Each of the four departments is split into a number of sections, which are managed by section managers. These act as line manager to staff in their section and carry responsibility for day-to-day activities. Senior store managers at Retailco have relatively secure conditions of employment, with structured career paths and a higher than average reward package for the retail sector. In contrast, section managers are more likely to join Retailco as school leavers, or from other retail organisations, and are promoted to their position from the shop floor with comparatively low earnings.

The nature of HRM

While little written evidence of HR strategy at Retailco exists, there is a commitment to strategic-level HR with the personnel director having full director status. Reporting to the personnel director is the retail personnel director who oversees HR activities in the retail division. The retail personnel director believes there are a number of HR challenges for Retailco including:

- Increasing productivity at minimum cost to the organisation, but minimising work intensification for employees.
- Maintaining a constructive relationship with the recognised trade union.
- Balancing the ratio of full- and part-time staff effectively.

The retail personnel director believes that improved workforce stability through the management of an optimum ratio of part-time to full-time workers is one solution to these challenges. The resulting policy is an aim to increase the number of full-time employees:

> **If we employ more full timers . . . we can better deliver our customer service promises**
> (Retail Personnel Director).

This policy is based on the belief that employees who work longer hours are more committed and so will deliver a higher quality of customer service than staff who only work a few hours each week for the company. Other HR policies include share option schemes, efforts to improve employee communication, a performance appraisal scheme for all staff, and corporate customer service training programmes.

The responsibilities of store-level managers

Store-level managers at Retailco hold substantial responsibility for the management of human resources, much of which is devolved to section managers. These managers are responsible for local HR decisions including recruitment and selection, on-the-job training, staff scheduling and performance management:

- Recruitment and selection
  Section managers hold responsibility for nearly all aspects of recruitment and selection of staff within their departments. A vacancy request is submitted to the general manager when they need to recruit a new member of staff. Subject to the vacancy request being approved, the personnel manager assists with the advertising and initial shortlisting of candidates using standard company application forms. Interviewing candidates is the sole responsibility of section managers unless they specifically

request support from the personnel manager, or if the personnel manager considers the section manager too inexperienced.

■ Training and development
The Riverside store has a training manager who is responsible for delivering the corporate customer service training packages and central induction programmes. However, day-to-day responsibility for training and development of new staff, particularly in the tasks of their job, is the duty of section managers.

■ Staff scheduling
Section managers are in charge of scheduling the working hours of all their staff.

■ Performance appraisal
Section managers hold responsibility for carrying out annual performance appraisals with all members of their staff.

■ Grievance and discipline
Section and senior store managers are involved in the initial stages of the grievance and disciplinary process. The personnel manager often adopts an advisory role and only becomes involved in the latter stages of any grievance or disciplinary process.

Human resource management at The Riverside

The decision-making process of store-level managers at Retailco is subject to the competing corporate strategies of cost reduction and quality enhancement:

> **The budget has been cut by 12 per cent this year even though we're opening for longer than we ever have before** (General Manager).

To deliver the cost minimisation strategy store-level managers at all levels are closely monitored by head office in terms of budgets and targets. In contrast, their HR responsibilities are not directly scrutinised or evaluated:

> **As long as we meet the targets set by head office and keep within our budgets they really don't bother us too much** (Senior Store Manager).

As a result there is difficulty securing store-level management commitment to HRM because of the limited incentives for managers to prioritise such activities. Store-level managers are more disposed to focusing on the quantifiable requirements of their job in order to be seen to be achieving pre-determined performance targets, while in turn neglecting more intangible activities such as HRM.

Store-level managers are conscious of the difficulties associated with the implementation of the seemingly conflicting corporate strategy focused on both quality enhancement and cost minimisation. As a consequence, local managers exercise their discretion and choose to circumvent or manipulate areas of company policy which they allege restricts their ability to fulfil performance targets. Examples of such manipulation include an increased use of non-standard labour; unauthorised recruitment freezes; the illicit deployment of staff; and undermining of the performance appraisal system.

To satisfy economic constraints section managers favour the employment of part-timers over full-timers. They attribute this tactic to their belief that the employment of full-timers makes it difficult to meet head office budgets and targets because full-timers attract premium rate overtime for working above their contracted weekly hours, compared with part-timers who do not. As a result many store-level managers, who are ultimately responsible for the efficient management of human resources, consider part-timers to be a more viable and attractive financial option. This is in contrast to central HR policy that aims to employ greater numbers of full-timers to deliver the customer service strategy. An additional consequence of this tactic is an increased demand for numerical flexibility from existing employees, particularly part-timers and a regular requirement for them to work additional hours or to change their shifts to accommodate business needs. All employees are expected to work at higher rates of efficiency to facilitate the delivery of corporate strategy:

> The company expects more from its employees to improve customer service and beat off the competition, but we are confined to the same, if not lower, budgets so we just have to work harder (Section Manager).

This is in contrast to the retail personnel director's aim to minimise work intensification for Retailco staff.

Recruitment levels at The Riverside are driven entirely by the budgets set by head office. The wage budget position is the key indicator as to whether there are the financial resources available to recruit new staff. In order to keep budgets under control the general manager at The Riverside often instigates a recruitment freeze, unbeknown to head office, in order to reduce costs. This restriction on recruitment is driven by the expectation that part-timers are available to offer numerical flexibility through working additional shifts to cover any staff shortfall:

> The Riverside is a strange animal when it comes to recruitment. Recruitment is financially controlled so you can look at the wage costs and look ahead to the budget squeeze and so you don't recruit and flex up the part timers. Then there is a desperate shortage of employees and so there is a mad rush to recruit (Training Manager).

Manipulation of HR policy to achieve performance targets can be seen through the deployment of customer service assistants at The Riverside. Customer service assistants are an initiative introduced by head office designed to deliver on customer service pledges and stores are provided with some additional financial resources to fund their employment. However, store-level managers at The Riverside view the employment of customer service assistants as somewhat extravagant at a time when they are attempting to implement competing corporate strategies of cost reduction and quality enhancement. Instead, customer service assistants at The Riverside are used as the ultimate in flexible labour with senior store managers often re-deploying them on to their own departments during peak trading or in times of staff shortages (usually prompted by the frequent recruitment freezes). The store's personnel records show these staff employed as customer service assistants, while in practice they are often to be found working in other roles as and when the budget dictates.

The preoccupation with tangible targets undermines and distorts HR initiatives at The Riverside. Attempts were made by head office to introduce performance appraisals for all staff to encourage greater emphasis on training and development. However, store-level managers complain about the excessive time demands of such initiatives, particularly in departments that employ large numbers of part-timers:

> I am expected to carry out annual performance appraisals on all my staff. I have 100 check-out staff alone because we only use part-timers so it's extremely difficult to

devote the time and attention needed to their appraisals when other demands are being made on you and your staff (Section Manager).

As a consequence, the performance appraisal system did not operate as head office envisaged.

The high devolution and low accountability of HR responsibilities at Retailco means that line managers can refrain from implementing any HR policies that might impede their ability to meet more tangible performance targets. The reality at Retailco is an undermining of HR policies to enable line managers to deliver on the quantifiable demands of their jobs within the constraints placed upon them. It raises concerns about the viability of corporate-wide HR strategy in large, branch-network organisations. The Case study illustrates how even the best conceived corporate strategies and policies can be mitigated by the actions of line managers. As a result, there are uncertainties about the consistency of handling day-to-day issues between different Retailco stores. The emphasis placed by Retailco on achieving tangible goals means that any manipulation of local HR invariably leads to a focus on 'hard' HRM techniques. The evidence suggests that the delegation of responsibility for HRM to line managers can negate the practice of 'soft' HRM, such as performance appraisal, due to a preoccupation with the achievement of tangible targets. This gives cause for concern about the execution and viability of high-commitment HRM in large complex organisations, which are pursuing a concurrent corporate strategy of cost reduction.

Questions

1. If line managers hold the main responsibility for HRM, how foreseeable is it that HR policy will always be undermined at store level in Retailco?

2. Is it inevitable that 'soft' HR practices will diminish in the foreseeable future in Retailco, regardless of any head office policies devoted to high-commitment human resource management?

3. How might the retail personnel director ensure that HR policies are fully converted into practice in Retailco stores?

CASE STUDY 8.2

LINE MANAGERS AND STAR EMPLOYEES

DOUGLAS RENWICK

This case examines the issues surrounding how managers handle fluctuating employee performance in high-performance work organisations – football clubs. The actors are football player David Beckham and manager Sir Alex Ferguson at Manchester United plc. The background to this case is the rise of Beckham as a football player at Manchester United from his displays as a player on the right-wing, and his specialist ability as a free-kick expert. His profile has been further enhanced by a number of high-profile displays for England, off-field commercial endorsements for leading companies, and his marriage to Victoria Beckham, a.k.a. the pop singer Posh Spice.

An alleged incident emerged between manager and player when Beckham's defensive performance was mentioned as a factor in Ferguson dropping him from starting a high-profile game in the Champions League with Real Madrid. Allegations between manager and employee were rife, Beckham allegedly being furious with Ferguson as he felt he was not the only player guilty of such a slip. Similarly, Ferguson was previously alleged to have kicked a boot across the dressing room hitting Beckham above the eye. A media scrum ensued as news of the alleged incident broke, and Beckham then completed a high-profile transfer to Real Madrid.

Questions

1. Do you feel that Beckham was harshly treated by Ferguson, or that Beckham let Ferguson down? What factors would you point to in support of your argument(s)?

2. Do you feel that the line manager (Ferguson) was right to discipline the player (Beckham), or that the player has a legitimate grievance to pursue against the manager?

3. What issues do you think this case raises in terms of performance management? If you were a manager, how would you manage highly paid star performers? If you were such a 'star' player, how do you think you would like to be managed?

References

Bach, S. (1995) 'Restructuring the personnel function: the case of NHS trusts', *Human Resource Management Journal*, Vol.5, No.2, pp.99–115.

Brewster, C. and Larsen, H.H. (1992) 'Human resource management in Europe: evidence from ten countries', *International Journal of Human Resource Management*, Vol.3, No.3, pp.409–34.

Brewster, C. and Larsen, H.H. (eds) (2000) *Human Resource Management In Northern Europe: Trends, Dilemmas and Strategy*, Oxford: Blackwell.

Budhwar, P.S. (2000) 'Evaluating levels of strategic integration and devolvement of human resource management in the UK', *Personnel Review*, Vol.29, No.2, pp.141–61.

Cassell, C., Nadin, S., Gray, M. and Clegg, C. (2002) 'Exploring human resource management practices in small and medium sized enterprises', *Personnel Review*, Vol.31, No.6, pp.671–92.

Cully, M., Woodland, S., O'Reilly, A. and Dix, G. (1999) *Britain At Work: As Depicted by the 1998 Workplace Employee Relations Survey*, London: Routledge.

*Cunningham, I. and Hyman, J. (1995) 'Transforming the HRM vision into reality: the role of line managers and supervisors in implementing change', *Employee Relations*, Vol.17, No.8, pp.5–20.

Cunningham, I. and Hyman, J. (1999) 'Devolving human resource responsibilities to the line: Beginning of the end or a new beginning for personnel?', *Personnel Review*, Vol.28, No.1/2, pp.9–27.

Cunningham, I., James, P. and Dibben, P. (2004) 'Bridging the gap between rhetoric and reality: Line managers and the protection of job security for ill workers in the modern workplace', *British Journal of Management*, Vol. 15, No. 3, pp.273–90.

*Currie, G. and Procter, S. (2001) 'Exploring the relationship between HR and middle managers', *Human Resource Management Journal*, Vol.11, No.1, pp.53–69.

Deeks, E. (2000) 'Self-service is hard work', *People Management*, Vol.26, No.23, p.9.

Dunn, C. and Wilkinson, A. (2002) 'Wish you were here: managing absence', *Personnel Review*, Vol.31, No.2, pp.228–46.

Eisenstat, R.A. (1996) 'What corporate human resources brings to the picnic: four models for functional management', *Organizational Dynamics*, Autumn, Vol.25, No.2, pp.7–22.

Edwards, C.Y. and Robinson, O. (2001) '"Better" part-time jobs? A study of part-time working in nursing and the police', *Employee Relations*, Vol.23, No.5, pp.438–53.

Fenton-O'Creevy, M. (1998) 'Employee involvement and the middle manager: evidence from a survey of organizations', *Journal of Organizational Behaviour*, Vol.19, pp.67–84.

Fenton-O'Creevy, M. (2001) 'Employee involvement and the middle manager: saboteur or scapegoat?', *Human Resource Management Journal*, Vol.11, No.1, pp.24–40.

Gibb, S. (2001) 'The state of human resource management: evidence from employee's views of HRM systems and staff', *Employee Relations*, Vol.23, No.4, pp.318–36.

Gibb, S. (2003) 'Line manager involvement in learning and development: small beer or big deal?', *Employee Relations*, Vol.25, No.3, pp.281–93.

Gratton, L., Hope-Hailey, V., Stiles, P. and Truss, C. (1999) 'Linking individual performance to business strategy: the people process model', in R. Schuler, and S. Jackson, (eds) *Strategic Human Resource Management*, Oxford: Blackwell.

Green, F. and James, D. (2003) 'Assessing skills and autonomy: the job holder versus the line manager', *Human Resource Management Journal*, Vol.13, No.1, pp.63–77.

Guest, D. (1987) 'Human resource management and industrial relations', *Journal of Management Studies*, Vol.24, pp.503–22.

Guest, D. and King, Z. (2001) 'HR and the bottom line', *People Management*, 27th September, pp.29–34.

Guest, D., King, Z., Conway, N., Michie, J. and Sheehan-Quinn, M. (2001) *Voices from the Boardroom*, London: Chartered Institute of Personnel and Development.

*Harris, L. (2001) 'Rewarding employee performance: line manager's values, beliefs and perspectives', *International Journal of Human Resource Management*, Vol.12, No.7, pp.1182–92.

Hutchinson, S, and Purcell, J. (2003) *Bringing Policies to Life: The Vital Role of Front-line Managers in People Management*, London: CIPD.

Hutchinson, S. and Wood, S. (1995) *Personnel and the Line: Developing the New Relationship*, London: Institute of Personnel and Development.

IRS Employment Trends (2001) *Managing Discipline at Work*, No.727, pp.5–11.

Jackson, S.E. and Schuler, R.S. (2000) *Managing Human Resources: A Partnership Perspective* (7th edn), London: International Thomson Publishing.

Kelly, J. and Gennard, J. (2001) *The Effective Personnel Director: Power and Influence in the Boardroom*, London: Routledge.

Larsen, H. and Brewster, C. (2003) 'Line management responsibility for HRM: what's happening in Europe?', *Employee Relations*, Vol.25, No.3, pp.228–44.

Legge, K. (1995) *Human Resource Management: Rhetorics and Realities*, Basingstoke: Macmillan.

Lowe, J. (1992) 'Locating the line: the front-line supervisor and human resource management', in P. Blyton and P. Turnbull (eds) *Reassessing Human Resource Management*, London: Sage.

Lynch, S. (2003) 'Devolution and the management of human resources: evidence from the retail industry', paper presented to the Professional Standards Conference, Chartered Institute of Personnel and Development, University of Keele.

MacNeil, C.M. (2003) 'Line managers: facilitators of knowledge sharing in teams', *Employee Relations*, Vol.25, No.3, pp.294–307.

Marchington, M. (1999) 'Professional qualification scheme: core personnel and development exam papers and examiners' reports, May 1999', Institute of Personnel and Development, paper given to the IPD Professional Standards Conference, University of Warwick, July, pp.1–12.

Marchington, M. (2001) 'Employee Involvement at Work', in J. Storey (ed.) *Human Resource Management: A Critical Text* (2nd edn), London: Thomson Learning.

Marchington, M. and Wilkinson, A.J. (2002) *People Management and Development: Human Resource Management at Work* (2nd edn), London: Chartered Institute of Personnel and Development.

Marsh, A.I. (1971) 'The staffing of industrial relations management in the engineering industry', *Industrial Relations Journal*, Vol.22, No.2, pp.14–24.

Marsh, A.I. and Gillies, J.G. (1983) 'The involvement of line and staff managers in industrial relations', in K. Thurley and S. Wood (eds) *Industrial Relations and Management Strategy*, Cambridge: Cambridge University Press.

McConville, T. and Holden, L. (1999) 'The filling in the sandwich: HRM and middle managers in the health sector', *Personnel Review*, Vol.28, Nos5–6, pp.406–24.

McGovern, P., Gratton, L., Hope-Hailey, V. and Truss, C. (1997) 'Human resource management on the line?', *Human Resource Management Journal*, Vol.7, No.4, pp.12–29.

Millward, N., Bryson, A. and Forth, J. (2000) *All Change At Work? British Employment Relations 1980–1998, as Portrayed by the Workplace Industrial Relations Survey Series*, London: Routledge.

Poole, M. and Jenkins, G. (1997) 'Responsibilities for human resource management practices in the modern enterprise', *Personnel Review*, Vol.26, No.5, pp.333–56.

Purcell, J., Kinnie, N., Hutchinson, S., Rayton, B. and Swart, J. (2003) *Understanding the People and Performance Link: Unlocking the Black Box*, London: Chartered Institute of Personnel and Development.

Redman, T. (2001) 'Performance appraisal', in T. Redman and A. Wilkinson (eds) *Contemporary Human Resource Management*, Harlow: Pearson Education, pp.57–95.

Renwick, D. (2000) 'HR–line work relations: a review, pilot case and research agenda', *Employee Relations*, Vol.22, No.1/2, pp.179–205.

*Renwick, D. (2003) 'Line manager involvement in HRM: an inside view', *Employee Relations*, Vol.25, No.3, pp.262–80.

Rollinson, D., Hook, C., Foot, M. and Handley, J. (1996) 'Supervisor and manager styles in handling discipline and grievance. Part 2: Approaches to handling discipline and grievance', *Personnel Review*, Vol.25, No.4, pp.38–55.

Sisson, K. and Storey, J. (2000) *The Realities of Human Resource Management*, Buckingham: Open University Press.

*Storey, J. (1992) *Developments in the Management of Human Resources*, Oxford: Blackwell.

Storey, J. (2001) 'Human Resource Management today: an assessment', in J. Storey (ed.) *Human Resource Management: A Critical Text* (2nd edn), London: Thomson, pp.3–20.

Taylor, S. (2002) 'A poor boss can be the last straw', *Basingstoke Gazette*, 20 December, p.56.

Thornhill, A. and Saunders, M.N.K. (1998) 'What if line managers don't realize they're responsible for HR? Lessons from an organization experiencing rapid change', *Personnel Review*, Vol.27, No.6, pp.460–76.

Tyson, S. and Fell, A. (1995) *Evaluating the Personnel Function* (2nd edn), Cheltenham: Stanley Thomes.

Ulrich, D. (1997) *Human Resource Champions: The Next Agenda For Adding Value And Delivering Results*, Boston, MA: Harvard University Press.

Ulrich, D. (1998) 'A new mandate for human resources', *Harvard Business Review*, January/February, pp.124–34.

Ulrich, D. (2001) 'The evolution of a professional agenda', *Financial Times, Mastering People Management*, 15 October, pp.2–3.

Walton, J. (1999) *Strategic Human Resource Management*, Harlow: Pearson Education.

Watson, T. (1986) *Management, Organisation and Employment Strategy*, London: Routledge & Kegan Paul.

*Whittaker, S. and Marchington, M. (2003) 'Devolving HR responsibility to the line: threat, opportunity or partnership?', *Employee Relations*, Vol.25, No.3, pp.245–61.

* Useful reading

Chapter 9

ORGANISATIONAL AND CORPORATE CULTURE

Alistair Cheyne and John Loan-Clarke

Introduction

In the study of organisations and their management, the concept of organisational culture (sometimes referred to as corporate culture) has become increasingly important, and the quantity of research in the area has increased dramatically since the early 1980s (Siehl and Martin 1990). This chapter outlines recent theory and research in organisational culture and the related concept of climate. In doing so it outlines definitions and categorisations of culture, discusses the assessment of culture and climate, investigates the links between culture and human resource management, and examines how organisations might attempt to manage culture.

The concept of culture

Culture as a concept derives from the fields of social anthropology and sociology. In general its description has been used to characterise an organisation or group of individuals within a social structure. Culture is, however, not a well-defined concept (Münch and Smelster 1992); it describes roles and interactions that derive from norms and values in the sociological tradition, or from beliefs and attitudes in the social psychological field (Wunthow and Witten 1988). In addition to these distinctions, there are at least two major approaches to the study of culture. The first views culture as an implicit feature of social life, and the second holds culture to be an explicit social construction (Wunthow and Witten 1988), in other words culture as the structure of a socio-political group or culture as a product of that group.

In the same vein, two models of culture have been proposed: that which defines culture in terms of behaviour and that which defines it in terms of meaning. The second of these models is supported by Trice and Beyer's (1984) assertion that culture is a system of publicly and collectively accepted meanings operating for a given group at a given time.

Such views of culture have been incorporated into organisational theory to give rise to the concepts of organisational culture (Brown 1998), and the similar corporate culture (Peters and Waterman 1982). The term 'organisational culture' tends to refer to a naturally occurring phenomenon that all organisations possess, whereas corporate culture is held to be more management driven, in an attempt to increase organisational effectiveness. Furthermore, it has been suggested (Shipley 1990) that culture is central to the understanding and control of and resistance to change in society, organisations and social groups.

Organisational culture

As noted earlier, the study of culture has been influential in the field of organisational studies for over 20 years (Denison 1996; Trompenaars and Hampden-Turner 1997). Its importance stems, in part, from the notion that it provides a dynamic and interactive model of organising (Jelinek *et al.* 1983; Smircich 1983) and as such can help explain how organisational environments might be characterised, assessed and ultimately controlled (Deal and Kennedy 1982; Schneider 1990). Furthermore, a number of authors have proposed that successful organisations have a strong or positive corporate culture (Deal and Kennedy 1982; Peters and Waterman 1982; Kilmann *et al.* 1985; Weick 1985). The notion of culture can, therefore, imply a practical way of explaining how and why particular organisations enjoy differing levels of success (Trompenaars and Hampden-Turner 1997; Brown 1998). The suggestion that organisational effectiveness is heavily influenced by a positive corporate culture has been particularly influential for practising managers. A key influence for the formation of this assumption was the 1982 book by Peters and Waterman, *In Search of Excellence*:

> Without exception, the dominance and coherence of culture proved to be an essential quality of the excellent companies. Moreover the stronger the culture and the more it was directed towards the marketplace, the less the need there was for policy manuals, organization charts or detailed procedures and rules (p.75).

However, as more systematic, longitudinal research (for example, Kotter and Heskett 1992) has indicated, the causal link between culture and organisational effectiveness is not necessarily easy to identify. We will come back to the potential link between culture and performance later in this chapter, after we consider what culture is, and how we might assess it.

DEFINING ORGANISATIONAL CULTURE

A number of definitions of culture have been proposed and it is possible to discern some common themes among these. Moorhead and Griffin (1995) suggest that organisational culture is a set of values that help people in an organisation to understand which actions are considered acceptable and which are unacceptable to the organisation and its members. Similarly, Schein (1985) has defined organisational culture in terms of employees' shared values and perceptions of the organisation, beliefs about it, and common ways of solving problems within the organisation. Schein (1985) has also described organisational culture in terms of an ongoing process through which an organisation's behaviour patterns become transformed over time, installed in new recruits, and refined and adapted in response to both internal and external changes. Culture helps an organisation's members to interpret and accept their world, and so it is not so much a by-product of an organisation as an integral part of it which influences individuals' behaviours and contributes to the effectiveness of the organisation.

Reviews of the concept of organisational culture (for example, Rousseau 1990; Furnham 1997) have detailed the abundance of definitions that have developed over the years. Examples of the range of definitions are detailed in Box 9.1.

While it is apparent that there have been a number of disagreements over the precise nature of organisational culture, the above definitions do bear some resemblance to each other. Several salient points emerge upon comparing these definitions. Emphasis, in many cases, is on values, beliefs and expectations that are shared within the group and/or organisation, and which, in turn, can help the members make sense of their environment, and direct behaviour. Rousseau (1990) agrees that it is not really the definitions of organisational culture that vary

Box 9.1: Definitions of culture

Kroeber and Kluckhohn (1952)	Culture consists of patterns of behaviour transmitted by symbols, embodied in artefacts, ideas and values.
Bowers and Seashore (1966)	The best way of doing things around here.
Becker and Geer (1970)	A set of common understandings.
Geertz (1973)	The fabric of meaning which allows the interpretation and guidance of action.
Van Maanen and Schein (1979)	Values, beliefs and expectations that members of organisations come to share.
Swartz and Jordon (1980)	Shared patterns of beliefs and expectations that produce norms shaping behaviour
Ouchi (1981)	The set of symbols, ceremonies and myths that communicate the organisation's values and beliefs to its members
Deal and Kennedy (1982)	A system of informal rules that spells out how people are to behave most of the time.
Louis (1983)	As having three aspects (1) some content (2) specific to (3) a group.
Martin and Siehl (1983)	The glue that holds together an organisation through shared patterns of meaning, consisting of core values, forms and strategies to reinforce content.
Uttal (1983)	Shared values and beliefs that interact with an organisation's structures and control systems to produce behavioural norms.

widely but the approaches to data collection and operation (see, for example, p. 235 below). Pettigrew (1990) offers one explanation of the problem in defining organisational culture. He suggests that it is, in part, due to the fact that culture is:

> not just a concept but the source of a family of concepts (Pettigrew 1979), and it is not just a family of concepts but also a frame of reference or root metaphor for organisational analysis (p.414).

Pettigrew's explanation reflects two very different understandings of the concept of culture. Brown (1998) suggests a clear distinction can be made between those who think that culture is a metaphor that helps understand organisations in terms of other entities (Morgan 1986), and those who see culture as an objective entity that distinguishes one organisation from another (Gold 1982). The view that culture is an objective entity can be subdivided, as pointed out by Rohner (1984), into something an organisation is (or its structure and meaning) or something an organisation has (for example, its behaviour) as embodied by most of the definitions summarised by Rousseau (1990) and detailed above.

LAYERS OF ORGANISATIONAL CULTURE

It may be that the use of culture as a concept can be seen to be too embracing, and some writers (Schein 1985; Morgan 1986; Rousseau 1990) describe culture as having a series of different layers. Schein (1985) suggests that there are three levels of culture: artefacts, values and basic assumptions. Figure 9.1 shows a representation of these layers of culture, organised from readily accessible, and, therefore, more easily studied, to difficult to access.

At the most accessible level are visible artefacts, or products of cultural activity. These might include patterns of behaviour (Cooke and Rousseau 1988), or the structures that reflect patterns of activity, observable to those outside the culture. Examples of these visible artefacts might include corporate logos and the physical layout of the organisation. The middle layer relates to values and priorities assigned to organisational outcomes. Such values might be reflected in group behavioural norms, or beliefs about what is acceptable and unacceptable behaviour within the organisation, similar to Moorhead and Griffin's (1995) definition of culture. This layer can be learned about through interaction with, and questioning of group members. Patterns of unconscious assumptions (Schein 1984) are the deepest of the layers of culture, and these may not be directly known by the organisation's members and therefore require a period of intensive interaction to uncover. An appreciation of layers of culture could, therefore, be important when considering whether culture can be managed (see below).

This type of representation of cultural layers has been further embellished, to present a more complex picture. Hatch (1997) has adapted Schein's (1985) original layers model to incorporate organisational symbols and processes in a more dynamic model. Similarly Hofstede *et al.* (1990) have divided the manifestations (or more accessible elements) of culture into values, at the deepest level, through rituals and heroes to symbols at the shallowest.

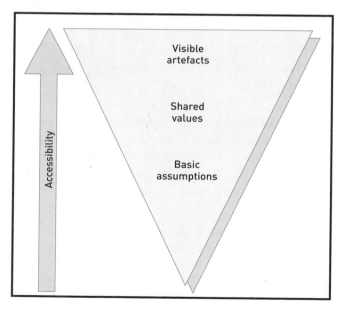

Figure 9.1 Schein's layers of organisational culture

In addition to the various definitions of culture and descriptions of level, several researchers have developed a number of classifications of organisational culture, allowing organisations to be described as different types of objective entity. These allow us to compare and evaluate different organisations in terms of their culture. There are many such categorisations; here we will examine three of the better-known examples, those of Deal and Kennedy (1982), Harrison (1972) and Hofstede (1980).

DEAL AND KENNEDY'S FOUR CULTURES

One of the most popular classifications of corporate culture was proposed by Deal and Kennedy (1982). Their categorisation of culture was the result of visiting hundreds of organisations and is based on two organisational environmental factors; the degree of risk associated with business activities, and the speed of feedback to the organisation and individuals about the success of those business activities. Deal and Kennedy (1982) identified four distinct culture types:

- Tough-guy macho culture – an organisation of risk takers who receive immediate feedback, examples include police, management consultants, media.

- Work hard/play hard culture – a low risk, quick feedback culture which encourages people to maintain high levels of activity, examples include sales companies, computer companies.

- Bet your company culture – the high risk, slow feedback culture, where ideas are given time to develop, examples include large multi-nationals engaged in research and product development.

- Process culture – the classic bureaucracy where feedback is slow and risks are low, so individuals focus on the processes, examples might include local government and heavily regulated industries.

Deal and Kennedy (1982) recognise that organisations might not precisely fit into these four types, or indeed perhaps not fit at all, but they propose that this model is still a useful tool for managers beginning to identify an organisation's culture.

HARRISON'S TYPOLOGY

An early, relatively simple, yet extremely influential classification of organisational culture was suggested by Harrison (1972). This classification has been elaborated on by other scholars, including Handy (1978) and Williams *et al.* (1993), and like the Deal and Kennedy model, includes descriptions of four main types of culture in organisations:

- Power culture – has a single source of power. Typically these types of organisation react quickly, but success often depends on those with the power at the centre and these organisations might be small, owner-managed businesses.

- Role culture – these types of organisations are more typically described as bureaucracies, with an emphasis on functions and specialities. These organisations are more likely to be successful in stable environments and could include public sector organisations.

- Task culture – the focus for these types of organisation is accomplishing goals, power is based on expertise and flexibility is important, for example management consultancies.

■ Person culture – these types of organisation exist primarily to serve the needs of their members, individuals are expected to influence each other through example and helpfulness, and have almost complete autonomy. This type of culture may be evident in those in professional practice, such as lawyers or doctors, or those involved in a collective organisation.

HOFSTEDE'S NATIONAL CULTURE DIMENSIONS

The consideration of organisational culture is complicated further when the effects of societal and national cultures upon individual organisations' cultures are considered. Hofstede (1980) studied these influences in relation to IBM, the American multi-national company, operating in over 40 countries worldwide. Hofstede collected survey data concerning work-related values from international affiliates and found evidence of national cultural differences. Hofstede (1991) demonstrated that managers in different countries varied in the strength of their attitudes and values regarding various issues. Four dimensions were identified including:

■ Power distance – the extent to which members are willing to accept an unequal distribution of power, wealth and privilege.

■ Uncertainty avoidance – the manner in which individuals have learned to cope with uncertainty.

■ Individualism – the degree to which individuals are required to act independently.

■ Masculinity – related to dominant values such as success and money.

A fifth dimension 'confucian dynamism' – the degree to which long-termism or short-termism is the dominant orientation in life, was added after further sampling and analysis of the data.

The results of this work suggest, for example, that organisations in the UK will have low power distance, be individualist, masculine and able to cope with uncertainty. Hofstede's work is not only deemed to be important for the identification of specific cultural differences (Hatch 1997) but it has also shown that organisational culture is an entry point for societal influence on organisations. This notion has been developed further in the work of Fons Trompenaars (Trompenaars and Hampden-Turner, 1977).

A number of similarities are apparent from these example classifications, for example, *Tough guy*, *Power* and *Power distance*, all seem to be tapping into similar types of culture, suggesting a degree of reliability in the observations of different research groups. However, while these typologies are a useful starting point in describing culture, as Deal and Kennedy (1982) acknowledge, we should remember that they represent ideal situations or models for us to compare actual organisations against, and no organisation will fit the types exactly. It is perhaps more useful for organisations to be able to describe the origin of their own cultures and the process by which they arise (Furnham 1997), and how they can enhance organisational effectiveness. A first step in achieving this might involve the detailed assessment of organisational culture.

It is clear from the literature examined above that there are certain inconsistencies in the way culture is defined. Many researchers agree that organisational culture involves beliefs and values, exists at a variety of different levels, and manifests itself in a wide range of artefacts, symbols and processes within any particular organisation. Culture helps an organisation's members to interpret meaning and understand their working environment. It is an integral part of an organisation and as such can influence individuals' behaviour and potentially contribute to the effectiveness or ineffectiveness of the organisation. The key issue for management is whether culture(s) will exist in the organisation irrespective of management action or whether management can proactively influence and change culture. These issues will be considered in more detail in the second half of the chapter; we now consider how an understanding of culture within an organisation can be acquired.

Assessing organisational culture

Meyerson (1991) has noted that:

> culture was the code word for the subjective side of organisational life . . . its study represented an ontological rebellion against the dominant functionalist or 'scientific' paradigm (p.256).

In other words organisational culture research came about in part as a reaction to the existing approaches to the study of organisations, focusing on systems (Brown 1998). Despite this reaction, both quantitative and qualitative methods persist in the study of organisational culture (Rousseau 1990; Brown 1998). Moorhead and Griffin (1995) trace these differences back to the historical foundations, or antecedents, of current organisational culture and climate research. These include methodologies influenced by economics as well as those from psychology, sociology and anthropology.

As we might expect from an examination of definitions, approaches to assessment vary widely. Rousseau (1990) argues that debates over organisational research methods are the result of the resurgence of qualitative methodologies, originally based in anthropology and sociology, and the perceived shortcomings of quantitative approaches. Smircich (1983) proposes that standardised, quantitative measures cannot describe a culture, which is essentially a frame of reference. Similarly, Schein (1984) suggests that, since each organisation is unique, it is difficult for an outside researcher to form a priori questions or measures to tap into its culture. Furthermore, Schein (1984) asserts that the use of such quantitative methods is unethical in its use of aggregated data and not the participants' own words. Given the definitions of culture discussed earlier, it is important for quantitative organisational culture research to address these criticisms.

Quantitative approaches to the assessment of culture are, however, still popular. Many similar dimensions appear on several culture and climate assessment instruments, suggesting that values and behaviours can be expressed, and in turn assessed, in similar terms (Rousseau 1990). Furthermore, Xenikou and Furnham (1996) found significant correlations between four instruments and went on to suggest a six-factor model based on the work of Cooke and Lafferty (1989), Glaser (1983), Kilmann and Saxton (1983) and Sashkin and Fulmer (1985; cited in Rousseau 1990). The factors uncovered related to:

■ openness to change;

■ values of excellent organisations;

■ bureaucratic culture;

■ organisational artefacts;

■ resistance to new ideas; and

■ workplace social relations.

Not surprisingly, these factors relate, almost exclusively to the more accessible layers of culture outlined in Figure 9.1, and bear more than a passing resemblance to some of the categorisations discussed above.

In addition to alternative research strategies and data collection methods, Pettigrew (1979, 1990) has identified several analytical issues, related to the complexity of the concept, that make the study of culture difficult. These include, among others, the fact that culture might exist at different levels (Schein 1985), is pervasive across the organisation, can include subcultures and is interconnected with the organisational system, subsystems and the external environment. These kinds of issues, together with varying data collection and research strategies, would seem to make a comprehensive study of organisational culture almost impossible. Rousseau (1990) suggests that different approaches and strategies may suit the investigation of different levels and aspects of culture. Few empirical researchers claim to uncover everything about an organisation's culture in their investigations; they mainly focus on one or two of the elements discussed above, or the more accessible manifestations. In many cases attempts to assess the social psychological environment of an organisation has led researchers to focus on the similar concept of organisational climate. Indeed much discussion of the concept and the study of organisational culture is related to that of organisational climate (Denison 1996).

ORGANISATIONAL CLIMATE

Climate has been held to be the individual descriptions of the social setting or context of which the person is part. James and Jones (1974) suggested that climate reflects employee perceptions of work and organisational practices. Investigations into organisational climate pre-date organisational cultural studies by at least a decade and some of the current interest in cultural perspectives of organisations is a result of the earlier research focus on climate (Brown 1998).

Moran and Volkwein (1992) have incorporated previous definitions of organisational climate and proposed that it is:

> a relatively enduring characteristic of an organization which distinguishes it from other organizations: and (a) embodies members' collective perceptions about their organization with respect to such dimensions as autonomy, trust, cohesiveness, support, recognition, innovation, and fairness; (b) is produced by member interaction; (c) serves as a basis for interpreting the situation; (d) reflects the prevalent norms, values and attitudes of the organization's culture; and (e) acts as a source of influence for shaping behavior (p.20).

The above definition makes reference to organisational culture and highlights the similarities between the two concepts.

Culture versus climate

Many authors have addressed the relationship between culture and climate. Denison (1996) has written:

> On the surface, the distinction between organizational climate and organizational culture may appear to be quite clear. Climate refers to a situation and its link to thoughts, feelings and behaviours of organizational members. Thus, it is temporal, subjective and often subject to direct manipulation by people with power and influence. Culture, in contrast refers to an evolved context (within which a situation may be embedded). Thus it is rooted in history, collectively held, and sufficiently complex to resist many attempts at direct manipulation (p.644).

Denison (1996) agrees that the research methods used by the earlier researchers could help distinguish most culture and climate studies. Studying culture required qualitative research methods and an appreciation for the unique aspects of individual social settings. Studying organisational climate, in contrast, required quantitative methods. A culture study would have been concerned with uncovering unit values and beliefs through on-going observations of the individual in their group. Climate research, on the other hand, would have been characterised by surveys of members' attitudes about their organisation.

Despite their distinct evolution, culture and climate are now often used as interchangeable terms (Denison 1996). However, distinctions can still be made between these concepts. Ashforth (1985) distinguishes between the shared assumptions of culture and the shared perceptions of climate and argues that culture informs climate by helping group members to define what is important. Reichers and Schneider (1990) suggest that culture and climate both deal with the ways by which members of an organisation make sense of their environment, and that both are learned through socialisation and interaction. However culture exists at a higher level and relates to longer-term and overarching policies and goals, whereas climate has been more generally described as the way things are done on a day-to-day basis (Furnham 1997). Thus, measures of climate generally focus on individual or 'group' perceptions of the prevailing organisational structures, and culture measures generally focus on the patterns of values and beliefs that lead to the emergence of these structures (Cooke and Szumal 1983). A further distinction is offered by Hofstede *et al.* (1990) who see climate as describing shorter-term characteristics of the organisation which indicate how it treats its members. Culture, on the other hand, reflects longer-term characteristics which describe the types of people that the organisation employs.

Researchers in the field have proposed various connections between culture and climate as described above. At the very least the two constructs are complementary (Schneider 1987), at most they provide different interpretations of the same phenomenon (Denison 1996). Schein (1985) proposes that climate can most accurately be understood as a manifestation of culture. In this way a 'positive' culture will be promoted and maintained by a 'positive' climate and vice versa. Culture and climate can be viewed as reciprocal processes in a cyclic relationship.

Denison (1996) offers a useful way of considering conceptual and research method differences between culture and climate, while recognising that the terms are often used interchangeably by many researchers. The definitional and assessment issues discussed above have proved particularly problematic when seeking to understand any relationships between culture and organisational performance.

Culture and organisational performance

Of particular interest to organisations and managers is the (assumed) link between organisational culture and organisational performance. Silverzweig and Allen (1976) were probably the first to claim such a link. Based on eight case studies of organisations seeking to change their culture in order to improve effectiveness, they identified that six of the organisations improved their performance. However, the real spur to popularity of the culture – performance link was Peters and Waterman's (1982) *In Search of Excellence*. Several researchers have sought to define and assess the link between culture and various organisational outcomes, often in the hope of identifying or nurturing the 'best' culture associated with those outcomes. One example of theoretical links being drawn between culture and outcome measures is given by the role for organisational culture and climate in productivity modelled by Kopelman and colleagues (1990). Their model is based on the influence of human resource management on productivity and individual satisfaction and motivation and illustrates how culture, management practices and climate can influence the outcome measure. Similarly, Bright and Cooper (1993) have proposed that quality management and organisational culture are closely aligned, with overall culture change being central to the development of quality management systems and essential to their functioning, although no empirical data is presented. Several attempts have also been made to link the assessment of organisational culture with financial performance (for example, Denison 1984; Gordon 1985; Gordon and DiTomaso 1992). Gordon and DiTomaso (1992) suggest that the appropriate culture for achieving results in the insurance organisations they examined may not be best described only as 'strong' in terms of consistency, but also as flexible. The organisational culture related to effectiveness may, therefore, best be conceived as a combination of several characteristics, which facilitate enhanced performance.

Petty and colleagues (1995) have endeavoured to link the assessment of organisational culture with broader performance measures. Their assessment of performance incorporated evaluations of operations, customer accounting, support services, marketing and employee health and safety into one overall performance measure. This study found evidence of associations between the measures of performance and organisational culture, with the strongest indication of the link being evident in the correlations between 'teamwork' and performance. They conclude that a culture that fosters cooperation may be the most effective in the organisations included in their study. However, in a recent review of studies purporting to have examined the culture – performance link, Wilderom *et al.* (2000) are not convinced that meaningful conclusions can be drawn from the evidence available. They argue that different measures of culture are used in different studies and the operationalisation of performance is inconsistent and lacks validity. This is particularly problematic in respect of the main claim made; that strong cultures lead to effective performance. They suggest that assessment of the culture gap, that is the difference between employees' preferred organisational practices and their perceptions of actual practices, is a more fruitful line of research, because of the inconsistency in the way that culture is defined.

Organisational culture and Human Resource Management

Having spent some time so far in the chapter outlining and debating conceptual issues relating to culture and climate in organisations, this section of the chapter will seek to explore the impact of the interest in culture on people management practices. Consistent with the trends within the 'people management' literature generally, this chapter will consider human resource management to be the most contemporary, if not the most common, general approach to the management of people in the workplace. As a number of commentators within the UK have noted, human resource management and organisational culture seem to be highly intertwined concepts. So, for example, Storey (1995) and Legge (1995) have articulated the centrality of organisational culture to the development and practice of human resource management. Storey (1995, p.8) suggests that managing culture change coincides so much with the movement towards HRM that they 'become one and the same project'.

Fundamental assumptions which reflect managerial perspectives on organisational culture are also central to the beliefs and assumptions of human resource management. As Storey (1995, p.6), observes, management does not merely seek compliance with rules and the implementation of procedures and systems as a way of controlling employee behaviour but seeks to develop high levels of employee commitment through the management of culture.

Mabey and Salaman (1995) comment that some have also welcomed the recognition that understanding culture changes the emphasis from focusing purely on formal/rational aspects of the organisation, for example, organisational structure, rules, procedures and technical processes. However, like Sackmann (1991) they feel that 'managerialist' perspectives on culture are simplistic and ignore the complexities of the anthropological concept from which it is derived. For example, Deal and Kennedy (1982) seem to equate culture within organisations to culture in societies, and assume that the same processes will occur.

Some researchers consider that culture cannot be controlled by management within the organisation, whereas others tend to believe that is at least possible. We shall return to this discussion later in the chapter. Nevertheless, there has been something of a convergence of approach to researching and understanding culture from those practitioners/consultants and academics who do believe that there is the potential to manage organisational culture. As Barley *et al.* (1988) have noted both groups are interested in identifying how culture can be used as a mechanism to enhance performance.

There have been extreme concerns expressed by some academics regarding this new approach to the management of employees. Whereas previous rational approaches overtly used rules, regulations and procedures as a way of ensuring behavioural compliance from employees, many see culture management as equally controlling but in a covert way. The difference is that culture management techniques focus much less on rational rather than emotive approaches to employee management. Therefore, the winning of 'hearts and minds' and the legitimacy of seeking to manipulate employee emotions has been questioned by writers such as Casey (1995), Keenoy and Anthony (1992) and Willmott (1993), highlighting the ethical dimension.

Recognising that there are different perspectives in respect of the ethics and practicalities of manipulating culture within work organisations, we shall now assume that there is at least the potential for management to manipulate culture and explore how this might be done.

CULTURE MANAGEMENT AND HRM PRACTICES

A range of HR activities might be used to either reinforce the existing culture within an organisation or support management initiated culture change efforts.

Recruitment and selection

Traditionally, organisations have sought to match individuals' abilities to job requirements, commonly known as person–job (P–J) fit. More recently, research has focused on the fit between the person and the organisation (P–O), particularly in respect of the organisation's culture. In this sense the individual's abilities/competencies are considered less important than their attitudes/values and the match of these with the organisation's culture. This is an interesting development and implies that it may be easier to change/enhance employees' abilities rather than their attitudes or values. Some of the latest research (Adkins and Caldwell 2004) explores whether the match of the individual with the subculture or group (P-G fit) of the organisation in which they are located, may be more important to factors such as job satisfaction. This matching of the individual's values with the organisation's culture can be assessed, for potential employees, during the selection process. However, it is also important for individuals to assess whether the organisation's culture matches their own preferences. Examples of how the management of culture has been used to attract and retain employees are shown in Box 9.2.

Employee induction

A key opportunity for the organisation to influence employee values is during the early stages of their employment. Marchington and Wilkinson (2005) suggest there is little evidence in

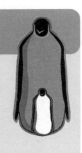

Box 9.2: Managing culture to attract staff

Madam Tussauds, which runs waxworks in various countries, as well as other visitor attractions, relies on seasonal labour for up to half its staffing, during peak periods. The company emphasises that it is a fun place to work as one of its mechanisms for (re)attracting staff. It uses beer and pizza evenings, Halloween balls and other events for staff to reinforce the culture it wishes to project (Arkin 2004)

A recent study by Cober *et al.* (2003) suggests that organisational websites that communicate clearly to possible job applicants regarding compensation, organisational culture and training opportunities can influence organisational attraction. However, culture is only one facet of attraction.

Recent research (Arnold *et al.* 2003) regarding recruitment and retention problems in the United Kingdom National Health Service (NHS) has also highlighted the importance of realistic job previews (Wanous 1989). Arnold *et al.* (2003) identified that some potential employees were put off by what they saw as unrealistic advertising and promotion campaigns which portrayed NHS work as rather more positive and attractive than candidates perceived it to be, and underplayed difficulties. Therefore, key cultural values participants wished to see associated with the NHS such as honesty and integrity appeared to be undermined by the recruitment campaigns which were simultaneously emphasising the high degree of expertise and professionalism expected of its staff.

A study by Van Vianen (2000) assessed new employees' perceptions of the organisational culture and whether this fitted with their personal preferences. Where new employees had a fit between their preference in respect of concern for people and this was shared with their supervisor, this was positively related to the newcomers' organisational commitment and (lack of) turnover intentions. However general perceptions of the organisational culture had little influence on new employees' affective outcomes, thus it was less important that newcomers perceived the organisational culture in the same way as their supervisor/peers, than that the culture fitted with the newcomers' preferences regarding value congruence.

Rather than seeking to ensure fit between applicants and the existing culture, Williams *et al.* (1993) identify the use of selection as a way of contributing to culture change. An electricity organisation increased the number of sales staff by 63 per cent over 5 years as part of a desired move from a technical to a sales culture. Iles and Mabey (cited in Stewart and McGoldrick 1996) have identified British Airways' use of Egyptian cabin crew and incorporation of Egyptian 'culture' on the London–Cairo route. As they point out this was done to attract more customers, not simply to introduce international diversification into the workforce. The evaluation by Iles and Mabey did not indicate complete success in either respect.

mainstream human resource publications to indicate that induction is used as a way of imparting the organisation's culture, and seeking to influence new employees in that respect. However, Harrison (2000, p.248) suggests that dialogic learning comprises a major component of induction programmes and 'should help [new starters] to understand and adapt to the vision of the organisation and its implicit values and norms'.

Dundon *et al.* (2001) have identified that an (unnamed) consultancy organisation employs a full-time culture manager, part of whose role is to ensure that new employees fit in with and are committed to the prevailing culture.

Trice and Beyer (1993) refer to different rites and identify induction and basic training as what they term a rite of passage, e.g., into the organisation. As they note, the manifest purpose of a rite of passage such as induction is to 'facilitate transition of persons into social roles and statuses that are new for them' (1993, p.111).

The extensive socialisation literature has referred to the impact of the socialisation process on organisational newcomers. For example, Ashforth (2001) identifies that formalised collective socialisation, for example in induction programmes can help reduce the anxiety of role/organisational entry for newcomers. Even if organisations commit considerable time and effort to the formalised socialisation process at the point of organisational entry, individuals will still, over time, be influenced by informal events which affect the newcomer's perspectives (for example, Ricks 1997). Gundry and Rousseau (1994) have identified that new organisational entrants come to understand their organisation's culture by decoding 'critical incidents'.

Therefore, unless the formalised institutional socialisation represented by induction programmes is reinforced by the activities and contacts newcomers encounter in day-to-day organisational life, it may not necessarily achieve the desired effect (from the organisation's perspective).

Training and development

A traditional personnel management approach to training and development would tend to focus individuals on learning job specific skills and knowledge rather than on personal development or broader career issues. However, Williams *et al.* (1993) indicate this may be a necessary first step as part of a culture change effort. For example, they suggest that it will not be possible to develop a customer-oriented culture if customer contact staff do not have the appropriate skills to interact effectively with customers. Equally, organisations such as building societies which have become privatised banks, for example Abbey National (now simply Abbey) have needed to develop business skills among their managers as part of a more commercial culture.

Lee (1996) proposes that learning and development activities can focus on different components of the individual. Some focus purely on the acquisition of knowledge ('head'), some focus on the development of skills ('hands') whereas some focus on affective aspects of the self and their relationships with others ('heart'). Some activities seek to integrate all these components.

Williams *et al.* (1993) suggest that training focused on employee behaviour is likely to be necessary in seeking to change employee values and attitudes. Indeed, Kunda (1992) argues that explicit attempts to change values can lead to employees feeling manipulated or brainwashed and therefore, becoming very cynical. Ogbonna and Wilkinson (1988) indicate that even behaviourally focused change efforts can lead to what they called resigned behavioural compliance. Hopfl *et al.* (1992) have followed British Airways long-term programme of culture management and highlight the need for consistency of message and practice from the organisation if employees are to consider the message credible. Perhaps more significantly they stress the differing reactions from individuals subjected to the same culture change process. Thus management cannot assume that all employees will respond in the way that management would wish.

Communication and integration activities

Communication is considered by many managers to be a central component of culture management (Williams *et al.* 1993). Manipulation of artefacts and symbols, Schein's (1985) top or surface level of culture, is the focus here. For example, Unisys used publications and audio cassette magazines as a way of reinforcing key cultural values such as customer orientation. Trice and Beyer (1993) identify two forms of rite which organisations may use to communicate culture. The rite of enhancement, for example the use of company newsletters, team briefings and employee of the month award schemes, can serve a number of purposes. It could be to spread good news about the organisation, equally it could focus on individuals, and provide public recognition for their accomplishments. At the same time this recognition of individual achievement is designed to communicate to others what is expected of them and act as a stimulus for effort and motivation.

The rite of integration again uses non-work activities as a way of influencing employees' emotions. For example, organised social events, e.g., barbecues, visits to bowling alleys, etc., can be used to try and foster a sense of binding employees to the social system, i.e., the organisation. This may be particularly the case where the organisation seeks to foster a high degree of teamworking and team commitment. Williams *et al.* (1993) identify the way that Marley tried to break down formal divisions between functions within the organisation through the use of inter-functional social activities.

Payment/rewards systems

Lawler (1990) has suggested that payments and reward systems need to take into account a range of internal and external factors and need to be consistent with the organisation's strategy and required behaviours of employees in order to achieve organisational goals. Armstrong (1999) suggests that the organisation's remuneration policy is one part of its human resource strategy and the different components of that HR strategy need to be complementary and not contradict each other. While reward strategy impacts on various HR activities, for example recruiting, retaining and motivating staff, Armstrong emphasises it can also be used as a way of communicating organisational values. Williams *et al.* (1993) stress that consistency is important if the organisation is not to send mixed messages to employees regarding management's preferred cultural values. For example, management may decide to reinforce the need for teamworking rather than individual 'stars'. However, if individually based performance-related pay, rather than team-based pay is used, employee behaviour is likely to respond to the greatest potential for financial reward rather than consistency with management-espoused cultural values. Therefore, it is important for organisations to think through how the different components of HR strategy fit together and reinforce each other.

Redundancies

When an organisation is seeking to achieve culture change it may find that certain individuals or groups of staff are particularly resistant to the proposed new culture. Williams *et al.* (1993) have noted the use by various organisations of redundancy programmes as a way of reducing resistance to culture change efforts. Similarly, after a merger, some individuals in the newly formed Unisys felt unable to be committed to the new organisation after long years of service with one of the merged organisations. In both instances, the importance of handling redundancy in a sensitive way is emphasised. More dramatically, Trice and Beyer (1993) talk about rites of degradation, the third example of which is the rite of removal. This is where an individual, for example the chief executive/managing director, or a group of people, e.g., the senior management team, are seen to be identified with failures within the organisation. Because of this it is considered appropriate to remove them from the organisation in order to move forward and introduce the required change. This is consistent with numerous models (see 'Leadership' section, below) where the role of leadership is considered crucial to cultural change. As Trice and Beyer (1993, p.115) note, the use of removal can 'can be dysfunctional if the person degraded did not contribute to the problems and if the degradation becomes a substitute for doing something more effective to deal with the problems'.

Performance management/appraisal

Stiles *et al.* (1997) undertook a study of performance management and its impact on perceptions of values. This study occurred in a distribution company, a telecommunications company and a bank, all of which had recently introduced values statements. While managers were aware of the corporate values being espoused by their organisations they still saw that their short-term demands were primarily focused around financial targets and the need to achieve other organisational objectives. In addition the setting of objectives was imposed from senior management without any negotiation. Perceptions were also influenced by the fact that organisational downsizing left managers in doubt whether even achievement of their objectives would be enough to facilitate career progression or, at worst, even job security.

We have already commented on the difficulty of identifying any relationship between culture and organisational level performance. Recent research in the UK by Ogbonna and Harris (2000) suggests that cultures which are externally-oriented, incline towards risk taking and readiness to meet new challenges and tend to be more strongly associated with organisational performance (which was operationalised using a range of measures), than cultures that are predominantly internally focused. However, as with other studies this work was cross-sectional and correlational and therefore it is difficult to identify whether culture was actually a cause of performance.

Williams (2002) suggests that the performance management process might be seen as a way of developing, at least in part, a 'performance culture'. However, certain advocates of performance management, e.g., Armstrong (1994) tend to associate performance management with a set of values reflecting openness, trust, employee participation, etc., in the performance management process. In contrast, a performance culture may not place any emphasis on these things and simply focus on increasing employee productivity, etc. For example, Fletcher and Williams (1992) identified that an organisation's performance culture placed particular emphasis on 'bottom line' results. Employees felt that fear was the driving force underpinning the performance culture rather than participation and openness.

In purely performance terms, many organisations may only be concerned with seeking to change employee behaviour rather than to change the deeper levels of cultural values and assumptions. Indeed Williams *et al.* (1993) recognised that behaviour change seems to be the central focus of many culture change programmes.

Leadership

In a useful analysis and evaluation of different models of culture change, Brown (1998) identifies the importance of leadership. The importance of leaders particularly at the top of the organisation, as figureheads of, and role models for, preferred culture and values is seen as crucial. A new leader is often associated with a new approach to culture. We referred earlier to the compulsory removal of leaders as a signal to employees of a state of change. Leaders at different levels in the organisation have influence and control over various organisational rites (Trice and Beyer 1993). We have referred already to some of these rites. The rite of enhancement is a clear and generally public activity that enhances the status of an individual. Mechanisms that may be used here include employee of the month award schemes, articles in company newsletters, commendations at team briefings.

At the most senior level leaders are often associated with charismatic qualities and considered to have the capacity to lead transformation of the organisation. There are links here with Bernard Bass' (1985) work on transformational leadership. Not only is the leader responsible for creating the vision for the organisation, but also being the embodiment of that vision and role-modelling it personally in order to influence others. Schein (1992) stresses the roles that leaders at all organisational levels have to play, and that this will vary depending upon the organisation's stage of development and require different types of culture management at different stages. He also stresses that different strategic issues lead to a focus on different cultural dimensions.

Employee relations

While much of the HRM approach tends to downplay the role of trade unions and formal mechanisms for employee representation, Williams *et al.* (1993) indicate that some organisations considered formal trade union involvement and support as essential. For example, Toshiba introduced a single union agreement with the EETPU, and employee representation on the 'company advisory board' was designed to achieve greater employee understanding of, and commitment to, organisational goals and values. Organisations may also use other mechanisms to foster involvement from employees. Employee suggestion schemes, quality circles and/or project groups can all be used as a way of indicating to employees that they have a voice and their ideas are valuable. However, some authors have been critical of some of these mechanisms in the way that they have excluded formal employee representation and downgraded the role for trade unions. For example Keenoy and Anthony (1992) have argued that HRM has often been used as a way of conducting anti-unionist policies. Indeed, they and others, for example Willmott (1993), see culture management as a way of increasing management control rather than empowering employees.

We have referred to a range of HRM practices that may be utilised as part of culture management efforts, however, as Williams *et al.* have indicated:

> It should not be assumed that culture can be changed simply by the introduction of, say, a new appraisal system, new reward practices or new methods of training. All of these are likely to have an effect on culture and each of these could be a crucial element of a culture change programme. In isolation though these personnel mechanisms are likely to be subordinated to the existing culture (1993, p.28).

Is culture change feasible?

There is considerable scepticism regarding the feasibility of management proactively changing organisational culture, particularly at the deep fundamental levels. For example Meek (1982) suggests that those who propose that culture change is feasible do not recognise that power differentials exist within organisations, that subcultures exist and that ultimately in seeking to change culture, management is seeking to control employees. However, she does accept that change over the artefacts or surface levels of culture is feasible. Ogbonna (1992) suggests that the espoused aim of many culture change programmes, that is to enhance employee commitment, is not achieved. In many senses change is focused purely on employee behaviours and achieved through compliance rather than the commitment which is sought. Sackmann (1991) suggests that cultures are highly complex, dynamic systems with individual and group variability within them. Therefore, they are not really amenable to direct management. For some writers attempts at culture management are ethically unacceptable. For example, Willmott (1993, p.517), argues that managers may like the idea of greater control over employees by using culture management to 'colonise the affective domain . . . promoting employee commitment to a monolithic structure of feeling and thought'. As he argues, the control has been transferred from managers to employees through high levels of self-monitoring and self-management. At one level employees are empowered to manage their own work, but in effect they have simply incorporated the organisation's desire for high standards of performance and behaviour and are only empowered to do what the organisation wants them to do. Thompson and McHugh (2002) reinforce this idea suggesting that by managing the meanings and values of employees, management seeks to manipulate employees' internalised sources of control and commitment.

Despite the cynicism about both the ethics of attempting, as well as the feasibility of achieving culture change, some writers have argued that culture change is feasible albeit with considerable difficulty. For example, Pettigrew (1990) has, on the basis of considerable research, proposed a number of factors for consideration in seeking to undertake culture change. He does note that this will be an arduous process and is more likely to affect surface levels of culture rather than core assumptions.

Harris and Ogbonna (1998) summarise the differing views on the feasibility of changing culture by suggesting three different perspectives; (a) culture can be managed, (b) culture cannot be managed, and (c) culture can be manipulated but only under certain conditions. They also stress that little research effort has been directed at understanding employee reactions to managerial culture change attempts. Therefore they conducted an empirical study in two contexts, one food and one clothing company in the British retail sector. They identified that employees could respond in a range of ways and that two key determinants seemed to be at play. One was willingness to change and the second was the existing strength of the particular subculture (for example, division of the organisation). Responses could range from active rejection through to active acceptance. Particularly interesting responses were reinvention and reinterpretation. Reinvention occurs where the attributes of the existing culture are recycled so that superficially at least, they appear to be in line with the new culture being espoused by management. Reinterpretation occurs where employee values and behaviour are modified to some extent but in a way which is consistent with both the existing culture and the desired culture. While there appears to be some adoption of the espoused culture this is filtered through the understanding of the existing culture and in that sense is not necessarily a predictable response. As we commented earlier individuals can and do respond to culture change efforts in widely different ways. As Harris and Ogbonna (1998) note there can be a range of responses between outright acceptance or rejection. This unpredictability of response makes culture change difficult to manage. Therefore Harris and Ogbonna suggest that attempts at culture change should not seek radical and transformational change but work on an incremental basis.

Conclusion

Based on the evidence reviewed in this chapter what can we say about organisational culture? First, despite the vast number of definitions and classification systems we can describe organisational culture as a phenomenon that involves beliefs, values and behaviours, exists at a variety of different levels, and manifests itself in a wide range of artefacts within any particular organisation. It is also apparent that culture is difficult to assess directly, given the varying data collection methods and the multi-level nature of the construct, but it is closely related to the concept of climate, which may be more easily assessed. Furthermore, culture might provide a useful description of organisational environments, which facilitate their comprehension, interpretation, acceptance and control, and might, but only might, help explain their success in terms of performance. Finally, if organisational culture is to be of use to managers and organisations, they must be able to adapt and change their culture when necessary.

It is clear from the research discussed in this chapter, however, that while culture change and the management of it by the organisation may appear feasible there are practical problems associated with it. A number of such issues can be identified:

1. At what level is culture change occurring – is it at the artefacts level or at the level of fundamental assumptions?
2. Even if behaviour is changed is this really culture change? If employee values and assumptions have not changed does this really matter if management is primarily interested in employees demonstrating appropriate behaviours?
3. Do organisations have unitary cultures, and if so is it feasible to change the culture of the whole organisation at once?
4. If it is accepted that organisations comprise subcultures, are strategies for culture change sophisticated enough to recognise the differential approaches required?

Martin (1992) has suggested that three differing perspectives can be adopted in seeking to understand culture and therefore interpret ways to approach culture change and its effectiveness. The integration perspective is most typical of management in that it assumes an organisation-wide consensus within the organisation and that consistency is feasible. The differentiation perspective assumes that there are likely to be subcultures within the organisation which will be inconsistent in their responses to culture change efforts. The fragmentation perspective assumes that there is such a multiplicity of views with little or no consensus that managing culture will be immensely complex.

UNDERSTANDING THE CULTURE OF AN ORGANISATION

JOHN LOAN-CLARKE AND ALISTAIR CHEYNE

Think about an organisation you know. This could be one you have worked in permanently (now or in the past), temporarily (e.g., vacation work) or during an industrial placement. Consider the following two questions about that organisation:

1. What do you consider the organisation's culture to be?

   Either use your own words to describe this or relate your understanding of the culture to one of the models we have covered in this chapter, e.g., Harrison, Deal and Kennedy, etc.
2. Does this culture apply equally across the whole of the organisation or just to a certain part(s) of it?

   You will initially need to think through these ideas on your own. Make some brief notes to help organise your thoughts. Having done this, exchange your ideas with others in a group.

LEVELS OF CULTURE

JOHN LOAN-CLARKE AND ALISTAIR CHEYNE

Various models of culture identify that it comprises a number of levels. For example, Schein's (1985) model comprises three. Choose one of these models and do the following:

Explain what each of the three levels means and what information would be needed to understand the culture at that level.

CULTURE AND CLIMATE ISSUES WITHIN A HEALTHCARE TRUST

JOHN LOAN-CLARKE AND ALISTAIR CHEYNE

The organisation

The case study organisation is a NHS community health care Trust (CHT) in England. It comprises two community hospitals and a number of health centres and clinics across a dispersed geographical region. Like all NHS Trusts in the UK over recent years, the organi-sation had been forced to react to a number of external pressures for change brought about by governmental reforms at a national level. The chief executive of the Trust, however, was proud to tell us that, despite the pressures and cuts in funding, no compulsory redundancies had been entailed and that he had fought hard behind the scenes to maintain funding and protect jobs. The Trust had recently achieved some of the best Patients Charter results in the region. This is an initiative introduced by the UK government which publicly announces the results of quantitative measures of Trust 'success' using criteria such as the length of time spent waiting for a consultation or operation and the numbers of patients seen. The Trust had also been awarded Investors in People status. This is another national initiative, which is granted to organisations which are able to demonstrate a high level of investment in their employees. Criteria used to judge the award include evidence of training and effective communication systems. In addition, two communications initiatives had recently been introduced by management; a monthly team briefing and a Trust newsletter. These were intended to help employees understand the broad implications of change for the Trust and, more specifically, to reassure staff about the relatively strong financial position of the Trust and the on-going policy of no compulsory redundancies.

The Trust management team originally commissioned research to assess employees' reactions to these communication initiatives and to provide feedback to management regarding employees' overall perceptions of working for the Trust. A second major management consideration was the impending introduction of a computerised information system for healthcare professionals working in the community, for example district nurses. Management was keen to assess the impact of the introduction of this system on staff work practices and attitudes, and wished to establish a benchmark for doing this, in its desire to introduce what it termed an 'information-led culture'.

As Cavanagh (1996) has noted, the impact of UK NHS reforms has led to a need to investigate and possibly change the culture of UK healthcare organisations, and management at CHT was keen to gather information from staff because of this.

Activity

Assume you have been commissioned by the management team at CHT to assess reactions to the communication and information change initiatives. They are also interested in gathering data regarding employees' overall perceptions of working for the Trust.

Outline how you would go about conducting this assignment.
1) What sort of questions would you ask and why?
2) Who would you seek to gather information from and why?
3) What data collection and analysis methods would you use and why?
4) How and to whom would you report back your findings?

CASE STUDY 9.4

MANAGING CULTURE AT BRITISH AIRWAYS

IRENA GRUGULIS AND ADRIAN WILKINSON

The British Airways story

Even by the standards of modern management myths the British Airways transformation is impressive. At the end of the 1970s and the start of the 1980s BA was performing disastrously against almost every indicator. Its fleet was old, which meant journeys were uncomfortable and contributed significantly to the airline's record for unpunctuality; its productivity was considerably below that of its main overseas competitors; it was beset by industrial disputes; and it was recording substantial financial losses (£140 million or some £200 a minute in 1981). Staff discontent was more than matched by customer dissatisfaction and in 1980 a survey by the International Airline Passengers' Association put BA at the top of a list of airlines to be avoided at all costs. By the mid-1990s this picture was reversed. Not only had BA become the world's most profitable carrier, it was also voted the company that most graduates would like to work for and, in the year 2000, another survey declared it the second most admired company in Europe (Corke 1986; Warhurst 1995; Blyton and Turnbull 1998; *Financial Times*, 9 July 1997; *Financial Times*, 18 March 2000).

Much of the management literature attributes this turnaround to BA's own cultural change which remodelled staff attitudes and set customer care as the primary focus of activity. As Doyle (1999, p. 20) noted:

> In the 80s BA had been transformed from a disastrous loss-making state enterprise – the British Rail of the sky – into the world's largest and most profitable international airline. It was a triumph for management, showing that Britain could produce world-class companies that could beat the best of the competition. Its success was the result of the process and strategy that management introduced. The process focused on creating a vision that would inspire the BA staff and gain their enthusiastic commitment.

It is certainly true that a great deal of effort and energy went into shaping BA's culture. At the heart of this was the 'Putting People First' (PPF) training programme launched by Colin Marshall, the company's new chief executive, in 1983. Originally intended for staff who had direct contact with customers it was, in fact, attended by all 40,000 employees by 1986 and it aimed to revolutionise their attitudes. In a direct challenge to the hierarchical and militaristic culture which existed in BA at the time, staff were instructed not to attend in uniform and, once on the course, put into cross-functional and cross-grade groups. Attendees were encouraged to take a more positive attitude to themselves, taught how to set personal goals and cope with stress and instructed in confidence building and 'getting what they wanted out of life'. Lapel badges inscribed with the motto 'We're putting people first' provided a visible reminder of the course's message.

The approach was self-conciously 'indoctrinative' (Bate 1994, p. 195). As Colin Marshall said

'We . . . have to design our people and their service attitude just as we design an aircraft seat, an in-flight entertainment programme or an airport lounge *to meet the needs and preferences of our customers*' (cited in Barsoux and Manzoni 1997, p.14: emphasis added).

But the most impressive aspect of BA's cultural change was not so much the sophistication of the PPF programme itself, nor the commitment of executive time, but the extent to which other employment policies and practices were changed to fit the 'new' culture and the continued emphasis on these practices and programmes throughout the 1980s and 1990s. Three-quarters of the 100 Customer First teams, formed to propagate the message of PPF, survived into the 1990s. Not only were team briefings and teamworking introduced but these were developed and refined with TQM, autonomous teamworking and multi-skilling introduced in many areas. Direct contact with all staff was considered so important that 'down route' briefings were developed to ensure that mobile and isolated staff were not neglected and in 1996 BA became the first company to make daily TV broadcasts to its staff (Colling 1995).

The way cabin crew were rostered was also changed. 'Families' of staff were created to work the same shift patterns. These were intended to provide mutual support, make cabin crew feel happier about their work environments and, as a result, facilitate the production of emotional labour (Barsoux and Manzoni 1997). A new role of 'passenger group coordinator' was introduced and staff appointed based entirely on personal qualities. The importance of emotional processes was also reflected in the new appraisal and reward systems such that work was judged on the way in which it was performed as well as against harder targets (Georgiades and Macdonnell 1998; Höpfl 1993). Managerial bonuses could be as much as 20 per cent of salary and were calculated on a straight 50:50 split between exhibiting desired behaviours and achieving quantitative goals. 'Awards for Excellence' and an 'Employee Brainwaves' programme encouraged staff input. The personnel department was renamed 'human resources' with many decisions devolved to line managers and, in the first few years of the programme at least, a commitment was made to job security.

Closely following these developments, a 'Managing People First' programme targeted managerial employees and aimed to bring their behaviours into line with a list developed by two consultancy firms (see Table 9.1).

Other courses were developed to maintain the momentum created by 'Putting People First' and 'Managing People First'. These included 'Winning for Customers', 'A Day in the Life', 'To Be the Best', 'Leading in a Service Business' and 'Leadership 2000' and, while each was different, they all shared a focus on shaping staff emotions. The most dramatic form of this was probably the 'love bath' exercise in one of the early courses in which delegates took it in turns to sit in the centre of a circle while their colleagues complimented them (see Höpfl 1993). Nearly 20 years after the launch of PPF, BA managers attending a training course were still being told about understanding themselves and taking responsibility: 'understanding self is our starting point . . . That means that to make a change within the airline we need to start with you – what can *you* do differently'. In 1995, Bob Ayling, newly taken over from Colin Marshall as chief executive, continued this active management of company culture and said of his staff: 'I want them to feel inspired, I want

Table 9.1   The four factor menu of practices used in British Airways in 1984–85

THE MENU OF PRACTICES

FACTOR I

CLARITY AND HELPFULNESS

Establishing clear, specific objectives for subordinates

Helping subordinates to understand how their jobs contribute to the overall performance of the organisation

Clearly defining standards of excellence required for job performance

Providing help, training and guidance for subordinate

Giving subordinates a clear-cut decision when they need one

FACTOR II

PROMOTING ACHIEVEMENT

Emphasising and demonstrating commitment to achieving goals

Giving subordinates feedback on how they are doing

Communicating your views to others honestly and directly about their performance

Recognising people more often than criticising them

Recognising subordinates for innovation and calculated risk taking

FACTOR III

INFLUENCING THROUGH PERSONAL EXCELLENCE AND TEAMWORKING

Knowing and being able to explain to others the mission of the organisation and how it relates to their jobs

Communicating high personal standards informally through appearance and dedication

Noticing and showing appreciation for extra effort

Sharing power in the interest of achieving overall organisation objectives

Being willing to make tough decisions in implementing corporate strategy

FACTOR IV

CARE AND TRUST

Behaving in a way that leads others to trust you

Building warm, friendly relationships

Paying close attention to what people are saying

Responding non-defensively when others disagree with your views

Making sure that there is a frank and open exchange at work group meetings

Source: *Leadership for Competitive Advantage*, Georgiades N. and Macdonnell R. Copyright 1998, p.174. Copyright John Wiley and Sons Ltd. Reproduced with permission

them to feel optimistic, I want them to feel that this is a good place to be' ('Dangerous Company', BBC2 April 2000).

Such substantive change certainly seems to justify the plaudits heaped on it. But, as an account, it suffers from a number of flaws. Most significantly, as Anthony (1994) notes, together with other presentations of culture change it neglects structure. Yet the existence of cultural factors do not negate more material ones and there were certainly structural reasons for BA's success. Colin Marshall's emphasis on putting people first and caring for one another had been preceded by a rule of fear. BA's first response to its problems had been a massive series of redundancies, the largest in British history at the time, with staff numbers reduced by 40 per cent between 1981 and 1983 (albeit with generous severance).

More fundamentally, the company was well-provided with slots in Britain's prestigious Heathrow airport and faced little competition on many of the routes that it served. European markets were still tightly regulated and market share often depended on negotiation skills rather than competitive success. In 1987, just before privatisation, BA controlled some 60 per cent of the UK domestic market and only experienced competition on 9 per cent of routes into and out of the UK (Monopolies and Mergers Commission 1987). Post privatisation its position was actually strengthened when it gained a 75 per cent share of domestic routes (Colling 1995). Moreover, BA built up a series of alliances and mergers to consolidate this position.

While staff numbers were being drastically cut, the infrastructure was dramatically improved. The fact that new uniforms were provided is well-covered in the human resource and marketing literature. Less commonly noted is that BA invested in control systems, terminal facilities and aircraft. Between 1980 and 1985 BA replaced over half their fleet (Colling 1995). Computer reservations were introduced, a series of hub and spoke routes through first Heathrow and then Gatwick networked flights, and selectively focused competitive pricing served to limit what little competition the airline faced (Blyton and Turnbull 1996). Nor was this the only strategy deployed against competitors. In 1993 BA used shared booking information to persuade Virgin customers to transfer to BA, informing them (incorrectly) that Virgin flights were no longer available. The subsequent court case fined BA £610,000 damages and £3 million costs. It raised questions about the extent of knowledge and involvement of Lord King, the chairman, Sir Colin Marshall, the chief executive and Bob Ayling, the head of marketing as well as criticising the impact of the BA culture itself.

Not only can much of the BA turnaround be attributed to structural factors, but also the extent of the company's cultural transformation itself is open to question. While cultural change interventions seek to influence the thoughts, values, attitudes and norms of others, employees are not cultural dupes. Cooperation may reflect ambition or pride in work as much as (or instead of) a belief in the organisation itself. Despite the claims of the prescriptive literature, the existence of 'culture management' does not ensure either that employees trust management, or that management trusts employees. So, in BA, 'new' management practices varied in the extent that they were introduced in departments and conflict between employees and management did not cease.

Nor was the much vaunted job security quite as robust as it seemed. Alliances, mergers and franchising agreements with other airlines already supported what was, in effect a 'tiered' system of terms and conditions with employees based at Heathrow privileged over those in the regional airports. This emphasis on part-time, seasonal and subcontracted work was extended to most aspects of BA's operations. Its engine overhaul plant was sold off to GEC, data processing work was moved to Bombay, and job security for existing staff questioned (Colling 1995; Warhurst 1995; Blyton and Turnbull 1996). And all this at a time when BA was making record profits.

In short, BA, while putting a great deal of effort into encouraging certain behaviours from staff, did not base its employment policies and practices around the new culture in the way that many accounts suggest. Their array of human resource management techniques was certainly impressive but not everyone benefitted from them and those employed in partner, assoicate, merged or taken-over firms often experienced very different terms and conditions to the 'core' BA staff.

Staff reactions to 'culture change' included enthusiasm and acceptance but also doubt, concern, opposition and open cynicism. Such individual reactions were mirrored by the collective representations and the persistence of disputes even at the height of the 'cultural success'.

The 1997 dispute

By the end of the 1990s many of the structural factors that had provided the basis for the company's success were under threat. The emergence of low-cost carriers such as easyJet and Ryanair were undercutting BA's prices and, elsewhere, alliances between rivals Lufthansa and United Airlines ensured that cross-national traffic would be less likely to transfer to BA. The company's hold on Heathrow was also loosening under double pressure from Europe and the USA. In response, Ayling claimed BA needed a second revolution. BA sought its own alliance with a different US carrier, American Airlines as well as proposing £1 billion of cost savings from within the organisation, with the aim of doubling profits by the year 2000. Much of this was to come from staff savings including 5,000 voluntary redundancies with staff to be replaced by newly hired employees on lower pay (Blyton and Turnbull 1998). In addition, BA established links with a charter airline called Flying Colours intending to continue its policy of outsourcing to other operators.

This policy of reducing labour costs was also extended to 'core' BA staff. In early 1997, BA attempted to change the structure of payments to cabin crew. It was proposed that the existing employees would be 'bought out' of their series of allowances (petrol, overnight stay, etc.) by receiving a higher basic wage. BA offered a three-year guarantee that no crew member would earn less under the new system but nothing beyond that and it was clear to cabin crew staff that the measure was launched with the explicit aim of saving money. When these negotiations failed, one union, the TGWU, threatened strike action (Cabin Crew 89, a small breakaway union, had already accepted management's offer). Despite 14 years of espoused policy of caring for one another and putting people first, the tactics deployed by BA's management were described by two such different sources as the TUC and *The Economist* as bullying (*The Economist*, 27 July 1997; Taylor 1998). Members of the cabin crew were warned not to strike and BA managers were instructed to tell discontented staff that anyone taking industrial action would be summarily sacked, then sued for damages. Any who simply stayed away would face disciplinary action, be denied promotion and lose both pension rights and staff discounts on flights for three years.
BA were also reported to be filming pickets.

The subsequent strike ballot had an 80 per cent turnout with 73 per cent of employees voting in favour of strike action. The TGWU called a series of 72-hour strikes with the first action scheduled for 9 July 1997. In response, temporary staff and an alternative workforce of 'volunteer managers' were given a training to perform the key tasks of the ground handling staff and BA threatened to take legal action over claimed discrepancies in the ballot. On the eve of the first day of action airline cabin crew were telephoned at home and warned that 'they had a duty to cooperate with their employer'.

These managerial actions certainly influenced the impact of the strike. On the first scheduled day of action fewer than 300 workers declared themselves officially on strike but more than 2,000 called in sick. The company's threats and 'replacement workers' notwithstanding more than 70 per cent of flights from Heathrow were cancelled. It seemed that BA's macho approach had ensured only that collective action took the form of collective illness.

Ironically this 'mass sickie' served to make things worse for BA. Not only did the pre-strike ballots (conducted to comply with legislation designed to discourage union activities) compound the effects of the strike by providing customers with advance notice of it; but also those employees who had called in sick tended to stay away longer than the official 72-hour strike. BA insisted that sick employees provide a doctor's note within 48 hours instead of the normal seven days but many employees still stayed off for the full two weeks that their sick notes allowed and, throughout this period, services were cancelled and passengers turned away. The strike was costly. Airline seats are a particularly perishable form of consumer good and aircraft scheduling is easily disrupted. When Bill Morris, the General Secretary of the TGWU announced that he had written to Bob Ayling, suggesting that they resume negotiations, Ayling agreed before even receiving the letter.

The TGWU promised to save £42 million over three years. Catering was sold off but existing staff kept earnings and BA staff discounts, while sanctions against strikers were withdrawn and the TGWU increased its membership by 50 per cent to over 10,000. BA's management fared less well, despite Bob Ayling's claim that this agreement marked a 'new beginning and spirit of a cooperation'. The gulf between the managerial rhetoric on culture and official actions during the strike had a predictable effect on employee morale. One undercover employee publication, aptly named *Chaos* advised on ways of maximising payments by delaying aircraft. These included throwing duvet feathers into the engine, superglueing down the toilet seat and poisoning the pilot: 'a particularly obnoxious captain can be made to suffer all the symptoms of violent food poisoning by emptying eye drops from the aircraft medical kit into his salad or drink'.

Moreover, the agreement itself fostered further dissent. By the end of 1997, 4,000 staff had left, but 4,500 more were recruited including 2,000 in 1998. By the terms of the agreement, these new staff were employed on different contracts to existing employees. As a result, cabin crew working the same shifts on the same aircraft were (increasingly) on different payscales. The impact of this on both labour relations and BA's much prized teamworking was problematic and problems were fuelled by suggestions that staff on new contracts were favoured by BA in promotion to purser (first line manager).

Bob Ayling attempted to salvage the situation by placing more emphasis on managing the company's culture. Following Colin Marshall he addressed staff training sessions and held question and answer forums with groups of employees. This time there were few positive reactions. The strike cost BA £125 million; morale never entirely recovered and profits suffered. Between 1998 and 1999 they fell by 61 per cent and in 2000 British Airways announced losses of £244 million on its main business. While gains from disposals succeeded in keeping the company out of the red this was its worst performance (and first loss) since privatisation. The new logo Bob Ayling had launched (at great expense) during the 1997 dispute was unpopular and had to be withdrawn. These failures so coloured the public perception of the chief executive that even his attempts to refocus BA onto profitable routes and introduce a new seat for business class, long-haul passengers were not entirely welcomed. On 10 March 2000, Bob Ayling resigned as chief executive.

Source: Adapted from I. Grugulis and A. Wilkinson (2002) 'Managing culture at British Airways: hype, hope and reality', *Long-Range Planning*, Vol.35, No.2.

Questions

1. Explain employee reactions to culture change initiatives in this case.

2. What lessons can managers learn from this case about managing culture?

References

Anthony, P.D. (1994) *Managing Culture*, Buckingham: Open University Press.

Barsoux, J.-L. and Manzoni, J.-F. (1997) *Becoming the World's Favourite Airline: British Airways 1980–1993*, Bedford: European Case Clearing House.

Bate, P. (1994) *Strategies for Cultural Change*, London: Butterworth Heinemann.

Blyton, P. and Turnbull, P. (1996) 'Confusing convergence: industrial relations in the European airline industry: a comment on Warhurst', *European Journal of Industrial Relations*, Vol.2, No.1, pp.7–20.

Blyton, P. and Turnbull, P. (1998) *The Dynamics of Employee Relations* (2nd edn), London: Macmillan.

Colling, T. (1995) 'Experiencing turbulence: competition, strategic choice and the management of human resources in British Airways', *Human Resource Management Journal*, Vol.5, No.5, pp.18–32.

Corke, A. (1986) *British Airways: The Path to Profitability*, London: Frances Pinter.

'Dangerous Company', BBC2, April 2000.

Doyle, P. (1999) 'From the top', *The Guardian*, 4 December.

Financial Times, 9 July 1997.

Financial Times, 18 March 2000.

George Galloway, MP, 'Newsnight', BBC2, 10 July 1997.

Georgiades, N., and Macdonell, R., (1998), *Leadership for Competitive Advantage*, London: Wiley.

Grugulis, I. and Wilkinson, A. (2002) 'Managing culture at British Airways: hope, hype and reality', *Long-Range Planning*, Vol.35, No.2, pp.179–94.

Grugulis, I., Dundon, T. and Wilkinson, A. (2000) 'Cultural control and the "culture manager": employment practices in a consultancy', *Work, Employment and Society*, Vol.14, No.1, pp.97–116.

Höpfl, H. (1993) 'Culture and commitment: British Airways', in D. Gowler, K. Legge and C. Clegg (eds) *Case Studies in Organizational Behaviour and Human Resource Management*, London: PCP.

Kunda, G. (1992) *Engineering Culture: Control and Commitment in a High-Tech Corporation*, Philadelphia, PA: Temple University Press.

Legge, K. (1995) *Human Resource Management: Rhetorics and Realities*, London: Macmillan.

Monopolies and Mergers Commission (1987) 'British Airways plc and British Caledonian Group plc: A Report on the Proposed Merger 247', London:HMSO.

Peters, T. and Waterman, R. (1982) *In Search of Excellence*, London: Harper & Row.

Reed, M. (1992) *The Sociology of Organization*, London: Harvester Wheatsheaf.

Storey, J. (1992) *Developments in the Management of Human Resources*, Oxford: Blackwell.

Taylor, R. (1998) 'Annual review article', *British Journal of Industrial Relations*, Vol.36, No.2 pp.293–311.

The Economist, 27 July 1997.

Warhurst, R. (1995) 'Converging on HRM? Change and continuity in European airlines' industrial relations', *European Journal of Industrial Relations*, Vol.1, No.2, pp.259–74.

References

*Adkins, B. and Caldwell, D. (2004) 'Firm or subgroup culture: where does fitting in matter most?', *Journal of Organizational Behavior*, Vol.25, No.8, pp.969–78.

Arkin, A. (2004) 'Wax Works', *People Management*, 25 November, pp.34–7.

Armstrong, M. (1994) *Performance Management*, London: Kogan Page.

Armstrong, M. (1999) *Employee Reward* (2nd edn), London: CIPD.

Arnold, J., Loan-Clarke, J., Coombs, C., Park, J., Wilkinson, A. and Preston, D. (2003) *Looking Good? The Attractiveness of the NHS as an Employer to Potential Nursing and Allied Health Profession Staff*, Loughborough: Loughborough University.

Ashforth, B.E. (1985) 'Climate formation: issues and extensions', *Academy of Management Review*, Vol.4, pp.837–47.

Ashforth, B.E. (2001) *Role Transitions in Organizational Life*, Mahwah, NJ: Lawrence Erlbaum.

Barley, S., Meyer, G. and Gash, D. (1988) 'Cultures of culture: academics, practitioners and the pragmatics of normative control', *Administrative Science Quarterly*, Vol.33, No.1, pp.24–60.

Barrett, S. and McMahon, L. (1990) 'Public management in uncertainty: a micro-political perspective of the health service in the United Kingdom', *Policy and Politics*, Vol.18, No.4, pp.257–68.

Bass, B.M. (1985), *Leadership and Performance: Beyond Expectations*, New York: Free Press.

Becker, H.S. and Geer, B. (1970) 'Participant observation and interviewing: a comparison', in W. Filstead (ed.) *Qualitative Methodology*, Chicago, IL: Rand McNally, pp.133–42.

Bowers, D. and Seashore, S. (1966) 'Predicting organizational effectiveness with a four-factor theory of leadership', *Administrative Science Quarterly*, Vol.11, pp.238–63.

Bright, K. and Cooper, C.L. (1993) 'Organizational culture and the management of quality,' *Journal of Management Psychology*, Vol.8, No.6, pp.21–7.

*Brown, A. (1998) *Organisational Culture* (2nd edn), London: Financial Times/Pitman.

Casey, C. (1995) *Work, Self and Society: After Industrialization*, London: Routledge.

Cavanagh S.J. (1996) 'Mergers and acquisitions: some implications of cultural change', *Journal of Nursing Management*, Vol.4, pp.45–50.

Cober, R.T., Brown, D.J., Levy, P.E. and Cober, A.B. (2003) 'Organizational web sites: web site content and style as determinants of organizational attraction', *International Journal of Selection and Assessment*, Vol.11, Nos2–3 pp.158–69.

Cooke, R.A., and Lafferty, J.C. (1989) *Organizational Culture Inventory*, Plymouth, MA: Human Synergistics.

Cooke, R.A. and Rousseau, D.M. (1988) 'Behavioural norms and expectations: a quantitative approach to the assessment of organizational culture,' *Group and Organization Studies*, Vol.13, pp.245–73.

Cooke, R.A., and Szumal, J.L. (1983) 'Measuring normative beliefs and shared behavioral expectations in organizations: the reliability and validity of the organizational culture inventory', *Psychological Reports*, Vol.72, pp.1299–339.

*Deal, T.E. and Kennedy, A.A. (1982) *Corporate Cultures: The Rites and Rituals of Organisational Life*, Reading, MA: Addison-Wesley.

Denison, D.R. (1984) 'Bringing corporate culture to the bottom line', *Organizational Dynamics*, Vol.13, No.2, pp.4–22.

Denison, D.R. (1996) 'What is the difference between organizational culture and organizational climate? A native's point of view on a decade of paradigm wars', *Academy of Management Review*, Vol.21, pp.619–54.

Dundon, T., Grugulis, I. and Wilkinson, A. (2001) 'New management techniques in small and medium-sized enterprises', in T. Redman and A. Wilkinson (eds) *Contemporary Human Resource Management*, London: FT/Prentice Hall.

Fletcher, C. and Williams, R. (1992) *Performance Appraisal and Career Development* (2nd edn), Cheltenham: Stanley Thornes.

Furnham, A. (1997) *The Psychology of Behaviour at Work*, Hove: Psychology Press.

Geertz, C. (1973) *The Interpretation of Culture*, New York: Basic Books.

Glaser, S.R. (1983) *The Corporate Culture Survey*, Bryn Mawr, PA: Organizational Design and Development.

Gold, K.A. (1982) 'Managing for success: a comparison of the private and public sectors', *Public Administration Review*, Vol.42, Nov–Dec, pp.568–75.

Gordon, G. (1985) 'The relationship of corporate culture to industry sector and corporate performance', in R.H. Kilman, M.J. Saxton and B. Serpa (eds) *Gaining Control of the Corporate Culture*, San Francisco, CA: Jossey-Bass.

Gordon, G. and DiTomaso, N. (1992) 'Predicting corporate performance from organizational culture', *Journal of Management Studies*, Vol.29, pp.783–98.

Gundry, L.K. and Rousseau, D.M. (1994) 'Critical incidents in communication culture to newcomers: the meaning is the message', *Human Relations*, Vol.47, pp.1063–88.

Handy, C.B. (1978) *The Gods of Management*, London: Penguin.

Harris, L.C., and Ogbonna, E. (1998) 'Employee responses to culture change efforts', *Human Resource Management Journal*, Vol.8, No.2, pp.78–92.

Harrison, R. (1972) 'Understanding your organization's character', *Harvard Business Review*, Vol.5, pp.119–28.

Harrison, R. (2000) *Employee Development* (2nd edn), London: CIPD.

Hatch, M.J. (1997) *Organizational Theory*, Oxford: Oxford University Press.

Hofstede, G. (1980) *Culture's Consequences: International Differences in Work-related Values*, Beverly Hills, CA: Sage.

Hofstede, G. (1991) *Cultures and Organizations: The Software of the Mind*, Maidenhead: McGraw-Hill.

Hofstede, G., Neuijen, B., Daval Ohayv, D. and Sanders, G. (1990) 'Measuring organizational cultures: a qualitative and quantitative study across twenty cases', *Administrative Science Quarterly*, Vol.35, pp.286–316.

Hopfl, H.J., Smith, S. and Spencer, S. (1992) 'Values and valuations: corporate culture and job cuts', *Personnel Review*, Vol.21, No.1, pp.24–38.

James, L. and Jones, A. (1974) 'Organizational climate: A review of theory and research', *Psychological Bulletin*, Vol.18, pp.1096–112.

Jelineck, M., Smircich, L. and Hirsch, P. (1983) 'Introduction: a code of many colors', *Administrative Science Quarterly*, Vol.28, pp.331–8.

Kilmann, R.H. and Saxton, M.J. (1983) *The Kilmann-Saxton Culture-Gap Survey*, Pittsburg, PA: Organisational Design Consultants.

Kilmann, R.H., Saxton, M.J. and Serpa, R. (1985) *Gaining Control of the Corporate Culture*, San Francisco, CA: Jossey-Bass.

Keenoy, T. and Anthony, P. (1992) 'Metaphor, meaning and morality', in P. Blyton and P. Turnbull (eds) *Reassessing Human Resource Management*, London: Sage.

Kopelman, R.E., Brief, A.P. and Guzzo, R.A. (1990) 'The role of climate in productivity', in B. Schneider (ed.) *Organizational Climate and Culture*, San Francisco, CA: Jossey-Bass.

Kotter, J.P. and Heskett, J.L. (1992) *Corporate Culture and Performance*, New York: Free Press.

Kroeber, A.I. and Kluckhohn, C. (1952) *Culture: A Critical Review of Concepts and Definitions*, New York: Vintage Books.

Kunda, G. (1992) *Engineering Culture: Control and Commitment in a High-Tech Firm*, Philadelphia, PA: Temple University Press.

Lawler, E. (1990) *Strategic Pay: Aligning Organisational Strategies and Pay Systems*, San Francisco, CA: Jossey-Bass.

Lee, M. (1996) 'Action Learning as a Cross-Cultural Tool', in J. Stewart and J. McGoldrick (eds) *Human Resource Development*, London: Pitman.

Legge, K. (1995) *Human Resource Management: Rhetorics and Realities*, Basingstoke: Macmillan.

Louis, M.R. (1983) 'Organizations as culture-bearing milieux', in L.R. Pondy, P.J. Frost, G. Morgan and I.C. Dandridge (eds) *Organizational Symbolism*, Greenwich, CT: JAI Press.

Mabey, C. and Salaman, G. (1995) *Strategic Human Resource Management*, Oxford: Blackwell.

Marchington, M. and Wilkinson, A. (2005) *Human Resource Management at Work*, London: CIPD.

Martin, J. (1992) *Cultures in Organizations*, New York: Oxford University Press.

Martin, J. and Siehl, C. (1983) 'Organizational culture and counterculture: an uneasy symbiosis', *Organizational Dynamics*, Vol.12, No.2, pp.52–64.

Meek, V.L. (1982) 'Organisational culture: origins and weaknesses', in J. G. Salaman (ed.) *Human Resource Strategies*, London: Sage.

Meyerson, D. (1991) 'Acknowledging and uncovering ambiguities', in P. Frost, L. Moore, M. Louis, C. Lundberg and J. Martin (eds) *Reframing Organizational Culture*, Beverly Hills, CA: Sage.

Moorhead, G. and Griffin, R.W. (1995) *Organizational Behavior* (4th edn), Boston, MA: Houghton Mifflin.

Moran, E.T. and Volkwein, J.F. (1992) 'The cultural approach to the formation of organizational climate', *Human* Relations, Vol.45, pp.19–47.

Morgan, G. (1986) *Images of Organization*, Beverly Hills, CA: Sage.

Münch, R. and Smelster, N.J. (1992) *Theory of Culture*, Berkeley, CA: University of California Press.

Ogbonna, E. (1992) 'Organisational culture and human resource management: dilemmas and contradictions', in P. Blyton and P. Turnbull (eds) *Reassessing Human Resource Management*, London: Sage.

Ogbonna, E. and Harris, L.C. (2000) 'Leadership style, organisational culture and performance: empirical evidence from UK companies', *International Journal of Human Resource Management*, Vol.11, No.4, pp.766–88.

*Ogbonna, E. and Wilkinson, B. (1988) 'Corporate strategy and corporate culture: the management of change in the UK supermarket industry', *Personnel Review*, Vol.18, No.6, pp.10–14.

Ouchi, W.G. (1981) *Theory Z: How American Business Can Meet The Japanese Challenge*, Reading, MA: Addison-Wesley.

Peters, T.J. and Waterman, R.H. (1982) *In Search of Excellence: Lessons from America's Best Run Companies*, New York: Harper & Row.

Pettigrew, A. (1979) 'On studying organizational cultures', *Administrative Science Quarterly*, Vol.24, pp.570–81.

Pettigrew, A. (1990) 'Is corporate culture manageable?', in D. Wilson and R. Rosenfield (eds) *Managing Organisations*, Maidenhead: McGraw-Hill.

Petty, M.M., Beadles, N.A., Lowery, C.M., Chapman, D.F. and Connell, D.W. (1995) 'Relationships between organizational culture and organizational performance', *Psychological Reports*, Vol.76, pp.483–92.

Reichers, A. E. and Schneider, B. (1990) 'Climate and culture: an evolution of constructs', in B. Schneider (ed.) *Organisational Climate and Culture*, San Francisco, CA: Jossey-Bass.

Ricks, T.E. (1997) *Making the Corps*, New York: Scribner.

Rohner, R.P. (1984) 'Towards a conception of culture for cross-cultural psychology', *Journal of Cross-Cultural Psychology*, Vol.15, pp.111–38.

Rousseau, D.M. (1990) 'Assessing organizational culture: the case for multiple methods', in B. Schneider (ed.) *Organizational Climate and Culture*, San Francisco, CA: Jossey-Bass.

Sackmann, S. (1991) 'Managing organisational culture: dreams and possibilities', in J. Anderson (ed.) *Communication Yearbook*, Beverly Hills, CA: Sage.

Schein, E.H. (1984) 'Coming to a new awareness of organizational culture', *Sloan Management Review*, Vol.25, pp.3–16.

Schein, E.H. (1985), 'How culture forms, develops and changes', in R.H. Kilmann, M.J. Saxton, R. Serpa and Associates (eds) *Gaining Control of the Corporate Culture*, San Francisco, CA: Jossey-Bass.

*Schein, E.H. (1992) *Organizational Culture and Leadership: A Dynamic View* (2nd edn), San Francisco, CA: Jossey-Bass.

Schneider, B. (1987) 'The people make the place', *Personnel Psychology*, Vol.40, pp.437–53.

Schneider, B. (1990) *Organisational Climate and Culture*, San Francisco, CA: Jossey-Bass.

Shipley, P. (1990) 'The analysis of organisations as a conceptual tool for ergonomics practitioners', in J.R. Wilson and E.N. Corlett (eds) *Evaluation of Human Work*, London: Taylor & Francis.

Siehl, C. and Martin, J. (1990) 'Organizational culture: the key to financial performance?', in B. Schneider (ed.) *Organizational Climate and Culture*, San Francisco, CA: Jossey-Bass.

Silverzweig, S. and Allen, R.E. (1976) 'Changing the corporate culture', *Sloan Management Review*, Vol.17, No.3, pp.33–49.

Smircich, L. (1983) 'Concepts of culture and organizational analysis', *Administrative Science Quarterly*, Vol.28, pp.339–58.

Stewart, J. and McGoldrick, J. (1996) *Human Resource Development*, London: Pitman.

Stiles, P., Gratton, L., Truss, C., Hope-Hailey, V. and McGovern, P. (1997) 'Performance management and the psychological contract', *Human Resource Management Journal*, Vol.7, No.1, pp.57–66.

Storey, J. (1995) *Human Resource Management: A Critical Text*, London: Routledge.

Swartz, M. and Jordon, D. (1980) *Culture: An Anthropological Perspective*, New York: Wiley.

Thompson, P. and McHugh, D. (2002) *Work Organisations: A Critical Introduction*, (3rd edn), Basingstoke: Palgrave.

Trice, H.M. and Beyer, J.M. (1984) 'Studying organizational cultures through rites and ceremonials', *Academy of Management Review*, Vol.9, pp.653–69.

Trice, H.M. and Beyer, J.M. (1993) *The Cultures of Work Organisations*, Englewood Cliffs, NJ: Prentice-Hall.

Trompenaars, F. and Hampden-Turner, C. (1997) *Riding the Waves of Culture: Understanding Cultural Diversity in Business*, London: Nicholas Brealey.

Uttal, B. (1983) 'The corporate culture vultures', *Fortune*, Vol.108, No.8, 17 October, pp.66–72.

Van Maanen, J. and Schein, E. (1979) 'Toward a theory of organizational socialization', *Research in Organizational Behavior*, Vol.11, pp.209–59.

Van Vianen, A.E.M (2000) 'Person-organization fit: the match between newcomers' and recruiters' preferences for organizational cultures', *Personnel Psychology*, Vol.53, No.1, pp.113–49.

Wanous, P. (1989) 'Installing a realistic job preview: ten tough choices', *Personnel Psychology*, Vol.42, pp.117–33.

Weick, K. (1985) 'The significance of corporate culture', in P. Frost, L. Moore, M. Louis, C. Lundberg and J. Martin (eds) *Organizational Culture*, Beverly Hills, CA: Sage.

Wilderom, C.P.M, Glunk, U. and Maslowski, R. (2000) 'Organizational culture as a predictor of organizational performance', in N.M. Ashkanasy, C.P.M. Wilderom and M.F. Peterson (eds) *Handbook of Organizational Culture and Climate*, Thousand Oaks, CA: Sage.

*Williams, A., Dobson, P. and Watters, M. (1993) *Changing Culture: New Organizational Approaches* (2nd edn), London: IPM.

Williams, R.S. (2002) *Managing Employee Performance: Design and Implementation in Organizations*, London: Thomson.

Willmott, H. (1993) 'Strength is ignorance, slavery is freedom: managing culture in modern organizations', *Journal of Management Studies*, Vol.30, No.4, pp.515–52.

Wunthow, R. and Witten, M. (1988) 'New directions in the study of culture', *Annual Review of Sociology*, Vol.14, pp.49–67.

Xenikou, A. and Furnham, A. (1996) 'A correlational and factor analytic study of four questionnaire measures of organizational culture', *Human Relations*, Vol.49, pp.349–71.

* Useful reading

Part II CONTEMPORARY THEMES AND ISSUES

Chapter 10

INTERNATIONAL HUMAN RESOURCE MANAGEMENT

Geoffrey Wood

Introduction

International HRM is, quite simply, the management of people in an international environment. As such, it is distinct from *comparative HRM,* which simply compares how people are managed in different national contexts. In practice, international HRM concerns people management in firms that operate across national boundaries. There are two key questions in international HRM. The first concerns the extent to which it is possible to retain a uniform set of organisational attitudes, norms and values – and HR policies and practices – across national boundaries, or whether these will perforce be remoulded in fitting with individual national locales. Or will organisations inevitably mirror the paradigms and practices of the original country of origin? Second, there are a range of practical issues concerning the management of employees in different national contexts. These include the management of expatriates, and the role and relative importance assigned to nationals from the organization's parent country *vis-à-vis* local staffers.

Thinking about international HRM: uniformity or diversity?

A key debate in international HR management is the extent to which firms mould their HR policies and practices to suit specific national contexts, whether they keep them in line with the dominant ways of doing business in their parent country, or whether a new trans-global model of HR management is emerging.

CONVERGENCE THEORIES

The neo-liberal perspective is based on the view that organisational and wider social outcomes reflect the choices of rational individuals, who seek to maximise their personal gain. Throughout much of the 1980s and 1990s, this perspective not only dominated the discipline of economics, but also informed government policies in many Western countries. To neo-liberals, variations between national contexts would represent variations in regulations (or 'market imperfections') on a continuum towards a desirable minimalism. There is an extensive body of literature in the neo-liberal tradition, that suggests that modes of regulation and associated inter- and intra-firm practices are likely to converge towards the (largely free market) Anglo-American model. In other words, these perspectives assume that all economies – and associated institutional structures – will over time become more alike, more or less in line with US model (Fukuyama 2000; cf. Friedman 1999). Freed from the restraints imposed by misguided attempts at regulation, individuals' desire for self-actualisation and recognition will unlock creativity and enterprise; firms will be able to operate without being hampered by unnecessary restrictions (Fukuyama 2000, p.320). Again, it is argued that the capacity to make use of similar organisational practices within different national locales is likely to optimise the firm's capacity; greater homogenisation is likely to make for greater efficiency (Kostova and Roth 2002, p.215; cf. Zeira and Harari 1977, p.328). While the diffusion of HR practices across the trans-national firm may be uneven, it will gradually make for similarities in different national contexts; firms will try to enforce their own view of the most appropriate ways of handling HRM in other countries (Brewster *et al.* 2004).

Convergence: towards best practices?

Grounded in the above-mentioned rational choice tradition (in other words, neo-classical economics), convergence theories assume that firms pursue economic advantage through choices 'guided by unambiguous preferences and bounded rationality' (Gooderham *et al.* 1999, p.507). Hence, industries will adopt practices that promote the maximisation of economic goals; optimistic accounts suggest that this will result in a set of best practices diffusing across the parent economy and worldwide. The 'best-practice' approach to strategic HRM holds that the adoption of an internally consistent set of high-performance work practices will result in superior outcomes (Huselid 2000, p.107). Conversely, it should be possible to identify optimal HR practices from analysing winning firms (ibid.).

'High-value-added' approaches base competitiveness on mutually rewarding employer–employee interdependence, with considerable delegation to employees (Kochan and Ostermann 1994; Pfeffer 1994; Ulrich 1997; Applebaum *et al.* 2000; cf. Whitley 1999). Such approaches are characterised by high levels of investment in training and development, flat organisational structures, with broadly based employee participation, superior job security and innovative reward systems. In turn, these facilitate greater levels of participation and involvement (Applebaum *et al.* 2000; cf. Webster and Wood 2005). These interventions are likely to prove complementary: permanent employment reduces turnover, while investing in people and job redesign enhances organisational commitment, providing fertile ground for far-reaching involvement programmes (Lincoln and Kalleberg 1990). Again, leading multi-national companies (MNCs) – sometimes referred to as trans-national companies (or TNCs) – are likely to prove pioneers in the dissemination of best practice, given their greater resource bases, and an ability to identify which specific sets of policies yield optimal results on a global basis.

Critics have questioned whether there ought to be a single set of optimal practices (Huselid 2000, p.107); indeed, lower-value-added approaches may prove highly profitable in specific industries and locales. Moreover, individual interventions may elicit specific outcomes; a set of good practices may not necessarily result in an outcome that is coherent and mutually supportive.

Convergence: the low road

Alternatively, it can be argued that any pressures towards uniform practices are likely to be downwards; the range of pressures associated with globalisation – most notably, the intensification of competition, market break-up and the increased mobility of investor capital – have placed renewed pressures on firms to enhance their competitiveness through on-going rounds of cost-cutting (Duysters and Hagedoorn 2001, p.348; Wood and Brewster 2002). Intense competition forces successive rounds of competition; this has placed particularly severe pressure on labour costs. Indeed, it has been argued that through the use of subcontractors, or simple relocation, MNCs have reverted to strategies centring profitability on steadily worsening employment conditions, including low standards of health and safety, extremely low pay, arbitrary management, a near total lack of job security and the discounting of skill (Moody 1987; Greider 1997). Inevitably this involves a gradual shift of production to low wage, low cost, labour repressive economies, forcing employees within core regions to accede gradually to worsening pay and working conditions in return for staving off threats to relocate. Given the pressures associated with globalisation, managers worldwide are gradually moving towards 'efficiency-enhancing' approaches; there is a general convergence in the direction of the lowest possible standards (Streeck 1995; O'Hagan 2002, p.40).

THE PERSISTENCE OF DIFFERENCE: INSTITUTIONAL ACCOUNTS

As noted earlier, rational choice theories depict organisational and social outcomes as the result of the combined choices of rational, profit-maximising individuals. In contrast, institutionalist accounts see organisational and social behaviour as not only the product of individual actions, but wider social structures and accumulated practices. In other words, institutional theories hold that pre-existing informal social conventions, as well as the regulations imposed by more formally constituted governmental structures, mould – and are remoulded by – human actions. Hence, what organisations do reflects not only the decisions of their members, but also formal and informal rules governing what can and should be done. More formally speaking, institutions can be defined as 'normative complexes relating to major aspects of our social activity' (Anderson and Parker 1964, p.136). Configurations of norms are established, formalised and regularised to ensure conformity in behaviour, allow for complex social transactions, while imparting greater predictability into social life. Within any given society, the major aspects of social structures influence daily life (ibid.); institutions may coincide with formal structures such as a national education and training system, or be rather less tangible sets of shared ways of 'doing things'. An example of the latter would be the common organisational practices shared by leading manufacturing exporters in Japan, centring on high security of tenure, mutual collegiality and commitment, and the sharing and dissemination of skills.

Accounts within the broad institutionalist tradition suggest that within specific national contexts, firm-level practices will gradually become homogenous or 'isomorphic' with the national context (Kostova and Roth 2002, p.215; cf. Brewster *et al.* 2001). Three forms of isomorphism may be identified: coercive (where the firm is forced to adopt specific practices, such as through force of law); mimetic (specific practices associated with success in individual firms are copied by others) or normative (behaviour is tailored to fit what is considered suitable for the specific environment) (Haveman 1993, p.593; Kostova and Roth 2002, p.216; Brewster *et al.* 2004).

Recent institutional writings (cf. Whitley 1999; Gooderham *et al.* 1999; Brewster *et al.* 2004) have pointed to the emerging body of evidence that global economic pressures do not seem to have translated into uniform outcomes in terms of HR practices. In some national contexts, institutional structures have been weak for many years, with national competitiveness being grounded on purely cost grounds, translating into HR policies centring on low wages, low security of tenure and a lack of investment in training or development; good examples would include the Philippines and Nigeria. Others have been characterised by more active regulation backed up by coherent national industrial policies, aimed at encouraging firms to adopt policies aimed at maximising productivity through coherent investments in people; examples would include South Korea and Mauritius. Institutional configurations are adaptable, and may evolve over time. For example, in apartheid South Africa, work organisation in large areas of the economy centred on racial fordism – mass production coupled with a rigid racial division of labour, with Africans being confined to largely unskilled jobs and subject to the Pass Laws that made it difficult to switch employment or move between different areas of the country. However, the system proved increasingly inefficient and uncompetitive in the face of mounting global competition; hence, even prior to the formal end of apartheid, more skilled occupations gradually opened up to Africans, and HR strategies based more around cooperation and less around coercion gradually diffused.

Towards trans-national institutional models?

As we have seen, theories of globalisation would suggest that specific national practices are unlikely to prove durable given pressures towards trans-national convergence. An alternative account would suggest that while specific institutional factors are likely to continue to mould firm-level practices in different parts of the world, national institutions will increasingly give way to regional and trans-national institutions. The most commonly cited example is that of the European Union. It is suggested that a broad social model is gradually diffusing, making a region of highly competitive firms, based around high-value-added HR practices (cf. O'Hagan 2002, p.6). Examples would include the *European Works Council Directive,* which compels firms with more than 1,000 employees operating in at least two EU states, with a workforce of 150 at least to have a 'European Works Council' (EWC). However, EWCs are relatively weak, primarily consultative bodies.

Indeed, as writers such as Whitley (1999, p.133) have pointed out, the limited significance of pan-European agencies and European systems of economic organisation, despite 40 years of the existence of the EEC and it successors, underscores the tenacity of national institutional arrangements and practices. Within the European context, MNCs are more likely to tailor their HR policies to national locale, or in line with prevailing international trends, than one that is specifically in tune with emerging trans-EU norms and practices.

Theories of ethnocentricity

In growing up in a particular social context, individuals are socialised into thinking that specific norms and values are the 'best' or the 'most proper'. Hence, as Anderson and Parker (1964, p.50) note, it is difficult for members of any specific society to be objective about ways of thinking and acting other than their own. A devotion to cultural norms reinforces in-group attitudes, strengthening customs and making change difficult (ibid.).

Consequently, originating within a specific national context, the core staff of an MNC is likely to have originated from a shared social context. They may learn to adapt to the ways of doing business in other contexts, but shared socialisation – both on the individual and corporate levels – is likely to reinforce embedded beliefs that the ways of the parent country are the most appropriate, and should be disseminated to subsidiaries abroad. Hence, ethnocentric theories argue MNCs will tend to mirror the dominant practices of the country of origin (cf. Zeira and Harari 1977, p.327). Based on comparative survey evidence, Mayrhofer and Brewster (1996) argue that, in practice, the vast majority of MNCs are ethnocentric.

THE PERSISTENCE OF DIFFERENCE: CULTURAL ACCOUNTS

In contrast to institutional accounts, cultural explanations believe that national differences can be ascribed not to regulatory structures and norms, but rather to the content of the relevant social environment as a whole. Culture can be defined as the integrated, interdependent sum of socially produced and socially inherited patterns constructed around a corpus of socially created physical and biological materials (Anderson and Parker 1964, p.40). In other words, culture is not just about the effect of social structures, but also about localised patterns of human interactions that reproduce themselves and develop over time, reflecting the effects of earlier interactions and the physical environment.

Cultural accounts would assume an even greater path dependence to nations – and firms located within them – than would the institutionalist tradition. Indeed it is argued that assimilation of one culture by another is a relatively uncommon process. It is far more likely that at best, representatives of different cultures can learn to collaborate (Sparrow and Hiltrop 2000, p.73). Hence, in MNCs, the 'corporate diplomat' who is experienced in the ways of diverse foreign climes has an invaluable role (Ferlie and Pettigrew 2000, p.204). Indeed, recent culturalist accounts have suggested that the world is irrevocably divided into rival cultures, leading to endemic clashes of belief systems at macro and micro levels, clashes that may prove difficult to resolve (cf. Huntington 1996).

Within management studies, some of the most influential accounts on the effects of national cultures include Hofstede (1991), Fukuyama (1995) and Sako (1998). Cultural theories concede that specific cultures do not coincide with national boundaries – common distinctions are drawn between the Western and Chinese traditions, for example. However, what firms do in different national locales will gradually shift into line with the dominant cultural context (Lao and Ngo 2001, p.95). This allows for prior knowledge to be harnessed most effectively, and for shared expectations, making for more efficient exchange relations. Specific national cultures mould behaviour and shape the perceptions managers have of the world (Sparrow and Hiltrop 2000, p.73). Not only does HRM impact on national ways of doing things, but also local conditions and cultures mould the processes and problems of national models (ibid., p.73).

Cultural explanations can be divided into two broad categories. *Etic* approaches 'describe phenomena in constructs that apply across cultures' (Morris *et al.* 1999, p.782). In other words, there are certain universals to human behaviour. For example, in any context people may be more or less committed to their organisation; relative organisational commitment may be measured in objective terms. However, specific cultures may be associated with higher levels of organisational commitment, on account of specific attitudes, expectations and values.

More broadly speaking, different cultures have different characteristics that can be objectively identified and contrasted according to some or other external standard (ibid., pp.781–2). For example, Hofstede (1980) argues that different cultures vary according to certain objective dimensions, such as power-distance (the extent to which the least powerful accept their status), uncertainty avoidance (tolerance for risk), collectivism (group or individual orientation) and masculine/feminine dimensions (procedurality or intuition).

A limitation of *etic* approaches is that the objective yardsticks against which cultures are measured are somewhat arbitrary, and may be ethnocentric. At worst, categorising nations according to pre-determined standards may amount to little more than crude ethnic stereotyping, with inevitably some cultures being branded inferior, less desirable or less effective than others. Attempts to deploy *etic* approaches to understanding organisational failings in regions of the world characterised by poor economic performance, but where such performance can be directly traced to uneven natural resource endowments and a specific colonial legacy – an obvious example being Africa – are particularly problematic.

In contrast, *emic* approaches locate culture as an integral component of a broader social system (Parsons 1951; Giddens 1990). Within such systems, individual conceptualisations are defined by a specific historical–social trajectory; behavioural patterns cannot be understood according to objective measures. Rather, it is necessary to attempt to see things from the 'insider's point of view', aiming to understand why specific actions make the most sense to those with particular sets of experiences. This would suggest that attempts to manage people across national contexts are likely to lead to persistent misconceptions, unless managers adopt people-centred approaches that allow for open-ended employee involvement and constant feedback.

More recent work has suggested that emic and etic approaches are not necessarily mutually exclusive; aspects of behaviour may incorporate both emic and etic dimensions (Berry 1999, p.165; Helfrich 1999, pp.131–54). Again, all cultural approaches assume that culture is something of a given. In other words, it is not easy to transform cultures in such manner as to enhance 'social capital', and hence, promote higher-skilled and higher-value-added production paradigms (Fukuyama 1995; Lane 1998; Wood and Brewster 2002).

COMMONALITIES BETWEEN INSTITUTIONAL AND CULTURAL APPROACHES

Both institutional and cultural approaches argue that MNCs have adapted their activities in line with local practices (Kostova and Roth 2002, p.215). As noted earlier, this process does reflect a certain *path dependence* – countries or regions tend to follow distinct trajectories, *inter alia* associated with specific sets of managerial and specifically HR practices, which are not easily altered. MNCs entering a new country have perforce to tailor their policies in practices in line with local expectations and realities, even if it means departing from long-established organisational practices.

It should also be noted that most cultural theories define culture as part-and-parcel of wider social structures. In other words, although distinct from recent institutionalist writing, such cultural accounts are grounded in a shared recognition of the objective effects of formal and informal institutional frameworks. However, their interpretation is a relatively conservative one, in that structures are characterised as bodies that ensure continuity and order, rather than dynamic and ever-changing in response to internal and external pressures.

SIMILARITY AND DIFFERENCE: DUALITY PERSPECTIVES

Writing from within the institutionalist tradition, Whitley (1999, p.126) argues that MNCs are unlikely to change their existing practices unless foreign operations constitute a very large component of organisational activities, with these activities beings concentrated in a national business system very different from – but more developed than – that of the country of origin. Moreover, the 'foreign business system' must be cohesive with a high degree of institutional integration, while in the country of origin institutional agencies should not prevent significant changes (ibid., p.127). Again, the firm should be closely integrated across national boundaries. However, in such contexts, not only can multi-national firms switch their dominant way of doing business, but they may also disseminate new practices back to their country of origin.

Given the extent of barriers to the altering of corporate strategies and practices, it is likely that many firms will infuse elements of practices associated with the principle national contexts in which they operate. In other words, firms face conflicting pressures towards the homogenisation of practices around different national models, making for an uneven and dynamic integration process (Gooderham *et al.* 1998).

International HRM in practice

As Holden (2001, p.657) notes, there is some common ground between comparative and international HRM in that both are concerned with HRM issues in a global or regional context. However, international HRM exclusively concerns HRM in a trans-national context; this would encompass the factors moulding the HR policies and strategies of MNCs, and the manner in which they are operationalised (ibid.).

POLICIES TO STAFFING

There are four approaches to staffing in MNCs, commonly referred to as ethnocentric, polycentric, geocentric and regional/regiocentric (cf. ibid.; Perlmutter 1969).

Ethnocentric approaches

This approach involves filling all key positions with parent country nationals, that is, the MNC's country of origin and/or where its headquarters are located. On the one hand, posting existing staff from the parent country allows for similar cultural and practical expectations, and may facilitate communication and coordination (Dowling *et al.* 1999, p.71). On the other hand, any visible gap in terms of incomes or possibilities for upward mobility within the firm, between expatriates and locals in favour of the former is likely to prove bad for morale (ibid.) and may result in the firm losing touch with local realities. Again, wages of expatriates are likely to be higher than locals – as it is necessary to provide financial incentives to cover the inconvenience of location – and hence, more costly for the firm. A good example of ethnocentric approaches to staffing would be US oil firms in a number of West African petrostates, such as Equatorial Guinea, reflecting both local skills shortfalls, and a lack of an institutional environment that would encourage greater use of locals (Wood 2004).

Polycentric approaches

Polycentric approaches are where locals fill the managerial positions in subsidiaries, and parent country nationals those at headquarters. As Scullion (2001, p.298) notes, polycentric approaches reduce language barriers within any particular plant or locale, eliminates the adjustment problems experienced by recently relocated expatriates, allows continuity in management, is cheaper and opens up new career opportunities for locals, hence enhancing morale and organisational commitment. However, this can make communication between subsidiaries and headquarters more difficult, it may be harder to exercise firm control over subsidiaries, while a lack of genuine cosmopolitanism within the firm may make it more difficult to compete in global markets. Moreover, it precludes the possibility of managers gaining broader experience by a series of postings into different areas where the firm has a presence (ibid.).

Regiocentric approaches

These are becoming increasingly important. This represents a form of functional rationalisation on a multi-country basis, dividing operations into several geographical regions, freely transferring staff within each (Dowling *et al.* 1999, p.75). The advantage of this is that it allows a sensitivity to regional conditions, while allowing an interaction between regional and parent country nationals at regional headquarters (ibid.). However, this policy can result in an excessive federalism, with a lack of synergy between different regions. While many motor firms have, in the past, used aspects of this policy, increasingly a trend in the industry is to rationalise design and production across continents, resulting in a need for closer liaison and more effective communication between different regional entities.

Geocentric approaches

Here, the firm appoints staff on a worldwide basis, with the most suitable individual regardless of national origin being appointed to key jobs within the organisation (Dowling *et al.* 1999, p.72). Problems include the high costs of relocating staff, the need to train staff to fit in with local conditions, and the fact that most developed countries have placed increasing restrictions on the immigration and employment of individuals from the developing world (see ibid.); the latter problem has become particularly pronounced since the United States embarked on its so-called 'War on Terror'.

Towards a greater variety?

Recent research has suggested a tendency to greater variety in MNC staffing strategies reflecting a desire to tailor global strategies to local conditions and needs (Scullion 2001, p.300). More expatriates tend to be found in under-performing subsidiaries, and in greenfields developments, and less so in local subsidiaries that had been taken over by MNCs (ibid.). Finally, it seems that subsidiaries in Asian countries seem to make a greater use of parent country nationals, although this could also reflect the nature of investments (see ibid.).

MANAGING EXPATRIATES: RELOCATION AND LOCAL NEEDS

In practice, a central concern of the literature has been on managing expatriates (Bratton and Gold 2003, p.62). Expatriates can play a central role in the transfer of knowledge and information, the developing of the knowledge and skills base of staff and subsidiaries, and in ensuring that subsidiaries act in accordance with general group policies, strategies and procedures (Holden 2001, p.658). However, local managers may prove resistant to such processes, on account of blockages that the widespread use of expatriates may pose to their own upward mobility and/or persistent cultural differences. In short, the availability of expertise and the need for organisational solidarity have to be reconciled with local sensitivities and needs.

Relocating staff members abroad involves revisiting their reward system, provision of adequate training as to local conditions, the organising of a removal company, the provision of short-term or long-term housing, and assistance regarding driving licences, banking and the availability of social services in the new locale.

Given the immediate costs of relocation, and the need to ensure that the individual involved enjoys a commensurate standard of living abroad to what they had at home, which may involve either higher pay, or assistance with housing or education, the use of expatriates is likely to be costly. On the one hand, the gradual diffusion of a global culture centring on consumerism has eroded great cultural divides between many regions and nations. Western society has become more individually-oriented, with weaker extended family ties. On the other hand, the greater likelihood that spouses will have independent careers, and changing social expectations surrounding marriage or similar long-term relationships, has meant that fewer spouses are prepared to endure long separations. Again, the fact that fewer individuals are prepared to live relatively solitary lives abroad, makes the process of relocation more difficult. Indeed, one of the major causes of high failure rates – in other words, a situation where an individual fails to make the successful transition to the new locale and returns home – is family pressures.

Finally, there is the process of repatriating expatriates to their home country after they have served out their assignments abroad. First, there is the preparation phase, including briefing the relevant employee as to their new job requirements, and practical issues to be considered in moving between nations (banking, housing arrangements, settling bills). Second, there is the actually physical relocation process, although this can be facilitated by the use of specialised removal firms that offer a comprehensive service. Third, there is the transition phase, which may involve assistance with a range of issues such as the provision of bridging housing, finding of schools, new banking and financial service arrangements, and the re-issue of driving licences. (Dowling *et al.* 2004, p.206). Unfortunately, returning individuals may feel that their international experience is under-valued, and/or that their status, autonomy or career direction has been negatively affected (Scullion 2001, p.305). This may account for the relatively high turnover among returning staff experienced by MNCs (ibid.).

Even more difficult is dealing with the inevitable reverse culture shock (Dowling *et al.* 2004, p.206). It is common for expatriates to idealise their home country when serving long assignments abroad, and equally common for them to be seriously disillusioned on their return home. In Britain, conservative newspapers such as the *Daily Mail* and *Daily Telegraph* promote a vision of a golden age somewhere in the imagined past, sharply contrasted to a decayed, disorganised and disobedient present, a vision that is particularly closely tailored to the sentiments felt by elderly expatriates who have spent a lifetime abroad.

REWARD SYSTEMS

As Moorehead and Griffin (2004, p.212) note, when transferring a staff member to a different national locale they seek to at least match the relative compensation they previously enjoyed. Typically, this will involve increasing salary when they are transferred to a country where the cost of living is higher. More difficult is a transfer to a part of the developing world where the cost of living is substantially lower, but where there may be a lesser availability of suitable accommodation or social services, or where the physical or political climate is unpleasant. In the latter instances, firms commonly provide accommodation for expatriate staff, and, sometimes, a pay premium for overseas service. Unfortunately, both these may increase the divide between expatriates and locals, and make the former less sensitive to the latters' culture and conditions of life (Wood 2004).

In working out a reward system for expatriates, firms may divide the pay according to three components – taxes, consumption and savings – and make sure that the transferred employee enjoys equivalent coverage and benefits in each of these areas to that which they would have enjoyed in the parent country (Moorehead and Griffin 2004, p.212). In other words, they should have at least the same amount of money available for savings (as they will probably wish to retire to their country of origin), adequate compensation in those cases where the employee would be prejudiced by a different tax regime, and sufficient pay to enjoy the same standards of housing, transport, food and social provision as in the home country. Understandably, such a provision does not come cheap, even when an employee is transferred to a country where the cost of living seems very much lower (see ibid.).

PLANNING AND MANAGING INDIGENOUS CAREERS

As can be seen, MNCs face conflicting pressures towards greater use of parent country nationals and localisation; inevitably, this will involve certain trade-offs. It will be extremely difficult to secure the commitment of talented local staff if they perceive that more senior positions are dominated by expatriates, closing off their own prospects for upward mobility. Moreover, there is growing pressure on organisations to ensure that they are representative of the wider community in ethnic and gender terms (Tummala 1999, p.495). Moreover, many governments in the developing world place legislative or informal pressures on firms to develop and implement coherent affirmative action policies aimed at redressing the historical disadvantages suffered by women and/or specific ethnic groups through targeted employment, development and/or promotional policies (Serote *et al.* 2001, p.166).

HUMAN RESOURCE DEVELOPMENT IN A TRANS-NATIONAL CONTEXT

As Elger and Smith (2001, p.449–50) note, MNCs have the potential to be major carriers of innovations in managerial practices across the global economy, allowing for distinct competitive advantages associated with one part of the world to be diffused to another. However, while there is some evidence of specific sets of innovative practices spreading across very different national contexts, such practices will often require modification or adaptation to fit in with differing cultural or institutional realities.

In practice, Human Resource Development (HRD) in a trans-national context involves three distinct processes. First, there is the process of disseminating existing knowledge and best practices within the firm into subsidiaries operating in different national contexts. While new technologies – and the practical skills needed to make use of them – are relatively portable, innovations in organisational processes may be harder to transplant into a different environment (Elger and Smith 2001, p.450). In other words, it is relatively easy to train people how to make the best use of 'hard' technological innovations, such as the use of new machinery to make innovative new products, such as flat panel televisions. However, it is rather harder to infuse new forms of socially organising work, or implement new managerial strategies that challenge pre-existing local attitudes, norms and values. The latter requires a detailed understanding of the implications of differing cultural and institutional contexts, and the manner in which changes in organisational practice may be adjusted to meet the needs and expectations of a different society, and sold to affected employees. There is also the possibility for diffusing upwards existing knowledge from subsidiaries or 'junior' partners. For example, in its alliance with Nissan, Renault was not only able to impart its design expertise, allowing Nissan to make use of the running gear from some of its highly successful model lines, but gained access to Nissan's specific knowledge regarding key aspects of work organisation.

Second, given the need to fully develop the capacity of talented local employees and to meet possible equity targets, MNCs need to have coherent training policies and interventions for indigenous staff. Given possible shortfalls in local training, and the need to continuously develop and upgrade the skills of those earmarked for upward mobility, there been a growing emphasis on internal development, or the use of programmes that have been commissioned by an outside body to specifically suit organisational needs (Faversnec-Hery 1996, pp.665–74).

Third, there is the issue of training expatriates to work within a different country. The type of training is moulded by the type of job, country of assignment, time available and mode of delivery; such training may include language training, field experiences, areas studies programmes including briefings on the relevant national context and cultural and/or sensitivity training (Dowling *et al.* 1999, p.157).

Conclusions

At a policy level, it is important to understand the extent to which the policies of MNCs are moulded by specific national contexts. It has been variously suggested that MNCs mould their policies in the different locations they operate in according to the specific cultural and/or institutional setting, that they inevitably mimic the policies that predominate in their parent countries, or that they are gradually converging towards a common international model of HRM. However, there is a growing body of critical research that suggests that there remains considerable variety in the HR policies followed by MNCs, reflecting a combination of pressures towards localisation, internationalisation or ethnocentricity.

At a practical level, people management in MNCs poses specific problems and challenges. These include the management of both expatriate and local staff careers, the development of skills and knowledge bases both within and across specific national settings, and the design of functional reward systems for an international environment. Again, while it is possible to implement specific policies and procedures across an entire enterprise, the nature and implementation of specific HR practices are likely to be shaped by the socio-economic contexts in which the firm operates. Clearly, there is insufficient evidence to conclude that there is an emerging international model of HRM. However, there is evidence that the most successful MNCs are those with a consistent track record of investing the people, and capable of reconciling the pressures of operating in a global market with those posed by specific national settings.

CASE STUDY 10.1

INTERNATIONAL HRM: THE PRACTICE OF OIL AND GAS COMPANIES IN WEST AFRICA

GEOFFREY WOOD

The West African microstate of Equatorial Guinea is one of the fastest growing economies on the African continent, owing to the discovery and exploitation of substantial offshore oil and gas reserves in the last decade. A former Spanish colony, the country has since independence been ruled a single family, the Nguemas; as such, its political development has been very much closer to the former Latin American family dictatorships, such as the Samosas in Nicaragua and the Batistas in Cuba, than other countries on the African continent. During the colonial era, the country developed a significant plantation economy, centring on the export of cocoa and, to a lesser extent, bananas. However, the founding president, Macias Nguema, systematically destroyed this sector, through his expulsion of the Nigerian contract labourers, and his wholesale personal expropriation, and subsequent poor management, of the plantations. Macias' excesses led to the death or exile of at least one-third of the population. Finally, he turned to murdering members of his own family, leading to his being overthrown, and subsequently executed, by his nephew and security chief, Obiang

Nguema Mbasogo. Initially, Obiang pledged to end the excesses of the Macias years. A multi-party constitution was later introduced. However, Obiang has won all subsequent elections with at least 98 per cent of the vote, thanks to systematic intimidation and fraud. The opposition is weak and divided, while Obiang is regularly ranked as one of the most brutal despots in the world. By the late 1980s, many aid agencies had left the country, owing to the voraciousness of the ruling elite, and death threats or attacks on both foreigners and locals who questioned the status quo. Finally, the United States withdrew its ambassador, after he had received death threats by members of the ruling elite. Owing to the termination of significant foreign aid, and the failure to rebuild the plantation economy, there is considerable evidence that the ruling elite turned to crime as a means of revenue generation, including trafficking in drugs, women and children, and allowing the country to serve as a base for arms smuggling and pirate fishing, and as a dumping ground for nuclear and chemical waste. President Obiang currently has very poor health, which has variously been ascribed to a cardiac or prostate condition.

The discovery of sizeable oil reserves ended the country's isolation. The ruling family has been courted by both major oil companies and foreign governments, and, under the Bush administration, full diplomatic relations have been restored with the United States. The oil industry is dominated by major US oil companies such as ExxonMobil and oil logistics companies such as Schlumberger. Recently, it transpired that oil companies were paying royalty payments directly into an account at Riggs Bank, New York, controlled by members of the ruling family. The oil reserves are all offshore, mostly in ultra-deep water (typically 7,500 foot below sea level, and a similar distance into the seabed); commercial exploitation has only been possible owing to very recent technological advances. Consequently, the development of the oil industry has been on highly capital-intensive lines, with skilled and managerial jobs being almost exclusively filled by expatriates; there are currently few opportunities for local employment, other than in a relatively small number of menial support tasks. There is no tertiary educational institution in the country, while the school system is in very poor condition; most of the population are functionally illiterate. When recruiting local labour, oil companies make use of labour bureaus controlled by members of the ruling family; wages are paid direct to the bureaus, who are responsible for disciplining labour. There is little evidence of significant firm-based internal training programmes aimed at upgrading the skills of local employees.

In contrast, in Angola, another West African petrostate with an exclusively offshore oil industry and persistent governance and transparency problems, locals have managed to gain access to a wide range of skilled and managerial positions. While in part this has resulted from a decision by the Angolan government to encourage and support a limited number of Angolans to gain engineering training abroad, it has also reflected decisions by a number of major foreign investors to make significant use of local staff, on account of their better understanding of local conditions, and to promote sustainability.

All oil companies investing in Equatorial Guinea centre their staffing policies around the use of parent country nationals. Expatriate oil workers are housed in closed and largely self-sufficient compounds, with almost all supplies being imported from abroad. However, while in many respects the compounds accurately reproduce suburban America, the persistence of a particularly severe strain of malaria has deterred foreign recruitment, leading to proposals to spray large proportions of the country with DDT. Recently, direct commercial flights have been introduced to Houston, Texas, in order to facilitate the exchange of staff and leave breaks. The offshore nature of the industry makes much of the development 'invisible' to locals despite the glow flaring from the offshore fields in the night sky. There is currently no refinery, and oil is simply exported on an unrefined basis. Meanwhile, in a goodwill gesture, ExxonMobil recently donated large numbers of mosquito nets to the Ministry of Health; it is commonly held that most were then resold in a neighbouring country by members of the ruling family.

The rich pickings from the oil industry have led to bitter feuds over the division of spoils within the ruling family. In March 2004, a bizarre coup attempt mounted by a grouping of foreign mercenaries, ostensibly to replace the family with an exiled opposition leader, Severo Moto, seems really to have been aimed to secure the succession for the President's brother Armengol, rather than his appointed heir, the notoriously unstable Teodorin, best known for his pretensions as a Hollywood rap artist and producer. It has since transpired that both the United States and British governments had prior knowledge of the attempt, as did senior management of at least one major US oil company.

There is little doubt that the present policies and practices of major oil companies investing in Equatorial Guinea raise a range of ethical and practical HR questions.

Questions

1. What alternative HR policies could oil companies investing in Equatorial Guinea adopt?

2. What are the practical, training, development and resourcing implications of shift to the alternative policies identified in question 1?

3. What benefits could the oil companies gain from a move away from the near exclusive use of parent company nationals in skilled and managerial posts?

4. Why do you think the oil companies investing in Equatorial Guinea chose the HR policies identified in the case?

CASE STUDY 10.2

STAFFING IN MULTI-NATIONAL ORGANISATIONS

GEOFFREY WOOD

Think of any multi-national organisation you know well.

1. Identify what approach you think it employs in staffing its national subsidiaries (e.g., convergence models, ethnocentric, emic, etic, etc.)
2. Why do you think this approach has been adopted?
3. Could organisational effectiveness be enhanced by the adoption of an alternative approach?

References

Anderson, W. and Parker, F. (1964) *Society: Its Organization and Operation,* Princeton, NJ: Van Nostrand.

Applebaum, E., Bailey, T., Berg, P. and Kalleberg, A. (2000) *Manufacturing Advantage: Why High Performance Work Systems Pay Off,* Ithaca, NY: Cornell University Press.

Berry, J.W. (1999) 'Emics and etics: a symbiotic conception', *Culture and Psychology,* Vol.5, No.2, pp.165–72.

Bratton, J. and Gold, J. (2003) *Human Resource Management: Theory and Practice,* London: Palgrave.

Brewster, C. (1995) 'Towards a "European" model of human resource management', *Journal of International Business Studies,* Vol.26, No.1, pp.1–21.

Brewster, C., Sparrow, P. and Harris, H. (2001) *Globalization and HR,* London: Chartered Institute of Personnel and Development.

Brewster, C., Brookes, M. and Wood, G. (2004) 'Convergence, Isomorphism or Duality?: Recent Survey Evidence on the HRM Policies of MNCs', Henley Management College Occasional Papers, Henley on Thames: Henley Management College.

*Dowling, P., Welch, D. and Schuler, R. (1999) *International Human Resource Management.* Cincinnati, OH: South West Publishing.

Dowling, P., Schuler, R. and Welch, D. (2004) *International Human Resource Management,* Cincinnati, OH: International Thomson.

Duysters, G. and Hagedoorn, J. (2001) 'Do company strategies and structures converge in global markets? Evidence from the computer industry', *Journal of International Business Studies,* Vol.32, No.2, pp.347–56.

Elger, T. and Smith, C. (2001) 'The global dissemination of production models and the recasting of work relations in developing societies', in J.K. Coetzee, J. Graaff, F. Hendricks and G. Wood (eds) *Development: Theory Policy and Practice,* Cape Town and Oxford: Oxford University Press.

Faversnec-Hery, F. (1996) 'Work and training: a blurring of the edges', *International Labour Review,* Vol.135, No.6, pp.665–74.

Ferlie, E. and Pettigrew, A. (2000) 'Managing through networks', in C. Mabey, G. Salaman, and J. Storey (eds) *Strategic Human Resource Management,* London: Sage.

Friedman, T. (1999) *The Lexus and the Olive Tree,* New York: Farrar & Strauss.

Fukuyama, F. (1995) *Trust: Social Virtues and the Creation of Prosperity,* New York: Free Press.

Fukuyama, F. (2000) 'One journey, one destination', in R. Burns and H. Rayment-Pickard (eds) *Philosophies of History,* Oxford: Blackwell.

Giddens, A. (1990) *The Consequences of Modernity,* Cambridge:Polity Press.

*Gooderham, P., Nordhaug, O. and Ringdal, K. (1998) 'When in Rome, do as the Romans? HRM practices of US subsidiaries in Europe', *Management International Review,* Vol.38, No.2, pp.47–64.

Gooderham, P., Nordhaug, O. and Ringdal, K. (1999) 'Institutional and rational determinants of organizational practices: human resource management in European firms', *Administrative Science Quarterly,* Vol.44, pp.507–31.

Greider, W. (1997) *One World, Ready or Not,* Harmondsworth: Penguin.

Haveman, H. (1993) 'Follow the leader: mimetic isomorphism and the entry into new markets', *Administrative Science Quarterly,* Vol.38, pp.593–627.

Helfrich, H. (1999) 'Beyond the dilemma of cross-cultural psychology: resolving the tension between emic and etic approaches', *Culture and Psychology,* Vol.5, No.2, pp.131–54.

Hofstede, G. (1980) *Culture's Consequences: International Differences in Work-Related Values,* Beverly Hills, CA: Sage.

*Hofstede, G. (1991) *Cultures and Organizations,* London: McGraw-Hill.

Holden, I. (2001) 'International human resource management', in I. Beardwell and L. Holden (eds), *Human Resource Management: A Contemporary Approach,* London: Pearson.

Huntington, S. (1996) *The Clash of Civilizations and the Remaking of the World Order,* New York: Touchstone.

Huselid, M. (2000) 'The impact of human resource management practices on turnover, productivity, and corporate financial performance', in C. Mabey, G. Salaman and J. Storey (eds) *Strategic Human Resource Management,* London: Sage.

Kochan, T. and Ostermann, P. (1994) *The Mutual Gains Enterprise,* Boston, MA: Harvard Business School.

*Kostova, T. and Roth, K. (2002) 'Adoption of an organizational practice by subsidiaries of multinational corporations', *Academy of Management Journal,* Vol.45, No.1, pp.215–33.

Lane, C. (1998) 'Theories and issues in the study of trust', in C. Lane and R. Bachmann (eds) *Trust Within and Between Organizations,* Oxford: Oxford University Press.

Lao, C. and Ngo, H. (2001) 'Organizational development and firm performance: a comparison of multinational and local firms', *Journal of International Business Studies,* Vol.32, No.1, pp.95–114.

Lincoln, J. and Kalleberg, A. (1990) *Culture, Control and Commitment: A Study of Work Organization in the United States and Japan,* Cambridge: Cambridge University Press.

Mayrhofer, W. and Brewster, C. (1996) 'In praise of ethnocentricity: expatriate policies in European multinationals', *International Executive,* Vol.38, No.6, pp.749–78.

Moody, K. (1987) *Workers in a Lean World: Unions in the International Economy,* London: Verso.

Moorehead, G. and Griffin, R. (2004) *Organizational Behaviour: Managing People and Organizations,* Boston, MA: Houghton-Mifflin.

Morris, M., Leung, K., Ames, D. and Lickel, B. (1999) 'A view from the inside and the outside: integrating emic and etic insights about culture and judgement', *Academy of Management Review,* Vol.24, No.4, pp.781–96.

O'Hagan, E. (2002) *Employee Relations in the Periphery of Europe: The Unfolding of the European Social Model,* London: Palgrave.

Parsons, T. (1951) *The Social System,* Glencoe, NY: Free Press.

Perlmutter, H. (1969) 'The tortuous evolution of the multi-national company', *Columbia Journal of World Business,* Vol.4, pp.9–18.

Pfeffer, J. (1994) *Competitive Advantage Through People,* Cambridge, MA: Harvard University Press.

Sako, M. (1998) 'Does trust improve business performance?', in C. Lane and R. Bachmann (eds) *Trust Within and Between Organizations,* Oxford: Oxford University Press.

*Scullion, H. (2001) 'International Human Resource Management', in J. Storey (ed.) *Human Resource Management: A Critical Text* (2nd edn), London: Routledge.

Serote, P., Mager, A. and Budlender, D. (2001) 'Gender and Development', in J.K. Coetzee, J. Graaff, F. Hendricks and G. Wood (eds) *Development: Theory Policy and Practice,* Cape Town and Oxford: Oxford University Press.

*Sparrow, P. and Hiltrop, J-M. (2000) 'Redefining the field of European human resource management', in C. Mabey, G. Salaman and J. Storey (eds) *Strategic Human Resource Management,* London: Sage.

Streeck, W. (1995) 'Neo-voluntarism: a new European social policy regime', *European Law Journal,* Vol.1, No.1, pp.31–59.

Tummala, K. (1999) 'Policy of preference: lessons from India, the United States and South Africa', *Public Administration Review,* Vol.59, No.6, pp.495–508.

Ulrich, D. (1997) *Human Resource Champions,* Cambridge, MA: Harvard University Business School Press.

Webster, E. and Wood, G. (2005, forthcoming) 'Human Resource Management Practice and Institutional Constraints', *Employee Relations,* Vol.27, No.4.

Whitley, R. (1999) *Divergent Capitalisms: The Social Structuring and Change of Business Systems,* Oxford: Oxford University Press.

Wood, G. (2001) 'Globalization and Human Resource Development', in J.K. Coetzee, J. Graaff, F. Hendricks and G. Wood (eds) *Development: Theory Policy and Practice,* Cape Town and Oxford: Oxford University Press.

Wood, G. (2004) 'Business and politics in a criminal state: the case of Equatorial Guinea', *African Affairs,* Vol.103, No.413, pp.547–67.

Wood, G. and Brewster, C. (2002) 'Decline and Renewal in the British Labour Movement', *Society in Transition,* Vol.33, No.2, pp.241–58.

Zeira, Y. and Harari, E. (1977) 'Genuine multinational staffing policy: expectations and realities', *Academy of Management Journal,* Vol.20, No.2, pp.327–33.

* Useful reading

Chapter 11

CAREERS

Laurie Cohen and Amal El-Sawad

Father Tadeusz was sixty-two years old, tall and thin. He had spent a career in the priesthood in small parishes, despite a lifelong desire for an assignment in a city, with libraries and museums and theatres . . . he thought of his career as a priest – as measured against his early ambitions – as a lackluster disappointment, if not an outright failure (*In the Memory of the Forest*, Powers 1997, p.41).

When my children grow up I don't want them to have a job, I want them to have a career (Prime Minister Tony Blair on a visit to the Sheffield Job Centre, *Sheffield Star*, 5 February 1998, p.1. Cited in Mallon 1998, p.48).

Introduction

This chapter is about career: how we can understand the concept of career, and how we might go about managing our own careers and other people's. Academics have examined career in a whole range of ways: from psychological and sociological perspectives, as objective realities or subjective constructions, from individual and organisational points of view. Similarly, in everyday language career has a number of different meanings and is used in a variety of contexts: the career of the footballer, the bureaucrat, the politician or the patient; career education, career breaks, career mentoring. If we were to analyse what career means in each of these cases, we would come up with a rich, diverse and probably ambiguous picture. In spite of this diversity, though, what many of these examples have in common is a relationship between an individual and an organisation. The nature of this relationship is a fundamental issue within HRM.

This chapter has five sections. The first focuses on the concept of career, considering a number of academic and popular definitions and usages, while the second examines changing work contexts and raises questions about the implications of these changes for people's thinking about career, and for career management. The mainstream careers literature has been widely criticised for its failure to account for the different ways in which people from diverse groups construct their careers. In light of such critique, the third section focuses on careers and diversity. The next section explores the way in which academic thinking about career has developed, considering traditional psychological and sociological approaches, as well as inter-disciplinary and interpretive perspectives. Finally, the chapter examines organisational interventions in career management, considering these in the context of current debates about changing careers.

Definitions of career: diverse understandings

The term 'career' conjures up an array of images. We might use it to refer to a lifetime of service in a bureaucracy, or to a professional career like law or medicine. In contrast, we could talk about the much more temporary career of a professional sports person. In years gone by 'career girl' was used to differentiate a woman in paid employment from housewives and mothers. We could refer to the career of a drug addict or of a patient. We could also consider a career in crime as 42-year-old Razor Smith (2004) has done in the published account of his life to date entitled *A Few Kind Words and a Loaded Gun: The Autobiography of a Career Criminal*. In contrast, we might also talk about the career of an academic subject, for example, the career of organisational analysis. In short, it is a term we use every day, unproblematically, in a whole variety of situations and contexts. But what do we actually mean by career? Is it just another way of talking about paid employment? Could any job be described as a career, or is the term exclusive to a particular type of position? And what role, if any, does one's life outside work play in the definition of career? An academic analysis of career and its management clearly requires some consideration of these questions.

A traditional view of career is illustrated in Wilensky's (1961) classic definition:

> Let us define career in structural terms. A career is a succession of related jobs arranged in a hierarchy of prestige, through which persons move in an ordered, (more or less predictable) sequence (p.523).

Implicit within this definition is the idea of career as paid work. The reference to 'hierarchy of prestige' suggests a bureaucratic context. Notably, Wilensky describes career as a structural phenomenon, that is, it seems to have its own existence independent of the individual. This view implies that careers are real things, prescriptions, available for people to take part in, in a particular, set way. A more recent take on this perspective is introduced by Leach and Chakiris (1988):

> Careers flow from jobs . . . jobs need not lead anywhere, it is just something a person gets paid for. Careers, on the other hand, are continuous behavioural episodes, leading to a path or ladder that ends, optimally, in some sort of career capstone experience (p.50).

Paths and ladders are familiar metaphors in talk about careers. While the path suggests career as a journey towards an ultimate destination, implicit in the ladder image is the notion of career as hierarchical and, again, oriented to a goal. Other popular metaphors for describing careers include tracks and arrows (and of course, the much more cynical rat race).

In contrast are those definitions of career which extend beyond the domain of paid employment, to the sequence of an individual's life experiences more generally. In the 1930s Chicago sociologist Hughes (1937) explained:

> A career consists, objectively, of a serious of statuses and clearly defined offices . . . subjectively, a career is the moving perspective in which the person sees his [sic] life as a whole and interprets the meaning of his various attributes, action, and the things that happen to him (p.413).

While acknowledging the structural, objective dimension of career, Hughes' definition also highlights the notion of the career as situated within the individual, thus emphasising its subjective dimension. Thus it is not the case that a person simply acts out a prescribed career pattern, instead, they construct their career in dynamic negotiation with their social, economic and cultural context. Hughes' work stimulated research into career in a whole variety of social situations: from funeral directors to tubercular patients and marijuana users. Goffman (1961) further developed Hughes' notion of career, subverting conventional definitions which equated career with occupational advancement.

> Traditionally the term career has been reserved for those who expect to enjoy rises laid out within a respectable profession. The term is coming to be used, however, in a broadened sense to refer to any social strand of any person's course through life . . . Such a career is not a thing that can be brilliant or disappointing; it can no more be success than a failure. One value of the concept is its two-sidedness. One side is linked to the internal matters held dearly and closely, such as image of self and felt identity; the other side concerns official position, jural position and style of life and is part of a publicly accessible institutional complex. The concept of career, then, allows one to move back and forth between the personal and the public, between the self and its significant society (Goffman, 1961, p.127).
>
> How does this compare to other definitions introduced thus far?
>
> Would you say that Goffman places more value on certain kinds of careers?
>
> How might a researcher go about studying the 'two sides' of career?

More recent definitions, particularly those put forward by academics writing in the fields of HRM and career guidance, tend to reflect this broader, more inclusive approach: 'the individual's development in learning and work throughout life' (Collin and Watts 1996, p.393).

Finally, different subject disciplines lead to and often explain variations in definitions of career. For example, economists may define career as 'the vehicle through which human capital is accrued through a lifetime of education and experience' whereas those from the discipline of politics might understand career as 'the sequence of endeavours to maximise self-interest, through successive attempts to gain power, status and influence' (Adamson *et al.* 1998, p.253).

Changing contexts of work and career

There is a growing consensus that careers are changing, from traditional, hierarchical, linear and organisationally bound models to more fluid arrangements, based on the accumulation of skills and knowledge and the integration of personal and professional life. It is notable that, in spite of the very different ways in which individuals' careers develop, much of career theory remains staunchly bureaucratic in its orientation, emphasising (albeit implicitly) linearity, hierarchy and the division of work and home life.

Kanter (1989), in a challenge to this traditional perspective, offers a very different model for understanding career development and change. Her starting point is that as bureaucratic forms of organising are beginning to wane, so too are bureaucratic careers. Kanter identifies three career forms: bureaucratic, professional and entrepreneurial. To Kanter, a bureaucratic career is characterised by: 'the logic of advancement. [It] involves a sequence of positions in a formally defined hierarchy of other positions' (1989, p.509). The bureaucratic career has been the basis of much HRM thinking about career management.

Kanter defines professional careers as: 'craft or skill, with monopolisation of socially valued knowledge the key determinant of occupational status, and "reputation" the key resource for the individual' (pp.510–11). She argues that a professional's relationship with their organisation is more complex than that of a bureaucrat. For Kanter, the entrepreneurial career is: 'one in which growth occurs through the creation of new value or new organisational capacity . . . the key resource in an entrepreneurial career is the capacity to create valued outputs' (1989, pp.515–516). There is a significant body of research which investigates the relationship between professional work and management (Raelin 1985; Cohen *et al.* 2002) although there is a striking neglect of entrepreneurship in the careers literature.

Kanter takes a broad, macro-view and does not examine in detail the processes through which these career forms are constructed. Furthermore, although she identifies three principal forms, there could of course be more. Nevertheless, Kanter's model provides a very valuable starting point for examining career in the early twenty-first century, and her suggestion that we need to know more about these forms and the ways in which they are enacted in organisational contexts is a significant issue for HRM.

CHANGE AND CONTINUITY IN CAREER CONTEXTS

There is an emerging consensus that we are experiencing an irreversible change in the organisation of our working lives and the structures and cultures of our working environments. This raises important questions about the ways in which these changes are impacting on our perceptions and experiences of career.

> Today the phrase 'flexible capitalism' describes a system which is more than a permutation on an old theme. The emphasis is on flexibility. Rigid forms of bureaucracy are under attack, as are the evils of blind routine. Workers are asked to behave nimbly, to be open to change at short notice, to take risks continually, to become ever less dependent on regulations and formal procedures. This emphasis on flexibility is changing the very meaning of work (Sennett 1998, p.9).
>
> What might be some implications of these changes for career development and management?

Arnold (1997a) cites a number of key changes which he sees as particularly relevant to individuals' understandings of career and career management, including macro-level changes in demography and the labour market, as well as at the level of the organisation. As regards the former, he highlights the significance of growing numbers of women in the labour force. The proportion of women who are economically active has risen from 66 per cent in 1984 to 73 per cent in 2003 while the proportion of men has fallen from 88 per cent to 84 per cent (National Statistics, *Labour Market Trends,* October 2003). At the same time, our labour force is ageing. The average age of those in employment in Britain increased from 37.5 to 39 years between 1991 and 2001 (National Statistics, *Labour Market Trends,* February 2003). Economic activity of both women and men in the 50–64 age bracket is forecast to increase until at least 2011 (Office for National Statistics 2000). Service sector work has increased and manufacturing and production decreased. Gender splits in sectoral patterns of employment have persisted over the last decade. Women are more likely to work in services and men are more likely to work in manufacturing and production (National Statistics, *Labour Market Trends*, October 2003).

According to the Labour Force Survey 2001, nearly 1 in 5 people of working age have a long-term disability – 3.7 million men and 3.4 million women. Of these, just 3.4 million were in employment in autumn 2001. The employment rate for those without a disability is 81 per cent compared to 48 per cent for those with a disability, and 36 per cent for those with a disability and from an ethnic minority.

Legislation to protect against sex and race discrimination has been in place for some 30 years and yet women and ethnic minorities remain disadvantaged in the labour market. Despite equal pay legislation, in 2001 women earned 81 per cent of equivalent male earnings. Both men and women from ethnic minorities experience higher levels of unemployment than whites (National Statistics, *Labour Market Trends*, October 2003). Individuals of Pakistani and Bangladeshi origin are even more disadvantaged than other ethnic groups. Interestingly though, self-employment varies significantly by ethnic group. Numbers of those in self-employment rose from around 2.2 million in the late 1970s to around 3.8 million in the late 1980s with little change since. As of December 2003 the figure remains at around 3.8 million. Except for those of Black African and Black Caribbean origin with a self-employment rate of 7 per cent, rates among all other ethnic groups are higher than the rate for whites. One wonders if self-employment offers minority groups an escape route from workplace discrimination and the subsequent disadvantage this creates.

As the labour force becomes more diverse, the structures of opportunity afforded to people are changing significantly. With more people involved in paid work, and changing structures of employment opportunities, it follows that individuals' and organisations' expectations of career and career development are also undergoing some transformation.

At the level of the organisation, widespread restructuring initiatives have had a significant impact on large numbers of people (see Chapter 14). For individuals these changes have meant working in a whole range of contexts, with different people, and requiring the acquisition of new skills. At the same time, from a cultural dimension it has been argued that within organisations traditional paternalistic relationships between employers and employees are being eroded in favour of more contractually based arrangements (Heckscher 1995).

CHANGE AND CONTINUITY IN CAREER FORM

The causes and extent of change in today's world of work is still a subject of vigorous debate. Nevertheless, in contrast to the (mythical?) job for life, careers today are characterised by uncertainty and frequent change – of organisation, role, colleagues and required skills. It is a world of movement.

Scholars have argued that not only are bureaucratic careers seen as less and less likely, but they are also less and less appealing. In the literature on emerging careers, organisations are frequently depicted as 'stultifying individuals' initiative and creativity and promoting an unhealthy dependence on organisations for the conduct of one's working life' (Cohen and Mallon 1999, p.333). People are encouraged to weaken their links with organisations, and to develop relationships based on short-term contracts and financial arrangements. Mirvis and Hall (1994) introduced the term 'boundaryless career' to describe career patterns based on cyclical rather than linear patterns of movement, periods of re-skilling, of lateral rather than upward movement and of change – of job, company, even occupation. Within such careers identity is no longer organisationally determined, but is constructed through 'cumulative work experiences and career achievement, [and] also through "work" as a spouse, parent and community member' (p.387).

While the idea of the new career is widely celebrated, voices have been raised about their potentially negative implications for both individuals and organisations. And questions are raised about the concept of 'boundarylessness' itself: 'the stories we heard were less about breaking free than about *reconstructing* the boundaries. . . It appeared that participants were attempting to establish new employment contexts which in some ways approximated those that they had only recently left' (Cohen and Mallon 1999, p.346).

There is an emerging consensus that individuals can no longer expect a job for life. Whether this kind of arrangement was ever available to the majority of workers is a moot point. However, a recognition of increasingly short-term employment arrangements has consequences for both individuals and organisations. It has been suggested that in today's world of movement, diversity, flexibility and short-term relationships, organisations need to re-think their approaches to human resource development and career development.

Gender and ethnicity in career debates

DIVERSE CAREERS: WOMEN'S CAREERS AND MEN'S THEORIES

A persistent criticism of mainstream career theory is its exclusivity: its central concern with those most privileged in traditional career terms (Sullivan 1999): white, middle-class and usually male-dominated occupational groups. Through such a focus, career theory has effectively constructed women, as well as people from minority ethnic groups, blue-collar workers, the disabled, the poor, the uneducated, as 'the other', as deviations from a dominant pattern (Marshall 1989; Thomas and Alderfer 1989). In what follows we consider how (if at all) career scholars have sought to redress this imbalance, in relation to gender and ethnicity.

Turning first to gender, career theorists mindful of the exclusion of women from the mainstream career canon have sought to develop understandings which more adequately reflect women's lives. Taking career development as an example, apart from a few early studies which suggested that the process of career development is essentially the same for women and men (Fitzgerald and Crites 1980), there is now a general consensus that women's lives are fundamentally different from men's, and that they construct their careers in different ways. Feminist psychologists take issue with theories of adult development based on male experiences (Gilligan 1982), while feminist sociologists emphasise the significance of gender in an individual's experience of life's choices and chances (Evetts 2000).

In recent years research on gender and careers has focused on a whole array of issues including constructions of career success (Sturges 1999; Höpfl and Hornby Atkinson 2000); family roles and responsibilities (White 1995; Hite and McDonald 2003), women's careers in management (Marshall 1985, 1995; Cassell and Walsh 1992), and women's experience of career transition (Mallon and Cohen 2001); work and leisure careers (McQuarrie and Jackson 2002) and women's involvement in 'non-traditional' and new careers (Whittock 2000; Belt 2002). These studies offer illuminating insights into the day-to-day issues which women confront as part and parcel of their unfolding careers.

To understand the ways in which career theory has or has not engaged with women, Marshall (1989) identified three overlapping phases of feminist thought. She describes the first as a consciousness-raising period, whereby the absence of women from career theory was noted and calls for more inclusive approaches were made. The second is identified as a reform period whose central purpose was to facilitate women's access to the career world, hitherto dominated by men. Arguably, much career theory remains in that phase (Brett and Stroh 1994; Hakim 2000). Finally Marshall discusses the emergence of a radical voice, which elucidates women's subordination through patriarchal social structures and cultural meaning systems. The intent of this phase is not so much to fit women into existing structures, but to assert women's perspectives, and in so doing, to challenge the status quo. The aim is emancipation and social transformation.

On one hand, it could be argued that the new and emerging definitions of career discussed above are particularly appropriate to women's career experiences, in so far as they blur out paid work as a distinguishing feature of career, celebrating instead a greater variety of career forms and lifestyle choices. Through the mobilisation of such discourses, women could be seen as deriving a sense of social legitimacy for their 'non-linear' career choices, and need not see themselves as falling off a career path.

On the other hand, though, current research evidence suggests that these new meanings do not simply eclipse the old in such neat ways (Pringle and Mallon 2003). Rather, so embedded are traditional notions of career development and success that they continue to resonate, even when they appear to no longer 'fit' the lives and experiences of many people. Similarly, within these new career discourses, important questions about power relations and inequality (questions central to researchers working in Marshall's third phase) are sometimes lost from view in the wide-open definitions of what now constitutes a career.

ETHNICITY AND CAREERS

While career scholars have at last begun to tune in to the experiences of women, they remain largely deaf to the voices of other marginalised groups. There is a dearth of work which explores the career experiences of individuals from ethnic minority groups. It is telling, for example, that in the recent edited book contributions to the mainstream careers literature – Peiperl *et al.* (2000), Collin and Young (2000), and Peiperl *et al.* (2002) – not a single chapter is devoted to exploring the experiences of ethnic minorities (though all three books do devote one chapter to the experiences of women). It is difficult to fathom why such neglect, noted some 15 years ago by Thomas and Alderfer (1989), persists. Thomas and Alderfer (1989) recall two interest groups set up by the Academy of Management in the 1970s – one on women in management which evolved into a division, the other on minorities and management which disbanded within five years. They offer a number of possible explanations for why so many people seem so uninterested in race-related issues: the under-representation of ethnic minorities in the academic community; a belief that race only becomes a pertinent issue worthy of attention when overt acts of discrimination occur; and the difficulties of researching a sensitive and potentially 'controversial' issue 'fraught with tension' (p.153).

Ethnic minorities who make up 8 per cent of the UK population, some 4.6 million people or one in twelve of the population, are without doubt disadvantaged in the workplace. According to figures published by the Office for National Statistics in 2001–02 the percentage of the working-age population in employment is far higher for whites than for other ethnic groups. There is enormous diversity of experience. Statistics do seem to demonstrate, however, that some ethnic groups, notably those of Indian and Chinese origin, fare better than others (Cabinet Office Strategy Unit 2003). Pakistanis and Bangladeshis (particularly women) come off worst, disadvantaged not only in relation to white people but frequently also in relation to other ethnic minorities (Modood 1997). This disadvantage is not merely a feature of the UK labour market. For example, Lamba (2003) examined the employment experiences of refugees living in Canada and found that many were held back by structural barriers and experienced downward occupational mobility.

The UK government has recently set itself the goal of ensuring that within 10 years ethnic minority groups living in Britain will 'no longer face disproportionate barriers to accessing and realizing opportunities for achievement in the labour market'. Measures to track progress towards this goal will include 'increased employment rates and earnings' and 'improvements in the career profiles of ethnic minorities' (Cabinet Office Strategy Unit 2003). The government has its work cut out.

Once in employment individuals from ethnic minorities face considerable hurdles in their attempt to pursue career. This is perhaps best documented in the UK police service. Bland *et al.* (1999) studied the career progression of ethnic minority police officers in order to assess whether and in what ways the careers of ethnic minority and white officers differed. Though the career aspirations of all groups were found to be similar, ethnic minority officers were significantly disadvantaged. For example although they applied at roughly the same time, ethnic minority officers took on average 12 months longer than their white colleagues to secure promotion to sergeant. For promotion to inspector black officers took on average 23 months longer and Asian officers 16 months longer than their white colleagues despite Asian officers being more likely to have 'A' levels and graduate qualifications than their white colleagues.

Following the inquiry into the death of Stephen Lawrence and the subsequent publication of the MacPherson report in 1999, police forces across the country were directed to take action to tackle the 'institutional racism' inherent in their policies and procedures. After five years there is little sign of improvement. An investigation by the Commission for Racial Equality found that police forces are failing to implement race equality regulations; 90 per cent of police race equality schemes do not meet the minimum legal requirements. Just one of the fifteen police force schemes investigated was seen to be fully compliant with the Race Relations Act.

In research terms what is needed to begin to plug the gap in our understanding of the relationship between ethnicity and careers? Pringle and Mallon (2003) point to the paucity of research conducted in non-Western industrialised cultures. There is thus a need for research which is carried out in different national and cultural contexts where ethnic groups who are a minority group in one context are studied in contexts where they represent the majority. We also need studies which focus specifically on the career experiences of all minority groups, not just ethnic minorities. Without such studies career theories will become increasingly detached from the experiences of these groups and the millions of people which they represent.

Career lenses and approaches

Traditional studies of career tended to approach career from the perspective of a single academic discipline: typically sociology or psychology: 'While psychologists say "people make careers", sociologists claim "careers make people" and the careers literature shows a dearth of cross referencing between these two frames of reference' (Derr and Laurent 1989, p.454). Although these approaches have been criticised for being partial and fragmented, given their prominence within career theory, they are a really useful and important starting point.

Sociological approaches see the career as something which is organisationally based, planned, progressive and enacted by rational individuals (Inkson 1995). This literature typically explores careers in terms of particular occupational paths, focusing on issues such as turnover patterns, organisational demographics and internal labour markets. Such perspectives are based on the concept of the career as objective, external to the individual. 'Individuals are portrayed as if they join the organisation practically as lumps of clay, ready to be shaped by all those around them' (Bell and Staw 1989, p.232). This view emphasises social structures over individuals' ability to act and affect change. It sees the career as something with its own prescribed existence, as something real and external to the individual.

In contrast, early psychological work on career focused on the individual, and on the notion of the career as situated within the individual. This literature is concerned with issues such as personality traits and their implications for occupational choice, and the importance of person–environment 'fit' for occupational stability (Super 1957; Holland 1973). Psychological approaches were influenced by trends in developmental psychology. Consistent with psychologists' interest in adult change and development (Hall 1976; Levinson 1978) career development theorists study the ways in which careers develop over the span of an individual's adult life. Here the work of Super (1957) has been particularly influential. His 5-stage model (re-worked in 1985): from 'growth' to 'decline', though criticised for its exclusivity and its apparent lack of flexibility, has been the basis of much thinking and theorising about career development over the last 40 years. (This revised model is illustrated in Table 11.1.)

Such models continue to influence academic and popular thinking about career and indeed available computer packages which help people to make career decisions are typically based on psychological models of person–occupation fit and career development. Nevertheless, questions have been raised about the adequacy of psychological models of understanding. Scholars have criticised personality traits approaches for being too static and determining, and for their failure to account for social processes and contexts (Nicholson and West 1989; Potter and Weatherell 1987). As regards life-stage models, academics have taken issue with the male orientation of much of this research. In addition, they have been criticised for their over-emphasis on age, and their lack of attention to social and organisational change.

Table 11.1 Typology of adult career concerns derived from Super *et al.* 1985 framework

Exploration phase

Clarification	Development of one's ideas about suitable and meaningful employment
Selection	Move from general ideas to specific choices
Enactment	Execution of plan for entering chosen occupation

Establishment phase

Becoming secure	Settling into occupation and adoption of a lifestyle consistent with its imperatives
Cementing	Process of gaining security in occupation
Advancement	Progression: in terms of position/earninigs/responsibility

Maintenance

Retention	Holding of position in context of internal and external pressure and change
Keeping up to date	Proactively keeping abreast of developments in field
Creativity	Finding innovating ways of performing roles

Disengagement

Slowing down	Easing off of workload and pace
Ideas for retirement	Financial and lifestyle planning
Retirement	Establishing alternatives to

MORE DYNAMIC, LESS STATIC APPROACHES?

Seeking to understand what gives a career its continuity, Schein (1978, 1993, 1996), Driver (1982) and Derr (1986) all attempt to look at careers as they unfold and develop through time: for Schein it is the anchor, for Driver enduring shapes and patterns, and Derr's work focuses on 'career logics'. Schein used the anchor image to describe what he saw as those fundamental ideas around which individuals construct their careers. Through his research into American male Master's students, he identified eight such anchors: technical/functional competence, general management competence, autonomy/independence, security/stability, entrepreneurial creativity, service/dedication, pure challenge and lifestyle (Schein 1996). In contrast to the anchor's solidity, Driver's 'concept' model is about shapes and patterns: transitory, steadystate, linear and spiral, while Derr's five 'career logics': getting ahead, getting secure, getting free, getting high and getting balanced, is based on the idea of career development as an essentially rational process.

It could be argued that these approaches are now somewhat dated, reminiscent of an employment context which offered more choice and opportunity than many experience today. Nevertheless we find them interesting in their attempt to integrate the individual and the organisation, and their radical departure from the idea of career as hierarchical. Instead, they acknowledge the diverse ways in which individuals construct their careers, and recognise the significance in non-work aspects of life in the experience of career.

INTERPRETIVE APPROACHES

As discussed in the section on definitions, Hughes and the Chicago sociologists were interested in the ways in which people make sense of their careers. While these interpretive approaches were to some extent eclipsed by more mainstream sociological and psychological research, they have nevertheless persisted, providing an illuminating – and often missing – perspective. Examples of interpretive work include Cohen and Mallon's research into individuals' transition from organisational employment to self-employment (Cohen and Mallon 1999), Fournier's (1998) on careers and the discourse of enterprise, Collin and Watts' (1996) study into career guidance and El-Sawad's (2002) research into career sense-making of graduate employees in a blue-chip multi-national, against a backdrop of large-scale change.

Recently attention has turned to using constructivist and social constructionist approaches in careers research. Common to both perspectives is the idea of social reality as subjectively constructed. However, while the former derives from development and cognitive psychology and sees social experience as subjectively constructed by individuals through cognitive processes, the latter is more inter-disciplinary, with roots in sociology, literary studies and cultural anthropology, focusing on the construction of reality as a fundamentally social process (Piaget 1969; Bruner 1990; Burr 1995; Gergen 2001; Young and Collin 2004).

In a special issue of the *Journal of Vocational Behaviour* dedicated to the use of constructivist and social constructionist perspectives in career theory (Young and Collin 2004), the editors argue that both offer challenges and opportunities to the career field. In particular the articles highlight how these perspectives move beyond static, individualised analyses, providing understandings which take account of the processes through which careers are developed, the dynamic contexts in which individuals enact and make sense of their careers and illuminating, in particular, patterns of dominance and subordination played out within these contexts. Furthermore, it is argued that the narrative and discursive approaches characteristic of constructionism, provide access into the 'unique interaction of self and social experience' (2004, p.381) which career represents, but which is difficult to tap through positivistic, survey-based methodologies.

HOLISTIC PERSPECTIVES: NEW METAPHORS FOR THINKING ABOUT CAREER

In contrast to scholars who see career as either external or internal, residing within the organisation or within the individual, are those who seek to explore career more holistically, as an on-going process central to which is the relationship between the individual and the organisation. To this end, metaphor analysis has been argued to offer a powerful tool in the study of careers (e.g., Gunz 1989; Mignot 2000, 2004; Inkson 2002, 2004; El-Sawad 2005).

The language we use to describe careers is often metaphorical: successful careers are described in terms of climbing to the top, reaching targets and being at the pinnacle, while unsuccessful careers are attributed to losing one's sense of direction, getting lost or hitting glass ceilings. It has been suggested that metaphors 'are used to make sense of the situations we find ourselves in' (Grant and Oswick 1996, p.1); they are 'a way of thinking and a way of seeing' (Morgan 1986, p.12). These familiar metaphors which we use to talk about career are no accident. Rather, underpinning them are fundamental assumptions about what a career is and is not, about career success and failure. These assumptions are typically based on notions of career as external to the individual, organisationally based and prescribed, linear and hierarchical.

Within the careers literature the dominant metaphors which scholars have used to talk about careers fall into four broad groups: spatial, journey, competition and horticultural metaphors (El-Sawad 2005). Spatial career metaphors draw attention to entrenched notions of vertical mobility with frequent reference to hierarchies, pyramids, career ladders, high-flyers and so on (Gunz 1989; Barley 1989). Journey metaphors frame careers as, for example, travel along paths. Competition metaphors represent careers as uphill struggles or rat races on fast tracks. Gunz (1989) notes the use of horticultural metaphors in the careers literature conjuring both positive career images of growing, flowering, blossoming as well as negative ones such as being pruned and cut back. But what of the metaphors employed by those having rather than studying careers? What do these tell us about the ways in which people make sense of their careers and the contexts in which they are played out?

In a study of the careers of graduates employed in a large blue-chip organisation, El-Sawad (2005) analysed the metaphors contained in their career accounts. Like career scholars, graduates drew on 'established' metaphors to describe their careers. In addition they drew on other essentially disciplinary metaphors not reflected in the careers literature – imprisonment, military, school-like surveillance, 'Wild West' and nautical metaphors. Through imprisonment metaphors graduates likened their careers within the organisation to serving a life sentence. Military metaphors included references to political battles, fighting, tending wounds and the need to wear body armour for protection. Through 'school-like surveillance' metaphors graduates presented themselves as children and their managers as the parental figures who could reward good behaviour with the opportunity to get involved in more responsible and interesting 'grown-up' work. Such metaphors highlight the graduates' understanding of the power held by managers to determine their career fates. The imagery conjured up by 'Wild West' type metaphors was of good and bad guys (rather than children). Through nautical metaphors, graduates described feelings of anxiety and insecurity created by the pursuit of career progression. They spoke of their experiences of floundering and even drowning and of their desire to bail out. Taken together these metaphors present a rich and textured reading of career, uncovering disciplinary dimensions of career and career contexts which, except for a handful of notable exceptions (Grey 1994; Savage 1998; Fournier 1998) are currently under-explored in the mainstream careers literature. Indeed, issues of power have been largely neglected in studies of career to date (Collin and Young 2000). There is clearly a need for more research in this area.

Managing careers: implications for HR practice

Assumptions about how we might define career are embedded within organisational approaches to career management and development. Indeed, current debates on organisational change have thrown the issue of HR intervention in career management into sharp relief. Some scholars have argued that traditional approaches to career management, based on notions of lifelong employment and hierarchical development, have become obsolete. However, others maintain that employees continue to attach real importance to managed career development initiatives and the concept of employment security.

Notwithstanding the current emphasis on self-managed careers, many organisations do make an attempt to intervene in individuals' career development. Arnold (1997a) identifies a number of such interventions, illustrated in Table 11.2.

Table 11.2 Career management interventions in organisations

Internal vacancy notification. Details about jobs available within the organisation prior to external advertising. Should include necessary experience and qualifications, and a job description.

Career paths. Information about the sequence of jobs that people can do, or competencies they can acquire within the organisation, with details of how high the path goes, potential lateral moves, required qualifications/skills/experience.

Career workbooks. Exercises designed to guide individuals in analysing their own strengths and weaknesses, identifying opportunities and assessing action necessary to achieve goals.

Career planning workshops. Deal with similar issues as workbooks, but in a more 'managed' way, offering opportunities for discussion and feedback. Sometimes includes psychometric testing.

Computer-assisted career management. Packages which help employees to assess their skills, interests, and values, and translate these into employment options. Sometimes these are organisationally-specific.

Opportunities for training and development. Information, financial support and sometimes delivery of courses. Could be within or outside of the organisation. Designed to enable employees to update, or to acquire new skills and knowledge. Often used in preparation for seeking promotion.

Personal development plans. Statements of how an individuals' skills and knowledge might develop, given a particular employment context and timescale. Often arise from performance appraisal or development centre assessment.

Career action centres. Resources (paper, video and electronic) available to employees on a drop-in basis. Sometimes also offer counselling.

Development centres. Employees are assessed on the basis of their performance in a number of different exercises and tests. Focus on identifying an individual's strengths and weaknesses for the purpose of development.

Mentoring programmes. Attaching employees to more senior colleagues who act as advisors, advocates, counsellors.

Job assignment/rotation. Careful use of work tasks can help a person to stay employable. Organisation will benefit from staff adaptability, flexibility.

Outplacement. Purpose is to support people who are leaving organisation, to help them clarify future plans. May include a variety of the above interventions.

Source: Adapted from Arnold 1997a. Reprinted by permission from Arnold, J., *Managing Careers into the Twenty-first Century*, copyright © Sage Publications ltd, 1997

Baruch (2002) presents a list of career management practices in order of the level of implementation which an earlier survey (Baruch and Peiperl 2000) found. These are: advertising internal job openings; formal education as part of career development; performance appraisal as a basis for career planning; career counselling by direct manager; career counselling by HRM department; lateral moves; retirement preparation programmes; succession planning; mentoring; common career paths; dual ladders; booklets on career issues; written personal career planning; assessment centres; 360-degree appraisals; career workshops; induction; special programmes, e.g., for high-fliers; creating psychological contracts; and secondments. Greenhaus *et al.* (2000) also offer a summary of typical career management practices: anticipatory socialisation via, e.g., apprenticeships; realistic recruitment; employee orientation; individual learning and development; on-the-job experiences; performance feedback and coaching; mentoring and supportive alliances; dual promotion ladders; dealing with career plateau; late career activities; redeployment and outplacement programmes; pre-retirement programmes.

This chapter does not offer the scope for a full debate on organisational career interventions. However, it is important to point out that there is still considerable uncertainty about how often these interventions are used and to what effect.

Arnold (1997a) concludes that career management interventions are most likely to have most impact in situations where, first, there is openness and trust. Although one could argue that these are becoming increasingly rare in these days of flexibility and changing psychological contracts, Macauley and Harding (1996) maintain that it is precisely in this context that such qualities are needed most. They report on the development of a career management programme in a computer software firm, the first step of which was a diagnosis of employees' perceptions and expectations. Macauley and Harding argue that where psychological contracts are being re-defined, an understanding of employees' perspectives is vital if motivation and commitment are to be maintained, and if career management interventions are to achieve their desired results – in this case increasing learning and development opportunities.

Second, Arnold suggests that the goals of career management processes must be explicit, and that this will be most easily achieved if there is a limited number of compatible interventions. Furthermore, it is important that interventions stay in existence long enough to become established.

Third, the way in which these processes are managed and delivered is crucial. On a theoretical level, Arnold (1997b) suggests that given current changes in career patterns and expectations, providers of careers guidance need to be more aware of process, rather than focusing exclusively on outcomes. Not only do Arnold's propositions relate to individual career management, but they likewise have implications for those involved in managing the careers of others.

On a more practical level, managers should themselves be appraised on how well they carry out career interventions, and top management should be seen as actively supportive of such initiatives (Mayo 1991). Here it is vital that career management programmes are seen as integrated in the organisation's daily practices, and consistent with its more general strategic orientation. Finally, it is essential that career management interventions are not perceived as only available to a select few: rather, organisations should be seen to take an interest in the careers of all their employees, including minority groups.

It is interesting to consider HR interventions in career management in light of current debates on changing careers. As noted earlier, traditional approaches to career management were based on the notion of the career as lifelong, existing within and defined by the organisation, and sought to establish the right 'fit' between the person and the position. In this case the role of the HRM practitioner 'became one of defining position requirements, identifying and selecting individuals capable of meeting those position requirements and assisting organizational members to progress through a sequence of positions within the organization' (Templar and Cawsey 1999, p.72). However, the emerging discourse on new careers sees the career as situated within the individual, focusing on individual choice, self-development and 'employability' (see also Ball and Jordan 1997). From this perspective, career management is contract-oriented, concerned with defining core competencies and identifying the 'core' workforce, and is short-term in focus. Templar and Cawsey describe these, respectively, as 'position centred' and 'portfolio centred' career development procedures. Whereas the former sees HR practitioners as having a central role to play the employees' long-term training and development, within a portfolio perspective individuals are responsible for their own training and career growth. In this case, HR managers must ensure that individuals have the requisite skills needed to fulfil the terms of a specific contract.

Given these two perspectives, we can then ask where the interventions outlined in Table 11.2 can be situated. Although certain interventions (such as career planning workshops and job assignment/rotation) are often associated with an individual's long-term relationship with the organisation, this does not have to be the case (Ball and Jordan 1997). Taking opportunities for training and development as an example, such programmes could be offered by the organisation to help individuals prepare for promotion. However, in other cases individuals might opt into particular training courses as a way of updating their knowledge and skills – thus enhancing their personal portfolio. Thus, it is not the intervention per se which is significant, but the way in which it is understood and used.

There is a cynical view that from the point of view of the organisation the self-managed career is a cheap option. However in their research into self-development, Mackenzie Davey and Guest (1994) found that some organisations take a much more proactive stance, sponsoring a range of activities from career workbooks to mentoring schemes and career workshops. The common view of 16 'leading career scholars' expressed in a survey conducted by Baruch (2002) was that popular career practices, while focusing on individual development, simultaneously retain a high degree of organisational involvement. Similarly, in their evaluation of two open learning career management initiatives, Ball and Jordan (1997) describe a high level of organisational involvement and commitment. Indeed, participants in these programmes felt that the support they received from highly trained and skilled tutors was an 'essential ingredient in the process' (1997, p.515). Likewise, although the programme described by Macauley and Harding (noted above, 1996) is based on the principle of individual career management and self-development, this is not to suggest that employers can simply duck out of their responsibility. Rather, their key point is that employers have a vital role to play in facilitating this development.

Summary

This chapter began with two quotes about career: one poignant and retrospective, the other looking ahead, full of promise and opportunity. In the first, career is seen as the sum of an individual's working life. Here, an elderly priest looks back on this life and finds it lacking. He has not fulfilled his youthful aspirations. He has had a disappointing, unsuccessful career.

Conversely, in the second quote Tony Blair uses the word career *in contrast* to a job to express his high hopes for his son's future. There is a sense of purpose and meaning embedded in the term. Together these quotes raise some fascinating questions about what careers are, the relationship between personal and worklife, about where careers are located and the extent to which (and by whom) they can be managed. While not aiming to provide definitive answers, this chapter has explored these questions, considering in particular emerging debates on changing careers, and the implications of these debates for HR practice.

The chapter began by discussing the changing contexts in which careers are enacted. While the precise nature and extent of change is still an open question, there is a growing consensus that careers are increasingly characterised by uncertainty and instability. One way of engaging with these debates is by considering how career thinking has developed – examining traditional definitions and the extent to which these are being reproduced/challenged or transformed in current employment contexts. While some might argue that conventional definitions are outdated, metaphors of ladders, arrows and getting to the top continue to send powerful messages about career success and failure. In addition to these traditional conceptualisations, broader, more inclusive definitions were introduced, emphasising both subjective and objective dimensions of career, and the integration of professional and personal life.

The chapter then briefly discussed the theoretical frameworks on which these definitions are based, with particular reference to the experiences of women and ethnic minorities. Not only were conventional definitions found to be wanting in their failure to adequately account for the diverse patterns of different individuals' working lives, but also within these approaches there is often an implicit assumption that careers take place in large organisations and are based on bureaucratic notions of success. Alternatives to this traditional model were introduced. The final section of the chapter focused on organisational intervention in career management, in light of current ideas about changing psychological contracts between individuals and organisations. In particular this section considers the role of the HR practitioner in the context of current debates on changing careers.

CASE STUDY 11.1

MAKING SENSE OF CAREERS

LAURIE COHEN AND AMAL EL-SAWAD

Understanding careers

1. Working in a group, make a list of 20–30 jobs – make your list as wide-ranging as possible.
2. Which of these jobs would you consider to be 'careers'? Which would not be careers? Why?
3. Construct a definition of career that justifies your categorisation. How does this definition compare to those introduced in the chapter?
4. Apply this definition to your own experiences. Which aspects of your life would it include? Which aspects would be excluded from this definition? Based on this definition, would you say that your experiences constitute a career?

Reflecting on career experiences

1. Make a 'time-line' of your career to date. Choose an appropriate shape, and include significant events, decisions, people, transitions. Should aspects of personal life be included? What about voluntary or community activities, education, training? Who have been the key stakeholders in your career development?

2. Consider this time-line in terms of the theoretical approaches introduced in this chapter.

   ▪ Do you see your career as objective or subjective? Who 'owns' your career?
   ▪ To what extent do sociological/psychological approaches shed light on your career experiences?
   ▪ Explore the relevance of career anchors, shapes or logics. What are the relative merits/weaknesses of these approaches in relation to your own experience of career?
   ▪ Consider the issue of career diversity in terms of your experience of career? To what extent do feminist calls for 're-visioning' the career concept have resonance for you?
   ▪ How does your career compare to traditional, bureaucratic conceputalisations?
   ▪ Consider Kanter's model in light of your career time-line. Would you say that your career could be described in terms of one of her career forms? Could more than one of these forms apply? Simultaneously or at different times? How might you account for movement between these career forms?

3. Describe any career interventions you have experienced (in terms of your own career, or in terms of managing the careers of others). Critically examine the apparent strengths/weaknesses of this intervention, for the individual and the organisation.

4. Using your accumulated understanding of careers, develop a metaphor that describes your career and reflects key concepts introduced in the chapter.

5. Based on your experience and observations, to what extent and in what ways do you think careers are changing? What are the implications of these changes for individuals and organisations?

CASE STUDY 11.2

MOVING FROM EMPLOYMENT TO SELF-EMPLOYMENT: YASMIN'S STORY

LAURIE COHEN AND AMAL EL-SAWAD

Yasmin is 35 years old, the single mother of two young daughters. At the time of interview, she had been working as an independent management consultant for two years. Yasmin never considered her career in terms of a single organisation, or indeed a single occupation. Instead, she explained how she had always envisaged her working life as an on-going developmental process: acquiring a range of skills, knowledge and experiences, and applying these to a whole variety of employment contexts. Since obtaining her degree and training as a teacher, Yasmin has had various positions within several different local authorities, working in the field of race relations. In addition, she had a short stint of self-employment, running a small clothing business together with her former husband. Her last organisational position, before embarking on her work as a management consultant, was a senior role within the policy department of a northern local authority.

Yasmin described how after two and a half years in this post, she began to feel stuck. It was a highly politicised local authority, both internally and publicly, and the issue of race relations was contentious and deeply sensitive. Her brief was to initiate policy change, and although she was given considerable responsibility, she felt largely ineffective. As a black woman coming from another city to work in a largely white, male organisation, an 'outsider' in an organisation in which many senior managers had spent their entire working lives, she described her feelings of marginalisation and powerlessness. In addition to these frustrations with the work itself, Yasmin described the incompatibility of her roles and responsibilities as a local authority employee and as a mother. In particular, she explained how the excessively bureaucratic culture within that organisation did not allow her the flexibility she needed to manage her domestic life, and to care for her children. Not only was she 'failing to thrive' professionally, but she felt that her daughters were likewise stifled by the arrangements. As her levels of stress and frustration grew, she realised that it was time to leave. 'I got to a point where I thought I'm becoming de-skilled here, I'm not developing further and I'm not getting a sense of achievement . . . Then I looked at where am I going to go, and I looked around at the organisation, I mean the next tier up would have been applying for director level, and it just seemed that people had to work so hard . . . I mean there's worklife, and there's the rest of your life, and there are your children. The balance would've been all wrong.'

During her notice period, Yasmin enrolled in a Masters course in Organisational Development, a programme oriented to management consultancy. Although she had not made a decision to become a consultant, she felt that such a course would give her the opportunity gain a more theoretical understanding of organisation in light of her own employment experiences. She explained how during that time she reflected on her career achievements and considered where to go next. 'What the course did for me is it made me realise that I had a lot of good experience, it made me realise that I'd already got consultancy skills, in fact, I was already a consultant. Without realising it I had been working as an internal consultant for several years. Only I called it something different then.' Upon completing the course, Yasmin decided not to go back into organisational employment, and to embark on a portfolio career as a consultant in organisational development.

Yasmin did not describe the move to portfolio work as a radical change; rather it was part of an on-going process, a way in which she could build on her experience and knowledge, continuing to grow and learn, as she has striven to do throughout her working life. 'It's interesting about my life. I grew up with the idea that I would have an education, that I would have a degree. I grew up with the idea that I'd be self-sufficient regardless of whether I was married or not . . . But I never really had a career plan as such. I knew I'd be working, but I didn't know where. So I mean, even now I don't really have a career plan beyond the next year or two . . . I couldn't tell you now what I'll be doing in ten years' time.'

Yasmin thus described her career as 'emergent' rather than 'planned'. However, she insisted that this did not mean that it was in any way ad hoc. Rather, at the time of interview she had in place firm plans for continued professional development (which is often problematic for consultants and other portfolio workers), and a network of contacts that she saw as a crucial resource. Notwithstanding these networks, however, Yasmin said that at times her new arrangements can be lonely and isolating, that she does miss the sense of belonging that can develop when one is a member of a department within an organisation.

On a personal level, Yasmin explained how her domestic responsibilities are more easily accommodated within the flexible patterns of portfolio employment. In charge of her own schedule, she can organise work to fit around her daughters' school year. While such arrangements were untenable within the local authority, among portfolio workers a greater integration of personal and professional life is seen as the norm. However, she maintained that this sort of synthesis does have its costs. In particular, there is no strict delineation between work and home life, each encroaches on the other, resulting in a lack of clarity and feelings of underachievement in both. In addition, she explained that when one is based at home, it is very difficult to stop working. However, Yasmin explained that as she has become more used to the rhythm of management consultancy, she has been able to find ways of managing the tension between these two contexts.

Although she is satisfied at the moment, Yasmin insisted that OD consultancy would definitely not be her last career move. She spoke of herself as 'essentially a change person. I've always had this willingness to take risks with my career. I'm not one of these people who has a clear plan, I have a sense that I'll always be working, and I'll always be doing something that I'm interested in, but I don't know what it is. As far as management consultancy goes, I'll probably do it for a couple of years, then I'll move on to something else. That's just how I am.'

Questions

Having read Yasmin's account, consider the following questions.

- Would you say that Yasmin's career could be described as external, having an objective existence, or internal, subjectively constructed by Yasmin herself?

- To what extent can Schein's career anchors be applied to this story?

- Examine Yasmin's story in light of Kanter's bureaucratic, professional and entrepreneurial career forms. Does Kanter's model work? To what extent to you think it can accommodate the transitions she described? Is there a fourth (or even a fifth) career form which you feel would enhance Kanter's framework?

- To what extent would you say Yasmin's career has been affected by changing social/economic and organisational contexts?

- Would you say Yasmin's story is more about change or continuity?

ORGANISATIONAL INTERVENTIONS IN CAREER MANAGEMENT: Experiences of performance appraisal schemes

LAURIE COHEN AND AMAL EL-SAWAD

These two case studies are adapted from the work of Paul Borton, Vince Elder and Debbie Hodge, MBA students at The Business School, Loughborough University.

Debbie

My first experience of performance appraisal was when I was working in the retail sector. The organisation I was employed by at that time used performance appraisal as a key tool in their performance related pay scheme. However, rather than being seen as part of an on-going developmental process, in that firm performance appraisal was a one-off yearly event, conducted in an almost tokenistic way, with no objectives or development plans. It was a really frustrating and demotivating experience, which I think had a lot to do with my decision to resign.

My current organisation, an insurance company, has been using performance appraisal for at least a decade, but in my view it has only become effective in the past five years. A corporate-wide framework has been adopted by all managers responsible for conducting half-yearly appraisals, part of this framework is the personal development plan (PDP). This plan is used to address an individual's development needs beyond their specific group or department, in the context of the whole organisation. Alongside the PDP are performance objectives, devised by the individual in consultation with their line manager. Objectives are intended to be both task and behaviorally oriented, designed to fulfill the needs both of the individual and the organisation. I think that when it is conducted well, performance appraisal is a valid and beneficial intervention.

However, I must say that my experience of this process has been erratic. The people who conduct the appraisal are really pivotal to its success. Unfortunately, though, I do not think that my company has fully appreciated the importance of this role, and as yet has not invested enough time and money into ensuring that managers are adequately prepared for it. This is disappointing, particularly given that salary increases are typically based on the outputs of the performance appraisal.

In addition, in order for the potential of the appraisal process to be realised, they need to be used regularly and consistently. Where they have become established, and where they are used thoughtfully, conducted by well-trained managers, they can be an extremely effective performance management tool. In particular, as project and contract work increase, the performance appraisal can be a useful way to align organisational and individual objectives.

Paul

The process of career management intervention in my organisation, a leading aeronautical engineering firm, involves four distinct, but inter-related phases: staff appraisal, the development cell (the management follow-up of the appraisal), personal development plans and the 360-degree appraisal.

As regards staff appraisal in particular, the system used in my firm, and in fact most of the engineering departments of the civil airline business, has been in place for many years. The appraisal typically takes place in the form of a private discussion between the individual and his or her immediate supervisor or functional manager. The structure of this discussion is directed towards the completion of a formal appraisal form which, upon completion, is entered into the individual's company record. Following this discussion, the appraisal form is passed on to the departmental senior manager for comment. Finally, the individual adds any relevant comments, and signs the form in acceptance. In cases where problems or discrepancies arise, these are discussed by the relevant individuals, and hopefully resolved.

In the past, the frequency of appraisals, and both the quality of the initial discussion and subsequent activities have been somewhat erratic. This, I think, resulted in some degree of cynicism amongst the participants in the process. However, project leaders have recognised these problems, and have worked to rectify them, and to provide a more coherent and consistent process. It is intended that everyone should be formally appraised on an annual basis. Individuals' performance is measured against the targets outlined through the appraisal process, and this information is made available to all project members, in an attempt to raise the status of the scheme, and to signal the importance placed upon it by senior managers. In addition, in an attempt to create greater coherence between appraisals, the form itself has been modified, such that it now provides an opportunity to reflect on an individual's success at the year end, as well as setting clear goals for the future. In contrast to those who argue that evaluation of past performance and the review of development needs should be separated, I think that the way in which these are synthesised in the current appraisal scheme is a real strength. However, the appraisal mechanism is seen as totally independent from the pay review process, a split that in my view is very important. Likewise, I agree entirely with my department's policy of not using appraisal to rank members of staff. Thus, within the appraisal there is no mechanism for comparing one individual's performance with another's. This is a real strength, as the appraisal does not get stuck on whether a certain individual should be given a 4 instead of a 3, but instead can develop into a meaningful and constructive dialogue.

The development cell is the next step in the staff appraisal. In this forum, the individual is excluded. Instead, it comprises the appraiser, the function manager and the HR representative aligned with that function. The focus of this discussion is the individual's career, in particular issues such as training and development needs, readiness for promotion, and possible job rotations and options. In addition, an assessment is made as to where in the organisation the individual might eventually aspire (e.g., staff technologist, management, company senior staff). Although in the past members of staff felt that this process was too secretive, it has become more open. The individual can now view their completed form, although they can not remove it from the HR department.

As regards my own experience of the development cell, in the very early years of my career I was, somewhat naively, satisfied if the front-page summary reflected a successful year. However, after the novelty of a manager's 'nice words' wore off I, like many others, became somewhat cynical that regardless of the contents of the appraisal, nothing seemed to ever happen as a result. In those days, the development cell seemed more of a 'smoke and mirrors' exercise carried out by management, with the individual excluded from many of the key issues and conclusions. However, I feel that there has been some improvement – although this change in my perception could be a result of the fact that I am now involved in conducting appraisals and development cells myself, and thus have new insights into the process. As an appraisee as well as an appraiser, I am sure there is still room for improvement. In particular, the form should be less prescriptive, and mechanisms should be put in place to ensure that the target of at least one yearly appraisal for all members of staff is realised.

Questions

Having read these accounts, consider the following:

■ Compare and contrast the stories of Debbie and Paul. If you have been involved in performance appraisal processes, to what extent do these stories resonate with your own experiences?

■ What would you say are the key advantages and disadvantages of these schemes?

■ Would you describe these performance appraisal schemes as 'position' or 'portfolio-centred' career management interventions?

AN ORGANISATIONAL CAREER AT COMPUCAN

AMAL EL-SAWAD AND LAURIE COHEN

Alison is 28 years old, is married with no children and no plans for any. She has worked for Compucan for the last six years. After graduating from university Alison struggled for some months to find a job. Having applied for a number of management training schemes without success, she decided to apply for programming roles in order to try to get her foot in the door of a company and was delighted when Compucan finally offered her a position as a computer programmer. Though she did not enjoy programming work (she felt she was no good at it) she hoped that eventually she would be able to move into a management role. The turning point for her came after two years when she worked on a programming project which enhanced her visibility by bringing her into contact with senior managers in the company. Soon after the project ended, she was promoted to the position of team leader, responsible for managing a small team of programmers. Following this she was appointed to a first line manager position with responsibility for a whole department. Recently she has secured another promotion to a second-line manager role. Alison now has several managers reporting to her and assumes overall responsibility for a number of different departments. While she describes her first role as a programmer as 'just a job' she is clear that what she has now is a career. She explains:

> I've been here six years and in the six years I've done five jobs. Each job has been a step up the career ladder. I know where I'm going next. I can see the natural steps,

the sort of stepping-stones to get more responsibility. That's what I believe a career is. I think I'm very fortunate because I happen to have got on a very nice path and was recognised early and have been given lots of opportunities.

Beyond attributions to luck, Alison is hard-pressed to explain her meteoric rise at Compucan. She is surprised at how well she has done and struggles explain her success:

I was offered the team leadership job after two years and that came as a surprise to me. I really wasn't expecting it then. I seem to have just fallen into things, you know? I didn't plan to become a first line manager but it, sort of, just happened. I certainly didn't plan to get this job as a second line manager. I was just offered it.

Alison suspects that her promotions may be connected to the visibility she secured within the organisation early on. She wonders whether the senior managers she met at this time have, behind the scenes, acted as her career sponsors:

I think if you've been recognised then I think you continue to be recognised. I think the senior management look after you quite heavily and worry about what you're doing, that kind of thing.

Now in a senior managerial role herself, Alison describes how she now keeps a look out for younger employees who she feels to be 'rising stars'. She instructs the managers who report to her to scout for stars on her behalf so that she can collate a list of high potential employees. A committee of senior managers meets regularly at Compucan and the lists which managers have drawn up are discussed. A small number of employees considered to have the highest potential are singled out for special attention and are placed on the 'high-flier database'. Their progress is monitored closely and they are often given extra projects to work on over and above their daily roles to help increase their visibility within the organisation. As Alison puts it:

We grow our people by giving them opportunities.

While many employees, in particular graduate recruits, aspire to be placed on the high-fliers database, only some of those that are on the database are actually informed of the fact. Ambitious employees therefore know not whether they are being 'watched' because their name is on the database or 'watched' because someone somewhere deems them to have the potential to be placed on the database. The net effect is to make them feel as though they are under constant surveillance. To be seen to ease off work is to jeopardise one's chances of being identified as a high-potential employee. This in turn ensures that the maximum effort goes into their work.

When it comes to promotion decisions, there are no set criteria written down. Indeed, like Alison, Compucan employees are not really sure what qualities and abilities are required to achieve promotion which makes it difficult for them to know how best to attract the attention of selectors. Alison is particularly drawn to enthusiastic employees. She explains:

I think the thing that I notice with people and what I appreciate in people and would encourage is enthusiasm because I think if somebody is enthusiastic then you can teach them anything and you can get them to do anything.

Despite acknowledging the role that senior managers have played in her own promotion, and the role that she plays in identifying and grooming the next generation of 'stars', Alison is frustrated by the views held by some employees that what matters at Compucan is 'not what you know but who you know' and that promotion decisions are political ones. Alison protests:

> I don't think [career progression] is political. To be promoted in Compucan you need to do your job, plus you take on extra responsibilities round it. The people who call it political are the people who just do their job and who are only willing to do their job. They're only willing to do the nine to five and that is their choice. You know, it's *no pain no gain*.

Alison works very long hours and twelve-hour days are the norm. For her, employees who have chosen to devote time and effort to commitments outside of work – for example to family life – should not expect to achieve the kind of career progression available to those prepared to 'devote all' to Compucan. Alison is attempting to communicate this message to the employees she is responsible for. She is currently mentoring two junior staff, passing on to them what she has learnt about the company and advising them what to do if they want to follow in her footsteps. She reflects on this:

> I've only ever worked at Compucan. I've got no other experience, nothing else to go on other than my experience here. It does worry me sometimes that I'm re-creating models of my own career rather than leaving people to find their own way of doing things. I don't think my way is the only way of doing it but it's the way I know and that's the way I'm going to encourage people. Well, it's what I know worked for me.

Alison feels proud of what she has achieved at Compucan and describes herself as 'incredibly loyal' to the company. She is committed to a long-term career at the company. There is one thing however which troubles her and which she would like to try and tackle:

> I would like to change the culture at Compucan with regards to women, to make it easier for women to gain promotion, to help women feel able to apply for this kind of work – technical work and managerial work. One thing that I miss is female company. My previous department had 25 people in it. I was the manager and there was just one other woman in it.

Though she is clear about what she would like to change, she does not know how to go about it.

Questions

1. How does Alison's conception of career compare with the numerous definitions presented earlier in the chapter? Which definition is closest to her conception of career?

2. What metaphors does Alison employ to describe her career? In what ways do her career metaphors help us to understand how she makes sense of career?

3. What does Alison mean when she says 'no pain no gain'? To what extent do you believe that in order to achieve career success there must be an element of 'pain'?

4. The 'high-flier database' offers managers at Compucan a highly effective disciplinary device in disguise. Explain.

5. Alison is adamant that 'getting on' at Compucan has nothing to do with politics. Do you agree with her?

6. Women are currently under-represented at Compucan in both technical and managerial roles. What evidence in Alison's account helps explain why this might be the case?

7. Through the mentoring process, Alison is attempting to 're-create models' of her own career at Compucan by encouraging others to do as she has done. How might this approach affect attempts to secure cultural change at Compucan?

References

Adamson, S.J., Doherty, N. and Viney, C. (1998) 'The meanings of career revisited', *British Journal of Management*, Vol.9, pp.251–9.

*Arnold, J. (1997a) *Managing Careers into the Twenty-First Century*, London: Paul Chapman.

Arnold, J. (1997b) 'Nineteen propositions concerning the nature of effective thinking for career management in a turbulent world', *British Journal of Guidance and Counselling*, Vol.25, No.4, pp.447–62.

Arthur, M. and Rousseau, D. (1996) *The Boundaryless Career*, Oxford: Oxford University Press.

Ball, B. and Jordan, M. (1997) 'An open-learning approach to career management and guidance', *British Journal of Guidance and Counselling*, Vol.25, No.4, pp.507–16.

Barley, S.R. (1989) 'Careers, identities and institutions: the legacy of the Chicago School of Sociology', in M. Arthur, B.S. Lawrence and D.T. Hall (eds) *Handbook of Career Theory*, Cambridge: Cambridge University Press.

*Baruch, Y. (2002) 'Career systems in transition: a normative model for organizational career practices', *Personnel Review*, Vol.32, No.2, pp.231–51.

Baruch, Y. and Peiperl, M.A. (2000) 'Career management practices: an empirical survey and theoretical implications', *Human Resource Management*, Vol.39, No.4, pp.347–66.

Bell, N.E. and Staw, B.M. (1989) 'People as sculptors versus sculpture: the roles of personality and personal control in organisations', in M.B Arthur, D.T. Hall and B.S. Lawrence (eds) *Handbook of Career Theory*, New York: Cambridge University Press.

Belt, V. (2002) 'A female ghetto? Women's careers in call centres', *Human Resource Management Journal*, Vol.12, No.4, pp.51–66.

Bird, A. (1994) 'Careers as repositories of knowledge: a new perspective on boundaryless careers', *Journal of Organisational Behaviour*, Vol.15, pp.325–44.

Bird, A. (1996) 'Careers as repositories of knowledge: considerations for a boundaryless Careers', in M.B. Arthur and D.M. Rousseau (eds) *The Boundaryless Career: A New Employment Principle For A New Organizational Era*, New York: Oxford University Press.

Bland, N., Mundy, G., Russell, J. and Tuffin, R. (1999) *Career Progression of Ethnic Minority Police Officers*, Police Research Series, Paper 107.

Brett, J.M. and Stroh, L.K. (1994) 'Turnover of women managers', in M.J. Davidson (ed.) *Women in Management: Current Research Issues*, London: Paul Chapman.

Bruner, J. (1990) *Acts of Meaning,* Cambridge, MA: Harvard University Press.

Burr, V. (1995) *An Invitation to Social Constructionism,* London: Routledge.

Cabinet Office Strategy Unit (2003) *Ethnic Minorities and the Labour Market: Final Report,* March, http://www.cabinetoffice.gov.uk/publications/

Cassell, C. and Walsh, S. (1992) 'Being seen but not heard: barriers to women's equality in the workplace', *The Psychologist,* Vol.5, pp.55–60.

*Cohen, L. (1997) 'Women's move from employment to self-employment: understanding the transition', Unpublished PhD Thesis, Sheffield Hallam University.

Cohen, L., Finn, R., Wilkinson, A. and Arnold, J. (2002) 'Professional work and management', *International Studies of Management and Organization,* Vol.32, No.2, pp.3–24.

Cohen, L. and Mallon, M. (1999) 'The transition from organisational employment to portfolio working: perceptions of boundarylessness', *Work, Employment and Society,* Vol.13, No.2, pp.329–52.

Collin, A. and Young, R.A. (2000) *The Future of Career,* Cambridge: Cambridge University Press.

Collin, A. and Watts, A.G. (1996) 'The death and transfiguration of career–and of career guidance?', *British Journal of Guidance and Counselling,* Vol.24, No.3, pp.385–98.

Commission for Racial Equality (2004) *A Formal Investigation of the Police Service in England and Wales,* London: Commission for Racial Equality.

Derr, C.B. (1986) *Managing the New Careerists,* San Francisco, CA: Jossey-Bass.

Derr, C.B. and Laurent, A. (1989) 'The internal and external career: a theoretical and cross-cultural perspective', in M.B Arthur, D.T. Hall and B.S. Lawrence (eds) *Handbook of Career Theory,* New York: Cambridge University Press.

Driver, M.J. (1982) 'Career Concepts: a new approach to career research', in R. Katz (ed.) *Career Issues in Human Resource Management,* Englewood Cliffs, NJ: Prentice-Hall.

Eaton, S. and Bailyn, L. (2000) 'Career as life path: tracing work and life strategies of biotech professionals', in M. Pieperl, M. Arthur, R. Goffee and T. Morris (eds) *Career Frontiers: New Conceptions of Working Lives,* Oxford: Oxford University Press.

El-Sawad, A. (2002) 'Playing the game: re-creational careers: a qualitative study of working lives in context', Unpublished PhD thesis, Loughborough University.

*El-Sawad, A (2005) 'Becoming a "lifer"? Unlocking career through metaphor', *Journal of Occupational and Organizational Psychology,* Vol.78, pp.23–41.

Evetts, J. (2000) 'Analysing change in women's careers: culture, structure and action dimensions', *Gender, Work and Organization,* Vol.7, No.1, pp.57–67.

Fitzgerald, L.F. and Crites, J.O. (1980) 'Toward a career psychology of women: what do we know? What do we need to know?', *Journal of Counselling Psychology,* Vol.27, pp.44–62.

Fournier, V. (1998) 'Stories of development and exploitation: militant voices in an enterprise culture', *Organization,* Vol.5, No.1, pp.55–80.

Gallos, J.V. (1989) 'Exploring women's development: implications for career theory, practice and research', in M.B Arthur, D.T. Hall and B.S. Lawrence (eds) *Handbook of Career Theory,* New York: Cambridge University Press.

Gergen, K. (2001) *Social Construction in Context,* Thousand Oaks, CA: Sage.

Gilligan, C. (1982) *In a Different Voice. Psychological Theory and Women's Development,* Cambridge, MA: Harvard University Press.

Goffman, I. (1961) *Asylums,* New York: Anchor.

Grant, D. and Oswick, C. (eds) (1996) *Metaphor and Organization,* London: Sage.

Greenhaus, J.H., Callanan, G.A. and Godshalk, V.M. (2000) *Career Management,* Orlando, FL: Harcourt.

Grey, C. (1994) 'Career as a project of the self and labour process discipline', *Sociology,* Vol.28, No.2, pp.479–97.

*Guest, D. and Mackenzie Davey, K. (1996) 'Don't write off the traditional career', *People Management,* 22 February, pp.22–5.

Gunz, H.P. (1989) *Careers and Corporate Cultures: Managerial Mobility in Large Corporations,* Oxford: Blackwell.

Gutteridge, T.G., Leibowitz, Z.B. and Shore, J.E. (1993) *Organisational Career Development,* San Francisco, CA: Jossey Bass.

Hall, D.T. (1976) *Careers in Organizations,* Pacific Palisades, CA: Goodyear.

*Hakim, C. (2000) *Work–Lifestyle Choices in the Twenty-First Century,* Oxford: Oxford University Press.

Handy, C. (1996) *Beyond Certainty,* Boston, MA: Harvard Business School Press.

Heckscher, C. (1995) *White Collar Blues: Management Loyalties in an Age of Corporate Restructuring,* New York: Basic Books.

Herriot, P. and Pemberton, C. (1995) *New Deals,* Chichester: Wiley.

Herriot, P. and Pemberton, C. (1996) 'Contracting careers', *Human Relations,* Vol.49, No.6, pp.757–90.

Hite, L. and McDonald, K. (2003) 'Career aspirations of non-managerial women: adjustment and adaptation', *Journal of Career Development,* Vol.29, No.4, pp.221–35.

Holland, J.L. (1973) *Making Vocational Choices,* Englewood Cliffs, NJ: Prentice-Hall.

Höpfl, H. and Hornby Atkinson, P. (2000) 'The future of women's career', in A. Collin and R.Young (eds) *The Future of Career,* Cambridge: Cambridge University Press.

Howard, A. (1992) 'Work and family crossroads spanning the career', in S. Zedeck (ed.) *Work, Families and Organisations,* San Francisco, CA: Jossey-Bass.

Hughes, E.C. (1937) 'Institutional Office and the Person', *American Journal of Sociology,* Vol.43, pp.404–13.

Hutton, W. (1995) *The State We're In,* London: Cape.

Inkson, K. (1995) 'Effects of changing economic conditions on managerial job changes and careers', *British Journal of Management,* Vol.6, pp.183–94.

Inkson, K. (2002) 'Thinking creatively about careers: the use of metaphor', in M. Peiperl, M. Arthur and N. Anand (eds) *Career Creativity: Explorations in the Remaking of Work,* Oxford: Oxford University Press.

Inkson, K. (2004) 'Images of career: nine key metaphors', *Journal of Vocational Behavior,* Vol.65, pp.96–111.

Kanter, R.M. (1989) 'Careers and the wealth of nations: a macro-perspective on the structure and implications of career forms', in M.B. Arthur, D.T. Hall and B.S. Lawrence (eds) *Handbook of Career Theory,* Cambridge: Cambridge University Press.

Lamba, N.K. (2003) 'The employment experiences of Canadian refugees: measuring the impact of human and social capital on quality of employment', *Canadian Review of Sociology and Anthropology,* Vol.40, No.1, pp.45–64.

Leach J.L. and Chakiris, B.J. (1988) 'The future of work, careers and jobs', *Training and Development Journal,* April, pp.48–54.

Levinson, D. (1978) *The Seasons of a Man's Life,* New York: Knopf.

London, M. and Stumpf, S. (1982) *Managing Careers,* Reading, MA: Addison-Wesley.

Macauley, S. and Harding, N. (1996) 'Drawing up a new careers contract', *People Management,* 4 April, pp.34–5.

Mackenzie Davey, K. and Guest, D. (1994) 'Self-development and the career: a review of some issues', paper prepared for the Careers Research Forum. Available from the authors at Birkbeck College, University of London.

Mallon, M. (1998) From managerial career to portfolio career: making sense of the transition, Unpublished Phd Thesis, Sheffield Hallam University.

Mallon, M. and Cohen, L. (2001) 'Time for a change? Women's accounts of the move from organizational careers to self-employment', *British Journal of Management,* Vol.12, No.3, pp.217–30.

Marshall, J. (1985) *Women Managers: Travellers in a Male World,* Chicester: Wiley.

Marshall, J. (1989) 'Re-visioning career concepts: a feminist invitation', in M.B Arthur, D.T. Hall and B.S. Lawrence (eds) *Handbook of Career Theory,* New York: Cambridge University Press.

Marshall, J. (1995) *Women Managers Moving On,* London: Routledge.

Mayo, A. (1991) *Managing Careers in Organisations,* London: IPM.

McQuarrie, F.A.E. and Jackson, E.L. (2002) 'Transitions in leisure careers and their parallels in work careers: the effect of constraints on choice and action', *Journal of Career Development,* Vol.29 No.1, pp.37–53.

Mignot, P. (2000) 'Metaphor: a paradigm for practice-based research into "career"', *British Journal of Guidance and Counselling,* Vol.28, No.4, pp.515–31.

Mignot, P. (2004) 'Metaphor and "career"', *Journal of Vocational Behaviour,* Vol.64, No.3, pp.455–69.

Mirvis, P.H. and Hall, D.T. (1994) 'Psychological success and the boundaryless career', *Journal of Organisational Behaviour,* Vol.15, pp.365–80.

Modood, T. (1997) 'Conclusion: ethnic diversity and disadvantage', in T. Modood and R. Berthoud (eds) *Ethnic Minorities in Britain: Diversity and Disadvantage,* London: Policy Studies Institute.

Morgan, G. (1986) *Images of Organization,* London: Sage.

Musson, G. and Cohen, L. (1998) 'Making sense of enterprise: identity, power and the enterprise culture', in M. Ram, D. Deakins and D. Smallbone (eds) *Small Firms: Enterprising Futures,* London: Paul Chapman.

Nicholson, N. and West, M. (1989) 'Transitions, Work Histories and Careers', in M.B Arthur, D.T. Hall and B.S. Lawrence (eds) *Handbook of Career Theory,* New York: Cambridge University Press.

Office for National Statistics (2000) *Labour Market Trends,* April.

Office for National Statistics (2003) *Labour Market Trends,* February.

Office for National Statistics (2003) *Labour Market Trends,* October.

Office for National Statistics (2004) *Labour Market Trends,* January.

Peiperl, M., Arthur, M., Goffee, R. and Morris, T. (2000) *Career Frontiers,* Oxford: Oxford University Press.

Peiperl, M., Arthur, M. and Anand, N. (eds) (2002) *Career Creativity: Explorations in the Remaking of Work,* Oxford: Oxford University Press.

Piaget, J. (1969) *Judgement and Reasoning in the Child,* London: Routledge & Kegan Paul.

Piore, M.J. and Sabel, C.F. (1984) *The Second Industrial Divide: Possibilities for Prosperity,* New York: Basic Books.

Potter, J. and Wetherell, M. (1987) *Discourse and Social Psychology,* London: Sage.

Powers, C. (1997) *In the Memory of the Forest,* London: Anchor.

*Pringle, J.K. and Mallon, M. (2003) 'Challenges for the boundaryless career odyssey', *International Journal of Human Resource Management,* Vol.14, No.5, pp.839–53.

Raelin, J., (1985) *The Clash of Cultures: Managers and Professionals,* Boston, MA: Harvard Business School Press.

Robinson, S.L. and Rousseau, D.M. (1994) 'Violating the psychological contract: not the exception but the norm', *Journal of Organisational Behaviour,* Vol.15, pp.245–59.

Savage, M. (1998) 'Discipline, surveillance and the "Career": employment on the Great Western Railway 1833–1914', in A. McKinlay and K. Starkey, (eds) *Foucault, Management and Organization Theory,* London: Sage.

Schein, E.H. (1978) *Career Dynamics,* Reading, MA: Addison-Wesley.

Schein, E.H. (1993) *Career Anchors: Discovering your Real Values,* London: Pfeffer.

Schein, E.H. (1996) 'Career Anchors Revisited: implications for career development in the 21st century', *Academy of Management Executive,* Vol.10, pp.80–8.

Sennett, R. (1998) *The Corrosion of Character: The Personal Consequences of Work in the New Capitalism,* New York: W.W. Norton & Co.

Smith, R. (2004) *A Few Kind Words and a Loaded Gun: The Autobiography of a Career Criminal,* London: Viking.

Sparrow, P. and Marchington, M. (1998) *Human Resource Management: The New Agenda,* London: FT/Pitman.

Still, L. (1993) *Where to From Here? The Managerial Woman in Transition,* Sydney: Business and Professional Publishing.

Sturges, J. (1999) 'What it means to succeed: personal conceptions of career success held by male and female managers at different ages', *British Journal of Management,* Vol.10, pp.239–52.

Sullivan, S. (1999) 'The changing nature of careers: a review and research agenda', *Journal of Management,* Vol.25, No.3, pp.457–84.

Super, D.E. (1957) *The Psychology of Careers,* New York: Harper & Row.

Super, D.E., Thompson, A.S. and Lindeman, R.H. (1985) *The Adult Careers Concern Inventory,* Palo Alto, CA: Consulting Psychologists Press.

Templar, A.J. and Cawsey, T.F. (1999) 'Rethinking career development in an era of portfolio careers', *Career Development International,* Vol.4, No.2, pp.70–6.

Thair, T. and Ridson, A. (1999) 'Women in the labour market: results from the spring 1998 Labour Force Survey', *Labour Market Trends,* March, pp.103–13.

Tharenou, P. (1997) 'Explanations of managerial career advancement', *Australian Psychologist,* Vol.32, No.1, pp.19–28.

Thomas, D.A. and Alderfer, C.P. (1989) 'The influence of race on career dynamics: theory and research on minority career experiences', in M. Arthur, B.S. Lawrence and D.T. Hall (eds) (1989) *Handbook of Career Theory* Cambridge: Cambridge University Press.

Van Maanen, J. (ed) (1977) *Organisational Careers: Some New Perspectives,* New York: Wiley.

White, B. (1995) 'The career development of successful women', *Women in Management Review,* Vol.10, No.3, pp.4–15.

Whittock, M. (2000) *Feminising the Masculine: Women in Non-traditional Employment,* Aldershot: Ashgate.

Wilensky, H. (1961) 'Work, Careers and Social Integration', *International Social Science Journal,* Vol.12, No.4, pp.543–74.

Young, R. and Collin, A. (2004) 'Constructivism and Social Constructionism in the Career Field', *Journal of Vocational Behaviour,* Vol.64, No.3, pp.373–88.

*Useful reading

Chapter 12

MANAGING DIVERSITY

Catherine Cassell

Introduction

Within the management and organisation literature there has been an increased interest in managing diversity as a way of addressing equal opportunity issues. A broad term that encompasses a number of concepts, managing diversity refers to the systematic and planned commitment on the part of organisations to recruit and retain employees from diverse demographic backgrounds (Thomas 1992). Building on the notion that all differences between groups and individuals within an organisation should be recognised and valued, managing diversity essentially presents a business case for equal opportunities. Noon and Ogbonna suggest that the concept of equal opportunities is increasingly being replaced with the notion on management of diversity: 'It has been a gradual drift, emanating from writers and organizations in the USA, traveling across the UK and seeping into mainland Europe' (2001, p.1). A key issue here is that in linking equal opportunities initiatives directly in with business strategy, the concept of managing diversity has similarities to the notion of strategic HRM.

The aim of this chapter is to outline the principles behind the managing diversity approach and examine some of the key issues and tensions around diversity debates. The chapter begins by outlining the context in which managing diversity has arisen. The principles of managing diversity strategies are then discussed, together with some of the techniques and tools that managers can use to this end. A series of key issues and debates are then outlined. These include a consideration of the research evidence upon which managing diversity initiatives are based; the integration of managing diversity initiatives with HR policies and practices; and a critique of the business case within which managing diversity initiatives are located.

The managing diversity context

To understand why managing diversity has become a pertinent issue now, rather than having a history in HRM and personnel generally, one needs to understand the context in which it has arisen. Two particular factors are important here: changing demographic trends, and the state of equal opportunities.

DEMOGRAPHIC TRENDS

The development of managing diversity strategies is clearly located within the context of shifting demographic trends. It is now almost a cliché within HRM that the composition of the workforce in many countries is changing, with an increased number of women and members of ethnic minority groups entering those workforces. Additionally the age profile of the working population is changing with an increase in the average age of employees. Prasad and Mills (1997) point out the impact that these shifts have had within North America:

> Few trends have received as much publicity or gained as much attention in management circles as the recent interest in managing diversity. It can be argued that much of this interest can be traced back to Johnston and Packard's (1987) influential report, *Workforce 2000*, which alerted organizations to the dramatic demographic changes that were in the process of transforming the North American workforce. . . . Confronted with the prospect of these major imminent changes, management practitioners, business educators, and organizational consultants quickly began preparing to meet the challenges of a new and diverse workforce in a number of ways (p.4).

Kandola (1995) in summarising changes in the UK and Europe suggests that similar demographic changes to those that have occurred in North America are anticipated. He summarises the changes that specifically relate to the nature of the workforce as:

1. Sex – increasing numbers of women entering the labour market.
2. Ethnic minorities – they will be forming an increasing part of the workforce.
3. Age – the ageing of the working population (p.138).

Therefore demographic trends have created the necessity to expand the labour pool to include those groups traditionally disadvantaged in the employment market. This, together with the increasing internationalisation of markets means that, as Kandola points out, organisations will have to deal with managing diversity not just in their own countries, but also in other countries.

THE STATE OF EQUAL OPPORTUNITIES

A further contextual issue is important here. Within the field of equal opportunities (EO) there has been an increasing disillusionment among activists, practitioners and employers alike about the effectiveness of equal opportunities policies and practices. Despite the existence of equal opportunities legislation, Wilson (1995) suggests that the notion that equal opportunity now exists is a myth. Indeed, there seems considerable disappointment and disillusionment about the current state of equal opportunities for disadvantaged groups, given 30 years of British EO legislation. Despite the initial high expectations of such legislation, in comparison to other equality legislation in Europe and the United States, it has been found to be lacking. Moreover, such legislation does little to rectify the more indirect forms of discrimination as by their very nature they do not appear discriminatory, but rather as part of normal everyday working patterns (Townley 1994).

Another concern about developments in equal opportunities surrounds the language within which such policies are framed and their appropriateness or attractiveness to employers. Ross and Schneider (1992) suggest that employers have resisted EO legislation precisely because it has been imposed upon them. They suggest that the law has enshrined the moral case for equal opportunities and has therefore given employers the responsibility to create a fair and equal society. Indeed, if they do not do this then they end up facing legal action. They argue that we all know that imposed change is likely to be resisted and causes a 'backlash' (p.50) therefore as equal opportunity policies rely on the law and ethics, and are externally driven and imposed, it is inevitable that employees will respond unfavourably towards them. As they suggest:

> So long as equal opportunities was equated simply with complying with legislation, then it's always going to be about group parity, and getting the numbers 'right'. This was a recipe for inertia over the last fifteen years, this is pretty much what we experienced (Ross and Schneider 1992, p.36).

They recommend that EO needs to be seen as business-driven in order to be attractive to employers, clearly a different case from that of fairness, justice or group parity. Davidson and Fielden (2003) suggest that one of the criticisms of the equal opportunities approach is that it is seen as a negative attempt to address issues of inequality because the focus is on punitive measures for those employers who do not comply with legislation. Diversity policies, on the other hand, are likely to be seen as more positive with regard to their recognition and celebration of the characteristics of diverse groups.

The debate about equal opportunities versus managing diversity is not that clear-cut. For example Liff and Dickens (1999) argue that a comparison between the two approaches can lead to an over-emphasis of the creation of a false dichotomy between them. Indeed, other authors such as Kaler suggest, 'what is unclear is whether they are two entirely separate approaches to employee management or whether diversity is offering a new and potentially more successful way of achieving the moral objectives of equal opportunity' (2001, p.58). There is, however, some consensus within the literature that managing diversity is an alternative approach due to its being located within the business case argument. This is outlined in the next section.

An alternative approach to equal opportunities: the business case

Given the problems outlined with the equal opportunities approach, it is not surprising that an alternative approach has emerged. Managing diversity is based very clearly on a business case. The business case focuses on the business benefits that employers accrue through making the most of the skills and potential of all employees. The argument is that the loss or lack of recognition of these skills and potential, usually as a result of everyday discriminatory practices, is very costly. Consequently the business case is fundamentally linked to the principles of strategic HRM where the human resource and its full utilisation is seen to give a company the competitive edge (Storey 1995). Additionally, it is crucial that equal opportunities initiatives are seen to tie in with the overall strategic direction of a company. A business case sees achieving equality as essential to achieving organisational goals. Again in the same way that HRM is linked into the general strategy of a firm, so equal opportunities pervades every aspect of business policy, rather than being an add-on.

In 1995 the Equal Opportunities Commission launched a campaign to highlight the business case for equal opportunities. The aim was to demonstrate that in economic terms, equality made good business sense. A leaflet produced at the time outlines the 'Benefits of Equality' and 'Costs of Inequality'. The benefits of equality include:

- Best use of human resources.

- Flexible workforce to aid re-structuring.

- Workforce representative of the local community.

■ Improved corporate image with potential employees and customers.

■ Attracting ethical investors.

■ Managers can integrate equality into corporate objectives.

■ New business ideas from a diverse workforce.

The costs of inequality include:

■ Inefficiency in use of human resources (high staff turnover; low productivity; and restricted pool of talent).

■ Inflexible workforce limiting organisational change.

■ Poor corporate image with prospective employees and customers.

■ Management time spent on grievances.

■ Losing an industrial tribunal case.

These costs and benefits are linked in to the demographic trends outlined earlier.

To summarise it is worth examining the differences between the diversity model based on the business case and traditional models of equal opportunity. Kandola and Fullerton propose that whereas EO is externally initiated, legally driven, and focuses on numbers and problems, diversity is internally initiated, business-needs driven and focuses on qualitative and opportunity outcomes. EO approaches tend to assume assimilation and are reactive, whereas diversity approaches assume pluralism and are proactive. Finally, EO approaches focus on a particular set of differences, usually race, gender and disability, whereas diversity approaches focus on all differences. Therefore diversity approaches based on a business case represent a different way of looking at equal opportunities. Ross and Schneider (1992) sum up the advantages of the business case with the following list:

> Equal Opportunities makes business sense. It enables organizations to: manage change by attracting people with new and different ways of thinking; create a working environment where total quality can take root; anticipate and meet the changing needs of customers; recruit and promote the best people by widening the traditional sources of candidates; retain the best people by ensuring that their needs are fully taken into account; increase productivity by raising motivation and commitment; increase profitability by reducing attrition and recruitment costs (p.109).

Managing diversity

The management of diversity presents a business case for moving towards a diverse workforce where the skills of all groups are recognised. The application of the business case through the management of diversity will now be explored in more detail.

GENERAL PRINCIPLES

The general argument behind managing diversity initiatives is that given the current shortage of skilled labour the effective use of diverse skills within an organisation makes good business sense. Diversity management is particularly popular in the United States where the skill shortages are more pronounced than in Britain. Management of diversity is based on the notion of difference and the effective management of difference. Valuing difference is seen as an important concept because it is specifically linked to an organisation's culture and values. A key element is to move towards 'cultures of inclusion' (Thornberg 1994) recognising that various organisational practices often lead to certain groups feeling left out or unwelcome. Exponents of the management of diversity perspective (Thomas 1990; Cox 1992; Jackson and Associates 1992; Kandola and Fullerton 1994; Montes and Shaw 2003) argue that all differences must be valued including those of white males. Kandola and Fullerton provide a useful working definition of managing diversity:

> The basic concept of managing diversity accepts that the workforce consists of a diverse population of people. The diversity consists of visible and non-visible differences which will include factors such as sex, age, background, race, disability, personality and work style. It is founded on the premiss that harnessing these differences will create a productive environment in which everybody feels valued, where their talents are being fully utilized and in which organizational goals are met (p.8).

The concept of managing diversity has become very popular, particularly in North America. The language surrounding diversity initiatives focuses on the notion of celebrating differences as Prasad and Mills (1997) suggest:

> Diversity is celebrated with the help of evocative metaphors such as the melting pot, the patchwork quilt, the multicolored or cultural mosaic, and the rainbow. All of these metaphors evoke enormously affirmative connotations of diversity, associating it with images of cultural hybridity, harmonious coexistence, and colorful heterogeneity (p.4).

Robinson and Dechant (1997) suggest that developing a business case for diversity is more difficult than for other business issues, mainly because 'evidence of diversity's impact on the bottom line has not been systematically measured and documented for easy retrieval and use' (p.21). They suggest that in putting the case, a number of business reasons can be suggested. These include cost savings such as decreased turnover and absenteeism and the avoidance of lawsuits. More positively they outline a range of ways in which diversity can drive business growth. These include improving marketplace understanding; increasing creativity and innovation; producing higher-quality problem solving; enhancing leadership effectiveness; and building effective global relationships. The authors report a survey where human resource executives from 15 Fortune 100 companies were asked to identify the main business reasons for engaging in diversity management. The top reasons given were better utilisation of talent (93 per cent); increased marketplace understanding (80 per cent); enhanced breadth of understanding in leadership positions (60 per cent); enhanced creativity (53 per cent); and increased quality of team problem solving (40 per cent). As Robinson and Dechant suggest, the executives focus more on the added value that emerges from diversity initiatives rather than the more negative penalties of mis-management, such as the avoidance of lawsuits for example.

Kandola and Fullerton (1994) suggest that, if it is to be successful, managing diversity must pervade the entire organisation. They propose a **MOSAIC** vision, which summarises the key characteristics of the diversity-oriented organisation. MOSAIC is used here as an acronym for **M**ission and values, **O**bjective and fair processes, **S**killed workforce: aware and fair, **A**ctive flexibility, **I**ndividual focus, and **C**ulture that empowers. Wheeler (2003) provides a model that links business strategy to diversity objectives and metrics. Where, for example, the business strategy is one of increased globalisation, then the diversity link is that of 'cultures working together effectively' and the metric of assessment 360 degree performance appraisal and employee attitude surveys (2003, p.63).

In highlighting these key characteristics it is clear that the managing diversity approach is considerably different from previous conventional approaches to equal opportunities. The focus becomes that of ensuring that all individuals within an organisation can maximise their potential, regardless of any groups they may belong to. It is an all-embracing concept where the focus is cultural change and learning, rather than promoting fairness and avoiding discrimination. Crucially, managing diversity is seen as a key element of overall business policy, linked into an organisation's strategy, rather than a personnel or HR policy. Given that, the emphasis is clearly on the business benefits that the successful management of diversity can accrue for a company.

TECHNIQUES AND EXAMPLES

A whole range of initiatives can be subsumed under the heading of diversity initiatives. Arnold (1997, p.179) lists some of the interventions that characterise diversity initiatives. They include:

- Multi-cultural workshops designed to improve understanding and communication between cultural groups.

- Multi-cultural 'core groups' which meet regularly to confront stereotypes and personal biases.

- Support groups, mentoring and relationships and networks for women and cultural minorities.

- Advisory councils reporting to top management.

- Rewarding managers on the basis of their record on developing members of targeted groups.

- Fast-track development programmes and special training opportunities for targeted groups.

To take a case example, Walker and Hanson (1992) describe some of the components of the 'Valuing Differences' philosophy that has been introduced and implemented at DEC (Digital Equipment Corporation), a company with 120,000 employees in 64 countries throughout the world. The philosophy:

> Focuses employees on their differences. Employees are encouraged to pay attention to their differences as unique individuals and as members of groups, to raise their level of comfort with differences, and to capitalize on differences as a major asset to the company's productivity (p.120).

The 'Valuing Differences' work is done in a variety of ways including awareness and skills training; celebrating differences events (e.g., Gay and Lesbian Pride week, Hispanic Heritage month); and leadership groups and support groups. A particularly radical intervention is that of the establishment of an informal network of small on-going discussion groups, known as core groups described as 'groups of 7–9 employees who commit to coming together on a monthly basis to examine their stereotypes, test the differences in their assumptions, and build significant relationships with people they regard as different' (p.121). The authors conclude that 'capitalizing on diversity means helping employees become their very best by learning to accept, trust and invest in others' (p.136). They propose that Digital have yet to learn how to quantify the impact of the valuing differences programme on profitability but evidence would suggest that the company has some specific concrete advantages from the programme so far. The authors outline these as:

1. A solid reputation as one of the best places to work – not just for women and minorities, but for everyone.
2. Empowered managers and leaders who empower others.

3. Greater innovation.
4. Higher employee productivity.
5. Effective global competition.

Clearly the authors see the programme as being highly beneficial to the organisation on a number of criteria.

Another example which is perhaps more typical is outlined by Ellis and Sonnenfeld (1994) in their review of corporate diversity programmes. They describe how National Transportation Systems (NTS) run a one day 'Diversity' workshop that is mandatory for all full-time managers and supervisors. The aim of the workshop is:

> To increase managers' awareness of the growing diversity of the workforce, to teach them the necessity of learning how to manage that diversity, and to help them identify personal biases that may interfere with their ability to manage cultural diversity (p.85).

The workshop begins with an introductory video which features the CEO explaining the importance of diversity and its link with the bottom line. A discussion then takes place about each participant's race and gender biases. As Ellis and Sonnenfeld suggest, for the workshop to be successful, individuals have to feel safe enough to reveal sensitive information about themselves. They suggest that the two key criteria that impact upon this are the quality of the facilitator and the cultural mix of participants. The authors summarise the overall impact of this diversity initiative:

> NTS is making great strides in enhancing its ability to manage diversity and promulgating the message that the firm values cultural differences, but its biggest hurdle in this area may be the cultural homogeneity of top level management, virtually all of the corporate leaders are white males. This homogeneity leaves subordinates to diverse backgrounds with few top level role models and inadvertently sends out the message that to make it to the top of the firm, one needs to be a white male (p.88).

This highlights that diversity initiatives in themselves maybe limited in the extent to which they can convey positive messages regarding differences and how difference is valued.

Increasingly within the literature there are recommendations about creating the appropriate climate and programme for managing diversity. Gilbert and Ivancevich (2000) identify five factors related to the success of diversity initiatives. These are the initiation and support of the chief executive; human resource initiatives; organisational communication; corporate philosophy; and measures of success. Friday and Friday (2003) focus upon another issue: that of how the change strategy associated with the diversity initiative is planned. They provide a framework for using a 'planned change – corporate diversity strategy' based on Lewin's (1951) unfreezing model, arguing that any strategy needs to be carefully planned.

Another key intervention strategy is diversity training. Kay and Stringer (2003) provide a range of suggestions about how diversity training can be designed to meet the needs of the organisation. They report that there are now hundreds of private management consultants who provide diversity training, and selecting the right one for the organisation is one of the key issues that needs to be addressed.

Despite some of the problems with implementing such initiatives, the benefits of the successful management of diversity are seen to be very rich. Cox (1992) for example describes them as 'better decision-making, greater creativity and innovation, and more successful marketing to different types of customers' (p.34). Thornberg (1994) outlines three phases which represent a company's evolution towards a more diverse heterogeneous culture. The first is to bring in more women and minorities, the second to emphasise working on problems of individual and group behaviour associated with race and gender, that is, to begin to understand how people are different and why; and the third a focus on company culture which involves evaluating all of the organisations policies and procedures. Therefore diversity interventions are characterised as comprehensive and inclusive.

Although most case studies of diversity initiatives are North American-based, British-based research is beginning to emerge. Rather than assessing the success of comprehensive diversity initiatives, a couple of studies have looked at comparisons between firms that have elements of a diversity policy and those that do not. Shapiro (2000) describes research designed to explore the link between organisational approaches to employee involvement and managing diversity. Using eight case studies from five European countries she argues that employee diversity can be seen as the missing link that can encourage the success of innovations such as TQM and employee involvement. Indeed, Shapiro suggests that unless organisations take explicit consideration of the differences that exist between employees then they will have difficulty in meeting their key corporate improvement objectives. Research conducted in Britain (Hicks-Clarke and Iles 2000) has also demonstrated that positive employment attitudes (e.g., job satisfaction and employee commitment) are related to a company having a positive climate for diversity (as indicated by perceptions of policy support; organisation justice; support for diversity and recognition of the need for diversity).

Key issues and tensions

The account above has outlined the key principles in managing diversity and described some typical examples of diversity interventions. Although diversity initiatives are sometimes presented in an unproblematic way in the literature, in practice there are a number of key issues that need addressing in this area. These are explored in the next section.

THE RESEARCH EVIDENCE

A key question about managing diversity initiatives is to what extent do they actually work? The search for empirical evidence to validate the success of managing diversity programmes can be a fairly frustrating exercise. One of the problems is that many of the case studies of diversity programmes that are reported in the literature do not contain any evaluative element. Indeed, sometimes these case study reports focus more on promoting a particular company approach with evangelical zeal, rather than assessing and evaluating the success of a given programme. Dick (2003) argues that the evidence linking management of diversity initiatives to different types of both achievement and affective outcomes is limited. An additional source of concern is that most of the studies that do look at diversity interventions are American-based. This in itself is not a problem, but there is the issue of how transferable the context is, given that the demographic trends experienced in the USA are a considerably exaggerated version of what is currently happening in the UK labour market. Jones *et al.* (2000) point out the paradox that as managing diversity develops as a worldwide vocabulary for examining or celebrating difference, US cultural dominance maybe reinforced by a US model of difference being applied globally.

As was suggested earlier, the impact of diversity on the business bottom line is difficult to assess. There are a couple of studies that consider the financial benefits of diversity programmes. One such analysis is provided by Wright *et al.* (1995). Using data from 1986 to 1992, they examined the impact that announcements of US Department of Labor awards for exemplary affirmative action had upon the stock returns of winning corporations, together with the effects that announcements of damage awards from the settlement of discrimination lawsuits had on the stock returns of guilty corporations. Their results indicated that announcements of quality affirmative action programmes were associated with an increase in stock prices, and conversely, announcements of discrimination settlements were associated with significant negative stock price changes. The authors conclude from this study that:

> the prevalent organizational ethnic and gender bias (Hitt and Barr, 1989) should be eradicated not only because such bias is not ethical or moral, but also because it does not make economic sense. As the climate of competition becomes more intense, no enterprise can afford the senseless practice of discrimination. In fact, America's cultural diversity may provide a competitive advantage for unbiased US corporations over both domestic rivals that discriminate and European and Japanese companies in the world marketplace (p.284).

Other discussions of diversity programmes focus on particular companies. Totta and Burke (1995) outline the processes by which the Bank of Montreal became committed to workforce diversity. The aim was to integrate issues of diversity and equality into the day-to-day working life of the bank, so that each and every business decision was influenced by diversity issues. The leaders of the organisation recognised that this would require a cultural transformation, at the centre of which would be a climate of workplace equality where individuals felt welcomed. A series of interventions were created to further these aims, including changes in a wide range of procedures and practices, and 26 action plans: 'initiatives that would dramatically transform every aspect of the way business was conducted at the bank, from hiring practices to performance review criteria, from approaches to learning to the definition of corporate values' (p.35). Totta and Burke's account is that of work in progress, rather than a systematic evaluation of the programme, but it provides an example of many of the cases that are published about the introduction of diversity programmes. Other examples which provide case studies or good practice guidelines include: American Express (Woolfe Morrison and Mardenfeld Herlihy 1992); Pepsi-Cola (Fulkerson and Schuler 1992); DEC (Walker and Hanson 1992); International Distillers and Vintners (Kandola and Fullerton 1994); the police force (Dick and Cassell 2002); the construction industry (Gale *et al.* 2003); and Royal Mail (Foster 2004).

A different approach is taken by Kandola and Fullerton (1994). After reviewing a range of managing diversity models from the literature they produced their own strategic implementation model that focuses on eight processes (the clarity of the organisation vision; the extent of top management commitment; the auditing and assessing of needs; the setting of clear objectives; the degree of accountability; the degree of communication within the organisation; the extent of coordination; the degree to which the strategy and actions are evaluated). The authors then conducted two surveys. The first was a study of 285 organisations examining the initiatives that each had put in place to manage diversity, and how successful they were perceived to be. The second survey was conducted with 49 organisations to test out the model proposed. The results from the surveys validated the model proposed, which, as the authors suggest, make it the 'first ever to have been empirically tested and validated' (p.97).

Results from their survey demonstrate that the initiatives perceived to be the most successful by HR managers were those that were related to equalising treatment between staff actions 'for universal benefit,' as Kandola and Fullerton describe them. This is important given the focus of the managing diversity philosophy on all individuals rather than specific groups. Such initiatives include eliminating age criteria from selection procedures and introducing the same benefits for part-time workers as full-time workers. The initiatives perceived to be the least successful were those focused on specific groups in the workforce. Such measures included setting targets for the composition of the workforce and using positive action in recruitment training. Additionally, 'Including equal opportunities as part of business plans', was also seen as unsuccessful by 53 percent of the organisations that had sought to implement it. The authors point out that this result could be an indication that the importance of diversity as a central business issue has not yet been recognised by many UK organisations.

The Kandola and Fullerton work is an asset to the literature in that it does have an empirical base. The limitations of the study are that its focus is the views of one senior manager within each of the companies studied, rather than the impact of diversity initiatives on the ground. It is, however, a useful starting point for those keen to evaluate the success or otherwise of diversity initiatives.

A number of authors have pointed to some of the problems that emerge when trying to implement diversity initiatives in organisations. Ellis and Sonnenfeld (1994) review three pioneering diversity programmes currently operating in US companies. They conclude that although it makes sense that the benefits of such programmes may translate into higher productivity and lower turnover, few organisations actually measure the transfer of the educational interventions into actual changes in human resource practices such as recruiting, management development and promotion. Their article highlights some of the emerging pitfalls with new corporate diversity programmes. They suggest that the programmes:

> are positive in tone, yet often lack systematic firm-wide integration into other human resource policies and do not tap the passionate disagreement that often rages beneath a platitudinous facade (p.80).

One of the problems they highlight is the lack of time actually spent on training in some diversity initiatives:

> These programes seem to be based on the premise that contact with members of different ethnic groups – if only for a few hours – or propaganda announcing the benefits of diversity, will clear up any misperceptions or ill will that some employees feel towards certain ethnic groups. Evidence often shows the contrary; simply pointing out differences among various groups, if not handled sensitively, can increase hostility and misunderstanding (p.83).

Of significance here is the danger that diversity training may actually reinforce old stereotypes, or create new tensions. Ellis and Sonnenfeld point out that when evaluating a 'Valuing Diversity' seminar they found that a minority of respondents disliked it. In particular white males complained that they were 'vilified' in the training materials which depicted bias and miscommunication in their interactions with women and minorities. The authors suggest that leaders need to continuously monitor the messages that are being put across through diversity initiatives. They also conclude that studies of the effects of managing diversity programmes are rarely conducted. So although an individual may be asked to evaluate the training they have received through an evaluation questionnaire, the impact is rarely measured at the level of the firm, for example, through the business benefits accrued.

Kossek and Zonia (1992) describe the importance of the diversity climate in an organisation, suggesting that climate and context, not numbers, are the real issues pertaining to the implementation of diversity policies. They conducted a study based on intergroup theory to examine relationships between perceptions of diversity climate and group and organisational characteristics. Their results suggest that diversity initiatives were more embraced by white women and ethnic minorities, most of who were not high up enough in the company hierarchy to effect any change. Their results also point to:

> The need to better understand issues of backlash and perceptions of equity regarding employer activities to promote a diverse workforce. In an era of shrinking resources and

downsizing, the competition between groups for scarce organizational resources will intensify . . . Our results suggest that conducting cosmetic diversity activities in an organization that is still overwhelmingly dominated by white males may, in fact, exacerbate negative intergroup processes such as hostility and splitting (p.77).

There is evidence within the literature that a more critical approach to managing diversity is emerging. Cassell and Biswas (2000) suggest that much of the literature that exists on the subject is largely atheoretical. Prasad and Mills (1997) suggest that management academics have adopted an approach which they describe as 'distant cheerleading' (p.5) where although they endorse the importance of managing diversity, it is not treated as a serious research area. Their own book: *Managing the Organizational Melting Pot: Dilemmas of Workplace Diversity* (Prasad *et al.* 1997) represents a refreshing attempt to address some of the more difficult issues surrounding diversity. As they suggest:

> Metaphorically speaking, the melting pot may well have become a cauldron (Nash, 1989), the quilt may have been torn, cracks may have begun to appear in the mosaic, and the rainbow may have become twisted out of shape. Yet, much of the management literature on workplace diversity (with few exceptions) tends to ignore or gloss over these dilemmas while continuing to stress the potency of workshops and training to accomplish the goals of workplace diversity (p.5).

Other authors suggest that structural change in itself may not be enough. Kossek, Markel and McHugh (2003) for example, propose that HR strategies that focus upon structural change without also focusing upon developing supportive group norms and an appropriate climate may be inadequate strategies for change in this area.

In conclusion it would seem that the jury is still out on whether or not diversity initiatives meet their long-term goals. To be fair, compared to other forms of organisational interventions, diversity initiatives are relatively new, which may account for the current lack of long-term evaluation studies assessing their impact.

INTEGRATING DIVERSITY MANAGEMENT WITH HRM POLICIES AND PRACTICES

Given the nature of managing diversity initiatives and their historical context one would expect that they would be clearly integrated into HRM policies and practices in organisations. One of the prime aims of managing diversity is to ensure that all the talent within a company's workforce is appropriately harnessed towards the company's objectives. Therefore the HR professional should, in theory, have a key role in the implementation of such initiatives. Jackson and Associates (1992) suggests that making the most of workforce diversity is a key challenge for HR professionals. She suggests that it is those professionals who are 'best able to educate business leaders about the strategic importance of working through diversity to mobilize them to take immediate actions' (p.27). She also suggests that HR professionals have a wide range of tools available to them for changing the attitudes and behaviours of their organisation's employees. Such tools include recruitment and selection systems, performance evaluation and appraisal, compensation and reward, training and development. Celebrating diversity could, therefore, be reinforced through the use of these tools. This approach sees diversity as a strategic imperative and therefore clearly linked into HRM.

However, there is little evidence yet that managing diversity practices and policies are integrated into HRM. Within the current textbooks on HRM for the UK market there are few references, if any, to managing diversity. Even discussion texts about HRM seem to neglect the diversity theme (e.g., Mabey *et al.* 1998). This leads us into the thorny question of whether the effective management of diversity is really an HRM issue. As Kandola (1995) suggests, whereas equal opportunities is often seen as an issue for personnel and HR practitioners, managing diversity is seen as a central concern for *all* managers.

In considering the role of the manager, a key question here is the extent to which managing diversity is really anything new. Is it not just the appropriate use of general management skills? The role of the manager is clearly significant within the diversity process. In particular, there has been an emphasis on the role of the individual leader. Managing diversity initiatives, like other change initiatives, will inevitably fail without top management commitment. Joplin and Daus (1997) suggest that because diversity is a relatively new phenomenon in the workplace it is not a self-managing process. Given this, it is important that leaders take a dynamic stance. They suggest that there are six particular challenges that need to be managed. These are:

■ The changed power dynamics.

■ Diversity of opinions.

■ Perceived lack of empathy.

■ Tokenism, real and perceived.

■ Participation.

■ Overcoming inertia.

This seems like a daunting list and it is seen to be the role of the line manager rather than the HR team to translate managing diversity into everyday practice.

Arnold (1997) points out that there is a significant difference between learning to like diversity and learning to manage it. He suggests that much social psychological research has shown us that the former is difficult enough and that most of us tend to equate difference from ourselves as being worse or wrong. He proposes that even when we learn to appreciate difference, it does not mean that we necessarily know how to manage it. McEnrue (1993) has argued that the successful management of diversity at the interpersonal level requires the acceptance of the relativity of one's own knowledge and perceptions together with a tolerance for ambiguity and the ability to demonstrate empathy and respect while being willing to change one's own beliefs. This could, of course, be a list of skills required to be a good manager, rather than those explicitly linked with managing diversity.

Given the chequered history of the link between HRM and equal opportunities, perhaps it is not surprising that there is little evidence of the integration between HR practices and policies and managing diversity initiatives. Taking gender as an example, Biswas and Cassell (1996) argue that in some cases there is a conflict of interest between strategic HRM and the implementation of equal opportunities policies. Others have argued that the gender equality assumption within HRM is more rhetoric than reality. Dickens (1994a) argues that in a number of ways HRM has different implications for men and women at work and demonstrates how the implementation of apparently gender-neutral HRM concepts and policies perpetuates rather than challenges gender inequalities. HRM concepts and practices are of course gendered as Townley (1994) has highlighted.

So the extent of integration between HR policies and the management of diversity interventions, where they exist, is somewhat uncertain. Indeed, one could argue that the two are somewhat contradictory. Johnson and Gill (1993) point out that most HRM literature focuses on cultural homogenisation. This form of cultural management is seen as a way of as a way of securing employees' identification with, and sense of commitment to, the firm. Indeed Bisset (2004) refers to diversity initiatives as part of a 'corporate culture cloning' process. Homogenisation, in any format, seems a major contradiction to notions of celebrating cultural diversity.

CRITIQUING THE BUSINESS CASE

A final important issue to consider is the extent to which the business case on which managing diversity is based holds any weight in relation to equal opportunities. Prasad and Mills (1997) suggest that the economic showcasing of diversity is both credible and persuasive to the public. However, the underlying economic assumptions of that case are drawn from human capital theories where people are treated explicitly as economic resources with their skills, qualifications and characteristics having potential value for the firms that employ them. However this ignores alternative economic approaches. If we take women as a group for example, it could be argued that opportunities for women employees in the labour force are enhanced when the perceived economic climate necessitates it. Where historians have conducted studies on the changes in women's participation in the labour force, interesting information has emerged about the conditions under which women have been encouraged to leave their homes and work (Alpern 1994; Farley 1994). A key theme in many such accounts is the role of war. During the Second World War the employment of women from a variety of social, economic and racial backgrounds was legitimised (Chafe 1977). Campbell (1984) outlines how in the United States, women entered managerial positions in droves, yet once the war ended, an intense reaction towards working women created 'a devastating impediment to women's entrance into management' (Alpern 1994, p.39). The changes in the postwar period in the ideology around women and work have been well documented. In this context, in evaluating the business case, the key question must be what happens when demographic trends alter and skill shortages disappear? In other words, one can envisage a time when there is no business case for employing or promoting women and their diverse skills.

Examples of a sudden restriction in equal opportunities developments can be found as a response to the economic recession in Britain in the early 1990s. Donaldson (1993) documents how positive initiatives for women staff were cut when cost-cutting became the key business imperative. She describes how, for example, child-care has fallen down the agenda for some of the Opportunity 2000 companies. Perhaps the most high-profile casualty was the Midland Bank's famous programme of 200 creches which was halted halfway at 115. As she suggests:

> Cost factors have influenced these decisions, but the recession, high unemployment, and consequently the diminution of concern about the demographic timebomb have also played a part in reducing the attraction of childcare support as a recruitment initiative. In contrast, flexible, part-time working arrangements have grown in attractiveness to employers. Such arrangements are seen both as an effective retention measure and as a way of reducing business costs by matching staff more closely to demand peaks (p.11).

The problem with an economic case is that it is only persuasive within a given economic climate. Consequently its impact in facilitating long-term change must be seriously questioned. A further issue is put forward by Richards who highlights how the difficulties with employer-driven equal opportunities agendas are that the priorities they usually support are those seen as important by the employer. These tend to address the more visible aspects of equal opportunities such as the number of women in senior positions for example. In this context 'they are unlikely, therefore, to offer measures dealing with "stone floor" inequalities' (2001, p.29).

Within the literature on the business case and the management of diversity, the links between valuing diverse skills and business success tend to be discussed in a way that renders them unproblematic. However, there are some examples that complicate the notion that equal opportunities makes business sense. Adkins (1995) in her analysis of gender relations in the tourist industry outlines how women workers were recruited to a variety of jobs at the Funland theme park on the basis of their physical appearance. The reasons given for using such selection criteria were 'because of the customers'. Consequently, women deemed as sexually attractive were employed in order to please the clients, 'sexual servicing' as Adkins calls it. Similarly Biswas and Cassell (1996) outline a case study of a hotel where the work was clearly divided on gender lines. It was argued that it was crucial that receptionists were physically attractive, as they were the first point of contact for the customer, so they would have an impact on whether that customer used the hotel again. In this context it was argued that accentuating the sexuality of women employees through styles of dress, etc., made business sense, that is, it was perceived that there was a business case for women doing typically female jobs and men doing specifically male jobs, because the customers liked it.

Such examples render the perceived clear link between equal opportunities and business benefits problematic. Dickens (1994b) for example suggests that some organisations will benefit from the absence of equal opportunities in that discriminatory practices can contribute to the bottom line. As she puts it:

> Organizations can, and do, obtain cost benefits from the non-recognition (but utilization) of women's skills, the undervaluing of women's labour, and from the exploitation of women as a cheap, numerically flexible (easily disposed of) workforce (p.13).

Indeed, a business benefits argument could, in this context, be used to legitimise a gendered status quo.

A final point is that the business case may not apply equally to all diverse groups. Woodhams and Danieli (2000) suggest that there is very little written within the diversity literature about the business case for employing disabled people. They suggest that the rationality underlying the diversity approach falters in relation to the employment of disabled people in a number of ways. As a considerably heterogeneous group who are not segregated within the labour market, a managing diversity approach based on the identification of group based characteristics has little to offer. This leads us to the view that some diverse groups maybe more suitable to the business case than others. Arnold (1997) points out that the prevailing use of the business case could be more appropriate to workers at different levels of organisations. Thus although there may be a need to value diversity amongst middle and senior management where there is a need for innovative, skilled staff, the impetus may not be the same with casual or unskilled staff who maybe easily replaceable.

This leaves us with the question of whether there is actually a business case for equal opportunities at all. Dickens (1994b) is suspicious about this. She suggests:

> In practice in the UK, there is not a business case for EO, but rather a number of business arguments which have greater or lesser attraction for particular employers in particular circumstances. The business-case arguments, although valid, are contingent on, and made within, variable decision-making contexts. Receptiveness to them, therefore, is likely to be uneven and they will not guarantee action on the part of all employers, at all times (p.5).

This discussion highlights the complicated nature of the processes through which issues of power, fairness and equality are reformulated into issues of competitive advantage. The potential for fundamental change within such an approach becomes questionable.

Conclusions

To conclude, four key issues emerge from this analysis of the managing diversity literature. The first is the extent to which there is evidence that organisations that manage diversity are more successful than organisations that do not. As suggested earlier, there is clearly the need for more research in this area. Ideally, research needs to focus on longitudinal assessment of diversity programmes, using a range of criteria from impact on economic performance to the attitudes of those groups that the interventions have been designed to address. Only then can the claims made for the success of managing diversity be properly evaluated.

Second, there is the question of the extent to which a movement that originated in North America translates easily into the British and European context. It would seem that the business case for managing diversity is more partial in other economic contexts. A further issue in this context is the problematic nature of universalistic notions of managing diversity. In practice the term does not have a unitary meaning, it means different things to different people, and can mean different things in different cultures or organisations. Increasingly, there are challenges from other cultures about whether the Western model is appropriate, for example with regard to India (Wilson 2003), Australia (Strachan *et al.* 2004) and New Zealand (Jones *et al.* 2000). Jones *et al.* argue that the discourse of managing diversity emerging from the US management literature cannot simply be mapped on to organisations in other cultural contexts. Using Aotearoa/New Zealand as an example they highlight how notions of diversity based on US demographics and culture may obscure key local diversity issues. They argue for: 'a genuinely multi-voiced "diversity" discourse that would focus attention on the local demographics, cultural and political differences that make the difference for specific organizations' (p. 364).

A third issue that is rarely addressed is resistance to change. As with any change initiative we would expect some resistance to managing diversity programmes. Yet this resistance is rarely addressed within the literature as managing diversity is promoted as being in the interest of all groups, regardless of their differences. Arnold (1997) suggests that one of the risks with diversity initiatives is the white male backlash. Indeed Prasad and Mills (1997) suggest that the literature on managing diversity has paid little attention to a growing hostility towards policies that promote workplace diversity (for example, affirmative action and employment equity) within North America. They refer to a growing 'white rage' which is fueled by 'harsh economic conditions, increased immigration of non-European people, the polarization of cultural differences within Canada and the United States' (p.14). Wahl and Holgersson (2003) provide research evidence of male managers' reactions to gender diversity activities in Sweden. They argue that a number of factors impact on those reactions, including the numerical gender distribution, and the nature of job segregation in the companies concerned. Clearly there needs to be further consideration of the issue of resistance, why it occurs, and how it can be effectively managed, together with the consequences of that resistance for those traditionally disadvantaged groups who may be seen to gain from diversity initiatives.

A final, but significant issue, is the extent to which managing diversity is really new. Kandola (1995) suggests that much that has been written under the heading of managing diversity is striving to make it appear to be a new area. He suggests that at best this is naive, and at worst somewhat dishonest. He outlines how there have, for example, been generations of work looking at the impact of heterogeneity and homogeneity on the performance of groups in the workplace. Additionally the work on diversity-focused organisations has produced very similar sets of characteristics to those identified as the characteristics associated with learning organisations elsewhere in the literature.

Having said that, perhaps the extent to which the debate is new is of little significance, if, as an area of discourse and intervention, managing diversity can offer new hope for furthering equal opportunities. More impetus is clearly needed to further moves for equality for those groups within the labour force who are traditionally discriminated against. What managing diversity approaches highlight is the economic costs to organisations of losing talented staff through discriminatory practices: surely a crucial issue for HRM policy and practice.

CASE STUDY 12.1

MANAGING DIVERSITY AT HINCHCLIFFE CARDS, ATHERTON EDUCATIONAL PUBLISHERS AND COSMIC COSMETICS

CATHERINE CASSELL

Below are three different cases that draw on a range of diversity issues. Case study questions are given at the end of the case descriptions.

Hinchcliffe cards

Hinchcliffe Cards was started by William Hinchcliffe in 1874. Hinchcliffe had an artistic talent which he used for drawing individual greetings cards for his family and friends. As demand for the products he made increased, members of William's family joined him in creating the more intricately decorated cards. As the products of the firm grew in popularity, Hinchcliffe cards began to expand, investing in its first printing press in the early 1900s. The business continued to grow and moved into the mass production of greetings cards for the family market. William, who by then was managing director of the firm, was keen that some element of the origins of the company remained, and despite the focus on mass production, a small sideline in the design and production of handmade cards remained.

After William Hinchcliffe died in 1934 the firm remained in the family and is now managed by chief executive James Hinchcliffe who is William's great-grandson. The company headquarters, warehouse and packaging plant are housed in the same Lancashire town where William originally started the business in his own home. Indeed, the firm prides itself on being a family firm and having a paternalistic culture. James Hinchcliffe is often to heard to say 'Now what would great-grandfather do in this situation', when discussing any key strategic or problem issues. Despite the paternalistic culture, James is keen that the company moves with the times. Having recently completed an MBA at a local business school, he is keen to hear about new ideas and new methods of working that he can introduce in to the company.

The company employs about 250 people. Seventy per cent of the workforce are women who work mainly on the production line and 10 per cent are from ethnic minority backgrounds. All the managers and senior management team, except the human resource manager (a white woman) are white males. Turnover in the company is generally low, though James Hinchcliffe suspects that there is a growing unease amongst the workforce about a number of issues.

The cards produced by Hinchcliffe's feed in to two main markets. First, there is the mass production of greetings cards. In particular the firm recently won a couple of key contracts to produce Christmas cards for two of the larger chain stores. This has caused some problems in terms of work scheduling as production needs to be far higher in the spring months to meet the Christmas demand. In particular, some of the more sophisticated machines that are used occasionally, for foiling for example, are in 100 per cent use at this particular time. Putting coloured or silver foil on a card is an expensive process and the two men who work that machine are highly skilled. Currently there is a shortage of such skills within the printing industry. To deal with the increase in output required at this time of year, the firm has tended to employ around 20 casual workers for the spring period when these cards are produced. There is evidence however that the permanent production workers display animosity towards the temporary workers. As one suggested:

> They're just here to make a quick buck, they don't seem bothered about the quality of what they do, their mistakes affect all of our bonuses.

The production workers have also recently been complaining about some other issues to do with their opportunities in the workplace. Some of the female workers have been asking why they haven't been trained on the more complex machines, which seem to be used exclusively by the male workers. Indeed, it is the production jobs based on those machines that carry the highest remuneration. Additionally, there are concerns among the female workers that they are expected to work very long hours at short notice during peak production periods. This is seen to interfere with their family lives. As one suggested:

> They expect us to work into the evening at the drop of a hat but we don't get that flexibility in return. Cheryl who recently left to have a baby wanted to come back and work here part time, but they said they couldn't slot her in. It would be too difficult to have one person working different hours from everyone else.

Apart from these issues, the production workers are generally happy about their work. Hinchcliffe's has a good name in the local area for being a decent employer who pay the going rate for the job. They are almost an institution in the Lancashire mill town in which they are based.

The other market that Hinchcliffe's serves is the demand for handmade products. Orders for these cards come from all over the world. To tap these markets the firm has recently started a mail order business. In order to meet the increasing demand for handmade products, production has largely moved out of the factory. The cards are now made by a series of 50 homeworkers who make the cards in their own homes. These homeworkers are mainly women from ethnic minority groups. One issue that concerns the firm is the high rate of turnover among the homeworkers. They are generally perceived as having little loyalty to the firm and are unreliable in meeting agreed dates for production. There has been some talk within the firm of investing in a team of designers employed officially by the firm who can be based in the firm's headquarters. The plan is that some of the current homeworkers would be employed on this basis. Early evidence suggests that they may not be particularly interested in this option. Indeed, the majority of these workers are female who fit in their drawing work with looking after small children. Additionally their view is that the company often treats them with little respect. An example of this is the common complaint that the materials needs to make the cards are often dropped of at their homes later than promised, sometimes with incorrect specifications. One homeworker has hinted that there may be some covert racism in the way some of the homeworkers are treated.

There is a recognition within the senior management team that the company is in a position to expand. A couple of the directors believe that there would be a considerable market for Hinchcliffe products in the European Union. This diversification of markets would however require a more diverse set of skills from the sales and marketing staff. In particular there would be a requirement that sales staff can speak at least one other European language and be comfortable dealing with a set of managers from a range of European cultures. The mail order catalogues have generated a lot of interest in the handmade products that need to be followed up by the small team of sales staff that Hinchcliffe's employs. The current sales director is concerned that his sales team are lacking in these skills.

The prospect of diversification into Europe raises a number of issues for James Hinchcliffe. He is desperately keen to investigate the available avenues, but is also keen that the firm retains its Lancashire roots. He believes that the handmade products are just as good and as popular as the product his great-grandfather produced years ago. As he suggests:

> I think we have to diversify into European markets. One of our greatest challenges in doing that is to get those homeworkers on board. We could no longer deal with them dropping the cards off here at the factory a day late because the baby threw up or whatever. In fact we may have to abandon them altogether and go for an in-house design team. I know great-grandfather was always keen to support the local community but maybe things have to change at some point.

At a recent board meeting the HR director suggested that some of the issues the firm was facing were actually management of diversity issues. James Hinchcliffe is keen to get any advice he can. Though the other senior managers are uncertain, they have agreed to invite in a team of consultants to progress the issues further.

Atherton Educational Publishers

Atherton Educational Publishers was initially established in 1902 as a publisher of educational textbooks. Starting off in a small printing press in a back London street, by the 1920s the firm employed 20 people in the selling and production of high-quality educational texts. After the 1944 Education Act the demand for educational texts increased and Atherton became one of the leaders in the market, with a name for commissioning and publishing language texts. Initially focusing on English, the senior management team after the Second World War realised that there would be an increased demand for tuition in European languages. Their proactivity in addressing this new market led to the firm successfully developing a reputation as the leading publisher of foreign language texts. During the 1960s the senior management team, led by Dan Walker predicted a growth in multi-cultural texts aimed at schools. In advancing in this direction Atherton took a large share of what was to be an increasingly important market. At the same time Atherton was taken over by a large multi-national media corporation. Dan Walker and his senior management team felt they had done quite well out of the deal, retaining the major decision-making power as to the strategic direction of Atherton, while benefiting from the networks carried by the corporation.

The economics of the publishing environment have changed considerably during this century, and particularly during the last ten years. A move has clearly occurred towards a more business-oriented and market-focused culture with a reorientation in values away from an editorial focus towards marketing and sales. As one of the employees at Atherton said:

> Publishing is about making sound commercial decisions about what people need and want. It used to be a gentleman's profession, but now we have had to tighten up our act – we need to publish things cheaply and quickly.

Currently, Dan Walker still chairs the board of 18 directors at Atherton. He is a powerful, charismatic figure who is said to inspire his colleagues and staff. Atherton currently employs 870 employees. Although 53 per cent of the managers in the company are women, only three women sit on the board. Recently there has been considerable dissatisfaction among the female staff who perceive that there is a glass ceiling at senior management and board level. There is a clear consensus among the female staff that sexual discrimination at work is covert rather than overt:

> I've not directly experienced any prejudice, but I've seen evidence of it around. It's not easy to move higher in the organisation. If you're exceptional then you rise, but then women have to be a bit better than men in order to do that. It's still grey suits at the top.

Having children is one of the pertinent issues that is seen to influence the promotion prospects of women. Although the women managers recognised that Atherton had good maternity policies, they feel that covert messages are given about having children and its impact on a woman's career. Most of the female managerial staff do not have children. Combining a successful career with motherhood is seen to be a difficult option, given the long hours and travel often associated with the work. Recent company evidence from the HR department suggests that talented female managers are leaving the company to work freelance, an option seen to tie in more favourably with raising a family. One of the female managers summed up this issue in the following way:

> Women are not promoted to senior editor positions and it's clear that women have often left due to frustration about this. It's difficult to see obvious cases of discrimination. My predecessor went on maternity leave: why didn't she come back? Women just become frustrated.

The vast majority of employees at Atherton are white. This creates issues with regard to selling multi-cultural texts. In the last couple of years Atherton have tried to recruit a number of ethnic minority publishers and sales people. Dan Walker's view is that they will serve to keep the company on top of the growing multi-cultural educational market, therefore employing a more diverse workforce would make business sense. Indeed, a number of clients purchasing multi-cultural texts have commented on the lack of ethnic diversity amongst Atherton selling staff. This is particularly apparent in the schools market where Atherton's sales staff go out to meet mutli-cultural education coordinators in schools. Despite actively trying to recruit from the ethnic minority labour market, Atherton's have not had much success in both recruiting and retaining ethnic minority employees. Where ethnic minority workers have been employed, they have rarely stayed at Atherton long, commonly complaining about the lack of access to 'real' opportunities. One particular salesman expressed his feelings of tokenism in the following way:

> **I'm sick of being the black face of Atherton's, the guy who goes out just to get orders from the black customers. There doesn't seem to be any other role for me here other than that.**

Dan Walker is concerned that some of the smaller, newer publishing firms are making inroads into the multi-cultural market, and are enticing away those customers who were previously loyal to Atherton. He knows that the firm needs to do something soon to retain its place, if not expand, its position in this market, a key market for the future. He wonders whether the firm actually has a problem with its image as an employer of the white, well-spoken, middle classes. He is also concerned that some of the older members of the workforce who have been around for a long time are reinforcing this traditional image of the firm by their very presence. In such a competitive market, where sales is a primary driver, Dan is beginning to think that he needs some external business advice. Given these issues he has decided to invite a team of consultants into the organisation to assess whether there are 'any real diversity issues to worry about' or whether 'we're just like any other company'.

Cosmic Cosmetics

Cosmic Cosmetics design and distribute natural-based cosmetics and toiletries derived from vegetable and fruit ingredients. The company was founded in the 1960s at Glastonbury by two hippies dedicated to animal rights and environmentalism. They recognised that many of the visitors to Glastonbury at the time could benefit from the use of such products, but were concerned not to partake, nor invest in what were seen to be environmentally damaging products. With the benefits of a keen family investor, Sara Newsome and Thom Nolan toured the wilds of Europe and South America finding appropriate ingredients for their products. On return they set up Cosmic Cosmetics. At first they were keen to maintain a collective spirit within the company and the organisation efficiently ran as a collective of 15 people for the first five years. Demand for Cosmic products was increasing rapidly, and their base in Glastonbury was seen as a prime site for tourist visitors. In 1971 Sara Newsome married and her new husband Will Sonner became heavily involved in the company. Over the next couple of years the company went through a period of turmoil as Will built up a power base around his own concerns about expanding the company within a more commercial framework, including the development of a mail order business. In 1973, a key turning point emerged with a number of the initial members of the collective leaving, suggesting that they were unhappy that the collective spirit of the firm had somehow been lost. The next few years were times of considerable growth for the company. Moving to a larger shop in Glastonbury, they also opened outlets on Carnaby Street in London and in Brighton and Edinburgh.

Currently, Jo Wicox still has a major role in the company, responsible for marketing and HR issues. Thom Nolan is now in charge of research and development of new products and spends much of his time searching the globe for exotic ingredients on which to develop new products with his partner David. Meanwhile Will Sonner is MD of the ever-expanding firm. Those three key individuals still maintain much of the idealism of the 1960s and company policies are seen to be quite liberal. Recently, however, there have been a number of instances where staff have been complaining about their treatment. The company currently employs over 900 people at mail order distribution sites and shops all over Britain. Each of these sites is headed by a 'coordinator' whose job is to oversee the operation of the company in that outlet. Twice a year the trio meet regularly with the coordinators, but will also make site visits as necessary. In practice the top trio rely heavily on the coordinators to run their own outlets in line with the company's guiding philosophies. Consequently, HR policies in each of the outlets may be considerably different. The head office is still in Glastonbury, seen as the 'spiritual home' of the firm. About 20 per cent of the workforce are gay or lesbian. As a result of the company image and philosophy, and the open homosexuality of one of the founders, Cosmic was always seen as a relatively safe place to work free from discrimination. However, some members of this group are now asserting that they are treated less favourably than the hetero-sexuals when it comes to management opportunities. In particular, there have been suggestions that outside the Glastonbury headquarters there is considerable intolerance for gay and lesbian staff.

These allegations have been taken seriously by the senior management team. Sara Newsome is extremely concerned about this situation. Being deeply committed to equal opportunities she is considerably distressed that such discrimination may be happening within her firm. Additionally, this kind of allegation could threaten the good reputation of Cosmic, which is renowned for not just its products, but also its radical philosophy. She has therefore, in conjunction with Thom Nolan and Will Sonner, decided to approach a group of consultants to see if they can provide some advice on the way forward to address some of these issues. Specifically, she wants advice on developing an overall strategy on managing diversity for the company as a whole. She is keen that all employees feel that their talents are recognised and rewarded regardless of any differences that may exist between them.

Tasks

Stage one

You are a member of a team of consultants who has been called in by the firms outlined above to give advice on diversity issues. Specifically your task is to design a diversity intervention that will meet the diversity issues that are outlined in each of the cases. In designing the interventions you will find it useful to refer to the 'Diversity Interventions Checklist' in Box 13.1 at the end of this chapter. This will give you some pointers and issues to think through about the design, process and content of the intervention.

Stage two

Now you have designed your intervention consider the following questions:

Questions

1. What response do you think the plan will receive from the diverse groups in each of the organisations?

2. What response do you anticipate from the senior management teams in each of the organisations?

3. Are there any particular problems you would anticipate in the implementation of the plan/s?

4. How do the plan/s link in with the overall business strategy of the organisations?

5. What are the similarities and differences between the organisational situations?

6. What are the similarities and differences between the diversity plans?

7. What were the key difficulties you experienced in devising the diversity plans?

8. Can the demands of managing diversity interventions be effectively linked in with overall business strategy?

References

Adkins, L. (1995) *Gendered Work: Sexuality, Family and the Labour Market*, Buckingham: Open University Press.

Alpern, S. (1994) 'In the beginning: a history of women in management', in E.A. Fagenson (ed.) *Women in Management: Trends, Issues and Challenges in Managerial Diversity*, Newbury Park, CA: Sage.

Arnold, J. (1997) *Managing Careers into the 21st Century*, London: Paul Chapman.

*Bisset, N. (2004) 'Diversity writ large: forging the link between diverse people and diverse organizational possibilities', *Journal of Organizational Change Management*, Vol.17, No.3, pp.315–25.

Biswas, R. and Cassell, C.M. (1996) 'The sexual division of labour in the hotel industry: implications for strategic HRM', *Personnel Review*, Vol.25, No.5, pp.51–66.

Campbell, D. (1984) *Women at War with America: Private Lives in a Patriotic Era*, Cambridge, MA: Harvard University Press.

Cassell, C.M. and Biswas, R. (2000) 'Managing diversity in the new millennium', *Personnel Review*, Vol.29, No.3, pp.268–74.

Chafe, W.H. (1977) *Women and Equality*, New York: Oxford University Press.

Cox, T. (Jnr) (1992) 'The multi-cultural organization', *Academy of Management Executive*, Vol.5, No.2, pp.34–47.

*Davidson, M.J. and Fielden, S.L. (2003) *Individual Diversity and Psychology in Organizations*, Chichester: Wiley.

Dick, P. (2003) 'Organizational efforts to manage diversity: do they really work?', in M.J. Davidson and S.L. Fielden (eds) *Individual Diversity and Psychology in Organizations*, Chichester: Wiley.

Dick, P. and Cassell, C.M. (2002) 'Barriers to managing diversity in a UK constabulary: the role of discourses', *Journal of Management Studies*, Vol.39, No.7, pp.953–76.

*Dickens, L. (1994a) 'What HRM means for gender equality', *Human Resource Management Journal*, Vol.8, No.1, pp.23–40.

Dickens, L. (1994b) 'The business case for women's equality: is the carrot better than the stick?', *Employee Relations*, Vol.16, No.8, pp.5–18.

Donaldson, L. (1993) 'The recession: a barrier to equal opportunities?', *Equal Opportunities Review*, No.50.

Ellis, C. and Sonnenfeld, J.A. (1994) 'Diverse approaches to managing diversity', *Human Resource Management*, Vol.33, No.1, pp.79–109.

Equal Opportunities Commission (1995) *The Economics of Equal Opportunities*, Manchester: EOC.

Farley, J. (1994) 'Commentary', in E.A. Fagenson (ed.) *Women in Management: Trends, Issues and Challenges in Managerial Diversity*, Newbury Park, CA: Sage.

Foster, C. (2004) 'Royal Mail: delivering dignity at work', *Equal Opportunities Review*, No.132, pp.8–15.

Friday, E. and Friday, S. (2003) 'Managing diversity using a strategic planned change approach', *Journal of Management Development*, Vol.22, No.10, pp.863–80.

Fulkerson, J.R. and Schuler, R.S. (1992) 'Managing worldwide diversity at Pepsi-Cola International', in S.E. Jackson and Associates (eds) *Diversity in the Workplace: Human Resource Initiatives*, New York: Guildford.

Gale, A.W., Davidson, M.J., Somerville, P., Sodhi, D., Steele, A. and Jones, S.R. (2003) 'Managing racial equality and diversity in the UK construction industry', in M.J. Davidson and S.L. Fielden (eds) *Individual Diversity and Psychology in Organizations*, Chichester: Wiley.

Gilbert, J.A. and Ivancevich, J.M. (2000) 'Valuing diversity: a tale of two organizations', *Academy of Management Executive*, Vol.14, No.1, pp.93–107.

Hall, D.T. and Parker, V.A. (1993) 'The role of workplace flexibility in managing diversity', *Organizational Dynamics*, Vol.22, No.1, pp.5–18.

Hicks-Clarke, D. and Iles, P. (2000) 'Climate for diversity and its effects on career and organisational attitudes and perceptions', *Personnel Review*, Vol.29, No.3, pp.324–45.

Hitt, M.A. and Barr, S.H. (1989) 'Managerial selection decision models: examination of configural cue processing', *Journal of Applied Psychology*, Vol.59, pp.705–11.

Jackson, S.E. and Associates (eds) (1992) *Diversity in the Workplace: Human Resource Initiatives*, New York: Guildford.

Johnson, P. and Gill, J. (1993) *Management Control and Organizational Behaviour*, London: Paul Chapman.

Johnston, W.B. and Packard, A.H. (1987) *Workforce 2000: Work and Workers for the Twenty-first century*, Indianapolis, IN: Hudson.

Jones, D. (2004) 'Screwing diversity out of the workers? Reading diversity', *Journal of Organizational Change Management*, Vol.17, No.3, pp.281–91.

Jones, D., Pringle, J. and Shepherd, D. (2000) '"Managing Diversity" meets Aotearoa New Zealand', *Personnel Review*, Vol.29, No.3, pp.364–80.

Joplin, J.R.W. and Daus, C.S. (1997) 'Challenges of leading a diverse workforce', *Academy of Management Executive*, Vol.11, No.3, pp.32–47.

Kaler, J. (2001) 'Diversity, Equality, Morality', in M. Noon and E. Ogbonna (eds) *Equality, diversity and disadvantage in employment*, Houndmills: Palgrave.

Kay, R.Y. and Stringer, D.M. (2003) 'Designing a diversity training programme that suits your organization', in M.J. Davidson and S.L. Fielder (eds) *Individual Diversity and Psychology in Organizations*, Chichester: Wiley.

Kandola, R. (1995) 'Managing diversity: new broom or old hat?', in C.L. Cooper and I.T. Robertson (eds) *International Review of Industrial and Organizational Psychology*, Vol.10, Chichester: Wiley.

*Kandola, R. and Fullerton, J. (1994) *Managing the Mosaic: Diversity in Action*, London: Institute of Personnel and Development.

Kossek, E.E. and Zonia, S.C. (1992) 'A field study of reactions to employer efforts to promote diversity', *Journal of Organisational Behaviour*, Vol.14, pp.61–81.

Kossek, E.E., Markel, K.S. and McHugh, P.P. (2003) 'Increasing diversity as an HRM change strategy', *Journal of Organizational Change Management*, Vol.16, No.3, pp.328–52.

Lewin, K. (1951) *Field Theory in Social Science*, New York: Harper & Row.

*Liff, S. and Dickens, L. (1999) 'Ethics and equality: reconciling false dilemmas', in J. Marshall and D. Winstanley (eds) *Ethical Issues in Contemporary Human Resource Management*, London: Macmillan.

Mabey, C., Salaman, G. and Storey, J. (1998) *Strategic Human Resource Management: A Reader*, London: Sage.

McEnrue, M.P. (1993) 'Managing diversity: Los Angeles before and after the riots', *Organizational Dynamics*, Vol.21, No.3, pp.18–29.

Montes, T. and Shaw, G. (2003) 'The future of workplace diversity in the new millennium', in M.J. Davidson and S.L.Fielden (eds) *Individual Diversity and Psychology in Organizations*, Chichester: Wiley.

Nash, M. (1989) *The Cauldron of Ethnicity in the Modern World*, Chicago, IL: University of Chicago Press.

*Noon, M. and Ogbonna, E. (2001) *Equality, Diversity and Disadvantage in Employment*, Houndmills: Palgrave.

Prasad, P. and Mills, A.J. (1997) 'From showcase to shadow: understanding the dilemmas of managing workplace diversity', in P. Prasad, A.J. Mills, M. Elmes and A. Prasad (eds) *Managing the Organizational Melting Pot: Dilemmas of Workplace Diversity*, Thousand Oaks, CA: Sage.

Prasad, P., Mills, A.J., Elmes, M. and Prasad, A. (1997) *Managing the Organizational Melting Pot: Dilemmas of Workplace Diversity*, Thousand Oaks, CA: Sage.

Richards, W. (2001) 'Evaluating equal opportunities initiatives: the case for a transformative agenda', in M. Noon and E. Ogbonna (eds) *Equality, Diversity and Disadvantage in Employment*, Houndmills: Palgrave.

Robinson, G. and Dechant, K. (1997) 'Building a business case for diversity', *Academy of Management Executive*, Vol.11, No.3, pp.21–31.

Ross, R. and Schneider, R. (1992) *From Equality to Diversity: A Business Case for Equal Opportunities*, London: Pitman.

Shapiro, G. (2000) 'Employee involvement: opening the diversity Pandora's box?', *Personnel Review*, Vol.29, No.3, pp.304–23.

Strachan, G., Burgess, J. and Sullivan, A. (2004) 'Affirmative action or managing diversity: what is the future of equal opportunities policies in organizations?', *Women in Management Review*, Vol.19, No.4, pp.196–204.

Storey, J. (1995) *Human Resource Management: A Critical Text*, London: Routledge.

Thomas, R.R. (Jnr) (1990) 'From affirmative action to affirming diversity', *Harvard Business Review*, Vol.68, No.2, pp.107–17.

Thomas, R.R. (1992) 'Managing diversity: a conceptual framework', in S.E. Jackson and Associates (eds) *Diversity in the Workplace: Human Resource Initiatives*, New York: Guildford.

Thornberg, L. (1994) 'Journey towards a more inclusive culture', *HRMagazine*, February, pp.79–86.

Totta, J.M. and Burke, R.J. (1995) 'Integrating diversity and equality into the fabric of the organization', *Women in Management Review*, Vol.10, No.7, pp.32–9.

Townley, B. (1994) *Reframing Human Resource Management, Power, Ethics and the Subject*, London: Sage.

Wahl, A. and Holgersson, C. (2003) 'Male managers' reactions to gender diversity activities in organizations', in M.J. Davidson and S.L.Fielden (eds) *Individual Diversity and Psychology in Organizations*, Chichester: Wiley.

Walker, B.A. and Hanson, W.C. (1992) 'Valuing Differences at Digital Equipment Corporation', in S.E. Jackson and Associates (eds) *Diversity in the Workplace: Human Resource Initiatives*, New York: Guildford.

Wheeler, M.L. (2003) 'Managing diversity: developing a strategy for measuring organizational effectiveness', in M.J. Davidson and S.L.Fielden (eds) *Individual Diversity and Psychology in Organizations*, Chichester: Wiley.

Wilson, F.M. (1995) *Organizational Behaviour and Gender*, London: McGraw-Hill.

Wilson, E.M. (2003) 'Managing diversity: caste and gender issues in India', in M.J. Davidson and S.L.Fielden (eds) *Individual Diversity and Psychology in Organizations*, Chichester: Wiley.

Woodhams, C. and Danieli, A. (2000) 'Disability and diversity: a difference too far?', *Personnel Review*, Vol.29, No.3, pp.402–17.

Wright, P., Ferris, S.P., Hiller, J.S. and Kroll, M. (1995) 'Competitiveness through management of diversity: effects on stock price valuation', *Academy of Management Journal*, Vol.38, No.1, pp.272–87.

Woolfe Morrison, E. and Mardenfeld Herlihy, J. (1992) 'Becoming the best place to work: managing diversity at American Express Travel related services', in S.E. Jackson and Associates (eds) *Diversity in the Workplace: Human Resource Initiatives*, New York: Guildford.

* Useful reading

Chapter 13

FAMILY-FRIENDLY POLICIES AND WORK–LIFE BALANCE

Peter Ackers and Amal El-Sawad

Introduction

Family-friendly policies and work–life balance raise a whole new set of issues and opportunities for the HR manager. Their emergence as a central issue in the last decade reflect the growing feminisation of the workforce, concerns in the UK about lengthening work hours and stress, and EU policies designed to support the family unit as a key source of social stability and agent of socialisation. Nor are these issues just about 'women and childcare' in our increasingly diverse workforce. In recent years the role of fathers has come to the fore, while with an ageing population, elder care is an issue for many employees, including those without partners or children. Equally, with 'care in the community' the support of the disabled and mentally ill has increasingly devolved on people who also have to earn a living at work. In this respect, the work–life balance and family-friendly employment agenda has increasingly overlapped with managing diversity, while in all of these areas HR managers have looked for a 'business case' to encourage companies to draw these concerns into their mainstream business policies.

This chapter explores two levels of family-friendly policies and work–life balance: the impetus from EU and UK government regulations and policies at a state and supra-state level; and initiatives developed by HR managers themselves at an organisational level. A third crucial individual level concerns the coping strategies pursued by employees. The Case study 13.1 explores some of the difficulties that both women and men face in developing their careers and maintaining their families in a large multi-national company.

Why family-friendly policies and work–life balance?

Patterns of paid employment, on the one hand, and of family roles and responsibilities, on the other, are structurally connected, whether this is explicitly acknowledged by public policy and academic disciplines or not. In the case of economic and employment analysis it rarely is. Hence it still needs pointing out that the familiar norm of full-time, male, paid employment in advanced industrial societies has only been possible, historically and socially, because of women's role in the family and vice versa. Business and management disciplines, like HRM, employment relations and organisational behaviour, have been slow to recognise this 'hidden-from-view' social environment of the business organisation (Ackers 2002a). Thus Wilson

(1999) notes the neglect of women's 'reproductive' and 'maintenance' labour in the study of work. This chapter tries to bridge the gap between Social Policy and HRM.[1]

Terms such as 'work-life balance' and 'family-friendly policies' are both vague and controversial in their meaning. As Harker (1996, p.48) notes: 'Little consensus about the definition of "family-friendly" currently exists and establishing a working definition is difficult, particularly when a European perspective is taken'. 'Family-friendly' and 'work-life balance', are used here interchangeably, in a loose, common sense way to describe any policies by employers, trade unions, works councils or the state that facilitate the 'reconciliation' of paid employment and life (European Commission 2002, p.11). The same expressions can be employed in a second, narrower sense, however. In the UK, for instance, 'family-friendly' and 'work-life balance' usually describe policies offered by employers in consultation or negotiation with employees or their representatives, usually at the firm or establishment level. And this voluntarist tenor contrasts with universal, statutory, rights-based state provision in countries such as France and Sweden (see Duncan 2002). Finally, family-friendly and work-life balance policies do not always overlap, since individuals with no care responsibilities may seek work-life balance. However, the major debate in the UK unites the two and this is where our focus will be.

The EU level

The EU has pioneered the legal framework for family-friendly policies in the UK. UK maternity rights have existed since 1975 and a right to time off for antenatal care was introduced in 1980. But it was only after the adoption of the Social Chapter at Maastricht in 1992, that a broader set of provisions began to appear. 'New statutory entitlements to parental leave and time off work for family emergencies, required by EU Parental Leave Directive, were introduced by the Maternity and Parental Leave Regulations 1999 and the ERA 1999' (Dickens and Hall 2003, pp.132–3). These were accompanied by the 1998 Working Time Regulations 'including a 48-hour limit on the average weekly working hours, minimum daily rest periods, rest breaks, restrictions on night- and shift-work and the provision of paid annual leave' and the 1998 Part-time Workers Directive which provided for equal rights with full-time workers. Legal regulation is one thing, however, what happens on the ground in different countries is another. Genuine family-friendly employment is as much about family policies and deeper gender relationships, as it is about employment legislation from above.

All European countries can be situated at some point on a continuum that runs between two theoretical poles. At one hypothetical extreme, family policy and employment policy are effectively merged because gender roles at home and work are symmetrical and both partners combine paid work and child-care/housework. As a result, work-life balance and family-friendly policies become a central focus. At the other pole, gender roles are so different, with men working for pay and women staying at home, that the question of work-family reconciliation hardly figures (Drew et al. 1998; Drew and Emereck 1998). One Polish employer expressed such conservative assumptions (in spite of the large number of women actually working):

> A woman is less courageous, more rarely than a man risks opening a business. . . . Even today a woman is still bound to her home and gives priority to her home, home duties, children's upbringing. . . . A man and a woman have been different and will always be different, which results in the fact that certain professions are typically predestined for men while others are for women.

In reality, no EU country is at either extreme, and large numbers of women work in all countries, even those where cultural attitudes to gender roles are most polarised. Moreover, a generalised impetus exists for work–life balance policies arising from women's growing presence in the labour force, demands for genuine (rather than formal) equal opportunities and labour shortages. Recent research suggests that there are three main patterns: where employment and family policies are already intertwined and have strong legitimacy; where a clear policy agenda is emerging on work–life balance, especially for women; and where paid employment policy and family policy are still conceived largely as separate fields of policy activity.

INTEGRATED FAMILY AND EMPLOYMENT POLICY

Some countries already have an established, closely integrated family and employment policy, most notably France and Sweden (Fagnani 1998; Hirdman 1998). In France, for instance, there is a broad consensus in favour of government intervention in family matters, irrespective of party politics. The everyday lives of families and their well-being are legitimate topics for political and public debate. Family policy is financed by social insurance contributions from employers and wage earners. Employers and trade unions are, thereby, directly involved in the organisation of support for families and are treated as partners in family policy. They are implicated in policy decisions due to their participation in management committees of the family allowance funds. State provision (public nurseries and tax allowances for child-care) underpins the work–life balance of working women, though the tacit assumption remains that men will make a minor contribution to child-care and housework. *Comités d'entrepris*, unique, works council type institutions carry employment/family regulation down to workplace level (see p.335).

EMERGING FAMILY AND EMPLOYMENT POLICY

Other countries, such as Eire, Germany and the UK, have what can be described as an emerging family and employment policy. While employment policy has been predicated on a male breadwinner model, the sheer expansion of the female workforce has forced work–life balance issues onto the political agenda. Until recently, in the UK, most work–life balance policies, involving flexible working, parental leave and child-care, have occurred at the initiative and discretion of the individual employer. As we shall see, the Labour government has recently under-girded this patchy, voluntary provision with new employment rights, also giving a new impetus to the debate at company level.

While professional women have benefited most from formal company policies, the take-up of part-time work has reflected individual and household costing strategies to balance work and child-rearing. Figures published by the Office for National Statistics in October 2003 show that 67 per cent of working mothers with a child under the age of 5 worked part-time compared to 32 per cent of women with no dependent children. It is often assumed that the numbers of women working part-time in the UK has increased dramatically but this is not the case. According to the figures published by the Office for National Statistics in January 2004 between 1993 and 2003 the proportion of women in employment working part-time remained stable at 44 per cent. The rate for men during the same period increased from 7 per cent to 10 per cent. Evidence from the Labour Force Survey (www.statistics.gov.uk/) does show that in 2003, 18 per cent of men and 27 per cent of women worked some form of flexible working pattern, such as flexi-time, job-sharing, nine-day fortnights or annualised hours.

EMPLOYMENT AND FAMILY POLICY AS SEPARATE GENDERED SPHERES

Most southern and eastern European countries still conceive of employment and family policy as separate gendered spheres – even where large numbers of women are in the labour force.

The family (women) is seen as supporting employment, rather than as being in reciprocal relationship to it. In Greece, for instance, the family is considered as a self-supporting institution that is a substitute for labour market policies and institutions (see also Papadopoulos 1998). In other words, the family, with little state or employer support is expected to provide social cohesion for the economic and social system. The family is conceived as a 'social shock absorber', and employers are more interested in drawing on the resources of the family than developing an adequate social and labour market policy.

THE IMPACT OF EU LEGISLATION

The impact of EU legislation depends on the pre-existing state of national provision. Sweden and France are the most obvious cases of countries where national family–employment provision and regulation are well above EU standards. Elsewhere, EU regulation on equal opportunities and parental leave has played a central role in bringing the debate on family-friendly policies to the fore. In Britain, EU and government 'prompts' have set a base-line for poor employers and stimulated more employer activity. The EU Employment Guidelines have also helped to raise the employment rate for women, which is low in countries like Spain, where the 1999 Conciliation Law and 1989 Parental Leave Law both followed EU directives. However, across most of southern and eastern Europe, EU legislation has made little practical difference due to economic and cultural barriers or poor implementation. While gender equality has entered the letter of the law, little has changed in reality. In Greece, for instance, better implementation of laws and regulations intended to support the family is felt to be more important than additional legislation. Employers outside the public sector largely ignore existing equal opportunities and reconciliation laws. Likewise, family-friendly issues have yet to be included in collective agreements, because they are not regarded as a priority, either by employers or trade unions. Finally, throughout southern Europe the macro-economic prerequisites of the EMU have undermined the funding of social priorities like the family. In countries like Greece, this experience of economic austerity may be partly compensated by EU funding for 'National Plans on Employment', which specifically include new 'all-day' child-care provision; though these do not make the workplace itself any more family-friendly and familiar cultural problems of implementation remain.

EMPLOYER POLICY AND PROVISION

Employers in some countries are much more active than in others. This reflects state policy, the extent of labour shortages, the importance of women as a labour resource; and the strength and activity of trade unions. In the German case, skills shortages have encouraged individual businesses to take positive steps as regards child-care arrangements and workplace nurseries, and many works councils have been very active in this field. The level of educational attainment of German women is very high, and central requirements for drawing more women into the labour market are flexible working hours, child-care facilities, all-day schooling and part-time work. Employers in large companies and feminised sectors, such as the public sector and private services, are more likely to provide family-friendly policies. Larger companies offer more family support, such as child-care provision and schemes to encourage equal opportunities at work, while the public sector provides positive opportunities for parental leave. Germany has strong collective bargaining, but in sectors traditionally seen as being for men, this takes little account of family arrangements – a problem found in other countries. By contrast, in the clothing industry, with a very high proportion of female employees, the pay agreement includes a clause which entitles employees to take three days' leave in excess of the legal requirement for the purpose of looking after sick children, making a total of 13 days.

Collective bargaining now covers less than half the British workforce, which limits its efficacy as a mechanism for introducing family-friendly policies. In many other countries, union membership is a poor indicator of the level of employment regulation because statutory works council systems give employees and their union representatives a strong voice. The French *comité d'entreprise* is the most striking instance. All firms with more than 50 employees are legally obliged to have this body, which is responsible for managing the social activities of the firm. The firm funds it, at between 0.2 per cent and 3 per cent of the wages bill, and the funds are redistributed as either monetary benefits or services to the workers and their families. *Comités d'entreprise* have played an important role in supporting families and have extended their input from the distribution of food and clothing to children's holiday camps and leisure activities for families. They also subsidise elder and child-care services for families. These bodies operate alongside company human resources policies as mechanisms for family-friendly policies.

In the new EU countries, employers often see family-friendly policy as a luxury they cannot afford, and in this respect provision has become worse since the collapse of communism in the late 1980s. Stable employment, by one or more family members, is the main priority. A Hungarian union leader said:

> Not only our company but a lot of other companies put an end to their family-friendly institutions. The postal company used to have its own childcare facilities like kindergartens, but they don't exist any more. Economic arguments have priority. They want to get rid of the remaining social welfare institutions, too. They are selling the rest homes and holiday resorts.

There is a sense that 'family life will get in the way of worklife' and that 'I have more importance as an employee than as a parent'. In this view, the contribution of business consists of paying taxes to the state. The employee is conceptualised in the language of neo-classical economics as, 'an employee [who]. . . sells his/her skills and not marital status or family problems'. This reflects the rapid transition from communist economic forms to a cost-minimisation version of capitalism, which has yet to address the 'business case' for investing in employees.

THE EUROPEAN PICTURE

The relationship between paid employment and family life clearly varies greatly across Europe, depending on a number of historical influences. These include: the stage of economic development; long-standing religious and cultural influences; and different employment and welfare state regimes, be they neo-liberal (as in the UK between 1979–97), social market or post-communist. The EU has the authority to directly shape employment policy, but not family policy (see Hantrais 2004). Nonetheless some broad generalisations are possible.

The principal impetus for work–life balance policies comes from greater female labour market participation, whether actual or potential. Low birthrates and labour shortages are major drivers of voluntary employer policies. (Sometimes generous state-funded child-care and leave policies are driven by pro-natalist concerns about the decline of the indigenous population as in France during the 1950s.) Yet, the 'business case' for harnessing human resources through family-friendly policies only works for certain employment groups – for example the more skilled/educated – during periods of full employment and labour scarcity. Forms of state-initiated social regulation that 'ride the wave', and generalise or institutionalise these social and economic pressures are most likely to be successful in providing comprehensive family-friendly provisions in the long run. Without this policy consolidation, the tide of interest will ebb and policies may be abandoned.

All employers are concerned about the cost implications of family-friendly policies. Centralised employment systems and large, unionised employers are more likely to take a long-term HRM view (Healey 2004). In some former communist economies and companies, a genuine trade-off is made between company survival and employment on the one hand and social provision, including family-friendly policies, on the other. Complaints of 'red tape' and excessive social costs, however, are always a routine part of employer rhetoric. Even where employers accept the need for extra provision, they prefer systems funded by general taxation, except for voluntary, discretionary policies that accrue distinct labour market advantages in recruitment and retention.

A conservative emphasis on strong family values, found in some countries, might lead us to expect societal support for work–life balance policies. By and large, however, strongly religious, more traditional societies in transition, such as Spain and Poland, give little practical support to work–life balance and expect women to support men in paid work. An equality perspective suggests, instead, that the better equal opportunities are between men and women, the more support the family gains from the economic system. Hence Scandinavia leads the field. However, the weight of women in the labour market (and pressure from labour shortages) would seem to be more important than purely formal equal opportunities policies. The more women that are in paid work, the greater is the pressure to turn equal opportunities rhetoric into practical policies at all levels. Some employers, including the CBI, criticise the inflexibility of continental labour markets. They argue that the more flexible the labour market is, the easier it is for men and women to balance work and family life. Over-regulation, for example by prohibition of part-time employment – as in Greece until recently – may block women entering the labour market altogether. This is particularly true when it is combined with rigid and restricted school and shop-opening hours that assume women stay at home as full-time carers. In the Swedish case, regulation may struggle to impose a symmetrical family (full-time work and caring) on men and women who prefer a measure of asymmetry. For instance, Hakim (2000) argues that the characteristic UK pattern of full-time men and part-time women represents lifestyle choices rather than economic coercion, though her views are hotly contested by others (see McCrae 2003). On the other hand, flexibility purely on employers' terms may amount simply to overwork, stress, casualisation and low-paid, dead-end jobs.

The British case: The 2000 Green Paper and family-friendly debate

The 2003 Employment Act was a landmark in the development of a statutory framework for family-friendly policies in the UK. It provides new or enhanced employee rights and state support in six main areas. Maternity leave has been extended to 26 weeks, and all women are entitled to this regardless of how long they have worked for their employer. Paternity rights are provided, for the first time, so a father can take paid time off work around the time of the birth of his child. Adoption leave and pay is allowed to one member of an adoptive couple to take paid time off work when their adopted child starts to live with them, while paternity leave may be available for the other partner. Parents with children aged under 6 or disabled children aged under 18 have the right to request a flexible working pattern and their employers have a duty to consider their applications seriously, looking at the implication of this for the business organisation. Parents with one year's service are entitled to 13 weeks unpaid parental leave to care for their child. All employees are entitled to a 'reasonable amount' of time off for dependents (including elder care) in an emergency.

These statutory rights are only part of the story, however. Since the 2000 Green Paper, the government has developed a 'Work–Life Balance Campaign' designed to persuade employers of the 'business case' for family-friendly policies and help them to extend innovative voluntary provision. Equally, other parts of government social policy, like Working Family Tax Credits and extended nursery provision have targeted families, while part-time women have benefited disproportionately from the national minimum wage, introduced in April 1999. This last point must be interpreted with some caution, however. According to figures published in November 2003, in spring of that year 2.7 per cent of part-time jobs fell below the minimum wage, despite the legislation. Part-time workers are seven times more likely than full-time workers to be paid below the minimum wage. Jobs held by women are twice as likely to fall below the minimum wage as those held by men.

The 2000 Green Paper on parental leave was the focus for a vigorous public policy debate, particularly in the context of concerns over stress and the UK 'long-hours culture', and the influence of EU and Labour policies, especially on parental leave. The subtitle, 'competitiveness and choice' illustrates the three different rationales that the government tried to capture. First, they argued the 'business case' that family-friendly policies are good HRM and would improve the retention and motivation of employees – and ultimately competitiveness. Second, they wished to persuade employers and employees that they were providing 'choice' in the sense of prompting flexible local arrangement rather than imposing a single blueprint. Third, by their initial silence over 'rights' they were aware that they were proposing statutory measures and that they needed to do little to win over their natural supporters, the child-care lobby and trade unions.

In Britain, the policy debate had hitherto concentrated on female caring roles and the extension of maternity leave. However, the Green Paper introduced the topic of statutory paternity leave, which was implemented in the March 2001 budget, and stimulated a debate over whether the emphasis should shift to the equalisation of parental rights and responsibilities. It is interesting to see how personnel professionals, employers and trade unions responded to the Green Paper.

TRADE UNIONS

Trade unions recognise that family-friendly employment policies are central to their future, as they attempt to win members from an increasingly feminised workforce. As figures published by the Office for National Statistics show, 58 per cent of women were in employment in 1984 rising to 70 per cent in 2003. Trade unions strongly support further state regulation – supplemented by collective bargaining – in this area and emphasise both the rights and business case arguments. The unions have unanimously and strongly supported the government and EU initiatives on employment regulation and worked with the Maternity Alliance to make these as strong as possible. The woman national organiser of the large general union, T&G welcomed this extension of 'workers' rights':

Treating workers like people, rather than machines, is the way to get the best out of them. These proposals show that the Government is listening to the concerns of people struggling to balance work and family life. The proposals also show that the Government has been looking at what increases productivity and gets skilled and experienced employees back to work. The reality is that employers and the Government can either make having a baby and return to work a positive experience or an extremely difficult one. Having a child is a time of great transition for the whole family and we need workers to feel they will not lose out by taking leave.

The General Secretary of KFAT, the union for the highly feminised footwear and textile industry also welcomed the Green Paper. The union had commissioned research with women at six textile and shoe factories, conducted by the Labour MP, Harriet Harman, as part of its submission to the Government's Review of Maternity Pay and Leave. The union leader rejected claims that the government was placing excessive burdens on industry. Moreover, he felt the proposal in the Green Paper could actually benefit employers:

> These changes would help employers to hold on to skilled workers, saving them money on recruitment and training costs. We must remember that society is changing, with people starting families later in life. More women work than ever before, and an increasing number of men want to spend more time with their children. Our working environment must take account of this change.

EMPLOYERS

Employers' representatives are more concerned about the quantity of employment legislation over recent years, rather than family-friendly policies as an issue in its own right. The CBI director-general complained of 'the relentless build-up of new regulations'. Even where the state funds the welfare schemes, they incur costs for administering policies such as the Working Time Directive and Working Family Tax Credits. The Federation of Small Businesses (FSB) are particularly vociferous in their opposition to what they see as 'red tape' and are concerned about providing cover for employees on maternity/paternity leave. Whether these concerns are justified is questionable. Evidence from an in-depth study of SMEs conducted by Dex and Smith (2002) found that flexibility could in principle be introduced without adversely affecting productivity. Furthermore, employees of SMEs which have introduced flexible working arrangements display the greatest levels of trust and loyalty. The CBI would have liked more time to see how the legislation works and how employers find it. They felt that some of Green Paper proposals had come too soon and would have liked to have explored some of the non-legislative options before further statutory rights.

Employers were looking for a 'business-friendly' approach, with policies to suit particular employer and employee situations and the CBI fears that legislation would damage voluntary flexibility that already exists. The CBI deputy director-general argued that flexible employment practice needed to be 'encouraged not regulated'.

PERSONNEL PROFESSIONALS

The Chartered Institute of Personnel and Development (CIPD) became involved in the family-friendly agenda over ten years ago, when they published a report 'Work and Family'. This was conceived then in more traditional terms as 'career-friendly employment policies to support standard work patterns', mainly for women. Today they recognise that there are much more complex patterns of work as we move towards a 24/7 society, which rules out standard general solutions, such as workplace nurseries. Their view is close to the tenor of the Green Paper, seeing family-friendly employment policies as part of a 'managing diversity' agenda, which includes other issues such as elder care. This view accepts that not everyone works or lives in the same way and that employers and individuals are entitled to choice and individuality. The pressure for work–life balance policies comes from both individuals and the product market. The CIPD wants to develop dialogue between employers and employees about what each wants and how they can fit together. In this respect, family-friendly policies are part of a broader debate about the 'Future of Work' and the 'Psychological Contract' between employer and employee.

The CIPD argued that some employers' bodies were scared of state regulation per se and as a result bring a very negative mentality to the work–life agenda. The CIPD would prefer to see employers take voluntary action, but recognised that employment law may be necessary to act as a 'driver' to 'move' recalcitrant employers and to provide some base-line foundation for employees with less labour market power. However, as the case of the minimum wage shows, even with legislation in place, some employers will still refuse to comply.

FAMILY-FRIENDLY POLICIES AS GOOD HRM

Access to genuine family-friendly arrangements, provided by employer discretion or negotiated with trade unions, is more difficult to gauge than it first appears. As we have seen, part-time working is very prevalent in the UK, especially among women in the service sector. But much of this is employer-driven and may not be linked to employee family priorities. In other words, part-time work should not be automatically equated with flexible and family-friendly work. Moreover, part-time work may be associated with 'dead-end' jobs with no career prospects. Taking up family-friendly options while attempting to maintain career progression is difficult to achieve in many business organisations.

A study by El-Sawad (2002) of the career experiences of professional and managerial employees working in a large blue-chip organisation with seemingly progressive family-friendly policies found that female employees who had opted for part-time hours on return from maternity leave felt their careers within the organisation were effectively terminated as a result. Male employees who were keen to continue in full-time employment, but wanted to ideally reduce their working hours in order to spend more time with their families believed that to do so would harm the speed of their career progression (see the Case study, below). Those employees, with or without family commitments, who were prepared to work very long hours, reaped the greatest career rewards. As Mirvis and Hall (1994) have noted, even family-friendly firms still value most highly those who sacrifice family life. Similar findings have been reported elsewhere. Brandth and Kvande (2001) found that fathers in Norway felt reluctant when it came to the uptake of flexible working options because of their concerns about the effects this would have on their careers. Smithson et al. (2004) conducted a study of flexible working arrangements among chartered accountants in the UK and found gendered patterns of take-up. Women who worked part-time tended to do so to in order to fulfil caring commitments and their careers were as a result damaged, with a knock-on effect on current and future earnings. Men in contrast delayed taking up flexi-working options to a time when they had achieved considerable career progression.

The lead for practical family-friendly policies often comes from employers in the heavily feminised service sector, reflecting very immediate and yet long-running labour market needs. The CIPD argues that there is a strong 'business case' for family-friendly and diversity policies and that this needs to be developed. This includes the HRM case of investing in people and making the most of the available human resources, but there is also a 'bigger business case', linked to delivering flexibility for the customer in the 24/7 society. This connects employee diversity to employers' needs for flexibility. Other 'big drivers' for employers are increased individual litigation around stress, which puts the 'fear of God' into many of them; and concerns for recruitment and retention of employees in a tight labour market – 'the scramble for talent'. In addition, employees are developing new expectations of their employment and are beginning to ask for these things. Personnel managers regularly field questions about more flexible working from employees and national 'best-practice' programmes, like Investors in People, have encouraged them. In the past, such concerns were often short-lived and linked to state of the labour market, but we may be seeing the creation of more long-term expectations. In the CIPD's view, many UK employers are still locked into old thinking about employment patterns and have yet to catch up with these new expectations.

'Best practice' tends to be found in the female-dominated public and private service sectors, where employers have a much stronger economic incentive to deal with these issues, it is not exclusively located here, nor are the business benefits only to be found in this sector. For example, McKee et al. (2000) argue that within the in the oil and gas industry there are some exemplary 'trail-blazing' companies, as well as some which use family-friendly policy as a 'symbolic rhetorical device aimed at countering the industry's poor public image' – rhetoric which often fails to translate into practice.

PARTNERSHIP OVER FAMILY FRIENDLY POLICIES

Since 1979 the coverage of collective bargaining in the UK has fallen from 75 to perhaps 40 per cent of employees. So it is a far less significant channel for family-friendly polices than it used to be. Nevertheless, another feature of UK employment relations since 1997 has been a modest increase in union membership and influence allied to the development of voluntary 'social partnership' agreements between employers and trade unions, modelled on EU examples and encouraged by the Labour government. These new-style agreements go beyond old-style adversarial bargaining over wages and conditions and often include 'family-friendly' provisions. For example, the agreement between the finance union, UNIFI and Barclays includes new maternity and paternity rights, beyond the statutory proposals of the Green Paper. In this way, UK unions have adopted a twin-track approach of lobbying the government to raise the statutory platforms, while negotiating higher-level voluntary schemes with 'good' employers that have strong labour market needs to attract and retain women employees and can afford to pay. The public sector union, UNISON, with a large female membership, has 'bargaining support guides' on 'negotiating time off for dependants' and 'negotiating parental leave'. The TUC general secretary argued that, 'Britain's good employers already provide benefits in excess of those recommended in the Green Paper.' The trade unions, however, see little prospects of this virtuous minority spreading their example to the rest of the workforce. They value statutory regulation because they fear that labour market-driven policies may favour the employer over employees, be short-lived and only cover collectively or individually strong labour market groups.

EQUAL OPPORTUNITIES VERSUS FAMILY-FRIENDLY POLICIES?

Equal Opportunities between men and women, at least at the level of rhetoric, are now part of the conventional wisdom of UK employment. Employers are particularly aware of a potential tension between equal opportunities and family policies. This may involve tensions between male and female rights (maternity versus paternity provision) and between the rights of parents and the childless, some of who may be involved in elder care and/or have simply made a 'lifestyle choice' to remain single. Some employers and personnel professionals see a solution in stressing the importance of 'managing diversity' (whereby all the various groups bring their own particular contribution to the organisation) and by talking more generally of work–life balance to be customised for each individual in ways which suit their circumstances. A broader conception such as this might do more to meet the currently under-supported and oft-neglected needs of some groups, for example parents of disabled children, for whom, work–family pressures are more intense and long term than those of other parents.

The CIPD sees a real danger of an employee 'backlash' against family-friendly or mother-friendly policies from single people and those who have done it themselves without any extra help: the 'Queen Bees'. This will happen if employers are 'not smart enough to be inclusive' and present family-friendly as part of a 'choice' agenda linked to people's lives outside work, including sabbaticals and opportunities to vary work commitments and 'plug in and out'. In the CIPD's view, this needs more 'joined-up thinking'. The CBI also noted that company schemes have moved away from narrow family-friendly emphasis to broader work–life balance to avoid this. They prefer voluntary schemes that offer opportunities for everyone, whether to care for elders or to pursue hobbies, as long as effects on the business are at least neutral. Employees should be able to balance work and family life and this is good for business because, in theory at least, it means they are happier and more committed to the company.

The Work Foundation (former Industrial Society), a think-tank funded by employers and trade unions, has argued that the government should equalise maternity and paternity rights in order to close the gender gap. They argue:

> Every extension of maternity rights that is not matched by an equal extension of paternity rights is a step in the wrong direction. Every such move gives employers a rational reason to choose Bob over Mary and seals half the workforce in the woman=mother=carer trap.

In their view, the government, Equal Opportunities Commission and the TUC all 'make the mistake of thinking that that the pay gap between men and women is irrational' and not linked to real HRM issues. Men run most business organisations and there is 'little hope of attitudes changing if the men dictating cultures are not taking time off'.

Trade unions strongly support orthodox equal opportunities policies and see little tension, as yet, between these and family-friendly policies. This partly reflects their strong need and desire to develop a campaigning agenda that is attractive to the large and growing female workforce. The woman deputy general secretary of T&G strongly rejected the Industrial Society report, 'Mothers versus men' as 'out of touch with the real working agenda' and called for 'full steam ahead' on the extension of maternity rights:

> The reality is that women are still battling against discrimination to get what they deserve. Telling them to back down because they might damage their employability is the worst kind of scare-mongering. Women are the ones who go through labour and they are society's main child carers. That has to be recognised in the rights that they are given and those

rights must be enshrined in law. We have had centuries of delay over women's equality. This government has given new impetus for women's rights in the workplace. To kill the momentum now would be criminal.

What UK companies are doing at the organizational level

As Healey (2004, p.219) notes: 'Whilst there is much hype about the importance of family-friendly policies, there is very little evidence to inform our understanding of what happens in practice.' Research using WERS data suggests, predictably, that they are more common in large, public sector organisations, which recognise trade unions: the heartlands of full-time, professional women's employment throughout Europe. The DTI's current 'Work–Life Balance campaign' bears this out in its 100 case-studies of work–life balance, while dividing practices into five categories: (1) flexibility in the arrangement of hours, (2) flexibility in the number of hours, (3) flexible benefits, (4) breaks from employment, and (5) working from home.

The experiences of Margaret Hill, an assistant director in the Capital and Savings Division of the Inland Revenue, offers an example of flexibility in the arrangement and number of hours and working from home:

> I work 25 hours a week. I can work two days in the office and the rest from home, and I can be flexible about when I work. I started working part-time four years ago because I have MS and am finding full-time work too much – particularly the travelling. My department was very understanding and has been excellent in supporting me. They let me choose my hours, and set me up with computer networked to my office colleagues and fax. This means I can work from home on certain days. I'm not so tired and not so bound up in my job. Part-time work was forced upon me because of my health but I feel I've gained as a person.

Holme House Prison has introduced flexibility in the arrangement of hours by abandoning rigid central rosters and passing the responsibility for arranging shift patterns to individual teams. Like the fire service, this is an instance of a service traditionally organised around 'male breadwinners' adjusting to the needs of working mothers and men with parental responsibilities. It seems a promising and transferable approach. As Thornthwaite and Sheldon (2004) report, a similar system of employee self-rostering to achieve work–life balance has been successfully implemented in two leading Austrian firms.

Financial services are another major area of female employment. Lloyds TSB has offered a work options scheme since 1999, which allows employees flexibility in the number and arrangement of hours. Today 34 per cent of employees work flexibly, including 16 per cent of men and 18 per cent of managers, suggesting that it is possible to do so and still remain a mainstream career employee. Options include reduced hours, job sharing, variable hours, compressed work and teleworking. Two-thirds of Barclays Bank 57,000 UK employees are women and the bank 'recognizes that caring is not just a women's issue'. In addition to flexibility in the number and timing of hours, Barclays also allows for breaks in employment. An employee can apply for paid carer leave for up to five days, responsibility breaks for a maximum of six months and career breaks for up to five years. All employees can also request flexible working arrangements, not just those with young children. New fathers are eligible for two weeks' paid paternity leave, the first week at full pay. The provisions for maternity and adoption pay are well in excess of the statutory minimum. In addition, couples who both work at Barclays can swap maternity leave between them, for example, the mother may return to work early and her partner take any remaining leave. All parents with children under the age of 4 are eligible for parental leave.

Retail is often seen as a sector dominated by low-paid, part-time women who carry the burden of flexibility themselves, working around school hours and child-care responsibilities and trying to reconcile these with the 24/7 opening hours of their employers. There are however pockets of good practice. Nearly 80 per cent of Marks and Spencer's 75,000 employees are women and the company offers flexible working, home and part-time working, job share, educational sponsorship, secondments, career leave and flexible retirement options. A 'child break' scheme is available for those who do not want to return to work immediately after maternity. Asda also claims innovative work–life balance policies for its 120,000 employees, including leave for parents in the summer holidays, job sharing in managerial posts, and a shift swapping scheme for specific family and domestic reasons. The over-50s are also able to take up to three months' unpaid leave and maintain continuous service.

Manufacturing has often been regarded as a male breadwinner bastion with rigid working times. However, at Rolls Royce cars 'The Challenge Fund' project has encouraged a more flexible approach to job sharing and part-time working, including managers, targeted at making work there more attractive to women, within an 'overwhelmingly male organisation'. Fox's Biscuits already have a diverse workforce and have focused on flexible shift working to meet the needs of the varied workforce. IT-based organisations have particular opportunities to develop work–life balance around their central technology. IBM has a Global Work–Life scheme, funded to support projects such as daycare centres, eldercare schemes and children's summer camps. BT's 'Achieving the Balance' programme offers employees choice and flexibility in the way they work, including flexi-time, part-time and home-working.

The above samples from the DTI's 100 cases show that some companies are innovating in this area and that many employees are already benefiting. A number of questions remain, however, and much more detailed case-study research is called for. First, the DTI's campaign is founded on the 'business case' for family-friendly and work–life balance policies; what Peter Ackers refers to in Chapter 17 as 'the Golden Calf Fallacy' (see p.440). The cases are replete with claims about improved customer service, more efficient use of labour, better recruitment and retention, and lower turnover and absenteeism – all as a result of these policies. No doubt there is some truth in these claims. The analysis conducted by Dex and Smith (2002) of WERS98 revealed that around 90 per cent of organisations with some experience of family-friendly policies found them to be cost-effective and experienced increases in a number of performance indicators. There is also some evidence that the promise of improved staff retention is one driver for employers to introduce some form of family-friendly working arrangements. Bond *et al.* (2002) found this to be the case in the financial services sector in Scotland, and McKee *et al.* (2000) found the same to be true for the oil and gas industry. If employees and the company can agree on mutually agreeable patterns of work this provides an excellent impetus for voluntary initiatives. This said, the business case does not always work for parents who may not be able to justify absence or flexibility in these terms and there are many other companies that are not prepared to adopt these enlightened policies.

Second, it is hard to discern, at a distance, whether flexible working is really family-friendly working. Much of the care responsibility in the UK labour market is borne by women in low-paid, part-time jobs who cope by curtailing their work expectations – rather than by enlightened companies. Third, and related, how far is the above flexibility consistent with opportunities to develop a well-paid career? Clearly in some cases above, where these schemes have penetrated management, there are such prospects, but in many cases, part-time work is a cul-de-sac that removes women from the main road of career development. Case study 13.1 explores the case of a company that has the full range of family-friendly policies, but where those who take them do so at cost to their career prospects. This leads, finally, to the question of whether flexible re-arrangement of work and even home-working misses the main problem, Britain's long hours culture noted by, for example, Thomas and Dunkerley (1999) and Simpson (1998). While France has introduced a binding 35-hour working week, UK employers have fought the EU's 48-hour maximum and used the employee 'waiver' to cajole their workers to work longer. Indeed, the Office for National Statistics report that in spring 2000, one-third of men with dependent children usually worked 50 or more hours a week compared to just under one-quarter of men without dependent children. Sheridan (2004) argues that men in managerial and professional roles, rather than contemplating taking up the option of part-time work, are facing increasing pressures to work longer and longer hours. This is echoed in findings of a number of projects being carried out as part of the Economic and Social Research Council's 'Future of Work' programme. In a report entitled 'The Future of Work–Life Balance' published in 2002, which summarises the provisional findings of these projects, Robert Taylor (2002 pp.7, 18), calls for a far wider public policy debate than has been conducted to date. He argues:

> A focus on the difficulties of balancing paid work and parental responsibilities remains much too narrow an approach for our understanding of the importance of the work–life debate. We also need to encourage a much broader discussion and place the issue firmly within the context of the wider political economy. . . Any sensible approach to work–life policies cannot ignore the intractable phenomenon of occupational class in the amount and take-up of work–life balance entitlements. Women in managerial and professional jobs with higher incomes and benefits are in a much better position to achieve a balance than their much lower-paid and insecure counterparts.

Unless long hours and the poor pay and prospects of many part-timers are addressed, flexible working – to use an old cliché – may be yet another case of re-arranging the deckchairs on the Titanic of work and family life.

 Conclusions

To conclude, UK family-friendly employment policies remain tenuous for a number of reasons. At the company level, many have been introduced to attract women into the labour market during a period of near full employment. Similar policies, such as workplace nurseries, were introduced by firms in the economic boom of the late 1980s,

---

[1]The research quoted in this chapter was conducted in 2000-01 by participants in a Framework Programme 5 project, funded by the European Commission (ref HPSE-CT-1999-00031) entitled 'Improving policy responses and outcomes to socio-economic challenges: changing family structures, policy and practice'. See http://www.iprosec.org.uk, where free electronic versions of some published material are available, and Hantrais (2004) and Hantrais and Ackers (2005). The text quotes and research material on EU policy actors is drawn directly from Ackers (2002b) and (2003a) except where otherwise referenced. The material on responses to the 2000 UK Green Paper are drawn directly from Ackers (2003b) including material from interviews with the CBI and CIPD and from websites. The material on current company policies at an organisational level is taken from the DTI website as of June 2004: http://164.36.164/cgi-bin/wlb/cs_fulllist.pl.

but abandoned in the recession that followed. On the other hand, the current Labour government has embedded the new wave of family-friendly policies in a statutory framework of employment rights. This regulation is still contested, ideologically and politically, however, by the main Conservative opposition and by employers' representatives. This said, the Conservatives have already abandoned their initial opposition in principle to the national minimum wage, because they recognise this would be a major vote loser among those who have benefited from this. Likewise, it is unlikely they would rescind the support for parental leave. Nonetheless, they remain opposed to further state regulation of the labour market, and it is quite likely that a future Conservative government would dilute the existing modest measures (by continental European standards). Against this, the sheer number of women working and with expectations of reconciling working and family life may have created an important political constituency, which no government can ignore. To conclude, UK family-friendly policies are not yet deeply embedded, but they do have new economic and social momentum, supported by a statutory framework.

CASE STUDY 13.1

CAREERS AND WORK-LIFE BALANCE AT COMPUCAN

AMAL EL-SAWAD AND PETER ACKERS

Introduction and background to the company

Compucan is a multi-national, blue-chip IT company renowned for its progressive HRM policies. The company has declared its commitment to helping employees achieve work–life balance. It has conducted a number of company-wide surveys in order, first, to understand the experiences of its employees and then to design appropriate policies which both meet their needs and are compatible with business objectives. Various practices have been introduced, notably flexible hours, home- and tele-working. However, some job roles are far less suited to these kinds of flexible working initiatives. Consequently, some employees have more opportunities to take up flexible working options than others. Business needs and the demands of certain job roles can also dictate that these 'options' are not always optional for some employees. That said, there are a number of company initiatives designed to respond to employees' needs and preferences. Women returning from maternity leave, for example, have a right to a minimum of two-years' part-time employment. Those who elect to return full-time after maternity leave receive an uplift to their salary for a two-year period to help cover child-care costs. Men are not entitled to these benefits at present, nor are those who care for other dependents or have other major life commitments outside of work. The company does, however, allow employees to apply for a 12-month sabbatical and, if successful, will part fund their 'year out'. On the face of it then, and relative to many other employers, Compucan is working hard to create a family-friendly work environment in which its employees can achieve and maintain a healthy work–life balance.

This case study presents an opportunity to assess the difficulties which even the best-intentioned company can experience when attempting to put policy into practice. The following discussion draws from the accounts of a number of Compucan employees. The employees we hear from here are all graduates, aged around 30 years, working at various UK locations in a number of different job functions and levels. Attention is turned first to mothers, then fathers and finally single people without children.

Motherhood and career at Compucan

Molly is married with a young child. She has worked for the company for 10 years and opted for part-time hours on returning from maternity leave three years ago. Her husband also works for the company on a full-time basis. Comparing herself to others Molly feels relatively well off:

> I know a lot of women in this area who work, or did work for various different employers, who've got children, and I'm in a very, very good position. In terms of having the option of going back part-time and having flexible hours and flexible days. . . They're very good if she's ill, which happens rarely, and that sort of thing. As a part-time job for a working mother, it's an extremely good one, it really is.

Exercising her right to the company's family-friendly options, however, comes at a price.

> Before I had a child I had a career. . . I'm not prepared to put in the sort of time and effort that it takes to have a career – well I've got a young child. If I was prepared to do that then I would still see it as a career and I think I would still be treated as having a career.

Molly feels that because of her part-time hours she is no longer able to maintain a career at Compucan and, importantly, she feels that her colleagues no longer treat her as someone who has a career. It is as though there is a tacit rule that career is something that is reserved only for men and childless women, not for mothers with child-care responsibilities. Even if her husband wanted to do so, he would be unable to share the child-care responsibilities with Molly since the company do not offer men the option to return part-time following the birth of a child. Thus Molly is the primary carer for the couple's child.

Jasmine is 30 years old, married with two children and has worked at the company for nine years. She made good progress in her early years at the company, earning rapid promotion to a first line managerial position. However, her line management role ended when she first went on maternity leave.

> My career stopped with the birth of my first child. If I bring up anything to do with promotion with my manager it's very quickly squashed. I believe until I've stopped having children, until I walk in and say I'm definitely not having any more children, they won't even consider me for promotion.

Thus, like Molly, Jasmine not only feels that she no longer has a career but that she is not being treated as though she has a career. Despite all the efforts of the company to create a family-friendly work environment, there appears to be a widespread acceptance, however reluctantly, of the incompatibility of motherhood and career at Compucan.

Samantha, like Jasmine, achieved rapid promotion before she had her first child and also recently returned from maternity leave to work part-time:

> My career is coming to a bit of an end because of, you know, how my priorities have changed. . . I suppose I'm slipping now from being on the high-flying list to being on the mediocre list.

She describes a female colleague who went through a similar experience:

> There's a lass who used to be my manager when I first joined who's older than me. She went into management. Terribly career-minded. Really moved on very quickly took on some really difficult roles, loads of stress. Then she suddenly fell pregnant in her early 40s. She's gone from like the real high-flying sort to the mediocre bunch.

Though they don't like it, Molly and Samantha have all rationalised the end of their career as linked to their decision to work part-time. Jasmine, however, does not accept this explanation. Following the birth of her first child, she initially returned to work full-time and took up the enhanced pay incentive. She soon discovered that she was still prevented from continuing her career, even on a full-time contract. From this experience she concludes:

> There's no point in coming back full-time. One of the things about coming back full-time is that you keep your career going, but you don't, so there's really limited point. You do if you work 12 hours and work absolutely no differently to the way you worked before, then you're fine. But the fact that you're working an 8- to 9-hour day, no matter what you get done in that time, the fact that you don't have lunch, the fact that you literally don't chat to anyone, you're just head down working the entire time you're there just doesn't count. So therefore what's the motivation for me to come back full-time?

Such demanding long hours cultures put those with commitments outside work at a distinct disadvantage. This expectation that aspiring employees should work long hours, as well as the assumption that women should shoulder primarily child-care responsibilities, is deeply embedded in the company's history and values. Molly offers a comparison between the old system as was and the new system aspired to, along with the inherent difficulties in bridging the divide between the two:

> I think the company as a whole is now very keen to be flexible around families. . . but it also likes people to be quite devoted to it. It's a bit double-edged, I think. For a long time, particularly on the technical side, the company has employed mostly men who will work long hours. The company has expected their wives to not work. It's been a fact that most of the men have had wives who don't work and so if they have children, it's the wives who look after them.

Even a supposedly family-friendly company *still*, it seems, values most and offers greatest rewards to those prepared to sacrifice family life. New mothers find their career and their family life cast in opposition to each other. As they understand it, they must make a 'choice' between family on the one hand and career on the other.

Fatherhood and career at Compucan

Unlike new mothers, new fathers at the company report that career and family life are not in opposition, but they are experienced as in competition with each other. Fathers are able to retain their careers perhaps in large part because their wives shoulder most child-care responsibilities. New fathers do nevertheless report difficulties achieving a work–life balance. With fatherhood comes a desire to decrease the time devoted to work in order to free up time for family life (as distinct from primary child-care responsibilities). Fathers' dilemma is this: the more time devoted to work, the faster the speed of career progression; time spent on family life slows down career progression.

For Tom, who is 30 years old, married with a three-month-old son, first marriage and then fatherhood has meant he now devotes less time to work than before:

> Before I was married and certainly before I had my son the hours and the weekends that I was working. . . I mean I put in a lot of time. It was not unknown to get up in the middle of the night and do something because we'd just had a new order or I couldn't sleep or something like that. I don't do that anymore.

So it is not just mothers whose hours of work decline due to family commitments. But mothers suffer more profound effects on their careers. Perhaps this is because primary child-care responsibilities fall almost exclusively to women, leaving their husbands freer to meet the demands of their careers. For example, Tom's wife has given up entirely her own full-time career to care for their son full-time. Tom's concerns rest with minimising the time demands of his career in order that he can spend more time with his family. He believes that he may have to compromise the speed of his career progression in order to achieve the work–life balance he desires:

> My life outside of work has changed quite a lot over the past three months. I'm now looking at my career and thinking – I don't spend as much time as I always in my own mind said I would with my family. That didn't used to be a problem until my wife gave up work, because we were both working the same sort of hours. Now it is a problem. Or I can see it growing into one because I'm not doing what I always wanted to do. I wanted to be able to spend more time at home, not work on Sunday evenings. . . I can't see a step forward. I can't see a career progression without home life suffering a bit. I mean I don't want [my wife] to have to go back to work so I need to look for that next job now and look for a bigger salary, but that may have an implication on how much time I get to spend with [my wife] and [son].

Although men's careers are affected by parenthood, they are affected in different ways. The speed of a new father's career progression may be restricted if he wishes to cut back on working hours to spend more time with his family but, unlike new mothers, fathers do feel that they retain their careers. New mothers on the other hand feel that the advent of parenthood signals not just the end of opportunities for career progression but the end of their careers.

The single person and work–life balance at Compucan

Ruby, who has been with the company for seven years, is 30 years old, single and has no children. She has been seriously ill recently. She hoped that she would recover quickly but has been advised by her doctor that her health problems are likely to continue for the foreseeable future. She is back at work now following a period of sick leave and has taken on a new role which is less physically demanding and involves far less travel than her previous roles. The experience of illness has caused Ruby to reflect on the sacrifices she has made for the sake of her career. Her previous roles required her to be geographically mobile – an 'intergalactic traveller'. Responding to these work demands has taken its toll on her life outside work. Ruby is a keen and very talented athlete, but in pursuit of her work career she has all but abandoned her 'athletics career' as she puts it. She has been paid very well for her efforts – so much so that she was able to pay off her student debts and buy her first flat by the age of 25. Looking back, she recalls having little time to enjoy her success, hardly ever seeing the inside of her new home. She also regrets the impact work has had on her relationships:

> **Because I was never at home, I saw a couple of relationships flounder, simply because I just never was around.**

Ben is 28 years old, single and has been at the company for five years. He has been promoted much higher and faster than he expected and realises he could reach executive level within a relatively short space of time. This makes him wonder just how high up the corporate hierarchy he wants to go, given the high price which accompanies such success.

> **I'm perhaps beginning to realise that I need to think about (a) where my natural ceiling is and (b) what I want to sacrifice to get there. If you want to get to executive level you have to live to work. You have to expect that most weekends you might be travelling somewhere. You're always on call effectively. If you're on holiday, you're probably always looking at your mail. You'll be travelling all over the show away from your home and family and friends. You know, if you have children then you probably wouldn't be able to go and see their sports day. That sort of thing.**

What makes Ben's account interesting is that he is a senior member of the company's HRM department. While the department is undoubtedly working hard to create a family-friendly work environment in which employees can achieve and maintain a work–life balance, achieving this in practice is clearly far from easy.

Questions

1. How successful has Compucan been in its efforts to become a family-friendly employer? What are the benefits of being *seen* to be a family-friendly employer?

2. In what ways do the work–life experiences of new mothers and fathers differ? How would you account for this?

3. Currently male employees at Compucan are not given the option of returning to work part-time following the birth of a child. Indeed, in most EU countries legal paternity rights are much less than maternity rights. What, if any, might be the benefits of equalising the entitlement of men and women? What effect might the take-up by new fathers of the option to return to work part-time have on attitudes to women's roles at Compucan?

4. What are the barriers that hamper effective family-friendly and work–life balance policies at Compucan on

   a) an individual level?
   b) an organisational level?
   c) a societal level?

5. Mirvis and Hall (1994), have argued that supposed 'family-friendly firms' still value most highly those who sacrifice family life. What benefits do employees with full and active lives outside work bring to the workplace?

6. 'Family-friendly policy initiatives are of no relevance to single childless employees.' Discuss.

7. Some writers refer to the term 'presenteeism' to describe a long hours culture. Is 'presenteeism' good for organisational effectiveness? Evaluate the case for and against 'presenteeism'.

8. Compucan recently conducted an employee survey to evaluate the success of their family-friendly and work–life balance initiatives. The feedback is disappointing. Senior managers are perplexed. Considerable effort has been devoted to developing and implementing policy yet employees report experiencing little change on the ground. You have been hired as an HR Consultant. Your task is to advise the company where it is going wrong and what it can do to improve things. How would you approach this task? What further information would you want to collect? What recommendations would you make?

CASE STUDY 13.2

MOTION FOR DEBATE

AMAL EL-SAWAD AND PETER ACKERS

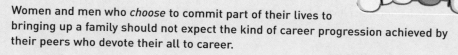

Women and men who *choose* to commit part of their lives to bringing up a family should not expect the kind of career progression achieved by their peers who devote their all to career.

Catherine Hakim has argued that only a minority of women consider their careers to be centrally important. In her view,

> even graduate wives who have well-paid professional jobs still regard themselves as secondary earners who are dependent on a man, whereas a man in the same occupation regards himself as the main breadwinner for his family. In the new scenario, self-classification as a primary earner or as a secondary earner is determined by *chosen identities* rather than imposed by external circumstance or particular jobs (Hakim 2000, p.275).

1. This notion of free choice is central to Hakim's ideas. Drawing on the evidence presented in this case-study, as well as your own experiences, discuss the notion of choice in relation to both women's and men's career experience (see also Hantrais and Ackers 2005).

2. Split into two groups. One group will argue for the motion, one against it. In groups, prepare your arguments drawing on evidence and examples to illustrate the points you want to make. Engage in a debate with the other group. Which group presents the most convincing arguments? Why?

FAMILY-FRIENDLY IN-TRAY EXERCISE FOR HRM MANAGER

AMAL EL-SAWAD AND PETER ACKERS

You are the HRM manager at large supermarket, which employs 200 part-time women, 100 students, 20 full-time men, and 10 full-time women. The store is open to customers 24/7, and a number of employees have raised family-friendly or work–life balance issues, which you have to resolve. Suggest how you would manage the following vignettes, allowing for the current legal situation, customer care and other business needs and employees' perceived sense of justice.

1. The bakery manager, a full-time, long-service employee, has divorced and become a single father with a 5-year-old son (his former wife has remarried and moved to New Zealand). He currently works an 8-hour shift, from 6am to 2pm, though overtime often takes him to 4pm. His son has just started school and the manager has requested a changed pattern of working that does not reduce his hours.

2. A young female, student check-out worker has become responsible for the care of her elderly grandmother who lives in the same town a short distance away. The old lady has mild dementia and needs regular checks every couple of hours. She also experiences periods of sudden, unexpected confusion and anxiety. The employee has a mobile phone (though written company policy insists that these are turned off during working time) and has to rush home once or twice a week for several hours.

3. You have two full-time employees who work regularly in the wine section. They are knowledgeable about the product and essential to the wine advice service you provide. One is a middle-aged mother with children; the other a single man in his 20s with no dependents. However, the latter is a very active Boy Scout leader. Both have applied for two weeks' holiday, in the first two weeks of July; a time when a major promotion of Australian wine is planned. The woman takes her family holiday with relatives in Italy every year at this time. However, the young man has a scout camp at the same time.

4. A group of part-time check-out operators, all of them mothers, who have been with the firm for several years complain that the company provides no career prospects for part-time women, whereas full-time men in the butchery area often move onto management positions. Indeed, while 70 per cent of employees are women only 10 per cent of managers are.

5. There are three applicants for the post of supervisor for the fruit and vegetable area. One, a young female graduate has been with the company only one year. She has 100 per cent attendance and is often prepared to work extra time to cover emergencies. This makes it easy for the store manager, since little pre-planning is needed the employee can be called in at a minute's notice. However, rumour says she may soon be getting married and having children. The other candidate is a 50-year-old family man, of 10 years' service, with a disabled, housebound wife and three children. He needs his shifts planned carefully ahead and occasionally has to take leave to deal with family problems.

CASE STUDY 13.4

STUDENT INTERNET RESEARCH PROJECT

AMAL EL-SAWAD AND PETER ACKERS

1. 'There is not one business case for family-friendly policies, but there are specific business cases for specific family-friendly policies directed at specific groups of employees.' Discuss.

2. Use the internet, beginning with the DTI, TUC and CBI websites, to discover what types of family-friendly policies companies are promoting and why. Choose several organisations in one sector or industry or type of work (e.g., IT companies, retailers, banks, public services, social workers) and compare what they are offering. Use this information to answer the above question.

Box 13.1: Diversity Interventions Checklist

1. Research

- What research do you need to conduct to design the intervention?
- What information do you need?
- How will you access that information?
- Who do you need to talk to?
- What do you need to ask them?
- What other research is necessary (e.g., audit of company culture)?

2. The context of the intervention

- What is the motivation behind the intervention?
- Is there a vision?
- What is the scope of the intervention (e.g., all diverse groups)?

3. Designing the intervention

- What are the objectives of the intervention?
- What will it consist of?
- Who will be involved?
- How will assumptions be addressed?
- How will systems or structures be addressed?
- How will the intervention be communicated?

4. Implementing the intervention
- ■ How will the intervention be implemented?
- ■ Who will be responsible for implementation?
- ■ What will be the timescale?

5. Evaluating the intervention
- ■ How will the intervention be evaluated?
- ■ What criteria will be used for the evaluation?

6. Issues in the long term
- ■ Who will be accountable for diversity issues in the future?
- ■ How will they be accountable?
- ■ What will be the role of the consultants in this process?

Source: Cassell 1999

References

Cassell, C.M. (1999) 'Managing diversity', in C. Clegg, K. Legge, and S. Walsh (eds) *The Experience of Managing: A Skills Guide*, Basingstoke: Macmillan.

References

Ackers, P. (2001), 'Business matters: how the character of the employment relationship shapes family life and the implications for public policy', *Management Research News*, Vol.24, No.10/11, pp.7–8. Employment Unit Research Annual Conference, Cardiff, September 2001.

*Ackers, P. (2002a) 'Reframing employment relations: the case for neo-pluralism', *Industrial Relations Journal*, Vol.33, No.1, pp.2–19.

Ackers, P. (2002b), 'Economic policy actors', in L. Appleton and L. Hantrais (eds) *Cross-National Research Paper*, Vol.6, No.3, *Comparing Family Policy Actors*, Loughborough: European Research Centre, Loughborough University, pp.14–28.

Ackers, P. (2003a) 'The work–life balance from the perspective of economic policy actors', *Social Policy and Society*, Vol.2, No.3, pp.221–9.

Ackers, P. (2003b) (ed.) *The Employment Relationship and Family Life*, Loughborough: European Research Centre, Loughborough University.

Ackers, P. and Wilkinson, A.J. (2003) (eds) *Understanding Work and Employment: Industrial Relations in Transition*, Oxford: Oxford University Press.

Bond, S., Hyman, J., Summers, J. and Wise, S. (2002) *Family-Friendly Working? Putting Policy into Practice*, Abingdon: The Policy Press.

Brandth, B. and Kvande, E. (2001) 'Flexible work and flexible fathers', *Work, Employment and Society*, Vol.15, No.2, pp.251–67.

Cully, M., O'Reilly, A., Millward, N., Forth, J., Woodland, S., Dix, G. and Bryson, A. (1998) *The 1998 Workplace Employee Relations Survey: First Findings,* DTI, London: HMSO.

Dex, S. and Smith, C. (2002) *The Nature and Pattern of Family-Friendly Employment Policies in Britain,* Abingdon: The Policy Press.

Dickens, L. and Hall, M. (2003) 'Labour law and industrial relations: a new settlement', in P. Edwards (ed.) *Industrial Relations: Theory and Practice* (2nd edn), Oxford: Blackwell.

Drew, E. and Emereck, R. (1998) 'Employment flexibility and gender', in E. Drew, R. Emereck and E. Mahon (eds) *Women, Work and the Family in Europe,* London: Routledge.

*Drew, E., Emereck, R. and Mahon, E. (1998) 'Introduction', in E. Drew, R. Emereck and E. Mahon (eds) *Women, Work and the Family in Europe,* London: Routledge.

Duncan, S. (2002) 'Policy discourses on "reconciling work and life" in the EU', *Social Policy and Society,* Vol.1, No.4, pp.305–14.

El-Sawad, A. (2002) 'Playing the game: re-creational careers–a qualitative study of working lives in context', Unpublished PhD thesis, Loughborough University.

*European Commission Employment and Social Affairs (2002) 'Family is not just a woman's affair', *Social Agenda,* No.1, Luxembourg: Office for Official Publications of the European Communities.

Fagnani, J. (1998), 'Recent changes in family policy in France: political trade-offs and economic constraints', in E. Drew, R. Emereck and E. Mahon (eds) *Women, Work and the Family in Europe,* London: Routledge.

Greene, A.-M., Ackers, P. and Black, J. (2002), 'Going against the historical grain: perspectives on gendered occupational identity and resistance to the breakdown of occupational segregation in two manufacturing firms', *Gender, Work and Organization,* Vol.9, No.3, pp.266–85.

*Hakim, C. (2000) *Work–life-style Choices in the Twenty-First Century: Preference Theory,* Oxford: Oxford University Press.

Hantrais, L. (2004) *Family Policy Matters: Responding to Family Change in Europe,* Bristol: The Policy Press.

Hantrais, L. and Ackers, P. (2005) 'Women's choices in Europe: striking the work–life balance', *Journal of Industrial Relations,* Vol.11, No.2, pp.197–212.

Harker, L. (1996) 'The family-friendly employer in Europe', in S. Lewis and J. Lewis (eds) *The Work–Family Challenge: Rethinking Employment,* London: Sage.

*Healey, G. (2004) 'Worklife balance and family-friendly policies: in whose interest?', *Work, Employment and Society,* Vol.18, No.1, pp.219–23.

Hirdman, Y. (1998), 'State policy and gender contracts: the Swedish experience', in E. Drew, R. Emereck and E. Mahon (eds) *Women, Work and the Family in Europe,* London: Routledge.

McCrae, S. (2003) 'Constraints and choices in mothers' employment careers: a consideration of Hakim's preference theory', *British Journal of Sociology,* Vol.54, No.3, pp.317–338.

McKee, L., Mauthner, N. and Maclean, C. (2000) 'Notes and issues – family-friendly policies and practices in the oil and gas industry: employers' perspectives', *Work, Employment and Society,* Vol.14, No.3, pp.557–71.

Ministry of Labour and Social Security (2001) *National Action Plan on Employment 2001: Greece,* April (see European Commission website).

Mirvis, P.H. and Hall, D.T. (1994) 'Psychological success and the boundaryless career', *Journal of Organisational Behaviour,* Vol.15, No.4, pp.365–80.

Papadopoulos, T.N. (1998) 'Greek family policy from a comparative perspective', in E. Drew, R. Emereck and E. Mahon (eds) *Women, Work and the Family in Europe,* London: Routledge.

Sheridan, A. (2004) 'Chromic presenteeism: the multiple dimensions to men's absence from part-time work', *Gender, Work and Organization,* Vol.11, No.2, pp.207–25.

*Simpson, R. (1998) 'Presenteeism, power and organizational change: long hours as a career barrier and the impact on the working lives of women managers', *British Journal of Management,* Vol.9, Special Issue, pp.S37–S50.

Smithson, J., Lewis, S., Cooper, C. and Dyer, J. (2004) 'Flexible Working and the gender pay gap in the accountancy profession', *Work, Employment and Society,* Vol.18, No.1, pp.115–35.

Taylor, R. (2002) *The Future of Work–Life Balance,* Swindon: Economic and Social Research Council.

Thomas, R. and Dunkerley, D. (1999) 'Careering downwards? Middle managers' experiences in the downsized organization', *British Journal of Management,* Vol.10, No.2, pp.157–69.

Thornthwaite, L. and Sheldon, P. (2004) 'Employee self-rostering for work–family balance: leading examples in Austria', *Employee Relations,* Vol.26, No.3, pp.238–54.

Wilson, F. (1999) *Organizational Behaviour,* Oxford: Oxford University Press.

*Useful reading

Chapter 14

DOWNSIZING

Tom Redman and Adrian Wilkinson

It was the best time (for stockholders), it was the worst of times (for employees).
The corporation was restructuring (DiFonzo and Bordia 1998, p.137).

Introduction

In this chapter we first introduce the subject of organisational downsizing by discussing its extent and potential for causing problems when mismanaged. The breadth and depth of organisational restructuring seen in the industrialised economies has been significant in recent years. Second, we review the methods by which downsizing occurs and consider a range of alternatives to its use. Third, we examine the processes involved and focus in particular on consultation, redundancy selection and support for both those made redundant and the survivors of downsizing. Lastly, we conclude by asking whether the costs of downsizing are worth it, and whether downsizing translates simply into 'increased stress and decreased job security' (De Meuse *et al.* 1997, p.168).

Downsizing: the reality of HRM?

Downsizing is the 'conscious use of permanent personnel reductions in an attempt to improve efficiency and/or effectiveness' (Budros 1999, p.70). Since the 1980s, downsizing has gained strategic legitimacy (Cameron *et al.* 1991; Boone 2000; McKinley *et al.* 2000). Indeed, recent research on downsizing in the US (Baumol *et al.* 2003, see also the American Management Association annual surveys since 1990), UK (Sahdev *et al.* 1999; Chorely 2002; Mason 2002; Rogers 2002), and Japan (Mroczkowski and Hanaoka 1997; Ahmakjian and Robinson 2001) suggests that downsizing is being regarded by management as one of the preferred routes to turning around declining organisations, cutting cost and improving organisational performance (Mellahi and Wilkinson 2004).

Downsizing and restructuring are often used interchangingly but organisations can restructure without shrinking in size and vice versa (Budros 1999). In the UK downsizing has been seen as an all too easy solution to management problems.

The lack of labour market protection, the weakness of unions and the intense pressure on private and public sector companies alike to improve their profitability and efficiency have meant that the fashionable doctrine of downsizing has spread like a contagion (Hutton 1997, p.40).

The above comment from Hutton reflects that organisational downsizing is thus now firmly established as a central aspect of HRM practice in the UK. However, after a perusal of the growing numbers of textbooks on HRM a reader could be forgiven for thinking that HRM practice is largely associated with a positively virtuous image in the organisation. Righteous HRM managers recruit, train, devise strategies, manage rewards and careers, involve employees, improve labour relations, solve problems, etc., for the mutual benefit of the organisation and workforce (see, for example, Torrington *et al.* 2005). Most management books take an upbeat tone with little reference to the more unpalatable aspects of downsizing and redundancy. Revitalising change is seen as an entirely positive process to do with 'rooting out inertia', promoting efficiency and fostering innovation. Change is to be achieved not incrementally but by 'big leaps' (Hamel 2000). Downsizing is more apparent in the Dilbert books (Adams 1996), the Doonesbury cartoons (Anfunso 1996) and Michael Moore's journalism (Moore 1997). When managers do discuss downsizing it tends to be couched in very euphemistic terms (see Box 14.1). However, an examination of managerial practice over the last decade or so also

Box 14.1: The sanitisation of dismissal: sacking goes out of fashion

Redundancy and dismissal are one area of HRM practice that particularly suffers from euphemistic jargon. Some of the terms HRM managers use include:

building down	downsizing	re-engineering
career re-appraisal	exiting	releasing
compressing	headcount reduction	resizing
decruiting	involuntary quit	re-structuring
de-hiring	lay-off	retrenchment
dejobbing	letting-go	rightsizing
de-layering	non-retaining	severance
demassing	outplacing	slimming
de-selection	payroll adjustment	streamlining
disemploying	rationalising	termination
downscoping	rebalancing	wastage

The motor industry seems especially afflicted in this respect, perhaps as a result of the large scale of workforce reductions For example, General Motors described one plant closure as a 'volume-related production schedule adjustment', Chrysler a 'a career alternative enhancement program' while Nissan introduced a 'separation program'. Two motor industry personnel managers interviewed about the effects of lean production methods talked of 'increasing the velocity of organizational exit' and 'liberating from our organization' those who could not accommodate the new system. One also talked of getting rid of the PUREs (Previously Unrecognized Recruitment Errors). In contrast the language of the shopfloor is much more direct and includes being: sacked, canned, given your cards, axed and being sent down the road.

finds a darker side to HRM in organisational downsizing and Worrall *et al.* (2000) note over 200,000 notified redundancies in the UK each year.

Despite its importance and growing prominence, this aspect of HRM rarely merits treatment in the texts. In those few texts that recognise its existence the focus is usually on a discussion of how to avoid the legal pitfalls when reducing the workforce or a simple attempt to quantify its use. Much rarer is any discussion that examines the nature, significance and aftermath of making people redundant. This neglect is a serious and somewhat puzzling one. As Chadwick *et al.* (2004) note, successful performance following downsizing requires HR practices that continue to promote discretionary efforts of employees, retain valuable human capital and reconstruct valuable organisation structures.

One possible explanation for the neglect of this issue lies in the view that workforce reduction is considered to be an isolated and unpleasant element of HRM practice and one that is best hurriedly carried out and quickly forgotten: the so-called 'Mafia model' of downsizing (Stebbins 1989). The statistics for redundancy and dismissal in Britain would, however, suggest that unpleasant though it may be workforce reduction is not an isolated event, rather it is a central aspect of HRM practice in recent years. Particularly worrying here is the numbers of organisations downsizing who are actually making healthy profits. As Cascio (2002) points out these are not sick companies trying to save themselves but healthy companies attempting to boost earnings. Organisational size is no longer a measure of corporate success. Western managers, it seems, have a bent for sacking employees. Jack Welch, for example, was known as 'neutron Jack' for his actions in getting rid of employees and leaving only the buildings intact (Welch 2001; Haigh 2004).

One trigger for increasing interest and attention for downsizing, above and beyond its greater extent and scale than in the past, is that as Sennett (1997, p.18) notes: 'Downsizings and reengineerings impose on middle-class people sudden disasters which were in an earlier capitalism much more confined to the working classes.' Effectively managing workforce reduction is thus of increasing importance in HRM practice not least because of its greater scale and frequency but also because of the potentially serious negative effects of its misman-agement (Thornhill and Saunders 1998; Wilkinson 2004). The mismanagement of Workforce reduction can clearly cause major damage to both the organisation's employment and general business reputations. Damage to the former can seriously effect an organisation's selection attractiveness with potential future employees by producing an uncaring, hire-and-fire image and affect the employer brand (Dewettinck and Buyens 2002). Similarly bad publicity over retrenchment can cause customers to worry that the firm may go out of business or give rise to problems in the continuity or quality of supplies and services.

There have also been increasing recent concerns about the organisational effectiveness of the post-downsized 'anorexic organisation'. The benefits, which organisations claim to be seeking from downsizing, centre on savings in labour costs, speedier decision making, better communi-cation, reduced product development time, enhanced involvement of employees and greater responsiveness to customers (De Meuse *et al.* 1997, p.168). However, some writers draw attention to the 'obsessive' pursuit of downsizing to the point of self-starvation marked by excessive cost cutting, organ failure and an extreme pathological fear of becoming inefficient. Hence 'trimming' and 'tightening belts' are the order of the day (Hancock and Tyler 2003).

Research suggests that downsizing can have a negative effect on 'corporate memory' (Burke 1997), employees' morale (Brockner *et al.* 1987), destroys social networks (Priti 2000), and causes a loss of knowledge (Littler and Innes 2003). As a result, downsizing could 'seriously handicap and damage the learning capacity of organisations' (Fisher and White 2000, p.249). Further, given that downsizing is often associated with cutting costs, downsizing firms may provide less training for their employees, recruit less externally, and reduce the research and development budget. Consequently, downsizing could 'hollow out' the firm's skills capacity (Littler and Innes 2003, p.93).

Paradoxically, restructuring has also been seen as a sign of corporate virility and stock market prices had boomed in the context of such plans. Barclays Bank shares soared after its announcement to axe 6,000 staff (Garfield 1999) and in the political arena, the Labour policy and the Conservative party have been attempting to outdo each other in announcing the number of civil service jobs they could reduce (BBC News, 12 July 2004), with the Labour government announcing the axeing of 104,000 civil servants' jobs and being accused by the Conservative party of failing to 'slim down its fat government'. As Haigh observes (2004, p.141) 'it remains the case that the quickest way for a CEO to obtain an ovation is to propose eliminating a layer of managers, as though dusting a mantelpiece or scraping off a coating of rust'. In the light of such reports it is interesting to note that in a 2002 CIPD survey on redundancy, 37 per cent of HR professionals felt organisations were too ready to make people redundant to meet short-term changes in demand.

Industrial conflict and workforce resistance (e.g., via strikes, sit-ins, work-ins, etc.) is also a potential problem that arises in periods of re-trenchment. However, given the unparalleled levels of workforce reductions, the relatively low level of disputes overall is perhaps more surprising. It may reflect not only reduced trade union and worker power but also that redundancy is now so commonplace and woven into the fabric of industrial life that it is seen as an inevitable consequence of work in hyper-competitive times (Turnbull and Wass 2004). The form of union resistance to redundancy has thus changed to one of attempting to secure the best deal possible for members via job security agreements which incorporate consultation mechanisms, severance payments and supportive measures, alongside a general lobbying and campaigning role, with industrial action a very rarely used last resort.

The potentially negative impact of downsizing is not restricted to those who leave but it has also a major effect on the remaining employees. Such employees are by their very nature now much more important to the employer but are often overlooked in downsizing situations. The impact of downsizing on the remaining employees is such that commentators now talk of ' the survivor syndrome' (Brockner 1992). This is the term given to the collection of behaviours such as 'decreased motivation, morale and loyalty to the organization, and increased stress levels and skepticism' that are exhibited by those who are still in employment following re-structuring (Doherty and Horstead 1995). It is interesting to note that the problems BA experienced in the summer of 2004 with angry travellers, people sleeping rough at airports, etc., was said by the unions to be the result of 13,000 redundant posts since 2001 leaving staff shortages in key areas (Inman 2004).

Methods of downsizing

There are a number of ways that organisations can reduce the size of the workforce. In this section we first examine the ones employers use the most; natural wastage, compulsory and voluntary redundancy and early retirement. Second, we consider a range of alternatives to dismissing workers, in particular redeployment and wage reduction.

NATURAL ATTRITION/WASTAGE

Natural wastage is often proffered as the most positive and humane method of workforce reduction. It is seen as giving individuals a free choice in whether to leave or stay and thus reduces the potential for conflict and employees' feelings of powerlessness. Evidence suggests that it is not the exact equivalent of normal labour turnover. It appears that in a redundancy situation both the rate and nature of labour turnover changes. Early research reported that labour turnover increases in retrenchment situations (Wedderburn 1965; Bulmer 1971) but this may reflect more on the nature of the labour market with alternative jobs easier to obtain during this period. This form of workforce reduction poses problems for management in that it is unplanned and uncontrollable. Some evidence also suggests that it depresses Workforce morale more than the short, sharp shock approach of redundancy. Natural wastage is also a form of job loss that is much more difficult for employees and unions to resist because of its incremental nature.

VOLUNTARY REDUNDANCY

This method is increasingly most employers' preferred method of downsizing. Some common concerns are that it is expensive, because employees with long service find it attractive, that the best workers leave because there is demand for their skills while poorer workers stay because they are less marketable. There is little evidence to make a judgement here but Hardy's (1987) research suggests the reverse actually occurs in practice. Marginal performers are more likely to take up voluntary redundancy packages because of either disillusionment with the job or the fear of dismissal without any financial cushion at a later date. Savery *et al.* (1998) report that high absenteeism and low commitment are associated largely with those who have expressed an interest in voluntary redundancy. The main advantages are that at least employees are given a choice and this de-stigmatises, to some extent, the loss of the job. Although voluntary redundancy is much preferred to compulsory forms it is sometimes seen by unions as 'selling jobs' .

There is, however, considerable evidence that voluntary redundancy is often far from a willing choice on the part of employees with many reports of managers 'leaning' on targeted employees leading to the question of did they jump or were they pushed? Research on teacher lay-offs, for example, found a wide range of informal and very threatening tactics used by managers to 'encourage' particular teachers to volunteer. In one case this included a manager threatening to disclose to an employee's spouse his extra-marital affairs if the teacher did not 'volunteer' for redundancy (Sinclair *et al.* 1995).

COMPULSORY REDUNDANCY

Compulsory redundancy – where no choice is presented to the departing employee – is normally a 'last resort' strategy for employers and is usually seen as the least acceptable face of downsizing. However, as it is based on managerial decision making, it gives employers the opportunity to design and implement criteria based on business needs. Compulsory redundancy is also more common where downsizings are large-scale or involve complete plant closures. According to WERS data compulsory redundancy is also much more common in the private sector than in the public sector (Cully *et al.* 1999). However, it has also been suggested that compulsory redundancy is rising in usage in the public sector as the potential for voluntary redundancy and early retirement has been exhausted and more generally because of doubts about the latter's effectiveness.

RETIREMENT

Early retirement schemes are usually utilised alongside other methods of workforce reduction although it may often be sufficient to generate the required cuts of itself. It is often seen less as a method of redundancy and more as a way of avoiding it. The mechanics differ from other methods in one key respect; employees opting for early retirement are less likely to seek to re-enter the workforce. The increasing use of early retirement can be detected in surveys, which measure the declining economic activity rates of older employees.

Ill-health is one cause for the increase in early retirement, but other developments at both company and national level also lie behind the increase. There has been a major increase in level of ill-health retirements in recent years. A commonly voiced argument is that this is a consequence of intensification of work and associated increases in stress levels which result in more long-term sickness.

At national level there has been a desire by governments in the US and Europe as well as other industrialised countries to increase work opportunities for younger workers. At company level the expansion of occupational pension schemes and the inclusion of standard arrangements for redundancy retirement has facilitated the use of early retirement as a method of Workforce reduction (McGoldrick and Cooper 1989). The use of enhanced early retirement benefit makes it more palatable. It would also appear that many managers, usually with little supporting evidence, associate increasing age with declining levels of productivity and poorer quality performance. Ageism in managerial circles, it seems, is rife and some companies even have formal 'first in first out' redundancy policies. The view that older workers have critical experience and expertise with 'seasoning', an asset not a liability, is not widely shared (Clabaugh 1997). The main exception here appears to be senior managers themselves. The increasing age profile of directors has caused some to question whether there should be a 'sell-by' date for such a group (Weyer 1994).

There are a number of advantages of early retirement ('downsizing with dignity' – Barbee 1986), in particular it is seen as carrying less stigma than other forms of redundancy; 'retired' is a much more socially acceptable 'r' word than 'redundant'. However, there are also a number of drawbacks. The decline of last in first out (LIFO) redundancy selection criteria, which protected older workers by virtue of seniority, has left them disproportionately vulnerable to enforced early retirement under employers' labour-shedding policies. People are now living longer and retiring earlier and thus need sound financial provision if demeaning financial dependency is to be avoided. The adequacy of early retirement benefits is under increasing question. It is now clear that the past trends in early retirement will not continue, not least because of uncertainty over the capacity of pension funds to sustain the costs. Forthcoming legislation on age discrimination and a changing policy on mandatory retirement look set to radically alter early retirement trends.

Alternatives to redundancy

Employers are often encouraged to consider alternatives to redundancies and to view compulsory redundancy especially, only as a last resort. There is a wide range of possible alternatives to redundancy. These include redeployment, freezing recruitment, disengaging contractors and other flexible workers, reducing overtime, secondments, career breaks, and introducing more flexible working patterns such as job-sharing and part-time work.

However, despite such calls there is little evidence for any widespread development of redundancy alternatives in Britain. For some commentators an explanation lies in the ease with which British employers can dismiss their workers without having to consider alternatives. Turnbull and Wass (1997) argue that deregulation has made redundancy, or what the European Union term 'collective dismissal', easier than other forms of reduction. A consequence of a more protracted dismissal process is that it seems other countries have a much greater emphasis on avoiding redundancy. Japan and Scandinavian countries have the most developed forms of employment protection with graded steps for cost reduction. In the case of Japan, this includes redeployment, relocation, retraining, transfer and even the suspending of dividends and cutting the salaries of senior managers. As Turnbull and Wass (1997) point out, this is the exact reverse of the British picture, where dividends and the bonus payments of senior managers are boosted by making workers redundant in the pursuit of short-term profit improvements.

Some of these main alternatives to redundancy are now briefly discussed.

WAGE REDUCTIONS

Wage cuts as an alternative to job cuts tend to be sparingly used, although there have been a number of prominent examples, as a method of cost reduction in the UK and elsewhere, such as Hong Kong. A particular use has been in the introduction of US concession-style bargaining arrangements wherein employees forgo a wage increase for some form of job security agreement. In the UK Thomas Cook in 2001 cut jobs by 1,500 and asked staff to take pay cuts of 10 per cent as business collapsed in the wake of terrorist attacks in the US. Senior executives cut their own pay by 15 per cent and all those earning more than £10,000 had salaries cut by 3–10 per cent (McCallister 2001)

The phenomenon that wages are 'sticky' downwards and labour markets respond to falls in demand by employment adjustments is well-established in economic theory. What Sullivan terms 'wage fix/employment flex' was found to operate widely with managers faced by a recession seeking to control labour costs (via redundancies), improve productivity and maintain employment reputation and workers' morale (Sullivan and Hogge 1987). The mechanisms that best achieved this were adjustments to employment rather wage levels. Neither management nor unions sought to negotiate on maintaining employment as an alternative to real wages as this would damage the 'implicit contract' between workers and managers. An alternative might be reducing hours as VW did in the early 1990s as part of a large cultural change which involved removing layers of management, introducing teamwork and raising skill levels (Pfeffer 1998, pp.189–92).

REDEPLOYMENT

Although employers' attempts to secure more flexible workforces have been subject to a great deal of debate of late, the concept of spatial flexibility and the redeployment of workers has received little attention. In the US redeployment – or 'inplacement' – is well-established. In the recession of the mid-1970s, Japanese corporations maintained as many as 4 million permanent employees despite the lack of work for them to do, with redeployment easier given the tendency to straddle several industries (Hill 1989, p.51). Even in the 1990s, when Japanese weaknesses were identified, plant closure and sell-offs were rarely carried out, and while the Japanese method of labour handling during a recession makes it difficult to instigate quick turnarounds on the other hand it also means that companies have resources at hand for a rapid expansion.

Redeployment is not an easy option for managers. It requires considerable cooperation between different divisions, plants and departments within a firm and brings a number of often costly implications. A common need is for redeployed workers to be retrained and reskilled. Relocation and/or travelling costs can be incurred. A key issue in supporting redeployment is the degree of pay protection given to such workers. The reality of redeployment is that most workers are redeployed to lower-graded posts. Many employers protect the existing income of redeployed workers for a specified period. Redeployment

Box 14.2: Redundant personalities

One controversial development in redundancy selection surrounds the use of psychometric tests, especially personality tests, in deciding who goes or stays. Tests have largely been used in redundancies involving white-collar jobs, for example, at Anglian Water, Southwark and Brent Councils, Coventry Healthcare NHS Trust and Wyeth Laboratories. Their use has caused considerable concern among the employees and trade unions involved.

At Anglian Water around a third of the staff (around 900 employees) were to be made redundant. Instead of keeping the staff whose jobs remained, all employees undertook personality testing designed to measure conceptual thinking, innovation, teamwork, initiative, people-orientation and flexibility. The test was said to influence around 30 per cent of the final redundancy decision but the union believes it carried more weight. Whatever weight the tests were given in eventual termination decisions and despite their 'objective' nature, they became a focus of staff resentment. Unison claimed that the company determined the competencies to be tested before it identified what characteristics and skills were needed. Those dismissed felt unfairly deprived of their jobs and tribunal claims for unfair redundancy have ensued. Concerns about racial discrimination have also arisen with the use of tests for redundancy and downgrading. At the Coventry Healthcare NHS Trust five nurses won an out-of-court settlement from their employer on these grounds. A similar out-of-court settlement was also reached in the Brent case where 53 workers lost their jobs after restructuring using aptitude tests. The particular tests used were found to be in error because they did not effectively take into account cultural differences.

A number of further concerns arise from the use of psychometric tests, which have been designed for other purposes, in downsizing decisions. Not least is the issue that effective testing relies on candidates behaving openly and honestly, and when some of the consequences of the test are redundancy and downgrading this is very difficult to achieve. Despite these problems, the use of tests for redundancy purposes is growing. It seems that managers like the idea of laying the blame for unpopular redundancy decisions on 'science' and the individual employee rather than accepting responsibility themselves.

Sources: Rich and Donkin, 1994; *Financial Times* 16 December, 1995: 13; Smith, 1996

can also be problematic for the employee and counselling, not least to help workers overcome a sense of loss, is helpful in such situations.

The redundancy process

Redundancy, despite the practice that managers have had in undertaking it of late, is often badly managed with many negative consequences. In part this may stem from the rarity of formal redundancy procedures. The large majority of employers do not have an agreed and written redundancy procedure. Recent interest in notions of partnership have begun to take on such concerns. Some have embodied no compulsory redundancy guarantees in such agreements. The recent WERS data reported 14 per cent of workplaces (with 25 or more employees) had a guaranteed job security or no compulsory redundancy policy (Cully *et al.* 1999).

There is much to be gained from a humane, planned and strategic approach to downsizing (Wilkinson 2004). According to Cameron (1994, 1998), the way downsizing is implemented is more important that the fact that it is implemented. He reports on three approaches to downsizing.

Workforce reduction strategies are focused primarily on reducing headcount and are usually implemented in a top–down, speedy way. However, the downside of such an approach is that it is seen as the 'equivalent to throwing a grenade into a crowded room, closing the door and expecting the explosion to eliminate a certain percentage of the workforce. It is difficult to predict exactly who will be eliminated and who will remain' (Cameron 1994, p.197), but it grabs the immediate attention of the workforce to the condition that exists. Because of the quick implementation associated with the workforce reduction strategy, management does not have time to think strategy through and communicate it properly to employees. This may result in a low 'perceived distributive fairness' (Brockner *et al.* 1987). As a result, employees may be negatively affected by the stress and uncertainty created by this type of downsizing and may react with reduced organisational commitment, less job involvement, and reduced work efforts.

Work redesign strategies are aimed at reducing work (in addition to or instead of reducing the number of workers) through redesigning tasks, reducing work hours, merging units, etc. However, these are difficult to implement swiftly and hence are seen as a medium-term strategy.

Systematic strategies focus more broadly on changing culture, attitude and values not just changing workforce size. This involves 'redefining downsizing as an on-going process, as a basis for continuous improvement; rather than as a programme or a target. Downsizing is also equated with simplification of all aspects of the organisation – the entire system including supplies, inventories, design process, production methods, customer relations, marketing and sales support, and so on' (1994, p.199). Again, this strategy requires longer-term perspectives than that of workforce reduction.

Sahdev (2003, p.72) suggests that the main focus of HR appears to be in implementing the procedural aspects of redundancy, including fair selection and provision of outplacement services for the leavers. While this is in keeping with the organisational justice approach, the contributions need to be directed towards managing the strategic aspects of decision-making processes with a view to managing survivors effectively. He suggests that HR practitioners need to be influential at both the strategic and operational levels, in order to manage survivors effectively and thereby enable the organisation to sustain competitiveness.

To what extent is such advice heeded in reality? Many problems relate to a low level of trust between those making decisions and those receiving them. A convincing rationale for downsizing

Box 14.3: Best of a bad job

Nearly half of organisations that have carried out redundancies in the past 18 months plan to make further cuts according to the CIPD/IRS report on redundancy workplace attitudes. The majority of organisations (52 per cent) also report a decline in employee morale in the aftermath of redundancies.

The main findings include:

■ A large proportion of organisations (45 per cent) believed that they would need to make further redundancies over the next 12 months.

■ Redundancies are concentrated in general manufacturing (17 per cent), engineering (10 per cent), retail (7 per cent) and financial services (5 per cent).

■ 37 per cent of HR professionals said that organisations were too ready to make people redundant to meet short-term changes in demand.

■ 53 per cent of HR professionals said that younger people were less worried about the prospect of redundancy while 32 per cent said that employees do not see redundancy as the threat it used to be.

■ 74 per cent of lay-offs were compulsory.

■ The main criteria used by employers for selecting people to be made compulsorily redundant included (where three criteria were selected by respondents):

1. the employee's role within the organisation (68 per cent)
2. job performance (62 per cent)
3. ability or flexibility (52 per cent)

■ Most organisations (95 per cent) sought to minimise the number of redundancies. The main alternative measures used included:

1. offering alternative employment to employees in affected posts (74 per cent)
2. placing a freeze on recruitment (56 per cent)
3. achieving workforce reduction through natural wastage (55 per cent)

■ Employers reported that the most common reaction of employees to the announcement that they were to be made redundant was acceptance (49 per cent).

■ The majority of employers (72 per cent) paid redundancy compensation above the statutory minimum. 50 per cent of organisations provided counselling whereas 44 per cent provided access to a specialist outplacement agency/consultancy.

■ HR professionals described the redundancy process as 'traumatic' although most considered the job cuts to be necessary.

■ Organisational restructuring is the most common reason given for making redundancies by employers (66 per cent).

Source: This material is taken from *Redundancy*, CIPD 2002, with permission of the publisher, the Chartered Institute of Personnel and Development, London

Three types of downsizing strategies			
	Workforce reduction	**Work redesign**	**Systemic**
Focus	Headcount	Jobs, levels, units	Culture
Eliminate	People	Work	Status quo
Implementation time	Quick	Moderate	Extended
Payoff target	Short-term payoff	Moderate-term payoff	Long-term payoff
Inhibits	Long-term adaptability	Quick payback	Short-term cost savings
Examples	Attrition	Combine functions	Involve everyone
	Layoffs	Merge units	Simplify everything
	Early retirement	Redesign jobs	Bottom–up change
	Buy-out packages	Eliminate layers	Target hidden costs

Source: *Human Resource Management* (1994), Vol.33, No.2, K.S. Cameron, copyright © (1994 John Wiley & Sons, Inc.); reprinted with permission of John Wiley & Sons, Inc.

is essential, as is a degree of planning. 'Good HR practice' suggests that three elements of the redundancy process are often critical: consultation with employees, the selection decision and pre/post-redundancy support for both those made redundant as well as those who remain. We deal with each of these in turn.

CONSULTATION

Consultation with unions and employees is emphasised in most accounts of downsizing. Employees need to understand the rationale for downsizing and also how the process will be managed. Breaks in communication are seen as sinister and lead to rumours (Kettley 1995). Consultation with unions over redundancies can make a difference to the nature of the redundancy process used, and occasionally the numbers of jobs lost (Edwards and Hall 1999). The downsizing process is often characterised by secrecy and swiftness and is thus often poorly planned and executed with little scope for employee involvement. To some extent this reluctance to consult over workforce reduction stems from its being seen as part of a deeply entrenched managerial prerogative about the right to hire and fire and close down businesses. The recent case of the deputies, supervisors and correction officers dismissed by the newly elected sheriff at Clayton County, Georgia is fortunately not that common. Staff who thought they were being invited to a swearing in ceremony had their badges, guns and car keys removed, were then dismissed and escorted to a ride home (in police vans) under the watchful eye of rooftop snipers who were there 'just in case someone got emotional' (Younge 2005).

Legislative restrictions on managerial prerogative in redundancy are extremely limited in the UK. First, the requirement is to consult rather than negotiate over redundancies (minimum of 30 days in cases of 20–99 redundancies and 90 days for greater than 100), although this should include examining ways of avoiding dismissal. Second, consultation was limited to recognised unions only and in the increasing non-union sector there was no such statutory requirement. However, following a ruling against the UK by the European Court of Justice in June 1994 under the *Acquired Rights* and the *Collective Redundancies* Directives, UK Regulations were issued in 1995 to provide for consultative mechanisms with 'appropriate' (employee) representatives in non-union organisations. The *Collective Redundancies and Transfer of Undertakings (Protection of Employment) Regulations,* which came into force in 1999 strengthened the 1995 regulations. The new regulations laid down specific requirements

Box 14.4: How employees were notified of potential redundancies

Means of notification	Employers using (n=563)%
Individual meetings	80.5
Line manager notification	61.4
Individual letters	57.0
Collective meeting	47.6
Meeting with trade union representatives	30.3
Notice board	13.3
Circular letter	10.1
E-mail	5.1
Press or other media	2.1
Other means	5.1

Source: Chartered Institute of Personnel and Development 2002

for electing employee representatives to be consulted in non-union organisations at times of redundancy. Third, redundancy consultation is often not complied with in practice, with managers choosing to make additional payments in lieu of notice so as to shed workers quickly via the short, sharp shock approach of a sudden announcement and a quick lay-off. Here the new regulations have buttressed and simplified the remedies that employees and their representatives may obtain in cases where employers fail to provide the required consultation. It remains to be seen how effective these new regulations are in practice. Most employers did not think the *Information and Consultation* Directive would have any effect on the way they currently consult with and inform staff in a redundancy situation (CIPD 2002).

Despite this lack of use, there is some evidence that extensive consultation and employee involvement, although it does little to reduce the stress caused by job loss, can help in its smooth implementation. US studies indicate that increased communication and participation of employees in the downsizing process were associated with improvement (Cameron 1994; DiFonzo and Bordia 1998).

SELECTION

Whatever methods are used to reach redundancy decisions the notions of fairness and 'organisational justice' are key issues. Here the process of the decision making on redundancy is equally if not more important than the outcome. Research on the perception of organisational justice by employees has been found to be related to both how the decision was made and how much 'voice' they felt they had in the process. The other important factors in the selection process, which also helps increase employees' perceptions of fairness, are that it should be clear and appropriate.

There are some noteworthy general trends within selection criteria. First, is the distinct move away from seniority and the reduction of LIFO and towards selection based on an assessment of skills and performance (IRS 2004). Despite the advantages of LIFO, which according to ACAS are that it is an 'objective, easy to apply, readily understood, and widely accepted' criterion, it now tends to be used as a criterion of last resort when others fail to produce a clear-cut decision. An IRS report found that less than a quarter used LIFO, fewer than 2 per cent used length of service exclusively with more than half using length of service as a factor alongside the job done by the employee or their level of skills and competencies. There can also be problems of unfair discrimination in its application. The issue of employers using sickness absences as a criterion for redundancy, has caused much concern among unions not least because of the worry that employees will now been frightened to take time off work when genuinely sick. In the IRS survey of those employers who use attendance as a criterion (60 per cent of the sample), certified absence appears to count against an employee in the selection process almost as much as unauthorised absence. Most employers (81 per cent) said that leave covered by a doctor's certificate would count against a worker, and 87 per cent said that self-certified leave would (IRS 2004).

Despite the outwardly 'objective' nature of many of these selection criteria and mechanisms, we can also find considerable evidence of subjective manipulation of a redundancy situation by managers. In the search for 'committed' worker employers appear to use workforce reduction for a variety of ends. Often it seems a redundancy situation is used, or in some cases even engineered, to weed out 'troublemakers' and periodically get rid of 'deadwood'. Troublemakers are variously defined as the shirkers, union activists and the non-believers in new managerial philosophies and programmes. For example, the personnel director of Co-Steel Sheerness, a British-based but Canadian-owned steel mill, described how they dealt with employees who were unhappy with the new practices of 'total team culture' and union de-recognition thus:

> When it became clear that there were employees who became increasingly dissatisfied with our new philosophies. . . . we bit the bullet with those employees and put in place termination programmes. About 5 to 6 per cent of employees were terminated. (Personnel Director, quoted in *The Guardian*, 6 September 1995, p.19).

EMPLOYEE SUPPORT

A wide variety of post-redundancy assistance can be offered to dismissed workers. There is considerable evidence to suggest that such help can have a very positive impact on the management of redundancy at a relatively low cost (e.g., Guest and Peccei 1992). The forms of support include redeployment centres, business start-up advice, training and loans, retraining, outplacement support, pre-retirement education, financial advice job search help, counselling, etc.

Redundancy counselling and stress management are emphasised to help employees overcome and come to terms with some of the intense damage to self-esteem, failure, loss of confidence, decreased morale, anxiety, bitter feelings of betrayal, debilitating shock and sense of loss that accompany downsizing. Real personal, social and financial problems also stem from redundancy situations. Studies of redundancy counselling and assistance programmes report it as being valued by the recipients but somewhat unproven in its actual benefits.

The availability of support is usually much greater the more senior the redundant employee is. Thus outplacement support is more often reserved for more senior grades and where it is provided for all employees senior managers usually receive external specialist services while lower-grade employees have in-house services. Surveys of outplacement reports its considerable growth in the UK since its import from the US in the mid-1970s (Doherty 1998). While most firms would claim expertise in wider career management advice, its main use is in downsizing situations. Its key aim is to help the redundant employee with the job search process by providing practical services such as office support and specific counselling and advice. At more senior levels this is often provided on a one-to-one basis involving psychometric tests and career counselling while for other levels of employee, group programmes of CV construction and job-search strategies are provided.

The most common support for operatives is the statutorily supported one of time off to look for work. Some employers have even advertised the availability of redundant employees in the national newspapers to facilitate their re-employment. The need for support in finding alternative work is a very real one. Redundant workers suffer particularly in their search for a new job, the so called 'lemon effect' (Turnbull and Wass 1997). Here recruiters become concerned about hiring an employee who has been discarded by another employer. Employers assume that a redundant worker must be of poor quality and potential. The labelling of redundant employees as inferior may well increase in the future as employers move to more performance-oriented selection criteria and away from seniority. Thus those most likely to be made redundant are least likely to follow a smooth path to re-employment.

SEVERANCE PAY

Arguably the acid test of support for redundant employees is the level of compensatory financial support or 'severance' pay. The CIPD survey noted that three-quarters of employers provide redundancy compensation above that required by law. Some companies provide little else in the way of support for redundant workers. For example, the financially-oriented Hanson Trust did not use outplacement but were said to 'use pound notes to staunch the blood' with generous severance packages. Most employers offer better severance terms than the base-line required by statute, with the main exception being public sector employers, except for senior managers. In part this reflects the paternalistic nature of British employers but also the pragmatic need for a form of inducement to encourage employees to volunteer. Severance is usually paid in the form of a lump sum to facilitate a 'clean break' rather than staged payments.

SURVIVORS

The needs of those who remain post-downsizing appear to be often overlooked. For example, a survey of financial services found 79 per cent of firms provided outplacement services for those employees who left but less than half gave support to the 'lucky' ones who remained (Doherty and Horsted 1995). Yet we have increasing evidence that such forgotten employees are often in need of support and counselling. For example, there is considerable evidence that remaining employees feel shocked, embittered towards management, fearful about their future and guilty about still having a job while colleagues have been laid off. The effects of such feelings are not difficult to predict. Such employees are more likely to have lower morale and increased stress levels, be less productive and less loyal with increased quit levels. Sennett describes survivors as behaving as though 'they lived on borrowed time, feeling they had survived for no good reason' (1997, p.125). Indeed, the threat of further downsizing may create difficulties in that the most able seek alternative employment. Moreover, employees may be asked to do jobs they are untrained or ill-qualified to do.

A number of downsized companies have recognised such problems and have set up training courses for managers in how to deal with downsizing effects, and by providing counselling programmes and help lines. One study found that the response of survivors is closely linked to the treatment received by those laid off (Brockner *et al.* 1987). Survivors react most negatively when they perceive their colleagues to have been badly treated and poorly recompensed.

Devine *et al.* note that job control is important in terms of occupational stress and employee outcomes when dealing with downsizing (see also Niehoff *et al.* 2001; Spreitzer and Mishra 2002). Being laid off and having to attain new employment is not necessarily more negative than 'surviving' the downsizing as displaced individuals who gain new employment have a greater sense of control and, subsequently, fewer negative strains. Survivors feel less in control due to witnessing past lay-offs and not knowing if they may be the next to go (Devine *et al.* 2003, p.121).

Conclusions: downsizing, rightsizing or dumbsizing

The last decade or so has witnessed unmatched levels of workforce reduction in many industrialised countries. Few organisations have not undergone some form of downsizing. A number of key questions remain about downsizing. These are not so much about its nature or the effects on the redundant or surviving employees, rather they are centred on whether organisations, and in turn whole economies, are now in better shape post-downsizing? Are such organisations leaner and fitter or understaffed and anorexic? Has downsizing resulted in increased competitive advantage for those companies who have undergone it? What are the drivers of continuing downsizing?

An increasingly popular view is that the effects of downsizing are the equivalent of an industrial nuclear war:

> **Below the chief executive and his cheer-leading human resources department, a number of companies resemble nothing so much as buildings blasted by a neutron bomb. The processes and structures are all there, but no human life to make them productive** (Caulkin 1995, p.19).

There is thus mounting evidence that all is not well in the downsized organisational form. As Pfeffer puts it: 'downsizing may cut labour costs in the short run, but it can erode both employee and eventually customer loyalty in the long run' (1998, p.192). However, as with all management tools, downsizing has unintended outcomes that could limit its presumed benefits such as cost reduction, removal of unnecessary layers of management, and better value for shareholders. Research has shown that downsizing has mixed effects on performance, Cascio (2002) showing no long-term financial payoff to downsizing, on average, and Hunter notes that while shares of downsizing companies have outperformed the stock market for six months there is little evidence to suggest that long-run performance or stock prices are improved by job cuts (Hunter 2000).

In some cases headcount may have gone down but labour costs have increased as companies were forced to re-hire, often ex-employees, as consultants, temps and interims.

HRM clearly has an important role in the process. Indeed, Chadwick *et al.* (2004) confirm that downsizing is more likely to be effective in the longer term when accompanied by practices that reinforce the contribution of HR to financial success (e.g., extensive communication, respectful treatment of redundant employees and attention to survivors' concerns over job security).

A possible explanation for this increasingly reported negative relationship between downsizing and economic performance can be found in Hamel and Prahalad's (1993) analysis of competitive advantage via resource productivity, both capital and human. They suggest that there are two ways to achieve this. First, via downsizing, and second, by the strategic discipline of stretch and leverage. This latter approach seeks to get the most from existing resources. Their view is that leveraging is mostly energising while downsizing is essentially the reverse, resulting in demoralised managers and work-forces. In the jargon, it appears that to achieve economic effectiveness downsizing is far from always 'rightsizing'. Strategic decision makers seem to have forgotten the benefits of growth strategies. Stephen Roach (chief economist, Morgan Stanley), the guru of downsizing business, has now disowned the practice of slash and burn restructuring (Carlin 1996). According to Roach, 'if you compete by building you have a future . . . if you compete by cutting you don't'.

Given such a grim picture of the effects of organisational downsizing, why then do managers persist in continuing with it? A number of explanations have been put forward. First, it is increasingly argued that managers have simply become addicted to downsizing because being lean and mean is now fashionable in itself. Downsizing, according to Brunning (1996) has become a corporate addiction and the 'cocaine of the boardroom'. Farrell and Mavondo (2004, p.396) suggest that:

> managers resort to downsizing because it is simple, generates considerable 'noise and attention' in the organisation, and may be viewed by some managers as tangible evidence of their 'strong leadership'. However, managers that pursue a reorientation strategy must necessarily engage in the much more difficult intellectual task of deciding how to reorient the organisation, combined with the associated challenges of building support, generating commitment and developing a shared vision.

Second, rather than a more 'acceptable' and appropriate use of downsizing because firms are now more productive or better organised or too bureaucratic and over-staffed, managers are often forced to do so by the market's demands for short-term boosts in profits. Depressingly, it seems downsizing acts a reassuring signal to markets that managers are 'in control' and acting to put things right. Third, Hitt et al. (1994) suggest that rage for 'mindless' downsizing is linked to the merger and acquisitions mania of the last decade as managers attempt to solve the problems associated with acquisitive rather than organic growth. Acquisition strategies are argued to promote conservative short-term perspectives among managers, hence downsizing as a solution rather than investing in human capital. Indeed, there is a case that with greater internal flexibility (e.g., wider jobs), there may be less necessity for external flexibility (e.g., via downsizing) as workers can cope more ably with adjustments and change. It is important to see security in the context of other policies. Workers are more likely to contribute ideas if they do not feel they are endangering their own colleagues' jobs, and both employer and employee are more likely to see investments in training as worthwhile.

Thus, despite the real sufferings of many workers in an era of redundancy there have been precious few long-term benefits to justify its level and severity nor an overwhelming economic justification for its continuing blanket use. The redundant find meaningful, well-paid and stable work difficult to come by while those who remain in employment are stretched thin, worried about their security and subject to considerable work stress in anorexic organisations. Questions may well be asked of MDs and

CEOs who are still rewarded with high and increasing salaries and perks (Haigh 2004). Lastly, it seems that the claim of HRM that people are an organisation's most valuable resource is difficult to sustain in this context. As Pfeffer argues, what we have seen in the era of widespread downsizing is simply an 'unplanned, haphazard management of the employment relationship' (1998, p.164).

DOWNSIZING DOWN UNDER: International Mining

ALLEN CLABAUGH

International Mining is an Australian company listed on the Australian stock exchange. The firm has developed and matured into a highly respected company with substantial assets and a growing international reputation as a successful mining resources explorer, developer and producer. International Mining was established in 1954 and began operations in the Gippsland area of south-east Victoria. Unable to locate resources in commercial quantities in this area, the firm began looking for fresh exploration opportunities elsewhere in Australia. By 1963, International Mining had acquired significant new exploration assets in the remote north-west of Western Australia. Because this was a vast, relatively unexplored area, the search for mining resources was a high-cost, high-risk business that required financial and technical support from other global mining companies. International Mining entered into a strategic alliance with several global firms but in return for this financial and technical assistance, had to align its strategic planning with input from its global partners.

By the early 1970s, the company had achieved financial success with the discovery of several lucrative mining resource fields near Western Australia's harsh Pilbara region. Delivery of the resources to customers in Western Australia commenced in 1984 under long-term contracts with the state government. Beginning in 1989, several 20-year contracts with energy providers in Japan enabled the company to begin overseas export. Since that time, spot sales of resources have been made to Spain, South Korea and Turkey. The company is actively exploring for mining resources in other areas, including Timor and Papua New Guinea.

International Mining underwent a series of restructurings, beginning in 1993 when comparisons with competitive organisations indicated shortcomings in profitability and revenue. Diminishing returns convinced higher management they should implement measures to improve efficiency. As a result, the firm decided to downsize, with a target of staff reduction in the size of the workforce from approximately 1,700 employees to 1,600 employees. It was thought that these reductions could be implemented through a reorganisation of service areas such as administration, security, building maintenance and information systems.

Having decided to reduce staff levels, the next decision was to determine just how to go about the process. Senior management felt that employees should not be provided too much time to consider the implications of the organisational restructuring and that the best option was to get the process over with as quickly as possible. Disgruntled employees who remained on the job for a long period of time, it was thought, would affect the morale of the survivors and this would result in a loss of organisational commitment and job satisfaction, thus the preferred downsizing strategies were to be voluntary redundancy and involuntary retrenchment. Targeted jobs in the firm would be made redundant, in which case the incumbent in that job would be retrenched. The policy of 'getting the process over quickly' resulted in several instances in which employees arrived at work that day to find a member of the security team at their desks and to be told they had only a few minutes to clear their work and leave the premises. As described by a manager at the time, 'We used a very heavy-handed approach.'

The second iteration of restructuring began in late 1994 and was handled very differently from the first. As a result of a series of meetings with the firm's global financial partners it was concluded that further cost savings were necessary. Planning then began with a 15-month technical study to determine where further efficiencies and cost savings could be realised. At the same time, a consultancy firm was commissioned to assist in the development of the restructuring process. These consultants facilitated the planning, provided advice during the implementation of the restructuring, and then left the organisation with a restructuring framework for later use if needed.

Analysis of the restructuring process began by classifying all jobs as 'core' and 'non-core' positions. One outcome of this analysis was the determination that the firm would eliminate the technical support divisions that provided mining exploration operations, as the company was shifting its focus away from an exploration role to one emphasising the operational side of mining. This would enable International Mining to outsource those technical and administrative functions not directly related to its core operation of mining. In order to further reduce costs, the company decided to scrutinise the operations of the entire firm in order to target areas of duplication and inefficiency. This resulted in the elimination of several administrative, technical support and security positions. In addition, the company decided to flatten the organisational structure through delayering which would result in a further reduction of staff numbers.

One of the outcomes of this planning stage of the process was the determination that some core positions had more employees than jobs. In order to reconcile these 'overstaffed core positions', a 'competency matrix' was developed in order to select which of these employees would be retained or retrenched. Production supervisors and the production manager provided most of this analysis, as these individuals were the direct supervisors of most of the targeted employees.

The competence matrix was based on the dimensions of technical competence, attitude, performance (based on supervisor perception), teamwork, achievement of outcomes, ability to work with others and understanding value. Professionals and managers were rated on the basis of performance reviews and potential. The evaluation of both employees and managers was based on the subjective perceptions of supervisors. On the other hand, evaluation of senior managers did not encompass a matching of the competencies of the individual to the needs of the job. Some key senior staff left the organisation and this had an effect on organisational performance. One of the senior HR managers described the process:

for non-award, higher level people there were a couple of mistakes that were made in that area which weren't really good for us (Interviewee, International Mining).

An after-the-event review by senior management of the downsizing processes used in the two restructuring processes evidenced two major issues. The first was the realisation that much of what had transpired was based very much on a preoccupation with cost reduction. As one senior manager put it,

> The consultants argued that the company needed to cut costs across the board and so we decided that the most expedient way of achieving this was to reduce the size of our workforce. We couldn't predict profits but it was obvious that we could control costs and downsizing immediately reduces costs. It wasn't so much a restructuring as we wanted to cut our costs. Our costs were too high compared to our competitors. It is quite well known that, for example, our costs in mining are always going to be higher than some of our competitors because of the way our ore is structured, we have to move more waste than our competitors because our ore body, although it's a fine ore body has a lot more rubbish on it. So if you've got to move 3 tons of waste to get 1 ton of ore and your competitors have to move 1 ton or less than 1 ton in some cases your costs are going to be higher. So the only way you can improve and be competitive is to make sure that your costs other than those uncontrolled ones are really spot on and that's what we set out to do (Senior manager, International Mining).

The second issue was based on negative feedback after the first restructuring from both retrenched employees and survivors as well. The result of this was a re-thinking of the idea of giving employees a minimal notification time for retrenchment, the establishment of a competence matrix to aid in the retrenchment selection process, and the establishment of an outplacement program to assist retrenched employees in the search for new jobs.

> The difficulty has been the fact that we've gone into this growth phase. Looking back now, we would've liked to have kept those people. Had we not had all this success this last year, had we had the same forward plans as when we went through the down-staffing, I don't think we would have been saying well let that person go (Interviewee, International Mining).

Questions

1. What were the over-riding issues that convinced International Mining it should restructure in each of the two episodes?

2. What was to be the desired outcome of the restructurings?

3. How did the company go about the process of downsizing in each of the two instances? How was the second restructuring different from the first?

4. What were the positive outcomes of the two restructurings? The negative ones?

5. What should the firm have done differently?

DOWNSIZING DOWN UNDER: Perth and Western Bank

ALLEN CLABAUGH

Perth and Western Bank is a regional bank founded in Western Australia. The bank was acquired by a nationally based organisation and was merged with the larger financial institution in 1996. The Western Australian organisation is self-contained within the larger corporate structure and maintains its own industrial relations, occupational health and safety, deployment, training, development, and finance functions. The organisational restructuring of Perth and Western Bank was precipitated by takeover by a larger, nationally based bank. The national bank had many branches in Western Australia, some of which were near those of Perth and Western Bank. The operation of the two systems side-by-side resulted in duplication of effort, administration and operations, so a rationali- sation of the two operations was seen to be a logical business move. All of the two sets of banks in Western Australia were to be fronted with the Perth and Western Bank name and logo, but some of both banks would be closed in order to avoid duplication. Perth and Western Bank was to function autonomously in the development of the amalgamation process for Western Australia and so it was decided that the national group would not participate in the integration process.

> When the two organisations merged a lot of functions were actually duplicated and once we identified which functions were duplicated and once you merged or amalgamated them together there was a surplus of people actually required to do those functions. A good example of that is probably the Human Resource Department where [the parent company] in WA had 12 people and [the national partner] had 45 people. The reason why there was such a disparity of numbers was because [the local firm] actually ran their whole operation out of Perth whereas [the parent company] had some of their operations centralised in Sydney. So when you brought the two functions together we had quite a number of HR people which was a lot more than we really required to go forward (Interviewee, Perth and Western Bank).

Another issue to be taken under consideration by the strategic planners was the merging of the two organisational cultures. Three different cultural points of view co-existed in the merged banking system. There was the local (state-level) Perth and Western Bank culture, the national banking culture of the corporate group, and the local culture of the corporate group.

> One of the things we did before we actually started the integration was that we did a cultural audit to actually see what makes up people from [Perth and Western Bank], and what makes up people from [the parent company]. Basically try and see where we can meld the two together. What we actually found is that there were three cultures running. There was the [Perth and Western Bank] culture, the [parent company] – Western

Australia culture and the [parent company] – Sydney culture operating in WA. People from Western Australia, their make up is very different from people in the Eastern Seaboard and we discovered that Western Australians operate best in an atmosphere of going against the tide, a little adversity, and that if they can make their decisions locally they will do them quicker and if they are a little more difficult, the task that you're asked to do, they will do it more vigorously and so we unashamedly took as much as we could out of that culture in order to use it to our advantage during integration and do so now. So the culture audit was probably one of the most important components that we did (Interviewee, Perth and Western Bank).

A survey of positions and jobs was undertaken in order to establish a base-line of integration between the two banking establishments:

The only jobs that were identified early on as being probably those that would go were those that were duplicated. We had two branches that were amalgamating and if they were duplicated at the branch next door then we decided that we would look at what the new branch would be, knowing that some jobs would go (Interviewee, Perth and Western Bank).

A second aim of the restructuring was to be a flattening of the organisational structure. It was felt that the removal of some layers of the organisation's structure would result in a more efficient operation. As described by one of the senior HR managers,

We didn't want to have seven or eight layers between the person who starts on the frontline counter and [higher management] (Interviewee, Perth and Western Bank).

Perth and Western Bank had learned from the downsizing pains of its parent company. The national organisation had recently restructured, and in the process, provided attractive redundancy packages to its employees. As a result, the parent company lost a large number of high-performing workers. In addition, many employees perceived the use of redundancy packages as rewarding employees for leaving the organisation. The feeling at Perth and Western Bank was that the use of attractive early retirement and redundancy packages was not cost-effective over the longer term. Indeed, the company set a 'no retrenchment policy' and actively communicated the message that no employees would be lost during the restructuring. Although some senior managers left the company, this was through resignation, rather than retrenchment or redundancy.

What happened during the last 5 or 6 years is that people, rather than resign because they want to go and do something different, will try their utmost to line up for a retrenchment. You get a maximum of 96 weeks payout which is quite a lot of money and this feeling was really running through the [Perth and Western Bank] network. During the integration we made a conscious decision to try and get a more community type atmosphere going, a community culture happening, that we would try to have a minimum amount of retrenchments as we possibly could and that we would actively as much as possible redeploy people to other areas. If you looked at it from a cost point of view, there is the cost of not only retrenching the person in the dollar and cent but it is also the cost of lost investment for the person walking out the door and there is also lost time from people then wondering, well this person's gone I wonder if I can go. So we actually tried to look at how we could best change that and we had basically a no retrenchment strategy happening since integration which really irked a lot of the more senior [Perth and Western Bank] managers who had been around for a long period of time. It now seems to have bitten so to speak and people now understand that there is no retrenchment, that if you do want to leave and look at a different lifestyle or a different job career then you make the decision to resign and go. What's helped us along on that is that [the parent company] has continued in other areas of the country to downsize using the retrenchment avenue whereas we have decided we won't do that. We've decided that when you look at the cost and the break even points of where the cost is there is a long time before you actually are starting to be in the red so to speak. We've found that we have been able to downsize using that approach and it brings a better feel to what's actually happening in the branch within the network (Interviewee, Perth and Western Bank).

At the organisational level, the determination of redundant positions began with a functional analysis of the organisation's positions with the aim of targeting areas of functional duplication. At the individual level, the organisation developed a functional job analysis of all its positions that then produced job descriptions and a set of employee competencies for each position. Each employee was subject to a process of performance appraisal and competency analysis and was evaluated on the basis of job-competency performance matching. Once the organisation's functional analysis was completed, the redundant positions were publicised throughout the organisation. Staff reduction was accomplished primarily through attrition (the organisation normally has an attrition level of around 35 to 45 employees per month) and voluntary redundancy. All employees who left the company underwent an outplacement process, designed to smooth the transition out of the company.

As described by the respondent:

We did a job description of what we wanted the role to be, we looked at the competencies of what all the people had, we then ranked the people based on the competencies, ability to go forward, and past performance, and then ranked them. We advised [the employees in those positions] that the positions which they were in had been made redundant, and [they were asked to decide who would like to stay and who would want to go] (Interviewee, Perth and Western Bank).

Employee selection for retention and retrenchment at Perth and Western Bank, therefore, was a competitive process, not unlike that used by many firms when hiring new employees.

Despite all of these efforts, some senior managers suggested that the downsizing was not as successful as it could have been. During the transition to the amalgamated bank's new accounting system, some accounts were mismanaged because of computer software errors. As a result, some accounts were not credited with automatic deposits from the customers' employers, and many accounts were not properly audited. Because of this, the company lost quite a few customers to its competitors during the transition period. As outlined by the respondent:

From a manpower point of view [the downsizing process] was successful. From a process point of view of profits and technology, it failed (Interviewee, Perth and Western Bank).

The company stated that it had lost some of its employees that it would rather have retained. As described by the respondent this was a result:

> . . . not of retrenchment though, [but] of resignation. There were some staff from the [Organisation] that were in more senior positions that decided to go because they really weren't certain whether this was an organisation for which they would want to work in but they went. We never retrenched any person who we would, in hindsight, rather have kept (Interviewee, Perth and Western Bank).

Questions

1. How did Perth and Western go about restructuring?

2. How was the downsizing process at Perth and Western Bank different from that of International Mining?

3. What were the positive outcomes of the restructuring? And what were the negative ones?

4. What could Perth and Western Bank have been done differently to ensure a more effective restructuring process?

References

Adams, S. (1996) *The Dilbert Principle,* London: Boxtree Press.

Ahmakjian, L.C. and Robinson, P. (2001) 'Safety in numbers: downsizing and the deinstitutionalization of permanent employment in Japan', *Administrative Science Quarterly,* Vol.46, No.4. pp.622–58.

Allen, T.D., Freeman, D.M., Russell, J.E.A., Reizenstein, R.C. and Rentz, J.O. (2001) 'Survivor reactions to organizational downsizing: does time ease the pain?', *Journal of Occupational and Organizational Psychology,* Vol.74, pp.145–64.

Amabile, T.M. and Conti, R. (1999) 'Changes in the work environment for creativity during downsizing', *Academy of Management Journal,* Vol.42, No.6, pp.630–40.

Anfunso, D. (1996) 'Strategies to stop the layoffs', *Personnel Journal,* June, pp.66–99.

Armour, J., Deakin, S. and Knozelmann, S. (2003) 'Shareholder primacy and the trajectory of UK corporate governance', *British Journal of Industrial Relations,* Vol.41, No.3, pp.531–55.

Barbee, G, (1986), 'Downsizing with dignity', *Retirement Planning,* Fall, pp.6–7.

*Baumol, J.W., Blinder, S.A. and Wolff, N.E. (2003) *Downsizing in America: Reality, Causes, and Consequences,* New York: Russell Sage Foundation Press.

Boone, J. (2000) 'Technological progress, downsizing and unemployment', *Economic Journal,* Vol.110, pp.581–600.

Brockner, J. (1992) 'Managing the effects of lay-offs on survivors', *California Management Review,* Vol.34, No.2, pp.9–28.

*Brockner, J., Grover, S., Reed, T., DeWitt, R. and O'Malley, M. (1987) 'Survivors' reactions to lay-offs: we get by with a little help from our friends', *Administrative Science Quarterly,* Vol.32, pp.526–41

Brunning, F. (1996) 'Working at the office on borrowed time,' *Macleans,* February, pp.8–9.

Budros, A. (1999) 'A conceptual framework for analyzing why orgnaizations downsize', *Organization Science,* Vol.10, No.1, pp.69–81.

Bulmer, M. (1971) 'Mining redundancy: a case study of the workings of the Redundancy Payments Act in the Durham coalfields', *Industrial Relations Journal*, Vol.26, No.15, pp.227–44.

Burke, W.W. (1997) 'The new agenda for organization development', *Organizational Dynamics*, Vol.26, pp.6–20.

*Cameron, K.S. (1994) 'Strategies for successful organizational downsizing', *Human Resource Management*, Vol.33, No.2, pp.189–211.

Cameron, K.S. (1998) 'Downsizing', in M. Poole and M. Warner (eds) *The IEBM Handbook of Human Resource Management*, London: International Thomson Press.

Cameron, K.S., Freeman, S.J. and Mishra, A.K., (1991) 'Best practices in white collar downsizing: managing contradictions', *Academy of Management Executive*, Vol.5, No.3, pp.57–73.

Carlin, J. (1996) 'Guru of "downsizing" admits he got it all wrong', *The Independent on Sunday*, 12 May.

Cascio, F.W. (2002) 'Strategies for responsible restructuring', *Academy of Management Executive*, Vol.16, pp.80–91.

Cascio, F.W., Young, E.C. and Morris, J.R. (1997) 'Financial consequences of employment-change decisions in major U.S. corporations', *Academy of Management Journal*, Vol.40, pp.1175–89.

Caulkin, S. (1995) 'Take your partners', *Management Today*, February, pp.26–30.

Chadwick, C., Hunter, L. and Walston, S. (2004) 'Effects of downsizing practices on the performance of hospitals', *Strategic Management Journal*, Vol.25, No.5, pp.405–27.

Chartered Institute of Personnel and Development (CIPD) (2002) *Redundancy Survey Report*, May.

Chorely, D. (2002) 'How to manage downsizing', *Financial Management*, May, p.6.

Clabaugh, A. (1997) 'Downsizing: implications for older employees', Working Paper, Perth, Australia: Edith Cowan University.

Cross, B. (2004) 'The times they are a-changing: who will stay and who will go in a downsizing organization?', *Personnel Review*, Vol.33, No.3, pp.275–90.

Cully, M., Woodland, S., O'Reilly, A. and Dix, G. (1999) *Britain at Work*, London: Routledge.

De Meuse, K.P., Bergmann, T.J. and Vanderheiden, P.A. (1997) 'Corporate downsizing: separating myth from fact', *Journal of Management Inquiry*, Vol.6, No.2, pp.168–76.

Devine, K., Reay, T., Stainton, L. and Collins-Nakai, R. (2003) 'Downsizing outcomes: better a victim than a survivor?', *Human Resource Management*, Vol.42, No.2, pp.109–24.

Dewettinck, K. and Buyens, D. (2002) 'Downsizing: employee threat or opportunity? An empirical study on external and internal reorientation practices in Belgian companies', *Employee Relations*, Vol.24, No.4, pp.389–402.

DiFonzo, N. and Bordia, P. (1998) 'A tale of two corporations: managing uncertainty during organizational change', *Human Resource Management*, Vol.37, pp.295–303.

Doherty, N. (1998) 'The role of outplacement in redundancy management', *Personnel Review*, Vol.27, No.4, pp.343–51.

Doherty, N. and Horstead, J. (1995) 'Helping survivors to stay on board', *People Management*, 12 January, pp.26–31.

Edwards, P. and Hall, M. (1999) 'Remission: possible', *People Management*, 15 July, pp.44–6.

Farrell, M. and Mavondo, F. (2004) 'The effect of downsizing strategy and reorientation strategy on learning orientation', *Personnel Review*, Vol.33, No.4, pp.383–402.

Fisher, S.R. and White, M.A. (2000) 'Downsizing in a learning organization: are there hidden costs?', *Academy of Management Review*, Vol.25, No.1, pp.244–51.

Garfield, A. (1999) 'Barclays shares soar as city welcomes job cuts', *The Independent*, 21 May.

Guest, D. and Peccei, R. (1992) 'Employee involvement: redundancy as a critical case', *Human Resource Management Journal*, Vol.2, No.3, pp.34–59.

Haigh, G. (2004) *Bad Company: The Strange Cult of the CEO*, London: Aurum.

Hamel, G. (2000) *Leading the Revolution*, New York: Harvard Business School Press.

Hamel, G. and Prahalad, C. K. (1993), 'Strategy as stretch and leverage', *Harvard Business Review*, March–April, pp.75–84.

Hancock, P. and Tyler, M. (2003) 'The tyranny of corporate slenderness: understanding organizations anorexically', paper presented at SOCS 21: 'Organizational Wellness', Robinson College, University of Cambridge, 9–12 July 2003.

Hardy, C. (1987), 'Investing in retrenchment: avoiding the hidden costs', *California Management Review*, Vol.29, No.4, pp.111–25.

Hill, S. (1989) *Competition and Control at Work*, London: Heinemann.

Hitt, M.A., Hoskisson, R.E., Harrison, J.S. and Summers, T.P. (1994) 'Human capital and strategic competitiveness in the 1990s', *Journal of Management Development*, Vol.13, No.1, pp.35–46.

Hunter, L. (2000) 'Myths and methods of downsizing', *FT Mastering People Management*, 2000, pp.2–4.

Hutton, W. (1997) *The State to Come*, London: Vintage.

Inman, P. (2004) 'Flying right in the face of logic', *The Guardian*, 28 August.

IRS (1998a) 'The 1998 IRS Redundancy Survey Part 1', *Employment Trends*, No.658, pp.5–11.

IRS (1998b) 'The 1998 IRS Redundancy Survey Part 2', *Employment Trends*, No.659, pp.9–16.

IRS (2004) 'The Changing Shape of Work: How organisations restructure', *Employment Review*, No.794.

Kettley, P. (1995) *Employee Morale During Downsizing*, Brighton: Institute of Employment Studies, Report No.291.

Littler, C. and Innes, P. (2003) 'Downsizing and deknowledging the firm', *Work, Employment and Society*, Vol.17, No.1, pp.73–100.

Mason, T. (2002) 'GSB top marketers exists as axe falls on budget', *Marketing*, Vol.31, p.6.

McCallister, T. (2001) 'Thomas Cook cuts jobs and pay', *The Guardian*, 1 November.

McGoldrick, A. and Cooper, C.L. (1989) *Early Retirement*, Aldershot: Gower.

McKinley, W., Zhao, J. and Rust, K.G. (2000) 'A sociocognitive interpretation of organizational downsizing', *Academy of Management Review*, Vol.25, pp.227–43.

Mellahi, K. and Wilkinson, A. (2004) *Downsizing and Innovation Output: A Review of Literature and Research Propositions*, BAM Paper 2004, British Academy of Management.

Moore, M. (1997) *Downsize This*, New York: Harper-Collins.

Mroczkowski, T. and Hanaoka, M. (1997), 'Effective downsizing strategies in Japan and America: is there a convergence of employment practices?', *Academy of Management Review*, Vol.22, No.1, pp.226–56.

Niehoff, B.P., Moorman, R.H., Blakely, G. and Fuller, J. (2001) 'The influence of empowerment and job enrichment on employee loyalty in a downsizing environment', *Group and Organization Management*, Vol.26, No.1, pp.93–113.

Peters, T. (1992) *Liberation Management*, London: Macmillan.

Pfeffer, J. (1998), *The Human Equation*, Boston, MA: Harvard Business School Press.

Priti, P.S. (2000) 'Network destruction: the structural implications of downsizing', *Academy of Management Journal*, Vol.43, pp.101–12.

Rogers, D. (2002) 'ITV digital culls staff to lure buyers', *Marketing*, April 25, p.1.

*Sahdev, K. (2003) 'Survivors' reactions to downsizing: the importance of contextual factors', *Human Resource Management Journal*, Vol.13, No.4, pp.56–74.

Sahdev, K., Vinnicombe, S. and Tyson, S. (1999) 'Downsizing and the changing role of HR', *International Journal of Human Resource Management*, Vol.10, No.(5), pp.906–23.

Savery, L.K., Travaglione, A. and Firns, I.G.J. (1998) 'The links between absenteeism and commitment during downsizing', *Personnel Review*, Vol.27, No.4, pp.312–24.

Sennett, R. (1997) *The Corrosion of Character*, New York: Norton.

Sinclair, J., Seifert, R. and Ironside, M. (1995) 'Performance-related redundancy: school teacher lay-offs as management control strategy', paper presented at British Universities Industrial Relations Association (BUIRA) Conference, Durham, July.

*Spreitzer, G. and Mishra, A.K. (2002) 'To stay or to go: voluntary survivor turnover following an organizational downsizing', *Journal of Organizational Behaviour*, Vol.26, No.6, pp.707–29.

Stebbins, M W, (1989) 'Downsizing with "mafia model" consultants', *Business Forum*, Winter, pp.45–7.

Sullivan, T. and Hogge, B. (1987) 'Instruments of Adjustment in Recession', *R & D Management*, Vol.17, No.4.

*Thornhill, A. and Saunders, M.N.K. (1998) 'The meanings, consequences and implications of the management of downsizing and redundancy: a review', *Personnel Review,* Vol.27, No.4, pp.271–95.

Torrington, D., Hall, L. and Taylor, S. (2005) *Human Resource Management,* London: FT/Prentice Hall.

Turnbull, P and Wass V (1997) 'Job insecurity and labour market lemons: the (mis)management of redundancy in steel making, coal mining, and port transport', *Journal of Management Studies,* Vol.34, No.1, pp.27–51.

Turnbull, P. and Wass, V. (2004) 'Job cuts and redundancy: managing the workforce complement', paper presented at the BUIRA Annual Conference, University of Nottingham.

Wedderburn, D. (1965) *Redundancy and the Railwaymen,* Cambridge: Cambridge University Press.

Welch, J. (2001) *What I've Learned Leading a Great Company and Great People,* New York: Headline.

Weyer, M.V. (1994) 'The old men on the board', *Management Today,* October, pp.64–7.

Wilkinson, A. (2004) 'Downsizing, rightsizing and dumbsizing: quality, human resources and sustainability', Invited keynote paper presented at the 9th World Congress for Total Quality Management, September, 2004, Abu Dhabi, UAE.

Worrall, L., Cooper, C. and Campbell, F. (2000) 'The impact of organizational change on UK managers' perceptions of their working lives', in R. Burke and C. Cooper (eds) *The Organization in Crisis,* Oxford: Blackwell.

Worrell, D.L., Davidson, W.N. and Sharma, V.M. (1991) 'Lay-off announcements and stockholder wealth', *Academy of Management Journal,* Vol.34, pp.662–78.

Younge, G. (2005) 'New black sheriff sacks opponents', *The Guardian,* 11 January.

* Useful reading

Chapter 15

EMPLOYEE PARTICIPATION

Tony Dundon and Adrian Wilkinson

Introduction

Employee participation has a long history in British employment relations. The changing political and economic climate has shaped both the demand (among employees and unions) and desire (by managers and employers) for the different types of practices. However, there is often a lack of clarity surrounding the term participation. The confusion is often made worse as some methods (such as team briefings or quality circles) tend to coexist and overlap with other techniques (such as joint union–management consultative committees or collective bargaining). The topic of employee participation is set against a new regulatory environment; in particular the influence of both European and British policy initiatives. In considering these issues, this chapter is structured in a number of ways. First, we define participation and consider the context in which participation has changed over time. We then review a framework against which to evaluate employee participation, and this is followed by an explanation of the types of schemes used in practice. Fourth is a consideration of the meanings and possible impact on organisational performance and employee well-being. Finally, we review some of the current influences and policy choices in the area of employee participation.

Defining participation

The literature surrounding participation can be confusing (Hyman and Mason 1995; Heller *et al.* 1998). Some authors refer to involvement as participation while others use empowerment or communications, often without fully extracting the key conceptual meanings or differences that are used in practice. For example in one organisation the term 'involvement' may be used to identify certain practices that in another organisation are regarded as 'participatory'. Differences can be further complicated depending on the presence or absence of a trade union. It is not uncommon for non-unionised companies to use the terms 'empowerment' or 'communications', even when they utilise representative forums such as European Works Councils (Benson, 2000; Ackers *et al.* 2005). The WERS survey reported that the majority of managers (72 per cent) preferred to consult with workers directly rather than via employee representatives (Cully *et al.* 1999, p.88), even though companies that utilise *only* direct schemes tend to involve their employees less then those that also consult with worker representatives (Wood and Fenton-O'Creevy 1999).

One way of making sense of the elasticity of the terms is to see participation as an umbrella term covering all initiatives designed to engage employees. However, there are two separate underlying ideologies behind the nature of participation. First, the concept of industrial democracy (which draws from notions of industrial citizenship), sees participation as a fundamental democratic right for workers to extend a degree of control over managerial decision making in an organisation. Second, the notion of economic efficiency, which implies it may make sense for employers to encourage greater participation in the organisation as it could help create more understanding (and hence commitment) and also allow employees to contribute more to the business. Although these are two different stances they are not polar opposites. As Cressey *et al.* (1985) usefully reminded us, no one wants a 'democratic bankruptcy'. This perspective is also useful in helping us chart the changing patterns and arrangements to do with participation over time. Much more important is what certain practices actually mean to the participants and whether such schemes can influence organisational effectiveness and employee well-being (Dundon *et al.* 2004). Brannen (1983, p.13) adopts a broad definition in this regard, defining participation as the processes by which 'individuals or groups may influence, control, be involved in, exercise power within, or be able to intervene in decision-making within organisations'. We define employee participation in a similarly broad way, following Boxall and Purcell (2003, p.162), as incorporating a range of mechanisms 'which enable, and at times empower employees, directly and indirectly, to contribute to decision-making in the firm'. As this chapter is also concerned with clarifying what is meant by different participation schemes, we will evaluate the extent to which various practices allow workers to have a say in organisational decisions. At times the extent of such a voice can be marginal, superficial and subject to managerial power; at other times it may be more extensive and embedded within an organisation.

The context for employee participation

Employee participation has a long history in the UK (and abroad for that matter). Notwithstanding oversimplification, a number of distinct phases can be traced to place the role of participation in a contemporary context. The 1960s was often preoccupied with a search for job enrichment and enhanced worker motivation. Managerial objectives tended to focus on employee skill acquisition and work enrichment. In the UK examples at ICI and British Coal included semi-autonomous workgroups to promote skill variety and job autonomy (Trist *et al.* 1963; Roeber 1975). In practice these schemes were more concerned with employee motivation as an outcome rather than the mechanisms that allowed workers to have a say about organisational decisions.

The 1970s witnessed a shift in focus toward industrial democracy which emphasised worker rights to participate. Participation reached its high point in the UK with the 1977 Bullock Report on Industrial Democracy which addressed the question of how workers might be represented at board level (Bullock 1977). This report emerged in a period of strong union bargaining power and the Labour government's 'Social Contact', an atmosphere which underpinned the Bullock approach to industrial participation. The Bullock Report was partly union-initiated, through the Labour Party, and based on collectivist principles which saw trade unions playing a key role, although it was not without controversy (Brannen 1983); in particular the general principle of employee rights established on a statutory basis (Ackers *et al.* 1992). Experiments with worker directors were initiated in the Post Office and the British Steel Corporation, although along with the Bullock Report itself, soon abandoned with the new neo-liberal agenda of the Thatcher government in 1979.

The 1980s saw a very different agenda for participation. Indeed, the vocabulary changed almost overnight. The term 'involvement' became more fashionable and associated with managerial initiatives designed to elicit employee commitment. During the 1980s the political climate was one of reducing union power and promoting more individualistic, anti-collectivist philosophies inspired by Thatcher's conservative government. Out went statutory blueprints for greater industrial democracy such as the Bullock Report, and in came a new wave of financial deregulation and managerial self-confidence for employee rather than union-centred communication channels. As Wedderburn summed up the general climate at the time:

> Those who opposed the new polices increasingly ran the risk of being seen not as critics with whom to debate and compromise (the supreme pluralist virtue), but as a domestic enemy within, which must be defeated . . . (quoting government spokesman). The mining dispute cannot be *settled*. It can only be *won* (Wedderburn 1986, p.85).

From the 1980s onwards the context for participation changed significantly. To begin with the whole philosophy was managerial-led, often from outside the institutions of industrial relations. Second, the rationale for employee participation stressed direct communications with individual employees which, in turn, marginalised trade union influence. Third, the new agenda for participation was anchored on business improvements through employee commitment (Ackers *et al.* 1992, p.272). Unlike notions of industrial democracy, employee involvement during the 1980s stemmed from an economic efficiency argument. This new wave of involvement was neither interested in nor allowed employees to question managerial prerogative (Marchington *et al.* 1992). In effect, this was a period of employee involvement on management's terms.

The 1990s saw a consolidation in the use of employee participation techniques. Tapping into employee ideas and drawing on their tacit knowledge was seen as one solution to the problems of managing in an increasingly competitive marketplace, in part due to globalisation and market liberalisation by governments, and also due to increasing customer demand for more choice, quality and design. The move to customised products with flexible speciali-sation, flatter and leaner structures was seen as the new route to competitive advantage which meant increasing attention to labour as a resource (Piore and Sabel 1983; Wilkinson 2002). Many of the specific mechanisms to tap into such a labour resource became crystallised in models of best-practice HRM and high commitment management developed in the USA in recent years (Huselid 1995; Becker and Huselid 1998; Pfeffer 1998). In the UK a series of studies sought to validate, in statistical terms, a link between a range of HR practices – including methods for employees to have a voice – and organisational performance (Patterson *et al.* 1997; Wood and De Menezes 1998). In this way the objectives for employee participation can be seen as unitarist in approach, often moralistic in tone, and predicated on the assumption that 'what is good for the business must be good for employees' (Claydon and Doyle 1996; Marchington and Wilkinson 2005).

At the same time as this is a continuing (and often complicated) policy dialectic that shapes management choice for employee participation (Ackers *et al.* 2005). The broader environment now seems more sympathetic to trade union recognition, individual employment rights as well as emergent collective-type regulations, such as the *European Directive on Employee Information and Consultation* (Ewing 2003). Arguably, the twenty-first century has ushered in a period of legal re-regulation, which can be divided between those policies that directly affect employee participation (the directive itself for example) and those than indirectly alter the environment in which employee participation operates (the competitive environment).

A framework for analysing employee participation

Before outlining various participation schemes, the purpose of this section is first to explain a framework that can be used to analyse the extent to which various schemes genuinely allow employees to have a say in matters that affect them at work. What is important here is to be able to unpick the purpose, meaning and subsequent impact of employee participation (Dundon *et al.* 2004). To this end a fourfold framework can be used: including the 'depth', 'level', 'scope' and 'form' of various participation schemes in actual practice (Marchington *et al.* 1992; Marchington and Wilkinson 2005).

First is the 'depth' to which employees have a say about organisational decisions (Marchington and Wilkinson 2005). A greater depth may be when employees, either directly or indirectly, can influence those decisions that are normally reserved for management. The other end of the continuum may be a shallow depth, evident when employees are simply informed of the decisions management have made (see Figure 15.1). Second is the 'level' at which participation takes place. This can be at a work-group, department, plant or corporate level. What is significant here is whether the schemes adopted by an organisation actually take place at an appropriate managerial level. For example, involvement in a team meeting over future strategy would in most instances be inappropriate given that most team leaders would not have the authority to re-design organisational strategy. Third is the 'scope' of participation, that is, the topics on which employees can contribute. These range from relatively minor and insignificant matters, such as car-parking spaces to more substantive issues, such as future investment strategies or plant re-location. Finally is the 'form' that participation takes, which may include a combination of both direct and indirect schemes. Direct employee participation, as noted earlier, has experienced a renewed focus since the 1980s and continued through the 1990s. Direct schemes typically include individual techniques such as written and electronic communications, face-to-face meetings between managers and employees, or team leaders with small groups of employees (such as quality circles or team briefing). Indirect participation, in contrast, is via employee representatives, either union stewards or employee works council representatives in consultation with management. Another form of participation is task-based (or problem-solving) participation, where employees contribute directly to their job, either through focus groups or attitude surveys. There is also financial participation through variable pay and/or bonus schemes, such as profit sharing.

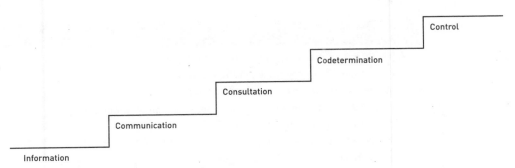

Figure 15.1 The depth of employee participation
Source: Marchington and Wilkinson 2005

Taken together this framework allows for a more accurate description not only of the type of involvement and participation schemes in use, but the extent to which they may or may not empower employees (Marchington and Wilkinson 2005). Figure 15.1 is more than a straight-forward continuum from no involvement (information) to extensive worker participation (control). It illustrates the point that schemes can overlap and co-exist. For example, the use of collective bargaining and joint consultation does not mean that management abandon communication techniques. Central to this understanding of participation is power within the employment relationship, differentiated by the methods used (direct or indirect classifications), the level at which participation takes place (individual to board room level), and the extent to which any particular technique is employee- or management-centred.

Employee participation in practice

The use of various employee involvement and participatory initiatives speeded up during the latter part of the 1980s and appears to have become more embedded and integrated with organisational practice during the 1990s (Marchington *et al.* 2001). A 'systematic use of the management chain' has been reported as one of the most frequent methods of communication between employer and employee (Millward *et al.* 1992, p.166). Regular meetings between managers and employees also grew, as did suggestions schemes and newsletters (Millward *et al.* 1992, p.167). In the 1998 *Workplace Employee Relations Survey* (Cully *et al.* 1999), direct employee involvement was evident through systems for team briefings (65 per cent of all workplaces), staff attitude surveys (45 per cent) and problem-solving groups such as quality circles (42 per cent) along with regular workforce meetings (37 per cent).

For the purpose of explanation and subsequent analysis, it is useful to break down the range of schemes in use into five broad classifications: communications, upward problem solving, task participation, teamworking and representative participation.

Communication is a weak form of participation but is a means by which management share information with employees, ranging from written memos, email or informal face-to-face communications. These have increased substantially in recent years (Millward *et al.* 2000), and are often regarded as a precursor to deeper forms of employee participation (Marchington and Wilkinson 2005). Of course, communication practices vary in frequency and intensity. Some

---

Table 15.1

Use of 'new' management practices and EI schemes	% of workplaces
Workplace operates a system of team briefing for groups of employees	65
Staff attitude survey conducted in the last 5 years	45
Problem-solving groups (e.g., quality circles)	42
'Single status' between managers and non-managerial employees	41
Regular meetings of entire workforce	37
Profit-sharing scheme operated for non-managerial employees	30
Workplace level joint consultative committee	28
Employee share ownership scheme for non-managerial employees	15

Source: Adapted from Cully *et al.* 1998, p.10 (base: all workplaces with 25 or more employees)

companies rely on their own internal newsletter to report a range of matters, from profits, new products to in-house welfare and employee development topics. More sophisticated techniques found by Marchington *et al.* (2001) included the use of electronic media, such as emails, company intranets and senior management on-line discussion forums.

The main problem with communications as a form of involvement is a lack of objectivity. Given that information is often political and power-centred, the messages managers seek to communicate to workers may be used to reinforce managerial prerogatives. The way information is communicated can also be ineffective as many line managers responsible for disseminating corporate messages lack effective communication skills, or information is conveyed in an untimely manner (often when bad news has already passed to the media before employees are told).

Upward problem-solving techniques seek to go one step further than communications by tapping into employee ideas for improvements. As with communications, problem-solving practices have increased, in part inspired by Japanese work systems which encourage employees to offer ideas (Wilkinson *et al.* 1998). Upward problem-solving practices are designed to increase the stock of ideas available to management as well as encourage a more cooperative industrial relations climate. Specific techniques can be either individual or collective, and range from employee suggestions schemes, focus groups or quality circles to workforce attitude surveys (Wilkinson 2002). The fundamental difference between these practices and communication methods is that they are upward (from employees to managers) rather than downward (managers disseminating information to workers).

In relation to the framework for analysing employee participation in the previous section, it is clear that upward problem-solving techniques do offer a greater degree of depth than managerial communications. However, they have also been highly criticised as being inherently unitarist in nature (Sewell and Wilkinson 1992). For example, the feedback in attitude surveys is essentially centred on a managerial agenda with the information asked for set by employers. Furthermore, in organisations where quality circles have been introduced, the take-up and enthusiasm among employees has often been found wanting (Collard and Dale 1989).

The third category of practices is *task-based participation*. The objective here has been to focus attention on the actual job rather than the managerial processes for participation. These practices have a longer pedigree in seeking to counter the degradation of work and associated employee alienation (Proctor and Mueller 2000), of which many schemes formed part of a series of work psychology experiments in the 1960s and 1970s (e.g., Tavistock Institute, Quality of WorkLife Programs in the USA and Sweden). More recently, task-based participation is celebrated as a root to sustained organisational performance via employee commitment and motivation (Patterson *et al.* 1997; Wood and De Menezes 1998). The types of practices include job enlargement and job enrichment whereby employees perform a greater range of task with a greater degree of job autonomy. The criticisms levelled at task-participation are that outcomes often result in work intensification rather than job enrichment. Arguably, devolving more and more responsibilities to employees can increase stress levels. In other words, employees simply work harder rather than smarter (Delbridge *et al.* 1992).

The fourth category is *teamworking*. Pfeffer's (1998) universal list of seven best practices includes, along other things, self-managed teams as integral to achieving better organisational performance through people. However, teamworking is one of the most imprecise of all the involvement and participation practices. More problematic is that teamworking is often portrayed in an upbeat, uncritical way. In the WERS98 survey, 65 per cent of managerial respondents indicated they have teamworking in their organisation, yet this figure reduced to 3 per cent when further questions probed the extent to which these teams were genuinely autonomous – such as deciding how tasks would be performed or appointing team leaders (Cully *et al.* 1999, p.43). Other commentators have reported a more subversive side to the effects of teamworking that result in forms of peer surveillance and control (Sinclair 1992; Barker 1993). For example, the pressure to conform to group norms and meet production targets is often policed by co-workers while simultaneously monitored by management (Geary and Dobbins 2001).

The final category is *representative participation,* most typically via trade union representation, collective bargaining and/or joint consultation. This category has experienced the most significant decline in recent years. Across the WERS survey data, the proportion of establishments with a recognised union presence has declined from over 70 per cent to 54 per cent of all workplaces, with collective bargaining coverage down from 70 per cent in 1980 to 41 per cent by 1998. Joint consultation is even lower with just 29 per cent of workplaces reporting the existence of a joint consultative committee in 1998 (Cully *et al.* 1999; Millward *et al.* 2000). It is often acknowledged that collective bargaining indicates a deeper and broader level of participation in organisational decision making through the act of negotiation between management and employee (union) representatives (Pateman 1970). However, the reality can be very different, as British managers have involved unions less and less as a legitimate participatory channel (Geary 2003; Ackers *et al.* 2005). Of all the workplaces that recognised a trade union, only 31 per cent said they involve unions through collective bargaining (Cully *et al.* 1999, p.109), with negotiation on pay and non-pay matters occurring in only one in every five unionised workplaces (Cully *et al.* 1999, p.110).

This may indicate that *representative participation* is not necessarily dependent on the existence of a trade union, but mediated through newer forms of involvement such as European Works Councils and/or non-union company committees (Ackers *et al.* 2005). In Marchington *et al.*'s (2001) study into employee voice and management choice, it was found that non-union consultative committees were more common than a decade ago, and considered a range of organisational issues including working conditions, capital investment expenditure and disciplinary procedures. At the same time, others have commented that non-union consultative committees are often weak on power and shallow in depth (Gollan 2002; Dundon and Rollinson 2004).

Inevitably, there are always dangers in seeking to locate discrete boundaries between certain practices. Some schemes are often unclear and ambiguous, ranging from the mechanistic descriptions of structures and procedures to more organic techniques that shape attitudes and behaviours. Other techniques limit participation to formal institutions and procedures, such as bargaining and joint consultation, while day-to-day interactions between employee and management may promote a more critical informal dimension to participation, particularly within the smaller workplace devoid of many formalised HR systems (Dundon *et al.* 1999). At the same time, there are questions about whether or not informality can survive as a viable mechanism for independent employee participation in the absence of formal structures, especially if market conditions or senior management philosophies change (Wilkinson *et al.* 2004). It is these dangers and uncertainties that warrant a consideration of the meanings and interpretations of how participation can impact organisational stakeholders.

The meanings and impact of participation

There are a number of problems with the meanings and definitions of the schemes outlined above. For example, in some organisations the full range of mechanisms – both direct and indirect – may be used simultaneously, while in other companies one or two techniques may be employed. There is no reason to assume that more is somehow better. It is also quite common for a particular label to be ascribed to very different practices (Wilkinson *et al.* 2004). For example, a joint consultative committee which takes place on a monthly basis at plant level, involving senior managers and shop stewards, may have a more significant impact on decision making than a European Works Council that meets once a year, even though both are consultative and indirect in nature. There is the possibility that the latter is regarded by participants as 'bolted-on' to other organisational practices, with little substance or meaning in reality (Marchington and Wilkinson 2005).

Arguably, the extrapolation of survey evidence about the use of various involvement and participation schemes tells us very little about the impact or extensiveness of such techniques within a particular organisation (Cox *et al.* 2003; Marchington 2005). Nor does this imply that certain schemes are an unwelcome intrusion into the lives of employees. For example, Geary and Dobbins (2001) suggest that while teamworking can lead to a reassertion of managerial authority this is not always as a brutal form of coercion. In this case, team participation was accompanied with autonomy and freedom, but also controls by granting workers a degree of discretion that served to protect managerial interests. In a study by Diamond and Freeman (2001), while employees tended to express satisfaction with the extent of involvement on matters such as the pace of work, a much wider participation gap was evident on a range of substantive employment matters, such as working hours or overtime rates.

The ambiguity and lack of clarity about certain involvement and participation schemes is evident in relation to the impact such techniques are claimed to have on enhanced organisational performance (Dundon *et al.* 2004). First, it is practically impossible to isolate cause and effect and demonstrate that participation can lead to better organisational performance given the whole range of other contextual influences. For example, labour turnover is likely to be influenced by the availability of other jobs, by relative pay levels and by the presence, absence or depth of particular participation schemes. Second is the unease associated with the reference to benchmarking: of assessing the date at which to start making 'before and after' comparisons. Should this be the date at which the new participative mechanisms (say, a quality circle or consultative committee) is actually introduced into the organisation, or should it be some earlier or later date? For example, the claim that a quality circle saves money through a new work practice does not take into account that such ideas may have previously been channelled through a different and even better-established route. This also leads on to a third concern, that of evaluating the so-called impact and on whose terms. Should assessments be made in relation to workers having some voice (i.e., the process) or in terms of how things may be changed due to participation (i.e., the outcomes)? If it is the latter, then who gains? It remains the case that it is usually managers who decide what involvement and/or participation schemes to employ, at what level, depth and over what issues (Wilkinson *et al.* 2004).

Employee participation and the EU

A more recent issue with regard to employee participation is the influence of European social policy. As noted earlier, in Britain the trend has been predominantly for employer-led schemes of a 'direct' nature, particularly since the 1980s. However the European Commission is beginning to promote what seems to be a favoured 'indirect' (i.e., more collectivist) route to employee participation. For example, the European Works Council Directive is currently under review at a European level with revisions expected in terms of the definitions and rights of employee representatives. Another development is the European Company Statute (ECS) with recommendations for a two-tier channel of participation for those companies that wish to avail of the EU Statute. It is envisaged that the participation structures will include a works council and employee representative at board level. These are similar to a range of employee participation schemes that are currently more common in other EU countries such as Germany, Denmark, Sweden and the Netherlands. Other European examples are the draft directives on temporary agency workers and company takeovers, all of which stipulate certain consultation rights for workers and worker representatives. Of more immediate significance is the recently adopted European Directive (2002/14/EC) on *Employee Information and Consultation,* and the remainder of this section will examine what this directive will mean in a British context.

The directive sets out the requirements for a permanent and statutory framework for employee information and consultation. These requirements stipulate that EU member states have to transpose the directive into domestic legislation by 23 March 2005, with the exception of the UK (and Ireland), where there will be an extended deadline up to 2008. This is because Britain and Ireland are the only two member states that do not have a statutory system for involvement and participation (Hall *et al.* 2002). The net effect is that British workers will have a legal right to be informed and consulted on a range of business and employment issues that may result in a significant departure from the traditional voluntarist system of British industrial relations (Sisson 2002).

The scope of the directive defines 'information' as the transmission, by the employer to employee representatives, of data in order to enable them to acquaint themselves with the subject-matter and to examine it. 'Consultation' means the exchange of views and establishment of dialogue between the employees' representatives and the employer, with a view to reaching agreement. Significantly, the explicit reference to 'employee representatives' in the directive is a clear indication of a preference for indirect (i.e., collectivist) forms of involvement and participation. This is not automatically via unions but rather employee representatives elected from and by the workforce – who may or may not be union stewards. Where this is likely to be more contentious is in those organisations that are either partly unionised, or have low union density levels. In all probability, companies that are highly unionised already have in place joint consultation arrangements that will suffice. Similarly, in completely non-union companies management and employees have the scope to design and implement information and consultation mechanisms in line with the directive without a union/non-union dichotomy. More problematic is in organisations with partial union membership as it is unclear whether there would have to be duplicate union and non-union employee forums, particularly if existing union representatives find it unacceptable to represent the interests of non-members. The directive states that organisations will have to inform and consult with employee representatives (whether union and/or non-union) on three general areas: the economic situation of the organisation; the structure and probable development of employment (including any threats to employment); and to inform and consult on decisions likely to lead to changes in work organisation or contractual relations (see Box 15.1 for a summary of the main features of the directive).

There are other aspects associated with employee participation contained in the directive. Article 6 (1) ensures confidentiality in that employee representatives (and experts that may assist them) cannot disclose commercially sensitive information provided to them. Article 7 stipulates that each of the EU countries has to ensure that employee representatives have adequate protection from managerial reprisals when carrying out their duties. This is likely to be particularly important given that employee representatives may not have the support and protection of a recognised trade union. Under Article 8, the governments of EU member countries must devise penalties for non-compliance: penalties that are 'effective, proportionate and dissuasive'. Article 5 of the directive has been receiving increasing attention in the media and among practitioners.

Box 15.1: Summary features of the EU Employee Information and Consultation Directive

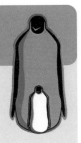

■ The Directive requires member states to establish a framework for the right to information and consultation for employees.

■ The government of an EU member state has to decide whether to apply these rights to all undertakings with 50 or more employees, or at an establishment level with 20 or more employees.

■ Information and consultation are defined as procedures that involve employee representatives according to national laws or practices. This means that the UK will have to ensure there is a right to employee information and consultation at either the undertaking and/or establishment level.

■ The Directive states that information and consultation rights must apply to:

  (a) Information on the recent and probable development of the undertaking's or the establishment's activities and economic situation.
  (b) Information and consultation on the situation, structure and probable development of employment, and on any anticipatory measures envisaged, in particular any threats to employment.
  (c) Information and consultation on decisions likely to lead to substantial changes in work organisation or in contractual relations.

■ Information must be given with sufficient time and in such fashion to enable employee representatives to conduct an adequate study of the information and prepare for consultation.

■ The arrangements can differ from those in the Directive provided they have been agreed by management and labour at the appropriate level in advance and in congruence with the general principles of the Directive.

■ Employee representatives will be required to treat certain information as confidential.

■ The Directive has been drafted in very general and broad terms to allow management and labour flexibility in respect of the practical arrangements at either the undertaking or enterprise level.

■ Sanctions for non-compliance must be effective, proportionate and dissuasive.

■ The Directive requires implementation by March 2005. However, countries with no 'general, permanent and statutory' system of information and consultation (i.e., the UK and Ireland) may apply the Directive in three phases:

  ■ Undertakings with at least 150 employees (or establishments with at least 100 employees) must be covered by March 2005.

  ■ Undertakings with at least 100 employees (or establishments with at least 50 employees) must be covered by March 2007.

  ■ Full application of the Directive (to undertakings with 50 or establishments with at least 20 employees) will be required from March 2008.

Source: Adapted from Hall *et al.* 2002

This provides the opportunity for management and employee representatives to define and negotiate their own voluntary arrangements; a principle that is not too dissimilar to voluntary arrangements contained in the European Works Council Directive.

The British government recently published regulations in relation to how the directive will be implemented in the UK (DTI 2005). Following discussions with the UK government, TUC and CBI, it is proposed that the regulations will be voluntary and apply to undertakings with 50 or more employees. The key features of the UK *Information and Consultation of Employees Regulations 2004* (ICE) are summarised in Box 15.2.

Box 15.2: Information and Consultation of Employees (ICE) Regulations 2004

- The regulations apply to undertakings in Great Britain with 50 or more employees. Equivalent legislation will be made in respect of Northern Ireland.

- The legal requirement to inform and consult employees is not automatic. A formal request has to be made by employees, or by an employer initiating the process (an employer notification).

- An employer must establish information and consultation procedures where a valid request has been made by employees.

- Such a request must be made in writing by 10% of employees in an undertaking (subject to a minimum of 15 and a maximum of 2,500 employees).

- Where the employees making the request wish to remain anonymous, they can submit the request to an independent body (such as the Central Arbitration Committee of ACAS).

- The employer would have the opportunity to organise a ballot of employees to endorse or reject the initial request.

- An employer can continue with pre-existing information and consultation arrangements, provided that such arrangements have been agreed prior to an employee written request and:

  (i) the agreement is in writing, including any collective agreements with trade unions;
  (ii) the agreement covers all employees in the undertaking;
  (iii) the agreement sets-out how the employer is to provide the information and seek employee views for consultation; and
  (iv) the arrangements have been agreed by the employees

- If an employee request is to change a pre-existing agreement already in place in an undertaking, then 40% plus a major of those voting must endorse the request. The employer is then obliged to reach a negotiated agreement with genuine employee representatives.

- Where fewer than 40% of employees endorse the request, the employer would be able to continue with pre-existing arrangements.

- The parties have 6 months to reach a negotiated agreement (extendable by agreement).

- Where a valid request (or employer notification) has been made, but no agreement reached, standard information and consultation provisions based on ICE Regulation 18 would apply.

- Where the standard information and consultation provisions apply, the employer shall arrange for a ballot to elect the employee representatives. Regulation 19 states that there shall be 1 representative per 50 employees, or part thereof, with a minimum of 2 and maximum of 25 representatives.

- Consultation should take place with a view to reaching agreement on decisions.

- Information must be given in such time, and in such fashion and with such content as are appropriate to enable the information and consultation representatives to conduct an adequate study and, where necessary, prepare for consultation.

- There are no prescriptive standard provisions and it is expected that these will vary from organisation to organisation. The standard provisions are based on Article 4 of the EU Directive. ICE Regulation 20 states that I&C representatives, once elected, must have the opportunity to meet with the employer and give their opinion on matters subject to consultation, with a view to reaching agreement. The employer must give a reasoned response to I&C representatives' views.

- Enforcement regulations do not apply to pre-existing agreements.

- A complaint regarding a negotiated agreement, or a failure to comply with standard provisions, must be brought to the CAC within 3 months of the alleged failure.

- Where the CAC uphold a complaint for failure to comply, the complainant may make an application to the Employment Appeal Tribunal (EAT). An appeal must be made within 42 days of the date on which written notification of the CAC declaration is sent.

- The maximum penalty for failing to comply with a declaration made by the CAC is £75,000.

- ICE Regulations 25 and 26 provide for the confidentiality of sensitive information given to I&C representatives.

- I&C representatives, and employees making a request, are protected against discrimination/unfair dismissal for exercising their rights under the ICE Regulations.

- I&C representatives are to be afforded paid time-off to carry out their duties.

Source: DTI 2005

 ## Conclusions

In this chapter we have outlined, briefly, the context of employee participation over the last few decades and pointed towards future directions through more recent European regulations. We have also considered the changing contours of management choice, public policy and that the adoption of various participation schemes is often uneven and complicated. In short, a range of schemes tend to co-exist within an organisation. Moreover, we have sought to stress that the meanings and interpretations of such schemes are much more important than the type or number of techniques adopted. What is important is the depth to which participatory mechanisms are integrated with other organisational practices, the scope to which workers have a genuine say over matters that affect them, and the level at which participation occurs.

These factors are now influenced and shaped by a new British and European policy environment for employee participation. The case for industrial democracy in the 1960s and 1970s gave way to a neo-liberal climate in the 1980s and early 1990s, with an assumption that the state would remain largely absent from the employment relationship. Since 1997, British and EU initiatives have introduced a new policy framework which is having an impact on the approaches to participation (Ewing 2003). However, this impact is complex, belying simplistic dichotomies between state regulation and management choice for certain involvement schemes. Public policy neither represents a continuation of management-led involvement of the 1980s, nor a rolling-back to the 1970s premise for industrial democracy. Instead, elements of a new regulatory dialectic are beginning to emerge with its own dynamics (Ackers *et al.* 2005).

At one level, the current practices of participation appear more embedded and less fragmented than they did in the early 1990s (Wilkinson *et al.* 2004). Attempts have been made to consolidate and integrate different involvement and participation mechanisms over time (Marchington *et al.* 2001). In some situations, the adversarial nature of shop floor relations appears to have partially diminished, with a new generation of union representatives willing and able to sit alongside non-union employee representatives on joint consultative forums. The dualism in 1980s, of separated direct (individual) and indirect (union) involvement channels seems to be more intermingled with a range of schemes that overlap in there approach.

According to Willman *et al.* (2003) employers choosing voice regimes prior to 1960 did so in circumstances where union-based participation regimes were common exemplars and where there were normative and mimetic pressures to avoid non-union only regimes. The risk-averse option was a dual-channel of voice. However, over time with the shift from manufacturing to services and inward investments, non-union examples have become much more commonplace (Beardwell 1994; Millward *et al.* 1992, 2000). Where union participation exists it is highly likely to do so as part of a dual-channel voice regime. In terms of choice, employers can 'make' voice through HR professionals or 'buy' voice through unions. As HRM professionals and the spread of HRM have become common the default option in the choice of voice regime has shifted over time in the UK from union to non-union, from make to buy or, in union-recognised establishments, negotiation has been relegated to consultation or communication (Marchington and Parker 1990). Switching costs, however, makes the options for participation 'sticky', with radical switching (from union to non-union and vice versa) rare (Willman *et al.* 2003).

Taken together, these developments suggest that the current policy environment holds better prospects for participation, partly as a result of greater EU regulation and partly because management has learned from the limitation of a weak form and a shallow depth to the participation initiatives of the 1980s. What remains problematic is that many managers find the European language of employment rights, with a renewed focus on more collectivist employee participation, unpalatable and even alien to newer organisational cultures shaped by flatter and leaner market environments. This tension is significant as managers play a key part in interpreting legislative requirements into practice in the workplace. In this regard employee participation is best understood not in terms of particular techniques or discrete typologies located along a static either/or continuum, but rather as a set of complex and uneven meanings and interpretations shaped by external regulation as well as internal stakeholder expectations for greater choice and voice. The challenges that lie ahead are how such a dynamic will be played out in practice, and whether existing multiple schemes for participation will be integrated or the whether a new policy framework will result in another 'missed opportunity' for British managers (Wilkinson *et al.* 1992).

CASE STUDY 15.1

EMPLOYEE VOICE AT COMPUCOM

TONY DUNDON, IRENA GRUGULIS AND ADRIAN WILKINSON

Compucom is a small to medium-sized enterprise. It is non-unionised, though uses a variety of participation techniques that might be found in a more traditional unionised manufacturing facility, including a non-union employee–management consultative council. The company was founded on the principle of designing and manufacturing microcomputers for dedicated purposes. It was started in 1982 on a £6,000 overdraft by three friends, and now employs around 220 people in five different countries with a turnover in excess of £30 million per annum. About 90 technical and IT staff work at the head office in the UK, with 100 employees based at a manufacturing plant in Malta. Another 30 employees work in the distribution and sales offices in the US, Belgium, Asia and Australia.

There are two main ways in which employee participation occurs at Compucom. First, direct systems for employees to be able to articulate their voice are channelled through **monthly team briefings** and **informal day-to-day communications** between staff and team leaders. This is facilitated to a large extent by a **matrix teamworking** structure. Staff members from different functions in the company are established into one team to decide how to complete a task or develop a new product. The team is then disbanded once the task has been completed. Management prefer this direct employee voice method, viewing it as appropriate where employees have a significant degree of professional freedom in their job. The second way employee voice is practised is indirect. Unlike most non-union companies, Compucom has a **works council** that meets on a bi-monthly basis (UK site only). There are ten 'elected' employee representatives and the personnel manager chairs the council. The council considers various work-and non-work-related matters, ranging from employee welfare programmes, staffing levels and health and safety. However, the council does not review pay or terms and conditions of employment. The personnel manager feels that the council is valuable in that it helps to reinforce company communications that add a degree of legitimacy to organisational change. For most of the time management regard the consultative council as a 'comfort blanket' for staff. Similarly, employees prefer to have the opportunity to express their concerns to management through a representative rather direct to their immediate supervisor on some occasions.

Compucom espouse the virtues of employee participation as a source of competitive advantage. There is a strong belief that obtaining employee views helps with product development, quality and better individual performance while also promoting trust. Examples of employee-led new initiatives include a new flexi-time attendance pattern, which corresponded to a reduction in absenteeism shortly after the introduction of flexi-time working. The suggestion emerged from employees themselves and was endorsed by the works council.

Barriers to employee participation at Compucom seem to be minimal. Some line managers felt they were less 'people-centred' than the company now expected, and this caused some tension when communicating at a team level. In other areas employees lacked interest in the works council and some employee representative seats remained vacant. Overall, team briefings are central employee participation, and actual decision making remains the prerogative of senior managers.

Questions

1. In relation to the framework for analysing employee participation described earlier in the chapter, where would you locate Compucom in terms of the 'depth' and 'scope' of their participation practices?

2. Do you think the use of a non-union consultative council helps Compucom management remain union-free? Why/Why not?

3. Do you think the size of the company is an important factor in the nature of employee participation practised at Compucom?

4. Why is it difficult to establish a relationship between employee voice and organisational performance?

ASSESSING PARTICIPATION

TONY DUNDON

Debating the case for and against participation

In Chapter 15 we reviewed the changing policy context for employee participation, in particular the on-going tension between management choices for employee participation and recent European regulations for consultation rights. Prepare an argument 'for' the legislation on employee information and consultation. Explain your argument in a class debate with co-students, who will speak 'against' your position.

Advising on employee participation

Imagine you are a management consultant. Your services have recently been retained by a large multi-national company (17,000 employees in the UK) to provide a report on the implications of the *Information and Consultation of Employees (ICE) Regulations 2004*. The company already has a European Works Council (EWC) and a union recognition agreement with AMICUS-MSF. Union membership is currently 38 per cent of the entire workforce. In particular, the company would like:

(a) a brief explanation of what the ICE Regulations mean,
(b) a timeframe for when the Regulations are likely to affect the company, and
(c) your considered opinion of any specific implications particular to this company.

Explain and justify the information you include in the report.

BEVERAGE CO.: employee participation in an SME

TONY DUNDON, IRENA GRUGULIS
AND ADRIAN WILKINSON

Introduction

Employee participation (EP) has retained a central role in HRM over the last two decades (Marchington *et al.* 2001; Marchington and Wilkinson 2005). It can be seen as a key component of best-practice HRM or high-commitment management (Pfeffer 1998). However, much of the research on employee participation has focused on 'large' or 'mainstream' organisations where a combination of techniques tend to coexist (Marchington *et al.* 2001). Here we report on EP in a small organisation. Because of the apparent absence of formalised relations within many SMEs, the role of EP may be qualitatively different from that in larger firms (Wilkinson *et al.* 1999). It can be less formal given the nature of communication flows together with the flexibility that is often associated with a small social setting (Scott *et al.* 1989; Dundon and Wilkinson 2003). While such informality has been a long-standing feature in the following case study, the range of EP techniques introduced was limited and at times problematic. In particular, the managerial motives for EP were not always understood among employees and the objective of greater employee commitment and loyalty was unsuccessful. The use of employee participation techniques tended to work against rather than with the informal character of relations that had existed previously in the company.

The Company

Beverage Co. manufactures intermediary products for the food and drink industry. It employs 150 workers between its head office in Manchester and a manufacturing site in Cheshire. There is union recognition for around 65 process operatives based at the manufacturing plant. Here, the nature of work is organised around distinct production cells. Each production cell comprises approximately 10 employees all of whom work on different production lines which make food and drink flavourings, including vanilla, coke, soup and meat additives. A similar team structure exists at the head office with clerical workers engaged in administration, sales and marketing. There is no union recognition for these employees and, despite several requests from the GMB union, management has decided to keep this side of the business non-unionised.

In the late 1990s Beverage Co. experienced a period of commercial uncertainty. It faced increasing UK competition for food and drinks flavourings, lost a few export contracts and, in 1997, made 10 workers redundant. This was the first time that Beverage Co. had ever experienced any form of job losses. The company had been owned by members of the same family for more than a century and their management style was characterised by benevolent paternalism. However, with increased market competition, declining profits and redundancy the company's owners decided to distance Beverage Co. from its informal industrial relations history. In its place they introduced a more strategic form of human resource management, much of which included several employee participation schemes.

EP techniques and management style at Beverage Co.

This new HR strategy had a profound impact on organisational culture and management style. In the past family-owners were highly paternalist and the industrial relations procedures were informal. Indeed, the previous chairman and managing director, descendants of the founding owner, were known for stopping production quite regularly and asking manual employees to help repair the family Bentley, Jaguar and collection of classic sports cars. This all changed when non-family members were appointed to senior management and board-level positions. A personnel department was established with the aim of formalising HR policies and practices across the two sites. Key performance targets for profits, quality and customer satisfaction were linked to staff appraisals. Merit pay was introduced and based on individual outputs, monitored and assessed by team leaders. In describing this approach the new MD regarded the strategy as 'a route to building a world class organisation'. The range of EP techniques that helped support this objective are summarised in Table 1.

Table 1   EP techniques introduced at Beverage Co.

EP Category	EP Technique Introduced
Downward communications	Staff newsletter Notice boards Electronic message boards (manual staff only) E-mail communications (clerical staff only) Site-wide meetings by MD Team/cell briefings by team leaders Personnel management surgeries Individual performance reviews/appraisals
Upward problem solving	Staff suggestion scheme Staff attitude surveys
Task participation	None
Financial involvement	Merit pay
Representative participation	Company Joint Consultative Committee

'Downward communication' was the most extensive of all forms of EP at Beverage Co. These included a quarterly staff newsletter, monthly team briefings, formal presentations by the MD to the whole workforce (held twice a year in the staff canteen), e-mail communications and electronic message boards informing employees about new products, quality initiatives and conveying financial information. The company-wide presentations by the MD explained company objectives, profit details and more general developments to staff, such as the company's Investors in People (IiP) accreditation.

However the introduction of these communication techniques was met with suspicion among some employees. Team leaders who held monthly briefings were regarded as 'supervisors on the cheap' by many staff. In effect, team leaders were the same grade as other workers but were also required to carry out briefing sessions without extra pay. The personnel manager compiled the information and team leaders then cascaded this down to shop floor level. In addition, the site-wide meetings introduced by the new MD were also questioned. Several workers suggested that the information presented was often partial with management controlling the agenda. One middle manager explained:

> There's a reluctance to show the whole picture. We have canteen meetings but they're controlled, the information is very selective. That's a general feeling; that not all the info is given out.

Across the manufacturing plant, electronic notice boards would regularly 'flash' with messages from the personnel department. Typical examples included the latest figures for customer complaints, current absenteeism rates or the volume of products made hour by hour and compared against the expected target. As one process operator commented during his lunch in the canteen:

> There's no getting away from them [i.e. management messages] here.

Other EP mechanisms included a 'weekly surgery' held by the personnel manager. The aim was to allow employees to discuss issues of concern in private without appointment. In addition, a staff suggestion scheme was introduced to encourage workers to make improvements to product quality. A financial payment ranging from £10 to £1,000 was given for adopted suggestions. Individual staff appraisals were also introduced for supervisors and workers to discuss objectives for the coming months.

In practice these EP techniques fell short of their intended objective, as few employees would attend such initiatives as the weekly surgery. According to the personnel manager, the time devoted to meeting staff in surgeries was often taken up discussing grievances with shop stewards. Several clerical employees were also critical of the staff suggestion scheme, especially the lack of any formal criteria for determining the amount of financial award. Further, employees at both sites commented that any 'discussion' about appraisal plans was a myth, as supervisors tended to 'inform' workers about new targets without any consultation. Overall, the range of EP at Beverage Co. can be seen to fit broadly those categories where management maintains greatest control, namely downward communications. Significantly, these 'newer' techniques tended to bureaucratise and formalise employee relations, as one production supervisor commented:

> Too much communications in one sense – we've forgotten to use general conversation. They try and make things too formal, thinking it's a better way, which isn't always the case.

Indirect forms of EP were reduced at Beverage Co. in favour of the more direct techniques described above. Representative participation remained with the GMB union for manufacturing employees, although a former bi-monthly joint consultative committee (JCC) met on a quarterly basis, and its remit was restricted to heath and safety matters. Previously it had dealt with all employment terms and conditions. Similarly, collective bargaining became the responsibility of two local shop stewards, the MD and personnel manager. Previously a full-time regional official had negotiated pay with family-owners. The pay rise for non-union clerical employees was reviewed by the personnel manager, and usually set in accordance with the negotiated settlement for manual workers. In addition, merit pay accounted for up to 10 per cent of the gross salary for most staff, determined on the basis of targets set by supervisors.

Table 15.3 provides a summary of employee responses to a survey conducted at Beverage Co. by the authors. While workers confirmed that management pass on information (52 per cent) and encouraged staff to make suggestions (82 per cent), only 15 per cent of respondents said that management acted on such suggestions. Overall there were few positive responses to the range of EP techniques introduced. One-quarter of employees suggested that management sought their views while over 80 per cent disagreed with the statement that management involved them in decisions.

Workplace sabotage at Beverage Co.

Shortly after these EP techniques were introduced a series of sabotage attacks were carried out at the manufacturing plant. The production unit in question manufactured food flavourings for a contract in the Far East. The company eventually lost the contract because of the sabotage incidents, which took a variety of forms. Flavouring products were labelled incorrectly, such that beef stocks were marked as vegetable soup ingredients and

Table 15.3 Employee responses (%) to EP at Beverage Co.

EP indicator	Agree	Not sure	Disagree
At Beverage Co. management regularly seek the views of employees	25	21	54
Employees are kept informed about changes at Beverage Co.	36	7	57
Management pass on information regularly	52	12	36
Management involve employees in decisions at Beverage Co.	9	10	81
Management encourage staff to make suggestions	82	13	5
Management at Beverage Co. act on staff suggestions	15	25	60

N = 67

garlic batches packaged as cola additives. Other acts included racial and sexual graffiti written inside cartons. The commercial impact of these events was highly significant. Beverage Co. flavourings form essential ingredients for food and drinks made by other organisations. Not only did this sabotage damage Beverage Co.'s reputation it also, owing to the intermediary character of the products, resulted in lost production of thousands of tonnes of food and drinks products. When incorrectly labelled food flavourings were used to produce final goods manufactured by Beverage Co.'s customers, these subsequently had to be destroyed.

Management were anxious to attribute these problems to the youth and immaturity of workers employed on the particular production line. One supervisor attributed the sabotage to the use of agency staff brought in to help meet sudden demand. For the shop steward, however, the sabotage was a form of resistance to increased supervisory pressures and poor working conditions. The nature of work was explained as dirty, dusty and intense. Interestingly, the system of cell working meant that management failed to identify the culprits. It was common for employees to work on several flavouring production lines simultaneously and switch to packaging duties during the same shift. As a result, management could not identify the employees who had been working on specific duties at the time of the sabotage.

Questions

1. What are the likely benefits for workers of employee participation as practised at Beverage Co.? Are these likely to differ in each of the union and non-union parts of the company? Why / Why Not?

2. The family owners of Beverage Co. have asked you to produce a report (or a short presentation) on the efficacy of EP in the company. Using the information in the case study identify the main barriers to EP, and make recommendations to help the new management team gain the commitment of staff to these (or other) techniques?

3. What influence has the small firm context had on EP at Beverage Co.?

4. Should trade unions be worried about the introduction of EP techniques? Why / Why Not?

5. To what extent has the change in management style and HR strategy exacerbated the tensions and contradictions in the employment relationship at Beverage Co.?

References

Dundon, T. and Wilkinson, A. (2003) 'Employment relations in smaller firms', in B. Towers, *Handbook of Employment Relations, Law and Practice* (4th edn), London: Kogan Page.

Marchington, M. and Wilkinson, A. (2005) 'Direct participation and involvement', in S. Bach, *Personnel Management in Britain* (4th edn), Oxford: Blackwell.

Marchington, M., Wilkinson, A., Ackers, P. and Dundon, T. (2001) *Management Choice and Employee Voice*, London: CIPD.

Pfeffer, J. (1998), *The Human Equation: Building Profits by Putting People First*, Boston, MA: Harvard Business School Press.

Scott, M., Roberts, I., Holroyd, G. and Sawbridge, D. (1989) *Management and Industrial Relations in Small Firms,* Research Paper, No.70, London: Department of Employment.

Schuler, R., and Jackson, S. (1987) 'Linking competitive strategies with human resource management', *Academy of Management Executives,* Vol.1, No.3, pp.206–19.

References

Ackers, P., Marchington, M., Wilkinson, A. and Goodman, J. (1992) 'The use of cycles? Explaining employee involvement in the 1990s', *Industrial Relations Journal,* Vol.23, No.4, pp.268–83.

*Ackers, P., Marchington, M., Wilkinson, A. and Dundon, T. (2005) 'Partnership and voice, with or without trade unions: changing UK management approaches to organisational participation', in M. Stuart and M. Martinez Lucio (eds) *Partnership and Modernisation in Employment Relations,* London: Routledge.

Barker, J. (1993) 'Tightening the iron cage: concertive control in self-managing teams', *Administrative Science Quarterly,* Vol.38, pp.408–37.

Beardwell, I. (1994) 'Managerial issues and the non-union firm', paper presented to the Centre for Economic Performance Workshop, London School of Economics, April.

Becker, B.E. and Huselid, M.A. (1998) 'High performance work systems and firm performance synthesis of research and managerial implications', in G.R. Ferris (ed.) *Research in Personnel and Human Resources,* Vol.16, Stamford, CT: JAI Press.

Benson, J. (2000) 'Employee voice in union and non-union Australian workplaces', *British Journal of Industrial Relations.* Vol.38, No.3, pp.453–9.

Boxall, P. and Purcell, J. (2003) *Strategy and Human Resource Management,* London: Palgrave.

Brannen, P. (1983) *Authority and Participation in Industry,* London: Batsford.

Bullock, A. (Lord) (1977) *Report of the Committee of Inquiry on Industrial Democracy,* London: HMSO (Cmnd. 6706).

Claydon, T. and Doyle, M. (1996) 'Trusting me, trusting you? The ethics of employee empowerment', *Personnel Review,* Vol.25, No.6, pp.13–25.

Collard, R. and Dale, B. (1989) 'Quality circles', in K. Sisson (ed.) *Personnel Management in Britain,* (1st edn), Oxford: Blackwell.

Cox, A., Zagelmeyer, S. and Marchington, M. (2003) 'The embeddedness of employee involvement and participation (EIP) and its impact on employee outcomes: an analysis of WERS98', paper presented at European Group for Organisation Studies (EGOS), Copenhagen.

Cressey, P., Eldridge, J. and MacInnes, J. (1985) *Just Managing: Authority and Democracy in Industry,* Milton Keynes: Open University Press.

Cully, M., O'Reilly A., Millward, N., Forth, J., Woodland, S., Dix, G. and Bryson, A. (1998) *The 1998 Workplace Employee Relations Survey: First Findings,* Department of Trade and Industry, London: HMSO.

Cully M., O'Reilly A., Woodland, S. and Dix, G. (1999) *Britain at Work: As Depicted by the 1998 Workplace Employee Relations Survey,* London: Routledge.

Delbridge, R., Turnbull, P. and Wilkinson, B. (1992) 'Pushing back the frontiers: management control and work intensification under JIT/TQM factory regimes', *New Technology, Work and Employment,* Vol.7, No.2, pp.97–106.

*Department of Trade and Industry (2005) *The Information and Consultation of Employees Regulations 2004: DTI Guidance,* January 2005, London: DTI. (http://www.dti.gov.uk/er/consultation/i_c_regs_guidance.pdf)

Diamond, W. and Freeman, R. (2001) *What Workers Want from Workplace Organisations: Report to the TUCs Promoting Unionism Task Group,* London: Trades Union Congress.

Dundon, T., Grugulis, I. and Wilkinson, A. (1999) 'Looking out of the black hole: non-union relations in an SME', *Employee Relations*, Vol.21, No.3, pp.251–66.

*Dundon, T., Wilkinson, A., Marchington, M. and Ackers, P. (2004) 'The meanings and purpose of employee voice', *International Journal of Human Resource Management*, Vol.15, No.6, pp.1150–71.

Dundon, T. and Rollinson, D. (2004) *Employment Relations in Non-Union Firms*, London: Routledge.

Ewing, K. (2003) 'Industrial relations and law', in P. Ackers and A. Wilkinson (eds) *Understanding Work and Employment: Industrial Relations in Transition*, Oxford: Oxford University Press.

*Geary, J. (2003) 'New Forms of work organizations: still limited, still controlled, but still welcome?', in P. Edwards (ed.) *Industrial Relations: Theory and Practice in Britain* (2nd edn), Oxford: Blackwell.

Geary, J. and Dobbins, A. (2001) 'Teamworking: a new dynamic in the pursuit of management control', *Human Resource Management Journal*, Vol.11, No.1, pp.3–23.

*Gollan, P. (2002), 'So what's the news? Management strategies towards non-union employee representation at New International', *Industrial Relations Journal*, Vol.33, No.4, pp.316–31.

Goodman, J., Earnshaw, J., Marchington, M. and Harrison, R. (1998) 'Unfair dismissal cases, disciplinary procedures, recruitment methods and management style', *Employee Relations*, Vol.20, No.6, pp.536–50.

Hall, M., Broughton, A., Carley, M. and Sisson, K. (2002) *Work Councils for the UK? Assessing the Impact of the EU Employee Consultation Directive*, London: IRS/IRRU.

Heller, F., Pusic, E., Strauss, G. and Wilpert, B. (1998) *Organisational Participation: Myth and Reality*, Oxford: Oxford University Press.

Huselid, M. (1995), 'The impact of human resource management practices on turnover, production and corporate financial performance', *Academy of Management Journal*, Vol.38, No.3, pp.635–72.

Hyman, J. and Mason, B. (1995) *Managing Employee Involvement and Participation*, London: Sage.

Lewis, P., Thornhill, A. and Saunders, M. (2003) *Employee Relations: Understanding the Employment Relationship*, London: Prentice Hall.

Marchington, M. (2005) 'Employee involvement: patterns and explanations', in B. Harley, J. Hyman and P. Thompson (eds) *Participation and Democracy at Work: Essays in Honour of Harvie Ramsay*, London: Palgrave.

Marchington, M. and Parker, P. (1990) *Changing Patterns of Employee Relations*, Hemel Hempstead: Harvester Wheatsheaf.

Marchington, M., Goodman, J. Wilkinson, A. and Ackers, P. (1992) *New Developments in Employee Involvement*, Research Paper No.2, London: Employment Department.

Marchington, M., Wilkinson, A., Ackers, P. and Dundon, T. (2001) *Management Choice and Employee Voice*, London: CIPD.

*Marchington, M. and Wilkinson, A. (2005) 'Direct participation', in S. Bach (ed.) *Personnel Management: A Comprehensive Guide to Theory and Practice* (4th edn), Oxford: Blackwell.

Millward, N., Stevens, M., Smart, D. and Hawes, W (1992) *Workplace Industrial Relations in Transition*, Aldershot: Dartmouth.

Millward, N., Bryson, A. and Forth, J. (2000) *All Change at Work: British Employment Relations 1980–1998 as Portrayed by the Workplace Industrial Relations Survey Series*, London: Routledge.

Pateman, C. (1970) *Participation and Democratic Theory*, Cambridge: Cambridge University Press.

Patterson, M., West, M., Lawthorn, R. and Nickell, S. (1997) *Impact of People Management Practices on Business Performance*, London: IPD, Report No.22.

Pfeffer, J. (1998) *The Human Equation: Building Profits by Putting People First*, Boston, MA: Harvard Business School Press.

Piore, M. and Sabel, C. (1983) *The Second Industrial Divide*, New York: Basic Books.

Proctor, S. and Mueller, F. (eds) (2000) *Teamworking*, London: Macmillan.

Proctor, S. and Ackroyd, S. (2001) 'Flexibility', in T. Redman and A. Wilkinson (eds) *Contemporary Human Resource Management: Text and Cases*, London: Prentice Hall.

Roeber, J. (1975) *Social Change at Work*, London: Heinemann.

Sewell, G. and Wilkinson, B. (1992) 'Empowerment or emasculation? Shopfloor surveillance in a total quality organisation', in P. Blyton and P. Turnbull (eds) *Reassessing Human Resource Management*, London: Sage.

Sinclair, A. (1992) 'The tyranny of a team ideology', *Organization Studies*, Vol.13, No.4, pp.11–26.

Sisson, K. (2002) 'The information and consultation directive: unnecessary "regulation" or an opportunity to promote "partnership"?', *Warwick Papers in Industrial Relations*, No.67, Industrial Relations Research Unit (IRRU), Warwick University, Coventry.

Tebbutt, M. and Marchington, M. (1997) 'Look before you speak: gossip and the insecure workplace', *Work Employment and Society*, Vol.11, No.4, pp.713–35.

Trist, E., Higgin, G., Murray, H. and Pollock, A. (1963) *Organisational Choice: Capabilities of Groups at the Coalface Under Changing Technologies*, London: Tavistock Institute.

Wedderburn, K.W. (Lord) (1986) *The Worker and the Law* (3rd edn), Harmondsworth: Penguin.

*Wilkinson, A. (2002) 'Empowerment', in M. Poole and M. Warner (eds) *International Encyclopaedia of Business and Management Handbook of Human Resource Management*, London: ITB Press.

Wilkinson, A., Marchington, M., Goodman, J. and Ackers, P. (1992) 'Total quality management and employee involvement', *Human Resource Management Journal*, Vol.2, No.4, pp.1–20.

Wilkinson, A., Redman, T., Snape, E. and Marchington, M. (1998) *Managing With TQM: Theory and Practice*, London: Macmillan.

Wilkinson, A., Dundon, T., Marchington, M. and Ackers, P. (2004) 'Changing patterns of employee voice', *Journal of Industrial Relations*, Vol.46, No.3, pp.298–322.

Willman, P., Bryson, A. and Gomez, R. (2003) 'Why do voice regimes differ?', paper presented at International Industrial Relations Association (IIRA) 13th World Congress, 8–12 September, Berlin.

Wood, S. and De Menezes, L. (1998) 'High commitment management in the UK: evidence from the Workplace Industrial Relations Survey and Employers' Manpower Skills Survey', *Human Relations*, Vol.51, No.4, pp.485–515.

Wood, S. and Fenton-O'Creevy, M. (1999) 'Channel hopping', *People Management*, 25 November, pp.42–5.

* Useful reading

Chapter 16

KNOWLEDGE MANAGEMENT

Donald Hislop

Introduction

While enormous quantities of ink have been spilled on the topic of knowledge management, and even though vast numbers of organisations have implemented (or attempted to implement) knowledge management initiatives, it can still be seen as a topic at a relatively young stage of development. Thus, within the knowledge management literature there are still many areas of debate (Can knowledge be codified? Can knowledge be managed? Do we live in a knowledge society? What are the best methods of persuading workers to share their knowledge with each other?), and many areas where understanding is somewhat limited. One of the areas where understanding is still relatively limited is in the linkages between knowledge management and the broad topic of human resource management. This is to some extent because HRM academics/writers have been more reluctant to engage with the topic than academics and writers in other disciplines. While the amount of writing on the linkages between these topics has grown from a trickle, the amount of contemporary published work on this area can best be described as a steady flow rather than a torrent. This is somewhat of a paradox given the way 'people management' issues have been identified as being fundamentally important in the knowledge management literature.

The objective of this chapter is to illustrate why HRM issues are of central importance to the topic of knowledge management, and to give an overview of the way that the topics have been linked thus far in the literature. In doing so, the chapter will give a flavour of the many active debates and disagreements which still exist. Before proceeding any further, however, it is necessary to define the term knowledge management. At one level this is a simple task. Putting to the side the difficulties of defining such ambiguous terms as 'knowledge' and 'management' (Alvesson and Karreman 2001), knowledge management can be defined as the attempt by an organisation to explicitly manage and control the knowledge of its workforce. However, the issue becomes more complex when it is recognised that there are a myriad number of ways by which such a task can be attempted. This can be illustrated by the number of typologies of knowledge management strategies that have been developed. One of the simplest, and most widely known is Hansen *et al.*'s (1999) distinction between personalisation and codification strategies, with a personalisation strategy focused on sharing knowledge between people, linked to a business strategy of knowledge creation. On the other hand, a codification strategy is focused on the codification of knowledge, linked to a business strategy of knowledge re-use. Hunter *et al.* (2002) and Alvesson and Karreman (2001) develop more complicated typologies, both of which produce four general knowledge management strategies. Of central significance to this chapter is that, as will be discussed in more detail later, the HRM implications of these different knowledge management strategies are quite distinctive.

The chapter begins by briefly examining the broad social context within which the growth of interest in knowledge management has occurred. Following this, subsequent sections consider why human motivation is key to making knowledge management initiatives successful, what general factors affect the willingness of workers to participate in knowledge management initiatives, and what specific HRM practices can be used to help persuade workers to participate in such initiatives. The chapter closes with an extended section looking at the more narrow and specific topic of knowledge workers, and how to manage them.

Social context: the growing importance of knowledge

The growth of interest in knowledge management that occurred in the mid-1990s can be to some extent explained by the growing significance of knowledge in contemporary economies. This has led many, both within and without the knowledge management literature to claim that we now live in a knowledge society (see for example Nonaka (1994), one of the 'gurus' of knowledge management). Thus, Littler and Innes (2003) suggest that the 'knowledge capitalism thesis' was one of the two dominant academic discourses during the 1990s and Tam *et al.* (2002) argue that such a belief has become 'conventional wisdom.' Bell's (1973) vision of a post-industrial service society with a workforce dominated by highly skilled knowledge workers thus, either explicitly, or implicitly casts a shadow over much of this writing.

To some extent empirical evidence backs up this claim , however, as will be seen later, this is one area of debate. The growing importance of knowledge to contemporary economies and organisations can be illustrated in a number of ways. First, since the 1950s there has been a growth of the proportion of knowledge workers in many economies. Reich (1991) showed that in the USA, between the 1950s and the 1990s, 'symbolic analysts' (his term for what contemporary writers call knowledge workers) grew from 8 to 20 per cent of the workforce. Contemporary evidence from other economies also supports this (Frenkel *et al.* 1999). Other claims that the knowledge intensity of all work has increased (see for example Harrison and Leitch 2000; Neef 1999) is supported by large-scale survey evidence which shows a general trajectory of upskilling to be evident (Gallie *et al.* 1998; Felstead *et al.* 2002).

Critics, however, suggest that such claims and evidence provide only a partial and distorted view of the changes in the nature of work, neglecting the extent to which there has been a simultaneous growth in low-skilled, routine service work, such as in call centres (Littler and Innes 2003; Mansell and Steinmueller 2000; Thompson *et al.* 2001). These writers suggest it is more accurate to talk of a bi-modal trajectory in the contemporary evolution of work, with there being a simultaneous growth in highly skilled knowledge work, and low-skilled, routine service work. Thus, even if a sceptical perspective is taken to the 'knowledge society' rhetoric, it is undeniable that, to some extent, there has been a growth in the importance of knowledge in contemporary economies.

Arguably, the enormous numbers of organisations which have been attempting to develop and implement knowledge management initiatives are inspired by the idea that their competitiveness and innovativeness is derived and sustained from the way they manage, facilitate and control their knowledge base, and that neglecting to do so is likely to have some negative consequences for organisational performance.

Why worker motivation is key to achieving participation in knowledge management initiatives

As the knowledge management literature has evolved and developed there has been a growing awareness that socio-cultural factors are key to such initiatives. For example, survey evidence consistently reveals this:

■ KPMG (2000) conducted a survey of over 400 organisations in the USA and western Europe and found the most important reason for the failure of knowledge management initiatives to be poor communication.

■ Edwards *et al.* (2003) in a survey of 25 academics and KM practitioners, identified 'people' and 'cultural' issues as the two key issues to be emphasised for knowledge management initiatives to be successful.

A plethora of case study evidence also reinforces this conclusion, with evidence of knowledge hoarding due to social factors not being uncommon (see example below, plus Hayes and Walsham 2000; Newell *et al.* 2000).

Functional conflict and knowledge hoarding

UK-Pharm, a large, specialised UK-based pharmaceutical company with sites and business units spread throughout the UK, Europe and the USA, attempted to introduce a change programme in the late 1990s to encourage cross-functional knowledge sharing, as this was perceived as being a way to improve the effectiveness of its R&D efforts. However, the success of the project was inhibited by a general lack of willingness among staff from different functions to share knowledge with each other. A significant proportion of staff were unwilling to participate in the project to some extent because there had been a historical culture of inter-functional rivalry, which tended to make staff unwilling to cooperate with staff from outside their functional group, and also because many senior managers in certain functional areas felt that the change programme would reduce their level of autonomy and lead to greater levels of standardisation.

Source: Hislop 2003

Part of the explanation for why workers cannot be assumed to be automatically willing to participate in knowledge management initiatives is due to structural factors which transcend individual organisations including the power and status workers can typically derive from possessing specialist knowledge, the nature of employment relationship, and the potential for inter-personal/group conflict that exists in all organisations. First, not only is much organisational knowledge tacit and personal in character, being acquired and built up by workers over time, but the possession of knowledge can also be a significant source of power and status in organisations (Horowitz *et al.* 2003; Hislop 2004). This fact alone means that workers may be unwilling to participate in organisational knowledge management initiatives if they feel this involves 'giving away' a source of their power and/or status.

Another structural factor affecting the willingness of workers to participate in knowledge management initiatives is the nature of the employment relationship, which results in the interest of workers and management not always being totally compatible. Thus, in relation to knowledge workers, there is potential conflict between workers and their employers both over who owns the knowledge of the worker, and how it is used (Scarbrough 1999). For example, Ciborra and Patriotta (1998) provide a clear example of such a conflict. Their research examined knowledge sharing among R&D staff in Unilever, via electronic discussion forums. When a very senior manager made a contribution to one particular forum, there was a '*panic reaction*' (p.50) among the R&D staff using the forum, which contributed to staff not using the system for some months. This reaction was due to a sense of unease by the R&D staff that their privacy was being invaded by management, which made them reluctant to express opinions which did not comply with managerial perspectives.

The potential for conflict in organisations also emanates from another structural factor: the real (and/or perceived) differences of interests between different workers and groups within organisations that inevitably exist (Marshall and Brady 2001). In relation to knowledge management initiatives, the fact that, as discussed above, power and knowledge are closely inter-related, means that knowledge management initiatives can be used to play out what Storey and Barnett (2000) refer to as 'micro-political battles'. Thus, the attitudes towards and participation (or not) by workers in organisational knowledge management initiatives are shaped by the way such behaviours affect, and link into the political battles that are a part of the fabric of organisations. For example, Storey and Barnett (2000) found inter-functional battles to control a knowledge management initiative were key to the eventual failure of the project they studied.

An unwillingness to share knowledge in a post-merger environment: fear of exploitation and contamination

Empson (2001) conducted detailed studies into three separate mergers undertaken by two UK accounting firms, and two pairs of UK-based management consultants. Empson found that in the immediate post-merger period in all three cases, staff were largely unwilling to share their knowledge with staff employed by the other partner to the merger. This unwillingness stemmed from the twin fears among workers of contamination and exploitation. The fear of exploitation stemmed from concerns related to perceptions that due to the knowledge possessed by the staff of their merger partners being of less value than their own, they would 'lose out' in any knowledge-sharing process. However, these fears were not based on any objective assessment of the value of the knowledge of those from the other organisation, and were more related to subjective, individual assessments. This was linked to the second fear, of contamination. As most staff in the mergers perceived the knowledge of staff from the organisation they were merging with to be of less value than their own, they were concerned not only that they would lose out in knowledge sharing processes, but that their knowledge would also be contaminated and somehow devalued in the process. Thus, in all three cases, the integration of the knowledge bases of the merging partners was inhibited by the concerns staff had regarding the outcome of such processes, which itself stemmed from perceived differences of interest between staff.

This section therefore shows how the participation of workers in organisational knowledge management initiatives cannot be taken for granted. The following two sections look at more specific factors within organisations which affect the attitudes of workers to knowledge management initiatives, and considers what HRM policies can be utilised to encourage the participation of workers in such initiatives.

The organisational climate and workers' attitudes to knowledge management initiatives

This section continues with the themes discussed in the previous section, why human motivation is key to the success of knowledge management initiatives, and why the participation of workers in knowledge management initiatives cannot be guaranteed. However, the focus here shifts from structural factors, which are to some extent beyond the control of organisational management, to factors affecting the general climate within organisations that are within the control of management. As outlined earlier, a lot of survey and case study evidence has shown socio-cultural factors to be key in shaping the attitudes of workers to knowledge management initiatives. This section provides an abbreviated summary of this literature. While this literature identifies an enormous diversity of factors that influence workers attitudes, these factors can be grouped into three general categories (see Table 16.1).

Table 16.1   Research data on organisational factors affecting the attitudes of workers to organisational knowledge management initiatives

Factor affecting workers' attitudes towards participation in knowledge processes	Supporting evidence/analysis	Conclusions/findings
The existence of inter-personal trust and good working relations among co-workers	Andrews and Delahaye 2000	Case study of knowledge sharing amongst scientists which showed trust to be necessary for knowledge sharing to occur.
	Storey and Barnett 2000	Case study of a single failed knowledge management project, with inter-group conflict being key to projects' failure.
	Bouty 2000	Study of inter-organisational knowledge sharing among R&D staff. Sense of fairness in inter-personal exchanges key to their success.
	Newell *et al.* 2000	Longitudinal case study of how inter-group conflict inhibited processes of knowledge sharing.
	De Long and Fahey 2000	Knowledge sharing between subcultures inhibited by differences in values, norms, etc.

Continued

Table 16.1 Continued

Factor affecting workers' attitudes towards participation in knowledge processes	Supporting evidence/analysis	Conclusions/findings
The existence of trust and good inter-personal relations between workers and their managers	MacNeil 2003	Suggests the role of line managers in facilitating team/group based knowledge sharing is key.
	Willman *et al.* 2001	Concerns that workers may be giving away key knowledge.
	Ciborra and Patriotta 1998	Concern by R&D scientists about expressing attitudes not deemed compatible with managerial perspectives in forums visible to management.
	Hayes and Walsham 2000	Concern by workers about expressing attitudes not deemed compatible with managerial perspectives in forums visible to management.
	Ribiere and Sitar 2003	The role of key leaders key to success in developing appropriate knowledge cultures: leading by example, etc.
	Pan and Scarbrough 1999	The role of key leaders key to success in developing appropriate knowledge cultures: leading by example, etc.
Proper recognition and reward for work efforts and use of individual knowledge	Robertson and Swan 2003	Case study of a single consultancy showing how reward and recognition contribute to willingness by workers to participate in knowledge management initiatives.
	McDermott and O'Dell 2001	Knowledge management Initiatives should be compatible with existing organisational culture.
	Hansen *et al.* 1999	Reward and recognition systems used required to be compatible with, and reinforce particular business strategy being pursued.
	Kim and Mauborgne 1998	Workers only likely to share their knowledge with others if they deem sense of 'procedural justice' to exist in decision-making processes.

The overall, somewhat general conclusion from this evidence is that workers are most likely to be willing to participate in organisational knowledge management initiatives when the general organisational climate/culture is fair and positive, for example where people feel their efforts are fairly rewarded and inter-personal relations between workers, and also between workers and managers, are based on trust. The following section looks at the type of HRM practices which can be used to create such a climate, and which are thus likely to help facilitate organisational knowledge management initiatives.

HRM practices to support knowledge management initiatives

Before considering the way HRM practices can be used to help motivate workers to participate in organisational knowledge management initiatives, it is necessary to take account of the diversity of ways that organisations can manage their knowledge. As discussed earlier, a number of writers have developed typologies to categorise the range of knowledge management strategies that exist (Hansen *et al.* 1999; Alvesson and Karreman 2001; Hunter *et al.* 2002). Each particular approach to knowledge management requires different behaviours from workers. Thus, using Hansen *et al.*'s (1999) framework, a codification-based strategy requires workers to focus their knowledge management activities around the use of IT systems, where they should codify their own knowledge, and use IT-based knowledge repositories (such as searchable databases) to search for any knowledge they do not possess. On the other hand, a personalisation strategy requires workers to be willing to share their tacit knowledge directly with other people. Therefore, as each knowledge management strategy requires different behaviours, their HRM implications are distinctive.

The diversity of knowledge management strategies that exist means that it is impossible to develop a 'one best way' checklist of general HRM practices to be used to allow an organisation to effectively manage its knowledge. Ultimately, the range and type of HRM practices required to underpin knowledge management initiatives depends upon the particular approach to knowledge management that is utilised.

One of the most common ways the literature suggests that HRM practices can be used to support knowledge management initiatives is through creating/supporting an organisational culture that is conducive to knowledge sharing/use/development (Pan and Scarbrough 1999; De Long and Fahey 2000; Robertson *et al.* 2000; Ribiere and Sitar 2003). However, one of the weaknesses of much of this literature is that it is relatively vague on exactly what such a culture looks like, and what organisations require to do to achieve one, although the role of organisational leaders is often argued to be important (Pan and Scarbrough 1999; Ribiere and Sitar 2003). However, within this literature there is a debate which mirrors debates in the broader culture literature, on the extent to which organisations can create and manage their cultures (Ogbonna and Harris 1998). Thus while the mainstream position in the knowledge management literature is that organisational cultures can be changed and controlled by management, others suggest that the resilience of an organisation's culture means that unless its knowledge management initiative is designed to be compatible with the existing culture it is likely to fail (Schultze and Boland 2000; McDermott and O'Dell 2001). Thus, both the lack of consensus, and lack of detail in this work makes it difficult to provide detailed advice on how appropriate knowledge cultures can be created.

However, in other areas there is more detail, and more specific advice regarding the type of HRM practices that can be utilised to support organisational knowledge management initiatives. Much of the discussion in this area takes place in the literature on knowledge workers, for example, on what can be done to help retain key knowledge workers, how providing autonomy at work as well as making work continually interesting and challenging can support knowledge management initiatives. The analyses developed by this literature are examined in the following section, which looks specifically at the narrower topic of knowledge workers and how to manage them. What is discussed here is the more general literature on knowledge management that does not have an exclusive focus on knowledge workers.

The commonest HRM policy areas where it is suggested practices can be developed to support knowledge management initiatives are training and development, pay and reward and performance appraisal (Hansen *et al.* 1999; Garvey and Williamson 2002; Hunter *et al.* 2002). The general advice is that these systems need to be designed to support the particular worker behaviours that are required for the specific knowledge management strategy being pursued. For example, Hansen *et al.* (1999) suggest that pay and reward systems can be used to do this, and that if a codification strategy is pursued the pay and reward systems should acknowledge employee efforts to codify their knowledge, and search for the knowledge of others, while with a personalisation strategy, pay and reward systems should recognise the efforts of workers to share their tacit knowledge with each other. Similarly, training and development activities should be structured to reinforce the knowledge management strategy being pursued. Thus Hunter *et al.* (2002), who develop a typology of knowledge management strategies, argue that the provision of appropriate training is most appropriate when the knowledge management strategy is focused on building the social capital of its employees. Garvey and Williamson (2002) suggest that the most useful sort of training to support and encourage a culture of learning and knowledge development is not investing in 'narrow' skills-based training, but training with a broader purpose to encourage reflexivity, learning through experimentation, and how to conduct critical dialogues with others. Such an approach fits most closely with Hansen *et al.*'s personalisation strategy, where knowledge management is achieved primarily through inter-personal interactions. Finally, as outlined in the example below, the importance of ensuring that all HRM practices are integrated and consistent is also important (Yahya and Goh 2002).

Integrating HRM practices to facilitate knowledge management

Garvey and Williamson (2002) describe how an oil company, Oil Company Co., used its HRM practices to support its efforts at developing a culture of knowledge creation and knowledge sharing. In terms of pay, Oil Company Co. staff were rewarded for both meeting commercial performance targets and for undertaking and utilising self-development activities. To signal the importance of both these elements they were embedded in the annual appraisal/pay scheme and together constituted 30 per cent of a worker's pay. Development needs were an intrinsic part of the annual appraisal/review, and staff were expected to provide evidence of the self-development activities they had undertaken. Thus, Oil Company Co. linked the objectives of its pay, appraisal and training and development systems together to create a coherent strategy for encouraging staff to take self-development and a culture of knowledge creation seriously. This scheme was successful, as it had a positive effect on the amount of time and effort staff devoted to development activities.

Managing knowledge workers

The remainder of this chapter takes a slightly narrower focus than has been taken up to now, specifically considering one category of workers whose knowledge is argued to be particularly key to organisational performance and of whom knowledge management initiatives need to take particular account: knowledge workers. As with the topic of knowledge management, an enormous amount has been written on knowledge workers, and their growing importance is closely tied to the knowledge society perspective discussed in the context section. Specifically it is argued that for those societies that are evolving in to knowledge societies, the number and importance of knowledge workers will increase significantly. Thus, as outlined, one of the key indicators used to establish whether a society can be characterised as being knowledge-based is the proportion of knowledge workers employed in it.

Writers on knowledge management and knowledge workers argue that the (growing) importance of knowledge workers to organisational performance means that managing them needs to be an intrinsic element of an organisation's knowledge management strategy. The management of knowledge workers is considered in a separate section partly because one argument made by those writing on knowledge workers is that they are a distinctive type of employee who needs to be managed in quite a different way from other workers. However, the end of this section concludes by critically discussing this assumption.

WHO ARE THE KNOWLEDGE WORKERS?

Defining the types of work that can be considered to constitute knowledge work is by no means easy, to a large extent because there is an enormous debate on the question. The extent of the debate on this topic is such that there is only space here to outline its general elements. The mainstream definition in the knowledge literature is that a knowledge worker is someone whose work is primarily intellectual in nature and which involves extensive and regular use of established bodies of formal, codified knowledge. From this perspective, knowledge workers represent an occupational elite: those workers who are in the vanguard of the knowledge economy, and whose work contributes significantly to the performance of their employers. Thus, as will be discussed later, they are typically regarded by their employers as workers who are worth retaining.

Based on such definitions, the range of occupations that are typically classified as knowledge work include:

- Lawyers (Starbuck 1993; Hunter *et al.* 2002)
- Consultants (Empson 2001; Morris 2001; Robertson and Swan 2003)
- IT and software designers (Schultze 2000; Horowitz *et al.* 2003; Swart and Kinnie 2003)
- Advertising executives (Beaumont and Hunter 2002)
- Accountants (Morris and Empson 1998)
- Scientists and engineers (Lee and Maurer 1997; Beaumont and Hunter 2002)
- Architects (Frenkel *et al.* 1995)
- Artists and art directors/producers (Beaumont and Hunter 2002).

Definitions of knowledge workers therefore overlap with and include the classical professions (such as lawyers, architects, etc.), but also extend beyond them to include a wide variety of other occupations (such as consultants, advertising executives, IT developers, etc.).

However, embedded in such definitions of knowledge work is the (arbitrary?) privileging of certain forms of knowledge (abstract, theoretical, scientific knowledge) over other types of knowledge (practical, skills-based knowledge). Critics of the mainstream definition of knowledge workers, which ring-fences the term to refer to an exclusive and elite range of occupations, argue that such definitions downplay, if not ignore the extent to which all work is knowledge work (Allee 1997; Grant 2000; Thompson *et al.* 2001). A response to this argument is that while all work to some extent involves the use of knowledge, different occupations have different degrees of knowledge intensiveness. However, as a term, knowledge intensiveness is somewhat vague, and its use to categorise certain jobs/occupations as knowledge intensive is open to debate (Alvesson 2001). Thus, while, as will be seen, much has been written about how to manage, motivate and develop the loyalty of knowledge workers, there still remains an element of debate and discussion over which occupations constitute knowledge (intensive) work.

KNOWLEDGE WORKERS AS THE IDEAL EMPLOYEES?

Until now the chapter has built from the assumption that workers' motivation to participate in knowledge management activities should not be taken for granted, as often workers are concerned, ambivalent and occasionally hostile to such initiatives, due to concerns related to the potential, perceived consequences from participating in them. However, a growing body of case study evidence suggests that this is not typically the case with knowledge workers, who appear to be prepared to invest significant amounts of time and effort into their work, and whose employers do not require major efforts to motivate them to do so (Kunda 1992; Alvesson 1995; Deetz 1998; Robertson and Swan 2003). Furthermore, these workers are typically prepared to make such efforts with minimal levels of supervision, and without regarding such effort as being problematic. Thus, motivating such workers to share their knowledge does not appear to be problematic. Moreover, knowledge workers appear on this evidence to be the ideal employee (Alvesson 2000).

Alvesson (2000) puts forward a number of reasons why knowledge workers are prepared to make such efforts: first, they find their work intrinsically interesting and fulfilling; second, such working patterns represent the norms within the communities they are a part of; third, they do it out of a sense of reciprocity, whereby they provide the organisation with their efforts in return for good pay and working conditions; and finally, such behaviours reinforce and confirm their sense of identity as a knowledge worker, where hard work is regarded as a fundamental component. Robertson and Swan (2003) suggest another reason: the structure of the employment relationship. Compared to other workers, they suggest that the employment relationship for knowledge workers is less clear, and the potential for conflict on the basis of it is thus less likely. Fundamentally, the employer/employee, manager/managed relationship is not as clear-cut in knowledge-intensive firms, as in other, more hierarchically based organisations, as in knowledge-intensive firms such boundaries are fuzzy, and evolve over time.

However, while knowledge workers generally appear to regard participating in organisational knowledge management initiatives as less problematic than other workers, this does not mean that the potential for conflict does not exist in knowledge-intensive firms, or that knowledge workers are ALWAYS willing to share their knowledge. Thus Starbuck (1993) described a knowledge-intensive company he examined as being, 'internally inconsistent, in conflict with itself . . . An intricate house of cards.' Furthermore, the Empson (2001) example outlined earlier, where, in a post-merger situation workers from the pre-merger companies were unwilling to share their knowledge with each other, occurred within knowledge-intensive firms (accountants and management consultants).

MOTIVATING KNOWLEDGE WORKERS: THE ROLE OF HRM PRACTICES

Embedded in the reasons put forward by Alvesson (2000), discussed immediately above, on why knowledge workers are typically willing to work hard and participate in knowledge management initiatives, are factors within the control of management and the personnel function, such as job design and the provision of good pay and working conditions. These issues are now examined in detail to consider how the HRM practices knowledge-intensive firms use can affect the attitudes and behaviours of knowledge workers to participate in knowledge management initiatives.

One of the key ideas developed in the mainstream literature on knowledge workers is that such workers have a number of features which distinguish them from other types of worker, and that consequently, they need to be managed in a fundamentally different way from other workers (Tampoe 1993; Alvesson 2000; Robertson *et al.* 2000; Horowitz *et al.* 2003). The previous section outlined one significant reason for this: that the nature of their employment relationship is different from other workers, and due to their importance to their employers the boundary between them and their managers is less clear than for 'conventional' workers. A number of other factors contribute to the distinctiveness of knowledge workers. First, they typically need to be very highly qualified, and also to continually develop their knowledge. For example, in the consultancy examined by Robertson and Swan (2003) one of the recruitment criteria was that prospective employees held doctorates. Second, their knowledge and expertise is typically of greater importance to their employers than that possessed by other workers. For example, in a law firm, such as that examined by Starbuck (1993), the knowledge possessed by the firm's lawyers represents arguably the key organisational asset. Third, their knowledge and skills are typically highly tacit and difficult, if not impossible to codify. For example one of the main reasons why the consultants researched by Morris (2001) were happy to participate in their organisation's attempts to codify their knowledge was that they were confident that such efforts could only be partially successful, and would allow them to retain key aspects of their accumulated expertise. A further example of important tacit knowledge that knowledge workers can possess, but that is impossible to codify, is social capital: the possession of good working and personal relations with particular individuals in client organisations (Fosstenlokken *et al.* 2003). Fourth, in labour market terms their knowledge is relatively scarce, and simultaneously highly valued, which thus typically provides knowledge workers with extensive opportunities to change job. Fifth, as discussed by Alvesson (2000), distinctive norms and expectations may have developed among knowledge workers with regard to factors such as pay, levels of autonomy, opportunities for development, etc. Finally, their work tasks, focused centrally as they are on processes of knowledge creation, utilisation and application, are highly specialised in nature.

Two consequences flow from these arguments. First, as outlined, knowledge workers need to be managed in distinctive ways. Second, as will be discussed separately in the final section, the topic of retention is key to organisations that employ knowledge workers.

In discussing the effectiveness of the HRM practices used to manage knowledge workers it has to be acknowledged, that much of the empirical research in this area is case study-based, focusing on only one or a small number of organisations (Deetz 1998; Schultze 2000; Morris 2001; Robertson and Swan 2003; Swart and Kinnie 2003). The most extensive research conducted to date in this area is the survey of 44 Singaporean organisations which employed knowledge workers conducted by Horowitz *et al.* (2003). However, while most of the research is survey based, its findings, and those of Horowitz *et al.* (ibid., p.23) are relatively consistent, and point towards what Horowitz *et al.* (ibid.) refer to as 'distinctive "bundles" of HR practices' that are effective for motivating and retaining knowledge workers. The cornerstones of such a bundle relate to having fundamentally interesting work, high levels of autonomy, significant opportunities for self-development and attractive levels of pay. Each of these elements is now examined in a little more detail.

Fulfilling work

In managerial decisions related to the nature of the tasks that knowledge workers conduct, empirical evidence suggests that a key motivating factor is that the work is intrinsically, and continuously satisfying and stimulating. Thus in Horowitz *et al.*'s (2003) survey, providing challenging work was ranked as the most important factor by the managers surveyed for helping to retain their knowledge workers.

Autonomy

As well as having work that is intrinsically interesting, the available evidence suggests that knowledge workers also typically regard having high levels of autonomy at work as important. For example, in the scientific consultancy examined by Robertson and Swan (2003) autonomy was found to be important to the consultants, and extended to areas as diverse as the projects they worked on (the consultants were free to choose, so long as they reached their annual revenue targets), the selection of the training and development activities they undertook (it was the responsibility of the consultants to identify their own development needs, and funding was available to support this), work clothing and work patterns (a wide diversity of work patterns, personalities and clothing styles were apparent, and a culture of heterogeneity rather than conformity was developed and encouraged).

Opportunities for personal development

As outlined, one of the distinctive characteristics of knowledge workers, compared to most occupational groups, is the need for continuous development. Research evidence suggests that knowledge workers regard the provision of such opportunities by their employers to be vitally important, and can be a key way to help both motivate and retain them. While the provision of such opportunities is potentially a double-edged sword for employers (as supporting such activities potentially makes it easier for staff to leave) without supporting continuous development, staff may be inclined to leave anyway.

Pay

The final key issue for the management and motivation of knowledge workers involves providing them with attractive and competitive pay and reward packages. For example, in Horowitz *et al.*'s (2003) survey, providing a 'highly competitive pay package' (p.32) was ranked as the second most effective way to help retain knowledge workers, and, as will be seen in the following section, the primary reason underlying the turnover of knowledge workers (see Table 16.2). Such findings reinforce Scarbrough's (1999) assertion that knowledge workers are relatively instrumental in their outlook, with issues of pay being one of their primary concerns.

Before moving on to the topic of retention, it is worth touching on a critique of the assumption made by the mainstream literature on knowledge workers that the best way to manage knowledge workers is to provide them with separate and distinctive pay and working conditions from other workers. This perspective has been criticised by a growing number of writers, who typically base their analysis on the assumption that all workers should be regarded as knowledge workers. The critique suggests that a potential problem with the 'distinctiveness' argument is that such approaches neglect the fact that if all workers are knowledge workers, then the knowledge of all workers is important to organisational performance (Allee 1997;

Table 16.2 Reasons for knowledge worker turnover	
Reason for knowledge worker turnover	**Percentage of organizations reporting this reason as most important**
Better Pay and Prospects	39
Personal Reasons	20
Career-Related Issues	13
Company-Related Issues	13
Market Factors	10
Job-Related Issues	5

Source: Adapted with permission from 'Finders, Keepers? Attracting, motivating and retaining knowledge workers', by Frank M. Horowitz, Chan Teng Heng and Hesan Ahmed Quazi, published in *Human Resource Manangement Journal*, Volume 13, Number 4, 2003, Figure 1

Beaumont and Hunter 2002; Garvey and Williamson 2002). Furthermore, organisations that utilise such an approach and treat knowledge workers as special and distinctive risk the development of a sense of resentment among the workforce that do not receive these favourable conditions, and that as a consequence these workers will potentially be less willing to participate in organisational knowledge management initiatives.

RETENTION: PREVENTING KNOWLEDGE LOSS THROUGH DEVELOPING LOYALTY

While motivating knowledge workers to participate in organisational knowledge processes appears to be less of a potential problem for their employers than motivating other employees, developing their organisational loyalty such that they remain working with their employers for extended periods, does appear to be more problematic. This is to a large extent because the labour market, where the skills and knowledge of knowledge workers are typically relatively scarce, creates conditions for knowledge workers which are favourable to their mobility (Scarbrough 1999; Flood *et al.* 2001). This idea is supported by much of the case study evidence as well as the Horowitz *et al.* (2003) survey. In this survey, the managers surveyed reported that the turnover levels of their knowledge workers were higher than for other workers, and many felt that the level of turnover of knowledge workers was at problematically high levels. The reasons knowledge workers gave their employers for leaving, and the proportion of cases where this was reported are outlined above, in Table 16.2. Thus, this survey found that by far the most important reason for knowledge worker turnover levels was pay and conditions. This therefore suggests that the most effective way to deal with retention problems is through offering good systems of pay and reward.

Having a high turnover rate of knowledge workers is a potentially significant problem for the organisations that employ them, due to some of the characteristics of knowledge workers outlined earlier (Lee and Maurer 1997; Alvesson 2000; Flood *et al.* 2000; Beaumont and Hunter 2002). First, their knowledge is typically highly tacit. As outlined, one key source of knowledge possessed by knowledge workers is social capital, their knowledge of key individuals in client firms. Thus, when such workers leave, there is a risk for their employer that they will lose their clients as well. Second, low retention rates may be a problem for knowledge-intensive firms as the knowledge possessed by knowledge workers is often a crucial element in organisational performance. Thus, retaining workers who possess valuable knowledge should arguably be as important an element in an organisation's knowledge management strategy as motivating workers to participate in knowledge activities. This is because the tacit and embodied nature of much organisational knowledge means that when employees leave an organisation, they take their knowledge with them. As Byrne (2001, p.325) succinctly puts it, 'without loyalty knowledge is lost'.

Alvesson (2000) argues that one of the best ways to deal with the turnover problem is to create organisational loyalty in staff, particularly through developing their sense of organisational identity. Alvesson identifies two broad types of loyalty: instrumental-based loyalty, and identification-based loyalty. Alvesson argues that the weakest form of loyalty is instrumental-based loyalty, which is when a worker remains loyal to their employer for as long as they receive specific personal benefits, with one of the most effective ways of developing such loyalty being through pay and working conditions. This conclusion is reinforced the findings of Horowitz *et al.*, as outlined in Table 16.2, which appear to present a general picture of knowledge workers displaying limited levels of organisational loyalty and being motivated to move jobs primarily by pay-related factors.

For Alvesson, the second, and stronger form of loyalty is identification-based loyalty, which is loyalty based on the worker having a strong sense of identity as being a member of the organisation, and where the worker identifies with the goals and objectives of their organisation. There are three strategies for developing identification-based loyalty. First, there is an institutionally based strategy, where the organisation develops a particular vision or set of values that the knowledge worker identifies with. Second is what Alvesson refers to as a communitarian-based strategy, where workers develop a strong sense of being part of a cohesive team, which is achieved partly through the use of social events which allow bonding and the development of good social relations between workers. Finally, there is socially integrative strategy, which is a combination of the institutionally based, and communitarian strategies. The case study below presents the case of a consultancy that primarily utilised a communitarian-based strategy.

Box 16.1: A communitarian-based strategy for developing loyalty: an HR consultancy

Cheshire Consultants is an HR consultancy based in the north-west of England specialising in the areas of recruitment & selection and employee development. Research was conducted on it by this chapter's author, and two colleagues from the Institute of Work Psychology at Sheffield. It is a small company, employing only 12 consultants plus some supporting administrative and management staff. The source of data on the company was based on interviews with one of its co-founders and seven of its consultants. Its consultants could be described as mobile teleworkers, as for much of their working week they are out of the office, visiting and working at various client locations. For example, one of their consultants described a typical week as involving two days based in the office and three days travelling to and visiting clients in different locations, spread throughout the UK. Thus extensive amounts of travelling were an intrinsic feature of their work. These work patterns therefore meant that during the course of their normal day-to-day work most communication was via phone calls and e-mails, with opportunities for face-to-face communication between consultants typically occurring on a weekly or twice weekly, rather than a daily basis. To counteract the potential isolation and weakened sense of team identity that such working practices could produce, a communitarian-based strategy was utilised to reinforce social relations and sustain a sense of community identity among staff. This fits with the articulated culture of the company, which one of its founders argued was to 'create a sense of community . . . like being part of a team'. Two primary mechanisms were used to achieve this. First, the managing director of the company (one of its co-founders) made efforts to maintain daily contact with all consultants. While such contacts had an element of surveillance to them they also helped to support the work of the consultants through the provision of advice. These contacts were regarded as typically positive and helpful by most consultants. The second strategy was to have monthly meetings which were primarily social in purpose, and which were never cancelled or compromised by demands of work. While most consultants attended these events to some extent out of a sense of duty, they also found them useful as they helped them to sustain good social relations with colleagues, and reinforced their sense of organisational identity.

DOMESTIC-POWERCO: SUPPORTING KNOWLEDGE SHARING AND USE AMONGST DISTRIBUTED WORK TEAMS

CASE STUDY 16.1

DONALD HISLOP

This case study examines the way management and HRM practices are used to support the work and knowledge activities in an organisation whose workers are geographically dispersed and isolated, with few opportunities to interact and meet on a face-to-face basis.

Organisational context

Domestic-Powerco is a UK-wide company whose main business is installing, repairing and servicing heating equipment into the homes of private individuals. During the 1990s Domestic-Powerco management implemented a large-scale cost-cutting and restructuring programme, as such changes were believed necessary to allow the company to remain commercially competitive.

The research this case study is based on was carried out during the first half of 2003, with two colleagues of the author from Sheffield's Institute of Work Psychology. The research was looking into the characteristics, knowledge sharing and communication dynamics of work that could be described as mobile telework, where people make extensive use of information and communication technologies as a central part of their work, and whose work requires geographic mobility between sites. The research study was small-scale, and exploratory in nature, and in Domestic-Powerco involved extended, semi-structured interviews with six people who worked in the service, repair and installation division, in Lincolnshire and South Yorkshire.

Before the restructuring process it would have been inappropriate to describe the service engineers as mobile teleworkers, as while their work required them to be geographically mobile, the engineers were not required to use ICTs, and they all operated out of central depots, from which they started and finished their daily activities. During this period, while the engineers were required to work in customers' houses on their own, the fact that they began and finished work each day from a central depot, and had to return to the depot if they needed particular spare parts, meant that there were extensive opportunities to interact with, and share knowledge between engineers. This can be illustrated by the following quotation, from one of the engineers interviewed,

> I can remember just before the depot shut, we had some outside assessors come in to look at our training, and . . .the best training they saw was the informal training, with everyone stood around the locker, you know, and someone's got a part in their hand, and it's 'oh don't take the right side off, do it from the left, it's a lot easier'.

The transformation of service engineers into mobile teleworkers

The changes involved in the restructuring project were extremely radical in nature, and involved reducing the workforce from approximately 10,000 to 4,000. Further, there was also a programme to close an enormous number of the 450 depots that existed in the UK at that time, with offices and depots being rationalised into regional centres. As part of this process the service engineers lost their bases in local depots. These workers no longer had any physical location from which they were based. While historically they had gone to the depot to be allocated jobs, under the new system this process was no longer necessary. Instead, each engineer, who had their own van and set of equipment, laptop and mobile phone, received their work instructions electronically. Thus, in terms of knowledge sharing, this change in working practices significantly reduced the opportunities for the type of interaction and knowledge sharing among peers illustrated by the first quote. This was summed up as follows by one of the engineers interviewed,

> [Isolation] can be an issue. I think the one thing we have lost is the word of mouth to engineers, the group gathering in the morning. It is like taking a part of the social life off you . . . A lot of the engineers would say the main thing they have lost is the contact with other engineers [about] this job.

As will be seen in the following section, Domestic-Powerco have recognised the consequences of these changes and have dealt with the loss of this informal means of knowledge sharing relatively successfully, through a number of mechanisms. However, among the engineers interviewed it was apparent that the organisational means to support interaction, communication and knowledge sharing did not totally satisfy their needs, and many of them developed their own informal means of doing this out of working hours, as illustrated in the following quotation,

> We all go . . . to pick up our parts, and there's a canteen there and there's often four or five of us in the morning, so we'll go up and have a cup of tea and a chat, so we've gone together – we still do meet each other, you know go in half an hour before the shift starts.

Managerial and HRM-related support for Domestic-Powerco's service engineers

Domestic-Powerco was relatively successful at providing support for its service engineers. Despite the fact that many of the engineers felt their work did not give them adequate formal opportunities to interact with colleagues, which were substituted for by the type of informal meeting described above, those interviewed were relatively happy with their work. Further, there was no evidence that they were unwilling to do their work, utilise their knowledge and share their knowledge with colleagues where appropriate.

Categorising Domestic-Powerco's strategy for managing the knowledge of its workers is difficult, as it does not fall neatly into any of the categories developed by the academic literature. For example, in terms of Hansen et al.'s (1999) framework, as will be seen, there are elements of both a codification-based strategy, where electronic means are used to collect and disseminate codified knowledge, and a personalisation-based strategy, where means are used to facilitate and encourage interpersonal knowledge sharing.

There are three broad knowledge processes that Domestic-Powerco's engineers needed to utilise in order to be able to do their job effectively. First, they needed to utilise and apply their acquired knowledge. For example the diagnosis of problems is one important task they carry out, going into customers' homes with a vague description of a problem, which necessitates their identifying the precise problem and sorting it. Second, they need to continually acquire new knowledge, for example, learning how to install and repair new types of equipment. Finally, as with the photocopy engineers studied by Orr (1996), there is a need for engineers to search for and share knowledge with their peers. The following subsection outlines the range of processes Domestic-Powerco management utilised to facilitate and support these activities.

Training

There were a number of aspects to the training provided by Domestic-Powerco that supported the work activities and knowledge processes of their service engineers. First there was a formal apprenticeship scheme, which was the basic training programme that new recruits with no previous experience were put on to learn the basic skills and knowledge of the job. This programme ran for a year, with half of it being classroom-based, and half of it being on-the-job training in the region where the apprentices would finally be working. For the on-the-job part of the training apprentices went out with specific engineers and learned through both observing the engineers at work, and also by being allowed to do some tasks themselves.

The second aspect of Domestic-Powerco's training scheme, a buddy system, follows immediately after the formal training programme, and is an extension and continuation of the engineers' on-the-job training with new engineers working full-time with experienced engineers. Thus in this period, new engineers do not visit any customers homes without a more senior engineer with them. This process serves two purposes. First, it helps the new engineers develop their diagnostic skills in applying their formal learning to specific domestic situations. Second, it also allows new engineers to develop good working and social relations with a number of more experienced engineers, which helps them develop a network of people they can contact if they require support and advice in the future, as most engineers do.

Third, to provide the engineers with opportunities to update their skills and knowledge when necessary, there are a number of mobile training centres that tour the country, which groups of engineers take turns to go to. These centres are customised, articulated lorries, of which there are eight in the UK. For example, when a manufacturer launches a new piece of equipment, the mobile training centres may be used for this, as it allows the engineers to get hands on experience looking at and working with the new equipment.

Finally, there is a system for providing staff with regular technical updates, in the form of codified knowledge and information that can be uploaded onto their laptops. This is discussed more below, in the section on codified knowledge.

Managerial support

An intrinsic and important element of the support system for the service engineers is provided by their managers. Groups of engineers are organised into geographically based teams of between 30 and 60, with one area manager being responsible for all the engineers in a particular area. For the 'small' areas that have only 30–40 engineers, the area manager is likely to have sole responsibility. For larger areas with over 50 engineers, the area manager will usually also have a supporting assistant manager working for them. With these supervisory ratios, the managers interviewed emphasised the importance of trust. Managers support and supervise their engineers through a combination of phone calls, team meetings (see below), and face-to-face meeting (close to customers' homes, or when they are picking up parts from distribution depots). However, supervisory ratios mean that managers are only typically able to see and/or contact each of their engineers once a week. Therefore, a hands-off style of management is a necessity rather than a positive choice by managers. The day-to-day performance of engineers can be examined by managers via the performance management system that exists, which requires engineers to complete weekly, electronic activity sheets detailing what jobs they have been working on (see below).

Team meetings/social events

Another mechanism used to bring teams of engineers together, which provides the manager with an opportunity to interact with them face-to-face, and allows the engineers to share relevant knowledge and information, and retain a sense of team spirit, are monthly team meetings. These are coordinated by the area manager, are typically relatively informal and ad hoc in nature, providing engineers with a forum to raise and discuss issues they regard as important. The staff interviewed also attended regular, team-based social events, organised outside working hours, but these were not a formal part of the management system, and were organised at the discretion of area managers.

Codified knowledge

A lot of codified knowledge was also used to support the engineers in their work. For example, their laptops had extensive, step-by-step lists of instructions, supported by relevant diagrams, for how to do most types of repair, on most types of equipment. Thus, theoretically, whatever model of equipment the customer had (with the exception of very old and outdated equipment), the engineer had, through their laptops, the resources to help them repair them. There were also regular (quarterly) updates of technical information sent to engineers on CD-roms. Finally, engineers also received some technical information as paperwork, via the postal system.

Technical support

The final form of support provided to the engineers 'in the field' was access to a 'technical helpline', which they could call up at any time if they found problems that they were unfamiliar with, or their laptops did not have. Thus, a lot of formal mechanisms existed to support the service engineers in their work, which acknowledged the isolated nature of their work, and provided mechanisms to search for and share knowledge and ideas when necessary.

Pay/performance management

The final issue examined is the pay and performance management system that the service engineers had. While searching for, sharing and effectively utilising knowledge were key aspects of their work, there were no direct pay-related incentives or rewards for doing so. These activities were assumed to be an intrinsic element of the engineers' work, and it wasn't therefore deemed appropriate to provide bonuses for conducting such activities. The main aspect of variability in pay that existed was where extra pay was available for working weekends, or holidays, and where engineers had to work overtime. The main way their performance was measured and monitored was on the quality of their work, and on their work-rate. Thus, each engineer had to complete a weekly activity sheet detailing all the jobs they had done. Every type of job they could do was allocated an amount of time to complete, and engineers had to ensure that they carried out enough jobs so that the time allocated to the total number of jobs they had done added up to the amount of hours they were meant to work in a particular week.

Questions

1. Is there more that Domestic-Powerco could have done with its payment and reward system to encourage/reward appropriate knowledge-sharing behaviours among engineers?

2. What would be the benefits and disadvantages of Domestic-Powerco providing formal support, within work time, for the informal, pre-work meetings that many engineers used to organise? Is it better to leave these meetings to be managed by staff informally, or for management to play a more formal role.

3. Is the ratio of managers to engineers adequate, or too high? Reflect on the benefits and disadvantages of either increasing or decreasing this ratio, for both managers and engineers. Is changing this ratio significantly likely to have any impact on the knowledge-sharing behaviours of the engineers?

4. Such engineers are not usually part of the mainstream definition of knowledge workers. On the basis of the case study, can Domestic-Powerco's service engineers be said to be knowledge workers? Does this case suggest that definitions of knowledge workers need to be modified to include such workers?

References

Allee, V. (1997) *The Knowledge Evolution: Expanding Organizational Intelligence,* Oxford: Butterworth-Heinemann.

Alvesson, M. (1995) *Management of Knowledge Intensive Firms,* London: de Gruyter.

Alvesson, M. (2000) 'Social identity and the problem of loyalty in knowledge-intensive companies', *Journal of Management Studies,* Vol.37, No.8, pp.1101–23.

Alvesson, M. (2001) 'Knowledge work: ambiguity, image and identity', *Human Relations,* Vol.54, No.7, pp.863–86.

*Alvesson, M. and Karreman, D. (2001) 'Odd couple: making sense of the curious concept of knowledge management', *Journal of Management Studies,* Vol.38, No.7, pp.995–1018.

Andrews, K. and Delahaye, B. (2000) 'Influences on knowledge processes in organizational learning: the psychosocial filter', *Journal of Management Studies,* Vol.37, No.6, pp.797–810.

Beaumont, P. and Hunter, L. (2002) *Managing Knowledge Workers,* London: CIPD.

Bell, D. (1973) *The Coming of Post-industrial Society,* Harmondsworth: Penguin.

Bouty, I. (2000) 'Interpersonal and interaction influences on informal resource exchanges between R&D researchers across organizational boundaries', *Academy of Management Journal,* Vol.43, No.1, pp.50–65.

Byrne, R. (2001) 'Employees: capital or commodity?', *Career Development International,* Vol.6, No.6, pp.324–330.

Ciborra, C. and Patriotta, G. (1998) 'Groupware and teamwork in R&D: limits to learning and innovation', *R&D Management,* Vol.28, No.1, pp.1–10.

Deetz, S. (1998) 'Discursive formations, strategized subordination and self-surveillance', in A. McKinlay and K. Starkey (eds) *Foucault, Management and Organization Theory,* London: Sage.

De Long, D. and Fahey, L. (2000) 'Diagnosing cultural barriers to knowledge management', *Academy of Management Executive,* Vol.14, No.4, pp.113–27.

Edwards, J., Handzic, M., Carlsson, S. and Nissen, M. (2003) 'Knowledge management research and practice: visions and directions', *Knowledge Management Research and Practice,* Vol.1, No.1, pp.49–60.

Empson, L. (2001) 'Fear of exploitation and fear of contamination: impediments to knowledge transfer in mergers between professional service firms', *Human Relations,* Vol.54, No.7, pp.839–62.

Felstead, A., Gallie, D. and Green, F. (2002) *Work Skills in Britain 1986–2001,* Nottingham: DfES Publications.

*Flood, P., Turner, T., Ramamoorthy, N. and Pearson, J. (2001) 'Causes and consequences of psychological contracts among knowledge workers in the high technology and financial services industry', *International Journal of Human Resource Management,* Vol.12, No.7, pp.1152–65.

Fosstenlokken, S., Lowendahl, B. and Revang, O. (2003) 'Knowledge development through client interaction: a comparative study', *Organization Studies,* Vol.24, No.6, pp.859–80.

Frenkel, S., Korczynski, M., Donohue, L. and Shire, K. (1995) 'Re-constituting work: trends towards knowledge work and info-normative control', *Work, Employment and Society,* Vol.9, No.4, pp.773–96.

Frenkel, S., Korczynski, M., Shire, K. and Tam, M. (1999) *On the Front Line: Organization of Work in the Information Economy,* London: ILR Press.

Gallie, D., White, M., Cheng, Y. and Tomlinson, M. (1998) *Restructuring the Employment Relationship,* Oxford: Clarendon Press.

Garvey, B. and Williamson, B. (2002) *Beyond Knowledge Management: Dialogue, Creativity and the Corporate Curriculum,* Harlow: FT/Prentice Hall.

Grant, R. (2000) 'Shifts in the world economy: The drivers of knowledge management', in C. Despres and D. Chauvel (eds) *Knowledge Horizons: The Present and the Promise of Knowledge Management,* Oxford: Butterworth-Heinemann.

Hansen, M., Nohria, N. and Tierney, T. (1999) 'What's your strategy for managing knowledge?', *Harvard Business Review,* Vol.77, No.2, pp.107–16.

Harrison, R. and Leitch, C. (2000) 'Learning and organization in the knowledge-based information economy: initial findings from a participatory action research study', *British Journal of Management,* Vol.11, pp.103–19.

Hayes, N. and Walsham, G. (2000) 'Safe enclaves, political enclaves and knowledge working', in C. Prichard, R. Hull, M. Chumer and H. Willmott (eds) *Managing Knowledge: Critical Investigations of Work and Learning,* London: Macmillan.

Hislop, D. (2003) 'The complex relationship between communities of practice and the implementation of technological innovations', *International Journal of Innovation Management,* Vol.7, No.2, pp.163–88.

*Hislop, D. (2004) *Knowledge Management in Organizations: A Critical Introduction,* Oxford: Oxford University Press.

*Horowitz, F., Heng, C. and Quazi, H. (2003) 'Finders, keepers? Attracting, motivating and retaining knowledge workers', *Human Resource Management Journal,* Vol.13, No.4, pp.23–44.

Hunter, L., Beaumont, P. and Lee, M. (2002) 'Knowledge management practice in Scottish law firms', *Human Resource Management Journal,* Vol.12, No.2, pp.4–21.

Kim, W. and Mauborgne, R. (1998) 'Procedural justice, strategic decision making and the knowledge economy', *Strategic Management Journal,* Vol.19, pp.323–38.

KPMG (2000) *Knowledge Management Research Report,* London: KPMG Consulting.

Kunda, G. (1992) *Engineering Culture: Control and Commitment in a High-Tech Corporation,* Philadelphia, PA: Temple University Press.

Lee, T. and Maurer, S. (1997) 'The retention of knowledge workers with the unfolding model of voluntary turnover', *Human Resource Management Review,* Vol.7, No.3, pp.247–75.

Littler, C. and Innes, D. (2003) 'Downsizing and deknowledging the firm', *Work, Employment and Society,* Vol.17, No.1, pp.73–100.

MacNeil, C. (2003) 'Line managers: facilitators of knowledge sharing in teams', *Employee Relations,* Vol.25, No.3, pp.294–307.

Mansell, R. and Steinmueller, W. (2000) *Mobilizing the Information Society: Strategies for Growth and Opportunity,* Oxford: Oxford University Press.

Marshall, N. and Brady, T. (2001) 'Knowledge management and the politics of knowledge: illustrations from complex product systems', *European Journal of Information Systems,* Vol.10, pp.99–112.

McDermott, R. and O'Dell, C. (2001) 'Overcoming cultural barriers to knowledge sharing', *Journal of Knowledge Management,* Vol.5, No.1, pp.76–85.

Morris, T. (2001) 'Asserting property rights: knowledge codification in the professional service firm', *Human Relations,* Vol.54, No.7, pp.819–38.

Morris, T. and Empson, L. (1998) 'Organization and expertise: an exploration of knowledge bases and the management of accounting and consulting Firms', *Accounting, Organizations and Society,* Vol.23, No.5–6, pp.609–24.

Neef, D. (1999) 'Making the case for knowledge management: the bigger picture', *Management Decision,* Vol.37, No.1, pp.72–8.

Newell, S., Scarbrough, H., Swan, J. and Hislop, D. (2000) 'Intranets and knowledge management: de-centred technologies and the limits of technological discourse', in C. Prichard, R. Hull, M. Chumer and H. Willmott (eds) *Managing Knowledge: Critical Investigations of Work and Learning,* London: Macmillan.

Nonaka, I. (1994). 'A dynamic theory of organizational knowledge creation', *Organization Science,* Vol.5, No.1, pp.14–37.

Ogbonna, E. and Harris, L. (1998) 'Managing organizational culture: compliance of genuine change', *British Journal of Management,* Vol.9, pp.273–88.

Orr, J. (1996) *Talking About Machines,* Ithaca, NY: ILR Press.

Pan, S. and Scarbrough, H. (1999) 'Knowledge management in practice: an exploratory case study', *Technology Analysis and Strategic Management,* Vol.11, No.3, pp.359–74.

Reich, R. (1991) *The Work of Nations: Preparing Ourselves for Twenty-first Century Capitalism,* London: Simon & Schuster.

Ribiere, V. and Sitar, A. (2003) 'Critical role of leadership in nurturing a knowledge-supporting culture', *Knowledge Management Research and Practice,* Vol.1, No.1, pp.39–48.

Robertson, M. and O'Malley Hammersley, G. (2000) 'Knowledge management practices within a knowledge-intensive firm: the significance of the people management dimension', *Journal of European Industrial Training,* Vol.24, Nos2–4, pp.241–53.

*Robertson, M. and Swan, J. (2003) 'Control–what control?' Culture and ambiguity within a knowledge intensive firm', *Journal of Management Studies,* Vol.40, No.4, pp.831–58.

Scarbrough, H. (1999) 'Knowledge as work: conflicts in the management of knowledge workers', *Technology Analysis and Strategic Management,* Vol.11, No.1, pp.5–16.

Schultze, U. (2000) 'A confessional account of an ethnography about knowledge work', *MIS Quarterly,* Vol.24, No.1, pp.3–41.

Schultze, U. and Boland, R. (2000) 'Knowledge management technology and the reproduction of knowledge work practices', *Journal of Strategic Information Systems,* Vol.9, pp.193–212.

Starbuck, W. (1993) 'Keeping a butterfly and an elephant in a house of cards: the elements of exceptional success', *Journal of Management Studies,* Vol.30, No.6, pp.885–921.

Storey, J. and Barnett, E. (2000) 'Knowledge management initiatives: learning from failure', *Journal of Knowledge Management,* Vol.4, No.2, pp.145–56.

*Swart, J. and Kinnie, N. (2003) 'Sharing knowledge in knowledge-intensive firms', *Human Resource Management Journal,* Vol.13, No.2, pp.60–75.

Tam, Y., Korczynski, M. and Frenkel, S. (2002) 'Organizational and occupational commitment: knowledge workers in large Corporations', *Journal of Management Studies,* Vol.39, No.6, pp.775–801.

Tampoe, M. (1993) 'Motivating knowledge workers: the challenge for the 1990s', *Long Range Planning,* Vol.26, No.3, pp.49–55.

Thompson, P., Warhurst, C. and Callaghan, G. (2001) 'Ignorant theory and knowledgeable workers: interrogating the connections between knowledge, skills and services', *Journal of Management Studies,* Vol.38, No.7, pp.923–42.

Willman, P., Fenton O'Creevy, M., Nicholson, N. and Soane, E. (2001) 'Knowing the risks: theory and practice in financial market trading', *Human Relations,* Vol.54, No.7, pp.887–910.

Yahya, S. and Goh, W.-K. (2002) 'Managing human resources towards achieving knowledge management', *Journal of Knowledge Management,* Vol.6, No.5, pp.457–68.

* Useful reading

Chapter 17

EMPLOYMENT ETHICS

Peter Ackers

Ethics: The philosophical study of the moral value of human conduct and the rules and principles that *ought* to govern it (Collins Dictionary, my emphasis).

Introduction

Employment ethics, as a subdivision of business ethics (see Chryssides and Kaler 1993; Crane and Matten 2004), involves the application of general moral principles to the management of employees' wages and conditions. In the same way as, say, sports or medical ethics, it begins with a concern about human relationships and how we treat other people. There are two dimensions to this: personal ethical issues at work; and broader questions of business social responsibility. The first addresses the way you or I should behave, as responsible individuals, towards other employees and our employer. This might include questions like personal honesty in completing expenses forms, using the work telephone or internet facilities (see Mars 1973), resisting the temptation of bribes, or simply kindness and consideration towards our workmates. Without a culture of personal ethics, high standards of business ethics are inconceivable. For this reason, many organisations now have an ethical code of practice to guide employee behaviour. The focus of this chapter, however, is on the second category, where you act as a management agent for the business organisation. In this case, while there is still scope for personal discretion, your approach to other employees will be heavily circumscribed by business policy. For instance, if 'the company' decides to close a factory – as Ford did at Dagenham – you will be left, as an individual manager, to implement a decision whether or not you agree with it.

In this light, the chapter aims to guide the student through employment ethics as it applies to real business management practice in the United Kingdom, past and present. Following some discussion of the complexities of applying ethics to business, various ethical theories are introduced by applying them to a real-life ethical problem. An employment ethics agenda is then established, contrasting a right-wing emphasis on the free market with left-wing social regulation. These are then linked to two competing unitarist and pluralist conceptions of management as an ethical agent in employment relations. The next section sketches the history of ethical employment management, followed by an assessment of a critical development of recent decades, the advent of HRM as a new way of talking about labour management. The chapter closes by advocating a left-wing, stakeholder view of employment ethics as an antidote to three fallacies of recent HRM theory and practice.

To begin with, however, the process of translating ethics from personal behaviour to business practice is not straightforward. As we have seen, one initial complication to business ethics is that decisions about right and wrong are made by an impersonal organisation, rather than a single identifiable individual, as in some other spheres of moral decision making. A further apparent difficulty, compared this time to other fields of management activity, is that ethics is about what ought to be, rather than what is. In short, it involves value judgements and differences of opinion rather than just technical decisions. In truth, the same is true of almost all organisational policy affecting human beings; only elsewhere these value-judgements are hidden behind technical sounding words like 'efficiency'. As Fox (1966) has argued, employment relations are always viewed through competing frames of reference leading to different interpretations of the situation. In this sense, 'ethics' should be seen as part and parcel of everyday personnel policy, not some entirely different realm of activity.

Employment ethics is still a highly problematic issue for two further reasons. While modern business seeks the moral high ground, often for public relations purposes, sceptics retort that business ethics in general is an oxymoron, a contradiction in terms. Is not the main goal of business, after all, to maximise profits, with all other considerations, such as the treatment of employees, coming a poor second? On the other hand, the employment relationship, between employer and employee, can become an especially deep-rooted and durable bond, evoking ethical notions of trust and loyalty. Paid work occupies many of our working hours and shapes our life chances, while HRM theory suggests that employees are a crucial resource to be nurtured, developed and retained by the business organisation (see Legge 1995). Some argue that good ethics is, in fact, good business and, therefore, that no serious conflict exists between doing the right thing towards employees and improving business performance. This may be true for some businesses, some of the time. But more often 'being ethical' involves making difficult choices between expedience and principle.

While all ethics starts with common-sense claims about what is 'right' and 'fair', we soon find there are very different views about what these words mean. For this reason, we cannot say whether some employment policy is ethical or unethical, without referring back to which ethical theory we are applying. One central employment issue is how much we pay people. Let me imagine for a moment that I am the main shareholder and senior manager of a business organisation. A group of manual workers have asked for a 20 per cent wages increase, to provide 'a fair day's pay for a fair day's work'. Their language asserts an ethical claim. I want to act 'ethically', but how can I decide whether their claim is a just one? To take the matter further, we must enter what is popularly known as a 'moral maze'. While the detailed facts of the case are always important, the way we interpret them will be shaped by which ethical theory we choose to follow as the road to truth (see Chryssides and Kaler 1993, pp.79–107; Winstanley and Woodall 1999).

Ethical theories: enter the moral maze

One common-sense starting point is to look to the costs and benefits of awarding a pay rise and to enter the passage to the maze marked 'Consequentialism'. Almost immediately, I begin to wonder how to weigh and measure these consequences. For instance, a pay increase will benefit these workers, but it will cut into my income as owner, perhaps reducing the amount I invest in new plant and machinery, spend on myself, or give to charity. How do I know which consequence is more beneficial? By now, however, my path has branched into another fairly wide thoroughfare entitled 'Utilitarianism', which claims to answer this question. Accordingly, whichever action gives the greatest happiness or utility is to be preferred. Since my employees are more numerous than me and on lower incomes, it may seem that a wage increase would be the most ethical course. But what of the broader consequences for happiness in society, if higher labour costs raise the cost of living for customers, or cut the incentive of entrepreneurs, like me, to establish business and create jobs? Another problem is that I do not know what the actual consequences will be, and can only guess. For instance, higher wages may benefit the business in the long run by improving employee performance and reducing labour turnover. Alternatively, higher labour costs may reduce competitiveness and lead to job loss. Thus, utilitarianism can nearly always provide good ammunition for both sides in an employment argument. More worrying, perhaps, it seems to provide a ready rationale for any employer seeking to wriggle out of any social responsibility – which of course, I am not.

A little discouraged, I retrace my steps to another, narrower passage, with the strange off-putting title of 'Deontology'. On closer inspection, however, we discover that this merely means that I should act out of duty and choose to 'do the right thing' irrespective of consequences. Indeed, this way purports to lead to a 'kingdom of ends' with two cardinal principles to guide my sense of duty. One is that I should be prepared to generalise or universalise my decision. So that if I give these manual employees an increase, we will also have to consider the situation of office workers and whether they are being treated consistently. The second principle is that we must show a respect for persons, by treating them as an end in themselves and not a means to an end. In practical terms, this could mean that I should not sacrifice my present duty towards these employees – by rejecting their wage claim – in order to pursue the long-term best interests of my business and society. Indeed, one path branches off, called Human Rights, announcing that all employees have a 'right' to a decent living wage and so on. In this way, Kant's ethic of duty can appear so high-minded that it prevents business management from even considering economic factors, which may affect the long-term viability of the firm. Moreover, the assumption that we must act out of a sense of duty to be genuinely ethical appears to outlaw any considerations of economic self-interest. What happens, for instance, if my motive is disinterested, but I am also aware that granting an increase will solve the firm's labour turnover problems? Am I still acting ethically?

But how do I know that my primary duty lies towards these employees? Suddenly I notice two less obvious paths leading in diametrically opposite directions, each also departing from the deontological mainstream. The first states boldly, 'Your primary duty is to the shareholders who own and invest in the company.' Indeed, it turns out that their property rights can only be protected by keeping costs to a minimum, maximising profits and returning the best possible dividend. It is hard to see how a pay increase for employees can match these goals, unless it has

Table 17.1 Fitting the ethical theories together

Consequentialist	Non-consequentialist
Utilitarianism	Kantianism
Happiness of the greatest number	Human dignity an end in itself
The end justifies the means	Universal moral rules
Language of economic utility	Language of human rights

a sound economic basis such as labour shortages or increased productivity. In this view, business efficiency must serve the shareholder, first and foremost. An alternative way, termed 'Stakeholding', argues that shareholders or investors are just one of several interest groups represented in the business corporation, including employees, customers, suppliers and the wider community. Accordingly, my ethical duty is to balance the needs of these different groups. Hence, if the pay and conditions of employees have been neglected in recent years, a pay award may be a justifiable piece of 'rebalancing'. On the other hand, if pay is already very high compared to elsewhere, and has been passed on in high prices to customers – as in Premier League football – it will not be the right thing to do. The general problem remains of how to adjudicate ethically between the claims of the competing stakeholders. By this point, many passages have begun to merge and overlap, as stakeholding and shareholding each blur into utilitarianism on the one side, and human rights on the other, at some point on the way.

At a clearing in the maze, however, a broad new passage begins, called 'Theories of Justice'. Yet within a few feet, this has divided in two completely different directions. The first route, 'Justice as Entitlement', eventually runs into the shareholder path on which we travelled earlier (see Nozick 1993). This argues that human beings have a right to acquire and transfer property freely, providing they follow due process and avoid fraud and theft. Neither the government, nor any other organised pressure group, has a right to interfere in this free, and therefore fair, exchange. Seen in this light, my employees should conclude individual deals with me over wages and conditions, and accept whatever is the commercial going rate. Although I may pay them more, through kindness and charity, this is an 'imperfect duty' or an act of gratuitous generosity and it remains quite just to pay them the bare market rate. If, by banding together in a trade union, my employees are trying to 'force' me to pay a higher rate than I would from free choice, this is unjust and I would be right to resist their efforts. This view of justice places little social responsibility on the business to protect the wages and conditions of employees and can lead to great economic inequality. It also demonstrates how far some ethical theories can depart from common-sense notions of fair treatment.

The other path, 'Justice as Fairness', leads to a table and chairs, where we all sit down, don blindfolds and think about what sort of society we would like to live in, without knowing what position we would occupy in it (see Rawls 1993). The conclusion drawn is that we would choose equal treatment except where differences work to the benefit of the worst off. We would not choose 'justice as entitlement' for fear that we might be born without talent or resources, and end up penniless and sleeping in the streets. Applied to my situation, this suggests that if the claimants are substantially poorer than I, or other shareholders and white-collar employees, I must either demonstrate that they benefit from these inequalities, or allow the pay claim. In defence, my unique skill and responsibility may be an adequate justification. Maybe to stay within the spirit of this social contract, I should give employees some say in the running of the business. This might involve establishing a consultation committee, including union representatives, having 'worker directors' or even turning the business into some sort of cooperative owned by the entire workforce, similar to the John Lewis Partnership. These options, if taken, lead into a common passage, shared with 'Stakeholding'. One linking way is 'Communitarianism' (see Etzioni 1995), whereby we ponder not just the distribution of economic resources in terms of poverty and inequality; but also the impact on social cohesion. In short, will high manual pay contribute to a more tightly knit workforce and community?

After all this wandering in the moral maze, it is easy to become confused and disheartened. And there are three wide avenues radiating from a clearing, each promising a quick route to a satisfactory ethical conclusion. One termed 'Divine Judgement', invites us to abandon all this confusion and buy a tried-and-tested set of moral rules off the religious shelf. My problem is that rules like the Ten Commandments were devised long before the genesis of modern business, and are too general to tell me what to do in this precise situation. In addition, many of my employees already have alternative sets of rules – which will make them hard to convince. Another path, 'Ethical Relativism', runs in precisely the opposite direction, reassuring me that such diversity of opinion is unavoidable in our postmodern society, and recommending that I avoid the sort of universal claims made by the deontologists earlier (see Smith and Johnson 1996). Far better, this approach suggests, to follow the shared opinion of my particular subculture. I belong, however, to many social circles each with different ethical views, while my business friends simply press a shareholder view that is quite unacceptable to my employees. Finally, I encounter 'Enlightened Self-Interest', a way that reassures me that I worry too much (see Pearson 1995). In the long term, good wages and conditions create loyal, productive, well-trained trustworthy employees, who, in turn, produce great rewards for all the stakeholders at the same time. This is the familiar human resource management (HRM) theory to which we return below. Yet still I wonder, how does this pay award help or hinder and what about the short term?

An employment ethics agenda

While the various ethical theories offer plenty of clues for what an ethical employment policy might look like, there are no straightforward and easy solutions that can be drawn from them. Moreover, most general ethical theories can be interpreted in very divergent ways. This said, the big debate in employment ethics concerns how far the state and social agencies, like trade unions, should be allowed to regulate the free market in order to protect workers' wages and conditions. And we can quickly see two main sides lining up and drawing together different elements from the above ethical theories. In general terms, this division bears an uncanny resemblance to the Right–Left political divide in Britain and America, between conservatives on one side and liberals or social democrats on the other. The right wing stresses the utilitarian benefits of free-market capitalism, duty to the shareholder, justice as the entitlement to own and freely dispose of property, and a paternalist version of enlightened self-interest which renders state intervention unnecessary. The left wing emphasises the disutilities of short-term, free-market capitalism for society, employee rights, stakeholding, justice as fairness and a sceptical view of enlightened self-interest which presupposes the need for substantial state regulation to ensure good employment practices. In these terms, the question of what is ethical employment practice transmutes into the question: how should employment be regulated and to what ends? But first, what sort of employment issues are we talking about?

Business ethics in general is already a major preoccupation of most large companies. Many corporate mission statements and ethical codes pay lip service to virtues such as integrity, fairness and loyalty and envision a variety of stakeholders, including employees. In some cases, this enthusiasm for ethics has been prompted by a scandal, which damaged a company's or industry's reputation, as with criticism of the banks for mis-selling pensions in the 1990s, the Enron case in the USA, or Shell's bad publicity over human rights in Nigeria. In other cases,

Table 17.2 Capitalism and theories of justice – an interpretation

	Theory of justice	Corporate responsibliity	Employment policies
Right-wing	Nozick (entitlement)	Shareholder (unitarist)	Free market
Left-wing	Rawls (fairness)	Stakeholder (pluralist)	Regulated market

ethics has been used as a marketing tool in a more proactive way. Hence, the Body Shop launched itself around a strong opposition to testing on animals for cosmetic purposes and has campaigned for fair trade with the Third World; while the Co-operative Bank has responded to customer objections to fur farming and investment in oppressive regimes (see Burchill 1994). By and large, these companies have concentrated their attention on external public relations and the customer as a stakeholder, with the often undeclared assumption that stakeholding will work directly to improve the position of the shareholder. In all this, employees often appear as a poor relation in the family of stakeholders, such that companies can flaunt their ethics to customers while making thousands of workers redundant. Any distinctively employment ethics agenda will revolve around the damage caused to workers' wages and conditions by unregulated, flexible, free-market capitalism. In so far as customers and shareholders benefit from this regime – high dividends and low prices at the expense of low wages, for instance – it may reflect a clash of stakeholder interests. As a consequence, employment ethics tends to deploy left-wing ethical arguments against free-market capitalism. Let us briefly rehearse four of these.

One points to just pay and the enormous gap that has opened up between executive pay and perks, on the one hand, and those of people in low-paid, temporary jobs on the other. In deciding whether these are 'just' rewards we can apply Rawls' test – for example, senior management rewards are much lower in Europe and Japan than in Britain and the USA – and explore issues of 'merit' and 'need'. The national minimum wage is prompted by an ethical assessment that the 'market rate' is not always a fair rate and that the state has to intervene to regulate bad employers. Another issue related to the flexible labour market concerns individual and family welfare associated with working time. Some workers today are trapped in such sporadic, part-time and temporary work that they find it hard to support themselves, let alone a family. Other, better-paid salaried workers find it hard to draw boundaries between their work and home lives, such that they suffer stress and their relationships and children suffer neglect (see Chapter 13 in this volume on family-friendly policies). In all these cases, as communitarians argue, the price for society may be family and community breakdown (see Ackers 2002). Once more, the European Union (EU) Working Time Directive, laying down a maximum 48-hour working week and minimum holiday provisions, rests on the assumption that in certain circumstances the free market can fail employees and society.

Two other issues are less directly economic in character. The first regards the right to employee participation, or the entitlement of workers (and the local community in cases of major plant closure) to have some say in the running of their business organisation. This relates to broader issues of corporate governance, and whose interests the business organisation should serve. Full-blown stakeholding or organisational pluralism demands some sort of representative structure by which workers can influence company decision making (see Ackers *et al.* 2005). In the past, trade unions played this role, and in many cases they still do. Legislation on statutory trade union recognition offers to bolster this union role. But this still begs the question of what happens across more than half of the economy where trade unions are completely absent. The European Social Chapter included a right to worker participation and European works councils already provide for this in large companies.

In addition to such positive rights, there is the issue of negative rights or civil liberties. For public sector workers these are now enshrined in the Human Rights Act. If left-wing thinking has often underestimated the threat of the state to individual freedom, right-wing thinkers are equally blind to the threat posed by the large business. Equal opportunities issues around race, gender, disability and sexuality are already established in law and public policy. Measures against age discrimination are likely to follow soon. But can an employer dismiss someone because they are fat, smoke, wear an earring or tattoo, or have eccentric religious or political views? In short, how far can a business, seeking to mould corporate culture, invade the private self of the individual employee or potential employee? This conundrum links to the question of whistle-blowers or workers who expose unethical practices in their company. Does the business own their conscience because it pays the wages, or do they have a higher obligation to society?

Here again, a pluralist or stakeholding view of the corporation demands forms of external regulation to underpin these rights. Enlightened companies may address these issues of their own accord, through voluntary agreements, procedures and codes of practice. But, from this perspective, business as a whole cannot be trusted to do so. And firms with bad employment practices may gain short-term cost advantages and undermine the high standards elsewhere. In several of the above examples, recent British government or EU regulation has been prompted by the decline of trade unions and collective bargaining, leaving many employees exposed to the full power of the employer. Moreover, as we shall see below, employers in general have failed to fill this 'ethical gap' by voluntary action. This said, the state can only secure minimum standards, leaving great scope for companies and managers to establish exemplary wages and conditions. Today, these may also include well-resourced efforts to train and involve workers, as well as 'family-friendly' policies such as extended maternity and paternity provision, flexitime or nursery facilities (see Chapter 13 in this volume).

Shaping an ethical workplace

If employment ethics is to mean anything in practice, we need to identify institutions or agencies capable of implementing it. Individual virtue is necessary, but not sufficient. Rarely does one person have the capacity to resolve a moral dilemma, as in the wages scenario earlier. Economic life is highly complex and beyond the scope of personal acts of goodwill. Only the state or substantial social institutions can impress some ethical pattern on the relationships that ensue. As Clegg's (1979) rule-making framework for employment relations suggests, three agencies can help to build an ethical approach into the very structure and process of economic life: from above, companies and their managers; from below, workers' own self-help organisations, most notably trade unions; and, finally, from without, the state as an expression of society's collective moral conscience.

Let us turn now to the most pervasive rule-making agent in most contemporary employment relationships: employers and the professional managers who act on their behalf. Even where the state and trade unions play a central part in framing the employment relationship, the chosen style of employers and managers is crucial in defining the experience of work. While some good practices can be imposed from outside – as with racial and sexual discrimination or minimum wages – the devil is in the detail, and management culture may become a major obstacle to the full realisation of an ethical workplace. In order to understand what role management can play, I will sketch the historical evolution of management practice, particularly in relation to the personnel function, and then look more closely at the experience of HRM since 1979. First, though, we need to understand what management is and how this shapes the ethical tone of the enterprise.

Today, employer regulation is only rarely exercised by the single owner in person, except in the small business. Management is the collective name for those specialist, technical workers who act as the employer's agents in day-to-day dealings with the workforce. As businesses grow in size, and as the personality of the individual owner fragments into the thousands of anonymous individual and institutional shareholders of the modern public limited company, managers become the visible hands and face of employer power. In line with modern rational-legal authority and scientific management, the extensive and ill-defined prerogatives of the individual master are broken down into a specialist management hierarchy. In large, complex organisations, this managerial division of labour is characterised by horizontal layers according to seniority, and vertical lines of function. At the apex, there are senior managers, headed by the managing director, who concentrate on business strategy; while, at the base, are line managers or supervisors who deal directly and regularly with ordinary workers. In between, lie various strata of middle managers who connect the two types of activity. Those at the two opposite ends of the management ladder tend to be general managers, but most of the intermediaries are allocated some specialist function, such as marketing, production or personnel. This management specialism is reinforced by some professional organisation and identity as is the case with groups like accountants, or more pertinently for us, HRM or personnel managers.

While few would dispute this general description of management, there is far greater controversy over who exactly managers are answerable to, and what their social responsibilities are. What we expect of managers in the business organisation depends largely on our chosen frame of reference and this is likely to dovetail with one of the competing ethical theories discussed above. For the unitarist, differences of management function and level are a purely technical issue, subordinate to his single purpose as the unquestioning agent of the shareholder owners. This 'stockholder' conception is enshrined in Anglo-American company law, though not in continental European stakeholder traditions. As the right-wing economist, Milton Friedman (1993) argues, once managers or companies take on goals and responsibilities which do not serve their ultimate aim of higher profits, they betray their ultimate employers and endanger the whole future of the enterprise, indeed of capitalism itself. In short, absolute adherence to market principles outside the business, and to the single line of authoritarian command within it, are but two sides of the same unitarist coin.

By contrast, pluralists are likely to perceive and welcome much greater diversity of allegiance and objectives among modern managers for two main reasons. First, from a purely sociological point of view, this conforms to their image of the business as fractured by competing interest groups, including various management levels and functions. Thus, senior company directors often belong to the Institute of Directors, while line managers join supervisory trade unions, like Amicus. Personnel specialists seek professional status and accreditation through the Chartered Institute of Personnel and Development (CIPD) courses and exams – modelled on other professional bodies such as the British Medical Association and the Law Society. Second, from a more normative perspective, this view of managers also provides them with some scope to exercise independent ethical action, as is implied in the ethical codes of bodies like the CIPD. They are no longer just servants of the shareholders, at their every beck and call. Rather, they hold responsibilities to all the stakeholders in the organisation, including workers, customers and the local community, and to society as a whole. As always, observed fact and value judgement become intertwined. Postwar pluralist industrial relations thinkers like Flanders (1974) found hope in the growing separation between the ownership and control of large public limited companies, precisely because it created new scope for professional managers to exercise a more spacious and socially responsible role. For them formal ownership no longer mattered, since *de facto* pluralism reigned even where, as in Britain, company law did not provide for this. In this they have been proved mistaken, for under Margaret Thatcher a free-market government rolled back the blanket of state protection and trade union influence to reveal the short-term shareholder model beneath. For these reasons, the ethical role of management must be closely related to the responsibilities of business and the way in which society defines these.

The greatest burden of pluralist hope lay upon the shoulders of personnel, the company function and department that specialises in dealing with employees and their representatives. This aspiring management profession seemed to personify the broader social concerns of management, as in the old conception of personnel managers as enlightened umpires, bringing management and workers together, and creating industrial relations concord. As we shall see, the history of personnel management has parallels with the growth of social work, beginning as a predominately female caring profession concerned with people. Below, I ponder whether the new title of HRM marks a rediscovery of this ethical mission, as some suggest, or an irrevocable break from any emphasis on workers as social beings, towards a calculating image of them as mere economic counters. But the management of people has never been the exclusive mandate of personnel. So it is important to set personnel's fluctuating role in the broader context of the overall management style adopted by the business towards employees, from the senior managers who attempt to shape the culture of the organisation, down to the line managers who actually conduct most relations between management and ordinary workers (see Fox 1974).

The history of ethical employment management

In *History and Heritage* (1985, pp.1–30), Alan Fox identifies two competing systems of labour control as, from the eighteenth century onwards, British society adjusted to the modern, capitalist employment relationship. Each operated at the level of state policy and law and through the strategies of individual business units. In this, there is much that is familiar today. The first strategy, paternalism, was carried over from the pre-industrial past, and combined notions of worker deference and a rigid social hierarchy with a sense of ruling class social responsibility. Hence, for many years, wage levels and customary rights were underwritten by law, partly for fear that a desperate and dispossessed poor would prove dangerous to the rich and powerful. The second strategy, market individualism, was informed by the new capitalist economic order that was breaking free of these semi-feudal bonds. This challenged the notion of a fixed social order and focused on the rights of individuals in politics, while reinterpreting the employment relationship as a private economic contract. Either approach was a mixed blessing for ordinary working people. While paternalism locked workers into a position of permanent subordination, as a price for some moral concern and social protection; market individualism threatened to cast them adrift with no reliable source of income or living, in exchange for the opportunity to freely sell their labour at the best price and better themselves.

Today, the balance between these two strategies has been largely reversed, at least at the level of the firm, with market individualism being regarded as the normal economic relationship and paternalism a noteworthy and deviant one (see Ackers 1998, 2001). Nonetheless, the same tension in management strategy continues and connects with the central right-wing–left-wing ethical divide outlined above. Should the business manage labour as an economic commodity, to be bought on the market at the cheapest possible price; or seek a long-term social relationship with their employees that transcends instant economic calculation? In most cases, the solution is a compromise between market and managerial relations, for, while labour may be hired in an outside marketplace, it can only be put to work in the social context of the workplace. For these reasons, though market individualism may be in the driving seat, it can rarely control the vehicle without some element of paternalism seated alongside. The development of management in general, and personnel management in particular, reflects this need to control and motivate the workforce as a social group, and passed through two main stages prior to 1979.

Stage one, roughly from 1850 to 1945 in most large companies, saw a new social hybrid, paternalist capitalism, emerge from the anti-social anarchy of early capitalism (see Joyce 1980;

Ackers and Black 1991; Greene *et al.* 2001). It is not surprising, therefore, that the birth of personnel management, as a distinctive profession, with its own authoritative body, code of practice and range of qualifications, coincided with the late Victorian movement towards a more socially conscious, if paternalist, employer style of management. As Britain settled down into more stable work communities, some large employers, influenced by Christian ideas about social responsibility, sought to shape a stronger social dimension to their businesses and the communities in which they operated. Many work towns of the early industrial revolution were merely factories surrounded by cheap housing for their workers. They lacked the most basic facilities, such as schools and sewage systems. To a large extent, the new working classes began to create their own civilisation through self-help bodies like trade unions, local religious congregations and cooperative societies. However, enlightened employers also played an important part, for a mixture of motives including disinterested public service, personal self-aggrandisement, and a concern for work discipline and social cohesion. Through involvement in local government or by personal direct donations, they sponsored the creation of social and cultural amenities like parks, chapels and libraries. At the turn of the century, the Quaker, George Cadbury, built the chocolate factory and garden city of Bournville, Birmingham for his workers and the local community, and it remains an impressive spectacle today. In the midst of acres of pleasant houses with large gardens, stood the model factory, with its exemplary working conditions, splendid playing fields and welfare facilities.

Personnel management emerged from large-scale Victorian paternalist capitalism, as direct personal contact between master and servant declined, and the employer families sought more institutional expressions of their ethical calling. According to Torrington and Hall's (1991) rather idealised seven-stage taxonomy, social reformers were the first on the scene, notably the Quaker chocolate manufacturer's wife, Elizabeth Fry, who conducted social work outside the factory and campaigned for legislation to protect health and safety. Next, during the full flowering of Christian paternalism, on the Bournville scale, came the welfare officer, again usually a woman, who conducted industrial social work within the workplace. This brought social concern in line with the modern management division of labour then emerging in large factories. Thus, in 1913, the Institute of Welfare Officers was formed at Rowntree's York chocolate factory. In this respect, personnel began with the same high ideals of caring for employees as the best representatives of paternalist capitalism, and travelled with them from a personal to a professional and institutional expression of these values.

However, a number of factors began to unpick the fabric of paternalist capitalism, so that from the 1930s onwards a new modern bureaucratic company emerged associated with a more scientific and less moralistic personnel outlook. By 1945 the sense of religious mission had entered into decline, as part of the general secularisation of mid-twentieth-century Britain. Trade unions had advanced during 'the people's war', which itself had eroded the spirit of worker deference. A comprehensive welfare state, meanwhile, superseded many company provisions. Otherwise, the main reason for the retreat of religious paternalism was the demise of the owner-manager and the private family company. This presents something of a paradox for pluralist advocates of social responsibility, since the growing separation of ownership and control destroyed the personal moral responsibility of individual or family ownership. Business owners moved away from the dirty towns they had created to live as country gentlemen, passed the running of the business completely to professional managers, and, ultimately, sold their shares to the highest bidder. Their children were educated at exclusive schools, and most preferred a genteel lifestyle to managing an ugly factory or busy store. As ownership of the new joint stock companies devolved to a multitude of passive shareholders and pension funds, only interested in a return on their investment, the guiding hand of employer paternalism slipped from view. To many employees this was welcome, since company beneficence had often gone with a desire to interfere in and shape their private lives outside work.

In this new era of rational-legal authority, when professional, career managers ran business and trade unions represented workers' interests, the religious language of calling and service appeared condescending and redundant. The emerging professions of teaching, social work and personnel reflected a new spirit of value-free social engineering. At work, social science theories of behaviour, such as scientific management and human relations, supplanted ethical idealism. During this phase, most employers withdrew from an active ethical role in both their business and the local community, as the welfare state and local government supplanted many of their earlier roles. Workers became more independent of their employers, preferring higher pay to cricket pitches, sermons and company picnics, and trade unions to consultative arrangements. In the long run, however, there would be a price to pay for this, as the business corporation was able to divest itself of any social responsibility beyond the efficient pursuit of profit.

Torrington and Hall (1991) identify four new and overlapping personnel roles which arose in this second period. The humane bureaucrat, a management specialist with skills in selection and training, first appeared during the interwar years at public limited companies like the chemical giant, ICI. Later, after the Second World War, a company-level industrial relations role gained increasing importance. From the 1950s onwards, collective bargaining with trade unions was pulled down to the workplace, calling for negotiating expertise at that level. This saw the arrival of the consensus negotiator, or contracts manager, a tough masculine part, involving new skills of conflict resolution. At the same time, the organisation person was concerned with the effectiveness of the whole organisation, and not just employee welfare, linking together other management activities through their role in management development. Meanwhile, the manpower analyst set about quantifying human resources, for instance, by measuring the cost of labour turnover and planning the labour supply. A concern for workers still lingered on in these roles, though not as an end in itself, even in theory. Even the consensus negotiator restricted his relations with employees to the arm's length, institutionalised relationship with trade union representatives. If the soul had gone out of personnel management, it seemed that at least a disinterested profession had been created with an apparently social scientific knowledge base linked to practical skills.

Before turning to contemporary developments associated with HRM, it is important to qualify this generalised image of British business. Sophisticated modern companies, such as Cadbury's, were far from the norm in the history of British industrial relations. What we have seen so far is the best parts of British business putting their best face forward. For, as Fox (1985) argues, market individualism remained the dominant preference of British employers, tempered only by the often uninvited presence of trade unions that forced businesses to confront the collective nature of the employment relationship through detailed personnel policies. These standard modern employers embraced trade unions as a short-term and pragmatic response to organised labour, rather than as a principled, long-term social vision of the employment relationship (Fox 1974). Most industrial relations commentators see this dual view of labour – a commodity in the external market and a cost within the firm – as conducive to a relatively low-skilled, low-waged and poorly trained labour force, in contrast to the best continental practice in economies like Germany. Arguably, too, this mentality has denied personnel its proper status in the business organisation, creating a ragbag of low-status administrators and industrial relations firefighters, rather than a cohesive profession of influential employment architects (see Sisson 1994). This, in turn, has stymied the development of distinctively ethical employment policies.

The advent of HRM

The third period, from 1979 to 1997, presented a remarkable opportunity for business to demonstrate its concern for employees, unhindered by state or trade union regulation. For two decades, the right-wing ethical perspective reigned supreme. During these years, management was cast as the principal agent of social change, and the rhetoric of the enterprise culture spoke eloquently of employee involvement and commitment, while remaining strangely silent about justice and rights at work (see Ackers 1994). For personnel, HRM was the big new theme in management thinking that tied together these various initiatives, and promised a new constructive role for people management in the workplace. It is to this that we now turn. Hitherto, the academic debate over HRM has revolved around the poles of 'rhetoric' and 'reality' (Legge 1995). In other words, has business lived up to the promises it has made? We begin, therefore, with the claims of HRM in theory and then turn to what this has meant for the employment relationship in practice.

The ethical rhetoric of HRM is everywhere in contemporary business and society. Some variation on the phrase – 'this business regards employees as its number one resource' – has become part of the ritual of company reports and briefings, tripping easily from the lips of chief executives. The CIPD's magazine, *People Management,* is now subtitled '*the magazine for human resources professionals*'. The sleek new HRM model is boldly contrasted with the 'bad old days' of personnel past, much as a born-again Christian celebrates his new creation by darkening his own past (see Clark 1993; Ackers and Preston 1997). Before, labour was a cost to be controlled; now, a resource to be nurtured. Before, personnel was a routine administrative activity; now, a strategic champion of people management for heightened business performance. Before, industrial relations was adversarial and arm's length; now, founded on consensus and employee consent. Before, personnel coveted people management; now, a human relations gospel for all. Rather than chase all these hares, as so many others have already, let us concentrate first, on HRM's central claim – to have made human resources more central to today's businesses than they were a generation ago. This, after all, is one key test of the ethical employment credentials of contemporary business.

Sisson's (1994, p.42) authoritative summary of the survey and case study evidence on the free-market experiment in Britain, concludes that 'personnel management in many organisations in Britain is locked into a vicious circle of low pay, low skill, and low productivity'. This is surprising, as he recognises, since HRM had promised exactly the opposite, arguing that people are the key to competitive advantage for Western economies where Third World low-cost labour is not an option. Old, rigid and authoritarian forms of management control were supposed to yield to 'the development of a highly committed and adaptable workforce willing and able to learn new skills and take on new tasks'. At face value, British business appeared to be placing a new stress on human resources, and this is the conventional wisdom taught in many business schools. However, the research paints a much more depressing picture. Following Fox (1985) and MacInnes (1987), this suggests that the enterprise culture has exacerbated the laissez-faire, short-term, cost-reduction employer attitudes to labour, endemic in the British employment relations tradition. Moreover, the definitive Workplace Industrial Relations surveys, suggest that HRM in practice has been largely a chimera (Millward *et al.* 1992; Cully *et al.* 1999). Yes, some HRM techniques, like employee involvement, are widespread in mainstream companies where trade unions remain a factor; no doubt partly as a means of countering their influence. Yet, where management has a free hand, in the now majority non-union sector, there is little evidence of a new 'ethical' HRM approach to managing labour.

The obvious conclusion is that union representation and effective joint consultation was replaced, not by a new enlightened HRM, but by a tough 'Bleak House' hire-and-fire employment policy. Overall, the evidence supports the view of labour as a disposable commodity, a cost to be controlled rather than a resource to be developed. At this level, employment ethics is mainly about good public relations towards customers and staying on the right side of the law. Accordingly, this Anglo-American share or 'stockholder' model concentrates on short-term costs, profits and dividends, dictated by city and financial markets. As in the past, British capital is short-term and cost-minimising in outlook, and has failed to invest in labour as a resource, while management remains attached to crude, cost-effective, payment-by-results systems. Within this framework, there is very little space for active employment ethics. For this to change, Sisson (1994, pp.42–4) argues,

> There would have to be a fundamental reappraisal of the way in which British companies are run . . . A policy of laissez-faire not only sends the wrong signals, above all to small and medium-sized businesses, it also fails to take into account that, left to their own devices, many UK companies will find the 'high pay, high skill, high productivity' route quite simply beyond them.

Writing before the 1997 general election, when the prospects were 'extremely remote', Sisson (1994) proposed the following stakeholding initiatives:

> overhauling the regulatory framework of companies and their relationships with the city; developing an appropriate training system; and introducing a legal framework of rights and obligations that would help to raise standards . . . the kind of framework that our partners in Europe are anxious to introduce in the form of the Social Charter.

Since then, New Labour has made some modest but significant moves in this direction. Overall, though, HRM rhetoric still has to translate into a management approach that values people, even in its own economic terms, as a resource. If the reality of HRM has proved a disappointment so far, maybe the idea at least is worthwhile. It is to this that we now turn.

Conclusion: three fallacies of HRM ethics

Much of this analysis presupposes that HRM has failed because British institutions have frustrated the managerial reforms that could have made it a reality, not that HRM itself presents a positive barrier to any progress towards a more 'ethical' workplace. Only rarely has anyone asked whether the rhetoric, let alone the practice, offers an attractive and credible vision of the world of work and management's place in this (see Hart 1993; Torrington 1993). We might, for instance, regard HRM as some do as organised religion, and conclude that, despite all the bad things done in its name, there remains a valuable ethical essence that is worth retaining. Some academics and trade unionists have approached HRM in this spirit, arguing that we can 'play back' promises about 'people being our number one resource' and ask management to live up to these. In purely pragmatic terms, there is much to be said for this approach in a business environment where HRM is unlikely to go away, as I have argued elsewhere (see Ackers and Payne 1998; Ackers and Wilkinson 2003). On the other hand, if we do not go beyond such necessary opportunism, there is a danger of becoming ensnared within the HRM worldview. For once we peel away the layers of HRM hyperbole, we reach a hollow core: an impoverished ethical vision of the employment relationship. This rests upon three ethical fallacies, which I will term 'golden calf', 'enlightened self-interest' and 'happy family'.

The golden calf fallacy assumes that all human values should be subordinated to business considerations and calculations. At the heart of the HRM worldview stands the claim that the human resource is a business's most valued asset. This appears, at first glance, a noble belief, even if it flies in the face of the manner in which many employers actually treat their workers. In particular, it suggests a culture in which companies invest in workers' long-term development, instead of regarding them as merely costs, to be cut and controlled. Yet, there is a dangerous flaw in this ethical vision, and this relates to the broader stream of right-wing ethical thinking, which redefines human beings with their complex social, spiritual and material needs, as mere rational economic categories, be these consumers or human resources. Such language assumes that business and its economic terminology should shape human aspirations, and not the other way round. From a practical management point of view, enlightened employment policies will always require a business case. Ethics should not be a recipe for economic suicide or ridicule. But to have a long-term competitive advantage at the back of your mind is not to subordinate every decision to short-term economic calculus, as HRM implies. For workers, the choice is between being a most valued economic asset, and being a rounded human being whose dignity should be respected by all – in Kant's terms, a subject that should never become an object. This has grave implications for the role of managers, since they are asked to lead the worship at the altar of false values. They too are required to treat their subordinates as merely a means to economic ends, to count the cost of every act of kindness. To personnel management in particular, HRM offers a Faustian pact within the enterprise culture. The prize advertised is an ever-growing personnel influence inside the business organisation; the price is personnel's professional soul and its total commitment to goals defined by senior executives and large shareholders, over and above all other stakeholders.

The enlightened self-interest fallacy takes the heresy a stage further, by pretending that business considerations alone are sufficient for companies to look after their employees, without outside regulation from the state or trade unions. As Pearson (1995) argues, a business needs to build long-term trust relationships with employees, customers and other companies in order to thrive, and therefore it needs to behave with integrity towards all these groups. Thus HRM theory fosters the seductive idea that it is in the self-interest of business to treat workers well, and that, for this reason alone, they no longer need to fear for their own protection. Yet numerous businesses, large and small, thrive on short-term, one-sided relationships, as the evidence for the failure of HRM shows. Perhaps, as Sisson suggests, this is against the long-term interests of Great Britain PLC, but there is little reason why that thought should detain for long the mobile, well-rewarded, modern business executive. The significance for workers' pay and conditions is that their entitlements are entirely contingent upon what makes business successful. If profitability demands investment in the human resource, employers will undertake this; if it entails exploiting cheap disposable labour, and breaking trade unions to this end, they will do the same. Once more, an economic theory that makes human rights entirely conditional on business convenience, and puts a price on human dignity, lies at the heartless centre of HRM's view of the world.

The happy family fallacy assumes that the state and trade unions are unwelcome intrusions into a fundamentally harmonious, unitarist employment relationship. Most American-style HRM theory is unitarist in outlook and either silent about or actively hostile to trade unions as representative bodies (Guest 1989). This approach to HRM claims to place this happy paternalist conjunction of self-interest and employee well-being on a new, harder, more calculative footing. However, it does so against all the evidence that the tradition went into decline long ago, and has collapsed in the postwar period. The way we live now, in postmodern Britain, talk of company loyalty is as specious and insincere as easy appeals to 'community' and calls for street parties to mark national anniversaries. The break-up of occupational communities, founded on steel, coal, cotton, tin, fishing or carpets, where large extended families all worked for the same firm, has created a much greater occupational and social fragmentation and a far more mobile workforce. When the HRM 'good news' hit British business in the early 1980s, most large companies had already shed their family benefactors, faded out the welfare provisions, sold off their leafy garden villages to middle-class professionals, turned their consultative committees into a branch line on which hardly anyone travelled, and begun building on their playing fields. Like the Cheshire Cat, too often all that remains of paternalism is the smile. Management can still make a central contribution in the creation of a more cooperative and cohesive employment system. However, it will not do so by pretending that one exists already, if only we could see it.

The sheer ambiguity of HRM may pose the biggest ethical problem, leading to charges of misrepresentation and bad faith. What so often sounds like a species of left-wing ethical thinking, promising something extra for employees, turns out on closer examination to be a sugar-coated edition of right-wing moral and economic philosophy. Milton Friedman (1993), from the latter perspective, suggests that such spurious claims to added 'social responsibility' are better left unsaid and merely detract from the strong, unvarnished case for capitalism. And it is true that right-wing ethical thinking has a firm grounding in certain business, economic and social realities. Most of us recognise, to some degree, the utilitarian benefits of a capitalist economic system, wherein countless selfish, individual market transactions produce unprecedented living standards for most people. In our personal lives, we expect this 'hidden hand' (Smith 1993) to be allowed considerable freedom, in order to ensure that our pensions keep pace with inflation and our supermarket groceries are as cheap as possible. We also want to be free to use our own money and property as freely as possible without undue interference from the state. We probably regard this economic freedom from state control (including the freedom to change job when we wish) as one essential freedom in a liberal democratic society. For all these reasons, any framework of employment ethics which, like full-blooded socialism in the past, threatened to 'kill the goose that laid the golden egg' is likely to be unacceptable to us. The problem with right-wing ethical thinking is that it forces these genuine concerns to an extreme, so that only the most minimal, individual ethics, such as honesty and trust in contracts, is deemed either necessary or possible. By denying the reality of a long-term employment relationship and presenting the labour contract as a spot-market transaction, like buying a bag of apples, right-wing ethics sends HRM managers into the workplace naked. They either have to imagine new clothes, like the emperor, and hope their employees will believe them; or else they have to look else where.

Perhaps the crucial distinction here then is between employment ethics as a public relations façade and rationalisation for what business already does out of short-term economic self-interest; and employment ethics as an active commitment to employees above and beyond this. For managers can and should play a crucial role in constructing socially responsible, business organisations at the heart of a decent society. This would require, however, a pluralist institutional framework which placed the long-term employment relationship and the wages and conditions of employees, alongside other stakeholders, at the heart of the business organisation. In these circumstances, we could speak meaningfully of social partnership, loyalty and commitment. Within a framework of relationship capitalism, managers could regain their professional autonomy and integrity, as public servants with a stakeholder ethos, rather than the handmaidens of private capital (see Hutton 1995). In communitarian language, the workplace would become a genuine 'moral community' responsive to society as a whole. HRM presents us with a paradox, because it talks of developing people, while considering its subjects as human resources. The reversion to economic language, and the lack of evidence for modern welfare capitalism (see Jacoby 1997), leads to the suspicion that when push comes to shove, the calculator will always take priority over the human being. Although the rhetoric of HRM contains elements that appeal to ethical employment principles, it fails to meet its promises on two counts. First, it bears little relation to the main developments in British employment relations, and thus presents itself as a mystifying ideology, a false promise of a better life in another world which will never arrive. Second, it abdicates any autonomous, ethical role for management, beyond doing whatever makes large shareholders and senior executives richer.

CASE STUDY 17.1

EMPLOYMENT ETHICS AT A&B STORES

PETER ACKERS

Introduction

A&B is a chain of department stores, selling clothes, food and hardware. It employs 10,000 UK workers in retail, distribution and office positions, mostly on permanent, full-time contracts. In addition, around 1,000 manufacturing workers, employed by its main subcontractor, are highly dependent on A&B's success and employment policy. The case study presents an opportunity to assess the ethics of the business at all stages in its development (was it doing the 'right thing' towards employees?), and to address a major contemporary dilemma between remaining competitive as a business and retaining a reputation as an ethical employer. It allows you to explore various ethical theories and to consider this business dilemma as a choice between different ethical frames of reference.

In the beginning

A&B was founded in 1900 as a small store in a medium-sized Scottish town by an austere, very religious Presbyterian (with his elder brother as a 'sleeping partner'). In the early days, the founder knew all his employees by their first name and exercised a strong 'fatherly' influence over their lives in and out of work. This had both benign and harsh aspects. The company was generous at times of family sickness, with the founder often visiting in person, though sometimes employees wondered if he was really checking up on them. And any employees who were caught with the smell of alcohol on their breath at work, or even drunk outside work, were summarily dismissed. The founder also promoted a strong sense of family values, organising (alcohol-free) works picnics and providing a free hamper every Christmas and at the birth of any child (up to three in number) and 200 cigarettes to the 'employee of the month'. Christian prayers were compulsory before each morning's work began. He also initiated and contributed towards various 'self-help' savings and mortgage schemes. Wages were generally slightly above the industry norm, according to the discretion of the founder, who liked to quote the parable of 'The Workers in the Vineyard' and reward those who he thought deserved and needed most. Women employees who married were required to leave, in order to fulfil their family duties, and all managerial positions were reserved for men with families. The firm promised lifetime job security for male employees and encouraged children to follow their parents into the trade. For many years, jobs were only rarely advertised externally.

Growth

The founder died in 1940 and ownership and control passed completely into the hands of his two sons. The boys had been educated at an English public school and lived in the Home Counties. But the founder's personal control had declined long before, as the company grew first into a Scottish chain in the 1920s, and then a nationwide chain during the Second World War. He had always strongly opposed trade unions as inimical to the family atmosphere of the firm, and in 1923 the firm fought off an organising campaign by the shop workers' union which was already well-established in the stores of the strong Scottish cooperative movement. As a result, 20 'ringleaders' were dismissed. During the 'hungry thirties' A&B gained a good reputation for maintaining employment when other businesses were laying people off. This was partly due to good business performance, but it was also widely believed that the owning family accepted lower profits in order to continue both to keep the loyal workforce and invest in the expansion of the firm.

The workforce was now counted in thousands rather than tens, so it was impossible for senior managers to retain personal, face-to-face contact – though local store managers were encouraged to do so. In response, the company developed a professional personnel department to create a more systematic set of provisions and policies. These included a non-union, representative company council that operated monthly at store level, and biannually across the whole company. Representatives were elected from every work group, and both negotiated with management over wages and consulted over any issues affecting the welfare of the workforce. There was also a welfare and sports society, which was heavily subsidised by the company and provided local A&B social clubs – initially on a strict temperance basis. These organised competitions for football, cricket, ballroom dancing and so on. Company developments and these social activities were reported in

Voice of A&B, a monthly company newspaper produced by the personnel department. The firm also pioneered a number of other welfare benefits, including a contributory pension scheme for all employees, and a seniority and promotion system called Growing Our Own, which meant that nearly all middle and senior managers were recruited from the shopfloor. Following one year's service, all employees joined the company profit-sharing scheme, which, in most years, added a further 10 per cent to their income.

PLC

In 1965, A&B became a public limited company (PLC), and within a few years family shareholdings had been dwarfed by those of pension funds and other outside investors. No senior managers now belonged to the original family, and many were being recruited from outside the business, rather than rising through its lower ranks as they had in the past. A new graduate recruitment programme had short-circuited the old seniority systems, though most middle managers had still risen from below. The business had also had to adapt to outside social trends, such as legislation for sexual and racial equality, and relaxed social mores – leading, among other things, to the serving of alcohol in A&B Clubs. A&B was still perceived by workers, customers and the general public as a family-run business with a strong ethical commitment to fair play. This was reflected in the trust and loyalty of long-service employees (and very low labour turnover), as of customers who repeatedly told surveys that they would not buy their clothes anywhere else. A&B continued to play a high-profile public charitable role, both in the town of its origin, where the head office remains, and in the wider community. In the latter case, the company sponsored a City Technology College in inner-city Glasgow during the 1980s and actively supported 'Business in the Community'. It also funded the first professorship in Business Ethics at a leading British business school.

The company had developed another long-term business relationship since its first major expansion in 1920, with a large clothing manufacturing firm situated in the town where the founder was born and A&B originated. Although Smiths & Co is an independent firm, 70 per cent of its output is contracted to A&B – whose letters also prefix the name of the local football team. Company head office and the local store employ between them 750 people, while the founder had presented to the town a park and art gallery, as well as a row of cottages for long-service company pensioners. The founder's wife had played a prominent charitable role in the interwar town, including organising youth clubs and holidays for children of the local poor and unemployed.

Today

A&B's personnel policy has remained fairly stable since the main structures were set in place in the 1930s. In line with 1960s and 1970s labour law and 'best practice', however, the company council system had been supplemented by a more formal (but still non-union) grievance and disciplinary procedure. Employees have shown no further interest in union membership, partly because wages and conditions are as good as those of most comparable unionised firms, and partly because they know A&B senior management are strongly anti-union and fear they might lose existing benefits if they push the issue. A new company interest in equal opportunities for women was partly inspired by the national policy mood, but also by labour shortages and recruitment difficulties in the postwar retail labour market. As a result, there has been a small influx of women graduates into managerial and supervisory roles, and the old distinction between 'men's' and 'women's' jobs has been replaced by a formally nondiscriminatory, A–G grading system. Equally, criticism that internal recruitment reproduced an 'all white' workforce, even in cities with large ethnic minorities, has led the company to advertise all vacancies in job centres and local newspapers, followed by a formal interview. Once again, outside policy influences have dovetailed with business concerns that its workforce should reflect the stores' potential customer base. Notwithstanding these developments, personnel policy still cultivates a long-term relationship with both the directly employed workforce and the manufacturing subcontractor. In the latter case, A&B has insisted on exercising substantial 'quality control' over the subcontractor's production process, while offering Smith & Co employees access to its social clubs and welfare provisions (though wages and conditions are handled separately). The company's commitment to high-quality, British-made products was a major attraction for its traditional customer base.

Until recently, A&B has interpreted the new wave of HRM thinking as largely an extension of its existing personnel practices. For instance, it has added team briefing, quality circles and a modest element of performance-related pay to its existing communications, consultation and reward structures. In some respects, like profit sharing, the firm was already a pioneer. Today, however, major changes in the retail market are forcing the company to reassess all elements of its activities. After years as a market leader, with steadily rising profits, A&B is now in some commercial difficulty. In particular, it faces competition from a new generation of fashion shops, which threaten its core clothing market. These firms source their products from low-cost Third World suppliers and are happy to switch these where and when the market justifies. They also employ a raw, if enthusiastic UK workforce of students and young people, almost entirely on short-term and temporary contracts. Their wages are close to the national minimum, often about 25 per cent less than A&B, and they spend far less on training and welfare. A&B has already responded to this threat by shedding 10 per cent of its workforce through natural wastage, early retirement and voluntary redundancy, while terminating one major contract with Smith & Co.

The ethical and business dilemma

A new managing director has been appointed to 'turn around' A&B. He has asked all the main functional directors to present a root-and-branch analysis of how the business can regain its market position and restore stock market confidence. These papers will be presented to and discussed at a 'Retail 2050: Future Directions' seminar, the outcome of which will determine the new business strategy to be presented to the next company Annual General Meeting.

The recently appointed head of marketing has already stolen a march on the others by circulating radical plans for a new, marketing-led, customer-focused, flexible firm that breaks almost completely with the traditional shape of the business, including its much-vaunted ethical employment policies. She proposes a new 'culture of entrepreneurship' which will withdraw the 'comfort zone' and 'time-serving' of current employment practices. Using a cricket metaphor, she argues that the point is 'not to occupy the crease but to score runs'. This will include establishing specialist boutiques and other facilities (including restaurants) within the stores, run on a franchise basis, using external subcontractors wherever possible, transferring all remaining direct employees to part-time contracts, except for a core of 'enterprise managers and supervisors' who, in future, will be paid largely according to performance. In addition, she moots the closure of the Scottish company headquarters and complete withdrawal from the town to smaller, more convenient facilities in an English new town; and the ending of the contract with Smith & Co to enable A&B to buy on the open market and benefit from low labour costs in south-east Asia. In the marketing director's view, the traditional paternalist approach is now completely archaic and untenable in the fast-moving retail market.

To further complicate matters, a whistleblower, within either senior management or the marketing department, has leaked these plans to the media. Rumours are circulating that A&B has been negotiating with a military dictatorship in the Far East for access to its labour force. Concerns about the abandonment of existing employees and the exploitation of Third World 'cheap labour' have been tabled by the founder's family for the company AGM. There have been demonstrations by employees in the original 'company town', addressed by outside trade union leaders, who called for union recognition for A&B employees under the new legislation and an effective European works council. A petition has been presented to the Scottish Assembly by local MPs and church leaders, describing A&B as 'the unacceptable face of capitalism' and urging a consumer boycott of stores nationwide.

Historically, the personnel function, now renamed HRM, has been seen as the custodian of the company's ethical employment policies. As we have seen, these centre on a long-term relationship with a stable workforce. Concerned at the bad publicity the business is attracting, the managing director has asked you, as personnel director, to frame an explicitly ethical employment policy which overcomes the difficulties you are facing and draws on some of the business' existing strengths. There are signs that the adverse publicity is affecting customers and undermining their trust and loyalty towards the company. No options are barred, but the managing director has asked you to specifically consider the following questions:

Note: While A&B is a fictional ideal-type company, it incorporates many real-life elements from a number of leading British manufacturing and retail organisations. These all began as paternalist family firms with their own ethical ideas about how employment should be managed and adapted and developed these as they grew into large, modern businesses.

Questions

1. How far was A&B's original employment policy 'ethical' in modern terms? What sort of ethical principles did it draw upon? Which elements would be acceptable today, and which would not?

2. How justified was the decision to prevent trade union organisation and is it still appropriate today? Consider the arguments *for* and *against* and the principles involved.

3. Construct an ethical case in favour of the flexible firm solution proposed by the director of marketing, explaining which principles you draw on.

4. Devise an alternative, HRM-driven business and ethical case for maintaining the existing long-term relationship with employees, customers and subcontractors.

5. Which stakeholder groups should take priority when push comes to shove? What duty, if any, does the company owe to its employees and shareholders in a modern free-market society?

6. Design an up-to-date and realistic, *ethical employment code of practice,* consistent with your answers to the above questions, which can be issued by the personnel department to all employees and used for external public relations purposes. Begin with some general principles and then identify key areas of business and employee rights and responsibilities.

CASE STUDY 17.2

APPLYING THE 'VEIL OF IGNORANCE'

PETER ACKERS

1. In the spirit of Rawls' 'veil of ignorance', imagine how it would feel to occupy someone else's role in society. Consider the following roles:

   (a) Rover carworker

   (b) Black civil servant

   (c) Hospital cleaner

   (d) Female junior doctor

   (e) Supermarket manager

   (f) Social worker

2. What workplace issues might concern you? What would justice mean to you? Think of both issues specific to your new situation and more general issues affecting workers and employees.

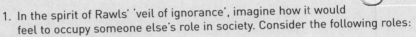

References

Ackers, P. (1994) 'Back to basics: industrial relations and the enterprise culture', *Employee Relations,* Vol.16, No.8, pp.32–47.

Ackers, P. (1998) 'On paternalism: seven observations on the uses and abuses of the concept in industrial relations, past and present', *Historical Studies in Industrial Relations,* Vol.6, pp.173–93.

*Ackers, P. (2001) 'Paternalism, participation and partnership: rethinking the employment relationship', *Human Relations,* Vol.54, No.3, pp.373–84.

*Ackers, P. (2002) 'Reframing employment relations: the case for neo-pluralism', *Industrial Relations Journal,* Vol.33, No.1, pp.2–19.

Ackers, P. and Black, J. (1991) 'Paternalist capitalism: an organisation culture in transition', in M. Cross and G. Payne (eds) *Work and the Enterprise Culture,* London: Falmer.

Ackers, P. and Payne, J. (1998) 'British trade unions and social partnership: rhetoric, reality and strategy', *International Journal of Human Resource Management,* Vol.9, No.3, pp.529–50.

Ackers, P. and Preston, D. (1997) 'Born again? The ethics and efficacy of the conversion experience in contemporary management development', *Journal of Management Studies,* Vol.34, No.5, pp.677–701.

Ackers, P. and Wilkinson, A.J. (2003) 'Introduction: the British industrial relations tradition – formation, breakdown and salvage', in P. Ackers and A.J. Wilkinson (eds) *Understanding Work and Employment: Industrial Relations in Transition,* Oxford: Oxford University Press, pp.1–27.

Ackers, P. Marchington, M., Wilkinson, A.J. and Dundon, T. (2005) 'Partnership and voice: with or without trade unions – changing UK management approaches to organisational participation', in M. Stuart and M.M. Lucio (eds) *Partnership and Modernisation in Employment Relations,* London: Routledge, pp.23–45.

Ackers, P., Smith, C. and Smith, P. (eds) (1996) *The New Workplace and Trade Unionism,* London: Routledge.

Armstrong, P. (1989) 'Limits and possibilities for HRM in an age of management accountancy', in J. Storey (ed.) *New Perspectives on Human Resource Management,* London: Routledge.

Burchill, J. (1994) *Co-op: The People's Business,* Manchester: Manchester University Press. (Reviewed by this author in *Review of Employment Topics,* Vol.5, No.1, (1997) pp.206–9.)

Carroll, S.J. and Gannon, M.J. (1997) *Ethical Dimensions of International Management,* London: Sage. (Reviewed by this author in *Human Resource Management Journal,* Vol.9, No.1, (1999), pp.89–91).

*Chryssides, G.D. and Kaler, J.H. (eds) (1993) *An Introduction to Business Ethics,* London: Chapman & Hall. (Reviewed by this author in *Human Resource Management Journal,* Vol.5, No.1, pp.103–5.)

Clark, J. (1993) 'Procedures and consistency versus flexibility and commitment in employee relations: a comment on Storey', *Human Resource Management Journal,* Vol.3, No.4, p.79.

Clegg, H.A. (1979) *The Changing System of Industrial Relations in Great Britain,* Oxford: Blackwell.

Crane, A. and Matten, D. (2004) *Business Ethics,* Oxford: Oxford University Press.

Cully, M., Woodland, S., O'Reilly, A. and Dix, G. (1999) *Britain at Work, As Depicted By the 1998 Workplace Employee Relations Survey,* London: Routledge.

*Etzioni, A. (1995) *The Spirit of Community: Rights, Responsibilities and the Communitarian Agenda,* London: Fontana.

Flanders, A. (1974) *Management and Unions: The Theory and Reform of Industrial Relations,* London: Faber.

Fox, A. (1966) 'Industrial sociology and industrial relations', *Royal Commission on Trade Unions and Employers' Associations, Research Paper No.3,* London: HMSO.

Fox, A. (1974) *Beyond Contract: Work, Power and Trust Relations,* London: Faber.

Fox, A. (1985) *History and Heritage: the Social Origins of the British Industrial Relations System,* London: Allen & Unwin.

Friedman, M. (1993) 'The social responsibility of business is to increase its profits', reprint of 1973 article in G.D. Chryssides and J.H. Kaler (eds) *An Introduction to Business Ethics,* London: Chapman & Hall.

Greene, A. M., Ackers, P. and Black, J. (2001) 'Lost narratives? From paternalism to team working in a lock manufacturing firm', *Economic and Industrial Democracy,* Vol.22, No.2, pp.211–37.

Guest, D. (1989) 'HRM: its implications for industrial relations and trade unions', in J. Storey (ed.) *New Perspectives on Human Resource Management,* London: Routledge.

Guest, D. (1999) 'Human resource management: the workers' verdict', *Human Resource Management Journal,* Vol.9, No.3, pp.5–25.

*Hart, T.J. (1993) 'Human resource management: time to exorcise the militant tendency', *Employee Relations,* Vol.15, No.3, pp.29–36.

Hutton, W. (1995) *The State We're In,* London: Cape.

Jacoby, S.M. (1997) *Modern Manors: Welfare Capitalism Since the New Deal,* Princeton, NJ: Princeton University Press. (Reviewed by this author in *Historical Studies in Industrial Relations,* Vol.8, pp.188–94.)

Joyce, P. (1980) *Work, Society and Politics: the Culture of the Factory in Later Victorian England,* Brighton: Harvester.

Legge, K. (1995) *Human Resource Management: Rhetorics and Reality,* London: Macmillan.

*Legge, K. (1996) 'Morality bound', *People Management,* 19 December, pp.34–6.

MacInnes, J. (1987) *Thatcherism at Work: Industrial Relations and Economic Change,* Milton Keynes: Open University Press.

Marchington, M. and Wilkinson, A. (1996) *Core Personnel and Development,* London: Institute of Personnel and Development.

Mars, G. (1973) 'Hotel pilferage: a case study in occupational theft', in M. Warner (ed.) *The Sociology of the Workplace: An Interdisciplinary Approach,* London: Allen & Unwin.

Millward, N., Stevens, M., Smart, D. and Hawes, W.R. (1992) *Workplace Industrial Relations in Transition: The ED/ESRC/PSI/ACAS Surveys,* Aldershot: Dartmouth.

Nozick, R. (1993) 'Anarchy, state and utopia', (extract) in G.D. Chryssides and J.H. Kaler (eds) *An Introduction to Business Ethics,* London: Chapman and Hall.

Pearson, G. (1995) *Integrity in Organisations: An Alternative Business Ethic,* London: McGraw-Hill. (Reviewed by this author in Employee Relations, Vol.18, No.6, (1996), pp.97–8.)

Priestley, J.B. (1934, 1977) *English Journey,* London: Penguin.

Rawls, J. (1993) 'A theory of justice' (extract) in G.D. Chryssides and J.H. Kaler (eds) *An Introduction to Business Ethics,* London: Chapman & Hall.

Sisson, K. (1989) (ed.) *Personnel Management,* Oxford: Blackwell.

Sisson, K. (1994) (ed.) *Personnel Management* (2nd edn), Oxford: Blackwell.

Smith, A. (1993) 'The wealth of nations' (extract) in G.D. Chryssides and J.H. Kaler (eds) *An Introduction to Business Ethics,* London: Chapman & Hall.

Smith, K. and Johnson, P. (1996) (eds) *Business Ethics and Business Behaviour,* London: International Thomson. (Reviewed by this author in *Human Resource Management Journal,* Vol.8, No.2, 1998, pp.97–8).

Storey, J. (1989) (ed.) *New Perspectives on Human Resource Management,* London: Routledge.

Storey, J. and Sisson, K. (1993) *Managing Human Resources and Industrial Relations,* Milton Keynes: Open University Press.

Torrington, D. and Hall, L. (1991) *Personnel Management: A New Approach,* Hemel Hempstead: Prentice Hall.

*Torrington, D. (1993) 'How dangerous is human resource management?: A reply to Tim Hart', *Employee Relations,* Vol.15, No.5, pp.40–53.

Warren, R.C. (1999) 'Against paternalism in human resource management', *Business Ethics,* Vol.8, No.1, pp.50–60.

*Winstanley, D. and Woodall, J. (1999) (eds) *Ethical Issues in Contemporary Human Resource Management,* London: Macmillan.

* Useful reading

Chapter 18

EMOTION AT WORK

Philip Hancock and Melissa Tyler

Commit to your business. Believe in it more than anybody else. I think I overcame every single one of my personal shortcomings by the sheer passion I brought to my work. I don't know if you're born with this kind of passion, or if you can learn it. But I do know you need it. If you love your work, you'll be out there every day trying to do it the best you possibly can, and pretty soon everybody around will catch the passion from you – like a fever (Walton, 1992 p.3).

Introduction

Consider the following extract from a recent job advertisement:

> You will need to be full of energy and want to add to the fun . . . if you want to start work with a great cast of characters then telephone . . .

You might be forgiven for assuming that this advert is for a job in what Robin Leidner (1993) calls 'interactive service provision' – work involving direct contact with customers or clients. In fact it is advertising vacancies for warehouse staff at a European distribution centre; for workers who handle 'things' rather than 'people'. Why is it important, then, for applicants to want to 'add to the fun', and why are potential colleagues and co-workers described as 'a great cast of characters'? Emotion is now thought of as central to business success; whether that business is selling fast food or sorting boxes. As management writers such as Robert Cooper (1998, p.48) have argued:

> Emotion has been rejected for many years as the messy, effeminate counterpoint to masculine logic and objectivity, but now it has become the latest business buzzword.

This raises the questions, then, why emotion, and why now? And of course, what exactly are emotions? Can they be managed, and if so, how and with what consequences? As sociologist Simon Williams (2001, p.132) has observed, 'emotion is a moving or slippery target'. As he goes on to note:

> The very term emotion, it seems, is far from settled (being many things to many people); a trend exacerbated perhaps, by the recent upsurge of interest in this domain. What is fair to

say, given these differing viewpoints, is that emotion is a complex, *multidimensional, multifaceted human compound*, including *irreducible* biological and cultural components, which arise or emerge in various socio-relationship contexts (original emphasis).

Broadly speaking, emotions are human responses to a whole range of socio-relational events relating to how we feel and how we express and make sense of those feelings, either individually or socially. Emotions are largely intersubjective (experienced or made sense of with reference to others) and communicative (used to convey how we feel – see Crossley 1998). They are often complex and contradictory – we might hear people saying that they have 'laughed until they cried' or 'wept tears of joy', for instance. As sources of (sometimes simultaneous) pleasure and pain, they are clearly central to who and what we are. Emotions can operate at many different levels, and can be highly reflexive or calculated strategies; they can be habitual or routine practices, as well as unconscious or involuntary responses), varying across time, place and culture (Lupton 1998).

Traditionally the province of psychology – with its emphasis on studying emotions largely as psychosomatic responses – it has increasingly been sociology that has dominated debates on the social nature of emotions, considering their expression and function, and also the way in which socio-cultural milieux shape the experience of emotion. In this sense, sociologists have argued that no emotion is ever an 'entirely unlearnt response' (Elias 1991), and that the emotional experiences of individuals – our ability to think about, feel and express emotions (relating to what sociologists call 'agency') are linked to enduring social institutions and arrangements such as power and status (what sociologists call 'structure'). In this sense, as Peter Freund (1990, p.453) has put it, '*emotions represent a juncture between society and the most personal realms of an individual's experiences. They also straddle both the mental and physical aspects of our being*' (emphasis added). That emotions act as something of a 'pivot' in this respect, between the individual and the structural or the personal and the social, explains, in part at least, why management theorists and practitioners alike have begun to take an interest in emotions, focusing (at least relatively recently) on emotion as central to understanding and controlling organisations respectively.

To complicate matters further, emotions are often thought about and expressed metaphorically – as if they were fluids in a container that might spill out or overflow at any moment. This fluid metaphor has been a strong theme in organisation and management studies, in which the workplace is often talked about as if it were an 'emotional cauldron' (Albrow 1992) beneath the surface of which a toxic brew is thought to bubble away. Others have thought of emotions with reference to a weaving metaphor, arguing that emotions are 'woven' into the very fabric of organisational life (Fineman 1994). For Fineman, the centrality of emotions is reflected, for instance, in the evocation of work organisations as families, communities or as social groups; ideas perpetuated by managerial attempts to conflate formal and informal aspects of organisational culture, so that 'stage-managed meetings and reward ceremonies, "graduation" ceremonies and "away days" all have *a distinct evangelical tone, intended "to keep spirits high"*' (Fineman 1993, p.20 [emphasis added]).

Not that such allusions to the spiritual needs of employees are always entirely metaphorical, however. Many organisations are increasingly supporting employees' participation in very real spiritually-oriented programmes and events as a means of encouraging personal well-being and emotional contentment (Bell and Taylor 2003). This is a trend which itself is likely to continue as more and more organisations embrace the idea that valuing employees' spirituality and the emotional benefits that this brings can also provide a powerful impetus to workplace productivity (Konz and Ryan 1999; Neck and Milliman 1994). Consider, for instance, the following (anecdotal) example:

> ### Example:
>
> The Vice-Chancellor of Scotia University recently introduced a series of 'Sparkle Days' when all staff (including academic, administrative and support personnel) could make suggestions about how the University could develop. Staff were encouraged to suggest 'Sparkle Projects' – ideas, ranging from the simple to the complex – and to post these on Sparkle Boards located at various points throughout the campus. Prizes were awarded for those ideas the senior management team decided to adopt. Staff were also encouraged to nominate particular 'Sparkle Words' (such as 'dynamic', 'creative', 'committed' and so on) that they felt summed up the University, its staff and its culture and these were displayed at random around the campus as an inspiration to staff and students.
>
> **Why might it be argued that the Sparkle Projects (and the Sparkle Words) were an attempt to manage emotions at Scotia University?**
>
> **What might have been the positive effects of this exercise (from the point of view of the University's senior management team)?**
>
> **What might have been the negative effects of a project such as this (and how might senior managers have dealt with any potential problems)?**

Significantly, many such 'emotional' and 'spiritual' events occur outside of normal working hours and so blur the boundaries between work and non-work, between who and what 'belongs' to the organisation and what does not, and hence many would argue, extends the scope of HRM into relatively uncharted, emotive territories. Obligations on organisational members to participate in social events, outside of the organisation's 'normal' time and space, are often seen as opportunities to share 'real' (disorganised, unmanaged) feelings safely within a receptive audience of peers. Thus, 'apart from being individually cathartic, the social sharing of normally hidden feelings creates a subculture through which organisational members can emotionally bond and feel at one' (Fineman 1993, p.21) – a central theme in contemporary HRM. In this sense, potentially anti-organisational emotions become subject to 'strategic renegotiations' (1993, p.22) so that the possibility for emotional leakage (to continue the 'fluid' metaphor) *within* the organisation's time and space, is minimised. For Fineman (1994), then, by effectively organising out 'bad' (unprofitable) feelings, by implication, the productive energy associated with 'good' feelings can be channelled into the labour process – a theme that has underpinned the turn to emotion in HRM.

The emotional turn: key concepts and issues

Although the presence of emotion and its organisation has long since been recognised by management practitioners and academics, it seems to be only relatively recently (in the last two decades or so) that specific and sustained attention has been paid to the emotional aspects of organisations and their management; it is only relatively recently that emotion has become both an academic and a practitioner 'buzzword'. As Sharon Bolton (2000) has noted, emotions now seem to be 'here, there and everywhere'. Several reasons can perhaps be identified for this relatively recent turn to emotion in organisation and management studies.

Much of the academic interest in emotion was inspired by US sociologist Arlie Russell Hochschild's book *The Managed Heart*, published in 1983. As Bolton and Boyd (2003, p.292) have put it, 'there is little that has been written concerning the subject of emotions and organizations in the last 20 years that does not take *The Managed Heart* as a reference point'. Hochschild's introduction of the term 'emotional labour' to describe the ways in which emotions are incorporated into the labour process illuminated an aspect of paid work that that has since beeen recognized as central to the lived experience of many workers, particularly those employed in the service sector, but that had been relatively obscured by dominant theoretical approaches both to management and to the study of management. Conceptualising some of the distinctive aspects of work in this way opened up fruitful avenues of investigation and analysis, and facilitated the on-going reformulation of both academic and managerial conceptions of work necessary to keep pace with transformations in the nature of work, and in the economy in general.

One such transformation is that increasingly 'people's working lives are shaped overwhelmingly by the experience of delivering a service' (Allen and Du Gay 1994, p.255). This increase, over the last three decades or so, in the proportion of jobs in which people are employed specifically to work as front-line, 'customer facing' service providers has meant that sustained managerial attention has been paid to customer relations as a vital contributor to competitive advantage and hence particularly to the stage management of what Jan Carlzon (1987) called 'moments of truth': when customers interact with organisations through inter-personal encounters with service providers. This recognition has increased the importance accorded to emotion and its management, particularly for those employees in direct contact with customers; those 'making a difference at the margins' (Peters and Austin 1985, p.45). Consequently, 'a key component of the work performed by many workers has become the presentation of emotions that are specified and desired by their organisations' (Morris and Feldman 1997, p.987).

Certainly in contemporary (what we might call 'post-Excellence') managerial discourse, that is, managerialism inspired largely by Peters and Waterman's (1982) *In Search of Excellence* and concerned particularly with the management of the cultural and subjective aspects of work – emotion has come to be viewed as an important resource that managers should harness in the service of organisational performance. In their book *A Passion For Excellence*, Peters and Austin (1985, p.287) argue that organisational emotions (the feelings, sensations and affective responses to organisation) 'must come from the market and the soul simultaneously'. In later work (Peters 1989, p.457), managers themselves are called upon to harness their own emotional energies by developing a 'passionate public hatred for bureaucracy'.

The turn to emotion, in management and organisation theory particularly, has also been fuelled by something of a challenge brought about by the impact of postmodern, feminist and post-structuralist ideas to the dominant, disengaged and largely disembodied traditions of Western thought and practice that have traditionally neglected emotion in favour of reason (Dale 2001; Williams 2001). This development relates, broadly speaking, to a revived interest in the body brought about in part, by recent developments in the biological and human sciences – in genetic engineering and reproductive technologies, for instance (Martin 1994; Hancock *et al.* 2000). It has also been fuelled by the expansion of consumer culture in most market societies (Falk 1994), and by the increasing organisational commodification of various forms of emotional experience ranging from new-age spirituality to Holocaust museums and theme parks. As Lupton (1998) notes, ours is an era characterised by an intense, voyeuristic and largely commercial interest in how others experience and express emotion.

In sum, the turn to emotion has been fuelled by various recent developments, including:

(i) *conceptual developments* in the way in which we describe and understand the emotional aspects of work organisations and their management;

(ii) *empirical changes* in the way in which we experience work; and

(iii) *theoretical trends* in the way in which ideal forms of management are defined, largely in managerial texts and 'how to' guides, as well as in the ways in which social scientists and management academics have tried to make sense of contemporary organisational life.

Cumulatively, each of these developments has amounted to something of a 'challenge' to rationality in Western thought (including managerialism), involving a renewed preoccupation with the body in management theory and practice, a concern with consumer culture and emotional labour (a concept to which we return below), and a largely commercial and mediated interest in emotions and their expression as we will now reflect, however, it is not the case that management and emotion have always been seen as ideal business partners.

Emotion in management theory and practice

EMOTION, BUREAUCRACY AND SCIENTIFIC MANAGEMENT

Modern organisations have been hailed since their inception as incarnations of rationality and as instruments of rationalisation. Bureaucracy – as the typically modern (advanced) mode of organising – has been defined largely according to an autonomous, impersonal, procedural rationality that has no place for emotion. What Rosabeth Moss Kanter (1977, p.22) in her now classic critique of bureaucracy refers to as 'the passionless organisation', one that strives to exclude emotion from its boundaries, does so in the belief that efficiency should not be sullied by the 'irrationality' of personal feelings.

In her account of the development of this modern, bureaucratic organisation, Kanter (1977) argues that the 'corporation' began to emerge as the dominant organisational form in the late nineteenth century, when what she calls the 'administrative revolution' (the successor to the industrial revolution) took place. By this she means that an increasing number of organisational functions were brought together and merged into a single corporate adminis-tration in order to gain control over a range of disparate activities that would otherwise have continued to be subject to a high degree of uncertainty. Hence, the need to coordinate complex operations made management a specialised occupation and, as she notes, managerial skills began to be more rewarded in business than technical ones. However, as managers were neither owners nor a traditional 'ruling class', they were required to establish their legitimacy and did so through the language of rationality and efficiency.

Control by managers was therefore presented as the most 'rational' way to run a corporate enterprise. Early twentieth-century management theory – such as Taylor's (1911) 'principles of scientific management' – therefore enshrined rationality as the central ideal of organisation, and defined it as the special province of managers. As Kanter (1977, p.22) notes in this respect, 'the very design of organisations thus was oriented toward and assumed to be capable of suppressing irrationality, personality and emotionality'.

For Max Weber, whose sociological analysis focused largely on the rationalisation of Western societies, the suppression of emotion gave bureaucracies their advantage over other organisational forms. Indeed, Weber built his critique of the spirit of capitalism – 'that attitude which seeks profit rationally and systematically' (Weber 1989 [1921], p.64) – on the belief that it is anchored in deeply held religious and emotional attitudes of affect control; in other words, on the exclusion of emotions from organisational life. Thus, as contemporary commentators have noted, privileging rationality and marginalising or excluding emotion 'means that bureaucracy perpetuates the belief that rationality and the control of emotions are not only inseparable but also necessary for effective organisational life' (Putnam and Mumby 1993, p.41).

Returning to Weber for a moment, it would be incorrect to say that his ideal type of bureaucracy is based on a total exclusion of emotion, however (Albrow 1992). As the following passage from his book *Economy and Society* indicates, Weber's account does allow for emotions within modern organisations, but only in so far as their rational calculation is perceived as an intrinsic aspect of their constitution; it is not emotion per se that Weber admits into the organisation, then, but rationalised emotion, ensuring

> First, that everything is rationally calculated, especially those seemingly imponderable and irrational, emotional factors – in principle, at least, calculable in the same manner as the yields of coal and iron deposits. Secondly, devotion is normally impersonal, oriented towards a purpose, a common cause, a rationally intended (Weber 1978, p.1150).

In sum, then, emotion was seen as irrational and unreasonable in Taylorism and bureaucracy, as the antithesis of organisation and in need either of exclusion or rational calculation.

EMOTION AND HUMAN RELATIONS

From the 1930s onwards management theorists and practitioners had begun to realise that even within the confines of organisational life, emotions cannot be excluded or ordered in any meaningful way. In management terms, this meant a significant shift from a view of 'ideal' organisations as based on the exclusion or 'rational calculation' of emotion to an emphasis on the idea that work is meaningful and motivating only if it offers security and opportunities for achievement and self-actualisation (Herzberg 1974; Maslow 1943). In what came to be known as the Human Relations school of management, emotion therefore became 'in', so to speak, as affectivity began to be recognised as being of central importance to the pursuit of organisational performance. It became increasingly emphasised, therefore, that the management of work organisations should be based on 'articulating and incorporating *the logic* of sentiments' (Roethlisberger and Dickson 1939, p.462, emphasis added).

Elaborating on this recognition of emotions within organisational life, Chester Barnard (1938, p.235) argued that 'feeling', 'judgement', a 'sense' of 'proportion', 'balance' and 'appropriateness' are all vital attributes of the executive. Participative styles of management, deemed to engender loyalty and commitment and so increase worker satisfaction and productivity, increasingly perceived emotion as an important aspect of organisational life to be managed.

Elton Mayo (1933), for instance, emphasised the importance for productivity of primary, informal relations among workers and developed the concept of the 'informal organisation' to include the emotional, non-rational and sentimental aspects of organisational behaviour. In Mayo's view, workers were controlled by their sentiments, emotions and social instincts – a phenomenon that he argued needed to be taken into account when devising, executing and evaluating management strategies. As Kanter (1977) notes in her critique, however, in emotional management terms Human Relations continued to rely on a relatively simplistic formula according to which managers were viewed as those who were able to control their own emotions as well as those of their workers, but not vice versa. According to a management training manual written in 1947 for instance,

> He [the manager] knows that the master of men [sic] has physical energies and skills and intellectual abilities, vision and integrity, and he knows that, above all, the leader must have emotional balance and control. The great leader is even-tempered when others rage, brave when others fear, calm when others are excited, self-controlled when others indulge (cited in Bendix 1956, p.332).

While the Human Relations emphasis on informal social factors may appear to diverge from those organisational traits considered important by scientific management, therefore, both approaches shared in common a similar (Kipling-esque) conception of the role of in the HR movement management heroism vis-à-vis emotion. As Hancock and Tyler (2001a) note, this meant that in the HR movement management education continued to be thought of largely as a vehicle for learning how to master, not unleash, emotional factors counter-productive to the organisation. In other words, Human Relations may have 'modified the idea of rationality but preserved its flavour' (Kanter 1977, p.22) – often in highly gendered terms. As feminist writer Rosemary Pringle notes in this respect,

> While the Human Relations theorists added an informal dimension, they did not challenge the theorising of the formal bureaucratic structures. In some ways they reinforced the idea of managerial rationality: while *workers* might be controlled by sentiment and emotion, *managers* were supposed to be rational, logical and able to control their emotions. The division between reason and emotion was tightened in a way that marked off managers from the rest (Pringle 1989, p.87, original emphasis).

HRM: MANAGEMENT GETS EMOTIONAL?

More recently, however, management practitioners and theorists have come to recognise that effective emotional management is a pre-requisite for successful organisational interaction. Consequently, recent managerial accounts of the importance of, say, successful service interaction place a considerable premium on the role of emotion and its contribution to organisational success. Thus it might be suggested that while broadly modernist approaches to management including Taylorism, bureaucracy and Human Relations were concerned largely with the *organisation of emotion,* more contemporary managerial orientations appear to be preoccupied largely with the reverse, that is, with the *emotion of organisation.*

Hence, management writers, consultants and practitioners have begun to advocate a less 'rationalistic' approach to the management of emotion and have emphasised instead the extent to which

> emotions, properly managed, can drive trust, loyalty and commitment and many of the greatest productivity gains, innovations and accomplishments of individuals, teams and organisations (Cooper 1998, p.48).

According to Cooper 'the ability to sense, understand and effectively apply the power and acumen of emotions as a source of human energy, information, trust, creativity, connection and influence' (Cooper 1998, p.48) represents that 'really crucial ingredient' for organisational success in the contemporary era, or as Jack Welch (former Chair of General Electric), has put it 'soft stuff with hard results' (cited in Cooper 1998). The 'proper' management of emotions, in this context, is often framed in terms of the deployment of *emotional intelligence.*

The term 'emotional intelligence' (EQ) is associated most notably with the work of Harvard psychologist Daniel Goleman (1997, 1999) and his colleagues (Goleman *et al.* 2002) who have argued that the effective management of EQ involves:

1. knowing one's emotions (emotional self-awareness);
2. controlling one's emotions (emotional self-regulation);
3. recognising emotions in others (social awareness);
4. controlling emotions in others (relationship management), and
5. self-motivation.

Goleman (1996) argues that emotions play a far greater role in decision making and individual success than is commonly recognised. In his best-selling book *Emotional Intelligence* (which, he claims, can be read as an update on Aristotle's *Nicomachean Ethics*), he argues that *the* contemporary challenge is to manage our emotional life with intelligence. In other words, our emotions:

> when well exercised, have wisdom; they guide our thinking, our values, our survival. But they can easily go awry, and do so all too often. As Aristotle saw, the problem is not with emotionality, but with the appropriateness of emotion and its expression. The question is, how can we bring intelligence to our emotions – and civility to our streets and caring to our communal life? (Goleman 1996, p.xiv; cited in Williams 2001).

The answer, for Goleman, lies in effective emotional management. With the right training and development, he argues (1998, p.24), emotionally intelligent managers can achieve a high level of *emotional competence* which he defines as 'a learned capability based on emotional intelligence that results in outstanding performance at work'. Goleman argues that EQ matters more to organisational performance than cognitive abilities or technical skills and impacts particularly, he argues, at the top of the 'leadership pyramid'.

In *Primal Leadership: Realizing the Power of Emotional Intelligence* (Goleman *et al.* 2002, p.3) he emphasises that 'great leadership works through the emotions'. Echoing particularly Mayo's earlier work on the importance of managing the informal organisation, they distinguish between leaders who drive emotions positively (achieving *resonance*) and those who spawn emotional *dissonance*, 'undermining the emotional foundations that let people shine'. Here management is re-defined as 'the emotional art of leadership' (ibid., p.13) and emotionally intelligent management is deemed to make effective use of the EQ competencies outlined above.

In a similar (albeit more collective) vein, Thomson (1997), then Chair of the UK Marketing and Communication Agency, argues that an organisation's most important asset is its *emotional capital:* 'the combination of emotions, feelings, beliefs and values that are held around an organisation'. Management writers Kandola and Fullerton (1995), known for their conception of the contemporary organisation as a 'mosaic', have also highlighted the organisational benefits of incorporating emotions into the management of diversity, including improved access to talent, enhanced organisational flexibility, promotion of team creativity and innovation, improved customer services, the fostering of satisfying work environments, enhanced morale and job satisfaction, greater productivity and sustained competitive advantage.

Not that such strategies are entirely without risk, however. Peter Frost (2003), for instance, has warned of the dangers of what he terms 'toxic emotions' and, in particular, the threat they pose to emotionally engaged managers whom he refers to as 'toxin handlers'. This refers to those managers (and other employees) who possess high levels of EQ, and are able to 'recognize the emotional pain in other people and in a situation' and as a result either absorb or deflect it 'so that people can get back to their work' (Frost 2003, p.1). Yet while the endeavours of such figures are often vital to the success of an organisation, such individuals can themselves suffer from the absence of adequate support mechanisms or organisational recognition. Thus, as Frost (2003) observes, they are highly vulnerable to personal burnout unless they develop their own coping strategies or are provided with appropriate support from those within the organisation responsible for the well-being of its employees.

This concern notwithstanding, however, underpinning the championing of EQ is the broader perception that 'without an actively engaged heart, excellence is impossible' (Harris 1996, p.18). In this respect, contemporary approaches share much in common with the earlier advocates of Human Relations and their concern to conflate what are perceived as artificial (and unprofitable) boundaries between the corporation and the individual. They have emphasised, perhaps most notably, that organisational stability comes at the price of losing originality, flexibility and creativity. The identification of innovative solutions that might emerge from processes that mediate and negotiate between diverse groups is thought to be foreclosed in more bureaucratic or scientific approaches to management that prioritise rationality over emotion. Organisational input that might come from valuing diversity is also thought to be denied. Passionate commitment to organisational goals, to co-workers and to the organisation itself is also seen to be lost in the unemotional organisation. In her critical account of recent attempts to 'refashion' management as a passionate enterprise, Caroline Hatcher (2003, p.391) notes, for instance, that:

> Despite what has traditionally been historically recognized as the masculinity of the credentials required for successful business life, contemporary managers now face new challenges. They are required to be caring and relationship-oriented. The traditional masculine/feminine hierarchy of logic/emotion is being reshaped by the imperative to be 'passionate' about work.

The deployment of emotional intelligence competencies has also come to be seen as central to management consultancy. The role of intuition has been highlighted, for example, by recent research focusing on the change management process. In their account of the knowledge and facilitation conceptions held by operational research consultants at British Airways in supporting the decisions and management processes of their internal 'clients', Yeoman *et al.* (2000, p.121), for instance, found that:

> While the fundamental ethos of analytical rigour characterises the world-view that the OR consultants adopt, it may be the modifications to techniques and practices that consultants make in *intuitive and creative ways* that secure their effectiveness (emphasis added).

Critical perspectives on emotion

More critical perspectives on emotion have emerged primarily from the Marxist-inspired critique of capitalism and, particularly since the 1980s and inspired largely by Hochschild's *The Managed Heart*, out of attempts to synthesise elements of labour process theory, feminism and organisational sociology. Such approaches tend to emphasise that employees are increasingly required to personify an emotional ethos prescribed by their employing organisation and have drawn attention largely to the alienating, degrading and objectifying consequences of this, particularly in relation to the control mechanisms and surveillance techniques used by organisations in prescribing and monitoring the expression of emotion. In particular, critical accounts have drawn attention to the increasing commodification of emotion particularly within service-oriented industries, emphasising what sociologist Nicky James has described as 'the labour involved in dealing with other people's feelings' (James 1989, p.15).

EMOTIONAL LABOUR

Coined initially by Hochschild (1979, 1983, 1990) the phrase 'emotional labour' refers, broadly speaking, to the commodification of emotions within the labour process. In *The Managed Heart*, Hochschild (1983) made a fundamental distinction between two conceptually different if empirically related ways of managing emotions; namely, emotion work and emotional labour. *Emotion work* describes the act of attempting to change an emotion and how it is displayed in everyday life. In everyday social interaction emotions are thought to be governed by what Hochschild termed 'feeling rules' – 'a set of shared albeit often latent, rules' (Hochschild 1983, p.268) that define what is emotionally appropriate in any given situation. The effort involved in conforming to these rules is what she means by emotion work. So when we laugh at someone's unfunny joke, or express gratitude for an unwanted gift we are engaging in 'emotion work', in Hochschild's terms. *Emotional labour,* however, is what occurs when a profit motive underpins the performance of emotion work within the labour process – when someone pays us to manage our own emotions and those of others. As she puts it,

> by 'emotion work' I refer to the emotion management we do in private life; by 'emotional labour' I refer to the emotion management we do for a wage (Hochschild, 1990, p.118).

According to Hochschild, emotional labour 'requires one to induce or suppress feeling in order to sustain the outward countenance that produces the proper state of mind in others' (1983, p.7). Drawing on sociologist Erving Goffman (1959), Hochschild argues that producing the 'proper state of mind in others' involves techniques she describes as 'surface' and 'deep' acting. *Surface acting* involves pretending to experience emotions that aren't genuine; 'faking it', in other words. *Deep acting* involves something more sustained and potentially intrusive – actually changing what or rather, how we feel.

Hochschild argued that 'just as we may become alienated from our physical labour in a goods-producing society, so we may become alienated from our emotional labour in a service-producing society' (1979, p.571). This sense of alienation may cause emotional labourers to feel false and estranged from their own 'real' feelings, an experience Hochschild (1983, p.90) terms 'emotive dissonance'.

Example:

In her account of the emotional labour undertaken by hospice nurses, Nicky James (1989) outlines the various skills involved in the performance of emotional labour. These include:

Being able to understand and interpret the needs of others,

Being able to provide a personal response to those needs,

Being able to juggle the delicate balance of individual and group needs, and

Being able to pace work, and take account of other responsibilities.

Try to list other occupations in which these skills might be particularly important. Why might these occupations (and the skills they require) result in what Hochschild calls 'emotional dissonance'?

Research suggests that a wide range of organisational contexts exist in which employees are required to manage their own emotions and those of others in the service of an employing organisation. Empirical studies of emotional labour have appeared in a range of sociology and management journals in recent years. In sociology, the emphasis has primarily been on documenting the content of emotional labour, and to a large extent, noting its gendered aspects. Studies have also emphasised the impact of emotional labour on job satisfaction, and have drawn attention to the negative effects of performing work that involves managing one's own and others' feelings and to the ethical issues this raises. Such accounts have tended to examine jobs with the most obvious emotional labour content, particularly in what Leidner (1993) calls 'interactive service work'. These include studies of fast-food workers at McDonald's (Leidner 1993, 1999), of flight attendants (Hochschild 1983; Tyler and Abbott 1998), nurses (James 1989; O'Brien 1994), waiters and waitresses (Hall 1993; Paules 1996), hair stylists (Parkinson 1991) and sex workers (Sanders 2004).

In management journals the concern has largely been with highlighting the importance of managing emotion through effective recruitment, selection, socialisation and supervision in order to increase product or service quality and hence, raise profitability. Notable examples include studies of supermarket and convenience store cashiers (Sutton and Rafaeli 1988; Rafaeli 1989) and ride operators at Disneyland (Van Maanen and Kunda 1989). These studies emphasise that the successful performance of emotional labour typically requires 'a complex combination of facial expression, body language, spoken words and tone of voice' (Rafaeli and Sutton 1987, p.33). This combination seems to be achieved through a range of human resource management techniques including recruitment and selection, training, supervision and monitoring of employee presentation and performance.

MANAGING EMOTIONAL LABOUR

The importance accorded to emotion and particularly to emotional labour in recent years means that considerable efforts have been made to control both its experience and expression. Hence, whereas what Hochschild termed 'emotion work' is governed largely according to an informal network of rules, including social values, attitudes and expectations; emotional labour is subject to a complex range of direct and indirect management control techniques. The importance of recruitment and selection of individuals of appropriate emotional dispositions has been highlighted (Ashforth and Humphrey 1995), as has the role of induction and training in establishing group norms of emotional expression (Willetts and Leff 2003). The importance of increasing group solidarity by creating opportunities for shared emotion during communal activities has also been emphasised (Morris and Feldman 1997). In particular, the rationalisation of emotion has been highlighted, particularly through the use of managerial attempts to introduce an element of routine and uniformity into the performance of emotional labour (Leidner 1993, 1999).

Leidner's research suggests that employers introduce a variety of strategies intended to reduce unpredictable elements, in order to standardise the behaviour of workers and service recipients. Also, to overcome resistance to mass-produced service, employees are often required to find ways to personalise routines, or to appear to do so. Further, where too much unpredictability remains to make it possible to dispense with worker flexibility entirely, employers often undertake what Leidner (1993) calls 'routinization by transformation' – changing workers into the kinds of people who will make decisions and interact with customers in ways that management desire/approve of. Indeed, the organisations in her research (McDonald's and Combined Insurance) paid 'close attention to how their workers looked, spoke, and felt, rather than limiting standardization to the performance of physical tasks' (Leidner 1993, p.18).

Management writers Ashforth and Humphrey (1995 p.104) identify four overlapping mechanisms for the management of emotion. These involve: *neutralising, buffering, prescribing* and *normalising* emotion:

'neutralizing' is used to prevent the emergence of socially unacceptable emotions, while the remaining means are used to regulate emotions that are either unavoidable or inherent in role performance: 'buffering' is used to encapsulate and segregate potentially disruptive emotions from ongoing activities; 'prescribing' is used to specify socially acceptable means of experiencing and expressing emotions, and 'normalizing' is used to diffuse or reframe acceptable emotions to preserve the status quo.

In her recent account of stories collected from members of various organisations in the US following terrorist attacks on 11 September 2001, Michaela Driver (2003) found that all four of Ashforth and Humphrey's measures were deployed as behavioural controls governing the expression of emotion. While buffering, prescribing and normalising seemed to have a positive effect on employee morale, the use of neutralising controls appeared to be somewhat damaging to employee commitment. Driver argues that it is useful to think of the range of reactions to organisational control attempts along a continuum:

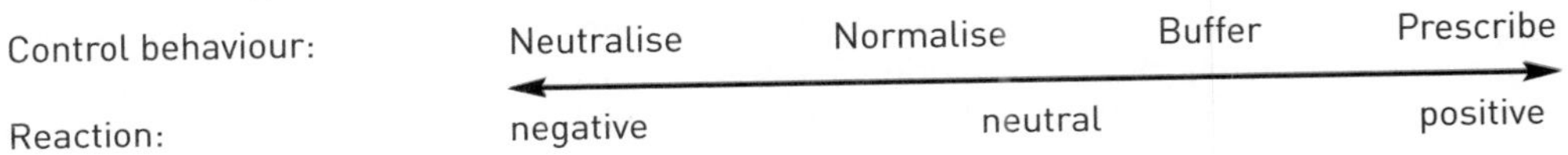

Control behaviour:	Neutralise	Normalise	Buffer	Prescribe
Reaction:	negative	neutral		positive

Figure 18.1

Source: Driver 2003, p.542, figure 1. Republished with permission, Emerald Group Publishing Limited (www.emerald insight.com)

In her research, buffering controls seemed to result in fairly positive reactions, somewhat above those that attempted to normalise emotion. Prescriptive controls, which 'refocused emotional expression from the horror of the events to acts of caring, seemed to result in the most positive reaction' (Driver 2003, p.542), as many employees were 'elated by how humane or family-like their organization appeared to be'. By the same token, employees perceived organisations that sought to neutralise or suppress emotional expression largely negatively, primarily because 'they would not grant space to express emotion but instead sought to return to business as usual'.

Driver's (2003) account highlights several themes in the management and study of emotion. First, it emphasises the importance of employee perceptions of the relationship between emotional control and organisational culture. As she puts it,

if organizational members view organizational control behaviours as indicators of their organization's culture, then the selection of control behaviours may be a critical process (Driver 2003, p.543).

Furthermore, such measures may be an important means by which employees assess whether they 'fit' with the values and culture of the organisation, and hence are important in terms of recruitment, selection and retention (this illustrates the point made above that emotions often act as a 'pivot' between the individual and the social or organisational).

Second, employees seemed not only to accept but to expect some level of organisational control of emotional expression – 'none of the stories indicated that the storytellers resented their organizations for attempting to control their emotions' (Driver 2003, p.544). Finally, her analysis emphasised the importance of developing a contingency approach to understanding the ways in which different employees respond to varying types of organisational controls on emotional expression in different circumstances and across different levels of organisational and occupational hierarchies.

Developing this contingency theme Sloan (2004) has recently highlighted the importance of occupational status for those who experience workplace frustration, noting how individuals working in highly esteemed occupations are more likely than lower-status workers to deal with anger directly, and hence experience less anger-induced, work-related stress. A similar finding has emerged from recent research on the relationship between emotion, management and learning which has emphasised the tensions that can exist between individual and organisational learning. Vince and Saleem (2004), for example, have highlighted the tensions created through repeated patterns of caution and blame within organisations. Their study shows how these tensions actually inhibit emotional processes of reflection and communication, undermining the implementation and further development of strategies explicitly designed for organisational learning.

Such contingencies, status inequalities and tensions are relatively neglected themes in the highly functionalist literature on emotional intelligence, which tends to emphasise that the successful harnessing of emotion leads unproblematically to increased identification, commitment, productivity and manageability. Yet recent research on service work has suggested that managerial efforts to secure employee identification and commitment through training, in the use of scripted and set-piece dialogue techniques for example, can actually have the opposite effect, engendering emotional dissonance and disharmony (Lashley 2002).

To avoid such 'emotional dissonance' and 'synthetic compassion', Ashforth and Humphrey (1993, p.108), in their account of what they term *bounded emotionality* (rationalised emotion), advocate 'job involvement and identification with the role and organisation'. An interesting issue, in this respect, is the considerable emphasis that they suggest should be placed on recruiting and selecting individuals predisposed to a particular emotional orientation as opposed to socialising and rewarding employees who appear to internalise an empathic approach. Similarly, Sutton (1991) has suggested that to the extent that emotional expression is 'dependent upon enduring dispositional factors', effective recruitment and selection is preferable to socialisation and reward.

Many of the studies of emotional labour also highlight the ways in which emotional labour is managed through the design of systems and routines ('scripts', for instance – see Leidner 1993), and through particular supervisory practices (Van Maanen and Kunda 1989), often involving self and peer surveillance (Tyler and Abbott 1998).

Example:

Consider the following instructions, given to flight attendants during a training course at an international airline:

Always walk softly through the cabin, always make eye contact with each and every passenger, and always smile at them. This makes for a much more personal service, and is what First Class travel and [we] as a company are all about. It's what we're here for (cited in Hancock and Tyler 2001b, p.31).

Why might these instructions have been given – what were the management team and the trainers trying to achieve?

How might the performance of emotional labour (through making eye contact, smiling and so on) have conflicted with other aspects of the flight attendant's job?

How might they manage (or avoid) this potential conflict?

When combined with the various demands of the work involved, techniques used to manage emotional labour can result in its performance becoming especially problematic for the individual. Such demands can involve, for instance, the requirement that a particular emotional display – such as smiling for the entire duration of a long flight – be maintained over long periods of time often in working environments that are entirely unconducive to maintaining such displays (Bain and Boyd 1998). Similarly, emotional labourers tend to be required to maintain an appropriate emotional display to customers who are being rude or offensive (Hochschild 1983; Filby 1992; Adkins 1995), resulting in many emotional labourers experiencing difficulties in performing this aspect of their work and, as such, devising various coping strategies.

COPING STRATEGIES

At their simplest, coping strategies may involve employees making use of 'back stage' areas (where customers and possibly co-workers are not present) to let off steam or simply 'switch off' (Van Maanen and Kunda 1989, p.67). Respondents in Bolton and Boyd's (2003, p.298) study emphasised the importance of camaraderie. According to one flight attendant

> The other crew are the best thing about this job and the only thing that keeps me going. We always manage to have a laugh during flights and that's what makes the long hours, annoying passengers and terrible working conditions bearable.

Indeed, humour appears to be a particularly important mechanism for diffusing the potentially negative aspects of emotional labour – when police officers have to deal with major disasters, for instance (Alexander and Wells 1991). In her account of humour as a coping strategy in the sex industry, for instance, Teela Sanders (2004) argues that sex workers consciously manipulate humour as a social and psychological distancing technique; humour contributes to a range of defence mechanisms that are necessary to protect the personal and emotional well-being of emotional labourers. She identifies six types of humour among sex workers that probably apply to many other forms of interactive service work requiring a range of emotional management skills and coping strategies. These are:

■ private jokes used to ridicule clients,

■ coded jokes that flow between sex workers in the presence of clients,

■ stories and anecdotes of personal disclosure framed in terms of jocularity and jest,

■ humour as a strategy to resist harassment and verbal aggression from community harassers and protesters,

■ humour as a source of communication with professionals (healthcare workers and police officers, for instance), and

■ humour as a signifier of conflict and group membership.

An alternative strategy is to retreat into the routine. Leidner (1993, 1999) suggests that workers resort to their scripts as a way of separation and that scripting is not more alienating therefore, but less so, because 'routines may actually offer interactive service workers some protection from assaults on their selves' (Leidner 1993, p.14). Another strategy identified involves a more empathetic form of deflection. For instance, in dealing with situations involving emotional conflict, Hochschild (1983, pp.105–8) reports that flight attendants are trained to perceive difficult or offensive passengers as people who are experiencing problems in their personal lives or who are afraid of flying, and to manage their emotions accordingly.

Underlying this aspect of their training, however, is the requirement for attendants to respond positively to emotional conflicts and to manage them in such a way as to always 'think sales' and so, essentially, to rationalise an otherwise 'irrational' organisational interaction.

EMOTIONAL LABOUR: A CRITIQUE

In her critique of Hochschild's use of the term emotional labour – a concept she suggests 'has now been stretched to its very limits', Sharon Bolton (2000) has offered a typology which distinguishes four distinct types of emotion management:

1. *Presentational* (emotion management according to general, social 'rules' – Hochschild's (1983) 'emotion work', see Bolton and Boyd 2003),
2. *Philanthropic* (emotion management given as a 'gift'),
3. *Prescriptive* (emotion management according to organisational/professional rules of conduct, but not necessarily in the pursuit of profit), and
4. *Pecuniary* (emotion management for commercial gain – Hochschild's 'emotional labour', see Bolton and Boyd 2003).

Bolton emphasises that emotional labour can be a source of pleasure as well as pain, and that many opportunities exist to engage in what Ackroyd and Thompson (1999) have called 'organisational misbehaviour'. For Yiannis Gabriel (1995), affective aspects of work are a fundamental part of what he calls 'the unmanaged organisation' – those spaces for resistance which are ultimately beyond the reach of managerial control. This may suggest, as Bolton argues, that an over-concentration on the 'pecuniary' category of emotional labour can lead to the neglect of vital parts of organisational life, in particular of 'the emotional management skills organizational actors possess' (Bolton and Boyd 2003, p.289), and of the potential for pleasure and job satisfaction in the performance of emotional labour.

Hence, despite its widespread and enduring influence, Bolton and Boyd (2003) note three central weaknesses in Hochschild's account of emotional labour. First, they argue that Hochschild over-emphasises the divide between the public and private performances of emotional self-management, and tends to use the terms 'public' and 'commercial' interchangeably, creating an oversimplified dichotomy. Bolton and Boyd argue that here (and elsewhere) Hochschild operates according to the assumption that there is no room for 'emotion work' within organisational life.

Second, they argue that Hochschild mistakenly equates a physical labour process with an emotional one. However, Bolton and Boyd argue that unlike the factory worker in Marx's analysis for instance, interactive service workers such as airline cabin crew 'own' the means of production (their bodies and emotions) and, therefore, ultimately control the capacity to present a 'sincere' or 'cynical' performance. What Hochschild fails to recognise, they argue, is that the indeterminacy of labour, and of managerial attempts to control it, is further exacerbated within the contested terrain of the emotional labour process as a result.

Third, Bolton and Boyd argue that 'Hochschild's concern with management attempts to seduce employees into "loving" the company, its product and its customers, creates an illustration of emotionally crippled actors' (Bolton and Boyd 2003, p.290). In contrast, they conclude that emotional labourers such as airline cabin crew demonstrate high levels of emotional dexterity as they are able to draw on different sets of feeling rules (commercial, professional, organisational and social) in order to match feeling to situation, thus rendering them multi-skilled emotional managers who are able to 'balance conflicting demands and still . . . effect polished performances' (Bolton and Boyd 2003, p.295).

Despite the efficaciousness of Bolton's critique, however, what remains the case is that emotional labour is relatively low-paid, low-status work. One of the main reasons for this is that it is predominantly carried out by women because women are deemed to be inherently skilled in its performance; in other words, the skill involved is 'essentialised'. In O'Brien's study of the UK nursing profession for instance, he argued that the skills possessed by nurses are often thought to derive 'not from the qualities of being a nurse, but from the qualities of being a woman' (O'Brien 1994, p.399).

Furthermore, work roles involving the performance of emotional labour may also include a sexual component itself often referred to as 'sexual labour' (Hall 1993; Adkins 1995). Secretaries, receptionists and waitresses are often expected, as part of the informal, everyday aspects of their jobs, to be flirtatious and to look sexually attractive, an aspect of the job that may result in sexual harassment – unwanted and unwelcome sexual attention from clients, customers or co-workers. In her study of restaurant employees for example, Elaine Hall found that management encouraged waitresses to smile, defer and flirt with male customers, carefully monitoring their body language and (sexual) displays of emotion.

Conclusions

In discussing emotion in organisations we have endeavoured to identify the various factors underpinning its emergence as an increasingly significant concern within HRM theory and practice. In sum, while traditionally emotion has largely been perceived as a relatively undesirable appendage to organisational rationality and, as such, to be excluded from organised life, in more recent approaches, particularly those associated with HRM, emotions have become increasingly valued as organisational resources in themselves. A prime example of this can be found in the idea of 'emotional intelligence'. Yet, as Fineman has noted, although HRM 'aims to harness positive emotion as a 'success' ingredient' (1994, p.86); emotion is still regarded as being in need of careful managerial rationalisation. As Fineman (1994, p.545) has put it, the dominant belief continues to be that

> Cool, clear, strategic thinking is not to be too sullied by messy feelings. Efficient thought and behaviour tame emotion. Accordingly, good organisations are places where feelings are managed, designed out or removed.

In the latter part of the chapter, however, we also outlined the insights of a range of more critical approaches to understanding organisations as 'emotional arenas' that demand the performance of emotional labour. Here, we drew largely on the work of those who have sought to understand organisational emotions in terms of their commodification. This approach has emphasised the extent to which the emotions of employees are considered fair game for employer intervention when self-presentation and interactive service style are integral parts of the labour process. As Simon Williams (2001, p.112) has put it, the contemporary era is one in which emotions appear to be 'managed if not manipulated and marketed if not manufactured, to an unprecedented degree'. Hence, the '(re)discovery' of the emotional has provided an important lever in terms of management practice and critique.

This led us to pay particular attention to the idea of emotional labour. While the definition first proposed by Hochschild just over 20 years ago has endured, we acknowledged how subsequent research has not only demonstrated how the contours and experiences of emotional labour are now thought to be more complex than those described in her account, but how much more widespread it is becoming across the contemporary organisational landscape. For as Steinberg and Figart (1999, p.23) have noted in this regard,

> **As our economy moves increasingly toward the provision of services and as the public–private distinction further blurs, the skills, effort and responsibilities associated with emotional labour will become more central to our understanding of what it means to work.**

In this chapter, then, we have tried to think critically about emotion in work organisations in terms of the management of emotion and the performance of emotional labour. In Case study 18.1 (based on Russell and Tyler 2002), we consider some of the concepts, ideas and debates introduced here with reference to the lived experience of emotion in the workplace, and reflect on some of the issues this raises for HRM theory and practice.

CASE STUDY 18.1

EMOTION MANAGEMENT AT GIRLIE GLITTER CO.

MELISSA TYLER AND PHILIP HANCOCK

The Girlie Glitter Co. concept and design

Girlie Glitter Co is a UK-based chain of retail outlets whose products and services are marketed primarily at 3–13-year-old girls. The team who designed the concept took the theme of 'girl power' as their starting point, and aimed to create a retail format catering specifically for young girls. The idea was to develop a retail store that stocked not only a range of (largely dressing up and party) clothes, hair styling products, cosmetics and fashion accessories, but also that provided the opportunity for girls to have a 'make-over' in store. The aim, as one of the co-founders of the company described it, was to create 'a girl friendly . . . pleasurable space . . . in which young girls could enjoy shopping together, and . . . mothers could enjoy shopping with their daughters'. In short, as the design team put it, the idea was to develop a retail experience that 'lets little girls live a dream'.

The format that was developed reflects a broader evolution in retail marketing towards stores as places to do more than just shop. With this in mind, a distinct design was developed – the stores are loud, bright and have a discernible colour and style theme that clearly differentiates them from other retail outlets in the shopping centres in which they are located. Indeed, colour was considered to be a vital component of their aesthetic and the design team decided that everything should be 'pink . . . and glittery, with lots of hearts'. This provided the style theme throughout the project and helped to bring to life the idea that the presentation of the products and services on offer should be a 'magical experience'. Much like other retail outlets and theme parks marketed particularly at children and families, the emphasis was upon the creation of an atmosphere of 'clean, wholesome, family fun'.

The Girlie Glitter Co. experience

Customers are enticed into the stores largely by the theatricality of what they have to offer. This is experienced through a combination of music, abundant use of glitter, bright lighting and white flooring, combined with distinctive chrome fittings, pink lettering and iconography (hearts and stars), as well as rows of sparkly costumes and make-up. Sales staff perform dance routines at the front of stores at regular intervals throughout the day creating 'an atmosphere of excitement' as one store manager put it. This reflects a broader performance ethos throughout the company that, at least in part, differentiates Girlie Glitter Co. from other retail outlets selling similar products. It has important implications for the recruitment, selection, training and monitoring of sales staff. As one of the co-founders of the company put it, 'staff don't see themselves as sales assistants but as performers'. Store managers are encouraged think of themselves as 'co-ordinators of a leisure experience'.

In this respect, the marketing team developed a number of other features designed to differentiate the Girlie Glitter brand from other retail 'experiences'. As the store's publicity puts it, 'not only does Girlie Glitter stock all things feminine and girlie, it provides its young customers with the opportunity to be transformed into a fairy princess in store'. At the front of the stores are located spaces called 'Princess Studios'. These are hair-styling and make-up areas where customers can have their hair and nails done, as well as a range of themed make-overs.

Because of this aspect of their work, sales assistants (or 'performers') function not only as dancers but also as hairdressers, make-up artists and nail technicians. Instructed to 'have fun while thinking sales' on the shop floor, they are also told to just 'do what comes naturally' as one sales assistant put it. This means that sales assistants 'need to look right because we are there for the girls [customers] to copy'. In this sense, 'standard presentation is important because they are like role models, they influence the kids, much like characters in kids cartoons or TV programmes, really' as one area sales manager said.

Aware of the potential pitfalls of standardisation and thematic repetition, however, the aim was to 'customise' the service provided, and to recruit staff capable of making individual customers feel special. Crucially, as the Girlie Glitter Co. marketing officer put it, 'this shop was not to be seen as an exploitation of children: it had to represent their dreams, and every girl who visited Girlie Glitter had to feel as though she had walked into a shop that was there just for her'. He goes on to say that this is because 'customers are no longer willing to accept that the shops they visit are just places to buy goods. They demand drama and deserve to be delighted by the experience. Shops have become destinations in themselves – not only a place to purchase, but as a place to be entertained, inspired and, in the case of Girlie Glitter Co., to have loads of fun. This means that the staff we select to work here, particularly on the shop floor, are absolutely crucial.'

Recruitment, selection and training at Girlie Glitter Co.

Recruitment at Girlie Glitter Co. can be likened to the formation of an all-girl pop group; potential employees are asked to sing and dance. Recruitment sessions are described not as interviews but as auditions. When a number of sales staff are being recruited for a new store, group interviews (or 'auditions') are held, followed by individual ones. As the HR officer responsible for recruitment and selection put it, 'group auditions allow you to see who shines through above the rest . . . and that's what we're looking for, people who really shine through and have that extra special something to offer'. Applicants, even those with relevant work experience, are often rejected because they don't look, sound or perform right. This is largely because 'personality is so important to what we do. It is vital for staff to really believe in the concept, so we recruit the personality not just the person.'

There is no specific training as such for sales staff, more an informal process of sociali-sation that involves, for those not skilled in hairstyling and make-up techniques, learning largely from each other. The make-overs are taught and practised much like 'painting by numbers', according to colour-coded charts and a pre-determined make-up palette. Dance routines are taught by store managers who act as choreographers and are practised by staff mainly before and after store opening hours. All staff are encouraged to socialise together and it is routine practice for staff at new stores or new staff at established ones to be taken out to a local bar by the store or area manager on group social events. There is a lot of informal pressure to attend these social gatherings and anyone who doesn't go along is thought to be 'not much fun' and so not really a Girlie Glitter person.

The sales and marketing director at Girlie Glitter Co. likens her role to that of a theatre director or a stage manager: 'responsible for managing the performers who work together like a cast'. She also suggested that she sees herself very much as a script writer, involved in the production of Girlie Glitter Co as a performance. This theatre metaphor carried through into other aspects of the format – store managers were likened to floor or 'front of house' managers, whose primary role is to stage manage those aspects of the store that are visible to the 'audience' [customers]; the till area was referred to by experienced staff as the 'box office', and the storerooms were described as 'backstage'. The opening of the store each day was called 'curtain call', and sales staff reported feeling 'stage fright' before the store opened and the 'performance' became subject to public scrutiny.

Emotional labour at Girlie Glitter Co.

Despite their nerves, staff were told it was 'more important to smile, and to look happy, than to be step perfect' in the dance routines. As one sales assistant put it, 'we're told it's more important to *look* happy than to *be* happy. ' For many staff, this meant either faking it or as one described it, 'going into robot':

sometimes I just look in the mirror, smile, and remind myself to hold that position during the day. At other times, when we've got the music on and we're dancing, I start thinking about messing around with my mates the night before and then I start to smile anyway. So I daydream quite a lot. It looks like I am really enjoying myself there and then, and the customers don't know any different, so there's no harm done really. At other times you don't really have to try, because it is such good fun. You see these really cute little girls come in and do their hair and make-up and they look so pretty, really cute and it's just great. I think how much I would've loved that when I was their age, all the dressing up and stuff. Some days I really love it here. Other days, if we're busy, or there are kids that are playing up, or older girls are in here just messing about and being a pain then it's not so great and you have to just put it on because that's what we're being paid for . . . that's what we're selling, big smiles and loads of fun.

Some sales assistants coped with the embarrassment or 'stage fright' of the dance routines by relying on each other, and by 'having a laugh': 'it is scary when you're out there and it's a really busy day and you maybe see someone you know going by, or people are pointing and laughing and you just look at each other and giggle. I couldn't do it out there on my own, but at least together we can have a bit of a laugh, and I mean, to be dancing about with your mates and getting paid for it, you can't really complain can you?'. New recruits particularly tended to feel anxious about performing in front of a crowd, however: 'I get very nervous before curtain call. But afterwards I get that coming off stage feeling and think, "Thank God, I did it", until the next time.'

Many of the staff are conscious that they are role models for their young customers, as well as the extent to which their uniform appearance (all shop floor staff wear fitted pink T-shirts with the Girlie Glitter logo on them – for sale in children's sizes in store, and black trousers) helped them to identify together as a group. The uniform appearance of staff is thought to be particularly important by the Girlie Glitter management team. One of the area sales managers (the only male employed by the company at the time of the research) also wore black trousers and a pink company T-shirt. He reflected '. . . I could wear a traditional suit and tie, but choose to wear the pink to fit in. It's not glittery and tight-fitting like theirs [the all-female sales staff], but at least we all look the same and that's important . . . so that we all fit in.'

Music is also particularly important to the management of Girlie Glitter Co., especially in terms of fostering employee and customer identification. Particular types of music (mainly by all-girl pop groups) or even specific songs come to be associated with the store, and these tend to provide a continuous soundtrack to the 'front stage' areas and, of course, to the dance routines performed at the store entrances. One particular store manager summed up the general effect of this when she said: 'every time I hear one of the songs we play, I am immediately reminded of the company, wherever I am or whatever I'm doing'.

Some sales assistants had experienced really rude or aggressive customers – either children playing up, or their parents shouting and being abusive. When this happens 'you just think, "oh well they're paying for it I suppose"'. It's their kid's birthday or whatever, or maybe they're divorced Dads and this is their only day with the children and so you think, "just let them get on with it". But it can be hard, sometimes. Some days when I've finished work all I can hear is the same music over and over in my head, and screaming, whining children saying "I want this . . . ." I don't think I'll ever have kids of my own, thanks very much. I've seen enough tantrums to last me a lifetime!'

Questions

1. In what ways is gender relevant to the performance and management of emotional labour at Girlie Glitter Co.?

2. How might the concepts of 'surface acting' and 'deep acting' (Hochschild 1983) be applied to the experiences of sales assistants?

3. Drawing on Bolton and Boyd's (2003) typology, identify the different types of emotion management performed by sales assistants at Girlie Glitter Co.

4. What techniques have the management team devised to encourage sales assistants to perform emotional labour?

5. What coping strategies do staff implement to alleviate the negative consequences of the emotional labour aspects of their work?

6. Draft a recruitment advertisement for sales assistants at Girlie Glitter Co. What key issues might you need to consider in recruiting, selecting and training new staff?

References

Ackroyd, S. and Thompson, P. (1999) *Organizational Misbehaviour,* London: Sage.

Adkins, L. (1995) *Gendered Work: Sexuality, Family and the Labour Market,* Milton Keynes: Open University Press.

Albrow. M. (1992) '*Sine ira et studio* – or do organizations have feelings?', *Organization Studies,* Vol.13, No.3, pp.313–29.

Alexander, D. and Wells, W. (1991) 'Reactions of police officers to body handling after a major disaster', *British Journal of Psychiatry,* Vol.159, pp.547–55.

Allen, J. and Du Gay, P. (1994) 'Industry and the rest: the economic identity of services', *Work, Employment and Society,* Vol.8, No.2, pp.255–71.

*Ashforth, B. and Humphrey, R. (1993) 'Emotional labour in service roles: the influence of identity', *Academy of Management Review,* Vol.18, No.1, pp.18–115.

*Ashforth, B. and Humphrey, R. (1995) 'Emotion in the workplace: a reappraisal', *Human Relations,* Vol.48, No.2, pp.97–121.

Bain, P. and Boyd, C. (1998) 'Once I get you up there where the air is rarefied: health, safety and the working conditions of airline cabin crews', *New Technology, Work and Employment,* Vol.13, No.1, pp.16–28.

Barnard, C. (1938) *The Functions of the Executive,* Cambridge, MA: Harvard University Press.

Bell, E. and Taylor, S. (2003) 'The elevation of work: pastoral power and the new age work ethic', *Organization,* Vol.10, No.2, pp.329–49.

Bendix, R. (1956) *Work and Authority in Industry: Ideologies of Management in the Course of Industrialization,* New York: Wiley.

*Bolton, S. (2000) 'Emotion here, emotion there, emotional organizations everywhere', *Critical Perspectives on Accounting,* Vol.11, pp.155–71.

Bolton, S. and Boyd, C. (2003) 'Trolley dolly or skilled emotion manager? Moving on from Hochschild's managed heart', *Work, Employment and Society,* Vol.17, No.2, pp.289–308.

Carlzon, J. (1987) *Moments of Truth,* New York: Harper Row.

Cooper, R. (1998) 'Sentimental value', *People Management,* April, pp.48–50.

Crossley, N. (1998) 'Emotions and communicative action', in G. Bendelow and S. Williams (eds) *Emotions in Social Life: Critical Themes and Contemporary Issues,* London: Routledge.

Dale, K. (2001) *Anatomising Embodiment and Organisation Theory,* London: Palgrave.

Driver, M. (2003) 'United we stand, or else? Exploring organizational attempts to control emotional expression by employees on September 11, 2001', *Journal of Organizational Change Management,* Vol.16, No.5, pp.534–46.

Elias, N. (1991) 'On human beings and their emotions: a process sociological essay', in M. Featherstone, M. Hepworth and B.S. Turner (eds) *The Body: Social Process and Cultural Theory,* London: Sage.

Falk, P. (1994) *The Consuming Body,* London: Sage.

Filby, M. (1992) 'The figures, the personality and the bums: service work and sexuality', *Work, Employment and Society,* Vol.6, No.1, pp.23–42.

*Fineman, S. (ed.) (1993) *Emotion in Organizations,* London: Sage.

Fineman, S. (1994) 'Organizing and emotion: towards a social construction', in J. Hassard and M. Parker (eds) *Towards a New Theory of Organizations,* London: Routledge.

Freund, P. (1990) 'The expressive body: a common ground for the sociology of emotions and health and illness', *Sociology of Health and Illness,* Vol.12, No.4, pp.452–77.

Frost, P. (2003) *Toxic Emotions at Work: How Compassionate Managers Handle Pain and Conflict,* Boston, MA: Harvard Business School Press.

Gabriel, Y. (1995) 'The unmanaged organization: stories, fantasies and subjectivity', *Organization Studies,* Vol.16, pp.477–502.

Gabriel, Y. (2000) *Storytelling in Organizations,* London: Sage.

Goffman, E. (1959) *The Presentation of Self in Everyday Life,* Harmondsworth: Penguin.

Goleman, D. (1996) *Emotional Intelligence: Why it Can Matter More Than IQ,* London: Bloomsbury.

Goleman, D. (1997) *Working with Emotional Intelligence,* New York: Bantham Books.

Goleman, D., Boyatzis, R. and McKee, A. (2002) *Primal Leadership: Realizing the Power of Emotional Intelligence,* Boston, MA: Harvard Business School Press.

Hall, E.J. (1993) 'Waitering/waitressing: engendering the work of table servers', *Gender and Society,* Vol.17, No.3, pp.329–46.

Hancock, P. and Tyler, M. (2001a) *Work, Postmodernism and Organization: A Critical Introduction,* London: Sage.

Hancock, P. and Tyler, M. (2001b) 'The look of love: gender and the organization of aesthetics', in J. Hassard, R. Holliday and H. Willmott (eds) *Body and Organization,* London: Sage.

Hancock, P., Hughes, B., Jagger, E., Paterson, K., Russell, R., Tulle, E. and Tyler, M. (2000) *The Body, Culture and Society: An Introduction,* Milton Keynes: Open University Press.

Harris, J. (1996) *Getting Employees to Fall in Love With Your Company,* New York: Amacom.

Hatcher, C. (2003) 'Refashioning a passionate ◀manager: gender at work', *Gender, Work and Organization,* Vol.10, No.4, pp.391–412.

Herzberg, F. (1974) *Work and the Nature of Man,* London: Crosby Lockwood Staples.

Hochschild, A.R. (1979) 'Emotion work, feeling rules and social structure', *American Journal of Sociology,* Vol.85, No.3, pp.551–75.

*Hochschild, A.R. (1983) *The Managed Heart: Commercialization of Human Feeling,* Berkeley, CA: University of California Press.

Hochschild, A.R. (1990) 'Ideology and Emotion Management: A Perspective and Path for Future Research', in T. Kemper (ed.) *Research Agendas in the Sociology of Emotions,* New York: SUNY Press.

James, N. (1989) 'Emotional labour: skill and work in the social regulation of human feeling', *Sociological Review,* Vol.37, No.1, pp.15–42.

Kandola, R. and Fullerton, J. (1995) *Managing the Mosaic: Diversity in Action,* London: Institute of Personnel Development.

Kanter, R.M. (1977) *Men and Women of the Corporation,* New York: Basic Books.

Konz, G.N.P. and Ryan, F.X. (1999) 'Maintaining an organizational spirituality: no easy task', *Journal of Organizational Change Management,* Vol.12, No.3, pp.200–10.

Lashley, C. (2002) 'Emotional harmony, dissonance and deviance at work', *International Journal of Contemporary Hospitality Management,* Vol.14, No.5, pp.255–7.

Leidner, R. (1993) *Fast Food, Fast Talk: Service Work and the Routinization of Everyday Life,* Berkeley, CA: University of California Press.

Leidner, R. (1999) 'Emotional labour in service work', *Annals of The American Academy of Political and Social Sciences,* No.561, pp.81–95.

Lupton, D. (1998) *The Emotional Self,* London: Sage.

Martin, E. (1994) *Flexible Bodies,* Boston, MA: Beacon Press.

Maslow, A.H. (1943) 'A Theory of Human Motivation', *Psychological Review.* Vol.50, pp.372–96.

Mayo, E. (1933) *The Human Problems of Industrial Civilization,* New York: Macmillan.

Morris, J. and Feldman, D. (1997) 'Managing emotions in the workplace', *Journal of Management Issues,* Vol.9, No.3, pp.257–75.

Neck, C.P. and Milliman, J.F. (1994) 'Thought self-leadership: finding spiritual fulfillment in organizational life', *Journal of Managerial Psychology,* Vol.9, No.6, pp.9–16.

O'Brien, M. (1994) 'The managed heart revisited: health and social control', *Sociological Review,* Vol.42, No.3, pp.393–413.

Parkinson, B. (1991) 'Emotional stylists: strategies of expressive management among trainee hairdressers', *Cognition and Emotion,* Vol.5, pp.419–34.

Paules, G. (1996) 'Resisting the symbolism of service', in C. Macdonald and C. Sirianni (eds) *Working in the Service Society,* Philadelphia, PA: Temple University Press.

Peters, T. (1989) *Thriving on Chaos,* London: Pan Books.

Peters, T. and Austin, N. (1985) *A Passion For Excellence,* New York: Random House.

Peters, T. and Waterman, R. (1982) *In Search of Excellence,* New York: Harper & Row.

Pringle, R. (1989) 'Bureaucracy, rationality and sexuality: the case of secretaries', in J. Hearn, D. Sheppard, P. Tancred-Sheriff and G. Burrell (eds) *The Sexuality of Organization,* London: Sage.

Putnam, L. and Mumby, D. (1993) 'Organizations, emotion and the myth of rationality', in S. Fineman (ed.) *Emotion in Organizations,* London: Sage.

Rafaeli, A. (1989) 'When cashiers meet customers: an analysis of the role of supermarket cashiers', *Academy of Management Journal,* Vol.32, No.2, pp.245–73.

*Rafaeli, A. and Sutton, R. (1987) 'Expression of emotion as part of the work role', *Academy of Management Review,* Vol.12, pp.23–37.

Roethlisberger, F.J. and Dickson, W.J. (1939) *Management and the Worker,* Cambridge, MA: Harvard University Press.

Russell, R. and Tyler, M. (2002) 'Thank heaven for little girls: "Girl Heaven" and the commercial context of feminine childhood', *Sociology,* Vol.36, No.3, pp.619–37.

Sanders, T. (2004) 'Controllable laughter: managing sex work through humour', *Sociology,* Vol.38, No.2, pp.273–91.

Sloan, M. (2004) 'The effects of occupational characteristics on the experience and expression of anger in the workplace', *Work and Occupations,* Vol.31, No.1, pp.38–72.

Steinberg, R. and Figart, D. (1999) 'Emotional labour since the managed heart', *Annals of the American Academy of Political and Social Sciences,* No.561, pp.8–26.

Sutton, R. (1991) 'Maintaining norms about expressed emotions: the case of bill collectors', *Administrative Science Quarterly,* Vol.36, pp.245–68.

Sutton, R. and Rafaeli, A. (1988) 'Untangling the relationship between displayed emotions and organizational sales: the case of convenience stores', *Academy of Management Journal,* Vol.31, No.3, pp.461–87.

Taylor, F.W. (1911) *Principles of Scientific Management,* New York: Harper & Row.

Thomson, K. (1997) *Emotional Capital: Capturing Hearts and Minds to Create Lasting Business Success,* London: Carstone.

Tyler, M. and Abbott, P. (1998) 'Chocs away: weight watching in the contemporary airline industry', *Sociology,* Vol.32, No.3, pp.433–50.

Van Maanen, J. and Kunda, G. (1989) 'Real feelings: emotional expression and organizational culture', in L.L. Cummings and B. Straw (eds) *Research in Organizational Behaviour,* Vol.11. Greenwich, CT: JAI Press.

Vince, R. and Saleem, T. (2004) 'The impact of caution and blame on organizational learning', *Management Learning,* Vol.35, No.2, pp.133–54.

Walton, S. (1992) *Made in America* New York: Bantham.

Weber, M. (1978 [1921]) *Economy and Society,* Berkeley, CA: University of California Press.

Weber, M. (1989 [1904]) *The Protestant Ethic and the Spirit of Capitalism,* London: Unwin Hyman.

Willetts, L. and Leff, J. (2003) 'Improving the knowledge and skills of psychiatric nurses: efficacy of a staff training programme', *Journal of Advanced Nursing,* Vol.42, No.3, pp.237–43.

Williams, S. (2001) *Emotion and Social Theory,* London: Sage.

Yeoman, I., Sparrow, J. and McGunnigle, F. (2000) 'Accessing knowledge at British Airways: the impact of soft OR', *Journal of Organizational Change Management,* Vol.13, No.2, pp.121–39.

* Useful reading

Chapter 19

FLEXIBILITY

Stephen Procter and Stephen Ackroyd

Introduction: what do we mean by flexibility?

Flexibility is a concept that can be understood in many different ways and at many different levels. At its broadest it is perhaps best understood as the quality by which an entity adapts itself to a change in the demands made upon it. The appeal of flexibility as a concept can be seen by a consideration of its opposites – inflexibility, rigidity, etc. – all of which carry a quite negative connotation. Before portraying flexibility as something which in all cases should be welcomed, however, we need to raise two simple questions: flexibility of what and flexibility for whom?

FLEXIBILITY OF WHAT?

In answer to the first question, we can identify four basic areas in which the idea of flexibility has been applied:

- **Flexibility of labour:** this in turn can be understood in two different ways: as the ability and willingness of individual workers to perform a wider range of tasks, jobs or skills; and as the ability of organisations to vary the amount of labour they use in accordance with fluctuations in demand.

- **Flexibility of technology:** technology here can include both physical technology and the broader ideas of technique and know-how; flexibility refers to both the range of things technology can do and the ease with which it can move between them.

- **Flexibility of organisations:** this might include the flexibility of both labour and technology, but refers to the more general ability of organisations to adapt themselves to the demands made upon them.

- **Flexibility of systems:** at a broader level still, we are concerned with the systems within which organisations operate. A system might thus be a national economy, a region or even the world economy as a whole. Again, to understand what form this might take, we must take into account the other forms of flexibility.

FLEXIBILITY FOR WHOM?

The nature of the present volume means that our focus is on the flexibility of labour. As we shall see, however, it is impossible to understand this in isolation from the other types of flexibility we have described. What we shall also see is that – in answer to our second basic question – flexibility is defined from the point of view of those who run and own organisations. In terms of the employment relationship, it is flexibility *for* the employer, which, in all likelihood, is likely to mean flexibility *of* the employee. The nature of the employment relationship means that, while in some circumstances this will mean flexibility *for* the employee, the fact that the interests of employee and employer will not always coincide means that from the point of view of the employee, flexibility cannot unequivocally be seen as a good thing (see also Legge 1998).

STRUCTURE OF CHAPTER

The chapter is structured as follows. We look first at flexibility in historical perspective, showing how the idea of the flexibility of labour needs to be understood against the background of longer-term trends in how work is organised. We turn then to how labour and organisational flexibility have been conceptualised in recent and current UK debates. We shall see that although the so-called 'flexible firm' model has much to commend it, it cannot offer a full explanation of the developments we observe. A consideration of technological flexibility leads us on to the 'new flexible firm' model, which combines labour, technological and organisational flexibility in a way that offers us much greater insight. The 'new flexible firm' is then compared to a rival configuration which is based on the idea that British organisations have attempted to achieve flexibility through the emulation of their Japanese counterparts. All this, as we shall see, involves a quite structural account of flexibility; one which emphasises the constraints within which HR and other managers are working. In the final main section of the chapter we therefore turn to areas in which managers are able to exercise more discretion.

Flexibility in historical perspective

Although we can trace the history of job or work design back to Adam Smith's (1776) enunciation of the benefits of a highly developed division of labour, it is only really since the end of the nineteenth century that these and other ideas have been applied systematically in organisations. According to Buchanan's (1994a) account, we can divide this more recent history very roughly into three phases:

- The period up to around 1950, which was dominated by the ideas of scientific management.

- The period from the middle of the century to around 1980, which, in reaction against scientific management, saw a concern to design jobs with workers' motivation and satisfaction in mind.

- The period since the late 1970s/early 1980s, in which we have seen the emergence of what Buchanan describes as team-based 'high performance work systems' (1994a, p.85).

Although it is in the last of these three periods that flexibility takes on a central role, we need to say something about the historical background against which this interest developed (for a fuller account, see Buchanan 1994a; Parker and Wall 1998; Parker *et al.* 2001).

SCIENTIFIC MANAGEMENT

The first of Buchanan's three periods centres on the development and influence of the ideas of Frederick Taylor (1856–1917; see Taylor 1911). Taylor's concern was to eliminate what he saw as systematic inefficiencies in the manner in which work was organised and managed. Under

Taylor's ideas of scientific management, work was to be fragmented into its most basic components, each of which would be undertaken in a manner deemed to be the most efficient. There was, in short, 'one best way' of organising work (see Kanigel 1997), and achieving this, it was argued, would benefit both workers and employers. Just as important was the idea that this organisation of work was to be the exclusive responsibility of managers: there was thus a separation between those who did the work – the workers – and those who determined how it should be done – the managers.

The extent to which these ideas were used, and the nature of their impact on people's work and lives, are issues which have generated a great deal of research and discussion. Much of this has centred around Harry Braverman's (1974) 'deskilling thesis', which was based on Marxist ideas of the 'labour process'. In this account, Taylor's ideas had proved to be overwhelmingly the dominant force in the organisation and control of work since the beginning of the century. Its fragmentation and the removal of worker responsibility for its organisation had thus led to work being progressively deskilled or degraded (see, for example, Noble 1977).

Subsequent research has sought to modify Braverman's basic thesis. Littler (1982), for example, showed how scientific management or Taylorism developed in different ways in different countries. McIvor (2001), surveying the period up to 1950, argues that UK employers still relied very heavily on such basic methods as the intensification of work. Most pertinent for our purposes is Friedman's (1977) distinction between 'direct control' and 'responsible autonomy'. His argument was that management interests would not in all cases be best served by the 'direct control' of the workforce which scientific management involved. Where workers were skilled and work was more complex, it might be better to acknowledge and exploit this through the pursuit of the more trust-based strategy of 'responsible autonomy'.

AWAY FROM SCIENTIFIC MANAGEMENT

New developments in thinking on how work should be organised were in any case already well-established by the mid-1970s. Problems associated with the simplified and repetitive nature of work under scientific management had from an early stage led to such measures as job rotation – the movement of workers between tasks – and job enlargement – the creation of jobs combining larger numbers of tasks (Parker and Wall 1998). From the 1950s onwards more fundamental concerns began to be addressed, as the design of jobs began more system-atically to take into account the motivation and satisfaction of employees (Parker and Wall 1998). Thus Herzberg's (1966) two-factor theory of worker motivation led to the idea that jobs should be not merely rotated or enlarged but 'enriched' by the provision of scope for personal achievement and development; while Hackman and Oldham's (1976) job character-istics model provided for the design of jobs on the basis of such principles as skill variety, task identity and task significance.

Also influential was the socio-technical systems approach. Of key importance here was the work of the London-based Tavistock Institute, whose principles, based on the idea of the 'joint optimisation' of the social and technical subsystems in organisations, gave rise to their proposing the development of autonomous working groups of employees (AWGs). Trist and Bamforth's (1951) study of the postwar British coal-mining industry showed how automation had brought with it the introduction of a version of scientific management, the 'longwall' method, which displaced the autonomous multi-skilled groups which had operated under the old 'hand-got' system. Later work (Trist *et al.* 1963) revealed the development of a compromise 'composite shortwall' method, based on multi-skilled, self-selecting groups, each responsible on one shift for the whole of the coal-getting cycle. Socio-technical ideas were picked up in several countries, most notably in Scandinavia (Benders and Van Hootegem 1999). It is here that we find the most celebrated and controversial examples of the use of AWGs: the Kalmar and Uddevalla plants of the automotive manufacturer, Volvo (Berggren 1993).

While the concept of the division of labour provides our initial point of reference, it is departures from this principle that we are more interested in. As we have noted, a focus on the adverse effects of scientific management is almost as old as scientific management itself. The policies pursued in the 1950s and 1960s are perhaps best thought of as attempts merely to ameliorate the worst of these effects. From the mid- to late 1970s on, however, we see a more fundamental challenge to the principle that the division of labour should be extended as far as possible. From this time onwards we see debate coalescing around the idea that work was undergoing a basic restructuring. What in many ways was the central theme running through these debates was that work was becoming more flexible. In the following section we look at the main models advanced both to explain and to encourage these developments.

The flexible firm

THE FLEXIBLE FIRM MODEL

In the period since the early 1980s, UK debates on the flexibility of work and organisation have centred on the model of the flexible firm. Put forward by John Atkinson and others (Atkinson 1984; Atkinson and Meager 1986; NEDO 1986), the model claimed that firms were increasingly seeking and achieving greater flexibility from their workforce. This flexibility was of two main kinds:

- **Numerical**: 'This is concerned with enhancing firms' ability to adjust the level of labour inputs to meet fluctuations in output' (NEDO 1986, pp.3–4). It thus covers such practices as the employment of part-time, temporary or contract workers.

- **Functional**: '[This] consists of a firm's ability to adjust and deploy the skills of its employees to match the tasks required by its changing workload, production methods and/or technology' (NEDO 1986, p.4). It is thus concerned with the ease with which employees can move or be moved between tasks or jobs.

As part of these developments, it was argued, the workforce was being divided into two basic groups. Represented diagrammatically in Figure 19.1, the two groups are:

- **Core workers**: members of this group would be expected to display functional flexibility in return for security of employment.

- **Peripheral workers**: members of this group would be expected to provide the firm with the numerical flexibility it required. This group would in fact be made up of a number of subgroups – part-time workers, contract workers, and so on – each of which would exhibit a particular type of numerical flexibility.

DEBATE OVER THE FLEXIBLE FIRM

Since the model of the flexible firm was first developed in the mid-1980s, it has been at the centre of an extensive and often heated debate. There certainly was enough evidence to offer the model at least *prima facie* support. With regard to numerical flexibility, besides the NEDO (1986) study itself, the work of Hakim (1990), Casey (1991), Marginson (1991) and Penn (1992) all contributed to establishing its continued importance. Evidence for functional flexibility was less easy to identify from survey data, but there was support for the idea that it

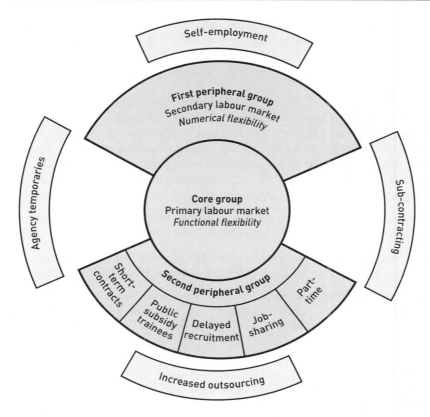

Figure 19.1   The flexible firm

Source: Atkinson 1984

was on the increase (Daniel 1987; Cross 1988; Elger 1991). Although applied originally to the UK, moreover, evidence pointed to the increasing use of flexible working practices across a range of countries. Brewster *et al.*'s (1994, p.189) conclusion from the Europe-wide 1992 Cranfield survey was that, 'despite the different legal, cultural and labour traditions around Europe there is a clear general trend amongst employers across the different sectors towards increasing their use of flexibility'.

What critics of the flexible firm took issue with was the idea that these developments were part of a deliberate or 'strategic' move on the part of employers. Analysis of the Cranfield study, for example, set out to establish 'whether the increase in flexibility is the result of a deliberate strategy by organizations or . . . just a reaction to circumstances' (Mayne *et al.* 1996, p.5; see also Friedrich *et al.* 1998). In a similar vein, Wood and Smith (1989) found that only around 11 per cent of a large sample of UK companies saw themselves as following a 'core-periphery' strategy.

As Procter *et al.* (1994) demonstrated, however, such an approach is based on a rather restricted view of what 'strategy' is. This view sees strategy as an explicit decision, made at the top of an organisation and then communicated to and implemented by managers at lower levels. This can be contrasted to more recent conceptions, in which strategy is a 'pattern' rather a 'plan', thus allowing account to be take of its 'emergent' as well as its 'deliberate' aspects (see, for example, Mintzberg 1978). As Hyman (1987, p.39) argued, while firms' attempts to accommodate fluctuations in demand might have led to the opening up of divisions in the workforce, 'this does not entail that such divisions were designed, let alone the primary motive'. If we take this view, what can we say about patterns of flexibility?

BEYOND THE FLEXIBLE FIRM: PATTERNS OF FLEXIBILITY

Looking first at patterns of functional flexibility, we can see that it was wildly optimistic to assume that this would involve the development of a core group of polyvalent super-craftspersons. As O'Reilly (1992, p.370) argued, there is a distinction between a functional flexibility 'accompanied by an increase in training and upgrading' and a functional flexibility 'used in an *ad hoc* manner to meet shortages and intensify work'. Functional flexibility in the UK has had two main characteristics:

- **Negative in nature**: it involves the breaking down of lines of demarcation rather than the more positive development of multi-skilled workers.

- **Limited in degree**: the most important thing from the employer's point of view is not that individual workers are fully flexible but that the workforce taken as a whole is flexible enough.

The negative nature of flexibility is shown in studies undertaken largely in manufacturing settings (Daniel 1987; Cross 1988; Kirosingh 1989). In this context, the employers' major concern has been to break down demarcations between production and maintenance work or between different areas of maintenance responsibility. This direct evidence on the nature of functional flexibility is consistent with other evidence on trends in training and skill. On training, Gospel (1995), for example, has pointed to the continued decline in traditional ways of training and recruiting skilled workers. On skill, Gallie's (1991) account of the findings of the Social Change and Economic Life Initiative (SCELI) shows that at first sight there is support for the idea of an upskilled workforce: in all but the lowest occupational classification, a majority of respondents reported an increase in skill. Interpretation of this data, however, very much turns on what we define as skill. As Gallie points out, those inclined to support the 'upskilling' thesis argue that skill should not be considered as synonymous with craft: account should also be taken of such things as general educational level and the ability to exercise responsibility.

As for the limited degree of flexibility, this in many cases is linked to its negative nature (Cross 1988). But even when flexibility is associated with a more positive attitude towards multi-skilling, its extent depends on the requirements of the employer rather than those of the employee. This is brought out clearly by Clark's study of Pirelli. As Clark expresses it, Pirelli 'achieved what they set out to achieve, namely full flexibility to do what they wanted. In practice, however, to do what they wanted they did not need full flexibility' (1995, p.153).

Turning now to patterns in numerical flexibility, we need to look at recent developments against the background of long-term labour market trends. The fourth Workplace Employee Relations Survey (WERS) showed part-timers to account for around 25 per cent of all UK employment in 1998 (Cully *et al.* 1999, p.32). The recent growth rate in part-time employment, however, has been nothing like that recorded in the 1960s and 1970s, and a large part of the growth can in any case be accounted for by changes in the sectoral composition of the economy (Emmott and Hutchinson 1998, pp.232–3). Similarly, looking at the period 1975–98, Gregg and Wadsworth (1999) showed that while average job tenure had remained almost the same at around 4.75 years, this in fact disguised significant changes for different parts of the workforce. In particular, although job tenure had risen for women with children, it had fallen for men and for women without dependent children – and Cappelli (1995) paints a similar picture of trends in the United States. The use of temporary workers did increase markedly in the 1990s, as employers moved out of the recession of the early part of the decade. Although the Labour Force Survey showed temporary workers to account for only around 7 per cent of the workforce by 1996, what was more significant was that temporary jobs accounted for almost one-third of all engagements since 1984 (Emmott and Hutchinson 1998, p.234).

Taken together with trends in functional flexibility, this could be regarded as at least *prima facie* evidence of the establishment of the flexible firm model. What the model is based on, however, is the association of each of the forms of flexibility with a particular group of employees: the protected core exhibits functional flexibility in return for employment security, while the peripheral workforce provides the necessary numerical flexibility. The difficulties involved in taking this line of argument are illustrated most clearly by the findings of WERS 4. 'It appears', Cully *et al.* (1999, p.38) conclude, 'that the use of the non-standard forms of labour is more closely related to employment *within* the core than outside it' (emphasis in original). Again, this is paralleled by developments elsewhere. Cappelli's (1995, p.591) review shows there is little sign of a core–periphery strategy being adopted in the US: 'there is no evidence that the current changes in the employment relationship in the USA are driven by an interest in buffering core employees'.

In other words, the boundaries between 'core' and 'peripheral' workers, in so far as they ever existed, are being broken down, and all workers are being made subject to a greater degree of insecurity. It is in this context that Legge (1998) offers up 'two cheers' for the security and predictability offered by the employment relationship characteristic of more traditional, bureaucratic organisations. This theme is explored in greater depth by Sennett (1998). In his view, the change in the nature of work means that it can now be said that, 'The qualities of good work are not the qualities of good character' (1998, p.21). The impact on individuals and society as a whole are profound: in the words of the title of Sennett's book, flexibility is associated with 'the corrosion of character'. Something of this can be seen in Box 19.1, which describes what flexibility can involve for those in an already vulnerable position.

Box 19.1: The abuse of flexibility

A report by the National Association of Citizens Advice Bureaux, *Flexibility Abused* (1997), shows how flexibility can too often take the form of 'worker insecurity'. Using evidence drawn from Citizens Advice Bureaux (CAB) throughout the country, the report identifies two broad categories of abusive action by employers: the introduction of contractual arrangements which severely disadvantage workers; and their withdrawal entirely from the responsibilities of the employment relationship. The former may take the form of variable hours contracts, fixed-term and casual employment, or the replacement of full-time by part-time work; withdrawal from the employment relationship might involve the imposition of 'self-employed' status on employees, the taking on of agency workers, and the use of 'contracting out'. The two broad categories are illustrated by the following cases, which are drawn directly from the report (pp.12–13, 36).

A CAB in Oxfordshire reported two typical clients. The first was looking for full-time work but had only been able to obtain a zero hours contract collecting and delivering cars for a car rental company. He had to ring every day to find out what work was available. His weekly earnings averaged £70 but some weeks he earned nothing. The second client worked as a chef. His written particulars stated his normal hours as 39 per week, but went on to say that 'your total hours of work and time of work may vary in accordance with the needs of the business'. The client came to the bureau because his hours had been cut drastically, to the extent that he had only been given one day's work in the last week, and the equivalent of two days per week over a full month.

A CAB in Dorset reported a client who had worked for a company as a skilled manual worker for several years. He had no written contract, but he had always worked regular hours for regular pay – so, although he paid his own tax and National Insurance, his pattern of work appeared to qualify him as an employee. He had now been presented with a contract which stated that he was an independent contractor; he was not guaranteed work at any time; he was not entitled to sick pay; and was not entitled to take any holiday. The employer was pressurising the client, and about ten colleagues, to sign the contracts, implying that there would be no further work if they did not do so.

Source: NACAB (National Association of Citizens Advice Bureaux) 1997

Labour-centred and technology-centred flexibility

TECHNOLOGY-CENTRED FLEXIBILITY

As Kalleberg's (2001) recent review argues, a deeper understanding of flexibility requires that we look more closely at the relationship between its functional and numerical facets. Although the flexible firm model has the merit of combining the two forms of flexibility, Kalleberg concurs with the view that there is simply not the evidence to support it. We can go further than Kalleberg, however, and say that, in addition, we need to look more closely at the relationship between labour-centred and technology-centred flexibility.

What we call here technology-centred flexibility refers to the flexibility of manufacturing systems. The study of such systems in the area of operations management is in some ways more sophisticated than the study of labour flexibility in employment relations and organisation theory. Among the conceptual tools that have been developed is Slack's (1987, 1990) distinction between the 'range' and the 'response' of flexibility. Upton (1995), in turn, developed this into a three-dimensional concept. As well as 'range', he argued, we need to look both at mobility, the cost involved in moving from one state to another, and at uniformity, the ability of a system to maintain a certain level of performance *within* the range of positions open to it.

A major concern of work in this area has been to identify the different forms that flexibility can take (see Beach *et al.* (2000) for a review, and Upton (1994) for a more sceptical viewpoint). Though there are significant differences between the many typologies put forward, technology-centred or manufacturing flexibility can be understood in five main senses:

■ The ability of a manufacturing system to adjust volumes of production.

■ The ability to produce a certain mix of products.

■ The ability of a system to change the mix of a certain set of products.

■ The ability to deal with changes in the design of existing products.

■ The ability to deal with new products.

As we move down this list, we can see that the issues faced by organisations become more complex and uncertain. In the terms used by Carlsson (1989), we see a move from Type 1 to Type 2 flexibility. Type 1 flexibility, which is based on quantifiable risk, refers to the ease with which firms can, say, alter the level of output of a product in response to changes in demand for it. As we move down the list, to consider, for example, how the manufacturing system might deal with the introduction of new products, the quantifiable risk is replaced by an unquantifiable uncertainty. While we will have some idea about how demand for existing products might fluctuate over the forthcoming year, in other words, we cannot say the same about what new products will need to be produced in five years' time.

While looking at flexibility in this way allows us to bring out some of the subtleties in the discussions surrounding technology-centred flexibility, a somewhat cruder classification might be considered adequate for our purposes here. We can distinguish between volume flexibility (which would include the first and possibly the second of our five forms) and product flexibility (which would cover the other three). This distinction appears quite encouraging for the flexible firm model. Might it not be the case that product flexibility can be achieved by the functional flexibility of the core and volume flexibility by the numerical flexibility of the periphery? A closer examination reveals that matters are nothing like so straightforward. The correspondence between volume and numerical flexibility might be a close one, but there is no necessary reason why producing a range of products rather than a single product should involve an individual employee in a wider range of skills and a more secure employment relationship.

In fact, the literature on manufacturing or technology-centred flexibility has almost nothing to say about its relationship with the flexibility of labour (Beach *et al.* 2000) For the most part, labour flexibility is ignored completely. Of the companies surveyed by Lim (1987), for example, none identified the use of labour as a way in which they conceived of flexibility. Where labour flexibility is referred to it assumes a position of subsidiary importance. In Slack's (1987, 1990) flexibility hierarchy, for example, flexible labour is found right at the bottom. Similarly, Gerwin (1987), although acknowledging the importance of 'social factors', says only that, 'In general, the critical workforce characteristic is multi-skilling but its nature varies depending upon the type of flexibility' (1987, p.47). How, then, might work-based concerns of labour-centred flexibility be brought together with the production-based concerns of technology-centred flexibility?

FLEXIBLE SPECIALISATION

One of the most important attempts to conceptualise and explain the restructuring of work and production is Piore and Sabel's 'flexible specialisation' thesis. As the title of their book, *The Second Industrial Divide* (1984), suggests, they argued that the capitalist world faced a fundamental choice between persisting with an economy based on mass production and returning to one based on craft production. In this account, the system of mass production which had established itself as dominant by the early part of the twentieth century had, from the end of the 1960s, found its existence under threat. It was at this point that craft production, in the shape of flexible specialisation, presented itself as the alternative.

Under flexible specialisation, production is based on flexible networks of technologically sophisticated manufacturing firms. The networks are situated in certain geographical areas, in which firms do not compete directly with each other on the basis of cost, and where industry is able to develop and draw on regional institutions. In some areas, argued Piore and Sabel, these arrangements were already emerging to challenge the dominance of mass production. The three most prominent and widely cited were the so-called 'Third Italy', the area around the city of Salzburg and the Baden-Württemberg region of Germany.

Although flexible specialisation is portrayed as the revival of craft production, Piore and Sabel did not explore in any real depth its implications for the nature of work. The assumption was that the use of more flexible capital equipment would be associated with the development of a highly flexible, multi-skilled workforce. As Piore and Sabel express it in their description of the restructuring of the steel and chemicals industries, 'the use of more flexible equipment grows out of and requires a more flexible use of labor' (1984, p.212).

Both Piore and Sabel themselves and subsequent commentators (see Elam 1990) have seen this in terms of the division of labour. For Piore and Sabel, Smith's concept of the division of labour had been augmented by Marx's insight that the importance of the specialisation of labour lay in the fact that it facilitated the introduction of special-purpose machinery. It was out of this transition to the situation in which, rather than vice versa, the worker was the adjunct of the machine, that mass production emerged. But it was in the spaces in and around the markets served by mass production – as well as in the provision of the special-purpose machinery itself – that craft-based production was able to persist.

The flexible specialisation thesis was at the centre of many of the debates concerning the restructuring of work and production in the 1980s and 1990s. Partly as a result of its appeal from a government policy point of view, it did attract a number of adherents in the UK (Hirst and Zeitlin 1989). A substantial part of the reaction it generated, however, was either sceptical or actively hostile (Williams *et al.* 1987; Amin 1994; Tomaney 1994). Among the concerns was the question of whether flexible specialisation was being put forward as a description of what was happening, a prediction of what was going to happen, or a prescription of what should happen. Like so many influential ideas, the fact that flexible specialisation was open to a number of different interpretations was a factor in the influence it enjoyed. For some, however, the lack of conceptual precision was a source of frustration. Elam (1990), for example, argues that although the flexible specialisation thesis was difficult to accept without also accepting that it was based on the idea of the saturation and fragmentation of mass markets, Piore and Sabel explicitly eschew the principle of market determinism.

Added to the conceptual difficulties are the more prosaic problems of lack of evidence. Even if taken as prediction rather than description, it is difficult to find examples of UK industries that have been restructured along the lines of flexible specialisation. This applies even in industries like ceramics, where the conditions for such a restructuring might be considered to be the most conducive (Rowley 1994, 1996).

TECHNOLOGY-CENTRED FLEXIBILITY IN THE UK

A wider review of the experience of UK firms reveals that they have not on the whole pursued a strategy of technology-centred flexibility. An examination of the adoption and operation of advanced manufacturing technology (AMT) shows that even in its more primitive forms it remains rare in British industry and, where it is used, it appears unable to achieve the level of flexibility expected of it. We concentrate here on four main areas:

- **Numerically controlled (NC) and computer numerically controlled (CNC) machine tools:** Tidd (1991) shows that the proportion of machine tools of this pre-programmed form was half in the UK what it was in Japan, and that no improvement in flexibility was evident.

- **Robotics:** Tidd (1991) paints a similar picture here: proportionate to the number of employees, the use of robotics was 10 times greater in Japan than in the UK. Their use, moreover, was often confined to the performance of a single task.

■ **Flexible manufacturing systems (FMS):** Rush and Bessant (1992) estimate that there were no more than 100 of these systems in the UK by 1990; while Jones (1988) reports on the difficulties firms had in using them to achieve greater flexibility.

■ **Computer-integrated manufacturing (CIM):** even the potential component parts of CIM – such as computer-aided design (CAD) – are difficult to detect (Edquist and Jacobsson 1988); while McLoughlin (1990) demonstrates the difficulties firms have encountered in the use of CAD.

EXPLAINING THE FAILURES OF TECHNOLOGY-CENTRED FLEXIBILITY

This catalogue of failure has not, of course, gone unnoticed. Attempts at explanation have focused on the 'barriers' or 'obstacles' to successful adoption – the implication being that if only these impediments could be overcome, the situation would resolve itself satisfactorily. The barriers or obstacles can be considered under three headings:

■ **Trade union or workforce resistance:** although a long-running theme in writings on British organisations (Nichols 1986), more recent evidence suggests that workers tend to welcome technical change for its association with progress and success (Daniel and Hogarth 1990; Hogarth 1993).

■ **The technological hardware itself:** this might refer to the technical limitations of such things as FMS (Tidd 1991) or to the initial design of systems (Jones 1989).

■ **Management failures:** at worst, the lack of success with technology-centred flexibility is put down to simple managerial incompetence (Burnes 1988); though a more sophisticated version of this argument is that AMT may require more flexible organisational structures (Lei and Goldhar 1991; Fjermestad and Chakrabarti 1993).

All this leaves a very dismal impression. Even if we accept that worker resistance plays little part, we still have a picture of widespread managerial incompetence in both technical and organisational matters. At worst, this is no more than a truism: if managers were more competent they would manage better. Even with a more sympathetic interpretation, it does not cut very deep: if the only barrier in the way of achieving success was the provision of managerial and technical training, why have firms not undertaken it?

In order to understand this we need to go beyond the level of the individual organisation and focus instead on the institutional constraints within which it operates and makes decisions. Of key importance in this regard is industry's relationship with finance. Hutton (1995) has provided a clear account of this relationship, placing emphasis on the financial system's need for liquidity and showing how this is reflected in its lack of commitment to industry. He sets out in detail how the operation of the banking system leaves industry dependent on expensive short-term funding; while reliance on the stock market forces it into the actions necessary to satisfy shareholders and fend off the threat of takeover.

This impacts on investment in flexible production technologies in a number of ways. The most basic argument is that conventional means of investment appraisal are inadequate for dealing with such technology because they have no way of taking into account its 'strategic' nature (Boer 1994). Thus the broader benefits of such systems are ignored because it is impossible to value them precisely (Pike *et al.* 1989). In any case, if this kind of investment does take place, it is likely that the technologies will be misused in order to make them financially viable. Thus, rather than being used for low-volume, high-variety manufacture, FMS, say, are pressurised by utilisation targets into producing on a mass, standardised basis.

Jones (1989, p.116), for example, points to the 'pronounced Fordist bias' of the objectives of British management and shows that it was in these terms, rather than in terms of flexibility, that the advantages of FMS were sought.

TECHNOLOGY-CENTRED AND LABOUR-CENTRED FLEXIBILITY

Our purpose here is not simply to provide an explanation of British firms' inability to introduce and operate flexible production technologies. Indeed, our primary concern is to explain why flexibility has taken on a labour-centred rather than this technology-centred form. The two issues are inextricably linked, since it is the same conditions that both discourage the latter and encourage the former. In Hutton's (1995) account, for example, the terms on which finance is offered are of direct implication for the way that labour is managed. Standards of employment need to be undemanding, he argues, 'because without that flexibility [British companies] are much more likely to get into financial difficulty than their competitors whose debt structure is more longterm' (1995, p.150). Though long-standing in nature, this labour-centred flexibility can be said to have intensified as short-term pressures on firms have increased over the last 20 or so years. At the same time, forces which might have militated against these pressures have been weakened. The analysis presented here is certainly in line with those such as Nolan (1989), who maintains that increased productivity growth needs to be seen against the background of a shift in the balance of power in industrial relations that encouraged the intensification of labour rather than the deployment of multi-skilled workers and advanced production techniques.

As we have seen, there has been little consideration of the link between labour-centred and technology-centred flexibility. To the extent that there has, the general presumption seems to be that the two go together. In Piore and Sabel's (1984) flexible specialisation, flexible production technologies are associated with a highly skilled flexible workforce. The analysis presented here, however, suggests that the two forms of flexibility should be regarded not as complementary but as substitutes for each other. The question of how we can represent this is the subject of our next section.

The new flexible firm

FLEXIBILITY THROUGH TECHNOLOGY AND LABOUR

As the previous section showed, there is very little evidence to suggest that flexibility in British industry is based on technologically sophisticated, flexible production systems. What appears to have emerged instead is a system of cell- or group-based production, in which factories are divided up into a number of 'mini-factories', each producing a particular product. Cellular working has quite quickly become widespread. In 1990 the Ingersoll Engineers (1990) consultancy's survey of engineering companies with turnovers in excess of £10 million found what they described as a 'quiet revolution': 51 per cent of their sample had introduced some form of cellular manufacturing, most of them in the previous few years. By 1993, they found that the proportion had increased to 73 per cent (Ingersoll Engineers 1994).

Cellular production will often be introduced on the initiative of production managers and for what seem largely technical reasons. A major advantage of organising production in this way is that it cuts down the time part-made products spend 'travelling' around the organisation from function to function (Hill 1991). Nonetheless, the implications from a human resource management point of view are likely to be profound. For one thing, the operation of cellular production will both encourage and be encouraged by the kind of flexibility in labour we explored in the previous sections. The introduction of a product 'focus' to the organisation of work will militate against too strong a reliance on functional specialisation, especially if the reorganisation of production is accompanied by reduction in workforce numbers, thus effectively forcing functional flexibility onto those remaining (Turnbull 1988). This relationship between cellular production and flexibility is shown in Box 19.2.

Box 19.2: Flexibility through cellular production

Cellular manufacturing was central to the programme of change introduced by 'Engineering Industries', a large UK-based manufacturing group, which, in common with many other manufacturing organisations, attempted to restructure itself in the aftermath of the recession of the early 1980s. Each business unit in the group had to submit its own 'Business Action Plan', which laid down business targets on the basis of the unit's leading international competitor. As part of this, each unit's products were to be divided into 'families'. These were translated, first, into broad categories known as 'modules', and then, within each module, into more tightly defined cells. Each cell, typically employing between 15 and 20 people, was to be given responsibility for its own scheduling, planning, quality control, set-up activities and maintenance diagnostics. The aim was that each cell would include members of a new breed of 'super-craftsmen', proficient in various skills and able to work in a highly flexible manner.

The introduction and operation of cellular production in two of Engineering Industries' business units was examined by Stephen Procter and his colleagues (Procter *et al.* 1995). In the first, Company A, cellular production demanded changes in working practices which some were unwilling to adopt. Some who saw themselves as, for example, millers or turners, were unwilling to perform other operations. With the removal of support staff, moreover, operators had to begin sweeping up around their own machines – something which caused great resentment. Flexibility was not absolute. One cell leader estimated that only 50 per cent of his cell had the level of ability necessary to perform the full range of tasks that flexible working demanded. The less able 50 per cent were thus restricted to a narrow range of relatively simple jobs.

A similar situation arose in Company B. Within each cell there were to be only two grades of worker – craftsmen and operators. This system was a major change for craftsmen who were used to specific job titles and numerous skill gradings. Under the cellular system, craftsmen, in addition to the specialist tasks, were required to do maintenance, inspection, cleaning, and to move the work around – all work which demarcation agreements had previously ruled out. What was achieved was not complete flexibility but a degree sufficient for the new system to work satisfactorily.

Source: Procter *et al.* 1995

A second major factor is the association of cellular production with teamworking. In the case of cellular production, what is important from a human resource management perspective is that when equipment is brought together, so too are the workers who operate it. As Benders and Van Hootegem (1999) argue, cellular production has been important in reintroducing the idea of semi-autonomous work teams into the UK, where, as we have seen, they were first identified. Certainly, the use of teamworking has extended beyond certain narrow areas of production. A survey of manufacturing companies undertaken by the Institute of Work Psychology found team-based working being used by 70 per cent of their respondents (Waterson *et al.* 1997); and this was backed up by the 1998 WERS, which, on its broadest definition, found 65 per cent of all workplaces reporting that most of those employed worked in formally designated teams (Cully *et al.* 1999, p.38).

If we broaden our perspective we can observe the reorganisation of production on the basis of product or customer taking place in other sectors of the economy. In the case of Business Process Reengineering (BPR), this would involve restructuring work so as to group together all the tasks necessary to satisfy a particular group of customers (Hammer and Champy 1993). The survey undertaken by Willcocks and Grint (1997) found nearly 60 per cent of large and medium-sized UK companies either planning or actually undertaking some BPR activity. In sectors involving direct 'front-line' contact with customers, a similar reorganisation might be based on the 'strategic segmentation' of customers into different 'revenue streams' (Frenkel *et al.* 1999; Batt 2000).

What is common to all these developments is that work design has come to be central to the way organisations deal with their customers and competitors (Buchanan 1994a). As Buchanan (1994a, p.86) expresses it, 'It has . . . become increasingly unrealistic to distinguish between work design on the one hand and organisational design on the other. The former now typically implies the latter.' Perhaps the most important aspect of this is that the team becomes the basic organisational unit. We have, in Jenkins' (1994, p.851) words, 'organizations *built around* – and not just including – autonomous teams' (emphasis in original). The implications of this for flexibility are taken up in Box 19.3, but the more general point is that as well as technology and labour, our account of flexibility needs to consider broader issues of organisation and management.

FLEXIBILITY THROUGH MANAGEMENT AND ORGANISATION

How, then, is flexibility managed and organised? The short answer is that this takes the form not of direct control based on high levels of surveillance – a line of argument to which we return below – but of indirect control based on the allocation of costs. From the second Company-level Industrial Relations Survey (CLIRS), carried out in 1992, we get some idea of how large British firms use a range of budgetary controls to manage the relationship between the corporate centre and the operating or business units (Armstrong *et al.* 1996). Perhaps most important for our purposes is the relationship Armstrong *et al.* establish between the use of budgetary controls based on labour cost and the extent of labour flexibility. Companies using these controls at business unit level were found to employ more part-time and female workers than those which did not. Using the original flexible firm model, Armstrong *et al.* argue that because of the relative ease with which it is possible to change the numbers or tasks of these 'flexible' workers, labour cost budgets were more likely to be used. 'The implication', they claim, 'is that these labour cost ratios are used to impose numerical and/or temporal flexibility on the workforces of large UK companies' (Armstrong *et al.* 1996, p.19).

But how do these corporate-level strategies translate into workplace-level decisions? Here, although the evidence is less systematic, a pattern can tentatively be identified. The survey data of Armstrong *et al.* (1996) shows a definite association between the use of

Box 19.3: Teamworking and flexibility

At first sight we might expect teamworking to be associated with a greater degree of specialisation among employees. The popular view of a team in such areas as medicine and sport is of a group that brings together individuals with complementary skills. The form of teamworking that has been introduced in many organisations in recent years is thus in some ways counter-intuitive, for what we see among team members is a tendency towards flexibility (see Procter and Mueller 2000).

Paul Edwards and Martyn Wright studied the operation of teamworking in Alcan's aluminium smelter in Lynemouth, Northumberland. One objective of their study was to see whether a 'continuous process' production technology was one that was suitable for teamworking. They observed what they described as a relatively advanced form of teamworking, 'which involved the eventual elimination of supervisors and the delegation of responsibility to teams, which were organized by team leaders who remained essentially part of the work group' (1998, pp.274–5).

Edwards and Wright found that the workforce responded to teamworking in a broadly positive way. A survey of workers revealed greater interest in the job, more scope to take decisions, and better relations with other workers. Workers, said Edwards and Wright (1998, p.278), were not more skilled in the sense of having new technical abilities. What workers did report was an increase in the number of tasks they performed, and this was backed up by more systematic approach to training. Although teamworking appeared on the whole to be working well at Lynemouth, a number of remaining tensions could be identified. Among these was that the work group were not ready to take on all new tasks. Production workers on the night shift, for example, would not take samples of metal for testing, something which was normally the job of a technician. As Edwards and Wright (1998, p.280) express it, 'There were thus limits to flexibility.'

Source: Edwards, P. and Wright, M. 1998

labour cost targets and the declaration of redundancies in operating units which fail to meet them. Other evidence is provided by Hunter *et al.* (1993), whose analysis of the flexible firm concluded that there was no tendency on the part of employers to effect horizontal segmentation by levels of skill. What we have instead is a vertical segmentation on the basis of teams. For each of these product-focused segments a calculation of costs and benefits can be made, and this allows firms to make decisions about discrete areas of activities. In other words, a form of numerical flexibility is achieved by taking on and dispensing with not sections of a peripheral workforce but sections of the workforce as a whole.

We can combine all these elements – labour, technology, management, organisation – into a model of the 'new flexible firm' (Ackroyd and Procter 1998). The main features of the model are summarised in Box 19.4. This is represented in diagrammatic form in Figure 19.2, which should be compared directly with the original flexible firm model portrayed in Figure 19.1. In the terms of the original flexible firm, the core of the new flexible firm is of almost negligible

Box 19.4: The new flexible firm: summary of features

- Production is organised through the arrangement of machines and workers as cells capable of producing 'families' of components or products.

- Advanced manufacturing technology is little used, except as an addition to existing configurations of equipment.

- Employed labour contributes to flexibility as teams of semi-skilled workers performing a range of specific tasks and given on-the-job training.

- Employees do not enjoy privileged status or high employment security, but compete with sub-contracted labour and alternative suppliers.

- Production operations are considered as dispensable separate 'segments', about which calculations of cost are regularly made.

- Management takes the form of intensified indirect control based on the allocation of costs.

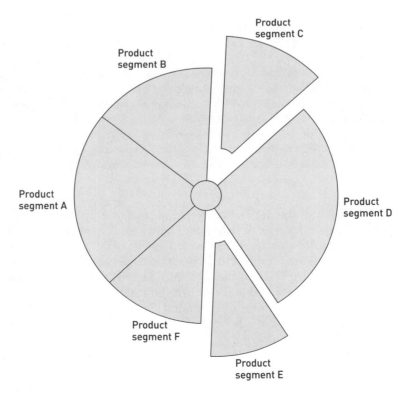

Figure 19.2   The new flexible firm
Source: Based on Ackroyd and Procter 1998

proportions; the distinction between core and periphery has disappeared; and flexibility is achieved through the manipulation of product-focused segments of activity.

Japanisation, the high-surveillance firm and lean production

Although the flexible firm model and flexible specialisation have been the main focuses of debate in the UK, and although the 'new flexible firm' appears to offer a better way of conceptualising the changes that have been taking place, we also need to look at other attempts to describe and explain the restructuring of work and organisation. One very popular idea is that British organisations have been restructuring themselves along the lines of their Japanese counterparts – a process known as Japanisation (see, for example, Oliver and Wilkinson 1992).

DIRECT AND INDIRECT JAPANISATION

Two main forms of Japanisation can be identified: direct and indirect (Ackroyd *et al.* 1988). Direct Japanisation refers to direct investment by Japanese companies in British industry. Although it is possible to identify certain high-profile cases such as Nissan, Toyota and Honda, the Japanese-owned sector remains very small. Even by the mid-1990s the number of people employed in Japanese manufacturing plants in the UK was 70,000, a figure that represented just 9 per cent of those employed in the foreign-owned manufacturing sector as a whole (Munday and Peel 1998). Moreover, there is little evidence to suggest that Japanese-owned plants offer an example to their British counterparts in terms of efficiency or effectiveness in management and organisation (Munday and Peel 1998).

In contrast to direct Japanisation, the indirect or mediated form refers to the adoption of Japanese-style policies and practices by indigenous UK companies. Surveys conducted at the end of the 1980s and the beginning of the 1990s did suggest that certain techniques were being picked up and used by British companies (Oliver and Wilkinson 1992). This data, however, carried with it a number of problems. The first was that it was never clear what exactly was 'Japanese' in this context. Thus cellular production, for example, could be included as part of the Japanese model, even though its origins and adoption could be explained in quite different terms. Even if these problems of definition could have been resolved, moreover, the way in which the surveys were conducted was itself a cause for concern (Procter 1995).

Most fundamentally, the idea of mediated Japanisation focused attention on how the conditions in which British companies were operating made anything but the most superficial adoption of Japanese methods very unlikely. Their effective adoption implies a high level of investment, the willingness and capacity to reconfigure technology on a continuous basis, and the commitment to high levels of training and employee involvement. As we have seen, the institutional conditions in which British companies operate are very different. In these circumstances they are likely to be very selective about which aspects of the Japanese model to adopt, taking only those that were cheap to implement and that would meet their immediate needs; or they would be even more pragmatic than this, making cosmetic use of Japanese ideas in order to introduce changes they would have made in any case (Ackroyd *et al.* 1988; Procter and Ackroyd 1998).

THE HIGH-SURVEILLANCE FIRM

What the focus on Japanese investment and Japanese practice has given rise to is a model of organisation and management we can call the high-surveillance firm. In this model, emphasis is put on the ability of specific procedures and techniques to secure increased quality and variety of production (Conti and Warner 1993; Delbridge *et al.* 1992; Sewell and Wilkinson, 1992). Control is exerted over individuals and groups by constantly monitoring, measuring and reporting their performance. This is achieved in part through the discipline imposed by such techniques as just-in-time production (JIT) and total quality management (TQM), but supplementing these are more recent developments which make use of the ability of IT-based systems to record and provide information on work performance. At the extreme, such systems are held to exercise an absolute control over employees. For some commentators, they represent the modern-day application of the all-seeing 'panopticon', the principles underlying which had previously applied to the design of prisons (Sewell and Wilkinson 1992).

These ideas are powerful ones and they have exerted a considerable influence on debates surrounding work and technology. They have been developed most recently in attempts to describe and understand the operation of telephone call centres. These have been portrayed as the apotheosis of panoptical control, the success of which is achieved ultimately by its 'internalisation' by workers as a result of its ubiquitous nature (Fernie and Metcalf 1997). There are, however, a number of reasons to cast doubt on such conclusions. Quite apart from the institutional conditions which we have already referred to on a number of occasions, there must still be doubts about the willingness and ability of British managers to condense, interpret and make use of the vast amount of information such systems can generate. Perhaps more importantly, the idea of absolute control assumes away the notion of worker resistance, ignoring the different forms such resistance can take and the effects it can have (Thompson and Ackroyd 1995; Taylor and Bain 1999). This is illustrated in Box 19.5.

Box 19.5: Flexibility, surveillance and resistance

Phil Taylor and Peter Bain's study of work in Scottish call centres set out to test the idea that the centres allowed management to exercise absolute control over employees. Their description of work in call centres is worth quoting in full (Taylor and Bain 1999, p.115):

> The typical call centre operator is young, female and works in a large open plan office or fabricated building, which may well justify the white-collar factory description. Although probably full-time, she is increasingly likely to be a part-time permanent employee, working complex shift patterns which correspond to peaks of customer demand. Promotion prospects and career advancement are limited so that the attraction of better pay and conditions in another call centre may prove irresistible. In all probability, work consists of an uninterrupted and endless sequence of similar conversations with customers she never meets. She has to concentrate hard on what is being said, jump from page to page on a screen, making sure that the details entered are accurate and that she has said the right things in a pleasant manner. The conversation ends and as she tidies up the loose ends there is another voice in her headset. The pressure is intense because she knows her work is being measured, her speech monitored, and it often leaves her mentally, physically and emotionally exhausted.

As Taylor and Bain make clear, however, all this does not mean that work in call centres is best understood as the application of a modern form of panoptical control.

▶

As well as being able to exert collective resistance through their membership of trade unions, workers have open to them a number of less formal, more individual courses of action. They find ways of removing themselves from waiting queues of calls, for example, or can merely pretend to be involved in making a call. Management, say Taylor and Bain, 'would certainly be surprised to discover that they exercise total control over the workforce' (1999, p.115). What the enhanced means of surveillance offers management is not a solution but a dilemma: while it cannot be abandoned altogether, 'intense surveillance can be counterproductive, costly in terms of workforce motivation and commitment' (1999, p.116).

Source: Taylor and Bain. 1999, pp.101–17. For a fictional account of work in a call centre see Matt Thorne's novel, *Eight Minutes Idle* (London: Sceptre, 1999)

GLOBAL JAPANISATION THROUGH LEAN PRODUCTION?

Perhaps the grandest claims made for a Japanese model of production and work are those made on behalf of 'lean production'. This term arose from the US-based International Motor Vehicle Program, a $5M, 14-country project which resulted in the publication of *The Machine that Changed the World* (Womack *et al.* 1990). Lean production, it was claimed, 'combines the advantages of craft and mass production, while avoiding the high cost of the former and the rigidity of the latter' (1990, p.13), or, more bluntly, it 'uses less of everything compared with mass production' (1990, p.13).

In the account provided by Womack *et al.*, mass production was a system based on an extreme division of labour, the 'visible hand' of organisation, dedicated or specialist machine tools, and highly standardised products. Lean production, on the other hand, had its origins in the system first developed in Toyota in the 1950s. Although mass production was at its zenith at this time, the argument runs that Toyota management did not consider it suitable for the conditions then prevailing in Japan. In particular, production volumes were not considered large enough to justify the use of dedicated machine tools. Instead, emphasis was placed on simplifying tool changes, with the responsibility given to production workers. This in turn reduced stocks and forced attention on improving product quality.

Womack *et al.* (1990) present the results of lean production in dramatic fashion. Taking the Toyota plant in Takaoka as representative of lean production and the GM plant in Framingham as representative of mass production, their comparison showed the former to have twice the level of productivity (or 'half the human effort'), three times the accuracy in terms of product defects, a 40 per cent greater efficiency in terms of space, and an average inventory equivalent to two hours' rather than two days' production.

The claims made by *The Machine that Changed the World* have been subject to challenge on a variety of grounds. Prime among the critics are Williams *et al.* (1992), who question almost all aspects of the Womack *et al.* thesis. For one thing, argue Williams *et al.* (1992), the polar opposition of 'mass' and 'lean' production is simply unsustainable. Their own historical analysis of Ford's Highland Park plant reveals its control of stock levels to be at least as good as that achieved by Toyota in more recent years. Moreover, the claim that lean production requires 'half the human effort' is based, argue Williams *et al.* (1992) on focusing on parts of the manufacturing process that together account for less than 15 per cent of the total value of the labour involved in making a car.

Two aspects of the claims made by the advocates of lean production are of particular interest to us here. The first is that the organisation of work – rather than the management of production – is placed centre-stage. A lean plant, it was claimed (Womack *et al.* 1990, p.99):

> transfers the maximum number of tasks and responsibilities to those workers actually adding value to the car on the line, and it has in place a system for detecting defects that quickly traces every problem . . . to its ultimate cause.

Thus, 'in the end, it is the dynamic work team that emerges as the heart of the lean factory' (1990, p.99).

But what kind of work team would operate under lean production? The idea of teamworking is usually associated with a group's ability to act with some degree of autonomy, but any control over the pace of production would be severely circumscribed by the removal of buffer stocks which lean production implies (Klein 1989). Delbridge *et al.*'s (2000) examination of teams in 'lean' plants in the automotive components sector found that the role of production workers was quite limited in the areas of maintenance and production management. More generally, Benders and Van Hootegem (2000) identify the key characteristics of the 'lean' team as: the focal position of foreman; the minute description and rigorous regulation of work through Standard Operating Procedures (SOPs); and the use of continuous improvement (*kaizen*) techniques to effect marginal improvement in these SOPs. Comparing this with the idea of scientific management that we examined earlier in this chapter, we see that while both might be based on a tightly defined division of labour, the main difference arises in the allocation of responsibility for changing the way in which work is organised. It is with this in mind that Kenney and Florida (1993) refer to the Japanese system as 'innovation-mediated Taylorism'.

The second aspect of lean production that we need to consider here is the claim that its principles are of universal application. Despite their argument that that it emerged in response to the particular conditions faced by the Japanese economy in the aftermath of the Second World War, Womack *et al.* (1990, p.88) maintain that 'lean production can be introduced anywhere in the world'. The response of Williams *et al.* (1992) was that neither American nor Japanese industry is inherently superior. Competition, they argue (1992, p.352) is 'not a contest between systems of inherently different efficiency; it is more like sumo where the off-balance wrestler is forced out of the ring'.

The claims of universalism made by the original advocates of lean production have also been the subject of more recent research work. A second phase of data collection in the automotive sector, in which the emphasis was placed on the human resource aspects of production, tried to assess what long-term trends were taking place (Pil and MacDuffie 1996; MacDuffie and Pil 1997). In particular, MacDuffie and Pil (1997) were keen to see whether practice across a range of countries was converging on the lean production model. Although their study does stress the idea of convergence, it recognises also that powerful forces were at work in the opposite direction. Thus although some – mainly European – automotive plants were classified as 'rapid move to lean', others were included under the headings of 'hybrid' and 'sticking with tradition'. A second major study, this time of the automotive components industry, also failed to find support for the idea that the principles of lean production were universally applicable (see Box 19.6)

Although the ideas underlying lean production and the high-surveillance firm deserve to be treated with respect, they offer little insight into the way British organisations are restructuring work and technology in order to achieve an enhanced flexibility of operation. A summary of the high-surveillance firm and our other two models of flexibility is presented in Table 19.1. As we have argued, the original model of the flexible firm is useful to the extent that it focuses attention on labour as the main route through which flexibility is achieved; less

Box 19.6: Flexibility through lean production?

Following on from the International Motor Vehicle Program, the Arthur Andersen 'Worldwide Manufacturing Competitiveness Survey' looked at the use of the principles of lean production by companies in the automotive components industry. Taking three areas – seats, exhausts and brakes – they explored what they defined as 'world-class performance' in terms of both productivity and quality. The key factor, it was argued, was whether a company was located in a supply chain that was operated in a disciplined manner. The study found no convincing evidence of the universal applicability and superiority of any particular systems of work organisation and human resource management. Although some of the world-class performers were operating under lean production principles, these were largely Japanese companies in Japan, and there were other world-class performers who were operating in quite different settings.

The Arthur Andersen study could thus not be used to support the universalist hypothesis. In the UK automotive components sector, for example, support was found for the idea that it was the supply chain that was the most important factor: significant differences were found between those supplying Japanese car assemblers and those not. Inventories were found to be high relative to those in Japan but there was some evidence of the adoption of the 'softer' aspects of the lean production model. At the same time, Japanese plants tended to follow the lean production model regardless of any linkage with performance. What all this suggested was that location and ownership were important explanatory factors in both performance and management practice. Oliver *et al.*'s (1996, p.S43) conclusion about the UK automotive components sector is quite stark: 'we are pessimistic about the prospects for building world-class manufacturing facilities in what may be basically a non-world-class economy'.

Sources: Lowe *et al.* 1997, pp.783–98; Oliver *et al.* 1996, pp.29–44

useful is its neglect of technology and its division of the workforce into core and peripheral elements. The 'new flexible firm' attempts to overcome some of these deficiencies. Although still focusing on the role of labour, this is combined with a low-technology, product-based organisational restructuring and an indirect, cost-based form of control. The high-surveillance firm shares some of this concern with technique and organisation, but stresses also the ability of high-technology IT systems to effect direct control over the workforce.

Human Resource Management and Human Resource managers

MANAGING HRM STRATEGICALLY

Our approach so far has been a rather structural one. In other words, rather than the options open to HR and other managers in the area of flexibility, we have stressed the constraints

Table 19.1 Dimensions of the three models: original flexible firm, high-surveillance firm and new flexible firm

	Labour	Technology in use	Sources of flexibility	Management	Network	Problems/sector
Original flexible firm (OFF)	*Requirements:* High-skill and low-skill groups *Policy:* Segmentation	Little or nothing specified	Labour	*Objective:* Rapid changes in direction and scale of production *Strategy:* Labour segmentation	Little or nothing specified; independent producer	Does it exist anywhere?
High-surveillance firm (HSF)	*Requirements:* Semi-skilled *Policy:* Progressive training	Medium to high investment in productive technology	Mix of technical and labour flexibility	*Objective:* Medium to large batch production *Strategy:* High quality/low price	Japanese parent	Electronics and automotives
New flexible firm (NFF)	*Requirements:* Mostly unskilled/ semi-skilled *Policy:* Limited on-the-job training	Low to medium technology; cell-working	Labour and selection of product markets	*Objective:* Medium batches of related products for specific niches *Strategy:* Short term profit	Specialist provider to supply chains	General manufacturing

within which managers operate, showing how these are more likely to give rise to certain courses of action than to others. While in the next section we want to shift the focus towards the discretion which managers can exercise in this area, we have first to explain and contextualise our overall approach.

The approach we have taken here is very much in line with that of Storey and Sisson (1993). As their work demonstrates, although the new models of HRM – especially in their insistence on its strategic importance – appeared to open up tremendous possibilities, few organisations could be said to have fully realised this potential. The question of why this ideal should be so difficult to attain carried with it a more specific question: 'what are the factors which limit its attainment in the British context?' (1993, p.73). As well as factors that relate to particular technologies and industries, Storey and Sisson identify what they call 'the more generic impediments' (1993, p.75). The first of these is the 'short-termism' which limits managerial performance horizons and encourages expedient solutions. This, in turn, is related to the way in which, in Goold and Campbell's (1987) terms, multi-divisional structures are used to effect a system of financial control rather than one of strategic planning. As we have seen throughout this chapter, it is these underlying conditions that encourage the adoption of particular forms of flexibility.

THE ROLE AND STANDING OF THE PERSONNEL PROFESSION

It is perhaps worth stressing one other aspect of the constraining structures within which decisions about flexibility are made. Reflecting and reinforcing the short-term, finance-driven mode of operation is the relationship between different professional groups. In many British organisations it is accountants who form the dominant group. Following Armstrong (1987a, 1987b, 1989), we can say that this results from their ability to capture the strategic functions of organisations. In the conditions we have described, it is accounting logic that has defined organisational performance and, therefore, it is accounting-based policies that provide the basis for organisational decisions. In decisions about the introduction and management of technology, for example, accountants are able to dominate the logic of engineers (Jones *et al.* 1994).

For the personnel or HR profession this is all part of a long-running debate about its role and standing. The origins of the personnel profession and its inability to exercise power in organisations have long been a matter of concern (Legge 1995). Thus even in areas like technological change, the success of which has been shown to depend on the manner of implementation and, in particular, the way in which organisational and human resource issues are dealt with, the personnel role is very much a subsidiary one (Clark 1993b).

The rise of HRM appeared to bring with it the opportunity to change this situation. Although the pessimistic interpretation was that the integration of HR issues into wider issues of business strategy would lead to HR managers losing what little specialist expertise and power they possessed, even this could be portrayed as the giving up of the more prosaic parts of personnel work in return for, in Storey's (1992) terms, the opportunity to act at the apex of the organisation as a 'strategic change-maker'. More recently, we have seen the work of Ulrich (1997) emerge as the focus for debate. His line is that HR professionals can – and should – take on multiple roles: they must be concerned with both strategic and operational matters and with both people and processes.

How this works out in practice is less clear. Within the constraints we have outlined, there is still scope for personnel managers to enhance their influence. Recent work by one of the present authors supports Ulrich's argument that this is best done through a consideration of the multiple roles the personnel function can perform (Procter and Currie 1999). What this work also shows is that two other things need to be taken into account: first, how these

Box 19.7: Managing flexibility

Among the issues raised by the case study attached to this chapter is the role played in flexibility initiatives by human resource or personnel managers (Case study 19.1). Flexibility in this case takes the form of the introduction of new, harmonised terms and conditions for two groups of staff – nurses and operational department practitioners or assistants – working in operating theatres in a large acute hospital. The two groups of staff worked closely together – and in some tasks were interchangeable – but their different terms and conditions posed immense problems for the management of the operating theatres.

For the hospital's human resources (HR) department, the so-called Theatres Project represented a pilot project for a system of local pay that they had intended – and still hoped – would apply to the hospital as a whole. They were involved in each stage of the process of implementation: the drawing up of the new pay scales; the calculation of the offers that were made to individual members of staff; the putting of the new terms and conditions to the operating theatres staff through a series of mass meetings; and the negotiation of agreements with individuals.

The Theatres Project thus involved the HR department in a variety of roles, some of which brought them into conflict with the operating theatres' management. It was felt, for example, that in negotiating deals with certain individuals, the HR department was more concerned with the financial implications for the hospital as a whole than with the day-to-day needs of the operating theatres. On the other hand, the presence of an HR adviser at the individual interviews was welcomed as providing an objective observer. The case thus illustrates the range of functions that personnel managers can be expected to take on and also how these functions depend on their relationships with other organisational actors (see also Procter and Currie 1999).

Source: Procter and Currie 'Organisational setting: the Theatres Directorate of Midland City Hospital NHS Trust' (Case study 19.1)

multiple roles relate to specific issues that personnel managers face within organisations; and, second, how these roles emerge from the process of interaction with other organisational groups. It is in this context that we can best understand the management of flexibility and the role of the personnel function within it. This is a theme explored in Box 19.7 and in Case study 19.1 at the end of this chapter.

Managing flexibility

NEGOTIATING FLEXIBILITY

Although in some eyes the effect of the shift in the industrial relations balance of power over the past 20 or so years has been to allow the reassertion of the 'managerial prerogative', there is little evidence to support the cruder versions of the idea that 'macho management' has emerged as dominant (Legge 1988). Certainly, we have seen no improvement in areas where traditionally there has been little legal or collective protection of employee interests, but, in other areas, settlements on such things as workforce flexibility have been the result of agreement rather than unilateral imposition. Marsden and Thompson (1990), for example, found that although the number of formal working practice agreements was fairly small, more significant were the associated changes in 'working methods', which were settled largely informally. Dunn and Wright (1994) also provided evidence to suggest that working practices were being negotiated through existing arrangements. In certain sectors at least, therefore, a traditional role in industrial relations negotiations is still open to personnel managers.

IMPLEMENTING FLEXIBILITY

In many cases, just as important as the content of work reorganisation is the process by which it is introduced. Using Fox's (1974) terminology, we can say that if flexibility is assumed to take on the characteristics of a 'high discretion syndrome' – trust, encouragement and participation – then its introduction as well as its operation require the use of high-trust management. As Geary (1994) argues, management in British organisations find it all too easy to adopt a strategy based on 'the availability of a cheap and dispensable workforce', one which is 'most likely to induce a low trust relationship' (1994, p.656). Procter *et al*.'s (1995) study of the introduction of flexible team-based working in two parts of a large engineering concern shows how its failure in one of these was associated with a closed and uncommunicative style of management.

While there is no necessary connection between success and the manner of introduction, the chances of successfully operating a work system based on a high-discretion syndrome will certainly not be reduced by a process based on the same assumptions. Studies of change episodes, however, suggest that personnel managers' involvement is often peripheral and, at best, only a belated response to foreseeable organisational problems (Legge 1993). Although this is itself explicable in terms of the constraints we have already identified, this process of introduction is one part of the management of flexibility in which personnel might take on a greater role.

PAYING FOR FLEXIBILITY

Paying for flexibility can be considered under two headings: the pay settlement associated with the introduction of flexible working arrangements; and the payments system under which they operate. On the first of these, Ingram (1991) looked at the extent to which changes in working practices were linked to pay settlements. Of a panel of 160 groups, 80 per cent of those with collective bargaining had experienced such change in working arrangements at some time over the period 1979–90. What this showed, he argued, was that change was more effective if linked to pay.

As for payment systems, those which might be thought to be most consistent with the development of flexibility have not proved the most popular and successful. If anything, the trend in payment systems has been towards the adoption of performance-related pay based on individual appraisal (Kessler 1994). While in itself this does not run contrary to the idea of flexible working arrangements, an explicitly skills-based system would appear to offer more positive encouragement. Such systems have proved difficult to operate. Mueller and Purcell's (1992) study of the European automotive engine industry found that it was in this area of work restructuring that firms had made the lowest rate of progress. Likewise, to the extent that flexibility is associated with teamworking, team-based systems of pay have been found to encounter severe problems. Ezzamel and Willmott's (1998) study of a UK-based clothing manufacturer shows clearly the conflicts and issues such systems can raise.

Conclusions

This chapter carries a mixed message for specialist HR managers and general managers with HR responsibilities. As we have seen, there are severe constraints within which they have to operate. This means that with regard to flexibility – as with other issues – some courses of action are more likely to be taken than others. Thus in their pursuit of flexibility, organisations are likely to place the emphasis on the flexibility of labour. The type of flexibility required of labour may be of a negative form: we are much less likely to see securely employed, highly trained, multi-skilled workers than we are their insecure, semi-trained, multi-tasked counterparts. At the level of the individual manager or the individual organisation, there is little opportunity to change the conditions which bring this situation about. This is not to say, however, that there is nothing at all that can be done. We have highlighted in our final section a number of areas in which HR managers might intervene in order to steer change in a particular direction. HR managers might at least be able to shift the emphasis of the employment relationship from areas in which the interests of employers conflict with the interests of employees, to areas in which the interests of the two coincide.

CASE STUDY 19.1

MANAGING FLEXIBILITY: The Theatres Project in Midland City Hospital NHS Trust

STEPHEN PROCTER AND GRAEME CURRIE

Organisational setting

The Theatres Directorate of Midland City Hospital NHS Trust

Our case study organisation, Midland City Hospital NHS Trust, is an acute NHS hospital based in a city in the English Midlands. It has an annual budget of over £100 million and employs around 5,000 staff. It is divided into between 30 and 40 departments or 'directorates'.

Within the hospital, our main focus is the Theatres Directorate, which consists of a total of 15 operating theatres. In addition to the eight theatres in the main block, there are more specialist facilities in the areas of urology, maternity, day surgery and burns. Over 200 people were employed in the directorate. Its annual budget was over £6 million, of which around half was accounted for by pay. The mission statement of the Theatres Directorate described its role as follows:

> **To provide a multi-disciplinary team using the holistic approach to care. To provide and maintain professional assistance in the anaesthetic, theatre and recovery areas within the resources available until patients are in a safe state prior to their return to intensive care or ward areas.**

Head of the directorate was the Clinical Director, who had taken up the post part-way through 1997, after 20 years in the NHS working as an anaesthetist. Two other key members of staff were the Theatre Manager and the Specialty Manager. The former, a senior nurse, had joined the hospital in the early 1970s, and her chief concern was staff management within the directorate. The Specialy Manager had been in the job eight years. His own role he described as 'really processes, money, ensuring things happen . . . I do lots of the linking with the rest of the hospital and linking with other directorates.'

The Human Resources Department

The trust's Human Resources (HR) Department has a total of around 20 staff. At its head is the Director of Human Resources, who sits on the trust's board. Among those reporting to the Director are the Management Development Manager and the Personnel Manager, who also serves as deputy to the director. Reporting to the Personnel Manager are three Personnel Advisers, each of whom is responsible for a particular area of the trust. It is these Personnel Advisers who are the main point of day-to-day contact with the trust's managers and staff

The trust's HR strategy for the period 1998–2003 was contained in a written document. The first of its 'key themes' was 'a competent and flexible workforce'. This and other key themes were each backed up by a series of more specific 'objectives'. In the case of flexible working, these included:

(a) To introduce new patterns of working appropriate to service needs, reducing overtime where necessary.
(b) To introduce local harmonised terms and conditions on a phased basis, linked with local need, robust costing procedures and affordability.
(c) To define roles through definitions based on competencies required to do the job. To review these competencies regularly and where appropriate, link progression within local pay scales to the acquisition of competencies.

Background to change

Local pay

From the point of view of the HR Department, local pay was an issue of great importance. The original intention had been to address this situation on a trust-wide basis. When the idea began to be encouraged by the Conservative government from 1995/96 onwards, local pay meant the operation of an 'X + Y' formula, under which the national pay awards (X) could be supplemented according to local discretion (Y). According to the Personnel Manager, Midland City's experience of this notion of local pay had not been a favourable one. Although financial scope to make discretionary awards was severely limited, it was decided to push forward with a corporate project. In consultation with the main trade unions, and with HR driving the process, a trust-wide programme of job evaluation was undertaken. This was followed by HR working closely with the Finance Directorate in order to arrive at a detailed idea of how this would translate into pay.

This whole process then became subject to the uncertainties surrounding the general election of 1997. It was felt that it was best to wait until the new government's position became clear. It was at this stage that the Theatres Project emerged. 'From there [Theatres],' as the HR Director expressed it, 'the managers were screaming.' 'So,' said the personnel manager, 'we developed what was a very corporate project into a Theatres project.'

Nurses and ODPs/ODAs

The problems faced by the Theatres Directorate arose from the co-existence of two groups of staff – nurses and Operational Department Practitioners or Assistants [ODPs/ODAs] – who worked very closely together and who, in some aspects of work, were interchangeable, but who were trained, paid, progressed, managed and organised quite separately from each other. The reason for this was that the nurses' role had been to assist the surgeons, and the ODPs' to assist the anaesthetist.

The two groups of staffs each had their own management and organisation within the directorate:

> [the ODP manager] used to meet with his team and he used to deploy them, agree training needs with them and agree a roster; and then there used to be the G grades [nurses] that are basically team leaders . . . and each month they'd get together and decide what they were going to do [Personnel Adviser].

Not only were there two different duty rosters, terms and conditions for the two groups of staff were very different. This could give rise to some anomalous situations. In particular, the relative position of the ODPs meant that it was felt they should be given greater opportunity to work at overtime rates of pay: 'you had to pay them overtime to make their pay up to the normal level,' said the Speciality Manager:

> . . . to allow ODPs to get equivalent earnings, all the overtime was in their favour . . . their normal shift would stop at 5.15 and they were allowed to stay until 6 o'clock in the evening. So each night they were picking up three-quarters of an hour overtime . . . and when they came at the weekends it was all as additional overtime [Personnel Adviser].

It was not just that this in itself caused managerial and organisational problems. The differences were held to generate conflict between the nurses and the ODPs:

> . . . you could have somebody working alongside each other, let's say for a Bank Holiday, and getting two entirely different rates of pay, one walking out saying, 'Thank you very much', and the other a little dissatisfied [Theatre Manager].

The Theatres Directorate began to take action by introducing a common work rota for nurses and ODPs at the beginning of 1997. Although this was seen as a move in the right direction, it did not address what were from the management point of view the more fundamental problems. With the situation a long-standing cause for concern, the prevarication over the organisation-wide local pay programme had led to demands from the Theatres Directorate that it be proceeded with at least in their area:

> A long time ago we wanted to do something about it, and we were told, 'Wait for local pay'. And we sat back and waited. There was a campus-wide group that looked at local pay, which then did not progress, but we said, 'Could we be the pilot for local pay, because we really need to sort it?' [Theatre Manager].

It was against this background that 'harmonised' terms and conditions for nurses and ODPs eventually came into effect. The process by which these terms and conditions were worked out, agreed upon and introduced was known as the Theatres Project.

The Theatres Project

Objectives

The official position on objectives was stated in the 'Harmonisation' document which set out the proposed new terms and conditions:

> **For some considerable time the Theatres Directorate has been wanting to recognise the contribution made by all the staff working within the service but who are paid on a range of different scales and allowances and are on different terms and conditions.**

The provision of a common pay scale and common terms and conditions would, it was claimed, have the following advantages:

■ an increase in flexibility of relevant staff

■ to enable a positive movement to equal pay for equal contribution to the service

■ to encourage the development of knowledge and skills among theatre staff

■ to ensure the most effective and efficient provision of cover at particular times during the week . . . ['Harmonisation']

The project's concern for flexibility was made clear in interviews with the directorate's managers. In reference to the nurses and ODPs, the Clinical Director said, 'we wanted to get them multi-skilled for flexibility'. 'The purpose of doing it,' said the Specialty Manager, 'was so that we could use the staff interchangeably . . . and so that we could make savings'.

Outcomes

The terms of the agreement eventually arrived at came into effect on 1 January 1998. The Clinical Director described its essence: 'We call everybody a theatre practitioner now; you're not a nurse, you're a theatre practitioner.' Its chief elements were:

■ single pay spine for nurses and ODPs

■ new seven-day single duty rota

■ common 37.5 hour week

■ pay enhancements for commitment to working 'non-core' hours

■ managers encouraged to avoid use of overtime

■ overtime rate of time-and-a-third

■ competence-based system of progression

The new 'harmonised' grades can be seen in Table 19.2. Alongside each of the eight grades are the basic salary range it covers, and the number and type of staff within it. As the table shows, the majority of trained theatre staff are to be found on Grade 6. This covers the old nursing grades of D and E and the equivalent grades on the ODPs' pay scales.

What did these changes imply for the two groups of workers? The 37.5-hour week, although leaving the hours of nurses unchanged, meant an increase in hours for the ODPs. At the same time, unsocial hours pay was abolished, managers were encouraged to 'continue to develop operational processes and policies which avoid using overtime', and the overtime rate was cut from the previous standard rate of time-and-a-half. As we saw

Table 19.2 The Theatres Project: new grades and their Whitley equivalents

Basic salary	Grade	Points/ bars	Scale	Whitley equivalent	No. staff
27,297–21,549	8	3/0	Operational manager		2
			Resources manager		1
			Pain control nurse		1
20,921–15,567	7	11/1	Team leader	G Grade nurse	13
			Relief team leader	F Grade nurse	6
			Assistant co-ordinator		1
16,515–12,289	6	11/2	Senior theatre practitioner	E Grade nurse/ MTO 2 + 3 ODP	58
			Theatre practitioner	D grade nurse/ MTO 2 ODP	45
13,428–11,246	5	7/1			
12,289–10,292	4	7/1			
10,918–9,144	3	7/1			
9,992–8,368	2	7/1	Theatre support worker	A Grade nurse	33
9,144–6,606	1	12/1	Student ODP		7

Notes:
1. Basic salary excludes 5 per cent and 8 per cent enhancements.
2. Staff numbers based on full-time equivalents.
3. MTO = Medical Technical Officer.
4. Full grid would also include eight clerical staff (three on grade 2 and five on grade 3) and nine ancillary staff (eight on grade 2 and one on grade 3).

above, it was the ODPs who had the most to lose in these respects as well. Against this, with 'core' hours defined as between 6am and 8pm, seven days a week, staff with a contractual commitment to work regularly outside these hours received a flat 5 per cent 'enhancement' of basic salary. Staff with a contractual commitment to work rotational shifts received an 8 per cent enhancement.

The competence-based system of progression was designed to replace a system in which progression had been based largely on time served. Under the new system, progression through a grade was to be done on the basis of 'performance/contribution/competency'. It was intended that this be fully in place by January 1999. For movement within Grade 6, for example, the general principles upon which the first bar could be crossed meant the new theatre practitioners would have to 'demonstrate competency in both areas of work – anaesthesia and surgery – and willingness to work flexibly in both' and 'demonstrate level of specialist knowledge in "base" area ['Harmonisation'].'

Financial implications

The trust, said the personnel manager, was under great pressure to break even financially: 'it's about the bottom line today; it's about this year's accounts and this year's income and expenditure'. In these circumstances it could be very difficult to make a case for this kind of flexibility agreement:

> If I said to you that by introducing harmonised terms and conditions in nursing, I believe that we could save hundreds of thousands of pounds over the next five or six years on recruitment, retention, induction, training etc., it's hard to put that up and show you, and say, 'Well, if we reduce turnover from 20 per cent to 10 per cent, that's 10 per cent less vacancies and that equates to [£]10,000 a vacancy and that means it's this amount of money' – it may be, but it isn't real money this year [Personnel Manager].

This trust's Director of Finance had called for this kind of justification. According to the HR Director, 'it was a very pure bottom-line approach to, "So, convince me of the benefits, HR", but the project was able to go forward on this basis:

> we went to the trust board with that Theatres Project fully costed, and it was £30,000 best case, £60,000 worst case; 1 per cent of the pay budget of [£]3,000,000, and it went in.' [HR Director]

Nonetheless, it was felt that a longer term, more strategic view should be taken:

> For me, the benefits of harmonised terms and conditions . . . are lost in the 'let's look at the bottom line cost' issue, are lost to a certain extent in the wider strategic view of what are the long-term benefits of actually doing certain things within the organization [Personnel Manager].

The change process

We thus have some idea of what flexibility looks like in this case and what its financial implications were. But how had all this come about? What, in other words, was the process of change? With the unified terms and conditions coming into effect on 1 January 1998, all new staff in the Theatres Directorate are appointed on that basis. For the directorate and trust management, of course, the main problem was how existing staff could be moved across. The principle contained in the official documentation was that staff transferring would be dealt with as follows:

> [they] will assimilate to the next point above their current salary within the appropriate section of the new grade. Where this assimilation is less than the individual's current salary, a personal offer may be made ['Harmonisation'].

Perhaps most importantly, there was no attempt to impose the new terms and conditions on employees; it was to be done through a process of consultation and negotiation. 'We said', said the Theatre Manager, 'You have a choice of remaining where you are or you take up the offer.'

Differences and issues

The Theatres Project had begun with the establishment of a working group. Consisting of representatives of the Human Resources Department and both management and staff of the Theatres Directorate, compromises had to be made. In particular, there was the issue of to what extent a scheme designed for the hospital as a whole should be modified so as better to fit the conditions in Theatres. 'There were times', said one Team Leader involved in the consultation process, 'when HR had very different ideas to us.' The Theatres Directorate felt themselves to be unique. '[Other directorates] don't have a similar situation', said the Clinical Director,

> . . . they have wards that are staffed by nurses. They don't have two separate groups of people working side by side on different conditions . . .

> They [HR] kept saying it was for the whole hospital, and we said, 'Well, it won't work for us. We'll have to be an exception on that one, and anyway you're not using it for the whole hospital' . . . there was the feeling that they'd designed it for the whole hospital and they didn't want us to come in and change it all, so it then was useless for the rest of the hospital – but equally it wasn't any use to us in the state it was in . . . [Clinical Director]

On this basis, for example, it was agreed that a permanent night-time staff, consisting of around 10 people, should be retained.

Another issue was the harmonisation of night-time breaks. Under the existing terms and conditions, both groups of workers had one hour's break but, while ODPs were paid for theirs, nurses were not. The original proposal was that there would be an hour's break, half of which would be paid and half unpaid. The initial reaction from staff was that they would make themselves unavailable for the half-hour for which they were not being paid, but in the end agreement was reached:

> The unions were involved, and said, 'You're not going to get very far here, because you're not actually entitled to any lunch-break time in the middle of the night, it's just that it happens to have evolved like that. If I were you, I'd take the half an hour and shut up.' I think that's what happened in the end, and in the end I think that is the sort of messy compromise, that everybody gets half an hour break in the night paid for and half an hour not paid for [Clinical Director].

This and other issues and compromises brought home the fact that the starting point for the project was not a blank sheet of paper but formal and informal practices built up over a number of years:

> We are still left with some anomalies which will fade away in about ten years, with retirement. You cannot substantially alter someone's earning capacity overnight, so I suppose the word is assimilation [Theatre Manager].

Mass meetings and individual offers

Once something approaching agreement had been reached, in the autumn of 1997, the proposed changes were put into booklet form and submitted to the Theatres staff as a whole. This was done in three stages, the first being a series of meetings –16 in number, according to the Specialty Manager – which were open to all staff. The meetings continued until it was felt that demand for them had been satisfied:

> we had big meetings, we had meetings at every time of day and night in small groups . . . You got down to as many as four people in a group or you had a room full of 20-odd

> . . . [The Specialty Manager] put out emails saying, 'Do you want to come any more?', and when we got the nil replies, we stopped [Theatre Manager].

The second stage was the drawing-up of each individual's terms and conditions:

> We had to get everybody's earnings over the last couple of years and then make decisions and decide on what we were going to offer people and what they were capable of [Theatre Manager].

Because nobody was being forced to move on to the new terms and conditions, said the Specialty Manager, 'everybody was made an offer that actually was slightly better or considerably better for them'.

The trade-off between the costs involved and the desire to extend the new terms and conditions as far as possible was most acutely felt in the cases of a group of around 12 key staff who did not come out well from the original calculations. Not only did they have a great deal of experience, it was argued, but there was a danger of their influencing other members of staff against accepting the new terms and conditions:

> They were people that we had to make sure were well provided for, but they didn't fit into the pay scale, so there were major arguments over that. And in the end we brought in a once-and-only, accept-it-this-time, if-you-decide-not-to-come-over-onto-local-pay-now-you-won't-get-as-good-an-offer-again, and we made them an off-the-scale offer of . . . I can't remember the figure but it was more than [£]1,000 [more] than they would have been normally offered . . . [Clinical Director]

In the third stage of this part of the project, the offers were discussed at in individual interviews with all staff. 'We interviewed about 240 people at 20 minutes a time,' said the Theatre Manager. The interviews could be quite fraught:

> A lot of the hassles we saved ourselves in the one-to-one by the open meetings, but there were still some that wanted every 'I' dotted. And although we kept saying, 'This is a personal offer to you', [they would say] 'Why has Joe Bloggs got . . .?' – 'We're not here to discuss Joe Bloggs, we're here to discuss you' [Theatre Manager].

The role of the HR Department

As the Theatre Manager recognised, the HR Department had a vested interest in the success of the Theatres Project:

> It was the project for the hospital; they were concerned that we sold it to the staff, we got the take-up. Otherwise we would have ended up with egg on our face . . . And the fact that as a directorate we wanted to do it, so it was their role to support us in getting it in, which they did.

We have already seen something of their role in the working group that thrashed out the terms and conditions that were to be put to Theatres staff; their involvement, however, did not end there. The Specialty Manager described the part they played in the series of open meetings:

> I tended to lead, but the Human Resources person was always there to answer any complex questions – which was rarely the case, but it's also quite good if you're leading it,

to say, 'We also have here . . .', so that they could see that the local management wasn't doing something just that they'd thought of, but it was the whole hospital [Specialty Manager].

They were also fully involved in the drawing up of individuals' offers:

> . . . they [HR] also, for every individual member of theatre staff, which is well over 200 – in conjunction with ourselves, people working in Theatres . . . – prepared individual offers for everybody, looking at their circumstances, how many years they'd worked there, what their incremental date was, etc. [Clinical Director].

In sorting out a number of special deals, the Clinical Director felt that Human Resources had been concerned with the financial rather than the operating implications:

> I got the feeling that they [HR] were coming from the organization's point of view that the cost had to be kept down, whereas we were coming from the point of view that these were people who we (a) rely on, and (b) work with . . . So there were two points to it: (1) we wanted to retain them so that Theatres didn't fall apart; and (2) they were people we worked with on a personal day-to-day basis, and we didn't want to see them done out of anything [Clinical Director].

The HR Department's input was carried into the individual interviews with staff. The Theatre Manager did most of the interviews on her own: 'But if there was a dodgy one I made sure I had a Personnel Adviser with me':

> People turned up with their pay slips. [The Personnel Adviser] sat there with his calculator and said, 'This is OK.' Some of the information we got from Finance was not easily interpretable and, yes, we did make some mistakes . . . [Theatre Manager].

The presence of the Personnel Advisor could be welcomed by the staff:

> I think some of them appreciated personnel being here . . . some of them wanted to know which would be the best advantage for them when they went on maternity leave – so, 'Over to you, [Personnel Adviser].' [Theatre Manager].

The Theatre Manager also described how she could be protected by personnel. She might be asked, for example, 'Is that the best deal if you have sickness?', to which her response was, 'I'm not allowed to advise you what to do. I can give you the options; you make up your own mind.' In these circumstances, said the Theatre Manager, the presence of the Personnel Adviser meant that, 'At least you had a witness to say that you had said that.' The Specialty Manager made similar observations about the individual interviews:

> . . . we always . . . had a Human Resources Adviser with us, to see fair play, . . . to answer any questions; but also to see that a totally consistent approach was taken along these lines. Then we had all the changes, after all the interviews, and then Human Resources did all the contract issuing.

Overall, it was held by some that the HR input had been essential to the success of the project: 'we could not have done all that without a great deal of support from HR,' said the Theatre Manager. The Clinical Director expressed similar views:

> We relied heavily on them to compose the pay scales, obviously, and to offer us advice about what we could and couldn't do. They did put a lot of effort into the individual

offer stage, so they played quite a big part in it. I think they also played a part of being an external body as well, rather than Theatres staff feeling that their pay depended on how [the Theatre Manager] viewed them . . .

Others were inclined to play down the role of the HR Department:

I think if the HR Department had just tried to introduce it themselves without negotiating with Theatres and without involving them, then it wouldn't have worked so well. It's very important for those people that are working within that environment to feel a part of it, to gain ownership of what's happening in their own workplace [Team Leader].

Evaluating the project

Take-up of new terms and conditions

As a first consideration, the project was judged to have been successful because of the proportion of Theatres staff that had elected to take up the new terms and conditions. Although there were small differences between the figures given by different respondents, it seemed that over 70 per cent of existing staff had moved over. Typical was the personnel manager: '75 per cent of people have actually moved over, so that was a real success story'. A 100 per cent take-up had not been expected. According to the Specialty Manager:

There are some that we never expected would [agree to the new terms and conditions]; the permanent night staff, you can't possibly offer them the sort of basic pay that they can get . . .

The Clinical Director made a similar point:

I thought it was probably quite a reasonable deal for a lot of people. But there were years' worth of bitterness from being underpaid and under-graded that all came out at the same time. I think for the organisation it was a success, and for most individuals it was [Clinical Director].

New working arrangements

It was not just a case of how many staff had moved over; more important to the trust and directorate management was what the Theatres Project implied for the way in which work was organised. The creation of the new position of Theatre Practitioner was seen by some to have facilitated a great improvement. Under the new structure, the ODP manager had disappeared, and the teams of Theatre Practitioners were each responsible to a Team Leader, who in turn reported to the Theatre Manager. What the changes had allowed was the much more effective operation of these teams:

Before the changes we would often have the right number of staff, but not the right mix of skills, so we had to cancel operations. Now it is a lot easier to fill gaps and we don't cancel lists as often because we can find someone either to scrub or to assist the anaesthetist, as staff do both on a regular basis. Throughput is smoother, there is more flexibility, we have better motivated teams and lower staff turnover [Clinical Director, professional journal].[1]

This echoed the Clinical Director's earlier comments to us:

> it has enabled us to be much more flexible with working, because you can ask people to do extra hours without worrying about what their conditions are. A team leader has a team of people and she can say who stays after six [o'clock]. Previously there were rules that the ODAs couldn't stay until after six o'clock or they had to stay until after six o'clock so many days a week to get their planned overtime [Clinical Director].

From the perspective of some those working in the teams, the changes in working arrangements had been welcomed or at least accepted. According to a team leader:

> teething problems seem to have sorted themselves out now, in that the rota certainly is running quite smoothly, and the staff seem to accept it; those who obviously signed over to local pay have accepted that.

In particular, it was felt that the distinction between the two main groups of staff was beginning to be broken down in practice:

> Certainly now we've got more nurses doing anaesthetics as well as the scrub side; and a lot more technicians working the scrub side. So, certainly, there's been a lot more of interchange between the roles . . . There was always, amongst some of the staff, this 'them and us' scenario. It's still there to a certain extent but not as much as it was before [Team Leader].

It was recognised that not all had welcomed the new arrangements and their implications. According to the Clinical Director, some of the senior nurses had regarded it as a 'levelling down' or re-grading exercise designed simply to cut costs. This she had found 'a bit annoying', given what she saw as the efforts that had been made to get as good a deal as possible for all staff. Nonetheless, even the fact that some would gain more than others might be the source of resentment:

> It wasn't a re-grading exercise at all; it was changing people onto a different set of scales, and some people got a couple of thousand [pounds] a year out of it and some people got £30. Because it depended on what level they were previously, they had to move across to the one up. They didn't all move across . . . they moved to the next point on the scale. So obviously some people who were nowhere near that point didn't get so much out of it. And that was where a lot of the bitterness came from [Clinical Director].

Later interviews with staff – carried out in late 1999 – revealed that, for some, divides between staff were still important: 'I think there's a nurse/ODA divide in theatre . . .', said one Theatre Practitioner, 'I don't know why it is but when you first come in you notice it.' This seemed to be felt particularly strongly by the former nurses:

> ODAs and nurses do exactly the same job now but with different training. And nurses are . . . I can't really explain it, but it's because we're no longer classed as nurses, morale has plummeted and that's the main thing [Theatre Practitioner].

Competencies and progression

As we have already noted, the new, unified pay spine was to be supplemented by a competence-based system of progression. These competencies, developed for introduction at the beginning of 1999, were the responsibility of the Management Development Manager. Interviewed towards the end of 1999, she pointed to the benefits this had brought:

> Where staff previously said that they didn't want to do something that was not part of their role, now they say they need that experience to progress on the pay scale. This means we now have a pool of people who can do two or three jobs. With better rostering, this means we have greater efficiency, and that is providing a payback on the costs incurred for training [Management Development Manager, professional journal].

Opinions were divided amongst those working in the new system. Some welcomed it as providing clear and achievable targets:

> It gives people direction to work in, and I think it is quite clear-cut what needs to be done to work your way up. Traditionally people have reached the top of the grade and they haven't done much for it, but with this scheme they really have got to work to achieve top of the grade [Theatre Practitioner].

Others felt it had made little difference or might even be counter-productive:

> You can get someone who's absolutely brilliant practically, you know, who could run rings round people practically . . . but can't get the qualifications. If they don't get them, they can't progress. You can get somebody who has just scraped through, who's wonderful with pen and paper, who will get up there. It's, as I say, too much reliance on some of the academic stuff [Theatre Practitioner].

Beyond the Theatres Project

As well as management in Theatres considering the project a success in terms of their ability to manage and deploy staff, the HR Department were keen to exploit its wider implications. The personnel manager said that it was now planned to apply the principles of the project in other areas of the trust. Previously, he said, the corporate project had not been seen as capable of meeting operational needs. The difference now was that:

> it's started to be bottom–up-driven, whereas when we set out with the project it was very HR–top-driven. It's started to be bottom–up driven because they've seen the benefits of the Theatres project [Personnel Manager].

The HR Director felt that the appeal of the project was further strengthened by its *not* being the result of central government initiative. It could be justified as concerted, long-term strategy, something that should not be dispensed with on the basis of political whim. If anything, he maintained, the rest of the NHS would now be following them.

Questions

1. From where did the Theatres Project emerge? What issues did it address? If you had been looking at the project at the time of its emergence, would you have said that it was likely to be a success?

2. How is flexibility understood by, respectively, the management of the Theatres Directorate, Theatres Directorate staff and the Human Resources Department?

3. What does the harmonisation agreement imply for the terms and conditions of the two main groups of staff involved? Would you welcome the new terms and conditions if you were formerly (a) a nurse, and (b) an ODP?

4. How well was the process of change managed?

5. What were the main concerns of the HR Department? What pressures and difficulties did they face? What role or roles did they take on?

6. On what criteria would you judge the Theatres Project? Would you say that it has been successful? Are there any lessons that might be learned by other NHS trusts and other organisations more generally?

Note

[1]Most of the research for this case study was carried out in 1998. The authors would also like to acknowledge two other sources of data: an article in a professional journal which was published in late 1999; and a small number of interviews with Theatres staff carried out by Nottingham University MBA student, David Giddings, at around the same time. Where data is drawn from the former, this is noted in the case study, although the precise reference is not given in order to preserve the anonymity of the case study organisation.

References

*Ackroyd, S. and Procter, S. (1998) 'British manufacturing organization and workplace industrial relations: some attributes of the new flexible firm', *British Journal of Industrial Relations*, Vol.36, No.2, pp.163–83.

Ackroyd, S., Burrell, G., Hughes, M. and Whitaker, A. (1988) 'The Japanization of British industry?', *Industrial Relations Journal*, Vol.19, No.1, pp.11–23.

Amin, A. (1994) 'Post-Fordism: models, fantasies and phantoms of transition', in A. Amin (ed.) *Post-Fordism: A Reader*, Oxford: Blackwell.

Atkinson, J. and Meager, N. (1986) 'Is flexibility just a flash in the pan?', *Personnel Management*, Sep., pp.26–9.

Atkinson, J. (1984) 'Manpower strategies for flexible organizations', *Personnel Management*, August, pp.28–31.

Armstrong, P. (1987a) 'Engineers, managers and trust', *Work, Employment and Society*, Vol.1, No.4, pp.421–40.

Armstrong, P. (1987b) 'The rise of accounting controls in British capitalist enterprises', *Accounting, Organizations and Society*, Vol.12, No.5, pp.415–36.

Armstrong, P. (1989) 'Limits and possibilities for HRM in an age of management accountancy', in J. Storey (ed.) *New Perspectives on Human Resource Management*, London: Routledge.

Armstrong, P., Marginson, P., Edwards, P. and Purcell, J. (1996) 'Budgetary control and the labour force: findings from a survey of large British companies', *Management Accounting Research*, Vol.7, No.1, pp.1–23.

*Batt, R. (2000) 'Strategic segmentation in front-line services: matching customers, employees and human resource systems', *International Journal of Human Resource Management*, Vol.11, No.3, pp.540–61.

Beach, R., Muhlemann, A., Price, D., Paterson, A. and Sharp, J. (2000) 'A review of manufacturing flexibility', *European Journal of Operational Research*, Vol.122, No.1, pp.41–57.

Benders, J. and Van Hootegem, G. (1999) 'Teams and their context: moving the team discussion beyond dichotomies', *Journal of Management Studies*, Vol.36, No.5, pp.609–28.

Benders, J. and Van Hootegem, G. (2000) 'How the Japanese got teams', in S. Procter and F. Mueller (eds) *Teamworking*, London: Macmillan.

*Berggren, C. (1993) *The Volvo Experience: Alternatives to Lean Production in the Swedish Auto Industry*, London: Macmillan.

Boer, H. (1994) 'Flexible manufacturing systems', in J. Storey (ed.) *New Wave Manufacturing Strategies*, London: Paul Chapman.

Braverman, H. (1974) *Labor and Monopoly Capital: The Degradation of Work in the Twentieth Century*, New York: Monthly Review Press.

Brewster, C., Hegewisch, A. and Mayne, L. (1994) 'Flexible working practices: the controversy and the evidence', in C. Brewster and A. Hegewisch (eds) *Policy and Practice in European Human Resource Management*, London: Routledge.

Buchanan, D. (1994a) 'Principles and practice in work design', in K. Sisson (ed.) *Personnel Management: a Comprehensive Guide to Theory and Practice in Britain* (2nd edn), Oxford: Blackwell.

Buchanan, D. (1994b) 'Cellular manufacture and the role of teams', in J. Storey (ed.) *New Wave Manufacturing Strategies*, London: Paul Chapman.

Burnes, B. (1988) 'New technology and job design: the case of CNC', *New Technology, Work and Employment*, Vol.3, No.2, pp.100–11.

Cappelli, P. (1995) 'Rethinking employment', *British Journal of Industrial Relations*, Vol.33, No.4, pp.563–602.

Carlsson, B. (1989) 'Flexibility and the theory of the firm', *International Journal of Industrial Organization*, Vol.7, No.2, pp.179–203.

Casey, B. (1991) 'Survey evidence on trends in "non-standard" employment', in A. Pollert (ed.) *Farewell to Flexibility?*, Oxford: Blackwell.

Clark, J. (1993a) (ed.) *Human Resource Management and Technical Change*, London: Sage.

Clark, J. (1993b) 'Personnel management, human resource management and technical change', in J. Clark (ed.) *Human Resource Management and Technical Change*, London: Sage.

Clark, J. (1995) *Managing Innovation and Change: People, Technology and Strategy*, London: Sage.

Conti, R. and Warner, M. (1993) 'Taylorism, new technology and just-in-time systems in Japanese manufacturing', *New Technology, Work and Employment*, Vol.8, No.1, pp.31–42.

Cross, M. (1988) 'Changes in working practices in UK manufacturing 1981–88', *Industrial Relations Review and Report*, No.415, pp.2–10.

Cully, M., Woodland, S., O'Reilly, A. and Dix, G. (1999) *Britain at Work: As Depicted by the 1998 Workplace Employee Relations Survey*, London/New York: Routledge.

Daniel, W. (1987) *Workplace Industrial Relations and Technical Change*, London: Pinter.

Daniel, W. and Hogarth, T. (1990) 'Worker support for technical change', *New Technology, Work and Employment*, Vol.5, No.2, pp.82–93.

Delbridge, R., Turnbull, P. and Wilkinson, B. (1992) 'Pushing back the frontiers: management control and work intensification under JIT/TQM factory regimes', *New Technology, Work and Employment*, Vol.7, No.2, pp.97–106.

Delbridge, R., Lowe, J. and Oliver, N. (2000) 'Worker autonomy in lean teams: evidence from the world automotive components industry', in S. Procter, and F. Mueller, (eds) *Teamworking*, London: Macmillan.

Dunn, S. and Wright, M. (1994) 'Maintaining the status quo: an analysis of British collective agreements, 1979–1990', *British Journal of Industrial Relations*, Vol.32, No.1, pp.23–46.

Edquist, C. and Jacobsson, S. (1988) *Flexible Automation: The Global Diffusion of New Technology in the Engineering Industry*, Oxford: Blackwell.

Edwards, P. and Wright, M. (1998) 'HRM and commitment: a case study of team working', in P. Sparrow and M. Marchington (eds) *Human Resource Management: the New Agenda*, London: Financial Times/Pitman.

Elam, M. (1990) 'Puzzling out the post-Fordist debate: technology, markets and institutions', *Economic and Industrial Democracy*, Vol.11, No.3, pp.9–37. Reprinted in A. Amin (1994) (ed.) *Post-Fordism: A Reader*, Oxford: Blackwell.

Elger, T. (1991) 'Task flexibility and the intensification of labour in UK manufacturing in the 1980s', in A. Pollert (ed.) *Farewell to Flexibility?*, Oxford: Blackwell.

Emmott, M. and Hutchinson, S. (1998) 'Employment flexibility: threat or promise?', in P. Sparrow and M. Marchington (eds) *Human Resource Management: the New Agenda*, London: FT/Pitman.

Ezzamel, M. and Willmott, H. (1998) 'Accounting for teamwork: a critical study of group-based systems of organizational control', *Administrative Science Quarterly*, Vol.43, No.2, pp.358–96.

Fernie, S. and Metcalf, D. (1997) '(Not) hanging on the telephone: payment systems in the new sweatshops', Centre for Economic Performance, London School of Economics.

Fjermestad, J. and Chakrabarti, A. (1993) 'Survey of the computer-integrated manufacturing literature: a framework of strategy, implementation and innovation', *Technology Analysis and Strategic Management*, Vol.5, No.3, pp.251–71.

Fox, A. (1974) *Beyond Contract: Work, Power and Trust Relations*, London: Faber & Faber.

Frenkel, S., Korczynski, M., Shire, K. and Tam, M. (1999) *On the Front Line: Organization of Work in the Information Economy*, Ithaca, NY: Cornell University Press.

Friedman, A. (1977) *Industry and Labour*, London: Macmillan.

Friedrich, A., Kabst, R., Weber, W. and Rodehuth, M. (1998) 'Functional flexibility: merely reacting or acting strategically?', *Employee Relations*, Vol.20, No.5, pp.504–23.

Gallie, D (1991) 'Patterns of skill change: upskilling, deskilling or the polarization of skills', *Work, Employment and Society*, Vol.5, No.3, pp.319–51.

Geary, J. (1994) 'Task participation: employees' participation enabled or constrained?', in K. Sisson, (ed.) *Personnel Management: a Comprehensive Guide to Theory and Practice in Britain* (2nd edn), Oxford: Blackwell.

Gerwin, D. (1987) 'An agenda for research on the flexibility of manufacturing processes', *International Journal of Operations and Production Management*, Vol.7, No.1, pp.38–49.

Goold, M. and Campbell, A. (1987) *Strategies and Styles: The Role of the Centre in Managing Diversified Corporations*, Oxford: Blackwell.

Gospel, H. (1995) 'The decline in apprenticeship training in Britain', *Industrial Relations Journal*, Vol.26, pp.32–44.

Gregg, P. and Wadsworth, J. (1999) 'Job tenure, 1975–98', in P. Gregg and J. Wadsworth (eds) *The State of Working Britain*, Manchester: Manchester University Press.

Hackman, J. and Oldham, G. (1976) 'Motivation through the design of work: test of a theory', *Organizational Behaviour and Performance*, Vol.16, pp.250–79.

Hakim, C. (1990) 'Core and periphery in employers' workplace strategies: evidence from the 1987 ELUS survey', *Work, Employment and Society*, Vol.4, No.2, pp.157–88.

Hammer, M. and Champy, J. (1993) *Reengineering the Corporation: A Manifesto for Business Revolution*, London: Nicholas Brealey.

Herzberg, F. (1966) *Work and the Nature of Man*, Cleveland, OH: World Publishing Company.

Hill, T. (1991) *Production/Operations Management* (2nd edn), London: Prentice Hall.

Hirst, P. and Zeitlin, J. (1989) 'Flexible specialisation and the competitive failure of UK manufacturing', *Political Quarterly*, Vol.60, No.2, pp.164–78.

Hogarth, T. (1993) 'Worker support for organizational and technical change: workplace industrial relations in UK manufacturing – the case study evidence', *Work, Employment and Society*, Vol.7, No.2, pp.189–212.

Hunter, L., McGregor, A., MacInnes, J. and Sproull, A. (1993) 'The "flexible firm": strategy and segmentation', *British Journal of Industrial Relations*, Vol.31, No.3, pp.383–407.

Hutton, W. (1995) *The State We're In*, London: Jonathan Cape.

Hyman, R. (1987) 'Strategy or structure? Capital, labour and control', *Work, Employment and Society*, Vol.1, No.1, pp.25–55.

IDS (Incomes Data Services) (1994) 'Multi-skilling', *IDS Study*, No.558.

Ingersoll Engineers (1990) *Competitive Manufacturing: the Quiet Revolution*, Rugby: Ingersoll Engineers.

Ingersoll Engineers (1994) *The Quiet Revolution Continues*, Rugby: Ingersoll Engineers.

Ingram, P. (1991) 'Changes in working practices in British manufacturing industry in the 1980s: a study of employee concessions made during wage negotiations', *British Journal of Industrial Relations*, Vol.29, No.1, pp.1–13.

Jenkins, A. (1994) 'Teams: from "ideology" to analysis', *Organization Studies*, Vol.15, No.6, pp.849–60.

Jones, B. (1988) 'Work and flexible automation in Britain: a review of developments and possibilities', *Work, Employment and Society*, Vol.2, No.4, pp.451–86.

Jones, B. (1989) 'Flexible automation and factory politics: the United Kingdom in current perspective', in P. Hirst and J. Zeitlin (eds) *Reversing Industrial Decline?*, Oxford: Berg.

Jones, B. (1991) 'Technological convergence and limits to managerial control: flexible manufacturing systems in Britain, the USA and Japan', in S. Tolliday and J. Zeitlin (eds) *The Power to Manage?*, London: Routledge.

Jones, O., Green, K. and Coombs, R. (1994) 'Technology management: developing a critical perspective', *International Journal of Technology Management*, Vol.9, No.2, pp.156–71.

Kalleberg, A. (2001) 'Organizing flexibility: the flexible firm in the new century', *British Journal of Industrial Relations*, Vol.39, No.4, pp.479–504.

Kanigel, R. (1997) *The One Best Way: Frederick Winslow Taylor and the Enigma of Efficiency*, London: Little, Brown.

Kenney, M. and Florida, R. (1993) *Beyond Mass Production: The Japanese System and its Transfer to the United States*, New York: Oxford University Press.

Kessler, I. (1994) 'Performance pay', in K. Sisson (ed.) *Personnel Management: a Comprehensive Guide to Theory and Practice in Britain* (2nd edn), Oxford: Blackwell.

Kirosingh, M. (1989) 'Changed working practices', *Employment Gazette*, August, pp.422–9.

*Klein, J. (1989) 'The human costs of manufacturing reform', *Harvard Business Review*, March–April, pp.60–6.

Lee, B. (1996) 'The justification and monitoring of advanced manufacturing technology: an empirical study of 21 installations of flexible manufacturing systems', *Management Accounting Research*, Vol.7, No.1, pp.95–118.

Legge, K. (1988), 'Personnel management in recession and recovery: a comparative analysis of what the surveys say', *Personnel Review*, Vol.17, No.2, pp.3–72.

Legge, K. (1993) 'The role of personnel specialists: centrality or marginalisation?', in J. Clark (ed.) *Human Resource Management and Technical Change*, London: Sage.

Legge, K. (1995) *Human Resource Management: Rhetorics and Realities*, London: Macmillan.

Legge, K. (1998) 'Flexibility: the gift-wrapping on employment degradation?', in P. Sparrow and M. Marchington (eds) *Human Resource Management: the New Agenda*, London: FT/Pitman.

Lei, D. and Goldhar, J. (1991) 'Computer-integrated manufacturing (CIM): redefining the manufacturing firm into a global service business', *International Journal of Operations and Production Management*, Vol.11, No.10, pp.5–18.

Lim, S. (1987) 'Flexible manufacturing systems and manufacturing flexibility in the United Kingdom', *International Journal of Operations and Production Management*, Vol.7, No.6, pp.44–54.

Littler, C. (1982) *The Development of the Labour Process in Capitalist Societies*, London: Heinemann.

Lowe, J., Delbridge, R. and Oliver, N. (1997) 'High-performance manufacturing: evidence from the automotive components industry', *Organization Studies*, Vol.18, No.5, pp.783–98.

MacDuffie, J. and Pil, F. (1997) 'Changes in auto industry employment practices: an international overview', in T. Kochan, R. Lansbury and J. MacDuffie (eds) *After Lean Production*, Ithaca, NY: Cornell University Press.

Marginson, P. (1991) 'Change and continuity in the employment structure of large companies', in A. Pollert (ed.) *Farewell to Flexibility?*, Oxford: Blackwell.

Marsden, D. and Thompson, M. (1990) 'Flexibility agreements and their significance in the increase in productivity in British manufacturing since 1980', *Work, Employment and Society*, Vol.4, No.1, pp.83–104.

Mayne, L., Tregaskis, O. and Brewster, C. (1996) 'A comparative analysis of the link between flexibility and HRM strategy', *Employee Relations*, Vol.18, No.3, pp.5–24.

McIvor, A. (2001) *A History of Work in Britain, 1880–1950*, London: Palgrave.

McLoughlin, I. (1990) 'Management, work organization and CAD: towards flexible automation?', *Work, Employment and Society*, Vol.4, No.2, pp.217–37.

Mintzberg, H. (1978) 'Patterns in strategy formation', *Management Science*, Vol.24, No.9, pp.934–48.

Mueller, F. and Purcell, J. (1992) 'The drive for higher productivity', *Personnel Management*, Vol.25, No.2, pp.28–33.

Munday, M. and Peel, M. (1998) 'An analysis of the performance of Japanese, US and domestic manufacturing firms in the UK electronics/electrical sector', in R. Delbridge and J. Lowe (eds) *Manufacturing in Transition*, London: Routledge.

NACAB (National Association of Citizens Advice Bureaux) (1997) *Flexibility Abused: A CAB Evidence Report on Employment Conditions in the Labour Market*, London: NACAB.

NEDO (National Economic Development Office) (1986) *Changing Working Patterns: How Companies Achieve Flexibility to Meet New Needs*, London: NEDO.

Nichols, T. (1986) *The British Worker Question: A New Look at Workers and Productivity in Manufacturing*, London: Routledge & Kegan Paul.

Noble, D. (1977) 'Social choice in machine design: the case of automatically controlled machine tools', in A. Zimbalist (ed.) *Case Studies in the Labour Process*, London: Monthly Review Press.

Nolan, P. (1989) 'The productivity miracle', in F. Green (ed.) *The Restructuring of the UK Economy*, London: Harvester Wheatsheaf.

Oliver, N. and Wilkinson, B. (1992) *The Japanization of British Industry* (2nd edn), Oxford: Blackwell.

Oliver, N., Delbridge, R. and Lowe, J. (1996) 'Lean production practices: international comparisons in the auto components industry', *British Journal of Management*, Vol.7, special issue, pp.29–44.

O'Reilly, J. (1992) 'Where do you draw the line? Functional flexibility, training and skill in Britain and France', *Work, Employment and Society*, Vol.6, No.3, pp.369–96.

Parker, S. and Wall, T. (1998) *Job and Work Design: Organizing Work to Promote Well-being and Effectiveness*, London: Sage.

Parker, S., Wall, T. and Cordery, J. (2001) 'Future work design research and practice: towards an elaborated model of work design', *Journal of Occupational and Organizational Psychology*, Vol.74, No.4, pp.413–40.

Penn, R. (1992) 'Flexibility in Britain during the 1980s: recent empirical evidence', in N. Gilbert, R. Burrows and A. Pollert (eds) *Fordism and Flexibility: Divisions and Change*, London: Macmillan.

Pike, R., Sharp, J. and Price, D. (1989) 'AMT investment in the larger UK firm', *International Journal of Operations and Production Management*, Vol.9, No.2, pp.13–26.

Pil, F. and MacDuffie, J. (1996) 'The adoption of high-involvement work practices', *Industrial Relations*, Vol.35, No.3, pp.432–55.

Piore, M. and Sabel, C. (1984) *The Second Industrial Divide: Possibilities for Prosperity*, New York: Basic Books.

Procter, S. (1995) 'The extent of just-in-time manufacturing in the UK: evidence from aggregate economic data', *Integrated Manufacturing Systems*, Vol.6, No.4, pp.16–25.

Procter, S. and Ackroyd, S. (1998) 'Against Japanization: understanding the reorganization of British manufacturing', *Employee Relations*, Vol.20, No.3, pp.237–47.

Procter, S. and Currie, G. (1999) 'The role of the personnel function: roles, perceptions and processes in an NHS Trust', *International Journal of Human Resource Management*, Vol.10, No.6, pp.1076–90.

*Procter, S. and Mueller, F. (2000) 'Teamworking: strategy, structure, systems and culture', in S. Procter and F. Mueller (eds) *Teamworking*, London: Macmillan.

Procter, S., Hassard, J. and Rowlinson, M. (1995) 'Introducing cellular manufacturing: operations, human resources and high-trust dynamics', *Human Resource Management Journal*, Vol.5, No.2, pp.46–64.

Procter, S., Rowlinson, M., McArdle, L., Hassard, J. and Forrester, P. (1994), 'Flexibility, politics and strategy: in defence of the model of the flexible firm', *Work, Employment and Society*, Vol.8, No.2, pp.221–42.

Rowley, C. (1994) 'The illusion of flexible specialisation: the case of the domesticware sector of the British ceramics industry', *New Technology, Work and Employment*, Vol.9, No.2, pp.127–39.

Rowley, C. (1996) 'Flexible specialisation: some comparative dimensions and evidence from the ceramic tile industry', *New Technology, Work and Employment*, Vol.11, No.2, pp.125–36.

Rush, H. and Bessant, J. (1992) 'Revolution in three-quarter time: lessons from the diffusion of advanced manufacturing technologies', *Technology Analysis and Strategic Management*, Vol.4, No.1, pp.3–19.

Sennett, R. (1998) *The Corrosion of Character*, London: Norton.

Sewell, G. and Wilkinson, B. (1992) 'Someone to watch over me: surveillance, discipline and the just-in-time labour process', *Sociology*, Vol.26, No.2, pp.271–89.

Slack, N. (1987) 'The flexibility of manufacturing systems', *International Journal of Operations and Production Management*, Vol.7, No.4, pp.35–45.

Slack, N., (1990) 'Flexibility as managers see it', in M. Warner, W. Wobbe and P. Brodner (eds) *New Technology and Manufacturing Management: Strategic Choices for Flexible Production Systems*, Chichester: Wiley.

Smith, A. (1776) *The Wealth of Nations*.

Sennett, R. (1998) *The Corrosion of Character*, New York and London: Norton.

Storey, J. (1992) *Developments in the Management of Human Resources*, Oxford: Blackwell.

Storey, J. and Sisson, K. (1993) *Managing Human Resources and Industrial Relations*, Buckingham: Open University Press.

Taylor, F.W. (1911) *The Principles of Scientific Management*, New York: Harper.

Taylor, P. and Bain, P. (1999) ' "An assembly line in the head": work and employee relations in the call centre', *Industrial Relations Journal*, Vol.30, No.2, pp.101–17.

Thompson, P. and Ackroyd, S. (1995) 'All quiet on the workplace front? A critique of recent trends in British industrial sociology', *Sociology*, Vol.29, No.4, pp.615–33.

Tidd, J. (1991) *Flexible Manufacturing Technologies and International Competitiveness*, London: Pinter.

Tomaney, J. (1994) 'A new paradigm of work organisation and technology?', in A. Amin (ed.) *Post-Fordism: A Reader*, Oxford: Blackwell.

Trist, E. and Bamforth, K. (1951) 'Some social and psychological consequences of the longwall method of coal-getting', *Human Relations*, Vol.4, No.1, pp.3–38.

Trist, E., Higgin, G., Murray, H. and Pollock, A. (1963) *Organizational Choice: Capabilities of Groups at the Coal Face under Changing Technologies: The Loss, Rediscovery and Transformation of a Work Tradition*, London: Tavistock.

Turnbull, P. (1988) 'The limits to "Japanization": just-in-time, labour relations and the UK automotive industry', *Industrial Relations Journal*, Vol.17, No.3, pp.193–206.

Ulrich, D. (1997) *Human Resource Champions*, Boston, MA: Harvard Business School Press.

Upton, D. (1994) 'The management of manufacturing flexibility', *California Management Review*, Winter, pp.72–89.

Upton, D. (1995) 'What really makes factories flexible?', *Harvard Business Review*, July–August, pp.74–84.

Waterson, P., Clegg, C., Bolden, R., Pepper, K., Warr, P. and Wall, T. (1997) *The Use and Effectiveness of Modern Manufacturing Practices in the United Kingdom*, Sheffield: Institute of Work Psychology.

Willcocks, L. and Grint, K. (1997) 'Reinventing the organization? Towards a critique of business process re-engineering', in I. McLoughlin and M. Harris (eds) *Innovation, Organizational Change and Technology*, London: International Thomson.

Williams, K., Cutler, T., Williams, J. and Haslam, C. (1987) 'The end of mass production?', *Economy and Society*, Vol.16, No.3, pp.405–39.

Williams, K., Haslam, C., Williams, J. and Cutler, T. (1992) 'Against lean production', *Economy and Society*, Vol.21, No.3, pp.321–54.

*Womack, J., Jones, D. and Roos, D. (1990) *The Machine that Changed the World*, New York: Rawson Associates.

Wood, D. and Smith, P. (1989) *Employers' Labour Use Strategies: First Report of the 1987 Survey*, Department of Employment Research Paper No.63, London: Department of Employment.

* Useful reading

INDEX

Page references in **bold** indicate chapters